Library of
Davidson College

MUSICAL PATRONAGE IN SEVENTEENTH-CENTURY ENGLAND:
CHRISTOPHER, FIRST BARON HATTON
(1605-1670)

MUSICAL PATRONAGE IN SEVENTEENTH-CENTURY ENGLAND: CHRISTOPHER, FIRST BARON HATTON (1605-1670)

JONATHAN P. WAINWRIGHT

© JONATHAN P. WAINWRIGHT, 1997

All rights reserved. No part of this publication may be reproduced, stored in a retrieval system, or transmitted in any form or by any means, electronic, mechanical, photocopying, recording, or otherwise without the prior permission of the publisher.

Published by
SCOLAR PRESS
Gower House
Croft Road
Aldershot
Hants GU11 3HR
England

Ashgate Publishing Company
Old Post Road
Brookfield
Vermont 05036-9704
USA

British Library Cataloguing-in-Publication Data:
Wainwright, Jonathan P.
    Musical patronage in seventeenth-century England: Christopher first Baron Hatton (1605-1670).
    1. Musical patronage—England—History—17th century.
    I. Title.
    780.7'9'42

Library of Congress Cataloguing-in-Publication Data:
Wainwright, Jonathan P.
    Musical patronage in seventeenth-century England: Christopher first Baron Hatton (1605-1670) / Jonathan P. Wainwright.
    Includes bibliographical references and index.
    1. Music patronage—England. 2. Music—England—17th century—History and criticism. 3. Music—England—17th century—Manuscripts. 4. Hatton, Christopher Hatton, Baron, 1605-1670.
I. Title.
ML286.2.W35 1997
780'.79'41—dc21
    97-2418
    CIP
    MN

ISBN 1 85928 278 4

Printed in Great Britain on acid-free paper at the University Press, Cambridge

For My Parents

CONTENTS

List of Plates	page x
List of Tables	xi
Preface and Acknowledgements	xiii
Abbreviations	xv
Miscellaneous	xv
Periodicals	xvi
Library Sigla	xvii

PART I

	Introduction	1
1	Christopher, First Baron Hatton: Biography	3
	The Hatton Family	3
	Christopher Hatton III	6
	Christopher Hatton IV	22
2	The Hatton Music Collection	25
	The Survival of the Hatton Music Collection	25
	The Dispersal of the Hatton Music Collection	41
	The Possible Extent of the Hatton Music Collection	43
3	John Lilly and Stephen Bing: Sometime Copyists for Christopher Hatton III	46
	John Lilly (1612-1678)	46
	Stephen Bing (1610-1681)	52
	The Christ Church Sets of Viol Consort Music	66
	Stephen Bing and the Oxford Court	90
	Stephen Bing's Copies of Italian Music	92
	Stephen Bing's Later Manuscripts	99
4	George Jeffreys (*c.*1610-1685): Steward to the Hatton Family	115
	George Jeffreys: Biography	115
	George Jeffreys' Copies of Italian Music	121
	Manuscripts of George Jeffreys' Compositions	132
	George Jeffreys' Compositions: An Historical Perspective	154
5	Christ Church, Oxford Mus. 877-880: 'A Strange Meddley'	160
	The Composite Partbooks Christ Church Mus. 877-880	160
	Music in Civil War Oxford	169
	Excursus I: Newly-Identified Motets by Richard Dering	178

6	Hatton-Related Manuscripts	186
	More Manuscripts from the Hatton Collection?	186
	The 'Tregian' Manuscripts	190
	Angelo Notari's Scorebook: British Library Add. MS 31,440	191
	Excursus II: The Dissemination and Influence of Italian Music in Restoration England	195
	Conclusion	208

PART II

	Manuscript Sources: Introduction	215
I	London, British Library Add. MS 10,338	217
II	London, British Library Add. MSS 17,816 & 30,829-30	233
III	London, British Library Add. MSS 27,550-4	235
IV	London, British Library Add. MS 29,282	238
V	London, British Library Add. MS 30,382	239
VI	London, British Library Add. MS 31,434	242
VII	London, British Library Add. MS 31,440	244
VIII	London, British Library Add. MS 31,460	251
IX	London, British Library Add. MS 31,479 & Madrigal Society MSS G 55-9	254
X	London, British Library Add. MS 33,234	260
XI	London, British Library Add. MS 33,235	264
XII	London, British Library Add. MSS 40,657-61	267
XIII	London, British Library Add. MS 59,869	275
XIV	London, British Library Egerton MS 2485	279
XV	London, British Library Egerton MS 2960	282
XVI	London, British Library Evelyn MS 189	285
XVII	London, Royal College of Music MS 920	286
XVIII	London, Royal College of Music MS 920A	288
XIX	London, Royal College of Music MS 2033	290
XX	London, Royal College of Music MS 2034	292
XXI	London, Royal College of Music MS 2039	293
XXII	Oxford, Bodleian Library Mus. Sch. MS C 9	297
XXIII	Oxford, Bodleian Library Mus. Sch. MS C 10	300
XXIV	Oxford, Bodleian Library Mus. Sch. MS C 11	302
XXV	Oxford, Bodleian Library Mus. Sch. MSS C 12-19	304
XXVI	Oxford, Bodleian Library Mus. Sch. MSS C 24-7	314
XXVII	Oxford, Bodleian Library Mus. Sch. MSS C 54-7	316
XXVIII	Oxford, Bodleian Library Mus. Sch. MS C 87	319
XXIX	Oxford, Bodleian Library Mus. Sch. MS C 204	321
XXX	Oxford, Bodleian Library Mus. Sch. MS E 451	326

XXXI	Oxford, Bodleian Library Tenbury MSS 973-6 & 1273	336
XXXII	Oxford, Bodleian Library Tenbury MS 1005	338
XXXIII	Oxford, Bodleian Library Tenbury MS 1009	339
XXXIV	Oxford, Bodleian Library Tenbury MS 1010	341
XXXV	Oxford, Bodleian Library Tenbury MS 1011	341
XXXVI	Oxford, Bodleian Library Tenbury MS 1012	342
XXXVII	Oxford, Bodleian Library Tenbury MS 1013	343
XXXVIII	Oxford, Bodleian Library Tenbury MS 1015	344
XXXIX	Oxford, Bodleian Library Tenbury MS 1016	346
XL	Oxford, Bodleian Library Tenbury MS 1017	347
XLI	Oxford, Bodleian Library Tenbury MS 1285	348
XLII	Oxford, Christ Church Mus. 2, 397-408 & 436	349
XLIII	Oxford, Christ Church Mus. 14	366
XLIV	Oxford, Christ Church Mus. 18	368
XLV	Oxford, Christ Church Mus. 21	370
XLVI	Oxford, Christ Church Mus. 43	374
XLVII	Oxford, Christ Church Mus. 48	376
XLVIII	Oxford, Christ Church Mus. 49	378
XLIX	Oxford, Christ Church Mus. 372-6	382
L	Oxford, Christ Church Mus. 417-18 & 1080	384
LI	Oxford, Christ Church Mus. 432 & 612-13	387
LII	Oxford, Christ Church Mus. 510-14	389
LIII	Oxford, Christ Church Mus. 621	391
LIV	Oxford, Christ Church Mus. 623-6	393
LV	Oxford, Christ Church Mus. 732-5 & London, British Library R.M. MS 24.k.3.	396
LVI	Oxford, Christ Church Mus. 747-9	401
LVII	Oxford, Christ Church Mus. 754-9	403
LVIII	Oxford, Christ Church Mus. 877-80	405
LIX	Oxford, Christ Church Mus. 1023	415
LX	Oxford, Christ Church Mus. 1151	416
LXI	Oxford, Christ Church Mus. 1155-61	417
LXII	Oxford, Christ Church Mus. 1178	418
LXIII	Oxford, Christ Church Mus. 1185	419
LXIV	Oxford, Christ Church Mus. 1215, Fascicle 3	421
LXV	EIRE, Dublin, Marsh's Library MS Z3.4.13, ff. 47-59	422

Appendix: The Hatton Music Collection	425
Bibliography	431
List of Music Soures Cited	431
Manuscript Sources	431
Printed Sources	434

Non-Music Manuscripts	445
Works Printed Before 1800	451
Works Printed After 1800	453
Index	467

LIST OF PLATES

1 Oxford, Christ Church Mus. 708
2 Oxford, Christ Church Mus. 432
3 Northamptonshire Record Office Finch-Hatton MS 2652
4 Oxford, Christ Church Mus. 317
5 Oxford, Christ Church Mus. 880, f. 1 second sequence
6 York Minster MS M.1.S, Medius Cantoris, f. 14^v
7 London, British Library Add. MS 31,434, f. 1
8 Oxford, Christ Church Mus. 436, f. 53^v

LIST OF TABLES

1	Christopher Hatton III's Associates, Musicians, Secretaries, etc.	22
2	Printed Music Bought by Christopher Hatton III from Robert Martin in November 1638	29
3	Glasgow University Library, Euing Music Collection R.c.28	31
4	Other Printed Sources used by Hatton's Musicians/Copyists	31
5	Annotated Prints and Manuscripts	33
	a. Covers annotated by Stephen Bing	33
	b. Covers annotated by George Holmes	34
	c. Covers annotated by George Jeffreys	34
	d. Covers annotated by Christopher Hatton III	35
6	George Holmes	35
	a. Manuscripts copied by Holmes	35
	b. Other examples of Holmes' hand	35
7	Prints Bound with the Hatton Purchases of 1638	37
8	Other Prints Bound with those used by Hatton's Musicians/Copyists	39
9	Other Martin Prints at Christ Church, Oxford	40
10	Miscellaneous Prints Associated with the Hatton Collection	40
11	Music Manuscripts Associated with the Hatton Family	41
12	Manuscripts Copied by John Lilly	47
13	John Lilly: Airs for Solo Lyra Viol	51
14	Stephen Bing	55
	a. Manuscripts copied by Bing	55
	b. Other examples of Bing's hand	56
15	Summary of Bing's and Lilly's Copies of Music for Viol Consort	68
16	Rastrum Rulings in Bing's and Lilly's Sets of Viol Consort Music	85
17	Textless Italian Madrigals in the Great Set	86
18	Stephen Bing's and George Jeffreys' Manuscripts of Italian Music: Watermarks and Rastrum Rulings	94
19	British Library Add. MS 31,434: Collation	97
20	A Proposed Chronology of the Surviving Manuscripts Copied by Stephen Bing	113

21	George Jeffreys	117
	a. Manuscripts copied by Jeffreys	117
	b. Other examples of Jeffreys' hand	118
22	George Jeffreys' Copy-Sources of Italian Music	124
23	George Jeffreys' Compositions	134
	a. Instrumental works	134
	b. Italian madrigals	135
	c. English secular music	135
	d. Latin sacred music	136
	e. English sacred music and devotional songs	138
	f. Doubtful works	139
24	A Proposed Chronology of the Copying of the Four-Part Pieces in British Library Add. MS 10,338	142
25	A Proposed Chronology of the Copying of the Three-Part Pieces in British Library Add. MS 10,338	146
26	A Proposed Chronology of the Surviving Manuscripts Copied by George Jeffreys	155
27	Music Manuscripts from Civil War Oxford?	175
	a. Manuscripts copied by George Jeffreys	175
	b. Manuscripts copied by Stephen Bing	175
28	Motets for Two- and Three Voices and Basso Continuo by Richard Dering	180
	a. Motets published in J. Playford ed., *Cantica Sacra* (London, 1662)	181
	b. Motets published in J. Playford ed., *Cantica Sacra.... The Second Sett* (London, 1674)	181
	c. Motets in manuscripts with firm attributions to Dering	182
	d. Anonymous motets found amongst attributable Dering motets	182
	e. Motets with questionable attributions to Dering	183
29	Popular pre-1638 Italian Pieces in English Restoration Manuscripts	201
30	A Provisional List of Unique Music Publications in the Library of Christ Church, Oxford	209
	a. *Unica*	209
	b. Sole Surviving Complete Copies	210

PREFACE AND ACKNOWLEDGEMENTS

This book, which began life as my doctoral dissertation, has been long in the making, and over the years numerous people have offered advice and encouragement. I owe my principal debt to Andrew Jones, my research supervisor, whose constant guidance and constructive criticisms have improved this study beyond measure. The late Peter le Huray and Iain Fenlon also offered invaluable advice and support, and my sincere thanks are also due to Peter Aston, Clifford Bartlett and Pamela Willetts for advice in the early stages of the project. I gratefully acknowledge the financial support of the British Academy and St Catharine's College, Cambridge; and awards from *Music & Letters* and the Royal Musical Association helped to finance research trips to Bologna and Venice. I am also grateful to St Catherine's College, Oxford, The Open University and York University for employing me, thus providing both the ideal environment for research and the financial security to enable me to complete the study.

My work would not have been possible without the co-operation and assistance of many librarians in both Great Britain and Italy. The staff of the following institutions must be singled out as having been particularly generous with their help: the Civico Museo Bibliografico-Musicale, Bologna; the Biblioteca Nazionale Marciana, Venice; the Pendlebury and University Libraries, Cambridge (Richard Andrewes); the British Library, London; the Public Record Office, London; the Royal College of Music, London; the Northamptonshire Record Office; the Bodleian Library, Oxford (Bob Bruce, Magosia Czepiel and Peter Ward Jones); and finally the staff of the Library of Christ Church, Oxford (in particular, Janet McMullin and John Wing) whose unfailing help and friendliness made my work in their library such a delight. The published work of David Pinto and Robert Thompson is constantly referred to in the following pages, but it is my pleasure to acknowledge that the debt is even larger than it appears: I have been privileged to engage in a long series of correspondence with both scholars concerning the Hatton collection and related issues, and their arguments and suggestions have been a constant source of inspiration. Individual thanks must also be extended to Andrew Ashbee, Sarah Boyer, Christopher Field, Peter Holman, Gunter Morche, Ricki Scalway, Ian Spink and Magnus Williamson. I am also extremely grateful to Rachel Lynch of Scolar Press for her advice and patience.

The greatest debts of all are due to my parents without whose support this study would never have been started, let alone finished.

Plates 1-2, 4-5 and 8 are reproduced by kind permission of The Governing Body of Christ Church, Oxford; Plate 3 by kind permission of The Trustees of the Winchilsea Settled Estates; Plate 6 by kind permission of the Dean and Chapter of York; and Plate 7 by kind permission of The British Library.

The jacket illustration is Christ Church, Oxford, Plate 27 from David Loggan's *Oxonia Illustrata*, 1675 (Bodleian shelfmark Arch. Antiq. A.11.13), reproduced by kind permission.

In the following pages the texts of quotations have been transcribed literally: the original orthography, punctuation and capitalisation (or non-capitalisation) is maintained; it has not been possible, however, to indicate such typographical refinements as the relative sizes of upper and lower case letters. Any realisations of abbreviations or editorial additions are given in square brackets. Dates are new style unless stated.

ABBREVIATIONS

Miscellaneous

S	soprano (g'-2 clef)
C	cantus (c'-1 clef)
M	mean (c'-2 clef)
A	alto (c'-3 clef)
T	tenor (c'-4 clef)
B	bass (f-4 clef)
CI, CII, etc.	first cantus, second cantus, etc.
bc	basso continuo
tr.vl	treble viol
b.vl	bass viol
org	organ
vl	viol
vln	violin
vla	viola
Add.	Additional (British Library MSS)
arr.	arranged (by) / arrangement
attrib.	attributed to
b.	born
b(b).	bar(s)
Bk	book
c.	*circa* (about)
d.	died
ed.	edited by
edn	edition
f(f).	folio(s)
FH	Finch-Hatton MSS (Northamptonshire Record Office)
fl.	*floruit* (flourished)
inc.	incomplete
insts	instruments
Mad. Soc.	Madrigal Society (manuscripts housed in the British Library)
mm.	millimetres
MS(S)	manuscript(s)
Mus. Sch.	Music School (Bodleian Library MSS)
n.d.	no date given
n.p.	no place of publication
NRO	Northamptonshire Record Office

NS	new style
Op.	*opus*
p(p).	page(s)
PRO	Public Record Office, London
pt	part
_r	recto
repr.	reprinted
rev.	revision / revised / reversed
s.n.	*sine nomine* (without name)
theo	theorbo
Tr	treble
trans.	translated by
v(v)	voice(s)
_v	verso
vol(s)	volume(s)
=	married

DNB	*The Dictionary of National Biography*, ed. L. Stephen & S. Lee (London, 1885-1900), 66 vols
New Grove	*The New Grove Dictionary of Music and Musicians*, ed. S. Sadie (London, 1980), 20 vols
RISM	*Répertoire Internationale des Sources Musicales: Einzeldrucke vor 1800*, A/I (Kassel, 1971-) *Recueils Imprimés, XVIe-XVIIe Siècles: Listes Chronologique*, B/I/1, ed. F. Lesure (Munich & Duisburg, 1960)
VdGS	G. Dodd ed., *Thematic Index of Music for Viols*, The Viola da Gamba Society (London, 1980-)

Periodicals

AcM	*Acta Musicologica*
AnMc	*Analecta Musicologica*
EM	*Early Music*
JAMS	*Journal of the American Musicological Society*
JRMA	*Journal of the Royal Musical Association*
MD	*Musica Disciplina*
ML	*Music and Letters*
MMR	*Monthly Musical Record*
MQ	*Musical Quarterly*
MR	*Music Review*
MT	*Musical Times*
PRMA	*Proceedings of the Royal Musical Association*
RCRMA	*Research Chronicle* [of] *The Royal Musical Association*

Library Sigla

B-Bc	Bibliothèque du Conservatoire Royal de Musique, Brussels, Belgium
B-Br	Bibliothèque Royale, Brussels, Belgium
EIRE-Dm	Archbishop Marsh's Library, Dublin, Ireland
F-Pc	Bibliothèque du Conservatoire, Paris, France
F-Pn	Bibliothèque Nationale, Paris, France
Bu	Barber Institute of Fine Arts, University of Birmingham
CA	Cathedral Library, Canterbury
CAR	Cathedral Library, Carlisle
Cfm	Fitzwilliam Museum, Cambridge
Ckc	King's College, Cambridge
Cmc	Pepys Library, Magdalene College, Cambridge
Cu	University Library, Cambridge
DRc	Cathedral Library, Durham
Ge	Euing Music Collection, University Library, Glasgow
Gu	University Library, Glasgow
Lam	Royal Academy of Music, London
Lbl	British Library (formerly British Museum), London
Lcm	Royal College of Music, London
Lgc	Gresham College Library, London (housed in *Lgl*)
Lgl	Guildhall Library, London
Lsp	St Paul's Cathedral, London
Lwa	Westminster Abbey, London
LI	Cathedral Library, Lincoln
Mp	Central Public Library, Henry Watson Music Library, Manchester
Ob	Bodleian Library, Oxford
Och	Christ Church, Oxford
Y	Minster Library, York
I-Bc	Civico Museo Bibliografico Musicale, Bologna, Italy
I-Fc	Biblioteca del Conservatorio, Florence, Italy
I-Fn	Biblioteca Nazionale Centrale, Florence, Italy
I-Gu	Biblioteca Universitaria, Genoa
I-MOe	Biblioteca Estense, Modena, Italy
J-Tn	Nanki Music Library, Tokyo, Japan
US-Cn	Newberry Library, Chicago, U.S.A.
US-LAuc	William Andrews Clark Memorial Library, University of California, Los Angeles, U.S.A.
US-NYp	Public Library, New York, U.S.A.
US-R	Sibley Music Library, Eastman School of Music, Rochester, New York, U.S.A.

US-SM   Huntington Library, San Marino, U.S.A.
US-Wc   Folger Shakespeare Library, Washington D.C., U.S.A.

PART I

INTRODUCTION

This book examines the mechanics and structures of seventeenth-century English musical patronage in the form of a case study of one particular nobleman's activities. Christopher, First Baron Hatton is revealed as one of the most important and influential patrons of the period, and in demonstrating this I happily allow the study to burgeon-out to cover wider issues. Patronage was, by its very nature, vague and undefined. A patron was often an enabler rather than an activator, and although some idea of the creative and financial support which Hatton offered to musicians can be gleaned from surviving evidence, in the following pages Hatton is often no more than a shadowy figure hovering over the activities of his musicians and copyists. In the chapters concerning the Hatton scribes - John Lilly, Stephen Bing and George Jeffreys - it will be necessary to move beyond the direct influence of Hatton in order to examine related issues. These issues will help to put the musical patronage of Christopher Hatton in its cultural context, and indeed add to our general understanding of music in England in the seventeenth century.

It is a truism to state that patronage was of vital importance to English musicians in the seventeenth century. A musician could not operate as an isolated individual at that time; he was utterly reliant upon institutional or noble patronage. An individual's personal advancement could only take place through the assistance of a well-placed and well-disposed patron or sponsor, and the patron-client relationship was an essential part the social mechanism of the seventeenth century.[1] One only needs to look at the dedications in music publications of the period to see the debt musicians owed to royal or noble patrons. The greatest patron of all was, of course, the monarch, and the 'Royal Music' has been the subject of a number of studies.[2] The musical patronage of men of lesser standing has also come under scrutiny and has added greatly to our understanding of music in the Elizabethan, Jacobean and

---

[1] See *inter alia*, W. MacCaffrey, 'Place and Patronage in Elizabethan Politics', *Elizabethan Government and Society: Essays Presented to Sir John Neale*, ed. S.T. Bindoff, J. Hurstfield, & C.H. Williams (London, 1961), 95-126; L.L. Peck, '"For a King not to be bountiful were a fault": Perspectives on Court Patronage in Early Stuart England', *Journal of British Studies*, xxv (1986), 31-61; ibid., *Court Patronage and Corruption in Early Stuart England* (London, 1990); and L.L. Peck ed., *The Mental World of the Jacobean Court* (Cambridge, 1991).

[2] See for example, A. Ashbee, *Records of English Court Music* i-iv (Snodland, 1986-91) & v-ix (Aldershot, 1991-6); P. Holman, *Four and Twenty Fiddlers: The Violin at the English Court 1540-1690* (Oxford, 1993); H.C. de Lafontaine, *The King's Musick* (London, 1909); and G.A. Philipps, 'Crown Musical Patronage from Elizabeth I to Charles I', *ML*, lviii (1977), 29-42.

Caroline eras.³ However only recently, following a thorough examination of the printed music in the library of Christ Church, Oxford and a study of a related group of manuscripts, has Christopher Hatton been revealed as a musical patron of some importance. It will be shown that Baron Hatton was the owner of a substantial music library - perhaps one of the richest collections yet identified from the seventeenth century - and that much of it survives today in Christ Church, Oxford. The collection has important implications when considering: (*a*) music from court circles of the 1630s; (*b*) music at the Oxford Court (1642-6); and (*c*) the dissemination and influence of Italian music in England in the seventeenth century.

---

³ Most important is L. Hulse, 'The Musical Patronage of the English Aristocracy *c*.1590-1640' (Ph.D. dissertation, University of London, 1993). See also C. Monson, *Voice and Viols in England 1600-1650* (Ann Arbor, 1982); D.C. Price, *Patrons and Musicians of the English Renaissance* (Cambridge, 1981); L. Hulse, 'The Musical Patronage of Robert Cecil, First Earl of Salisbury (1563-1612)', *JRMA*, cxvi (1991), 24-40; J.A. Westrup, 'Domestic Music under the Stuarts', *PRMA*, lxviii (1942), 19-53; and W.L. Woodfill, *Musicians in English Society from Elizabeth I to Charles I* (Princeton, 1953).

CHAPTER ONE

CHRISTOPHER, FIRST BARON HATTON: BIOGRAPHY

The Hatton Family

The Cheshire family of Hatton first came to prominence in the reign of Elizabeth I when Sir Christopher Hatton I (1540-91) became Lord Chancellor. This first notable Christopher Hatton gained Royal favour - apparently due to his dancing skills[1] - and gradually obtained a substantial estate comprising lands in Northamptonshire, Dorset, Cheshire and Oxfordshire, and Hatton House and Gardens in London. From his father he inherited various Northamptonshire properties (an estate in Holdenby and five manors in Church and Chapel Brampton) and to these he soon added estates in Sulby and Wellingborough, the manors of Great and Little Weldon, Deenethorpe and Kirby, and, by grants from the Crown, the Lawn of Benefield, Corby, Cottingham, Gretton and Pipewell Woods and Middleton Thick; he also acquired the custody of other properties including Moulton Park and Warren, and the advowsons of Old (or Wold), Great Billing, Blisworth, Cottingham and Stoke Bruerne.[2] The most impressive of these was Hatton House in Holborn, London. In 1576 Christopher Hatton I had established himself in the gatehouse of Ely Place, the town house of the bishops of Ely since 1292, and then had petitioned the Queen for a lease of the grounds and some parts of the house; on the death of the bishop of Ely, in 1581, Hatton took over the whole of Ely Place and built Hatton House in the gardens.[3] When the Lord Chancellor died in 1591 his estates were worth over £5000 a year.[4] Christopher Hatton I died without issue and his estates passed to his sister's son Sir William Newport who took the name Hatton. On Newport-Hatton's death in 1597 many of the Hatton estates were inherited by Christopher Hatton II, a godson and second-cousin-once-removed to the Lord Chancellor Hatton (see Figure 1);[5] Hatton House, however, was retained by Newport-Hatton's widow, Elizabeth née

---

[1] According to Thomas Fuller in *The Worthies of England* (London, 1662), 285.
[2] *DNB*, ix, 159-62; G. Baker, *The History and Antiquities of the County of Northampton* (Northampton, 1822), i, 194-7; and H.D. Turner, 'Five Studies of the Aristocracy, 1689-1714' (M.Litt. dissertation, University of Cambridge, 1965), Chapter 1, *passim*.
[3] H. Marryat & U. Broadbent, *The Romance of Hatton Garden* (London, 1930), 25-7; the house was demolished around 1659 (see footnote 98 below).
[4] NRO FH 814: rents, etc. due to Sir Christopher Hatton (I or II) (n.d.); and NRO FH 3713 A & B: notes on the settlement of the affairs of Sir Christopher Hatton I after his death (n.d. [c.1598]).
[5] Christopher Hatton II was created a knight at the coronation of James I on 25 July 1603; W.C. Metcalfe, *A Book of Knights* (London, 1885), 150.

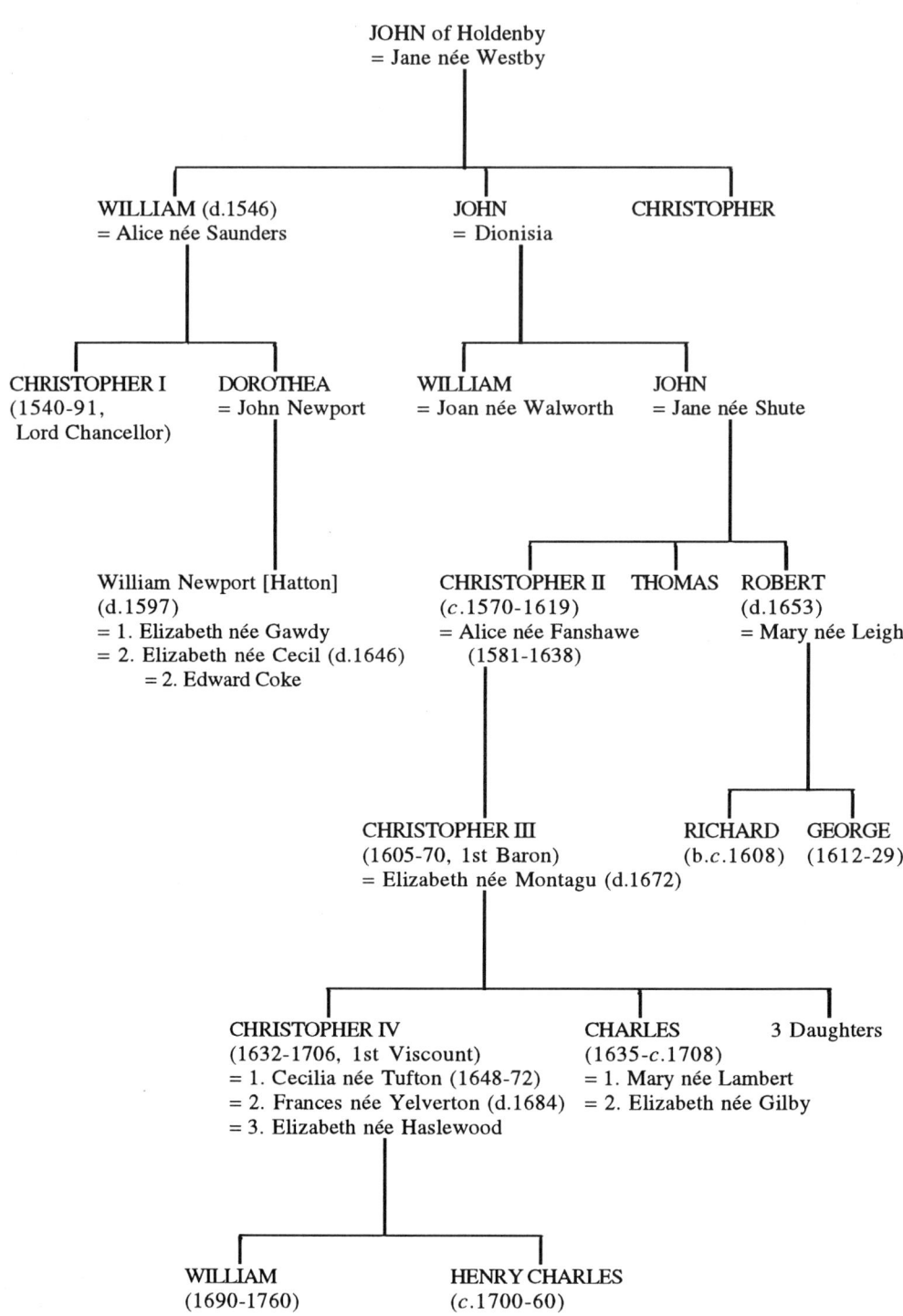

Figure 1 The Hatton Family

Cecil.[6] This arrangement caused some family disagreement and in 1616 Lady Elizabeth had to give evidence before the Privy Council concerning her ownership of Hatton House which was in danger of being handed over to Sir Christopher Hatton II. The Council acknowledged her claim and she remained in Hatton House until her death in 1646 when the property passed to Christopher Hatton III. Christopher Hatton II's only London residence was in Westminster.[7]

Sir Christopher Hatton II's attempts to claim Hatton House are perhaps understandable considering the enormous debts with which the Lord Chancellor had saddled his descendants. These debts, which were owed mainly to the Crown and amounted to approximately £40,000, were paid by the sale of the Oxfordshire estates and by an annual repayment of £1,500 on those remaining.[8] In 1607 the original Holdenby estate was sold to James I and the second Sir Christopher Hatton also appears to have dispensed with the Dorset estate.[9] (The lands in Cheshire had been bequeathed elsewhere.) Despite this financial burden Hatton II added two estates to his holdings: the Long Stanton estate in Cambridgeshire and Clayhall in Barking, Essex.[10] David Pinto has suggested that he may have gained the lease of Clayhall from his father-in-law, Sir Thomas Fanshawe I (1533-1601), who had been tenant of the estate in 1578.[11] Christopher Hatton II built a chapel there which was consecrated in 1616 by the Bishop of Chester and licensed for baptisms, marriages and burials of family members.[12] The Hatton family's principal residence was, however, Kirby Hall, an impressive Elizabethan/Jacobean building three miles north-east of Corby in Northamptonshire,[13]

---

[6] NRO FH 3545 and 3713 A & B. Lady Elizabeth also appears to have retained Sir Christopher Hatton I's collection of books; W.O. Hassall, 'The Books of Sir Christopher Hatton at Holkham', *The Library*, Fifth Series, v (1950), 1-13; and R.J. Roberts, 'Sir Christopher Hatton's Book-Stamps', *The Library*, Fifth Series, xii (1957), 119. In 1598, on the condition that she retained the name of Hatton, Lady Elizabeth married Sir Edward Coke, the Attorney General; she continued to receive a third of the income from the Hatton estates as jointure until her death in 1646.
[7] NRO FH 618: an appraisal of the contents of the Westminster house, 1619-22, after the death of Sir Christopher Hatton II.
[8] Historical Manuscripts Commission, *Calendar of the Manuscripts of the Most Hon. The Marquis of Salisbury Preserved at Hatfield House, Hertfordshire* (London, 1904), x, 429.
[9] NRO FH 3545: indenture dated 24 November 1608.
[10] On Hatton II's death in 1619 the Long Stanton property passed on to his two younger brothers, Thomas and Robert (see Figure 1).
[11] D. Pinto, 'The Music of the Hattons', *RCRMA*, xxiii (1990), 87.
[12] W.R. Powell ed., *The Victoria History of the County of Essex* (London, 1966), v, 195-6. David Pinto - (1990), note 40 - points out that the verse anthem 'Glorious and powerful God' by Orlando Gibbons, who was patronised by Christopher Hatton II (see below), is appropriate for the dedication of a church, and is the sole contemporary setting of the text.
[13] Begun in 1570 by Sir Humphrey Stafford of Blatherwick and based on the plans of the surveyor-architect John Thorpe; completed after Stafford's death in 1575 by Sir Christopher Hatton I, and important alterations were made between 1638 and 1640 by Sir Christopher Hatton III. There is no evidence to support the tradition that the 1638 remodelling was designed by Inigo Jones; rather the work was undertaken by Nicholas Stone, who was an associate of

and it was at Kirby that the Royal consort, Queen Anne of Denmark, and later her husband James I, were entertained on four occasions between 1605 and 1619.[14] Sir Christopher Hatton II is known to musicologists as the patron of Orlando Gibbons. Gibbons' single published collection of secular vocal music, *The First Set of Madrigals and Mottets of 5. Parts: Apt for Viols and Voyces* (London, 1612), is dedicated to Hatton, and in the preface the composer states that the pieces 'were most of them composed in your owne house... the language they speake you provided them'. It is possible, then, that Gibbons composed his madrigals at Kirby Hall to texts selected by Sir Christopher Hatton II[15] and, as will be shown in Chapter Two, a substantial part of the family's music collection probably dates from this period. To complete the picture of Sir Christopher Hatton II as a patron of the arts mention must be made of the partial dedication to him of Tobias Hume's *Captaine Humes Poeticall Musicke* (London, 1607),[16] which includes pieces entitled 'The Lady Hattons delight' (ff. 5v-6) and 'Sir Christopher Hattons choice' (ff. 21v-2); of William Sympson's *De Accentibus Hebraicis* (London, 1617) with a Latin 'Epistola Dedicatoria' to 'ILLUSTRI AC GENEROSO DOMINO CHRISTOPHORO HATTONO'; and to Hatton's appearance in the printed list of subscribers to John Misheu's polyglot dictionary *Ductor in Linguas* (London, 1617).

Christopher Hatton III

Christopher Hatton III was born at Clayhall in Barking, Essex on 28 June 1605 and was baptised on 11 July 1605; he was the eldest surviving son of Sir Christopher Hatton II and Alice, the eldest daughter of Thomas Fanshawe (1533-1601) of Dronfield, Derbyshire and of Ware Park, Hertfordshire.[17] Little is known about Christopher Hatton III's early years; he was no doubt brought up in a cultured environment and, not surprisingly, he developed his father's great interest in music and the arts. His father died in 1619 and, at the age of fourteen, Christopher Hatton III inherited what was still a substantial estate. He was educated at Jesus College, Cambridge,

---

Jones, and certain features of Stone's work do show the influence of Jones' designs (for details see footnote 45 below). See G.H. Chettle, rev. P. Leach, *Kirby Hall* (London, 1986).

[14] J. Nichols, *The Progresses... of King James the First* (London, 1828), i, 525; ii, 453-4.

[15] Clayhall, Barking could also have been the place of composition, but not the Westminster house as there is no reference to Hatton in Westminster before 1612. E.H. Fellowes, *Orlando Gibbons* (2/London, 1951; rev. 1970), 38-9 & 80, suggests that the madrigals were composed at Ely Place (Hatton House), Holborn; this is unlikely as, in 1612, the house was in the possession of Dowager Lady Elizabeth Newport-Hatton not Sir Christopher Hatton II.

[16] Copies of Hume (1607) survive in *Ge*, *Lbl*, *Mp* and *US-Wc*; the unsolicited dedication to Hatton is found only in the *Mp* copy and is an expanded form of the dedication to Philip, Earl of Arundel found in the *US-Ws* copy (Pinto (1990), note 42).

[17] Christopher Hatton III's precise date of birth, uncertain in *DNB*, can be worked out from his father's *Inquisition post mortem* (PRO SP 142/376/100) where Christopher III's age was given as exactly 14 years on 28 June 1619.

matriculating as a Fellow-Commoner on 12 January 1620 and graduating Master of Arts in 1622,[18] and he maintained links with Cambridge (both the city and the shire) throughout the 1620s and 1630s. He represented Peterborough in the Jacobean Parliament of 1625, was the Member for Clitheroe in 1626 and served as Justice of the Peace for Cambridgeshire almost continuously from 1628 to 1640.[19] The family links with Cambridge were, of course, strong: his father had been a native of Long Stanton near Cambridge where his uncle, Sir Thomas Hatton, still maintained an estate, and his other uncle, Sir Robert Hatton, lived nearby in Oakington. Sir Robert's two sons were also educated at Cambridge: Richard graduated Bachelor of Arts from Sidney Sussex College in 1623 and his brother George matriculated from King's College in 1628 and died shortly after being admitted as an Eton Scholar at the same college in 1629.[20]

The cultural circle of the Hatton cousins (Christopher III and Richard) included poets and playwrights such as Thomas Randolph (1605-35) and Peter Hausted (*c*.1603-45). Randolph was probably acquainted with Christopher Hatton before going up to Cambridge. The poet's father was steward to Lord Zouch of Harringworth, Northamptonshire and, until his death in 1625, supervised the Zouch-family estates at Harringworth and Bulwick near Kirby Hall; Christopher Hatton and Thomas Randolph were therefore virtual neighbours in Northamptonshire. At Cambridge Randolph got to know Hatton's cousin Richard who was himself a keen writer.[21] A manuscript of music copied and composed by George Jeffreys, Christopher Hatton's steward and secretary, offers other evidence of Richard Hatton's literary activity. British Library Add. MS 10,338 contains four 'Songs made for some comedyes. A 4 voc. 1631 S[i]r. R. Hatton': 'You that have been this Evening light', 'Fond Maydes, take warninge while you may', 'Cupid blushes to behold' and 'Hymen hath together tyed ye lusty bridegroome' set for four voices and basso continuo by Jeffreys.[22] These settings are preceded in the manuscript by settings of five poems by an unnamed author: 'Musicke thou Queene of Soules', 'Coy Cœlia dost thou see', 'Say Daunce how shall wee go' (*The Maskque of Vices*), 'Why sigh you swayne' (*Dialogue Nymphe & Sheaphard*) and 'Lovely Sheaphard' (*Dialogue Febisse Endimion*). The first four of these poems are by Randolph and were published posthumously in *Poems, with The Muses' Looking-Glass and*

---

[18] J. Venn & J.A. Venn, *Alumni Cantabrigienses* (Cambridge, 1922), Part 1, ii, 331.
[19] M.F. Keeler, *The Long Parliament* (Philadelphia, 1954), 208.
[20] Venn & Venn (1922), Part 1, ii, 331 describe Richard Hatton as the son of Sir Robert Hatton of Lambeth and state that he was educated at a school in Croydon.
[21] Richard Hatton had published a translation of Ovid's *Nux* (*Ovid's Walnut-Tree Transplanted*) in 1627.
[22] This section of *Lbl* Add. 10,338 was copied retrospectively as Richard Hatton was not knighted until 27 January 1645; Metcalfe (1885), 202. *Lbl* Add. 10,338, and the music and career of George Jeffreys are examined in detail in Chapter Four.

Amyntas (London, 1638),[23] and the fifth poem, the pastoral dialogue 'Lovely Sheaphard', may also be by Randolph.[24] These settings by George Jeffreys, Christopher Hatton's life-long servant (see Chapter Four), are an indication that Hatton acted as a patron to Randolph in Cambridge in the fifteen or so years before the poet's untimely death in 1635. In 1640 Hatton had a marble monument erected in memory of Randolph in the church where he was buried at Blatherwick, Northamptonshire; the memorial stone was made by Nicholas Stone and inscribed with a verse by Peter Hausted, the other Hatton protégé of this period.[25]

In March 1632 King Charles I and Queen Henrietta Maria visited Cambridge and were, in the time-honoured tradition, entertained by plays which were produced by individual Colleges but overseen and supported financially by the University.[26] On 19 March they attended a performance of Peter Hausted's comedy *The Rivall Friends* given in the hall of Trinity College by students from Queens' College, and a day later they witnessed a performance of Thomas Randolph's *The Jealous Lovers*, again in Trinity College hall but now given by the students of that college. Randolph's *The Jealous Lovers* was a great success and when the comedy was published, later the same year, one of its dedicatory poems was assigned 'To the truely noble Knight / Sir CHRISTOPHER HATTON.'[27] Peter Hausted's comedy, *The Rivall Friends*, performed the previous day by Trinity's rival college, Queens', had not been so well received.[28] George Jeffreys, perhaps already working for Christopher Hatton, composed some of the music for the performance. This has survived in his scorebook, British Library Add. MS 10,338; folio 43 is headed 'Songs made for Dr Hausteds Comedy called ye Rivall freinds [*sic*] Acted before ye Kinge & Queene An[n]o 1631. [NS 1632] 19. March', and then follow:

---

[23] *The Maskque of Vices* ('Say Daunce how shall wee go') is part of *The Muses' Looking-Glass*; 'Musicke thou Queene of Soules', 'Coy Cœlia dost thou see' and 'Why sigh you swayne' (*Dialogue Nymphe & Sheaphard*) are from the poems. See W.C. Hazlitt ed., *Poeticall and Dramatic Works of Thomas Randolph* (London, 1875), i, 587, 586, 193 & 585 respectively.
[24] G.C. Moore Smith, 'Some Unpublished Poems of Thomas Randolph (1605-1635)', *Palaestra*, cxlviii (1925), 244-57.
[25] W.L. Spiers, 'The Note-Book and Account Book of Nicholas Stone', *Walpole Society*, vii (1918-19), 129 & Plate XLIIb.
[26] A.H. Nelson ed., *Records of Early English Drama: Cambridge* (Toronto, 1989), 731-7 & 779.
[27] For a modern edition of the play see Hazlitt ed. (1875), i, 51-172. The only music surviving from the play is a song for Bbc by Thomas Holmes (?c.1580-1638) in *Lbl* Add. 11,608, f. 18: 'Oberon. (or) ye Madmans songe. / Sung in a Comedy at Cambridge before ye King, & Queene. by ye Author.'
[28] L.J. Mills, *Peter Hausted* (Bloomington, 1944), 17-37. A cast list for *The Rivall Friends* survives penned into a printed book in the British Library (664.b.45) once owned by Thomas Alston; the list is transcribed in Nelson ed. (1989), 641-2.

Folios
43-5   'Drowsy Phœbus com[e] away' 'Dialogue' CCBbc & 5vv chorus
45ᵛ   'Have pity greefe' Cbc
46   'Cruell but once againe' Cbc
46ᵛ-7   'Cupid if a God thou art' CCATBbc
47ᵛ-8   'To the Ladyes Ioy, delight' CCATBbc
48ᵛ-9   'But why do ye wing'd minutes fly so fast away?' CCATBbc
49ᵛ-51 'Haue you a desyre to see the glorious Heavens' CCATBbc

A note on folio 51 states that 'The Dialogue Drowsy Phebus & ye rest to this place we made to and sung in Dr Hausteds unfortunate Comedy at Cambridge before ye Kinge and Queene called ye Rivall Freinds. [16]31 [NS 1632].'[29] The title-page of the published version of the play (London, 1632) is as follows:[30]

> The Rivall Friends. A comœdie, as it was acted before the King and Queens Majesties, when out of their princely avour they were pleased to visite their Universitie of Cambridge, upon the 19. day of March. 1631 [NS 1632]. Cryed downe by boyes, faction, envie, and confident ignorance, approv'd by the judicious, and now exposed to the publique censure, by the authour, Pet. Hausted M[aste]r in Artes of Queenes Colledge. Non tanti est ut placeam insanire.

The Cambridge première of *The Rivall Friends* was doomed from the beginning; the comedy had first been prepared for a performance on 8 March 1632 but had been postponed due to an accident that had befallen the Chancellor, Lord Holland. The performance was rescheduled for the Royal visit but its contents, particularly the vivid portrayals of low-life, were deemed unbefitting for the Royal presence.[31] This, combined with intense rivalries surrounding the play and its competitor, Randolph's *The Jealous Lovers*, eventually led to the suicide of the Vice-Chancellor of the University, Henry Butts, on 1 April 1632.[32] Further links between Hausted

---

[29] The fact that Hausted is described as 'D[octo]r' when he was not created a Doctor of Divinity until 1642 (Venn & Venn (1922), Part 1, ii, 332) and that a marginal note to the song 'Cruell but once againe' states that 'This Song was made for the Comody but I thinke not sunge', are indications that these are retrospective copies; see Chapter Four for full details of Jeffreys and *Lbl* Add. 10,338. 'Drowsy Phoebus, come away', 'Have pity, grief; I cannot pay' and 'Cruel! but once again' are published in I. Spink ed., *English Songs 1625-1660*, Musica Britannica, xxxiii, (London, rev. 2/1977), Nos. 96-8, pp. 153-61. Other musical settings for the play can be found in Henry Lawes' autograph songbook (*Lbl* Add. 53,723: 'Haue pittye Greife', f. 43ᵛ and 'Cruell! but once againe', f. 44) although these may have been written for a later performance; W. McC. Evans, *Henry Lawes* (New York, 1941), 74-5, and P. Willetts, *The Henry Lawes Manuscript* (London, 1969), 46-7.
[30] For a modern edition see L.J. Mills ed., *Peter Hausted's The Rival Friends* (Bloomington, 1951).
[31] A.W. Ward & A.R. Waller ed., *The Cambridge History of English Literature* (Cambridge, 1932), vi, 324-5.
[32] PRO SP 16/215, f. 14: an anonymous letter concerning the suicide of Henry Butts; it is transcribed in Nelson ed. (1989), 641-2.

and Hatton will become apparent later in the chapter when we consider Hatton's religious affinities and his patronage of the High Church party.

Hatton's patronage of the arts continued throughout the 1630s. In 1638 Michael East dedicated *The Seventh Set of Bookes* to Hatton, 'the truely noble lover of learning, and patron of arts' and, as will be shown in Chapter Two, the known acquisitions of music date from this period. Music was just one of Hatton's many interests and, although the central concern of this study is Hatton's musical patronage, it should be noted that music was not Hatton's primary pastime. His main interests concerned the preservation of the past in the form of transcriptions of medieval records and genealogical research into the families of English knights.[33] On 1 May 1638, together with his colleagues William Dugdale (1605-86), Thomas Shirley (1597-c.1665) and Edward Dering (1598-1644), Hatton formed a private association called *Antiquitas Rediviva*.[34] The results of the research undertaken by this learned society have survived amongst the Cotton Manuscripts in the British Library and the Hatton Manuscripts in the Bodleian Library.[35] The 'Hatton Manuscripts' were bought - via a London bookseller - by the Bodleian in 1671 and consist of 112 medieval manuscripts of which twenty-three came from monastic or cathedral libraries; eleven of the twenty-three had been borrowed by Hatton from Worcester Cathedral, presumably in 1644, and never returned.[36] Most important of all is 'Sir Christopher Hatton's Book of Seals' which survives in the Northamptonshire Record Office.[37] This is a collection of 529 charters of which 240 are facsimiles of the original deeds transcribed by Hatton's copyists with extreme skill and accuracy.[38] The 'Book of Seals' appears to have been compiled between 1638 and about 1641 when Hatton's association of antiquaries was forced to disband due to the membership's differing political allegiances at the outbreak of Civil War.

In comparison with his exalted status as a patron of the arts, Hatton's political and court career was frankly unspectacular. He had been admitted to Gray's Inn on 18 March 1620[39] and had been created a knight at Charles I's

---

[33] Sir Symon Archer described Hatton as 'a generall sercher of all antiquityes concerning the whole kingdome, but chiefelye Northamptonshire his own country [*sic*]. It doth cost him an hundred poundes per ann. in abstracting Records. - Sr Christopher hath almost an hundred bookes of his own abstracting, of very choyce antiquityes generally for the whole Kingdome.'; draft of a letter to Thomas Habington (26 December 1637) quoted in W. Hamper ed., *The Life, Diary, and Correspondence of Sir William Dugdale* (London, 1827), 171 footnote.
[34] For more on Dugdale's antiquarianism see G.Parry, *The Trophies of Time: English Antiquarians of the Seventeenth Century* (Oxford, 1995), 217-48.
[35] C.G.C. Tite ed., [Thomas Smith] *Catalogue of the Manuscripts in the Cottonian Library 1696* (Cambridge, 1984), 6; and F. Madan, H.H.E. Craster & N. Denholm-Young ed., *A Summary Catalogue of Western Manuscripts in the Bodleian Library* (Oxford, 1937), ii/2, 801-63.
[36] I. Philip, *The Bodleian Library in the Seventeenth and Eighteenth Centuries* (Oxford, 1983), 56-8.
[37] NRO FH 170.
[38] L.C. Loyd & D.M. Stenton ed., *Sir Christopher Hatton's Book of Seals* (Oxford, 1950).
[39] J. Foster, *The Register of Admissions to Gray's Inn, 1521-1889* (London, 1889), 159.

Coronation on 2 February 1626.[40] In 1636 he became Steward of Higham Ferrers and of the manors of Warrington, Irchester, Rushden and Raunds,[41] and he was Member of Parliament for Higham Ferrers in the 'Long Parliament' of 1640.[42] Until 1642 he remained, in fact, 'a country rather than a court luminary'.[43] The late 1630s proved to be an expensive period for Hatton: between 1635 and 1639 he was fined £7,386 for encroaching on the royal forest of Rockingham;[44] between 1638 and 1640 he had Kirby Hall extensively remodelled by Nicholas Stone;[45] in 1638 he supplied the stone for the refacing of his *alma mater*, Jesus College, Cambridge;[46] and he is known to have spent a great deal of money in pursuing his leisure-time activities.[47] His manner of living meant that by 1642 he was £18,600 in debt and his zealous support of the Royalist cause certainly did not help his dire financial situation.[48] In 1641, in an attempt to rectify an immediate financial crisis, he mortgaged his manors and advowson in Church and Chapel Brampton to his uncle, Sir Thomas Hatton, and the Hatton estates were diminished still further over the following decade.[49] In some respects the outbreak of war in September 1642 was, for Hatton, 'a godsend in heavy disguise'[50] as it meant he could throw himself wholeheartedly into the King's cause and ignore his own financial plight. The Civil War period, disastrous for so many noblemen, was actually the high point of Hatton's career; not since the time of the first Sir Christopher had the Hatton family played such an important rôle in the monarch's affairs.

Charles I entered Oxford on 29 October 1642 accompanied by four Princes and parading Parliamentarian colours captured at the battle of Edgehill six days earlier. The welcome was a warm one and, after being

---

[40] Metcalfe (1885), 186.
[41] *DNB*, ix, 163.
[42] Keeler (1954), 208.
[43] Pinto (1990), 87.
[44] P.A.J. Pettit, *The Royal Forests of Northamptonshire: A Study in their Economy, 1558-1714*, Northampton Record Society, xxiii (1968), 88.
[45] For full details see Spiers (1918-19), 119 & 125. Nicholas Stone, Charles I's master mason, was influenced by Inigo Jones in his use of Italianate features in the remodelling at Kirby: e.g., the south-east staircase was copied from Palladio, and busts of Apollo and Marcus Aurelius were incorporated into his design (the bust of Marcus Aurelius still survives above the north loggia and bears the date 1638 on its base).
[46] Royal Commission on Historical Monuments, *The City of Cambridge* (London, 1959), i, 86.
[47] See footnote 33 above.
[48] NRO FH 4106: catalogue of Hatton's debts in 1642.
[49] Moulton Park and Warren were mortgaged in 1647, as were Gretton manor, Cottingham Woods, Pipewell Woods and Middleton Thick a year later, and in 1649 both the Wellingborough and Sulby estates were sold. The Bramptons were finally sold to William Gore in 1657; Turner (1965), Chapter 1, *passim*. Hatton's dealings were not always strictly legal: following an agreement with Thomas, Lord Brundell of Deene 'for a generall division and inclosure' of land at Deenethorpe (16 September 1637), the scheme faltered for 'the Lord Hatton (contrarie to his agreement under his hand) sould his lands there unto the tenants and many others whosoever would buye'; M.E. Finch, *The Wealth of Five Northamptonshire Families* (London, 1956), 157.
[50] Pinto (1990), 88.

presented with a bag of money by the mayor and listening to a speech from the University's deputy orator, the King took up residence in Christ Church.[51] Hatton joined the King at Oxford; at first he took rooms in Hart Hall but later moved into Christ Church with the Court.[52] His support of the Royalist cause was recognised on 29 July 1643 when he was raised to the peerage as Baron Hatton of Kirby. On 26 December of the same year he was sworn as a privy councillor and on 29 December he became the Comptroller of the King's Household; during the same year he was made keeper of Olney Park, Buckinghamshire.[53] Hatton played an active part in the politics of the Civil War: he was a signatory to the peers' 'Letter to the Council' in Scotland in November 1643,[54] acted as a joint commissioner for the King at the conference of Uxbridge from 28 January to 22 February 1645[55] and undertook a number of 'diplomatic' missions.[56]

Despite the upheavals of the time, Hatton continued to patronise writers, theologians and musicians. William Dugdale was in Oxford between 1642 and 1646 and continued his association with Hatton; it is not clear how much time Hatton found for his own antiquarian research but he certainly encouraged others in their work. Dugdale, who was to be knighted and created Garter Principal King of Arms in 1677, had been commissioned by Hatton to survey the monuments of England's principal churches and cathedrals; Hatton had apparently foreseen the mass destruction of monuments by the 'Presbyterian contagion'.[57] Dugdale dedicated his *History of St. Pauls Cathedral* (1658) to Hatton and specially acknowledged his obligation to his patron in the second dedication of his *Antiquities of Warwickshire* (1656). Here he thanks Hatton for 'procuring for me, both accesse to most of the publique records in this Nation, and affording me the chief support I then had, whilst I laboured therein', and in his autobiography Dugdale states that Hatton 'made him soon acquainted with Sir *Thomas Fanshawe*, (his near Kinsman) at that Time the King's Remembrancer in the *Exchequer*, (afterward Lord Viscount *Fanshawe*,) by Means of which great Office he had the Custody of divers Leiger-Books, and other choice

---

[51] P. Gregg, *King Charles I* (London, 1981), 369-70.
[52] Dugdale, 24 May 1644: 'My Lo[rd] Hatton removed from Hart hall to his lodgings in Christchurch'; W. Hamper ed. (1827), 68.
[53] *DNB*, ix, 163.
[54] W.D. Macray ed., *Clarendon's The History of the Rebellion and Civil Wars in England* (Oxford, 1888), iii, 287-8, note 6 (Clarendon's Book VII, § 369).
[55] C.H. Firth & R.S. Raith, *Acts and Ordinances of the Interregnum, 1642-1660* (London, 1911), i, 609 & 612.
[56] Dugdale, 15 January and 3 February 1645: 'Lo[rd] Hatton went to Banbury'; Hamper ed. (1827), 77. A long stay in Banbury with Dugdale in March 1645 was noted by Secretary Nicholas who asked Hatton if it was his intention 'to goe to London & quitt the king, & it seemes by yo[u]r long absence you care little for o[u]r company here' (Nicholas in Oxford to Hatton in Banbury, 30 March 1645); *Lbl* Add. 29,549, f. 54, quoted in Pinto (1990), note 49.
[57] W. Dugdale, *The History of St. Pauls Cathedral in London* (London, 1658), 'Epistle Dedicatory' (to Hatton); see also Parry (1995), 217-48.

Manuscripts of great Antiquity; specially that notable record called the *Red Book*; as also *Testa de Nevill, Kirby's Quest. Nomina Villarum*, and others: to all which by his Favour he had free access'.[58] Perhaps more important was the reconvening in Oxford of Hatton's religious coterie: Peter Hausted, Jeremy Taylor (1613-67) and Peter Gunning (1614-84).

Hatton's patronage of this group of High Church clergymen had its roots in Cambridge in the early 1630s and revolved around the eminent Arminian, Edward Martin (d.1662), one-time chaplain to Archbishop Laud and President of Queens' College, Cambridge. Hatton was probably acquainted with Martin from at least October 1631, the date of Martin's appointment as Rector of Uppingham; in 1634 Martin appointed Peter Hausted as his curate. Hausted has already been mentioned in connection with the 1632 Royal visit to Cambridge; he was a native of Oundle, less than ten miles from Kirby Hall, and in 1636 he dedicated his *Ten Sermons* to Christopher Hatton. These sermons hint at his extreme Laudian views - views which had, in November 1634, caused a scandal following a sermon he preached at Great St Mary's, Cambridge in which he attacked the university puritans and advocated the use of Arminian ceremonies.[59] Edward Martin was one of those who spoke in Hausted's defence; during his presidency at Queens', Martin had himself introduced various ceremonies into the chapel services which, in 1641, resulted in the college being accused of covert Catholicism.[60] Hausted's appointment as Vicar of Gretton in 1639 was the direct result of Hatton's patronage, as was the additional sinecure of the Hatton advowson of Wold which Hausted held from 26 February 1643 to his death in 1645.[61] At Uppingham, in 1638, Hausted and Martin had been replaced by Jeremy Taylor, another one-time chaplain to Archbishop Laud and a Fellow of Caius College, Cambridge; Taylor, 'a great favourer of popish doctrines and ceremonies',[62] carried on the reforms instigated by Martin and Hausted which included the installation of an organ at Uppingham for use in divine worship.

In 1642 Taylor and Hausted moved to Oxford with Hatton, but Martin was prevented from joining them by the Parliamentarians who imprisoned

---

[58] [W. Dugdale], *The Life of that Learned Antiquary, Sir William Dugdale, Kt..... Published from an Original Manuscript* (London, 1713), 8.
[59] *Lbl* Harley 7019, f. 54: report on Hausted's 'Scandalous Sermon'; Mills (1944), 38-52.
[60] I owe many of the expressed ideas concerning Hatton's religious affinities and his patronage of the High Church party to Dr Lynn Hulse (unpublished paper presented at the Fourth Biennial Baroque Conference on Baroque Music at Royal Holloway and Bedford New College, University of London, July 1990); concerning the Cambridge Laudian/Arminian movement see H. Trevor-Roper, 'Laudianism and Political Power', *Catholics, Anglicans and Puritans* (London, 1987), 40-119, and J.G. Hoffman, 'The Puritan Revolution and the "Beauty of Holiness" at Cambridge: The Case of John Cosin, Master of Peterhouse and Vice-Chancellor of the University', *Proceedings of the Cambridge Antiquarian Society*, lxxii (1982-3), 94-105.
[61] Mills (1944), 49-51.
[62] *Lbl* Harley 7019, f. 79; actually a description of Taylor's Cambridge College, Caius, rather than of Taylor individually.

him in London until 1648. Both Taylor and Hausted were created Doctors of Divinity of the University of Oxford on 1 November 1642 and both continued their religious writings in Civil War Oxford.[63] Taylor accompanied the Royal army as Chaplain in Ordinary to Charles I and was captured at Cardigan Castle in 1645. At the end of the 'First Civil War' Taylor retired to Wales where he found a patron in the Earl of Carbery, then living at Golden Grove, Carmarthenshire; this house was immortalised in the title of Taylor's popular manual of devotion of 1655.[64] Taylor had written *The Sacred Order and Office of Episcopacy* in Oxford in 1642 and dedicated it to Hatton; during his enforced seclusion (1647-60) Taylor produced some of his great religious works, of which *A Discourse of The Liberty of Prophesying* (1647) and *The Great Exemplar of Sanctity and Holy Life* (1649) are dedicated to Baron Hatton. (For the sake of completeness, mention should be made of Taylor's *A New and Easie Institution of Grammar* (1647) which includes two dedicatory epistles: the first, in Latin by William Wyatt, is dedicated to Baron Hatton and the second, in English, is dedicated to Baron Hatton's son, Christopher Hatton IV.)[65] It is now generally accepted that Taylor was also responsible for Hatton's *The Psalter of David with Titles and Collects according to the Matter of Each Psalme* which was published in Oxford in 1644. Hatton undoubtedly superintended and paid for the edition; the engraving that precedes the title-page depicts King David with two horses bearing banners containing the Hatton coat-of-arms. There are two copies of the work in the Bodleian Library in Oxford.[66] One was presented to the library by Hatton on 2 May 1644 (probably the day of issue) and the other includes an inscription in Hatton's hand: 'For my noble & much honored friend S[i]r John Culpeper K[nigh]t Master of the Roles from Your affectionate & obliged servant Chr. Hatton. 7º May 1644'. Hatton's signature is crossed through and replaced with the signature of Edward Wood; this is explained in another appended note, this time in the hand of the antiquarian and writer, Anthony Wood: 'S[i]r John Culpep[er] K[nigh]t then lodging in my mothers house against Merton Coll. Christop. L[or]d Hatton then in Oxon sent him this book, w[hi]ch after Culpep[er']s departure, came into the hands of my brother Edw. Wood'. Wood also states that 'These Psalmes with Devotions at the end, were collected & published by Christopher L[or]d Hatton But written by Dr. Jer. Taylor of All S. Coll.'

The third member of Hatton's religious circle was Peter Gunning, a prominent Royalist divine, who preached regularly before the exiled Court at Oxford. Again it is likely that Hatton knew Gunning from Cambridge as

---

[63] J. Foster, *Alumni Oxonienses* (Oxford, 1891-2), Early Series, 673 & 1459.
[64] *DNB*, xix, 422-9.
[65] For full transcriptions of the dedicatory epistles to all Taylor's mentioned publications, see R.R. Herber ed., rev. C.P. Eden, *The Whole Works of the Right Rev. Jeremy Taylor* (London, 1847-54): v, 9-12; v, 341-64; ii, 1-4; & i, 62-3 respectively.
[66] *Ob* 8º A 25 Th. BS, and *Ob* Wood 811.

Gunning was a student and later Fellow of Clare Hall in the early 1630s.[67] He took holy orders and was appointed, as curate, to Little St Mary's in Cambridge by the Master and Fellows of Peterhouse, the Cambridge college most closely associated with the High-Church party. He preached against 'the rebellious League' in Great St Mary's, Cambridge, was imprisoned by the Parliamentarians for a short period and in 1644 retired to Oxford along with many of his Royalist friends.[68] On 10 July 1644 he was incorporated Master of Arts at the University of Oxford and was conferred with the degree of Bachelor of Divinity on 23 June 1646, the day before Oxford finally succumbed to Fairfax's forces.[69] In September 1646 Hatton appointed Gunning as his son's tutor[70] and surviving letters from 1647 indicate that Gunning acted as Hatton's agent in supplying books from London.[71] During the Commonwealth Gunning managed to maintain some kind of High-Church worship in the chapel of Exeter House in the Strand; the significance of this will become apparent later when the music of George Jeffreys is examined (Chapter Four). Finally, mention must be made of Hamon L'Estrange's *The Alliance of Divine Office*, a history of the liturgies and ceremonies of the Anglican Church, which was dedicated to Hatton in 1659. Hatton's patronage of the High-Church party will prove significant when examining the contents of his music library and the activities of his musicians.

Hatton's precise duties as Comptroller of the King's Household at the Oxford Court are difficult to determine. In London the Comptroller's duties had been well defined and the post was part of an elaborate administrative hierarchy.[72] Just how different things were in Oxford it is difficult to say, but we should perhaps remember that the act of leaving Whitehall was nothing new for the staff of the household departments, and that they were well used to attending the King and Queen (or the Royal children) on summer progresses and on the Court's moves between the palaces of Whitehall, Greenwich, Hampton Court and Windsor. It seems that no radical step was involved in the Court's move from London.[73] Even so, it appears that the court musicians did *not* move to Oxford *en masse*[74] and, for reasons

---

[67] Bachelor of Arts 1632, Master of Arts 1635; Venn & Venn (1922), Part 1, ii, 274.
[68] *DNB*, viii, 788-91; and P. Bliss ed., [Anthony Wood] *Athenae Oxoniensis* (1813-21), iv, 140-5.
[69] Foster (1891-2), Early Series, 619.
[70] Dugdale's diary entry for 9 September 1646: 'Mr Gunning came to Kirby as Tutor to Mr. Ch. Hatton'; Hamper ed. (1827), 93.
[71] *Ob* Bodley 878, ff. 10, 11, 13 & 22: letters from Gunning to Hatton dated: n.d., 10 February 1647, n.d., and 16 March 1647 respectively; and ff. 8 & 17-18: lists of books in Gunning's hand.
[72] See K. Sharpe, 'The Image of Virtue: The Court and Household of Charles I, 1625-1642', *The English Court from the Wars of the Roses to the Civil War*, ed. D. Starkey (London, 1987), 226-60.
[73] G.E. Aylmer, *The King's Servants* (London, 2/1974), 409.
[74] A. Ashbee, *Records of English Court Music* (Snodland, 1988), iii, pp. xii-xiii & 115-29.

which will become clear, I shall suggest that Hatton's duties - perhaps unofficially - included the overseeing of music. It is my contention that music played a small but significant part in life at the Oxford Court and that Hatton's musicians acted as 'replacement' court musicians; this hypothesis is examined in detail in Chapter Five.

Official information concerning the Court between 1642 and 1646 is scarce and only a small number of Royalist records - including the Bankes Papers and the records of the Royal secretaries, Nicholas and Walker[75] - survived the decision, in June 1646 by the Royalist remnants, to destroy all their papers before surrendering.[76] The memoirs of Edward Hyde, First Earl of Clarendon (1609-74), John Aubrey (1626-97), William Dugdale, Lady Ann Fanshawe (1625-80) and Anthony Wood (1632-95) do, however, supply much information concerning Civil War Oxford.[77] Secretary Nicholas lodged at Pembroke College; Clarendon, then Sir Edward Hyde, Chancellor of the Exchequer, lodged at All Souls' College; other members of the Privy Council were housed in Postmasters's Hall opposite Merton College; and Prince Rupert returned to St John's where, in Laud's time, he had been created Master of Arts of the University. The footsoldiers of the Royalist army were billeted in villages around Oxford, the cavalry headquarters were at Abingdon, ammunition was stored in the cloisters and tower of New College, the Law and Logic Schools of the Bodleian Library became granaries and cloth was cut for the Royalist Army's uniforms in the Music and Astronomy Schools, and the great quadrangle of Christ Church was converted into animal pens. Despite the chaos, inside Christ Church the King managed to maintain some splendour: the master of the revels organised entertainments, William Davenant (1606-68) continued to write verse and

---

[75] The papers of Sir John Bankes (1589-1644) - Attorney General 1634-44, present at the Oxford Court 1642-4 - were discovered at Lydney Park Estate Office, Gloucestershire in 1949 and are now on deposit in the Bodleian Library Oxford; correspondence of Sir Edward Nicholas: *Lbl* Egerton 2533-62 (see G.F. Warner ed., *The Nicholas Papers. Correspondence of Sir Edward Nicholas* (1886), i); and Edward Walker, *Historical Discourses Upon Several Occasions* [1664] (London, 1705) reissued as *Historical Collections... Relating to the... Rebellion and Civil War in England* (London, 1707).

[76] J.F. Larkin, 'Royal Proclamations of King Charles I 1625-46', *Stuart Royal Proclamations*, ii (Oxford, 1983), p. vi.

[77] Clarendon, *The History of The Rebellion and Civil Wars in England* (Oxford, 1702-4), 3 vols; and [R. Scrope and T. Monkhouse ed.,] *State Papers Collected by Edward, Earl of Clarendon, Commencing from the Year MDCXXI, Containing the Materials from which his History was Composed* (Oxford, 1767-86), 3 vols (see also W.D. Macray ed., *Calendar of the Clarendon State Papers Preserved in the Bodleian Library* [1649-57] (Oxford, 1869-76), ii & iii); the papers and correspondence of John Aubrey: *Ob* Aubrey MSS (see J. Walker ed., [J. Aubrey] *Letters Written by Eminent Persons in the Seventeenth and Eighteenth Centuries, to which are Added Lives of Eminent Men* (London, 1813)); [W. Dugdale], *The Life of that Learned Antiquary, Sir William Dugdale, Kt..... Published from an Original Manuscript* (London, 1713) (see Hamper ed. (1827)); the memoirs of Lady Ann Fanshawe: *Lbl* Add. 41,161 (see J. Loftis ed., *The Memoirs of Anne, Lady Halkett and Ann, Lady Fanshawe* (Oxford, 1979)); and Anthony Wood's diary: *Lbl* Harley 5409 and *Ob* Tanner 102, ff. 1-69 (see A. Clark ed., *The Life and Times of Anthony Wood* (Oxford, 1891-1900), 5 vols).

William Dobson (1610-46) even managed to paint court portraits.[78] There must also have been at least some music at the Oxford Court. Queen Henrietta Maria, who for safety's sake had been in Holland since February 1642, returned to England in January 1643; she was finally reunited with her husband in Oxford on 14 July 1643 and took up residence in the Warden's lodgings at Merton College. It is likely that the Chapel was given over to the Queen for the practice of her Roman Catholic faith and, as we shall see in Chapter Five, this raises some intriguing musical possibilities. The Queen remained in Oxford until 17 April 1644 when she escaped to France.[79] The increasingly beleaguered King continued to use Oxford as his headquarters until 27 April 1646 when, with the city under siege, he escaped under cover of darkness disguised as a servant. On 20 June 1646 Oxford surrendered to Sir Thomas Fairfax. The terms of surrender allowed Prince Rupert ten days in which to leave the country, the remaining 3,000 Royalist soldiers were dispersed peaceably and the ancient rights of Oxford were respected by the Parliamentarians (guards were even placed in the Bodleian Library to prevent looting). The King's unhappy story until his execution on 30 January 1649 is well known and need not be retold here. Christopher, First Baron Hatton left Oxford on 23 April 1646 and, after visiting Kirby and London, sailed from Dover on 24 November 1646 to join many other eminent Royalists in exile in Paris.[80]

Hatton's activities in Paris can be reconstructed fairly precisely from his letters - often under the pseudonyms Charles Parker or Simon Smith - to Sir Edward Nicholas[81] and from references in the diaries of William Dugdale and John Evelyn (1620-1706).[82] Evelyn visited Hatton in Paris a number of times[83] where he had comfortable quarters and was surrounded by his 'bookes and fiddles';[84] Hatton continued to collect books during this period

---

[78] J. Adair, *By the Sword Divided: Eyewitnesses of the English Civil War* (London, 1983), Chapter 5; C. Carlton, *Charles I* (London, 1983), 266; Gregg (1981), 369-70; M. Rogers, *William Dobson 1611-46* (London, 1983), 14-19.
[79] F.J. Varley, *The Siege of Oxford* (London, 1932), 6, 8 & 56-63.
[80] Dugdale's diary entries for 23 April 1646: 'Mr. Chr. Hatton went from Oxford', 24 November 1646: 'The Lord Hatton went from Dover'; and 27 November 1646: 'He arrived at Calice' (Hamper ed. (1827), 85 & 93). PRO SP 23/200, p. 143: printed pass issued by the Parliamentarian forces to enable Hatton to move around freely after the fall of Oxford (dated 25 June 1646). *Ob* Rawlinson Poet 62, f. 14^{r-v}: undated poem 'To my L[or]d Hatton at Calais' by the Royalist poet Martin Lluelyn (1616-82), 'Welcome on shore'.
[81] *Lbl* Egerton 2533-62, *passim*; see Warner ed. (1886-92).
[82] [Dugdale] (1713) (see Hamper ed. (1827)); and J. Evelyn, 'Kalendarium' [1620-1697], manuscript now in *Lbl* (see E.S. de Beer ed., *The Diary of John Evelyn* (London, 1955), 6 vols).
[83] de Beer ed. (1955), ii, 562; iii, 21-2 & 24.
[84] W.D. Macray ed. (1869), ii, 133: 17 May 1652, Hatton 'has changed lodgings, & moved all his books and fiddles... he lies as well as ever'; for other references to Hatton's intrigues in Paris see ibid., 6, 10, 40, 116 ('Lord Hatton's intelligence not always to be believed'), 143, 161, 229, 434 & 437.

and Peter Gunning appears to have acted as his book agent in London.[85] Hatton also maintained his links with various exiled High-Church clergymen; after his escape from prison in 1648 Edward Martin fled to Paris where he spent several years as Hatton's guest. Another clerical exile associated with Hatton at this time was John Cosin (1594-1672), one-time Master of Peterhouse, the Cambridge College most closely associated with the High-Church movement.[86] For almost a decade Hatton was involved in Royalist intrigues at the exiled Court of Queen Henrietta Maria and his efforts to restore the monarchy led to the Council of State in England requesting Sir Arthur Hesilridge to have him watched.[87]

Like most other prominent Royalists, Hatton had suffered various sequestrations and fines by the Parliamentarians;[88] his plottings in Paris meant that he was liable to lose all his estates so, in November 1651, he resolved to discontinue his visits to the exiled King and attempted to make peace with the Commonwealth administration.[89] Hatton's situation was undoubtedly helped by his wife's family connections: various members of the Montagu family had supported Parliament in the Civil War and were therefore well placed during the Commonwealth to plead Hatton's case. Elizabeth Hatton (née Montagu) remained in England during the Commonwealth and looked after the family's affairs;[90] her Steward and Secretary throughout this period was the musician George Jeffreys, and much correspondence exists between Jeffreys and Lady Hatton concerning the daily running of the estates.[91] During the 1650s Lady Hatton attended High-Church services held in the chapel of Exeter House on the north side of the Strand. These services were led by Peter Gunning, the Anglican divine so closely associated with the Hatton family, and were conducted strictly in accordance with the rites of the Church of England. Although frowned upon by the authorities, Cromwell connived at the practice and the Exeter House Chapel became a frequent resort for supporters of the High-Church movement. Occasionally there was some interference and the diarist John Evelyn records that on Christmas Day 1657 'The Chapell was surrounded

---

[85] *Ob* Bodley 878: papers relating to the formation of Hatton's library, 1646-9: lists of books offered to or purchased by him in England and France, bills and letters, including four from Peter Gunning (see footnote 71 above).

[86] *DNB*, iv, 1189-96; G. Ornsby ed., *The Correspondence of John Cosin, Together with other Papers Illustrative of his Life and Times*, Surtees Society, lii (London, 1869); Trevor-Roper (1987), 40-119, *passim*.

[87] R. Lemon & M.A.E. Green ed., *Calendar of State Papers, Domestic Series* (London, 1856-72), 1649-50: 184 & 461; 1650: 54.

[88] NRO FH 3981-4, 3987, 3989, 4000, 4002, 4011 & 4841; M.A.E. Green ed., *Calendar of the Proceedings of the Committee for Compounding, &c., 1643-1660* (2/Nendeln, Liechtenstein, 1967), 28, 31, 40, 42, 65, 88, 111, 233, 690, 1579-82, 1653 & 3305. His fine, set first at £4156, was reduced upon review to £3,226 (Keeler (1954), 208).

[89] *Calendar of State Papers, Domestic Series*, 1651-2, 3.

[90] Lady Hatton appears to have spent her time either at Kirby Hall or at Hatton House, Holborn which Baron Hatton had inherited in 1646 on the death of Elizabeth Newport-Hatton.

[91] *Lbl* Add. 29,548-96, *passim*; and NRO FH 1407, 3921 & 4180.

with Souldiers' and a number of the congregation, including Lady Hatton and Evelyn himself, were 'surpriz'd & kept Prisoners'.[92]

In September 1656 Baron Hatton was finally allowed to return to England.[93] Although Hatton had not suffered as badly as many Royalists his affairs were in chaos and, as usual, his debts were immense. Evelyn had visited Kirby Hall on 8 August 1654 and had found 'the seate naked'[94] and much of Hatton's precious library appears to have been dispersed. A requisition order dated 27 January 1644 instructs the authorities 'to bring away all such books in the library or study or any other place of Kirby House to Rockingham for the publick [use]'[95] and, in a document relating to household-sequestration assessments 1647-9, Hatton mentions that he has lost 'three cart loades of choyce bookes and manuscripts which I cannot value'[96] (it is not known whether music was included amongst these books and manuscripts). Hatton's attempts to rebuild his shattered estates were most unsuccessful; he had always been financially feckless and, although we must remember that the family had been saddled with enormous debts from the time of the Lord Chancellor Hatton, Christopher Hatton III's attempts to rebuild the family's fortunes were at best half-hearted and at worst incompetent. He leased parts of Hatton House and Gardens to Robert Smyth of Upton for £1,500 with a proviso for its speedy recovery, but before the redemption money could fall due he transferred the lease to Robert Johnson, making another £300 on the transaction; finding himself unable to repay the first instalment to Johnson, Hatton was finally forced to make the lease absolute.[97] Hatton also attempted to make money by building on the lands of Hatton Garden, and we read in Evelyn's diary for 7 June 1659 that he went to 'see the foundations now laying for a long streete, & buildings in *Hatton Garden* design'd for a little Towne: lately an ample garden:'[98] By 1664 things were becoming desperate and Hatton was forced to convey most of his Northamptonshire estates to his Lawyer, Richard Langhorne, and to a London merchant, John Clements. Arrangements were made for the gradual

---

[92] Evelyn, 'Kalendarium', 25 December 1657; de Beer (1955), iii, 203-4.
[93] *Calendar of State Papers, Domestic Series*, 1656-7, 116 & 583. *Lbl* Add. 29,586, ff. 14 & 15: permits for Baron Hatton to reside in London (1657-8); and *Lbl* Add. 29,548, f. 14: the same, signed by Oliver Cromwell (6 March 1658).
[94] Evelyn, 'Kalendarium', 25 August 1654; de Beer (1955), iii, 133-4.
[95] NRO FH 4841. Rockingham Castle is four miles west of Kirby Hall; it was the seat of Sir Lewis Watson until March 1643 when it was stormed by forces led by Lord Grey of Groby; thereafter it became a Parliamentarian garrison.
[96] PRO SP 23/200, p. 135.
[97] NRO FH 2044: concerning the mortgage of Hatton Gardens; Marryat & Broadbent (1930), 37.
[98] Evelyn, 'Kalendarium', 7 June 1659 (de Beer (1955), iii, 231). *Calendar of State Papers, Domestic Series*, 1661-2, 82: ?September 1661, 'Petition of Christopher, son and heir of Lord Hatton, to the King, for pardon for tenements already erected, and leave to build others on grounds already let for the purpose at Hatton House, Holborn, for which, till the Restoration, no licence could be obtained.'; and ibid.: 5 September 1661, 'Grant to the said Christopher Hatton of pardon of all forfeiture for building houses on the old foundations of Hatton House and licence to continue the buildings and erect new ones on the said ground.'

repayment of his debts and portions were secured for his younger son, Charles, and his three daughters, Alice, Mary and Jane.[99] When, in 1666, negotiations started concerning the marriage of his heir, Christopher Hatton IV, to Cecilia Tufton, daughter of the Second Earl of Thanet, he was still in debt to the tune of 'eight thousand and seven hundred pounds or thereabouts', and payment of the marriage portion of £5,000 was contingent upon the debts being cleared.[100]

At the Restoration the advancement which Hatton could quite justifiably have expected, as a loyal Royalist and previous Comptroller of the King's Household, was not forthcoming; although he was appointed as a Privy Councillor on 29 January 1662, high Court or Government office eluded him. The usual progression from Comptroller to Treasurer of the Royal Household was denied him,[101] his Viscountcy warrant, apparently signed at St Germain-en-Laye on 20 September 1649, was never ratified[102] and the rumour that he was to become Lord Privy Seal proved to be unfounded.[103] Clarendon, in his *History of the Rebellion*, described Hatton as 'a Person of great Reputation... which in a few years he found a way to diminish';[104] unfortunately Hatton lived up to Hyde's typically uncomplimentary remark. On 22 May 1662 he was appointed Governor of Guernsey, a difficult post and one for which he was totally unsuited. The island had supported Parliament and the Protectorate and, not surprisingly, there was a strong anti-monarchist feeling lingering; in 1662 the problems had been exacerbated when Anglicanism had been imposed on the Calvinistic islanders.[105] A Governor with patience and tact was clearly required. Hatton was not the man for the job: he was becoming increasingly morose and cantankerous, his judgements were erratic, he quarrelled with the island officers (he even imprisoned the Lieutenant-Governor), he taxed the island illegally, sold guns from Castle Cornet to the French and appropriated the pay of the garrison.[106] On 12 December 1664, less than a year after his arrival in Guernsey, Hatton was summoned home to face allegations of mismanagement. Hatton chose to ignore the command until, on 10 February 1665, Charles II ordered him to

---

[99] NRO FH 841: indenture dated 4 February 1664; Charles Hatton was to receive £1,000 and the daughters £2,000 each.
[100] NRO FH 2010: articles of agreement between Lord Hatton and the Dowager Countess of Thanet (4 July 1666).
[101] *Ob* Carte 74, f. 301: Hatton's unsuccessful petition to King Charles II to become 'Tresorer of your Royall Household'.
[102] The warrant of 21 December 1682 creating Christopher Hatton IV Viscount Hatton of Gretton records this fact; *Calendar of State Papers, Domestic Series*, 1682, 583.
[103] Historical Manuscripts Commission, *Fifth Report of The Royal Commission on Historical Manuscripts* (London, 1876), 156: letter from Andrew Newport to Sir Richard Leveson (25 September 1660).
[104] Clarendon (1703), ii (Book vi), 156.
[105] F.B. Tupper, *The History of Guernsey and its Bailiwick* (2/Guernsey, 1876), 363-6; and H.D. Turner, 'Viscount Hatton and the Government of Guernsey, 1670-1706', *Société Guernesiaise Report and Transactions 1969*, xvi (1970), 415-16.
[106] Turner (1965), Chapter 1, *passim*.

return to England and appointed Colonel Jonathan Atkins as Commissioner of Guernsey with the full powers of a Governor.[107] Despite various appeals for forgiveness Hatton was to remain under the King's deepest displeasure until his death in 1670, and he was never again to be trusted with government office.[108]

Hatton was a broken man. In the last few years of his life he deserted his family and, leaving his wife almost destitute at Kirby Hall, took lodgings in Scotland Yard where he continued to pursue his cultural - and not so cultural - activities oblivious to the needs of his dependants.[109] Even Hatton's faithful Steward and Secretary, George Jeffreys, despaired of his master and appears to have conducted the family's affairs through Christopher Hatton IV whenever possible.[110] (Jeffreys' position as Steward seems to have been taken in the 1660s by a 'Mr. Clough' who proved to be incompetent, as did his replacement William Neale; the Hatton stewards, secretaries, copyists and advisors are listed in Table 1.)[111] Despite all this, Hatton's patronage of the arts and sciences continued: he was one of the earliest Fellows of the Royal Society, and in 1667-9 he employed Dugdale's clerk Gregory King (1648-1712) to assist him in forming a heraldic collection.[112] Little is known about Hatton's patronage of musicians during this period although it is clear that by this time George Jeffreys pursued his musical interests quite independently of Hatton (see Chapter Four).[113]

---

[107] *Calendar of State Papers, Domestic Series*, 1670, & Addenda 1660-1670, 699; *Lbl* Add. 29,551, ff. 105-6: George Jeffreys to Hon. Christopher Hatton IV (24 November 1664); and Add. 29,577, ff. 48-9: Charles Lyttelton to Hon. Christopher Hatton IV (10 December 1664).
[108] *Calendar of State Papers, Domestic Series*, 1668-9, 643-4, & Addenda 1660-85, 150-1.
[109] The family correspondence is strangely sparse concerning Baron Hatton's personal affairs during this period - perhaps a later generation of the family had expurgated all embarrassing records? - but Roger North, Lady Hatton's nephew, gives a vivid account of the family's misfortunes at this time: *Lbl* Add. 32,516, f. 30^{r-v}. (*Lbl* Add. 32,516 is a draft of Roger North's 'Life of Dr Jno. North'; the passage is slightly watered down in the final manuscript version (dated 1728), *Lbl* Add. 32,514, § 41-2 (see P. Millard ed., [Roger North] *General Preface and Life of Dr John North* (Toronto, 1984), 116-17).)
[110] Letters from Jeffreys to Christopher Hatton IV: *Lbl* Add. 29,551, f. 35, 'at present a writt sued out against me to arrest me' unless he [Jeffreys] received payment from Lord Hatton (13 April 1663); Add. 29,552, f. 7, Jeffreys complains about 'their usage of me at Kirby' (10 January 1669); Add. 29,551, f. 259, copy of a defence by Jeffreys against complaints made by Lord Hatton (n.d.); and Add. 29,552, f. 302, Jeffreys describes an unexpected visit to Weldon by 'the great Don' (to collect some outstanding rents) but states that he was 'resolved not to stirr a foot towards him...' (25 April 1670).
[111] British Library and Northamptonshire Record Office Finch-Hatton Papers, *passim*.
[112] *DNB*, xi, 131.
[113] One scrap of evidence of Hatton's patronage of musicians in the 1660s comes in a letter from Hatton to Dean Barwick of St Paul's Cathedral (21 October 1661); Hatton recommends 'Henry Frost whom I have taken into my care from childhood' for a place in the cathedral choir: *Lgl* Arch. St P. 25,200/6.

Table 1   Christopher Hatton III's Associates, Musicians, Secretaries, etc.

Stephen Bing	occasional secretary and music copyist
William Bottomley	occasional secretary
George Bristoll	occasional secretary
William Bullock	occasional secretary
Thomas Checkley	occasional secretary
John Clements	financial advisor and creditor
[?] Clough	sometime steward
Henry Cooke	children's music tutor
Edward Dering	antiquarian associate
William Dugdale	occasional secretary and antiquarian colleague
Michael East	composer associate
James Freeston	occasional secretary
Henry Frost	singer
Joseph Glass	occasional secretary
William Goode	occasional secretary (G. Jeffreys's son-in-law)
Peter Gunning	children's tutor, book agent and clerical associate
Peter Hausted	clerical associate
George Holmes	secretary and occasional musician
Thomas Holmes	occasional secretary (cousin of G. Holmes)
Christopher Jeffreys	occasional secretary (G. Jeffreys's son)
George Jeffreys	steward, secretary and musician
John Jeffreys	occasional secretary (G. Jeffreys's brother)
William Jones	lawyer(?)
Gregory King	antiquarian colleague
Richard Langhorne	lawyer
John Lilly	occasional music copyist
John Mawson	London agent
William Neale	sometime steward
Thomas Randolph	poet/playwright associate
Thomas Shirley	antiquarian associate
Nicholas Stone	stonemason associate
Jeremy Taylor	clerical associate
Philip Willoughby	occasional secretary
Thomas Woodhall	occasional secretary

Christopher Hatton IV

Christopher Hatton III had married Elizabeth, the eldest daughter of Sir Charles Montagu of Cranbrook, Essex, on 8 May 1630 at Hackney, Middlesex.[114] The marriage connected the Hattons with other important and

---

[114] *DNB*, ix, 163.

influential families: Sir Charles Montagu was the younger brother of Edward, First Baron Montagu of Boughton (c.1562-1644) and of Henry, First Earl of Manchester (c.1563-1642), and one of Sir Charles' daughters, Anne, married Dudley, Fourth Baron North. Christopher Hatton III and Elizabeth had numerous children of whom there survived two sons, Christopher (1632-1706) and Charles (1635-c.1708), and three daughters, Alice, Mary and Jane. The two sons, although both interested in books and antiquarian studies, were of very different temperament to their father and showed no signs of Baron Hatton's instability. The 'incomparable' Charles Hatton,[115] a noted botanist and horticulturalist, had a particularly stormy relationship with his father; things came to a head in 1667 when Baron Hatton discovered that Charles had secretly married the daughter of General John Lambert (1619-83) who was Hatton's prisoner on Guernsey.[116] Charles Hatton was banished and never again spoke with his father.[117] Christopher Hatton III died at Kirby Hall on 4 July 1670 and was buried in Westminster Abbey. On succeeding to his father's titles and estates Christopher, Second Baron Hatton (later First Viscount Hatton) found that the late Lord had mortgaged 'all or most part of [the estates] for several great sums of moneys'.[118] Undeterred, Christopher Hatton IV set about rebuilding the 'shattered Estate'.[119] He proved to be a prudent and skilled financial manager and by 1677 he had been able to reach an agreement with his father's main creditor, John Clements.[120]

Hatton IV's career need only be described briefly: he became a Gentleman of the Privy Chamber of Charles II in 1662; he acted as Governor of Guernsey after his father's recall in February 1665; on 13 June 1667 he was made captain of the Lord Chamberlain's regiment of foot; in March 1670 he was appointed Deputy-Lieutenant of Northamptonshire; in July of the same year, on the death of his father, he became Governor of Guernsey; and on 13 December 1683 he was created First Viscount Hatton of Gretton.[121] It is a sad fact that perhaps the most significant factor contributing to Christopher Hatton IV's financial recovery was the death of his first wife in an explosion at Castle Cornet, Guernsey on 30 December 1672; lightning struck and ignited the gunpowder in the castle's storeroom and Hatton's wife, Cecilia, and his mother, Dowager Lady Elizabeth Hatton, were killed. Hatton himself miraculously escaped unharmed having been

---

[115] Roger North, 'The Life of Dr John North', *Lbl* Add. 32,514, § 42.
[116] *DNB*, xi, 458.
[117] *Calendar of State Papers, Domestic Series*, 1668-9, 643-4; for full details of Charles Hatton's life see H.D. Turner, 'Charles Hatton: A Younger Son', *Northamptonshire Past and Present*, iii/6 (1965-6), 254-61.
[118] NRO FH 2048: copy of a paper sent to John Clements by Lord Hatton (n.d. [?early 1670s]).
[119] North, *Lbl* Add. 32,514, § 42.
[120] NRO FH 2044: the case between John Clements and Lord Hatton (n.d. [1671-2]).
[121] *DNB*, ix, 163-4; Hatton's governorship of Guernsey is described in detail in Turner (1970), 416-26.

blown out of bed onto the battlements.¹²² The family lawyer, Richard Langhorne, was quick to advise a second marriage 'with a fortune of 8,000*l*. or thereabouts'.¹²³ In 1675 Hatton married Frances Yelverton, the daughter of Sir Henry Yelverton, Baronet of Easton Maudit, Northamptonshire and of Susan, Baroness Grey de Ruthyn (in her own right); in the event the marriage brought with it a fortune of £6,000.¹²⁴ Frances died in May 1684 leaving Hatton still without a male heir; in August 1685 he was married for a third time, to Elizabeth, daughter of Sir William Haslewood of Maidwell, Northamptonshire, and by this marriage had two sons, William (1690-1760) and Henry Charles (*c*.1700-60). William died unmarried and the title passed briefly to his brother with whom the title expired.¹²⁵

By the time of his death on 21 September 1706 Christopher, Viscount Hatton had restored the family's fortunes and had even begun to repair the damage done to the family library. It has been noted above that books and manuscripts from the library at Kirby were confiscated by the Parliamentarians and, as will be shown in Chapter Two, many other books were sold in the early 1670s in order to help the family's dire financial situation. Even so, in August 1694 the library was still important enough to be included in a catalogue of 'all ye Manuscripts in all ye private libraries in England' proposed by University College, Oxford.¹²⁶ We turn now to a detailed examination of the Hatton music collection.

---

¹²² C. Ozanne, 'Contemporary Accounts of the Explosion at Castle Cornet, December 1672', *Report & Transactions* [of] *La Société Guernesiaise*, xi (1930), 41-54.
¹²³ NRO FH 3845: letter from Richard Langhorne to Christopher Hatton IV (13 October 1673).
¹²⁴ NRO FH 3101: marriage settlement, Lord Hatton and Hon. Frances Yelverton (18 November 1675).
¹²⁵ *DNB*, ix, 164.
¹²⁶ *Lbl* Add. 29,574, f. 317: letter from Charles Hatton to Viscount Hatton (2 August 1694). Other references to the library at Kirby Hall: *Lbl* Add. 29,576, f. 134: letter from Charles Hatton to Viscount Hatton (12 October 1703), mentioning the addition of King Charles I's works and Clarendon's *The History of the Rebellion* to the library (the latter had been presented by Lord Clarendon, the son of the author); and NRO FH 4287: 'Books lent to Dr Stillingfleet, Deane of St Paules out of ye MSS belonging to ye L[or]d Hatton' (23 December 1683) and notes as to which had been returned (5 August 1705).

CHAPTER TWO

THE HATTON MUSIC COLLECTION

The Survival of the Hatton Music Collection

It has already been noted that music was just one of the Hattons' many cultural interests; even so, the few surviving references to music and musicians in the Hatton archives indicate that music did play an important part in family life. We know that Orlando Gibbons spent some time at one of the Hatton residences around 1612;[1] the organist and composer George Jeffreys was, for many years, Christopher Hatton III's Steward and presumably also had musical duties (see Chapter Four); and another of Baron Hatton's employees, George Holmes, also appears to have been a musician (see below). A letter of 11 December 1656 from George Jeffreys to Lady Hatton indicates that a Captain Cooke was employed to teach the Hatton children, and that he visited the Hatton residences regularly.[2] This was probably the Henry Cooke (*c*.1615-72) who, at the Restoration, was to make his name as Master of the Children of the Chapel Royal. During the Civil War Cooke joined the Royalist forces, eventually becoming a captain - a title which he used for the rest of his life - and throughout the Commonwealth period, like many Royalist musicians, he earned a living as a music teacher.[3] The likelihood that Cooke was associated with the Hatton family in the 1650s has important implications. As we shall see, Baron Hatton owned a substantial amount of Italian music and, as it was Cooke who, in the 1660s, introduced Italianate techniques of composition to the Chapel Royal and was himself a celebrated practitioner of the Italian style of singing,[4] it is tempting to suggest that Cooke's Italianate tastes were perhaps influenced by the Hatton music collection. Evidence that there was an organ at Kirby Hall comes in two undated letters from Christopher Hatton IV to his wife Cecilia which mention the shipment of organ pipes to Kirby;[5] this

---

[1] According to the dedication to Gibbons' *First Set of Madrigals and Mottets* (London, 1612).
[2] *Lbl* Add. 29,550, f. 275: '.... My Sweet Mistresses have been to ask Blessing and are very well, Capt: Cooke came into ye lodging yesterday to teach them, when he promised to do his utmost for them....'
[3] P. Dennison, 'Cooke, Henry', *New Grove*, iv, 710-11; ibid., *Pelham Humfrey* (Oxford, 1986), 13-17. Cooke's name occurs in a list of 'excellent and able masters' in the Rules and Directions prefixed to John Playford's *A Musicall Banquet* (London, 1651); his name is given under the heading for 'Voyce or Viol'.
[4] John Evelyn described Cooke as 'esteem'd the best singer after the *Italian* manner of any in *England*', 'Kalendarium', 28 October 1654 (see de Beer ed. (1955), iii, 144).
[5] *Lbl* Add. 29,571, ff. 64-5 & 68.

instrument was probably used at the family's private devotions as well as for secular music-making.[6]

The evidence for an extensive music library once belonging to the Hatton family is, on the face of it, sparse. With the exception of six manuscript fragments,[7] no music survives in the Hatton archives in the Northamptonshire Record Office and music does not feature in any of the numerous catalogues and lists of books once in the Hatton library.[8] However, a close examination of the printed music collection in Christ Church, Oxford and a related group of manuscripts has revealed that Christopher, First Baron Hatton was the owner of a substantial and important music library - perhaps one of the richest seventeenth-century collections yet identified - and that much of it still survives today at Christ Church. The collection has important implications when considering music at the Oxford Court (1642-6) and offers an excellent example of the dissemination and influence of Italian music at that time.

The reason that this collection has, until recently, remained unnoticed must be due partly to the general lack of direct archival evidence relating to music during the Caroline period (considering the background of civil war and regicide it is not surprising that the chroniclers concentrated on more important things than music). But perhaps the main reason that the Hatton collection has been overlooked is due to the traditionally accepted view that it was Henry Aldrich (1648-1710, Dean of Christ Church from 1689 to 1710) who collected most of the Christ Church Italian music on visits to Italy.[9] It is not in doubt that on his death in 1710 Aldrich bequeathed a substantial music collection to his college and that this included many of the Italian prints which concern us in the present study, but it can now be shown that it was not Aldrich who was responsible for the original purchase of much of this music.[10] It is in fact debatable whether Aldrich actually visited Italy at all.

---

[6] It should be noted that Kirby Hall does not have a chapel. However, it is noted in Chettle rev. Leach (1986), 8, that the room over the gateway in the north loggia was used as a chapel; no dates are given.

[7] NRO FH 1395, 1997, 2398, 3431A, & 3431B: melodic lines of dance movements copied by George Holmes; and NRO FH 3431C: dance movements in lute tablature copied by George Jeffreys.

[8] NRO FH 642, 2444, 2659, 2661, 4016, 4017, 4019-23, & 4025; and *Ob* Bodley 878. It should be noted that music was rarely included in general library catalogues of the period (except for theoretical music books); it seems that music was regarded as 'performing material' and was therefore separate from the main body of a library collection (possibly stored in moveable chests); see S. Jayne, *Library Catalogues of the English Renaissance* (Berkeley, 1956; rev. 2/Godalming, 1983), *passim*.

[9] H. Watkins Shaw, 'Aldrich, Henry', *New Grove*, i, 234-6; W.G. Hiscock, *Henry Aldrich of Christ Church 1648-1710* (Oxford, 1960), 13.

[10] In 1718 a small music collection was bequeathed to the college by the elder Richard Goodson (*c*.1655-1718) and the Aldrich and Goodson bequests together account for most of the printed and manuscript music in the Christ Church collection today; the only significant item to have been acquired in recent times is John Barnard's *The First Book of Selected Church Musick* (London, 1641) purchased in 1917 (*Och* Mus. 544-53).

Hiscock considers that Aldrich showed first-hand knowledge of Italy in his *Elementa Architecturae Civilis* (Oxford, 1789) and Humphrey Wanley (1672-1726), who first catalogued the Harleian Manuscripts in the British Library, also believed that Aldrich travelled in Italy; Sir John Hawkins quotes a note by Wanley once appended to Harley MS 1265 (which contains Carissimi's cantata 'Ferma lascia'):[11]

> This Giacomo Carissimi was in his time the best composer of church-music in all Italy. Most of his compositions were with great labour and expence collected by the late learned dean of Christ-Church, Dr. Henry Aldrige. However, some things of Carissimi I had the luck to light upon, which the great man could not procure in Italy, of which this Cantata was one. Carissimi living to be about ninety years old, composed much, and died very rich as I have heard.

It is known that Aldrich travelled to Cologne in the summer of 1673 but there is no archival evidence to corroborate the theory that he visited Italy.[12] Aldrich ordered his personal papers to be destroyed after his death so we do not have details of his musical acquisitions. However, it appears that soon after 1670 Aldrich obtained the Hatton music collection, probably in its entirety, and added it to an already existing library (see below).[13]

The most obvious surviving items from the Hatton collection at Christ Church are two sets of partbooks (Mus. 432/612-13 and 708-12) which both have sumptuous bindings containing the Hatton family crest or coat of arms. These bindings must have been specially commissioned by the Hatton family, and it is not surprising that one of the sets (Mus. 708-12) is Orlando Gibbons' *The First Set of Madrigals and Mottets* of 1612 which was dedicated to Sir Christopher Hatton II. It is possible that this very set was Gibbons' presentation copy to his patron. The dark-brown calf binding of each partbook is richly gilt and at the centre is the Hatton crest upon a torse: a hind statant or (see Plate 1).[14] Christ Church Mus. 432 and 612-13 are a set of manuscript partbooks (an organbook and two bass viol parts) bound in dark-blue morocco, again richly tooled in gold, but here containing the full Hatton coat of arms (azure, a chevron between three garbs or) flanked with

---

[11] Hiscock (1960), 13. Sir John Hawkins, *A General History of the Science and Practice of Music* (London, 1776), iv, 93 and quoted in A.V. Jones, *The Motets of Carissimi* (Ann Arbor, 1982), i, 81-2; Wanley's note in *Lbl* Harley 1265 - presumably once on a loose leaf - is now lost.

[12] *Calendar of State Papers, Domestic Series*, 1673, 478: letter from Dr Fell to Aldrich (4 August 1673).

[13] This theory has also been examined by David Pinto (1990). I am indebted to Mr Pinto for engaging in a long and complex correspondence concerning the Hatton music collection; although we disagree on a number of details we are united on the fundamental proposition that much of the Hattons' music survives today in Christ Church, Oxford.

[14] Pinto (1990), 79, notes that the corner-pieces have been identified as tools from the workshop of John Bateman (*fl.* 1567-1635), bookbinder by appointment to James I (see M.M. Foot, *The Henry Davis Gift: A Collection of Bookbindings* (London, 1978), i, 35-49).

the inscription 'CHR:HATTON DEO:ET PATRIÆ' and encircled by a riband from which hangs the ensign medallion of the Order of the Bath (see Plate 2). (The contents and copyists of the partbooks are examined in Chapter Three.) The evidence for the survival of the rest of the Hatton music collection in Christ Church is not quite so obvious, but is greatly helped by one important document in the Northamptonshire Record Office. Finch-Hatton MS 2652 is a bill of sale dated November 1638, from the London bookseller Robert Martin to Sir Christopher Hatton III (see Plate 3), with a quittance note signed by Martin and dated 9 November 1641. It lists twenty-five Venetian music prints of the period 1624 to 1638 (the very year in which Hatton bought them) and one non-musical item; the music prints are detailed in Table 2. All twenty-five prints survive today at Christ Church, Oxford.

Hatton's music supplier, Robert Martin, originally worked as 'journeyman' to the London bookseller Henry Fetherstone of St Anne's Parish, Blackfriars. Fetherstone had a successful business and was one of the Bodleian Library's main suppliers of books (many of which were bought in Italy). On 7 December 1618 the Court of the Stationers' Company ordered Fetherstone to 'avoid Robert Martin (which he keepeth disorderly in his house) within 8 dayes upon paine of the penaltye contayned in the ordinance for forrenors' (meaning simply foreign to the Stationers' Company?). Fetherstone paid a fine of forty shillings but did not dismiss Martin, and on the 18 January 1621 was ordered to pay twenty shillings for each week that he had employed a 'forrenor' beyond the original eight days' notice. Fetherstone refused and as a result was barred from having books from the English stock. It is not known how the dispute was eventually settled, but it is recorded that Fetherstone paid £6.13s.4d on 26 March 1622 'to have his man Robert Martin translated into this Company'. Fetherstone obviously held Martin in very high regard for when he retired in 1631/2 he left the import side of his business jointly to Martin and George Thomason.[15] Martin eventually went into business on his own and continued to supply the Bodleian Library with books.[16] He was successful enough to issue, between 1633 and 1650,[17] six printed catalogues of his purchases from abroad (chiefly from Italy) and five of these contain a section listing Venetian music.[18]

---

[15] W.A. Jackson ed., *Records of the Court of the Stationers' Company 1602-1640* (London, 1957), 105, 107, 131-2, 462 & 467; and H.G. Pollard & A. Ehrman, *The Distribution of Books by Catalogue to 1800* (Cambridge, 1965), 91-2.
[16] G. Hampshire ed., *The Bodleian Library Account Book 1613-1646* (Oxford, 1983), 92, 96, 105, 125 & 131.
[17] Martin probably died soon after the issue of his last catalogue in 1650.
[18] D.W. Krummel, 'Venetian Baroque Music in a London Bookshop: the Robert Martin Catalogues, 1633-50', *Music and Bibliography: Essays in Honour of Alec Hyatt King*, ed. O. Neighbour (London, 1980), 1-27; for a revision of Krummel's lists see J.P. Wainwright, 'The Musical Patronage of Christopher, First Baron Hatton (1605-1670)' (Ph.D. dissertation, University of Cambridge, 1993), i, Appendix III.

Table 2 Printed Music Bought by Christopher Hatton III from Robert Martin in November 1638

† Copy at Christ Church (†1: *unicum*; †2: only complete copy extant)
* Used by Bing and/or Jeffreys for their manuscript copies

	Price
G.B. Aloisi, *Contextus Musicarum Proportionum* Op. 4 (1637)†*	5s-0d
G.B. Aloisi, *Corona Stellarum* Op. 5 (1637)†2 *	2s-4d
F. Cauda, *Catena Sacrarum Cantionum* Bk 1, Op. 3 (1626)†1	5s-0d
A. della Ciaia, *Madrigali* Op. 1 (1636)†2	3s-0d
F. Costantini ed., *Motetti* Bk 4, Op. 12 (1634)†1	2s-6d
A. Cremonese, *Madrigali Concertati* Bk 1, Op. 1 (1636)†1	3s-6d
A. Facchi, *Motetti* Bk 2 (1635)†1 *	2s-6d
A. Facchi, *Madrigali* Bk 2 (1636)†2	3s-0d
B. Ferrari, *Musiche Varie* [Bk 1] (1633)†1	2s-6d
G. Filippi, *Concerti Ecclesiastici* Bk 1 (1637)†2	3s-0d
N. Fontei, *Bizzarrie Poetiche* [Bk 1] (1635)†1 &/or Bk 2 (1636)†1	2s-0d
N. Fontei, *Melodiae Sacrae* Op. 3 (1638)†2	4s-6d
A. Marastoni, *Madrigali Concertati* Op. 6 (1628)†	1s-6d
F.M. Marini, *Concerti Spirituali* Bk 1 (1637)†2 *	4s-6d
T. Merula, *Musiche Concertate* Bk 2, Op. 10 (1635†* [1/1633])	4s-0d
T. Merula, *Curtio Precipitato* Bk 2, Op. 13 (1638)†1	1s-6d
G. Monte dell'Olmo, *Applausi Ecclesiastici* Bk 1 (1636)†2	2s-0d
G. Monte dell'Olmo, *Sacri Affetti* Bk 2 (1637)†1	1s-0d
A. de Pisticci, *Motetti* Bk 3, Op. 6 (1633)†	2s-6d
A. de Pisticci, *Motetti* Bk 4, Op. 7 (1637)†1	2s-6d
O. Polidori, *Motetti* Op. 13 (1636)†	2s-0d
G.F. Sances, *Motetti* (1638)†*	4s-6d
C. Saracini, *Musiche* Bk 5 (1624)† & Bk 6 (1624)†	3s-0d
B. Tomasi, *Motecta* Op. 6 (1635)†2 *	2s-8d

Marini is given as 'Martini' on the bill; Pisticci's *Motetti* Bk 3 is erroneously described as 'il 3° Lib Mad[rigali]'; and it is not clear whether Book 1 or Book 2 of Fontei's *Bizzarrie Poetiche* was purchased, the fact that there are unique copies of both in Christ Church could indicate that both books were bought in November 1638 (although the price is perhaps too low for both).

In all there are 224 music prints listed in Martin's catalogues; most of them are Venetian and forty-nine are today unidentifiable (apparently lost). Of the 224 editions cited only 107 exist today in British libraries (74 at Christ Church), and it therefore seems unlikely that all the prints in the catalogues were actually on the shelves in Martin's shop. Perhaps the catalogues simply indicated that he was able to get hold of a print if a customer ordered it. It is unfortunate that no information is presently available concerning Martin's business links with the Venetian publishing houses.[19] Indeed, as yet we know very little about his customers.[20] One imagines that Hatton was not the only person who bought music from Martin, although he may well have been one of Martin's most regular customers. The only hint of Martin's other music customers is to be found in a composite Cantus partbook surviving in the Euing Collection at Glasgow University.[21] This bound partbook contains the Cantus I parts of ten Italian prints (see Table 3). All ten are listed in Martin's catalogues and, what is more, all the prints except one have the original prices marked on their title pages; as these prices basically correspond to the prices Hatton paid to Martin in 1638, it is not unreasonable to suggest that the ten prints were originally purchased from Martin by an as yet unidentified customer. The fact that the Glasgow copy of Rovetta's *Madrigali Concertati.... Libro Primo* is the second edition of 1636 (as listed in Martin's 1639 catalogue) rather than the first edition of 1629 (as listed in the 1633 and 1635 catalogues), and that the Glasgow prints were slightly more expensive than the prints which Hatton bought in 1638, leads to the suggestion that the 'Glasgow customer' was dealing with Martin in the 1640s. (Martin's 1640 catalogue does not specify an edition for Rovetta's *Madrigali* but presumably it refers to the second edition of 1636.)[22]

Returning to the Hatton purchases of 1638: the fact that there are copies of every one of the twenty-five prints at Christ Church today cannot be a coincidence. Nine of the twenty-five prints are unique copies, eight are the only complete copies in existence, and seven of the prints were used by Hatton's scribes, Stephen Bing and George Jeffreys, when they compiled their various manuscripts (see Chapters Three and Four). These twenty-five prints provide the nucleus of the Hatton music library surviving in Christ Church, Oxford. Table 4 lists other prints which were used by Hatton's musicians; perhaps these were also at one time part of Hatton's library.

---

[19] It is possible that Martin bought his Venetian stock at the Frankfurt book fairs rather than directly from Venice. Martin's erstwhile partner, George Thomason, is known to have travelled to Frankfurt several times before 1640; see F.J. Levy, 'How Information Spread Among the Gentry, 1550-1640', *Journal of British Studies*, xxi (1982), 17.
[20] One identified non-music customer of Martin's was Edward, Second Viscount Conway (see H.R. Plomer, 'A Cavalier's Library', *The Library*, Second Series, v (1904), 165).
[21] *Ge* R.c.28. The partbook does not contain any clues of provenance.
[22] It should be noted that two pieces from Gregori's *Sacrarum Cantionum* (Venice, 1635) were copied by George Jeffreys (Mad. Soc. G 55-9, see Chapter Four). The fact that the greater majority of the printed sources used by Jeffreys were owned by Hatton could lead one to suggest that the 'Glasgow partbook' was also once owned by Hatton. This is perhaps unlikely as it would mean that Hatton bought duplicate copies of five publications: he had already purchased copies of the Facchi (1636), Marini (1637), Ciaia (1636) and the two Aloisi prints (both 1637) in 1638 from Robert Martin and, as explained above, it seems that the Christ Church copies of these publications are those very prints. It is possible that Hatton once owned another copy of the Gregori which is now lost or that Jeffreys had access to the 'Glasgow' partbook quite independently of Hatton's patronage. (See Chapter Four for a full discussion of Jeffreys' copies of Italian music.)

Table 3   Glasgow University Library, Euing Music Collection R.c.28

Cantus I part to the following prints: Price   Hatton paid

A. Gregori, *Sacrarum Cantionum* Bk 3, Op. 8 (1635)   -   -
G.B. Aloisi, *Corona Stellarum* Op. 5 (1637)   2s-6d   2s-4d
A. Facchi, *Madrigali* Bk 2 (1636)   3s-0d(6d?)   3s-0d
A. Grandi / L. Simonetti ed., *Messa et Salmi* (1635-6)[a]   4s-6d   -
M. Scacchi, *Madrigali* (1634)   3s-6d   -
F.M. Marini, *Concerti Spirituali* Bk 1 (1637)   4s-0d(6d?)   4s-6d
G. Rovetta, *Madrigali Concertati* Bk 1, Op. 2 (1636)[b]   5s-0d(6d?)   -
G.B. Aloisi, *Contextus Musicarum* Op. 4 (1637)   5s-6d   5s-0d
A. della Ciaia, *Madrigali* Op. 1 (1636)   3s-6d   3s-0d
C. Gesualdo, *Madrigali* Bk 6 (1616)[c]   2s-0d(6d?)   -

[a] 2nd edition; first published in 1630 as *Raccolta Terza*
[b] 2nd edition; first published in 1629
[c] 2nd edition; first published in 1611

Table 4   Other Printed Sources used by Hatton's Musicians/Copyists

† Copy at Christ Church (†[1]: *unicum*)
‡ Listed in Martin's book catalogues
* No copy in U.K. today

G.B. Aloisi, *Coelestis Parnasus* Op. 1 (1628)†[1]
G.G. Arrigoni, *Concerti di Camera* (1635)‡
S. Bernardi, *Secondo Libro de Madrigali* Op. 7 (1616)†
S. Bernardi, *Concerti Accademici.... Libro Primo* Op. 8 1615-16)
A. Cifra, *Motecta* Bk 5, Op. 11 (1616† [1/1612])
R. Dering, *Cantica Sacra... Senis Vocibus* (1618)†(x2)
C. Gesualdo, *Madrigali* [Bk 1] (1603†, 1617 as Bk 2)†‡ [1/1594])
C. Gesualdo, *Madrigali* Bk 2 (1603†, 1616 as Bk 1)†‡ [1/1594])
C. Gesualdo, *Madrigali* Bk 3 (1619†‡ [1/1595])
C. Gesualdo, *Madrigali* Bk 4 (1604†, 1616†‡ [1/1596]
A. Grandi, *Il Primo Libro de Motetti* (1617†, 1628†‡ [1/1610])
A. Grandi, *Il Secondo Libro de Motetti* (1628†‡ [1/1613])
A. Grandi, *Madrigali Concertati* [Bk 1] (1626† [1/1615])
A. Grandi, *Il Quarto Libro de Motetti* (1628†‡ [1/1616])
A. Grandi, *Celesti Fiori... Libro Quinto* (1625†‡, 1638†‡ [1/1619])
A. Grandi, *Motetti... con Sinfonie* Bk 3 (1629)†

Table 4 concluded

A. Grandi, *Il Sesto Libro de Motetti* (1630)†‡
A. Gregori, *Sacrarum Cantionum* Bk 3, Op. 8 (1635)‡
G. Hayne (E. Hennio), *Motetti Sacri* Op. 4 (1646)*
T. Merula, *Il Primo Libro de Motetti* Op. 6 (1624)‡*
T. Merula, *Libro Secondo de Concerti Spirituali* (1628)
C. Monteverdi, *Il Quarto Libro de Madrigali* (1615†(x3),1622†(x2)‡
[1/1603])
P. Nenna, *Il Settimo Libro de Madrigali* (1624†‡ [1/1608])
D. Pecci, *Sacri Modulatus* Op. 3 (1629)†¹ ‡
F. Pio, *Liber Primus Motectorum* (1622-4)*
G. Rovetta, *Madrigali Concertati* Bk 1, Op. 2 (1629)†‡
E. Trabattone, *Concerti* Bk 2, Op. 4 (1629)†¹ ‡
F. Turini, *Madrigali* Bk 1 (1624†‡ [1/1621])

Again it is noticeable that most of the prints survive today at Christ Church, and that many appear in Martin's book catalogues, also that three are unique to Christ Church. It seems reasonable to suggest that most of the prints in Table 4 were also at one time part of the Hatton collection, particularly in view of the fact that George Jeffreys is not known to have worked for anyone except Hatton.

Another possible clue to the origins of some of the present Christ Church collection is given by various annotations on the covers of a number of prints and manuscripts. These annotations - usually a brief description of the contents of the volume - are in a variety of hands; some are as yet unidentified but others are definitely in the hands of Hatton's secretaries and musicians - Stephen Bing, George Jeffreys and George Holmes - and two appear to be in the hand of Hatton himself. (Table 5 is a list of the annotated covers and Plate 4 shows Stephen Bing's annotation on the cover of Christ Church, Oxford Mus. 317.)[23] The activities of Stephen Bing and George Jeffreys are examined in detail in Chapters Three and Four. George Holmes' handwriting can be identified from a number of letters surviving in the Hatton archives (see Table 6). Holmes was one of Hatton's many secretaries and, with his cousin Thomas, he appears to have served the Hatton family in various ways in the late 1640s, 1650s and 1660s. Nothing more is known

---

[23] It should be noted that the annotations on the listed prints and manuscripts are substantial enough to offer good examples of the handwriting in question. Concerning the identification of Stephen Bing's handwriting - both his secretary and italic hands - see Chapter Three; George Jeffreys' handwriting can easily be identified from his letters (see Chapter Four); concerning George Holmes' handwriting see above; and, although Christopher Hatton III's numerous letters (*Lbl* Add. 29,548-96, *passim*, etc.) are in the hands of his secretaries, Hatton's very characteristic signature corresponds closely with the annotations on *Och* Mus. 123-8 and *Och* Mus. 335 (Pinto (1990), 85), as does the handwriting of NRO FH 2133, a list of musical instruments, organ stops, musical terms, etc.

about George Holmes; his only importance to us is that he annotated various prints and manuscripts and thereby gave us some useful hints of provenance. (Holmes' surviving output is detailed in Table 6.)[24]

Table 5   Annotated Prints and Manuscripts

a. Covers annotated by Stephen Bing

Och Mus. 139: Ward, *The First Set of English Madrigals* (1613)

Och Mus. 147 & 151: Victoria, *Motecta* (1603)

Och Mus. 225-30 (& Jeffreys): East, *Madrigals to 3. 4. and 5 Parts* (1604); East, *The Second Set of Madrigals* (1606); East, *The Third Set of Bookes* (1610). Bing annotated the cover of *Och* Mus. 229 and added to Jeffreys' annotations on the covers of *Och* Mus. 225-8 & 230

Och Mus. 317: Philips ed., *Melodia Olympica* (1591); Philips, *Madrigali a Otto Voci* (1599)

Och Mus. 372 (& Holmes) (MS): Instrumental pieces and madrigals (some untexted) *a* 4-5 by Cato, Mason, Merulo and Rore

Och Mus. 442: Radesca di Foggia, *Madrigali* Bk. 1 (1615); Gentile, *Il Primo Libro de Madrigali* (1616); Missino, *Tirsi Doglioso Primo Libro di Madrigali* (1615); Pecci, *Madrigali* (1609); Bartolini, *Il Primo Libro de Madrigali* (1606)

Och Mus. 466 (MS): Madrigals, motets and In nomines *a* 4-6 by Anon., Clemens(?) and Ferrabosco I

Och Mus. 597: du Caurroy, *Meslanges de la Musique* (1610); du Caurroy, *Fantasies a III. IIII. V et VI Parties* (1610)

Och Mus. 796: Fornaci, *Amorosi Respiri Musicali* Bk 1, Op. 2 (1617); Caccini, *L'Euridice* (1615); Caccini, *Le Nuove Musiche* (1615); Cecchino, *Amorosi Concetti. Il Terzo Libro de Madrigali* Op 7 (1616); Monteverdi, *Scherzi Musicali a Tre Voci* (1615); Calestani, *Madrigali et Arie.... Parto Primo* (1617); Orlandi, *Arie a Tre Due et Voce Sola* Op. 2 (1616)

---

[24] He cannot be identified with the George Holmes (d.1721), organist of Lincoln Cathedral (1705-21), who appears to have published songs between *c*.1715 and 1721, and examples of whose church music survives in *Cu, Lbl, LI, Ob(T)* and *Och*. See W.H. Husk (rev.), 'Holmes, George', *New Grove*, viii, 657; A.R. Maddison, 'Lincoln Cathedral Choir A.D. 1700-1750', *Associated Architectural Societies' Reports and Papers*, xx/2 (1889), 213-26; and Watkins Shaw, *The Succession of Organists* (Oxford, 1991). (The catches by 'a George Holmes in Hilton's *Catch that Catch Can* (1652)' mentioned in *New Grove* are in fact by Thomas Holmes of Winchester (?*c*.1580-1638).)

Table 5a continued

Och Mus. 798: Barbarino, *Madrigali di Diversi Autori* (1609); Radesca di Foggia, *Il Primo/Secondo/Terzo/Quarto Libro delle Canzonette Madrigali et Arie* (all 1616); Radesca di Foggia, *Il Quinto Libro delle Canzonette Madrigali et Arie* (1617); Barbarino, *Il Secondo/Quarto Libro de Madrigali di Diversi auttori* (1611 & 1614); Barbarino, *Canzonette a una e due voci* (1616)

Och Mus. 806 (& Jeffreys): Morley, *The First Book of Consort Lessons* (1599)

Och Mus. 1028: Marenzio, *Cantiones Sacrae* (1603); Marenzio, *Madrigali a Quatro Voci* Bk 1 (1587); Marenzio, *Il Quarto Libro de Madrigali a Sei Voci* (1587); Turnhout, *Il Primo Libro de Madrigali a Sei Voci* (1589)

Och Mus. 1038: Marenzio, *Madrigali Spirituali a Cinque Voci* (1610); Graswinkel ed., *Nervi D'Orfeo.... a Cinque et Sei Voci* (1605)

Och Mus. 1044: Marenzio, *Il Primo, Secondo, Terzo, Quarto & Quinto Libro de Madrigali a Sei Voci* (1610); Marenzio, *Il Sesto Libro de Madrigali a Sei Voci* (1610)

Och Mus. 1063: Marenzio, *Il Primo, Secondo, Terzo, Quarto & Quinto Libro delle Villanelle et Canzonette alla Napolitana a Tre Voci* (1610)

b. Covers annotated by George Holmes

Och Mus. 84: d'India, *Le Musiche* [Bk 1] (1615)

Och Mus. 190-8: Pallavicino, *Sacrae Dei Laudes* (1605)

Och Mus. 207-14: Pallavicino, *L'Ottavo Libro de Madrigali a 5* (1612)

Och Mus. 254: Valentini, *Secondo Libro de Madrigali* (1616)*

Och Mus. 372 (& Bing) (MS): Instrumental pieces and madrigals (some untexted) *a* 4-5 by Cato, Mason, Merulo and Rore

Och Mus. 715: Barbarino, *Madrigali a Tre Voci* (1617)

Och Mus. 759 (MS): W. Lawes' 'The Royall Consort' (new version)

Och Mus. 867: Patta, *Motetti et Madrigali* (1614)

Och Mus. 1056: Marenzio, *Madrigalia a Quinque Vocum* (1601)

Och Mus. 1159 (MS): Variant version of part of Striggio's 'Il Cicalamento delle Donne al Bucato'

c. Covers annotated by George Jeffreys

Och Mus. 225-8 & 230 (and Bing): East, *Madrigals to 3. 4. and 5 Parts* (1604); East, *The Second Set of Madrigals* (1606); East, *The Third Set of Bookes* (1610)

Och Mus. 242-6: Morley, *The First Booke of Balletts to Five Voyces* (1595)

Och Mus. 301-5: Marenzio, *Madrigali a Cinque Voci Ridotti in un Corpo* (1593); de Castro, *Chant Musicale* (1597)

Och Mus. 806 (and Bing): Morley, *The First Book of Consort Lessons* (1599)

Table 5c continued

Och Mus. 1047-51: Marenzio, *Il Primo, Secondo, Terzo, Quarto & Quinto Libro de Madrigali a Cinque Voci* (1609)

d. Covers annotated by Christopher Hatton III

Och Mus. 123-8: Aux-Cousteaux, *Meslanges de Chansons* (1644)
Och Mus. 335: Metru, *Fantaisies a Deux Parties* (1642)

* The basso continuo partbook of Valentini's *Secondo Libro de Madrigali* (1616), *Och* Mus. 255, includes manuscript insertions copied by Stephen Bing. This is perhaps evidence for the practical use of the Hatton music: the continuo part of the Valentini was bound with its pages in the wrong order (1-15, 32-3, 18-31, 16-17, 34-50) and Bing's manuscript insertions were added to pp. 32, 17 and 34 in order to avoid awkward page turns for the continuo player.

Table 6   George Holmes

a. Manuscripts copied by Holmes

NRO FH 1395: treble parts only to two Gavottes (2nd incomplete)
NRO FH 1997: treble part only to a Saraband
NRO FH 2398: two strains of a Saraband (incomplete)
NRO FH 3431A: treble parts only to a Gavotte and Jigge (incomplete)
NRO FH 3431B: treble part only of a Courant by Holmes (incomplete)

b. Other examples of Holmes' hand

Lbl Add. 29,586, f. 29[r-v]: 'An Account of what goods received backe from my masters use from my cousin Thomas Holmes' (12 November 1661)
NRO FH 2416: Holmes' account of £5 travelling expenses (1 July 1647)
NRO FH 2631: letter from Holmes to Mr Clements at his lodgings in 'Charingcrosse' (*c*.1660)
NRO FH 2635: 'A note of clothes, etc. for myselfe' (n.d.)

The fact that a substantial number of prints and manuscripts - fifty-three prints and four manuscripts (Table 5) - were annotated by scribes who are known to have worked for Christopher Hatton III could indicate that they were all once part of the Hatton music library. However, it must be pointed out that, with one exception,[25] we have no idea exactly when the covers were

---

[25] *Och* Mus. 754-9, Stephen Bing's manuscript parts to William Lawes' 'The Royall Consort' (new version), were apparently copied in the Commonwealth period (see Chapter Three) and thus, in this case only, we have a clue to the date of Holmes' annotation.

actually annotated - when the prints and manuscripts were new or some years later - and the annotations do not in themselves indicate that the music originally belonged to the Hattons. The annotations merely indicate that the group of prints and manuscripts were connected with Baron Hatton at some stage. Indeed, an examination of the list of prints with annotated covers in Table 5 reveals that most of the prints are slightly older than those in Tables 2 and 4. David Pinto has suggested that these prints were originally from the library of Christopher Hatton II and were purchased before 1619.[26] Alternative theories could be proposed: perhaps these prints were already in the library at Christ Church when the Court came to Oxford in 1642, or other patrons and musicians - unconnected with Hatton - brought the prints to Oxford, and it was there that Jeffreys and the others came across the prints and added their annotations. Until more evidence is available this must remain speculation; it is possible, though, that - like the prints in Tables 2 and 4 - these annotated prints were once part of the Hatton music collection.

There are four further groups of prints in Christ Church which may originally have been part of the Hatton collection (Tables 7-10). Again the association of these prints with Hatton involves a degree of speculation; but the possibilities must be considered along with alternative hypotheses. The first groups of prints which need consideration are those in Table 7, a list of prints bound with the Hatton purchases of 1638, and Table 8, a list of other prints bound with those used by Hatton's musicians/copyists. It has already been noted that most of the prints which concern us in this study were part of Dean Henry Aldrich's bequest to Christ Church in 1710.[27] Many of the prints and manuscripts in the bequest were bound into uniform volumes of brown-speckled calf decorated with a characteristic floral stamp on the front and back and, thickness permitting, with Aldrich's logo on the spine. In organising his music collection Aldrich split the manuscripts and prints into three series: 'Fantasias', 'Madrigals' and 'Motets'.[28] Thus there are eight sets of instrumental parts, labelled *FANT*[asia] A-H, five *MAD*[rigal] sets (A-E), nine *MOT*[et] sets (A-I) and a number of outsized volumes which were not given a classification.[29]

When organising the binding Aldrich was obviously careful to keep the Hatton prints (Tables 2 and 4) together within each of his three series, and

---

[26] Pinto (1990), 85.

[27] The earliest surviving catalogue including the Aldrich bequest is dated 1717 (*Och* Library Record 15). However, items belonging to the Aldrich collection are marked '+' in *Ob* Mus. e 17: notes for a projected history of music made between 1708 and 1711 by Thomas Ford, Chaplain of Christ Church, Oxford.

[28] The vocal music in the 'MAD' and 'MOT' series is actually arranged as much by format as by genre; for example, fourteen of the eighteen prints in *MOT*[et] E (*Och* Mus. 881-6) are actually madrigal publications (for full details see Wainwright (1993), i, Appendix IV).

[29] Graziani's *Motetti* Op. 24 (1676) in *MOT* G (*Och* Mus. 887-9) provides a *terminus ante quem non* for the Aldrich bindings. Pinto (1990), note 21, points out that *MOT* G is the only set bound by Aldrich which contains items printed both before and after 1670.

with these 'likely' Hatton prints he also bound the prints listed in Tables 7 and 8. A substantial number of these are listed in the Martin catalogues, and as Hatton was a known customer of Martin's, and as his known purchases all ended up in Christ Church, it is not too far-fetched to suggest that the prints in Tables 7 and 8, and indeed those in Table 9 (other Martin prints at Christ Church) may also have come from the Hatton library, particularly as Aldrich appears to have kept prints of common provenance together.[30] All but seven of the Hatton prints detailed in Table 2 were distributed between *MAD* A (Christ Church Mus. 484-8), *MOT* A (Mus. 919-21), *MOT* B (Mus. 922-5), *MOT* C (Mus. 926-30), *MOT* D (Mus. 931-5), *MOT* E (Mus. 881-6) and *MOT* I (Mus. 893-9), and six of the seven prints which remained outside Aldrich's scheme are of folio format and were presumably too large for the series.[31]

Table 7 Prints Bound with the Hatton Purchases of 1638

†1 *unicum*; †2 only complete copy extant
‡ Listed in Martin's book catalogues
* Used as copy source by Hatton's Musicians/Copyists (see Table 4)

	Christ Church Mus.
G.B. Aloisi, *Coelestis Parnasus* Op. 1 (1628)†1 *	931-5
D. Bellante, *Concerti Accademici* Op. 1 (1629)†2 ‡	881-6
S. Bernardi, *Secondo Libro de Madrigali* Op. 7 (1616)*	881-6
S. Bonini, *Lamento d'Arianna* (1613)	448
S. Bonini, *Serena Celeste* Op. 8 (1615)†1	795
C. Burgh, *Hortus Marianus* (1630)†2	931-5
L. Calvi ed., *Quarta Raccolta de Sacri Canti* (1629)	922-5
G. Carrone, *Il Primo Libro delli Motetti* Op. 1 (1629)†1	931-5
G.M. Cesare, *Concerti Ecclesiastici* Bk 1 (1614)†1 ‡	931-5
A. Cifra, *Motecta* [Bk 1] (1614)	926-30
A. Cifra, *Motecta* Bk 2 (1611)	926-30
A. Cifra, *Motecta* Bk 3 (1614)	926-30
A. Cifra, *Motecta* Bk 4, Op. 8 (1613)	926-30

---

[30] This theory was first examined in print by David Pinto (1990), 83-6; a less well-developed form of the hypothesis had been suggested by the present writer in an unpublished paper to the Viola da Gamba Society, 'Civil War Oxford: a Centre for the Dissemination of Italian Music in England?' (London, February 1987).
[31] i.e. Fontei (1636), Merula (1638), Polidori (1636), and the two Saracini (1624) in *Och* Mus. 795, and Ferrari (1633) in *Och* Mus. 863. The remaining Hatton print not included in Aldrich's scheme is Fontei (1635) which is found, with four other prints, in *Och* Mus. 448. The composite volumes *Och* Mus. 448 and 795 were supplied with bindings of dark mottled calf (presumably by Aldrich?); Ferrari (1633) was left unbound (*Och* Mus. 863).

Table 7 continued

A. Cifra, *Motecta* Bk 5, Op. 11 (1616)*	926-30
A. Cifra, *Scherzi et Arie* (1614)	795
A. Cifra, *Madrigali a Cinque Voci* Bk 3 (1615)	484-8
B. Cossa, *Madrigaletti a Tre Voci* Bk 1 (1617)	922-5
M. Delipari, *I Baci. Madrigali* Bk 1 (1630)†² ‡	881-6
R. Dering, *Cantiones Sacrae Quinque Vocum* (1617)	881-6
R. Dering, *Cantica Sacra... Senis Vocibus* (1618)*	881-6
G. Ferrari, *Il Primo Libro de Madrigali* Op. 2 (1628)‡	484-8
L. Gallerano, *Ecclesiastica Armonica Concerti* Bk 1, Op. 6 (1624)†¹ ‡	931-5
A. Grandi, *Il Primo Libro de Motetti* (1628)‡*	926-30
A. Grandi, *Il Secondo Libro de Motetti* (1628)‡*	926-30
A. Grandi, *Motetti... con Sinfonie* Bk 3 (1629)*	926-30
A. Grandi, *Quarto Libro de Motetti* (1628)‡*	926-30
A. Grandi, *Celesti Fiori... Libro Quinto* (1625)‡*	926-30
A. Grandi, *Il Sesto Libro de Motetti* (1630)‡*	926-30
A. Grandi, *Madrigali Concertati* [Bk 1] (1626)*	484-8
A. Grandi, *Madrigali Concertati* Bk 2, Op. 11 (1626)	484-8
A. Gualtieri, *Motetti* Bk 3, Op. 10 (1630)†¹ ‡	931-5
S. d'India, *Villanelle alla Napolitana* Bk 1 (1610)	919-21
S. d'India, *Liber Secundus Sacrorum Concentuum* (1610)	881-6
S. d'India, *Il Terzo Libro de Madrigali a 5* (1615)†² ‡	881-6
S. d'India, *Le Musiche a Due Voci* [Bk 1] (1615)	795
S. d'India, *Le Musiche* Bk 4 (1621)†¹	795
S. d'India, *Le Musiche* Bk 5 (1623)†¹	795
S. d'India, *Liber Primus Motectorum* (1627)	926-30
L. Leoni, *Sacri Flores* (1619)	922-5
B. Marini, *Per le Musiche di Camera. Concerti* Op. 7 (1634)†¹ ‡	893-9
B. Marini, *Madrigaletti* Bk 5, Op. 9 (1635)†¹ ‡	922-5
R. Micheli, *Musica Vaga* (1615)	795
S. Molinaro, *Concerti Ecclesiastici* (1605)	919-21
F. de Monte, *Musica Sopra Il Pastor Fido* (1600)†²	893-9
C. Monteverdi, *Il Primo Libro de Madrigali* (1621)‡	881-6
C. Monteverdi, *Il Secondo Libro de Madrigali* (1621)‡	881-6
C. Monteverdi, *Il Terzo Libro de Madrigali* (1621)‡	881-6
C. Monteverdi, *Quarto Libro de Madrigali* (1622)‡*	881-6
C. Monteverdi, *Il Quinto Libro de Madrigali* (1620)‡	881-6
C. Monteverdi, *Il Sesto Libro de Madrigali* (1620)‡	881-6
C. Monteverdi, *Concerto. Settimo Libro de Madrigali* (1628)‡	881-6
C. Monteverdi, *L'Orfeo* (1615)	795
G.C. Monteverdi, *Delli Affetti Musici* Bk 1 (1620)	893-9
B. Pallavicino, *Il Primo Libro de Madrigali a 5* (1606)‡	484-8

Table 7 concluded

B. Pallavicino, *Il Secondo Libro de Madrigali* a 5 (1606)‡	484-8
B. Pallavicino, *Il Terzo Libro de Madrigali* a 5 (1606)‡	484-8
B. Pallavicino, *Il Quinto Libro de Madrigali* a 5 (1609)‡	484-8
B. Pallavicino, *Il Sesto Libro de Madrigali* a 5 (1611)‡	484-8
B. Pallavicino, *Il Settimo Libro de Madrigali* a 5 (1611)	484-8
B. Pallavicino, *L'Ottava Libro de Madrigali* a 5 (1612)	484-8
D. Pecci, *Sacri Modulatus* Op. 3 (1629)†[1] ‡*	919-21
G.B. Piazza, *Libro Secondo. Canzonette a Voce Sola* (1633)‡	448
G. Rovetta, *Madrigali Concertati* Bk 1, Op. 2 (1629)‡*	484-8
G.F. Sances, *Cantade* Bk 2 (1633)‡	448
H. Schütz, *Symphoniae Sacrae* (1629)‡	881-6
E. Trabattone, *Concerti* Bk 2, Op. 4 (1629)†[1] ‡*	931-5
R. Trofeo & G.D. Rognoni Taeggio, *Canzonette Leggiadre* (1600)†[2]	919-21
F. Turini, *Madrigali* Bk 1 (1624)‡*	922-5
L. Valvasensi, *Secondo Giardino d'Amorosi Fiori* Op. 8 (1634)†[1] ‡	448
F. Vitali, *Concerto... Madrigali* Bk 1 (1629)‡	881-6
F. Wynant, *Madrigali a Cinque Voci* Bk 1 (1597)	484-8

Table 8 Other Prints Bound with those used by Hatton's Musicians/Copyists

†[1] *unicum*; †[2] only complete copy extant
‡   Listed in Martin's book catalogues

	Christ Church Mus.
C. Gesualdo, *Madrigali.... Libro Sesto* a 5 (1616)‡	908-12
S. d'India, *Libro Primo de Madrigali* a 5 (1610)‡	908-12
S. d'India, *Libro Secondo de Madrigali* a 5 (1611)†[2] ‡	908-12
S. d'India, *Il Quarto Libro de Madrigali* a 5 (1616)†[2]	908-12
S. d'India, *Il Quinto Libro de Madrigali* a 5 (1616)	908-12
S. d'India, *Le Musiche e Balli* a 4 (1621)†[1]	908-12
P. Nenna, *Madrigali.... Quinto Libro* a 5 (1612)	908-12
P. Nenna, *Il Primo Libro de Madrigali* a 5 (1617)‡	908-12
P. Nenna, *Il Quarto Libro de Madrigali* a 5 (1617)‡	908-12
P. Nenna, *Il Sesto Libro de Madrigali* a 5 (1618)	908-12
P. Nenna, *Il Primo Libro de Madrigali* a 4 (1621)	908-12

Table 9 Other Martin Prints at Christ Church, Oxford

	Christ Church Mus.
A. Grandi, *Motetti a Voce Sola* (1628)	86
B. Pallavicino, *Il Quarto Libro de Madrigali a 5* (1607)	502-7
L. Simonetti ed., *Ghirlanda Sacra... Libro Primo* (1630)*	937-8

* Listed as 1631 in Martin's 1633 catalogue

Finally, the four prints listed in Table 10 should be mentioned as all have various associations with the Hatton collection. Orlando Gibbons' *First Set of Madrigals and Mottets* (1612), Christ Church Mus. 708-12, was referred to at the start of this section as one of the sets of parts in 'Hatton bindings' (see Plate 1) and it was suggested that this very set was Gibbons' presentation copy to his patron Sir Christopher Hatton II. Michael East's *Seventh Set* (1638), Mus. 455-8, has no obvious marks of ownership but, as the print was dedicated to Christopher Hatton III, it is possible that the set was of Hatton provenance.[32] Walter Porter's *Motetts* and John Wilson's *Psalterium Carolinum* (both of 1657) are bound with various manuscript sections in Christ Church Music 877-880, a collection which has close links with the Hattons; this 'strange meddley' is examined in detail in Chapter Five.

Table 10 Miscellaneous Prints Associated with the Hatton Collection

	Christ Church Mus.
M. East, *The Seventh Set of Bookes* (1638)	455-8
O. Gibbons, *The First Set of Madrigals and Mottets* (1612)	708-12
W. Porter, *Motetts of Two Voyces* (1657)	877-80
J. Wilson, *Psalterium Carolinum* (1657)	877-80

The publications listed in Tables 2, 4-5, and 7-10 together represent the hypothetical limits of the printed section of the Hatton music collection. To this already substantial collection could be added the various manuscripts

---

[32] Michael East (*c*.1580-1648) may have been connected with the Hatton family as early as 1606: his *Second Set of Madrigales* (London, 1606) is addressed as 'from Ely House Holborne' which was at that time occupied by Dowager Lady Elizabeth Newport-Hatton (P. Brett, 'East [Easte, Est, Este], Michael', *New Grove*, v, 801). East's *Second Set* is included in the composite volumes *Och* Mus. 225-30 (bindings annotated by Hatton scribes, see Table 5).

either copied or annotated by the Hatton family's copyists (Table 11).[33] Again, this list involves a certain amount of speculation. It is, for example, very difficult to distinguish between manuscripts copied for the Hattons and those copied for the scribes' own use quite independently of any Hatton patronage. Only in the case of the manuscripts Christ Church Mus. 612-13 and 432 (two bass viol parts and an organbook) can we be certain of Hatton provenance: it has already been noted that the bindings include the Hatton coat of arms (see Plate 2). The complete outputs of Hatton's copyists - John Lilly, Stephen Bing and George Jeffreys - are examined in Chapters Three and Four (see Tables 12, 14 and 21). However the only manuscripts included in Table 11 are those which survive today in Christ Church, Oxford. It is not unreasonable to suggest that the manuscripts in Table 11, which were all either copied or annotated by Hatton scribes, were at one time part of the Hatton music collection and followed the same path to Christ Church as the printed music.

Table 11   Music Manuscripts Associated with the Hatton Family

Och Mus. 2/397-408/436: copied by Bing and Lilly
Och Mus. 372-6: annotated by Bing and Holmes
Och Mus. 417-18 & 1080: copied by Bing
Och Mus. 432/612-13: Hatton binding and copied by Bing and Lilly
Och Mus. 463-7: annotated by Bing
Och Mus. 732-5: copied by Bing
Och Mus. 754-9: copied by Bing and annotated by Holmes
Och Mus. 877-80: copied by Bing and Jeffreys
Och Mus. 1023: copied by Bing and Jeffreys
Och Mus. 1155-61: annotated by Holmes
Och Mus. 1185: copied by Bing
Och Mus. 1215, fascicle 3: copied by Bing

The Dispersal of the Hatton Music Collection

The line of transmission of the Hatton music collection from the ownership of Christopher Hatton III to Dean Aldrich and Christ Church needs now to be considered. It is possible that the dispersal of the Hatton music collection started soon after 1646; it was noted in Chapter One that Hatton's precious library suffered at the hands of the Parliamentarian sequestrators although it is not clear if any of the music was lost. We also know that Hatton was

---

[33] These manuscripts are dealt with in detail in Chapters Three to Five.

surrounded by his 'bookes and fiddles' in exile in Paris,[34] so it is even possible that Hatton took some or all of his music with him to France. However, it is more likely that his music collection remained in England. The fact that Hatton was present at the Oxford Court leads to the intriguing possibility that he took his music collection with him to Oxford in 1642 and, at the fall of the city in 1646, left it in the safe-keeping of Christ Church where it has remained ever since. In this case Aldrich would have come upon an already intact music library which he added to, organised and bound, and which later became known as 'his' collection. David Pinto has argued convincingly against this idea, pointing out that all the 'later-generation' manuscripts containing 'Hatton repertoire' (music copied from the Hatton prints) date from after 1670.[35] The most likely hypothesis is that the collection remained in the possession of the Hatton family - probably at Kirby Hall - until the First Baron's death on 4 July 1670, after which it was sold in an attempt to rectify some of the family's appalling financial problems. It is known that in June 1671 the Hattons' main library was sold - via John Mawson, Christopher Hatton IV's London agent - to the bookseller Robert Scott of Little Britain near St Paul's Cathedral.[36] Scott was at that time the principal London agent for the Bodleian Library, Oxford[37] and Anthony Wood records that in September 1671 'most part of the lord Hatton's library came to Oxford.... Bought of Scot' and that 'the University bought 100 volumes of MSS. from the booksellers which they bought of the lord Hatton'.[38] An entry in the Bodleian Library's accounts for 1671, 'To Mr Scot for severall bookes and MSS. £156.', probably records the purchase.[39] It is possible that Robert Scott was also responsible for the dispersal of the music collection and found in Aldrich an eminently suitable buyer.[40]

---

[34] Macray ed. (1869), ii, 133.

[35] Pinto (1990), 89. These 'later-generation' manuscripts - those copied, for example, by Aldrich, Blow, Bowman and Lowe - are examined in Excursus II.

[36] *Lbl* Add. 29,553, ff. 226, 245 & 284; Philip (1983), 56-8.

[37] L. Rostenberg, 'Robert Scott, Restoration Stationer and Importer', *The Papers of the Bibliographical Society of America*, xlviii (1954), 49-76.

[38] Clark ed. (1892), ii, 231.

[39] W.D. Macray, *Annals of the Bodleian Library* (Oxford, 2/1890, repr. 1984), 137 & 141-2; Madan et al. (1937), ii/2, 801. In 1675 the Bodleian acquired four volumes of Anglo-Saxon Homilies from Christopher Hatton IV: *olim* Junian 22-4 and 99, now *Ob* Hatton 113-16; these volumes were lent by the Bodleian to Thomas Marshall soon after 1675, and by him to Francis Junius on whose death they were returned to the Bodleian (*DNB*, ix, 164; and Madan et al. (1937), ii/2, 967-9). Charles Hatton also donated three fifteenth-century manuscripts to the Bodleian: *Ob* Hatton donat. 1-3 (Madan et al. (1937), ii/2, 863-4).

[40] It is even possible that George Jeffreys acted as an intermediary in the deal between Scott and Aldrich, or even directly between the Hatton family and Aldrich, particularly given his links with Christ Church during the Civil War and the fact that his son, Christopher Jeffreys, was a student at the college in the 1660s (matriculated 9 December 1659, BA 1663, MA 1666; Foster (1891), ii, 805). A further examination of the non-music books and manuscripts bequeathed by Aldrich to Christ Church in relation to the surviving book catalogues in the Hatton archives (NRO FH 642, 2444, 4016-17, 4019-23 & 4025, and *Ob* Bodley 878, etc.) may reveal more about the links between the Hattons, Aldrich and Christ Church.

The above examination of the survival of the Hatton music collection has involved a certain amount of speculation. It would be foolish to assert that Hatton provenance has been proven beyond doubt in all cases. As an example of the dangers involved, attention should be drawn to a printed source listed, in Table 9, as a possible 'Hatton print': Grandi's *Motetti* of 1628 (Mus. 86). According to a catalogue of the Aldrich and Goodson bequests made by Johann Baptist Malchair (1730-1812) in July 1787, the print comes from the Goodson bequest of 1718 and not the Aldrich bequest of 1710.[41] This print does not, therefore, appear to fit the Hatton-Aldrich hypothesis as outlined above, unless some interchange - or even confusion - of ownership between Aldrich and Goodson can be believed.[42] This is not impossible as the two men were close colleagues. Alternatively Goodson could have bought some 'stray' Hatton prints quite independently of Aldrich.[43]

The Hatton-Aldrich-Christ Church line of transmission is just one possibility and it is quite easy to formulate alternative hypotheses. For example, Aldrich is known to have acquired music (both printed and manuscript) which was previously associated with various other patrons, collectors and musicians - such as John Browne, Clerk of the Parliaments, Sir Henry Fanshawe, Thomas Myriell, Angelo Notari and Francis Tregian[44] - so some of the prints may have been obtained from sources of which no traces remain. Despite the possibility of alternative theories, the Hatton-Aldrich-Christ Church hypothesis, as outlined above, is the best interpretation of the currently available evidence.

The Possible Extent of the Hatton Music Collection

Notwithstanding the above 'warning', a hypothetical reconstruction of the Hatton music collection has been attempted in the Appendix. This includes all the prints and manuscripts listed in Tables 2, 4-5 and 7-11 (together with

---

[41] *Lcm* 2125. Malchair also copied many of the contents lists which appear in the front of the composite volumes of prints in Christ Church, and two music manuscripts (*Och* Mus. 55 and *T* 900) include sections in Malchair's hand (Jones (1982), i, 81). Grandi's *Motetti* (1628) is also listed in an alphabetical 'Catalogue of Mr Goodson's Books contained in ye Archives 1747' at the reverse of *Och* Library Record 15.

[42] Malchair's catalogue is not always completely accurate: a number of items from the Aldrich bequest are omitted and his listing of the prints in the composite volumes is not always exhaustive (see Pinto (1990), note 24). In the case of Simonetti's *Ghirlanda Sacra* of 1630 (Mus. 937-8), Malchair assigns the print to the Goodson collection but Thomas Ford, in his notes for a projected history of music (*Ob* Mus. e 17, 1208-11), lists the print as Aldrich's and, what is more, the two partbooks are bound in standard 'Aldrich' bindings.

[43] This idea finds some support in the fact that, according to Malchair, the partbooks Christ Church Mus. 225-30 (East's *Madrigals*, Sets 1-3) were also part of the Goodson bequest; these books must - at some stage - have been connected with the Hattons as the bindings are annotated by Hatton scribes (Bing and Jeffreys, see Table 5). *Och* Mus. 1185, which was copied by Bing (see Chapter Three), also belonged to Goodson.

[44] These collections and some possible links with the Hattons are explored in Chapter Six.

ten other prints and manuscripts which are considered in Chapter Six).[45] A degree of 'likelihood of Hatton provenance' has been assigned to each print and manuscript as follows:

(a) definitely of Hatton provenance (prints bought by Hatton III from Robert Martin in November 1638; prints annotated by Hatton himself; prints and manuscripts in Hatton bindings).
(b) very likely of Hatton provenance (prints used by Hatton copyists).
(c) possibly of Hatton provenance (covers annotated by Hatton scribes; prints bound with the 1638 purchases; prints bound with those used by the Hatton copyists).
(d) less likely to be of Hatton provenance (problematic).[46]

Thus, twenty-nine prints and a single manuscript are categorised as 'definitely of Hatton provenance';[47] twenty-eight prints and five manuscripts as 'very likely'; 119 prints and six manuscripts as 'possibly'; and a further seven prints and seven manuscripts are classed as 'less likely' to be of Hatton provenance. (a) and (b) together total sixty-three prints and manuscripts; (a), (b) and (c) total 188; and (a), (b), (c) and (d) total 202 items.[48]

It is possible that my hypothetical limits are grossly exaggerated and that the true story is far more complex than the evidence suggests, but it is perhaps equally possible that, hidden amongst material of uncertain provenance in Christ Church and other libraries, there are many other items which were once connected with the Hatton family. The true extent of the Hatton music collection may never be known but, in examining the origins of the Christ Church music, the Hattons have been revealed as the owners of

---

[45] Only the Porter and Wilson publications (1657) and the manuscripts *Och* Mus. 754-9 and 1185 date from after 1646; the remainder of the Appendix could therefore represent the extent of the Hatton music collection in c.1646.
[46] These 'problem' prints and manuscripts are dealt with in detail in Chapter Six.
[47] The (a)-total of prints must be reduced by one if it is considered that Hatton bought only one book of Fontei's *Bizzarrie Poetiche* in November 1638; see Table 2 note. A manuscript set of partbooks is classed as a single item for the present purposes.
[48] 194 of the total 201 possible-Hatton items survive today at Christ Church, Oxford. There are approximately 460 pre-1800 music prints at Christ Church of which approximately 380 were printed before 1670. If the most extreme version of the hypothesis is to be believed - (a), (b), (c) and (d) - there are 182 music prints of Hatton provenance in Christ Church which represent almost 48% of the pre-1670 holdings today; if only (a) and (b) are accepted as evidence of Hatton provenance this still represents 15% of the pre-1670 Christ Church prints. (The Christ Church totals have been calculated using only the prints bearing the 'Mus.' shelfmark and therefore exclude plainchant collections and liturgical books with music notation, etc. With the exception of John Barnard's *The First Book of Selected Church Music* (1641) which was purchased in 1917 (now Mus. 544-53), no significant items have been added to the Christ Church music collection since 1800. A number of items of music were missing by the mid-nineteenth century (it appears that E.F. Rimbault (1816-76) purloined a number of music prints, see W.G. Hiscock, *A Christ Church Miscellany* (Oxford, 1946), 128-33) and other items listed in Malchair's catalogue, such as books of airs by Campion, Corkine, Danyel and Dowland, are no longer extant.)

a substantial and important library of music. Indeed the Hatton collection may prove to be one of the richest seventeenth-century music libraries yet identified. The significance of this collection is examined in the following chapters.

CHAPTER THREE

JOHN LILLY AND STEPHEN BING: SOMETIME COPYISTS FOR CHRISTOPHER HATTON III

John Lilly (1612-1678)

It was noted in Chapter Two that one of the most obvious items to have survived from the Hatton collection is the set of three manuscript partbooks, Oxford, Christ Church Mus. 432 and 612-13. The three volumes (an organbook and two bass viol parts) are bound in dark-blue morocco and bear the Hatton coat of arms, crest and family motto 'Deo et Patriae' (see Plate 2). The partbooks, which contain untitled and unascribed fantasias and ayres for two bass viols and organ by Coprario, Jenkins and Ward (see Part II, MS LI),[1] were copied by the musician and copyist John Lilly. The music-hand of John Lilly was first identified by John Wilson from a note in a manuscript in the Bodleian Library, Oxford: an inscription on the first folio of Mus. Sch. MS C 57 (Part II, MS XXVII), in the hand of Edward Lowe (the organist of Christ Church, Oxford and Professor of Music from 1662 to 1682), reads 'Thes[e] 4 Bookes were prickt by Mr John Lillye, who had of mee 5£ for the prickinge them 29th of December. 1688: besides my Charge of paper & bindeinge. Ed. Lowe'.[2] This has enabled the identification of twenty-two partbooks or organbooks in the hand of John Lilly (see Table 12).[3]

Until recently all the known sources of information relating to John Lilly [Lely, Lillie, Lylly] concerned his career after 1650. However, Pamela Willetts' research has now filled-out the details concerning his early life.[4] John Lilly was born in the Cambridgeshire village of Croydon cum Clopton (Clapton) in January 1612 to Henry Lilly, the vicar of Croydon, and his wife Elizabeth. The next probable reference to John Lilly appears in relation to William Johnson's university play *Valetudinarium*, which was performed at Queens' College, Cambridge on 6 February 1638: the college bursarial accounts for this Latin comedy, although not specifically listing musicians,

---

[1] The organbook (*Och* Mus. 432) also contains Mico's three-part fantasias added by Stephen Bing (see below and Part II, MS LI).
[2] J. Wilson ed., *Roger North on Music* (London, 1959), 37-8.
[3] Descriptions and inventories of all these manuscripts are given in Part II. It should be noted that Lilly's surviving manuscripts probably represent only a fraction of his total output as a copyist. (*Och* Mus. 1175 and 1185 are occasionally incorrectly identified as the work of Lilly.)
[4] P. Willetts, 'John Lilly, Musician and Music Copyist', *Bodleian Library Record*, vii (1967a), 307-11; and ibid., 'John Lilly: a Redating', *Chelys*, xxi (1992), 27-38.

Table 12 Manuscripts Copied by John Lilly

Lbl Add. 27,550, ff. 1-14: treble part of Jenkins' fantasia-ayre suites *a* 3. Dated 1674 by a contemporary hand. The set Add. 27,550-4 includes a number of different music-hands (including Stephen Bing's).

Lbl Add. 59,869, ff. 35^v-8: two sets of divisions for bass viol, one by Polewheele, added to a copy of Simpson's *Division-Violist* (1659). Bound with the Cartwright lyra viol manuscript.

Lbl Egerton 2485: organ-score to instrumental music by Coprario, Ferrabosco II, Lupo, Mico, White; and Madrigals *a* 5 (untexted) by Marenzio and Monteverdi.

Ob Mus. Sch. C 54-7: Simpson's 'Months and Seasons'. Copied in 1668 (C 54, ff. 1-4 were copied - on different paper - by an unidentified scribe).

Och Mus. 397-400: parts to instrumental music *a* 4 by Bull, Coprario, Ferrabosco, Jenkins, Ward. (Organ-score (Mus. 436) and full score (Mus. 2) copied by Bing.)

Och Mus. 401-2: parts, lacking 1st viol part, to instrumental music *a* 3 by Coprario, Gibbons, Lupo, Mico. (Score (Mus. 2) copied by Bing.)

Och Mus. 403-8: parts to instrumental music *a* 5-6 by Coleman, Coprario, Ferrabosco, Gibbons, Jenkins, Lupo, Mico, Ward, White; and Madrigals and Motets *a* 5 (untexted, but with titles added by Aldrich) by Lupo, Marenzio, Monteverdi, Pallavicino, Vecchi, Ward. (Organ-score (Mus. 436) and full score (Mus. 2) copied by Bing.)

Och Mus. 432, ff. 0^v-11: organ-score to instrumental music by Coprario, Jenkins, Ward; parts in Mus. 612-13 (see below). (Mus. 432, ff. 109-3 rev. were copied by Bing.) The bindings of both Mus. 432 and the associated parts Mus. 612-13 bear the Hatton arms, crest and motto 'Deo et Patriae'.

Och Mus. 612-13: parts to fantasias, for two bass viols and organ, by Coprario, Jenkins, Ward; the organ-score is Mus. 432 (see above).

---

include a payment to a 'Mr Lilly'.[5] This is significant because it places Lilly in and around Cambridge in the 1630s, at a time when Sir Christopher Hatton was closely associated with the city. John Lilly married his wife Frances probably in the early 1640s, and they had a son, also called John, who was baptised on 11 August 1644 at Croydon. It seems that some time

---

[5] See G.C. Moore Smith ed., 'The Academic Drama at Cambridge: Extracts from College Records', *Malone Society Collections* (n.p., 1923), ii/2, 192-3; and J.K. Wood, 'Two Latin Play Songs', *RCRMA*, xxi (1988), 47. Wood notes that the sole-surviving anonymous piece of music from *Valetudinarium* - the song 'Dulcis somne' for Sbc alternating with CATB chorus (*Cu* Dd.III.73, f. 23^{r-v}) - shares some stylistic traits with the songs written by George Jeffreys for Peter Hausted's play *The Rival Friends* (produced in the hall of Trinity College by Queens' College students on 19 March 1632; see pp. 8-9 above).

during the year after the birth of their son, John and Frances Lilly moved to Cambridge, for their two daughters, Elizabeth and Mary, were baptised in the Parish Church of St Michael's, Cambridge on 11 October 1645 and 26 June 1647 respectively.[6]

Roger North (c.1651-1734), the amateur musician and writer, is an important source of information concerning Lilly. In the biography of his elder brother - Francis North, First Baron Guilford (1637-85) - Roger North describes his family's patronage of the 'old soker' (old-timer) Lilly; he mentions his teaching and copying activities; and describes his move from Cambridge to London, after the Restoration, to take up a position at Court.[7] Lilly is also the subject of a poem, 'To Mr. Lilly, Musick-Master in Cambridge' by Nicholas Hookes (b. 1628), a student at Trinity College, Cambridge between 1649 and 1653, which was published in a collection entitled: *Amanda, a Sacrifice to an Unknown Goddesse* (London, 1653).[8] The poem pays tribute to Lilly's skill as a performer on the viol, but it was as a theorbo player that he gained a place in the King's 'private Musick' in 1660, a post he retained until his death on 25 October 1678. The Lord Chamberlain's papers, the Exchequer records and Treasury papers for the period 1660-1683 (now at the Public Record Office) give an indication of Lilly's activities as a member of the King's Musick:[9]

19 June 1660: Lilly sworn in by the Gentleman Ushers as a member of the 'private Musicke' '...in the place of Mr Kelley'. [PRO LC 3/2; 3/33]

9 November 1660: Warrant from the Lord Chamberlain to the Clerk of the Signet Office to prepare a bill for the King's signature granting Lilly a place as musician in ordinary (theorbo) in the place of John Kelly with wages of £40 p.a. [PRO LC 5/137, p. 244]

24 March 1663: Warrant from the Lord Chamberlain to the Treasurer of the Chamber to pay £12 to Lilly for a lute sold and delivered by him for the King's service. [PRO LC 5/137, p. 421]

4 January 1664: Letter from John Jenkins appointing Lilly, of St. Andrew's, Holborn, as his attorney. [PRO LC 3/33, p. 114]

8 November 1666: Accounts of the Great Wardrobe: 'Lent to Mr. Lilly, musician: £5.' [PRO LC 9/255/ix, p. 8]

'Liveries in Arrears & Onpayd from June 1660 to Mich[aelm]as 1667': Lilly is listed as being owed £32. 5s. 0d. for 1661 and 1666. [PRO LC 9/389/ii]

---

[6] Willetts (1992), 29.

[7] R. North, *The Life of the Right Honourable Francis North, Baron of Guilford* (London, 1742); the manuscript draft material survives as *Lbl* Add. 32,507 and Add. 32,509-10 . The section concerning Lilly is in *Lbl* Add. 32,510, f. 110^v.

[8] There may also be a rather less flattering reference to Lilly in a three-voice catch, 'If any so wise', by William Child, published in John Hilton's *Catch that Catch Can* (London, 1652): '... Soon as out of your bed, to settle your head, take a haire of his tayle in the morning, and be not so silly to follow old *Lilly*, for there's nothing but sack that can tune us...'

[9] See A. Ashbee, *Records of English Court Music*, i (Snodland, 1986), v (Aldershot, 1991b), and viii (Aldershot, 1995), *passim* for a comprehensive account of Lilly's career at Court.

25 March 1667: Letter from Dr. Charles Coleman assigning his livery of £16. 2s. 6d., due on 30 November 1665, to Lilly for deputizing for him. [PRO LC 3/33, p. 125]

28 November 1672: Petition of John Turner, a merchant of Cambridge, against Lilly for a debt of £29. [PRO LC 5/189, f. 104]

29 September 1673: Copy of articles of agreement between Lilly and Pelham Humfrey. Humfrey to pay Lilly £30 p.a. to 'teach and instruct fower of the aforesaid Children of his Ma[jes]ties Chappel royall (such as he the s[ai]d Pelham Humfries shall appoynt) on the violl and Theorbo after the best manner and way he can in the place and stead of him the s[ai]d Pelham Humfreys.'[10] [PRO LC 9/341, f. 30]

n.d.: Lilly listed as a theorbo player in 'the Masque' of 1674.[11] [PRO LC 5/141, pp. 547-8]

n.d.: Warrant from the Lord Chamberlain to the Treasurer of the Chamber to pay Lilly and thirteen other musicians £381. 10s. 0d. for being on duty in the Chapel at Windsor for 109 days, from 18 May to 3 September 1674, at the rate of 5s. per day each. [PRO LC 5/141, p. 124]

21 August 1676: Warrant from the Lord Chamberlain to the Treasurer of the Chamber to pay Lilly and seven other musicians £132 expenses for being on duty in the Chapel at Windsor for sixty-six days, from 7 July to 11 September 1675, at the rate of 5s. per day each. [PRO LC 5/141, p. 448]

n.d. [Arrears of liveries 1677]: Lilly is owed £16. 2s. 6d. [PRO LC 3/39, f. 11]

Debenture Book 29 September 1677 to 24 June 1678: Lilly's name is annotated 'ob. 25 Oct. 1678'. [PRO LC 9/199 (third section) 1677: St. Andrew]

27 September 1678: Warrant from Lord Chamberlain to Clerk of the Great Wardrobe to prepare a bill for the King's signature to provide a yearly livery to John Mosse in the place of John Jenkins, and Edmund Flower in the place of John Lilly, deceased. [PRO LC 5/143, p. 198]

23 March 1680: Letter from Andrew Hatley and William Browne (executors of the will of John Jenkins, deceased) appointing Frances Lilly of Baldwins Gardens, Middlesex (widow and executor of the will of John Lilly, deceased) and Johanna Wheeler of Stepney, to be their attorney to receive all sums of money due to Jenkins from the Exchequer or Treasury Chamber. [PRO E406/50, f. 158]

25 September 1683: Exchequer payment of £20 to Francis Lilly, widow and executor of John Lilly. 'Theire is but one q[ua]rter of a yeare nowe due to Mrs Lilly for Mr Lilly was Buried on ye 28th of October 1678'. [PRO E403/1801, p. 175]

---

[10] It is possible that one of the children was Henry Purcell; F. B. Zimmerman, *Henry Purcell, 1659-1695: His Life and Times* (Philadelphia, rev. 2/1983), 34.

[11] *Calisto* by John Crowne, music by Nicholas Staggins; W. van Lennep, *The London Stage 1660-1800* (Carbondale, Illinois, 1965), i, 228-9.

John Lilly was also an active member of the Westminster Corporation of Musicians, a guild representing, in particular, the interests of the court musicians.[12] Lilly's name appears frequently in the Corporation's minute book for the period 22 October 1661 to 2 July 1679 (British Library Harley MS 1911), and in 1664 and 1675 he served as one of the Wardens of the company.[13] Lilly died on 25 October 1678 and was buried in his parish church of St Andrew Holborn three days later.[14]

The picture presented above is of a typical professional musician of the period scraping together a living from performing, teaching and copying. It appears that even after the Restoration, when he had gained a court appointment, Lilly relied upon the patronage of noble families to supplement his court salary (which was constantly in arrears). Roger North states that Francis North 'was so great [a] patron to him [Lilly], as almost to support his family'[15] and in return Lilly taught Roger North the theorbo and copied music for Francis North 'and others'.[16] Lilly was obviously well acquainted with various members of the North family, particularly 'the tyranicall old lord' Dudley, third Baron North (1581-1666) of Kirtling, Cambridgeshire, who was also the patron of Lilly's friend and colleague, John Jenkins (1592-1678).[17] It should be noted that the North family was related by marriage to the Hatton family: Christopher Hatton III's wife, Elizabeth (née Montagu) was Dudley, fourth Baron North's sister-in-law, and therefore aunt to Francis and Roger North (see Figure 2); perhaps it was Hatton who introduced Lilly to the North family or *vice versa*. At this point, mention should be made of Lilly's extant compositions: twenty-five airs for solo lyra viol survive in various mid- to late-seventeenth-century manuscripts and two were published by Playford (see Table 13).

---

[12] The Corporation of Musick in Westminster claimed authority over the training and performance of musicians in London and was in direct opposition to the rival Company of Minstrel Freemen of the City of London. For accounts of the rivalries between the two guilds see Ashbee (1991b), 245-53; and J. Harley, *Music in Purcell's London: the Social Background* (London, 1968), 15-20.
[13] *Lbl* Harley 1911, f. 5 (24 June 1664) & f. 18 (24 June 1675).
[14] Willetts (1992), 32.
[15] See footnote 7 above.
[16] The 'others' included Edward Lowe (c.1610-82) - organist of the Chapel Royal and Professor of Music at Oxford - for whom Lilly copied Simpson's *Months and Seasons* in 1668 (*Ob* Mus. Sch. C 54-7; see Part 2, MS XXVII).
[17] See M. Crum, 'The Consort Music from Kirtling, Bought for the Oxford Music School from Anthony Wood, 1667', *Chelys*, iv (1972), 3-10; and A. Ashbee, *The Harmonious Musick of John Jenkins. Volume One: The Fantasias for Viols* (Surbiton, 1992), 67-104.

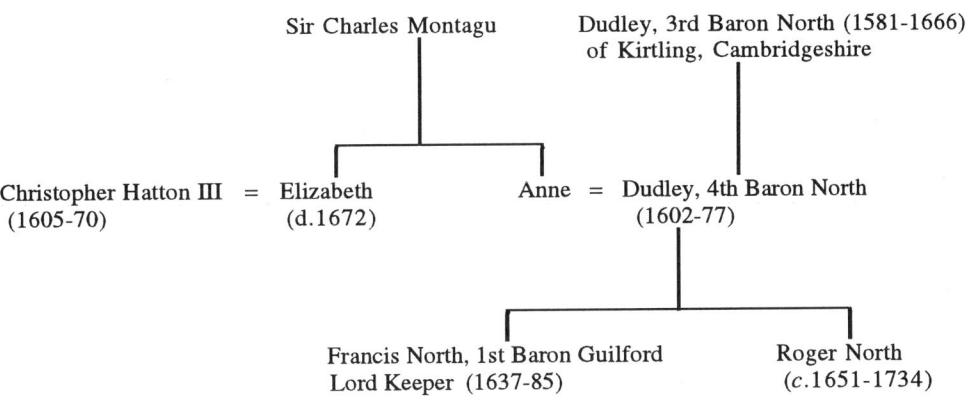

Figure 2 The North Family

Table 13 John Lilly: Airs for Solo Lyra Viol

VdGS
No.[18]

1 Alman in G: *Cu* Dd 6 48(F), f. 16ᵛ; *Lbl* Add. 59,869, f. 10: No. 1.
2 Corant in G: *Lbl* Add. 59,869, f. 10: No. 2.
3 Saraband in G: *Lbl* Add. 59,869, f. 10v: No. 1.
7 Alman in g: *Mp* BRm 832 Vu 51, XI, 15, p. 118: No. 2; Playford:[19] (1651[6]), No. 25; (1652[7]), No. 52 [56]; (1661[4]), No. 26; (1669[6]), No. 88; (1682[9]), No. 23 (misattributed to Jenkins).
8 [Alman in g]: *Lbl* Add. 59,869, f. 18ᵛ: No. 1

---

[18] I am indebted to G. Dodd ed., *Thematic Index of Music for Viols*, The Viola da Gamba Society (London, 1980-) for the manuscript concordances. *Cu* Dd.6.48(F): a manuscript of lyra viol music by Coleman, Lilly, Wilson, etc., dated 19 June 1671; *Lbl* Add. 59,869: the 'Cartwright lyra viol manuscript', music by Coleman, W. Lawes, Lilly, etc., copied in the second half of the seventeenth century (the collection also contains a few folios in Lilly's hand copied *c*.1659 (Willetts (1992), 35; see Table 12 above, and Part II, MS XIII); *Lbl* Add. 63,852: manuscript of lyra viol music by Coleman, W. Lawes, Lilly, etc., copied in the mid-/late-seventeenth century (the 'Griffith Boynton Manuscript'); *Mp* BRm 832 Vu 51: manuscript of lyra viol music by Coleman, Jenkins, Lilly, etc., copied in the mid-seventeenth century; *Ob* Mus. Sch. F 575: manuscript of lute songs and lyra viol pieces by Coleman, Gregory, Ives, Jenkins, W. Lawes, Lilly, etc., owned by William Iles and dated 1673 (but copied earlier); and *EIRE-Dm* Z3.5.13: manuscript of lyra viol music by Ives, Jenkins, W. Lawes, Lilly, etc., copied by Narcissus Marsh and dated 1666.

[19] 1651[6]: *A Musicall Banquet* (T.H., London, 1651); 1652[7]: *Musick's Recreation: on the Lyra Viol* (J. Playford, London, 1652); 1661[4]: *Musick's Recreation: on the Viol, Lyra-way* (J. Playford, London, 1661); 1669[6]: *Musick's Recreation on the Viol, Lyra-way* (W. Godbid, London 1669); 1682[9]: *Musick's Recreation on the Viol, Lyra-way* (W. Godbid & J. Playford, London, 1682).

Table 13 concluded

9 Saraband in g: *Lbl* Add. 59,869, f. 22: No. 3; Playford (1661[4]), No. 83 [86]; (1669[6]), No. 89.
13 Corant in D: *Ob* Mus. Sch. F 575, f. 25^v.
14 [Corant in D]: *Ob* Mus. Sch. F 575, f. 26 (anonymous but attributed to Lilly by virtue of its position in the source).
15 [Alman in D]: *Ob* Mus. Sch. F 575, f. 26^v (anonymous but attributed to Lilly by virtue of its position in the source).
16 Prelude in D: *Lbl* Add. 59,869, f. 27: No. 3 (misattributed to Young); *Ob* Mus. Sch. F 575, f. 26^v: No. 2.
17 Corant in D: *Lbl* Add. 59,869, f. 28.
18 Saraband in D: *Lbl* Add. 59,869, f. 28^v (anonymous but attributed to Lilly by virtue of its position in the source).
19 Corant in D: *Lbl* Add. 59,869, f. 29^v: No. 1 (anonymous); *Ob* Mus. Sch. F 575, f. 82^v rev.; *EIRE-Dm* Z3.5.13, f. 12 (anonymous).
20 [Corant in D]: *Lbl* Add. 59,869, f. 29^v: No. 2 (anonymous but attributed to Lilly by virtue of its position in the source).
21 [Corant in D]: *Lbl* Add. 59,869, f. 30 (anonymous but attributed to Lilly by virtue of its position in the source; a variant of VdGS No. 27, see below).
22 Alman in D: *Lbl* Add. 59,869, f. 30^v; *Ob* Mus. Sch. F 575, f. 83 rev.
23 Saraband in D: *Lbl* Add. 59,869, f. 31.
24 Corant in D: *Ob* Mus. Sch. F 575, f. 82 rev.: No. 1.
25 Saraband in D: *Ob* Mus. Sch. F 575, f. 82 rev.: No. 2.
26 Alman in D: *Ob* Mus. Sch. F 575, f. 81 rev.
27 Corant in D: *Ob* Mus. Sch. F 575, f. 80^v rev. (a variant of VdGS No. 21, see above).
31 Alman in d: *Lbl* Add. 63,852, f. 94 rev. (for lyra viol) and f. 34^v (for keyboard).
32 Alman in d: *Lbl* Add. 63,852, f. 93^v rev. (for lyra viol) and f. 35 (for keyboard).
33 Corant in d: *Lbl* Add. 63,852, f. 93 rev. (for lyra viol) and f. 35^v (for keyboard).
34 Saraband in d: *Lbl* Add. 63,852, f. 92^v rev. (for lyra viol) and f. 36 (for keyboard).

Stephen Bing (1610-1681)

An examination of Table 12 reveals that the copyist John Lilly often worked in conjunction with an associate copyist. For example, the instrumental parts of the 'Great Set' of consort music - Christ Church Mus. 397-408 - were copied by Lilly, but the score and organbook - Christ Church Mus. 2 and

436 respectively - were copied by the associate scribe. Pamela Willetts, in an important article in the *Journal of the Viola da Gamba Society*,[20] identified the 'Lilly associate' as Stephen Bing, a well-known scribe of the Restoration period.[21] This is borne out by a comparison of the manuscripts copied by the 'Lilly associate'[22] with those copied by Stephen Bing.[23] Plate 5 (Christ Church Mus. 880, f. 1 second sequence) represents a typical example of the Lilly associate's script and this should be compared with Plate 6 (York Minster MS M.1.S, Medius Cantoris, f. 14^v), a manuscript copied by Stephen Bing in the 1670s (see below). The hand is the same: the shape and formation of the note heads, the placing of the stems, the accidentals and *custos* marks are so similar as to make the possibility of two separate copyists most unlikely (for comment on the different text styles, see below).[24] Table 14 is a comprehensive list of Stephen Bing's output; the impressive range of his copying activities, together with his longevity, mark Bing as one of the most important music copyists of the seventeenth century.

Stephen Bing's career as a copyist spanned approximately fifty years; we should not, therefore, be surprised to find some variety or apparent inconsistencies amongst the detail of the manuscripts. For example, Bing used a wide range of clef-styles throughout his career. His g' clefs were particularly diverse; in British Library Add. MS 31,434 (see Plate 7) and Christ Church Mus. 2 and 754-9 he used a rather commonplace g' clef:

---

[20] P. Willetts, 'Stephen Bing: a Forgotten Violist', *Chelys*, xviii (1989), 3-17.

[21] See W.H. Cummings, *Purcell* (London, 2/1896), 112; E. Van Tassel, 'Purcell's *Give Sentence*: Two Purcell Discoveries - 1', *MT*, cxviii (1977), 381; J.A. Westrup, *Purcell* (London, rev. 4/1980), 25; H. Watkins Shaw, 'Bing, Stephen', *New Grove*, ii, 723; and ibid., *The Bing-Gostling Part-Books at York Minster: A Catalogue with Introduction* (London, 1986).

[22] The majority of the Lilly associate's manuscripts were identified by Pamela Willetts and David Pinto (Willetts, 'A Neglected Source of Monody and Madrigal', *ML*, xliii (1962), footnote 11; ibid. (1967a), 309-10; and Pinto (1990), 80-2 & Table 1); a few additional examples were identified by the present writer (see S. Boyer & J. Wainwright, 'From Barnard to Purcell: the Copying Activities of Stephen Bing', *EM*, xxiii (1995), 638-42, and Table 14 below).

[23] Stephen Bing's Restoration manuscript copies were identified by Watkins Shaw (1986), 4-8. The 1661-2 Warden's Accounts of the College of Minor Canons of St Paul's Cathedral (*Lgl* Arch. St P. 25,746) were copied and signed by Bing and thus provide a sample of his handwriting for comparison with manuscripts (see Watkins Shaw (1986), Plate IV).

[24] The Lilly associate's hand can also be seen in Plates 7 & 8. The writer is aware that the visual evidence offered by Plates 5-8 alone is insufficient proof that the Lilly associate and Stephen Bing are the same person. The limitations of space preclude the inclusion of numerous examples of Bing's hand - from his early incarnation as the 'Lilly associate' through to his later career as a Restoration copyist - but the reader is referred to the following publications which include plates of his hand: Hiscock (1960), Plate 35 (*Och* Mus. 2, f. 280^v) & Plate 38 (*Och* Mus. 436, f. 63, the titles were added by Aldrich and this led Hiscock to attribute the music-hand mistakenly to Aldrich); D. Griffiths, *A Catalogue of the Music Manuscripts in York Minster Library* (York, 1981), Plate 1 (*Y* M.1.S, Bassus Decani, f. 92); J. Harper, 'Introduction', *Orlando Gibbons: Consort Music*, Musica Britannica xlviii (London, 1982), pp. xxviii-xxix (*Och* Mus. 2, f. 272^v); Watkins Shaw (1986), Plate 1 (*Y* M.1.S, Medius Cantoris, f. 14^v) & Plate 2 (*Y* M.1.S, Bassus Cantoris, f. 76^v); Willetts (1989), Plate 1 (*Och* Mus. 754, No. 57) & Plate 2 (*Lgc* G Mus. 469, f. 20); and Boyer & Wainwright (1995), Plate 1 (*Lbl* Add. 31,434, f. 1), Plate 2 (*Och* Mus. 436, f. 53^v) & Plate 6 (*Lsp* 43.D, ff. 33^v-34).

in the Gresham College partbooks (Guildhall Library, London, Gresham Music MSS 469-71) and the 'Bing-Gostling Partbooks' (York Minster MSS M.1.S) he used the 'fragmented' type (similar to that used by John Playford in his early publications):

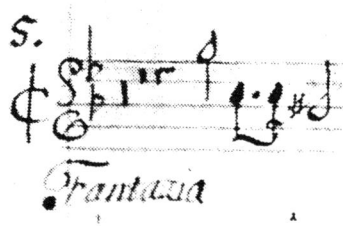

and in Christ Church Mus. 432 and 436 he used a more formal clef (see Plate 8). Pamela Willetts has suggested that Bing was here imitating the *g'* clef found in Thomas Morley's *A Plaine and Easie Introduction to Practicall Musicke* (London, 1597):

Table 14 Stephen Bing

a. Manuscripts copied by Bing

Lbl Add. 27,551: one of five partbooks copied by various hands (instrumental music *a* 3-4 by Jenkins).

Lbl Add. 31,434: parts to anthems, madrigals & motets by H. Lawes, [Notari?], Aloisi (1637 Op. 4), Merula (1624 Op. 6).

Lgc G Mus. 469-71: 'Fantazies & Aires' *a* 3 by Jenkins, Locke and Young; sonatas and airs by 'Sieterich Beckron' [Dietrich Becker?] added to the treble book at a later date.

Lsp Partbook 43.D: bass parts to English chants and services copied by Bing and others (also includes a printed psalter). (?)

Lsp Partbooks A 1: Contratenor and Tenor Decani parts to English services (later additions by Gostling, and some missing pages supplied by an 18th-century hand).

Lwa Partbooks: Triforium Set 1 (Alto Cantoris '1A' and Tenor Cantoris '4') contain sections in Bing's hand (English services and anthems).

Lwa Partbook: Triforium Set 2 (Tenor Decani '5') contains sections in Bing's hand (English services and anthems).

Ob Mus. Sch. C 87: Jenkins' 'fantazies of 3 parts' copied in conjunction with an anonymous scribe. (?)

Ob Mus. Sch. C 204, ff. 46-49^v: parts to motets *a* 3 by Antonelli. (?) (A few annotations added by Jeffreys?)

Ob Tenbury 1005: score to madrigals by Anon., Bernardi (1615-16), Monteverdi (1603).

Ob Tenbury 1009: score to madrigals *a* 5-6 by Anon. (with English texts, *contrafacta?*), Bernardi (1616), Dering, Gesualdo (1595, 1596).

Ob Tenbury 1017: score to Merula's 'Nominativo hic' and 'Nominativo quis' (1633). Some of the text underlay added by Jeffreys.

Och Mus. 2: score to instrumental music *a* 3-6 by Bull, Coleman, Coprario, Ferrabosco II, O. Gibbons, Jenkins, Lupo, Mico, Ward, White; and madrigals and motets *a* 5 (untexted, but titles added by Aldrich) by Lupo, Marenzio, Monteverdi, Pallavicino, Vecchi, Ward. (Associated parts: *Och* Mus. 417-18 & 1080, 436; and others copied by John Lilly: *Och* Mus. 397-400, 401-2, 403-8.)

Och Mus. 255: Bing copied the three manuscript insertions stuck into the basso continuo partbook of Valentini's *Secondo Libro de Madrigali* (1616).

Och Mus. 417-18 & 1080: parts to instrumental music *a* 3-4 found in score in *Och* Mus. 2. (The parts *Och* Mus. 397-400, copied by John Lilly, duplicate this set.)

Table 14a concluded

Och Mus. 432, ff. 109-3 rev.: organ-score to fantasias *a* 3 by Mico. (Parts in *Och* Mus. 401-2, copied by John Lilly. *Och* Mus. 432 ff. 0^v-11 were copied by Lilly with associated parts in *Och* Mus. 612-13.)

Och Mus. 436: organ-score to music *a* 4-6 found in *Och* Mus. 2.

Och Mus. 732-5: Bing added to the work of three other scribes by copying some of the parts for two fantasias *a* 4 by O. Gibbons.

Och Mus. 754-9: parts to 'The Royall Consort' (new version) by W. Lawes.

Och Mus. 878-880, 1st sections: parts to motets *a* 2-3 by Dering and anonymous (also Dering?): three layers: (*a*) anonymous scribe; (*b*) another anonymous scribe provided the music but with text underlay by Jeffreys and with occasional text alternatives added by Bing; and (*c*) Bing's music with underlay by Jeffreys.

Och Mus. 880, last section: basso continuo parts to motets and madrigals by Aloisi (1628, 1637 Op. 4), Arrigoni (1635), Facchi (1635), Ferrabosco I, Gallerano (from Aloisi 1628), Gesualdo (Madrigals Books 1, 2 & 4 complete), Grandi (1610, 1613, 1616, 1630), Mazzocchi (from 1643[1]), Merula (1624, 1628, 1633), Sances (1638), Tomasi (1635), Trabattone (1629).

Och Mus. 1023: basso continuo parts to the whole of Dering's *Cantica Sacra* (1618); text headings added by Jeffreys. (N.B. one of the two copies of *Cantica Sacra* in *Och*, Mus. 881-6, lacks the basso continuo book.)

Och Mus. 1185: organ part to fifteen fantasia-suites for violin, bass viol and organ by Coprario.

Och Mus. 1215, fascicle 3: organ part to verse anthems *a* 3 by Ward.

Y M.1.S: eight partbooks containing English cathedral music (later additions by John Gostling).

US-NYp Drexel 5624: incomplete score of four of Coprario's fantasia-suites for two violins, bass viol and organ.

US-R ML96 L814f, fascicle 3: short score to Coprario's eight fantasia-suites for two violins, bass viol and organ. Copied by Bing and Jeffreys in collaboration.

b. Other examples of Bing's hand

Lbl Add. 29,587, f. 47: 'The speech of Monsieur du Vain when he delivered the Seales to the King, translated out of French' (undated & unsigned, preserved amongst Hatton correspondence).

Lbl Egerton 2533, ff. 481-2: letter dated 16/26 March 1648/9 from Christopher Hatton to Edward Nicholas in Bing's hand.

Lbl Harley 3785, ff. 19, 20, 24, 27, 29 & 47: letters from Stephen Bing to William Sandcroft, Dean of St Paul's Cathedral (July-November 1665).

Table 14b concluded

Lgl Arch. St P. 25,650/2: St Paul's Cathedral acquittance book (receipts for salaries 1670-87) contains examples of Bing's signature and occasionally other comments in his hand.

Lgl Arch. St P. 25,746: the account book of the Warden of the College of Minor Canons of St Paul's Cathedral contains examples of Bing's signature (1642-3, 1647-9, 1661-6), and the accounts for the years ending midsummer 1661 and 1662 were copied by Bing.

Lwa Muniments 61,228A (Precentor's Book), f. 130: contains Bing's signature on his admittance as a Lay Vicar of Westminster Abbey (1 April 1672).

NRO FH 2659 & 2661: two bills (1657-1660) for books and bindings supplied by the London stationer William Searle, endorsed by Bing. (?)

NRO FH 4025: undated catalogue of manuscripts and printed books.

Cover annotations in Bing's hand (see Table 5a, above).

---

and she notes that the account book of the Warden of the College of Minor Canons of St Paul's Cathedral records that Bing borrowed a copy of Morley's treatise on 23 July 1647.[25] It would not be unusual for a professional music-copyist, such as Bing, to imitate notation from current publications. Although Bing's clef-styles differ considerably throughout the manuscripts listed in Table 14, other features of his notation remain relatively constant: the shape and formation of the note heads, rests (and the arrangement of series of rests), accidentals and *custos* marks are uniform; many pieces finish with a decorated ending consisting of a breve or a long surmounted by a fermata and concluding with a series of diminishing vertical lines:

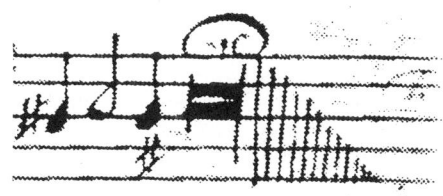

(*Lgc* G Mus. 469, f. 20)

---

[25] *Lgl* Arch. St P. 25,746, f. 29; Willetts (1989), 6.

and, in verse anthems and services, Bing uses two dots to indicate the end of verse sections.[26]

Bing's text-hand is rather more problematic and was perhaps the reason for the delay in identifying Stephen Bing as the 'Lilly associate'. The problem was caused by the fact that Bing appears to have used two distinct text-hands during his career. Stated simply - and thus risking a generalisation - it appears that in his earlier manuscripts he used an old-fashioned secretary hand and later (Commonwealth and Restoration periods) he used an italic hand. The most extensive example of Bing's secretary hand is to be found in British Library Add. MS 31,434 (see Plate 7) and this should be compared with the italic hand used in, for example, the 'Bing-Gostling Partbooks' (see Plate 6, above). Watkins Shaw has noted that Bing's italic text-hand was itself not entirely fluent and that certain letters, such as the minuscules 'g', 'w' and 'y', were particularly variable.[27] Pamela Willetts also commented upon the instability of the italic hand and postulated that some of the letter forms, such as the small 'g' (the type with a tightly curled descender) and the serifs on certain capital letters, were imitations of printed characters.[28] That Bing was not entirely happy in his use of the italic hand was probably due to the fact that, having being born in 1610, he had been educated at a time when two styles of handwriting were in regular use. During the first half of the seventeenth century the indigenous 'English' or 'secretary' hand was gradually supplanted by the imported 'Italian' or 'italic' hand that had first appeared in England around 1580.[29] A professional scribe, such as Stephen Bing, who had been trained in the second and third decades of the seventeenth century would certainly have learnt to use both styles of writing. It is noteworthy that even as late as the 1670s Bing occasionally reverted to his secretary hand: in the St Paul's Cathedral acquittance books (which contain receipts for salaries for the years 1670-87)[30] Bing occasionally supplied a few words of receipt as well as an obligatory signature. These short samples of Bing's secretary hand closely resemble his handwriting in

---

[26] See for example *Lbl* Add. 31,434; *Lsp* Partbooks A 1; and *Y* M.1.S. Willetts - (1989), 6 - notes that the same practice can be found in sources connected with St Paul's Cathedral, such as John Barnard's *The First Book of Selected Church Musick* (London, 1641) and a complementary set of manuscript partbooks (*Lcm* 1045-51) probably copied in part by Adrian Batten (see J. Bunker Clark, 'Adrian Batten and John Barnard: Colleagues and Collaborators', *MD*, xxii (1968), 207-29; and P.J. Willetts, 'John Barnard's Collections of Viol and Vocal Music', *Chelys*, xx (1991), 28-42); this is not surprising given Bing's links with St Paul's and with John Barnard (see below).
[27] Watkins Shaw (1986), 7-8.
[28] Willetts (1989), 7.
[29] See R.B. McKerrow, 'A Note on Elizabethan Handwriting', reprinted in P. Gaskell, *A New Introduction to Bibliography* (Oxford, 1972), 362-3; and H. Love, *Scribal Publication in Seventeenth-Century England* (Oxford, 1993), 106-16.
[30] *Lgl* Arch. St. P. 25,650/2.

early manuscripts such as British Library Add. MS 31,434 and Christ Church Mus. 754-9, 878-80 *passim*, and 1215 fascicle 3 (see below).[31]

The main outlines of Stephen Bing's life have been established by Watkins Shaw and Pamela Willetts;[32] the following discussion represents a comprehensive account of Bing's surviving manuscripts set within the context of this biographical framework. Stephen Bing, 'son of Stephan Binge', was baptised at the church of St George the Martyr, Canterbury on 20 September 1610[33] and gained his early musical training as a chorister at Canterbury Cathedral (1617/18-1624).[34] He was probably taught to play the viol by John Barnard who was a lay-clerk at Canterbury Cathedral from 1618 to 1622 (Barnard was paid 20s in 1620 for teaching the viol to the choristers).[35] It is highly probable that this Barnard can be identified with the John Barnard who was a collector and editor of viol and church music and later Minor Canon of St Paul's Cathedral, London;[36] as we shall see, Stephen Bing was to have many connections with John Barnard. Bing probably left Canterbury soon after his voice changed (his name does not appear in the Cathedral records after 1624). Although little is known of his activities between 1625 and 1640, it seems likely that he was in Cambridge sometime during the 1630s. This is revealed, in passing, in a letter dated 24 October 1666 from Michael Honywood, Dean of Lincoln Cathedral, to William Sancroft, Dean of St Paul's Cathedral, London.[37] The letter is concerned with events much later in Bing's life (see below for the full details), but it is important to us here because Honywood reveals that he knew Bing '30 or 40 years' earlier. Honywood was a Fellow of Christ's College, Cambridge from 1618 to 1643 and it is therefore likely that his previous acquaintance with Bing had been in the university town in the early

---

[31] It should be noted that, whilst his letter shapes often vary in his manuscripts, Bing's numerals remain remarkably uniform. Pamela Willetts' suggestion - (1989), 7 - that the headings and titles in *Och* Mus. 2 and 436 - and therefore also *Och* Mus. 403-8 - 'could be an earlier form of Stephen Bing's italic hand' is not accepted by the present writer. A comparison of these headings with the handwriting in *Ob* Lister 36, ff. 129-30^v and *Och* Mus. 18 & 43, etc., would seem to support Miss Willetts' original suggestion - (1967a), 309 - that they are in the hand of Henry Aldrich (1648-1710).

[32] Watkins Shaw, *New Grove*; ibid. (1986), 4-7; and Willetts (1989). See also R.F. Ford, 'Minor Canons at Canterbury Cathedral: The Gostlings and their Colleagues' (Ph.D. dissertation, University of California, Berkeley, 1984), 258-61.

[33] J.M. Cowper ed., *The Register Booke of the Parish of St. George the Martyr within the Citie of Canterburie* (Canterbury, 1891), 23. From other entries in the register we gather that Bing was the only son and second of five children born to Stephen Bing (presumably the 'Steven Bing', a beer-brewer, who was buried at St George's on 31 August 1632) and - probably - Mary Binge (who was buried on 3 February 1638 (NS) and described as a widow).

[34] *CA* Bound Papers of Accounts 1576-1642 (with gaps), and *CA* 26-47 Fair Copy Accounts 1617-42 (with gaps); references from Watkins Shaw (1986), footnote 7. Bing is first listed as a chorister in the accounting year ending Michaelmas 1618 and last mentioned in the year ending 1624 (his name is crossed through in the Fair Copy Accounts for 1624).

[35] *CA* Treasurer's Accounts 1620; I am indebted to Dr Andrew Ashbee for this reference.

[36] See J. Morehen, 'Barnard, John', *New Grove*, ii, 165-6; and Willetts (1991).

[37] *Ob* Tanner 130, f. 17.

to mid 1630s;[38] we should remember that Christopher Hatton III, George Jeffreys and John Lilly were all associated with Cambridge at this time.

There is one possible piece of evidence to support an early link between Bing and George Jeffreys (and therefore, by association, also with Hatton): a manuscript in the Bodleian Library, Oxford - Mus. Sch. MS C 204 (see Part II, MS XXIX) - contains, amongst miscellaneous sets of parts from the second half of the seventeenth century, parts to two three-part motets by the Roman composer Abundio Antonelli (section 'O', ff. 46-49^v).[39] According to an inscription on folio 47 the copyist had received the motets 'from Rome [on] the 11 of Novemb[er] 1634'; the paper-type (a Normandy-Pillars watermark) is consistent with a copying-date in the mid-1630s.[40] This manuscript may be the earliest identified exemplar of Stephen Bing's hand. A comparison with various manuscripts listed in Table 14a reveals that the music-hand of MS C 204, folios 46-49^v is slightly thinner and more untidy but, with the exception of the time signatures and the bass clefs, the details are very similar and the text-hand (including the inscription) seems to be Bing's secretary hand. What is more, a few annotations at the top of the pages appear to be in the hand of George Jeffreys.[41] This is supported by a later single-sheet index in the hand of Edward Lowe that lists the contents of a Music School bundle of papers;[42] some of the listed items correspond to fascicles in Mus. Sch. MS C 204. Amongst the 'Loose papers' listed by Lowe are '4 papers of an Italian[']s Latin Songe O [sic] dulcis Jesu. w[hi]ch I had of Mr Jeffreys'; this would appear to refer to folios 46-49^v of MS C 204 and thus links it with George Jeffreys.[43]

---

[38] Honywood spent the Civil War and Commonwealth periods in the Low Countries and at the Restoration returned to England, became Dean of Lincoln Cathedral (1660-81), and went on to assemble one of the most important library collections in the country (including a substantial number of English and Italian music prints). See J.H. Srawley, *Michael Honywood, Dean of Lincoln (1660-81): A Story of the English Church in Critical Times* (Lincoln, 2/1981); C. Hurst, 'Introduction', *Catalogue of the Wren Library of Lincoln Cathedral: Books Printed before 1801* (Cambridge, 1982), pp. ix-xiii; N. Linnell, 'Michael Honywood and Lincoln Cathedral Library', *The Library*, Sixth Series, v (1983), 126-39; and I. Fenlon, 'Michael Honywood's Music Books', *'Sundry sorts of music books' Essays on The British Library Collections Presented to O.W. Neighbour on his 70th Birthday*, ed. C. Banks, A. Searle & M. Turner (London, 1993), 183-200.

[39] I have been unable to identify a printed source for the motets; the pieces do not appear in Antonelli, *Liber Primus/Secundus/Tertius Diversarum Modulationum* (Rome, 1615/1615/1616).

[40] R. Thompson, 'English Music Manuscripts and the Fine Paper Trade, 1648-1688' (Ph.D. dissertation, University of London, 1988), 91-2, 218 & 220.

[41] It is conceivable that the clefs and the time signatures are in the hand of Jeffreys; as we shall see, Bing copied a number of manuscripts in conjunction with or under the supervision of Jeffreys.

[42] The index was found in *Ob* Mus. Sch. C 9 and is now kept in the folder *Ob* Mus. Sch. A 641 (the list is transcribed on p. 320 below).

[43] Lowe's reference to the motet as 'O dulcis Jesu' rather than 'Dulcis Jesu [pie Jesu]' appears to have been a simple mistake: the fact that he copied the basso continuo part of Antonelli's 'Dulcis Jesu' in *Ob* Mus. Sch. E 451 (see Part II, MS XXX) would seem to confirm that Lowe was referring to this piece in the index and not some other motet entitled 'O dulcis Jesu'. The only other concordance noted for Antonelli's 'Dulcis Jesu' is in Angelo Notari's score *Lbl* Add.

During the 1630s Stephen Bing took Holy Orders, for in 1640/41 he was appointed as a Minor Canon at St Paul's Cathedral, London: the statutes of the College of Minor Canons at St Paul's required a beneficiary to have been ordained and, as the duties were musical as well as liturgical, also to have a good voice.[44] Amongst Bing's colleagues at St Paul's were John Barnard, who was in the process of seeing his monumental *First Book of Selected Church Musick* through the press (1641), and John Woodington who was also a court violinist.[45] The association between Barnard, Bing and Woodington is apparent in a set of four manuscript partbooks in Christ Church, Oxford (Mus. 732-5) and a companion organbook in the Royal Music Library (MS R.M. 24.k.3 housed in the British Library, London; see Part II, MS LV). Whereas the Royal Music organbook is finely bound in black morocco and bears the arms of Charles I, the four Christ Church partbooks remain in their original paper covers.[46] The inside front cover of Mus. 732 contains the name 'John Wodenton', and the back cover of Mus. 734 - in a different hand and in very faded ink - is signed 'Woodington'; the latter inscription is very similar to Woodington's signature as found in the Whitelocke Papers at Longleat.[47] Christ Church Mus. 732-5 and Royal Music MS 24.k.3 (which contain Coprario's fantasia-suites for one and two violins, bass viol and organ, and Orlando Gibbons' fantasias for one and two treble viols, bass viol and 'great Dooble Basse') were copied by four scribes: the main scribe ('A') copied all the organbook and substantial sections of the four partbooks, and the three other scribes ('B', 'C' and 'D') - apparently working in collaboration with 'A' - completed the copying.[48] Of

---

31,440 (see Part II, MS VII), a source which has circumstantial links with the Hatton music collection (see Chapter Six).

[44] *Lgl* Arch. St P. 25,746, f. 19^v: Bing paid his Ingress money of 11s 8d sometime during the year 1640-1; and *Lgl* Arch. St P. 25,746, f. 22^v: Bing signed the Warden's accounts for the first time at midsummer 1642 when he collected his yearly dividend. It is possible that Hatton was influential in Bing's appointment at St Paul's. Hatton had various links with the cathedral: for example, he had commissioned William Dugdale to survey the monuments of England's principal churches and Dugdale had begun work on St Paul's Cathedral in 1640, the same year as Bing's appointment (Dugdale later dedicated his *History of St. Paul's Cathedral* (1658) to Hatton); and in 1661 Hatton was to recommend a singer, Henry Frost, for the choir - perhaps he did the same for Stephen Bing in 1640?

[45] In a petition to Charles I dated 12 May 1625 Woodington describes himself as 'Musician to K[ing] James 6 yeres, and to His Ma[jes]tie in Coperario[']s musique 3 yeres' (*Lbl* Add. 64,883, f. 57) and his name appears in court records until 1647 (see A. Ashbee, *Records of English Court Music*, iii (Snodland, 1988), *passim*). Woodington was a Vicar Choral at St Paul's from *c*.1628 to 1645; see Willetts (1991), 34-6.

[46] *Och* Mus. 732-5 are now contained in modern vellum bindings.

[47] Longleat, Whitelocke Papers, Parcel II, No. 9, Item 6, f. 5. Woodington's signature is reproduced in M. Lefkowitz, 'The Longleat Papers of Bulstrode Whitelocke; New Light on Shirley's *Triumph of Peace*', *JAMS*, xviii (1965), Plate 1, No. 5.

[48] An examination of the scribal layers in relation to the collations of the partbooks supports the suggestion that the four scribes were working in collaboration.

the four scribes, only 'C' has been identified for certain;[49] this is none other than Stephen Bing, who contributed a single piece to three of the Christ Church partbooks.[50] Scribe 'A' also contributed to the Royal College of Music MSS 1045-51 and Bodleian Library Tenbury MS 302, two sources closely associated with John Barnard.[51]

The evidence would seem to suggest that scribes 'A', 'B' and 'D' were from the 'St Paul's circle' of copyists Could Barnard or Woodington be amongst the copyists? The only positively identified exemplars of John Barnard's handwriting are signatures.[52] The sections of the Christ Church partbooks copied by hands 'B' and 'D' do not include text and so cannot be compared with Barnard's hand;[53] the text-hand of scribe 'A' can be seen in the Royal College of Music MSS 1045-51 and Bodleian Library Tenbury MS 302, but it bears no similarity to Barnard's signatures.

What then of John Woodington? As we have seen, it is possible that one of the Christ Church partbooks contains Woodington's signature. This must make him a prime candidate for one of the copyists 'A', 'B' or 'D' and this becomes even more likely given the fact that, on 15 February 1635, Woodington was paid £20 'for a whole sett of Musicke Bookes by him p[ro]vided & prickt w[i]th all Coperaries & Orlando Gibbons theire Musique, by his Ma[jesty's] speciall Com[m]and and Warr[an]t'.[54] The case would seem to be clear cut: the organbook and partbooks are the 'whole sett

---

[49] Pamela Willetts (1991), 35, has suggested that scribe 'A' (= Willetts' scribe 'B') may be John Tomkins (1586-1638), a court musician and also colleague of Bing's and Woodington's at St Paul's Cathedral. The circumstantial evidence makes this an attractive proposition.

[50] I cannot agree with Richard Charteris ('Autographs of John Coprario', *ML*, lvi (1975), 43-4) that the title - 'The great Dooble Basse' - on the front cover of *Och* Mus. 735 is 'almost certainly in Woodington's hand' and that scribes 'B' and 'C' (Bing) contributed to the titles and inscriptions on the paper covers of *Och* Mus. 732-4.

[51] See J. Morehen, 'The Sources of English Cathedral Music *c*.1617-*c*.1644' (Ph.D. dissertation, University of Cambridge, 1969), 244-304; and Willetts (1991). Mention should be made of two other 'sightings' of scribe 'A': Thurston Dart and W. Coates ed., *Jacobean Consort Music*, Musica Britannica ix (London, 2/rev. 1962) considered that *Lbl* R.M. 24.k.3 was copied by Coprario (p. 228); and D. Pinto ed., *William Lawes: Fantasia-Suites*, Musica Britannica lx (London, 1991) considered the same manuscript to be 'in the youthful hand of [William] Lawes... dating from the the mid-1620s' (p. xvi) (see also D. Pinto, *'for ye violls': The Consort and Dance Music of William Lawes* (Richmond, 1995), 15-16). The present writer is not in agreement with either identification, but Pinto's suggestion that scribe 'A' is William Lawes, and the 'knock-on' implications, needs careful consideration.

[52] Barnard's signatures appear in the account book of the Warden of the College of Minor Canons at St Paul's for the years 1624-44 (*Lgl* Arch. St P. 25,746); his signature in the 1636 Visitation Records at the House of Lords is reproduced in Willetts (1991), Plate 2a. It is possible that the correcting hand in the full score of Ward's first service at the reverse end of *Lcm* 1049 is that of Barnard, but the sample of music-hand is too limited for useful comparison.

[53] The headings 'Fantaziæ/Fantasie', 'Almaine/Almand' and 'Galliard' were not necessarily added by the scribes who copied the music, thus the titles are here not considered as evidence of the text-hands of scribes 'B' and 'D'.

[54] PRO AO1/394/72. See also PRO LC 5/134, p. 43: 'A Warr[an]t for paym[en]t of XXli unto Mr John Woodington for a new sett of bookes for Cooperarios Musique, by his Ma[jes]t[y']s speciall com[m]annd. Febr[uary]. 20. 1634 [NS 1635]'; Ashbee (1988), 81 & 150.

of Musicke Bookes' copied under the supervision of - and perhaps even in part by - John Woodington. However, it should be noted that (*a*) John Woodington's signatures cannot be reconciled with the handwriting of scribe 'A' (as found in Royal College MSS 1045-51 and Bodleian Tenbury MS 302) nor with that of scribes 'B' and 'D' (as no text exists to be compared with Woodington's signature);[55] (*b*) the organbook, although beautifully bound and stamped with the royal arms, is unfinished (no music has been entered on ff. 47^v-[96^v]) and, as Pamela Willetts has pointed out, it would have been most unusual for payment to have been made in advance of copying;[56] (*c*) the partbooks were copied rather untidily and do not 'come up to standard for a royal commission for which handsome payment was authorised';[57] (*d*) the Coprario fantasia-suites are numbered continuously 1-23 in the Royal Music organbook but are divided into three groups 1-8, 1-7 and 1-8 in the Christ Church partbooks; and (*e*) the Royal Music manuscript and the Christ Church partbooks are made up of different types of paper.[58]

Richard Charteris considered that, as the Royal Music organbook 'clearly adopts a system of numbering that streamlines the numeration in the partbooks, it can be confidently assumed that MSS. 732-5 antedate the compilation of the organ-book.'[59] David Pinto has suggested that the partbooks - 'probably the personal playing parts of the violinist John Woodington' - were the original rough copies used in February 1635 when Woodington produced new copies of music by Coprario and Gibbons.[60] This would mean that the Christ Church partbooks date from before 1635 and that the Royal Music organbook is all that survives of the 1635 royal commission for a 'whole sett of Musicke Bookes'. It is even possible that the Royal Music organbook, despite its regal binding, is not part of the 1635 commission; it was noted above that the organbook is unfinished and that it would have been most unusual for payment to have been made in advance of copying. Whatever the true case, the organbook remained in the Old Royal Library whereas Woodington's performing parts found their way to Oxford, possibly when the Court moved there during the Civil War, or perhaps as part of the music collection of Christopher Hatton III (in the manner outlined

---

[55] See note 53 above.
[56] Willetts (1991), 34-5.
[57] Ibid.
[58] The partbooks include three different types of paper. The physical evidence offered by the paper in *Och* Mus. 732-5 and *Lbl* R.M. 24.k.3 is no help in assigning a more exact date to the manuscripts; the four watermarks - small pot, pillars, grapes and encircled peacock(?) - are consistent with a date sometime in the 1630s.
[59] Charteris (1975), 45. Charteris' dating of both *Lbl* R.M. 24.k.3 and *Och* Mus. 732-5 as *c*.1625 must now be revised following the identification of Bing's hand in the partbooks (Bing would only have been 15 years old in 1625); an examination of the scribal layers in relation to the collations of the partbooks argues against the possibility that Bing could have made his contribution independently and at a later date to the other copyists.
[60] Pinto (1991), p. xvi.

in Chapter Four). In both these hypothetical cases the linking factor between the partbooks and Oxford and/or Hatton is Stephen Bing.

Another of Stephen Bing's manuscripts that reveals his London connections in the 1630s is Christ Church Mus. 1215, third fascicle. This is the organ part of two multi-sectional three-voice verse anthems[61] by John Ward based on the texts of Psalm 103 ('Praise the Lord O my soul') and Psalm 51 ('Have mercy upon me O God'). The only known concordances for these verse anthems are to be found in 'Will Foster's Virginal Book', a keyboard score dated 1624 (Royal Music Library 24.d.3), and in manuscripts copied in part by Thomas Myriell: the partbooks Christ Church Mus. 61-6 and the companion organbook Christ Church Mus. 67.[62] Stephen Bing's organ parts of the Ward verse anthems in Christ Church Mus. 1215/3 are very closely related to those in Myriell's organbook, Christ Church Mus. 67 folios 0^v-7; the two sources agree in almost every detail (even down to the repetition of accidentals).[63] Thomas Myriell, who was rector of St Stephen's Walbrook (close to St Paul's Cathedral) from 1616 to his death in 1625, is best known as the compiler of the manuscript-partbook anthology *Tristitiæ Remedium... 1616* (now British Library Add. MSS 29,372-7) which is one of the most important musical sources of the Jacobean period; Myriell was also the copyist of Brussels, Bibliothèque Royale MS II.4109, and British Library Add. MS 29,427 and Christ Church Mus. 44, 61-7 and 459-62 are partly in his hand. This is not the place for a detailed examination of Myriell's connections and musical tastes as represented in these manuscripts, but a few comments will help place Bing's copy of the Ward verse anthems in context, and also demonstrate a possible link between the Myriell manuscripts and the Hatton collection.[64]

Myriell's musical-circle centred around the St Paul's Cathedral area of London. He probably knew Nicholas Yonge (d.1619), the well-known editor of anthologies of Italian madrigals 'Englished',[65] who lived in Cornhill, and was a Vicar Choral at St Paul's Cathedral.[66] A section from the

---

[61] The verses are for cantus and altus and the bassus joins for the 'chorus'.
[62] The third and fourth sections of Psalm 51 are lacking in the organbook.
[63] Craig Monson - *Voice and Viols in England 1600-1650* (Ann Arbor, 1982), Chapter 2, note 33 - comments that the readings of *Och* Mus. 67, ff. 0^v-7 and *Och* Mus. 1215/3 are 'remarkably close' and suggests that *Och* Mus. 1215/3 was the 'rough copy' for *Och* Mus. 67. This is unlikely given that it is now known that Stephen Bing (b. 1610) was the copyist of *Och* Mus. 1215/3, and Myriell died in 1625; nor is it possible that *Och* Mus. 1215/3 was copied from *Och* Mus. 67 as the Myriell organbook lacks the third and fourth sections of Psalm 51 (which were copied in *Och* Mus. 1215/3). The explanation would seem to be that both *Och* Mus. 67, ff. 0^v-7 and *Och* Mus. 1215/3 were copied from a common source (possibly *Lbl* R.M. 24.d.3, but a comparison of readings is inconclusive).
[64] See P. Willetts, 'Musical Connections of Thomas Myriell', *ML*, xlix (1968), 36-42; ibid., 'The Identity of Thomas Myriell', *ML*, liii (1972), 431-3; ibid., 'Myriell, Thomas', *New Grove*, xiii, 6; C. Monson, 'Thomas Myriell's Manuscript Collection: One View of Musical Taste in Jacobean London', *JAMS*, xxx (1977), 419-65; and Monson (1982), 5-69.
[65] *Musica Transalpina* (London, 1588 & 1597).
[66] See Monson (1982), 7-9 & Plate 1: C & D.

oft-quoted 'Epistle dedicatorie' to his first anthology gives an impression of the vibrant musical life of the district:

> ...since I first began to keepe house in this Citie, it hath been no small comfort unto mee, that a great number of Gentlemen and Merchants of good accompt (as well of this realme as of forreine nations) have taken in good part such entertainment of pleasure, as my poore abilitie was able to affoord them, both by exercise of Musicke daily used in my house, and by furnishing them with Bookes of that kinde yeerely sent me out of Italy and other places, which beeing for the most part Italian Songs, are for sweetnes of Aire, verie well liked of all, but most in account with them that understand that language...

Myriell's manuscripts include a substantial number of Italian madrigals that are either 'Englished' - many copied directly from Yonge's anthologies - or left textless for instrumental performance. The manuscripts also include music by St Paul's musicians (such as Martin Peerson, Simon Stubbs and John Tomkins) and, as Craig Monson has noted, there appears to be a link between Myriell and John Barnard: 'virtually all Myriell's older anthem choices were also picked for inclusion in John Barnard's monumental *First Book of Selected Church Musick*'.[67] John Ward was another composer closely associated with Myriell and the St Paul's enclave: his compositions are well represented in Myriell's manuscripts; Barnard chose to include a service[68] and two anthems by Ward in his 1641 publication; and it is even possible that Ward's handwriting appears in two of Myriell's manuscripts (Christ Church Mus. 61-6 and British Library Add. MS 29,427).[69] John Ward was employed as a household musician to Sir Henry Fanshawe (1569-1616), the Remembrancer of the Exchequer, of Ware Park, Hertfordshire;[70] it is possible that after Myriell's death in 1625 his manuscripts found their way into the collection of John Ward or that of the Fanshawe family.[71] We should note that Sir Henry Fanshawe's half-sister Alice was married to Christopher Hatton II; could some of the Myriell manuscripts have come, via Alice, into the Hatton collection? The likelihood that Christopher Hatton III inherited a music collection from his father has already been suggested (see page 36) and this raises the possibility that the presence of Myriell sources at

---

[67] Monson (1982), 43.
[68] Indeed, Monson has noted (ibid., 40) that all Ward's extant service music survives in manuscripts associated with Barnard and/or his St Paul's colleague Adrian Batten (see R.T. Daniel & P. le Huray, *The Sources of English Church Music 1549-1660*, Early English Church Music, supplement i (London, 1972); Bunker Clark (1968); and Willetts (1991)).
[69] See I. Payne, 'The Handwriting of John Ward', *ML*, lxv (1984), 176-88.
[70] The Fanshawes also owned a London house in Warwick Lane close to St Paul's Cathedral; see Monson (1982), 40 & Plate 1: G.
[71] This speculation would probably have been over-stepping the mark of acceptability were it not for a piece of evidence cited in Monson (1982), 41: one of Myriell's manuscripts (*B-Br* II.4109) was, according to a note on its flyleaf, bought in 1784 by Isaac Reed at Ware in Hertfordshire - the seat of the Fanshawe family.

Christ Church, Oxford is due to the Hattons.[72] Further links between the Myriell manuscripts, Fanshawe manuscripts and the Hatton collection are explored in Chapter Six.

The Christ Church Sets of Viol Consort Music

The three Bing manuscripts examined above have no obvious connection with Christopher Hatton III. However, as Bing's first association with Hatton probably dates from the early to mid 1630s, it is not impossible that Hatton's influence lurks behind Bing's earliest copying activities in some, as yet, undemonstrable way.[73] (The alternative possibility that Bing was working for other unidentified patrons should not, of course, be discounted.) Christ Church Mus. 432, a large oblong-quarto organbook, has definite links with Christopher Hatton as its binding contains the Hatton coat of arms, crest and family motto (see Plate 2). Stephen Bing's handwriting appears in a section towards the end of the organbook (reversed), but the main copyist was John Lilly who also copied the two companion partbooks: Christ Church Mus. 612-13 (see Part II, MS LI). The 'Hatton Set' contains fantasias and ayres for two bass viols and organ by Coprario, Jenkins and Ward - copied by Lilly - and Mico's three-part fantasias - added by Bing to the organbook. The parts to the Mico fantasias were not copied into the companion partbooks (Mus. 612-13); they do, however, appear in another set of books: Christ Church Mus. 417-18 and 1080 (Part II, MS L) which were copied entirely by Stephen Bing. The 'Bing Set', which is incomplete (lacking the tenor-book for the four-part pieces), contains three- and four-part viol consort music by Bull, Coprario, Ferrabosco II, Orlando Gibbons, Jeffreys, Lupo, Mico and Ward. With the exception of the six three-part fantasias by George Jeffreys, the whole contents of the Bing Set are duplicated in another collection of instrumental music copied jointly by Bing and Lilly: Christ Church Mus. 2, 397-408 and 436 (Part II, MS XLII). This comprehensive collection of larger-scale viol-consort music from the earlier Stuart period is known by the apt sobriquet 'The Great Set'. The scorebook (Mus. 2) and the organbook (Mus. 436) were copied by Stephen Bing and the three sets of partbooks by John Lilly (Mus. 397-400: four-part works; Mus. 401-2: three-part works, incomplete;[74] and Mus. 403-8: five- and six-part works). Mention must also be made of a separate organbook copied by

---

[72] The author is aware of the dangers of building hypothesis upon hypothesis, particularly when dealing with such incomplete - and often circumstantial - evidence. However, I am of the opinion that, within limits, a certain amount of conjecture is worthwhile, if only to present ideas for testing by other scholars as more research is undertaken and new evidence unearthed.

[73] For example, Hatton's court connections should be borne in mind when considering a context for the copying of *Och* Mus. 732-5 and *Lbl* R.M. 24.k.3.

[74] The two books containing parts for fantasias *a* 3 (*Och* Mus. 401-2) were stamped '4.B[ooks]' on their spines by Henry Aldrich. This indicates that the set lacks not only a treble book but also an organbook; this is supported by the fact that the Great Set organbook (*Och* Mus. 436) does not contain any three-part works.

John Lilly: British Library Egerton MS 2485 (Part II, MS XIV); the contents of the 'Lilly Organbook' are, with the exception of ten pieces,[75] duplicated in the organbook to the Great Set (Mus. 436). Descriptions and inventories of manuscripts of viol-consort music copied by Bing and Lilly are given in Part II, and Table 15 presents a summary of the contents of the sets and details the relationships and duplications between the manuscripts.

Two obvious questions need to be answered concerning these manuscripts: when were they copied and why? Before attempting to throw new light on these matters, a number of points need to be made and a few misconceptions corrected. First it should be noted that the contents of the Great Set were originally left untitled, unascribed and unnumbered; the headings and numberings of the first twenty-four five-part pieces - untexted vocal works except for Ferrabosco II's 'Dovehouse Pavan' - were added by Henry Aldrich (see Plate 8).[76] The presence of Aldrich's text-hand in the Great Set led a number of commentators to identify incorrectly the music-hand of Christ Church Mus. 2, 436 and others as that of Aldrich.[77] It seems that when Aldrich acquired the Great Set, probably in the 1670s (see pages 41-3 above), the partbooks (Mus. 397-408) and organbook (Mus. 436) were without bindings, and the scorebook (Mus. 2) was bound in 'rugh calf' (according to Johann Baptist Malchair's 1787 catalogue of the Christ Church music collection).[78] Aldrich gave the partbooks and organbook their present uniform bindings of speckled brown leather with blind-tooled motifs of three pointed buds. The three sets of parts were incorporated into his

---

[75] Six of these ten pieces do, however, appear in either the scorebook (*Och* Mus. 2) or the partbooks (*Och* Mus. 404-8) of the Great Set; see Table 15.
[76] Aldrich mistakenly attributes No. 24 'O doloroso [*recte* dolorosa morte]' to Marenzio; it is in fact by Pallavicino (from *Il Settimo Libro de Madrigali a Cinque Voci* (1604)).
[77] For example: E. Walker, 'An Oxford Book of Fancies', *The Musical Antiquary*, iii (1912), 63-73; G.E.P. Arkwright, *Catalogue of Music in the Library of Christ Church, Oxford* (London, 1923), ii, 94; and Hiscock (1960), 33 & Plates 35-6. Pamela Willetts - (1962), 332, footnote 11; and (1967a), 309 - was the first to disengage the text-hand (Aldrich) from the music-hand (the 'Lilly associate', i.e. Bing). In (1989), 7, Willetts reconsiders the question of the text hand in the Great Set and states that 'the headings and titles in Och MSS 2 and 436 could be an earlier form of Stephen Bing's italic hand.' It is, however, the opinion of the present writer that the text hand *is* that of Henry Aldrich (by comparison with the handwriting in Aldrich's letters, e.g., Bodleian Library Lister MS 36, ff.129-30^v; and that which appears in Aldrich's music manuscripts: Christ Church Mus. 9, 16, 17 (ff. 1-29 & 48^v rev.), 18, 19, 55 (pp. 1-65), 521-4, 525 (ff. 1-11), 526 (1-13^v & 17-24), etc.). D.W. Krummel, *English Music Printing 1553-1700* (London, 1975), 134-8, notes that the Oxford printer Peter de Walpergen based his two music type faces on Aldrich's calligraphy. However, the surviving specimens of Walpergen's first music type-face (such as *Och* Mus. 1208, 'Specimen of Church Musick in Score, as Intended to be printed by Dean Aldrich') are remarkably similar to Stephen Bing's music-hand (see Krummel (1975), Plate 48); and his second music type-face (for example in *Musica Oxoniensis* (Oxford, 1698)) has many of the features of John Lilly's music-hand (Krummel (1975), Plate 50). (See also H. Carter, 'Peter de Walpergen, Punchcutter and Type-founder, 1646(?)-1703', *Gutenberg Jahrbuch* (1965), 48-52.)
[78] *Lcm* 2125, f. 37. The present binding of *Och* Mus. 2 is modern.

Table 15 Summary of Bing's and Lilly's Copies of Music for Viol Consort

Composer	Title	Scoring	VdGS No.	The Great Set 2 401 402 436	The Bing Set 417 418 1080	The Hatton Set 612 613 432
Coprario	Fantasia	2b.vl org	1			1 1 a^v
Coprario	Fantasia	2b.vl org	2			1^v 1^v 1
Coprario	Fantasia	2b.vl org	3			2 2 1^v
Coprario	Fantasia	2b.vl org	4			2^v 2^v 2
Coprario	Fantasia	2b.vl org	5			3a 3 2^v
Coprario	Fantasia	2b.vl org	6			3a^v 3^v 3
Coprario	Fantasia	2b.vl org	7			3 4 3^v
Coprario	Fantasia	2b.vl org	8			3^v 4^v 4
Coprario	Fantasia	2b.vl org	9			4 5 4^v
Coprario	Fantasia	2b.vl org	10			4^v 5^v 5
Ward	Ayre	2b.vl org	1			5 6 5^v
Ward	Ayre	2b.vl org	2			5^v 6^v 6
Ward	Ayre	2b.vl org	3			6 7 6^v
Ward	Ayre	2b.vl org	4			6^v 7^v 7
Ward	Ayre	2b.vl org	5			7 8 7^v
Ward	Ayre	2b.vl org	6			7^v 8^v 8
Jenkins	Ayre	2b.vl org	38			8^v 9 8^v
Jenkins	Ayre	2b.vl org	37			9^v 10^v 9
Jenkins	Ayre	2b.vl org	45			10^v 11^v 9^v
Jenkins	Ayre	2b.vl org	46			11^v 12^v 10
Jenkins	Ayre	2b.vl org	63			12^v 13^v 10^v
Jenkins	Ayre	2b.vl org	44			13^v 14^v 11
Coprario	Fantasia	a3	10	50 b^v b^v	17^v 17^v	
Coprario	Fantasia	a3	1	50^v 1^v 1^v	18^v 18^v	
Coprario	Fantasia	a3	2	51 2^v 2^v	19^v 19^v	
Coprario	Fantasia	a3	4	51^v 3^v 3^v	20^v 20^v	
Coprario	Fantasia	a3	3	52 4^v 4^v	21^v 21^v	
Coprario	Fantasia	a3	9	52^v 5^v 5^v	22^v 22^v	
Coprario	Fantasia	a3	5	53 6^v 6^v	23^v 23^v	
Coprario	Fantasia	a3	6	53^v 7^v 7^v	24^v 24^v	

Table 15 continued

Composer	Title	Scoring	VdGS No.	The Great Set				The Bing Set			The Hatton Set		
				2	401	402	436	417	418	1080	612	613	432
Lupo	Fantasia	a3	2	54	8ᵛ	8ᵛ	-						
Lupo	Fantasia	a3	3	54ᵛ	9ᵛ	9ᵛ	-						
Lupo	Fantasia	a3	4	55	10ᵛ	10ᵛ	-						
Lupo	Fantasia	a3	5	55ᵛ	11ᵛ	11ᵛ	-						
Lupo	Fantasia	a3	6	56	12ᵛ	12ᵛ	-						
Lupo	Ayre	a3	7	56ᵛ	13ᵛ	13ᵛ	-						
Lupo	Fantasia	a3	8	57	14ᵛ	14ᵛ	-						
Lupo	Fantasia	a3	9	57ᵛ	15ᵛ	15ᵛ	-						
Lupo	Fantasia	a3	10	58	16ᵛ	16ᵛ	-						
Lupo	Fantasia	a3	11	58ᵛ	17ᵛ	17ᵛ	-						
Lupo	Fantasia	a3	12	59	18ᵛ	18ᵛ	-						
Lupo	Fantasia	a3	13	59ᵛ	19ᵛ	19ᵛ	-						
Lupo	Fantasia	a3	14	60	20ᵛ	20ᵛ	-	3	3	3			
Lupo	Fantasia	a3	15	60ᵛ	21	21	-						
Lupo	Ayre	a3	20	61	21ᵛ	21ᵛ	-						
Lupo	Fantasia	a3	16	61ᵛ	22ᵛ	22ᵛ	-						
Lupo	Fantasia	a3	19	62	23	23	-						
Lupo	Fantasia	a3	17	62ᵛ	23ᵛ	23ᵛ	-						
Lupo	Ayre	a3	18	63	24ᵛ	24ᵛ	-						
Lupo	Ayre	a3	21	63ᵛ	25ᵛ	25ᵛ	-						
Lupo	Ayre	a3	23	64	26ᵛ	26ᵛ	-						
Mico	Fantasia	a3	1	64ᵛ	27ᵛ	27ᵛ	-	12ᵛ	12ᵛ	12ᵛ	-	-	109rev
Mico	Fantasia	a3	2	65	28ᵛ	28ᵛ	-	13ᵛ	13ᵛ	13ᵛ	-	-	108rev
Mico	Fantasia	a3	3	65ᵛ	29ᵛ	29ᵛ	-	14ᵛ	14ᵛ	14ᵛ	-	-	107rev
Mico	Fantasia	a3	4	66	30ᵛ	30ᵛ	-	15ᵛ	15ᵛ	15ᵛ	-	-	106rev
Mico	Fantasia	a3	5	66ᵛ	31ᵛ	31ᵛ	-	-	-	-	-	-	105rev
Mico	Fantasia	a3	6	67	32ᵛ	32ᵛ	-	16ᵛ	16ᵛ	16ᵛ	-	-	104rev
Mico	Fantasia	a3	7	68	33ᵛ	33ᵛ	-	-	-	-	-	-	103rev
O. Gibbons	Fantasia	a3	1	68ᵛ	34ᵛ	34ᵛ	-	3ᵛ	3ᵛ	3ᵛ			
O. Gibbons	Fantasia	a3	2	69	35ᵛ	35ᵛ	-	4ᵛ	4ᵛ	4ᵛ			
O. Gibbons	Fantasia	a3	3	69ᵛ	36ᵛ	36ᵛ	-	5ᵛ	5ᵛ	5ᵛ			

Table 15 continued

Composer	Title	Scoring	VdGS No.	The Great Set 2	401	402	436	The Bing Set 417	418	1080	The Hatton Set 612	613	432
O. Gibbons	Fantasia	a3	4	70	37ᵛ	37ᵛ	-	6ᵛ	6ᵛ	6ᵛ			
O. Gibbons	Fantasia	a3	5	70ᵛ	38ᵛ	38ᵛ	-	7ᵛ	7ᵛ	7ᵛ			
O. Gibbons	Fantasia	a3	6	71	39ᵛ	39ᵛ	-	8ᵛ	8ᵛ	8ᵛ			
O. Gibbons	Fantasia	a3	7	71ᵛ	40ᵛ	40ᵛ	-	9ᵛ	9ᵛ	9ᵛ			
O. Gibbons	Fantasia	a3	8	72	40aᵛ	41ᵛ	-	10ᵛ	10ᵛ	10ᵛ			
O. Gibbons	Fantasia	a3	9	72ᵛ	41ᵛ	42ᵛ	-	11ᵛ	11ᵛ	11ᵛ			
Lupo	Pavan	a3	4	-	42ᵛ	43ᵛ	-	1	1	1			
Lupo	Pavan	a3	3	-	43	44	-	1ᵛ	1ᵛ	1ᵛ			
Lupo	Pavan	a3	1	-	43ᵛ	44ᵛ	-	2	2	2			
Lupo	Pavan	a3	2	-	44	45	-	2ᵛ	2ᵛ	2ᵛ			
Jeffreys	Fantasia	a3	1					25ᵛ	25ᵛ	25ᵛ			
Jeffreys	Fantasia	a3	2					26ᵛ	26ᵛ	26ᵛ			
Jeffreys	Fantasia	a3	3					27ᵛ	27ᵛ	27ᵛ			
Jeffreys	Fantasia	a3	4					28ᵛ	28ᵛ	28ᵛ			
Jeffreys	Fantasia	a3	6					29ᵛ	29ᵛ	29ᵛ			
Jeffreys	Fantasia	a3	5					30ᵛ	30ᵛ	30ᵛ			

Composer	Title	Scoring	VdGS No.	The Great Set 2	397	398	399	400	436	The Bing Set 417	418	1080	The Bing Set 417	418	1080
Bull	Fantasia	a4	-	74	1	1	1	1	1	33	33	33			
Ferrabosco II	Fantasia	a4	1	74ᵛ	1ᵛ	1ᵛ	1ᵛ	1ᵛ	1ᵛ	33ᵛ	33ᵛ	33ᵛ			
Ferrabosco II	Fantasia	a4	2	75ᵛ	2ᵛ	2ᵛ	2ᵛ	2ᵛ	2ᵛ	34ᵛ	34ᵛ	34ᵛ			
Ferrabosco II	Fantasia	a4	3	76ᵛ	3ᵛ	3ᵛ	3ᵛ	3ᵛ	3ᵛ	35ᵛ	35ᵛ	35ᵛ			
Ferrabosco II	Fantasia	a4	4	77ᵛ	4ᵛ	4ᵛ	4ᵛ	4ᵛ	4ᵛ	36ᵛ	36ᵛ	36ᵛ			
Ferrabosco II	Fantasia	a4	5	78	5ᵛ	5ᵛ	5ᵛ	5ᵛ	5ᵛ	37ᵛ	37ᵛ	37ᵛ			
Ferrabosco II	Fantasia	a4	6	78ᵛ	6ᵛ	6ᵛ	6ᵛ	6ᵛ	6ᵛ	38ᵛ	38ᵛ	38ᵛ			
Ferrabosco II	Fantasia	a4	7	79	7ᵛ	7ᵛ	7ᵛ	7ᵛ	7ᵛ	39ᵛ	39ᵛ	39ᵛ			
Ferrabosco II	Fantasia	a4	8	79ᵛ	8ᵛ	8ᵛ	8ᵛ	8ᵛ	8ᵛ	40ᵛ	40ᵛ	40ᵛ			
Ferrabosco II	Fantasia	a4	9	80	9ᵛ	9ᵛ	9ᵛ	9ᵛ	9ᵛ	41ᵛ	41ᵛ	41ᵛ			
Ferrabosco II	Fantasia	a4	10	80ᵛ	10ᵛ	10ᵛ	10ᵛ	10ᵛ	10ᵛ	-	-	-			

Table 15 continued

Composer	Title	Scoring	VdGS No.	2	The Great Set 397	398	399	400	436	The Bing Set 417	418	1080
Ferrabosco II	Fantasia	a 4	11	81^v	11^v	11^v	12^v	11^v	11^v	-	-	42^v
Ferrabosco II	Fantasia	a 4	12	82^v	12^v	12^v	13^v	12^v	12^v	42^v	42^v	43^v
Ferrabosco II	Fantasia	a 4	13	83^v	13^v	13^v	14^v	13^v	13^v	43^v	43^v	44^v
Ferrabosco II	Fantasia	a 4	23	83^v	14^v	14^v	15^v	14^v	14^v	44^v	44^v	45^v
Ferrabosco II	Fantasia	a 4	14	84^v	15^v	15^v	16^v	15^v	15^v	45^v	45^v	46^v
Ferrabosco II	Fantasia	a 4	15	85^v	16^v	16^v	17^v	16^v	16^v	46^v	46^v	47^v
Ferrabosco II	Fantasia	a 4	16	86^v	17^v	17^v	18^v	17^v	17^v	47^v	47^v	48^v
Ferrabosco II	Fantasia	a 4	17	87^v	18^v	18^v	19^v	18^v	18^v	48^v	48^v	49^v
Ferrabosco II	Fantasia	a 4	18	88^v	19^v	19^v	20^v	19^v	19^v	49^v	49^v	50^v
Ferrabosco II	Fantasia	a 4	19	89^v	20^v	20^v	21^v	20^v	20^v	50^v	50^v	-
Ferrabosco II	Fantasia	a 4	20	90^v	21^v	21^v	22^v	21^v	21^v	51^v	51^v	-
Ferrabosco II	Fantasia	a 4	21	91^v	22^v	22^v	23^v	22^v	22^v	52^v	52^v	-
Ferrabosco II	Fantasia	a 4	22	92^v	23^v	23^v	24^v	23^v	23^v	53^v	53^v	-
Ward	Fantasia	a 4	1	93^v	24^v	24^v	25^v	24^v	24^v	54^v	54^v	-
Ward	Fantasia	a 4	2	94^v	25^v	25^v	26^v	25^v	25^v	55^v	55^v	-
Ward	Fantasia	a 4	3	95	26^v	26^v	27^v	26^v	26^v	56^v	56^v	-
Ward	Fantasia	a 4	4	95^v	27^v	27^v	28^v	27^v	27^v	-	57^v	-
Ward	Fantasia	a 4	5	96^v	28^v	28^v	29^v	28^v	28^v	-	58^v	-
Ward	Fantasia	a 4	6	97	29^v	29^v	30^v	29^v	29^v	-	59^v	-
Jenkins	Fantasia	a 4	1	97^v	30^v	30^v	31^v	30^v	30^v			
Jenkins	Fantasia	a 4	2	98^v	31^v	31^v	32^v	31^v	31^v			
Jenkins	Fantasia	a 4	4	99^v	32^v	32^v	33^v	32^v	32^v			
Jenkins	Fantasia	a 4	3	100^v	33^v	33^v	34^v	33^v	33^v			
Coprario	Fantasia	a 4	1	101^v	34^v	34^v	35^v	34^v	34^v			
Coprario	Fantasia	a 4	2	102^v	35^v	35^v	36^v	35^v	35^v			
Coprario	Fantasia	a 4	3	103^v	36^v	36^v	37^v	36^v	36^v			
Coprario	Fantasia	a 4	4	104^v	37^v	37^v	38^v	37^v	37^v			
Coprario	Fantasia	a 4	5	105^v	38^v	38^v	39^v	38^v	38^v			
Coprario	Fantasia	a 4	7	106^v	39^v	39^v	40^v	39^v	39^v			

Table 15 continued

Composer	Title	Scoring	VdGS No.	2	403	404	405	406	407	408	436	The Lilly Organbook
Marenzio	Arda pur sempre o mora	a5		108	-	1	1	1	1	1	49	43ᵛ
Marenzio	Rimanti in pace	a5		108ᵛ	-	1ᵛ	1ᵛ	1ᵛ	1ᵛ	1ᵛ	49ᵛ	
Marenzio	Ondei di morte	a5		109	-	2	2	2	2	2	50	
Marenzio	Caro dolce mio ben	a5		109ᵛ	-	2ᵛ	2ᵛ	2ᵛ	2ᵛ	2ᵛ	50ᵛ	
Marenzio	Che sei tu se'l cor mio	a5		110	-	3	3	3	3	3	51	
Monteverdi	Latral, Parte Prima	a5		110ᵛ	-	3ᵛ	3ᵛ	3ᵛ	3ᵛ	3ᵛ	51ᵛ	42ᵛ
Mico	Parte Seconda	a5		111	-	4	4	4	4	4	52	43
Monteverdi	Sovra tenere herbette	a5		111ᵛ	-	4ᵛ	4ᵛ	4ᵛ	4ᵛ	4ᵛ	52ᵛ	
Monteverdi	O come gran martire	a5		112ᵛ	-	5	5	5	5	5	53ᵛ	
Vecchi	Clorinda hai vinto	a5		113	-	5ᵛ	5ᵛ	5ᵛ	5ᵛ	5ᵛ	54	
W. White	Diapente	a5		113ᵛ	-	6	6	6	6	6	54ᵛ	39ᵛ
Ward	Cor mio deh non languire	a5		114ᵛ	-	6ᵛ	6ᵛ	6ᵛ	6ᵛ	6ᵛ	55ᵛ	
Pallavicino	Era l'anima mia	a5		115ᵛ	-	7	7	7	7	7	56ᵛ	
Marenzio	Ami Tyrsi e me'l nieghi	a5		116ᵛ	-	7ᵛ	7ᵛ	7ᵛ	7ᵛ	7ᵛ	57	
Marenzio	Deh poi ch'era	a5		117	-	8	8	8	8	8	57ᵛ	
Pallavicino	Come vivro	a5		117ᵛ	-	8ᵛ	8ᵛ	8ᵛ	8ᵛ	8ᵛ	58	
Marenzio	Quell'augellin	a5		118	-	9	9	9	9	9	58ᵛ	
Marenzio	Ma grideran per me	a5		118ᵛ	-	9ᵛ	9ᵛ	9ᵛ	9ᵛ	9ᵛ	59	
Lupo	Miserere mei Domine	a5		119	-	10	10	10	10	10	59ᵛ	
Lupo	O vos omnes	a5		119ᵛ	-	10ᵛ	10ᵛ	10ᵛ	10ᵛ	10ᵛ	60	
Pallavicino	O dolorosa morte	a5		120	-	11	11	11	11	11	60ᵛ	
Monteverdi	Voi pur da me partite	a5		-	-	11ᵛ	11ᵛ	11ᵛ	11ᵛ	11ᵛ	61ᵛ	28ᵛ
Monteverdi	Luci seren'e chiare	a5		-	-	12	12	12	12	12	62ᵛ	29
Ferrabosco II	Dovehouse Pavan	a5	1	-	-	12ᵛ	12ᵛ	12ᵛ	12ᵛ	12ᵛ	63	27ᵛ
Mico	Pavan	a5	1	-	-	13	13	13	13	13	63ᵛ	12
Mico	Pavan	a5	2	-	-	13ᵛ	13ᵛ	13ᵛ	13ᵛ	13ᵛ	64	11ᵛ
Mico	Pavan	a5	3	-	-	14	14	14	14	14	-	
Mico	Fantasia	a5	3	-	-	14ᵛ	14ᵛ	14ᵛ	14ᵛ	14ᵛ	-	
Mico	Fantasia	a5	4	-	-	15	15	15	15	15	-	
Mico	In Nomine	a5	-	-	-	15ᵛ	15ᵛ	15ᵛ	15ᵛ	15ᵛ	66ᵛ	23ᵛ

Table 15 continued

Composer	Title	Scoring	VdGS No.	2	403	The Great Set 404	405	406	407	408	436	The Lilly Organbook
Ferrabosco II	In Nomine	a 5	3	-	-	16^v	16^v	16^v	16^v	16^v	67^v	20^v
Ferrabosco II	In Nomine	a 5	1	-	-	17^v	17^v	17^v	17^v	17^v	68^v	21^v
Ferrabosco II	In Nomine	a 5	2	-	-	18^v	18^v	18^v	18^v	18^v	69^v	22^v
Ward	Fantasia	a 5	1	127^v	-	47^v	47^v	46a^v	47^v	47^v	101^v	
Ward	Fantasia	a 5	2	128^v	-	48^v	48^v	47^v	48^v	48^v	102^v	
Ward	Fantasia	a 5	3	129^v	-	49^v	49^v	48^v	49^v	49^v	103^v	
Ward	Fantasia	a 5	4	130^v	-	50^v	50^v	49^v	50^v	50^v	104^v	
Ward	Fantasia	a 5	5	131^v	-	51^v	51^v	50^v	51^v	51^v	105^v	
Ward	Fantasia	a 5	6	132^v	-	52^v	52^v	51^v	52^v	52^v	106^v	
Ward	Fantasia	a 5	7	133^v	-	53^v	53^v	52^v	53^v	53^v	107^v	
Ward	Fantasia	a 5	8	134^v	-	54^v	54^v	53^v	54^v	54^v	108^v	
Ward	Fantasia	a 5	9	135^v	-	55^v	55^v	54^v	54a^v	55^v	109^v	
Ward	Fantasia	a 5	10	136^v	-	56^v	56^v	55^v	55^v	56^v	110^v	
Ward	Fantasia	a 5	14	137^v	-	57^v	57^v	56^v	56^v	57^v	111^v	
Ferrabosco II	Fantasia	a 5	-	138^v	-	58^v	58^v	57^v	57^v	58^v	-	
Ferrabosco II	Fantasia	a 5	-	139^v	-	59^v	59^v	58^v	58^v	59^v	-	
Ferrabosco II	Pavan	a 5	9	140^v	-	60^v	60^v	59^v	59^v	60^v	114^v	25
Ferrabosco II	Pavan	a 5	4	141	-	61	61	60	60	61	115	24^v
Ferrabosco II	Pavan	a 5	3	141^v	-	61^v	61^v	60^v	60^v	61^v	115^v	26
Ferrabosco II	Alman	a 5	4	142	-	62	62	61	61	62	116	
Jenkins	Fantasia	a 5	8	142^v	-	62^v	62^v	61^v	61^v	62^v	-	
Jenkins	Fantasia	a 5	9	143^v	-	63^v	63^v	62^v	62^v	63^v	-	25^v
Jenkins	Fantasia	a 5	11	144^v	-	64^v	64^v	63^v	63^v	64^v	-	
Jenkins	Fantasia	a 5	12	145^v	-	65^v	65^v	64^v	64^v	65^v	-	
Jenkins	Fantasia	a 5	14	146^v	-	66^v	66^v	65^v	65^v	66^v	-	
Jenkins	Fantasia	a 5	10	147^v	-	67^v	67^v	66^v	66^v	67^v	-	
Jenkins	Pavan	a 5	1	148^v	-	68^v	68^v	67^v	67^v	68^v	-	
O. Gibbons	In Nomine	a 5	2	149^v	-	69^v	69^v	68^v	68^v	69^v	123^v	26^v
W. White	Fantasia	a 5	2	150^v	-	70^v	70^v	69^v	69^v	70^v	-	
W. White	Fantasia	a 5	3	152	-	71^v	71^v	70^v	70^v	71^v	-	
Pallavicino	[Cor mio]	a 5	-	-	-	72^v	72	71^v	71^v	72^v	125a^v	

Table 15 continued

Composer	Title	Scoring	VdGS No.	2	The Great Set 403	404	405	406	407	408	436	The Lilly Organbook
Coprario	[Leno]	a5	47	—	—	19^v	19^v	19^v	19^v	19^v	70^v	28
Coprario	[Cresce in voi]	a5	16	163	—	20	20	20	20	20	71^v	11
Coprario	[Deh cara anima mia]	a5	32	—	—	20^v	20^v	20^v	20^v	20^v	72	14 & 37^v
Coprario	[Crudel perche]	a5	1	120^v	—	21	21	21	21	21	72^v	2^v
Coprario	[Io son ferito amore]	a5	2	121	—	21^v	21^v	21^v	21^v	21^v	73^v	1
Coprario	[O voi che sospirate]	a5	48	163^v	—	22	22	22	22	22	74^v	
Coprario	[Per far una leggiadra]	a5	31	121^v	—	22^v	22^v	22^v	22^v	22^v	75^v	2
Coprario	[Gittene Ninfe]	a5	34	164^v	—	23^v	23^v	23^v	23^v	23^v	76^v	12^v
Coprario	[Rapina l'alma]	a5	3	122^v	—	24^v	24^v	24^v	24^v	24^v	77^v	5^v
Coprario	[Lume tuo fugace]	a5	4	123^v	—	25^v	25^v	25^v	25^v	25^v	78^v	4^v
Coprario	[Io piango]	a5	5	165^v	—	26^v	26^v	26^v	26^v	26^v	79^v	14^v
Coprario	[Luci beate e care]	a5	9	124^v	—	27^v	27^v	27^v	27^v	27^v	80^v	6^v
Coprario	[In voi moro]	a5	8	166^v	—	28^v	28^v	28^v	28^v	28^v	81^v	15^v
Coprario	[In te mio nove sole]	a5	6	167^v	—	29^v	29^v	29^v	29^v	29^v	82^v	16^v
Coprario	[Del mio cibo amoroso]	a5	7	168^v	—	30^v	30^v	30^v	30^v	30^v	83^v	17^v
Coprario	[Al primo giorno]	a5	10	169^v	—	31^v	31^v	31^v	31^v	31^v	84^v	18^v
Coprario	[Chi pue mirarvi]	a5	11	170^v	—	32^v	32^v	32^v	32^v	32^v	85^v	19^v
Coprario	[Lucretia mia]	a5	12	125^v	—	33^v	33^v	33^v	33^v	33^v	86^v	3^v
Coprario	Fantasia	a5	49	171^v	—	34^v	34^v	34^v	34^v	34^v	87^v	10^v
Coprario	[Fuggi se sai fuggire]	a5	38	172^v	—	35^v	35^v	35^v	35^v	35^v	88^v	
Coprario	[Occhi miei con viva speme]	a5	46	126^v	—	36^v	36^v	36^v	36^v	36^v	89^v	1^v
Pallavicino	[O come vaneggiate donna]	a5	—	—	—	37	37	37	37	37	90	
Coprario	[O sonno, della mia morte]	a5	21	174^v	—	37^v	37^v	37^v	37^v	37^v	90^v	13^v
Lupo	Fantasia	a5	4	—	—	38^v	38^v	38^v	38^v	38^v	91^v	29^v
Lupo	Fantasia	a5	5	—	—	39^v	39^v	39^v	39^v	39^v	92^v	
Lupo	Fantasia	a5	18	—	—	40	40	40	40	40	93^v	
Lupo	Fantasia	a5	2	—	—	40^v	40^v	40^v	40^v	40^v	94^v	30^v
Lupo	Fantasia	a5	11	—	—	41^v	41^v	41^v	41^v	41^v	95^v	33^v
Lupo	Fantasia	a5	12	201	—	42^v	42^v	42^v	42^v	42^v	96^v	34^v
Lupo	Fantasia	a5	13	201^v	—	43^v	43^v	43^v	43^v	43^v	97^v	35^v
Lupo	Fantasia	a5	14	202^v	—	44^v	44^v	44^v	44^v	44^v	98^v	36^v

Table 15 continued

Composer	Title	Scoring	VdGS No.	2	403	404	405	406	407	408	436	The Lilly Organbook
Lupo	Fantasia	a5	1	203ᵛ	-	45ᵛ	45ᵛ	45ᵛ	45ᵛ	45ᵛ	99ᵛ	31ᵛ
Lupo	Fantasia	a5	3	204ᵛ	-	46ᵛ	46ᵛ	46ᵛ	46ᵛ	46ᵛ	100ᵛ	32ᵛ
Coprario	[Dolce mia vita]	a5	14	173ᵛ	-	-	-	-	-	-	-	7ᵛ
Coprario	[Passa madonna]	a5	15	175	-	-	-	-	-	-	-	9
Coprario	[Illicita Cosa]	a5	13	175ᵛ	-	-	-	-	-	-	-	-
Coprario	[Caggia fuoco dal cielo]	a5	19	176ᵛ	-	-	-	-	-	-	-	-
Coprario	[Ite leggiadre rime]	a5	25	177ᵛ	-	-	-	-	-	-	-	-
Coprario	[De la mia cruda sorte]	a5	26	178ᵛ	-	-	-	-	-	-	-	-
Coprario	[D'un si bel fuoco]	a5	37	179	-	-	-	-	-	-	-	-
Coprario	[Dove il liquido argento]	a5	45	179ᵛ	-	-	-	-	-	-	-	-
Coprario	[Voi caro il mio contento]	a5	17	180ᵛ	-	-	-	-	-	-	-	-
Coprario	[Alma mia tu mi dicesti]	a5	18	181ᵛ	-	-	-	-	-	-	-	-
Coprario	[Fugga dunque la luce]	a5	20	182ᵛ	-	-	-	-	-	-	-	-
Coprario	[Dolce ben mio]	a5	22	183ᵛ	-	-	-	-	-	-	-	-
Coprario	[Qual vaghezza]	a5	23	184ᵛ	-	-	-	-	-	-	-	9ᵛ
Coprario	[Credemi]	a5	24	185ᵛ	-	-	-	-	-	-	-	-
Coprario	[Dammi o vita mia soccorso]	a5	27	186ᵛ	-	-	-	-	-	-	-	-
Coprario	[Sia maledetto amore]	a5	28	187ᵛ	-	-	-	-	-	-	-	-
Coprario	[Ninfa crudele]	a5	29	188	-	-	-	-	-	-	-	8ᵛ
Coprario	[Nel sen della mia Margherita]	a5	30	188ᵛ	-	-	-	-	-	-	-	-
Coprario	[Ohime la gioia e breve]	a5	35	189	-	-	-	-	-	-	-	8
Coprario	[O misero mio cor]	a5	33	189ᵛ	-	-	-	-	-	-	-	-
Coprario	[Lieti cantiamo]	a5	43	190ᵛ	-	-	-	-	-	-	-	-
Coprario	[Dolce tormento]	a5	40	191	-	-	-	-	-	-	-	-
Coprario	[Quando la vaga flori]	a5	42	191ᵛ	-	-	-	-	-	-	-	-
Coprario	[Ingiustitia d'Amore]	a5	41	192	-	-	-	-	-	-	-	-
Coprario	[La Primavera]	a5	39	192ᵛ	-	-	-	-	-	-	-	-
Coprario	[Se mi volete morto]	a5	36	193ᵛ	-	-	-	-	-	-	-	-
Coprario	[Io vivo in amoroso fuoco]	a5	44	194ᵛ	-	-	-	-	-	-	-	-
Anonymous	Fantasia	a5	-	-	-	-	-	-	-	-	-	37ᵛ
Lupo	Fantasia	a5	9	-	-	-	-	-	-	-	-	38ᵛ

Table 15 continued

Composer	Title	Scoring	VdGS No.	2	403	404	405	406	407	408	436	The Lilly Organbook
							The Great Set					
Ward	[Leggiadre sei]	a 5	13	214								40ᵛ
Ward	[Dolce languir]	a 5	1	215ᵛ								41ᵛ
Lupo	Fantasia	a 6	1	217	aᵛ	76ᵛ	72ᵛ	74ᵛ	77ᵛ	76ᵛ	—	
Lupo	Fantasia	a 6	2	218	1ᵛ	77ᵛ	73ᵛ	75ᵛ	78ᵛ	77ᵛ	—	
Lupo	Fantasia	a 6	3	218	2ᵛ	78ᵛ	74ᵛ	76ᵛ	79ᵛ	78ᵛ	—	
Lupo	Fantasia	a 6	4	219ᵛ	3ᵛ	79ᵛ	75ᵛ	77ᵛ	80ᵛ	79ᵛ	—	
Lupo	Fantasia	a 6	5	219ᵛ	4ᵛ	80ᵛ	76ᵛ	78ᵛ	81ᵛ	80ᵛ	147ᵛ	
Lupo	Fantasia	a 6	6	221	5ᵛ	81ᵛ	77ᵛ	79ᵛ	82ᵛ	81ᵛ	—	
Lupo	Fantasia	a 6	7	222	6ᵛ	82ᵛ	78ᵛ	80ᵛ	83ᵛ	82ᵛ	149ᵛ	
Lupo	Fantasia	a 6	8	223ᵛ	7ᵛ	83ᵛ	79ᵛ	81ᵛ	84ᵛ	83ᵛ	—	
Lupo	Fantasia	a 6	9	225	8ᵛ	84ᵛ	80ᵛ	82ᵛ	85ᵛ	84ᵛ	—	
Lupo	Fantasia	a 6	10	227ᵛ	9ᵛ	85ᵛ	81ᵛ	83ᵛ	86ᵛ	85ᵛ	—	
Ward	Fantasia	a 6	2	229	10ᵛ	86ᵛ	82ᵛ	84ᵛ	87ᵛ	86ᵛ	—	
Ward	Fantasia	a 6	3	230	11ᵛ	87ᵛ	83ᵛ	85ᵛ	88ᵛ	87ᵛ	—	
Ward	Fantasia	a 6	4	231	12ᵛ	88ᵛ	84ᵛ	86ᵛ	89ᵛ	88ᵛ	—	
Ward	Fantasia	a 6	5	232ᵛ	13ᵛ	89ᵛ	85ᵛ	87ᵛ	90ᵛ	89ᵛ	—	
Ward	Fantasia	a 6	6	233ᵛ	14ᵛ	90ᵛ	86ᵛ	88ᵛ	91ᵛ	90ᵛ	—	
Ward	Fantasia	a 6	7	235	15ᵛ	91ᵛ	87ᵛ	89ᵛ	92ᵛ	91ᵛ	155ᵛ	
Ward	In Nomine	a 6	1	236ᵛ	16ᵛ	92ᵛ	88ᵛ	90ᵛ	93ᵛ	92ᵛ	156ᵛ	
Ward	In Nomine	a 6	2	238	17ᵛ	93ᵛ	89ᵛ	91ᵛ	94ᵛ	93ᵛ	158ᵛ	
Ferrabosco II	Fantasia	a 6	1	239ᵛ	18ᵛ	94ᵛ	90ᵛ	92ᵛ	95ᵛ	94ᵛ	157ᵛ	
Ferrabosco II	Fantasia	a 6	2	241	19ᵛ	95ᵛ	91ᵛ	93ᵛ	96ᵛ	95ᵛ	159ᵛ	
Ferrabosco II	Fantasia	a 6	3	242ᵛ	20ᵛ	96ᵛ	92ᵛ	94ᵛ	97ᵛ	96ᵛ	160ᵛ	
Ferrabosco II	In Nomine	a 6	1	244	21ᵛ	97ᵛ	93ᵛ	95ᵛ	98ᵛ	97ᵛ	161ᵛ	
Ferrabosco II	Fantasia	a 6	4	245ᵛ	22ᵛ	98ᵛ	94ᵛ	96ᵛ	99ᵛ	98ᵛ	—	
Ferrabosco II	Fantasia	a 6	5	247	23ᵛ	99ᵛ	95ᵛ	97ᵛ	100ᵛ	99ᵛ	—	
Ferrabosco II	Fantasia	a 6	7	248ᵛ	24ᵛ	100ᵛ	96ᵛ	98ᵛ	101ᵛ	100ᵛ	162ᵛ	
Ferrabosco II	Fantasia	a 6	6	250ᵛ	25ᵛ	101ᵛ	97ᵛ	99ᵛ	102ᵛ	101ᵛ	163ᵛ	
Ferrabosco II	Fantasia	a 6	8	251ᵛ	26ᵛ	102ᵛ	98ᵛ	100ᵛ	103ᵛ	102ᵛ	164ᵛ	

Table 15 concluded

Composer	Title	Scoring	VdGS No.	2	403	404	The Great Set 405	406	407	408	436
Ferrabosco II	Fantasia	a6	9	252^v	27^v	103^v	99^v	101^v	104^v	103^v	165^v
Ferrabosco II	Fantasia	a6	10	253^v	28^v	104^v	100^v	102^v	105^v	104^v	–
W. White	Fantasia	a6	1	255	29^v	105^v	101^v	103^v	106^v	105^v	–
W. White	Fantasia	a6	2	256^v	30^v	106^v	102^v	104^v	107^v	106^v	–
W. White	Fantasia	a6	3	258^v	31^v	107^v	103^v	104a^v	108^v	107^v	–
W. White	Fantasia	a6	4	260	32^v	108^v	104^v	105^v	109^v	108^v	–
W. White	Fantasia	a6	5	261^v	33^v	109^v	105^v	106^v	110^v	109^v	–
W. White	Fantasia	a6	6	262^v	34^v	110^v	106^v	107^v	111^v	110^v	–
Coprario	Fantasia	a6	2	283	35^v	111^v	107^v	108^v	112^v	111^v	167^v
Coleman	Fantasia	a6	3	268	36^v	112^v	108^v	109^v	113^v	112^v	168^v
Coleman	Fantasia	a6	2	265	37^v	113^v	109^v	110^v	114^v	113^v	169^v
Coleman	Fantasia	a6	1	266^v	38^v	114^v	110^v	111^v	115^v	114^v	170^v
O. Gibbons	Fantasia	a6	1	269^v	39^v	115^v	111^v	112^v	116^v	115^v	171^v
O. Gibbons	Fantasia	a6	2	271	40^v	116^v	112^v	113^v	117^v	116^v	172^v
O. Gibbons	Fantasia	a6	3	272^v	41^v	117^v	113^v	114^v	118^v	117^v	173^v
O. Gibbons	Fantasia	a6	4	274	42^v	118^v	114^v	115^v	119^v	118^v	174^v
O. Gibbons	Fantasia	a6	5	275^v	43^v	119^v	115^v	116^v	120^v	189^v	175^v
O. Gibbons	Fantasia	a6	6	277	44^v	120^v	116^v	117^v	121^v	120^v	176^v
O. Gibbons	Variations on 'Go from my window'	a6	–	278^v	45^v	121^v	117^v	118^v	122^v	121^v	–
O. Gibbons	Pavan	a6	–	280^v	47^v	123^v	119^v	120^v	124^v	123^v	–
O. Gibbons	Galliard	a6	–	281^v	48^v	124^v	120^v	121^v	125^v	124^v	–

FANT[ASIA] series and the spines of the partbooks were inscribed: 'FANT[asia] G 4.B[ooks]' (Mus. 397-400), 'FANT E 4.B' (Mus. 401-2)[79] and 'FANT H VI.B' (Mus. 403-8); the scorebook (Mus. 2), which did not have an 'Aldrich Binding', and the organbook (Mus. 436) were left unclassified (perhaps because of their larger formats). The Bing partbooks (Mus. 417-18/1080) were probably also unbound when Aldrich obtained them, and one book appears to have been missing at the time as Aldrich classified the set: 'FANT D.3 B[ooks]'.[80]

All three sets of instrumental music mentioned above - the Hatton, Bing and Great Sets - are, to some extent, unfinished. The three books of the Hatton Set each contain a large number of blank - but ruled - pages (see Part II, MS LI); two of the three partbooks of the Bing Set are incomplete (Part II, MS L);[81] and the score of the Great Set (Part II, MS XLII) opens with forty-seven blank folios ruled and barred ready for two-part pieces which were not entered. The scorebook also lacks thirty-one pieces found in the partbooks Mus. 401-8 and/or Mus. 417-18/1080 (it does, however, contain twenty-seven of Coprario's five-part fantasias which do not appear in the partbooks Mus. 404-8, see Table 15).[82] Added to this we should note that (*a*) the order of the pieces differs occasionally between the score, the partbooks and the organbook; (*b*) there are a number of slight disagreements in readings between the score and the partbooks; (*c*) a number of obvious errors in the parts are corrected in the score; and (*d*) the organbook lacks sixty-six of the 209 four- to six-part pieces found in the score and/or parts (see Table 15).[83] The Great Set is not the uniform and coherent unit one would perhaps expect from a collection of this size and importance.

---

[79] 'FANT E 4.B[ooks]' (*Och* Mus. 401-2) lacks two books: the treble-viol part and a keyboard part (see footnote 74 above).
[80] Only *Och* Mus. 417 and *Och* Mus. 418 have the spine inscription 'FANT D 3.B' (the spine of *Och* Mus. 1080 is blank); this probably explains the shelfmark-numerical separation of *Och* Mus. 1080 from *Och* Mus. 417-18.
[81] *Och* Mus. 417 lacks the final three fantasias *a* 4 by Ward, and *Och* Mus. 1080 lacks three fantasias *a* 4 by Ferrabosco II and all six of the fantasias *a* 4 by Ward.
[82] The score (*Och* Mus. 2) lacks the following three-part pieces: Jeffreys, six fantasias (*Och* Mus. 417-18/1080) and Lupo, four pavans (*Och* Mus. 401-2 and 417-18/1080); and the following five-part pieces (all in *Och* Mus. 404-8): Coprario, 'Deh cara anima mia' and 'Leno'; Ferrabosco II, 'Dovehouse' pavan and three In nomines; Lupo, five fantasias; Mico, one In nomine, two fantasias and three pavans; Monteverdi, 'Luci seren'e chiare' and 'Voi pur da me partite'; and Pallavicino, 'Cor mio' and 'O come vaneggiate donna'.
[83] As noted in footnote 74, the lack of three-part pieces in the organbook *Och* Mus. 436 may be explained by the missing fourth book of the set 'FANT E 4.B' (Mus. 401-2) which was probably an organbook. David Pinto's statement - (1990), note 6 - that 'Mus. 436 appears to have been made up from the score' may be an over-simplification. There are a number of variants between *Och* Mus. 2 and Mus. 436 (particularly concerning accidentals) which cannot be easily explained-away as 'non-significant variants' or copyist's errors. What is more, eighteen five-part pieces included in the organbook do not appear in the score (Coprario, 'Deh cara anima mia' and 'Leno'; Ferrabosco II, 'Dovehouse' pavan and three In nomines; Lupo, five fantasias; Mico, one In nomine and two pavans; Monteverdi, 'Luci seren'e chiare' and 'Voi pur da me partite'; and Pallavicino, 'Cor mio' and 'O come vaneggiate donna'); it is possible that the organ-scores to

What is to be learnt from this bewildering series of facts and statistics? Do they tell us anything about the purpose or plan behind the copying of the three sets, how they relate to each other, or in what order they were copied? The Hatton Set (Mus. 432/612-13) can be considered separately from the other two sets as, with the exception of Bing's later additions in the back of the organbook, they are not related by repertoire. John Lilly appears to have been commissioned by Christopher Hatton III to copy music for two bass viols and organ and, although the project was left unfinished, the three partbooks were sumptuously bound and stamped with the Hatton coat of arms, crest and family motto. The fact that Stephen Bing added Mico's seven three-part fantasias to the organbook (Mus. 432) after it was bound[84] suggests that the Hatton Set predates the Bing Set (which contains the parts of the Mico fantasias and other three- and four-part viol-consort music). It has been noted that the Bing Set was left incomplete and that its contents - with the exception of the six three-part fantasias by George Jeffreys - are duplicated in the Great Set; this could suggest that the Bing Set became 'outmoded by a decision to recopy the three- and four-part works disjunctly into the separate sets in Lilly's hand that made up the grander design of the Great Set.'[85] It is even possible that Lilly had embarked on his copying project independently of Bing and, having completed the partbooks, was for some reason unable to copy the score and organbook; perhaps Bing was commissioned to complete the set, and did so using basically the same manuscript sources that Lilly had used, but without reference to Lilly's completed parts? This theory goes some way towards explaining the discrepancies between the parts and the score and organbook; it does not, however, explain the occasional differences between the score and the organbook (which were both copied by Bing). The picture is obviously too complex, and the surviving information too sparse, to reconstruct fully the events and chronology of copying.

The questions of provenance, dates of copying and the scribes' sources still need to be examined. The Great Set contains a large proportion of the three- to six-part English viol-consort repertoire written before the mid to late 1630s.[86] The scribes - or their organising patron(s) - would have needed

---

these pieces were made up from the partbooks (*Och* Mus. 404-8), but a comparison of the readings is inconclusive.

[84] This is made clear by the position of the additional pieces in relation to the gatherings of the book: they were copied 'across' gatherings S2 (f. 103) to T2 (f. 109); if the pieces were added before binding the scribe would surely have started on the first page of a gathering.

[85] Pinto (1990), 80.

[86] Five of the ten composers of viol consort music represented in the Great Set died before the third decade of the seventeenth century (Bull, Coprario, Ferrabosco II, Orlando Gibbons and Lupo); Ward died in 1638; and all the works of the younger composers in the set (Coleman, Jenkins, Mico and White) appear to be early works written before *c.*1640 (see e.g. A. Ashbee, 'The Four-Part Consort Music of John Jenkins', *PRMA*, xcvi (1969-70), 29-42; ibid., 'John Jenkins, 1592-1678: the Viol Consort Music in Four, Five and Six Parts', *EM*, vi (1978), 492-

access to a large number of manuscript sources in a relatively short period of time;[87] the most likely provenance for this would have been the Court or the household of a nobleman with strong links with the court musicians. A court origin is supported by the repertoire of the Great Set. Four of the most eminent composers of consort music represented in the set, Ferrabosco II, Coprario, Orlando Gibbons and Lupo, had been employed by Charles I when he was still Prince of Wales.[88] Charles was a most discerning patron of music and - if John Playford's report of 1683 can be trusted - was himself a skilled performer on the bass viol: '*Charles I... could play his part exactly well on the* Bass-Viol, *especially of those Incomparable Fancies of Mr.* Coperario *to the* Organ'.[89] It should be remembered that Christ Church Mus. 432/612-13 - the Hatton Set - include ten of Coprario's fantasias for two bass viols and organ, and that Christ Church Mus. 732-5 and Royal Music MS 24.k.3 (examined in detail above) contain Coprario's fantasia-suites for one and two violins, bass viol and organ. Mention should also be made at this point of Bing's copies of the Coprario fantasia-suites for two violins, bass viol and organ: MS ML96 L814f, fascicle 3 in the Sibley Music Library of the Eastman School of Music, Rochester, New York is a short-score (with organ cues) of all eight of the fantasia-suites copied by Bing and George Jeffreys in collaboration;[90] and New York, Public Library Drexel MS 5624 is a fragmentary score containing four of the fantasia-suites.[91]

500; J. Bennett and P. Willetts, 'Richard Mico', *Chelys*, vii (1977), 43-6; and E.H. Meyer rev. D. Poulton, *Early English Chamber Music* (London, 1982), *passim*).

[87] The regularity of both scribes' handwriting and the careful organisation (even taking into account the occasional differing order in the partbooks, score and organbook) would seem to indicate that the Great Set was compiled over a relatively short period of time.

[88] Orlando Gibbons was also patronised by the Hatton family in the second decade of the seventeenth century (see page 6 above).

[89] J. Playford, *An Introduction to the Skill of Musick* (London, 10/1683). This is the first edition to make reference to the King's performing ability; previous editions which contain the section, are concerned only with the King's musical preference: '*And for Instrumental Musick none pleased him like those incomparable Fantazies for one* Violin *and* Basse Viol, *to the organ, Composed by Mr.* Coprario' (4th-7th editions; 1664-1674). All editions subsequent to 1683 repeat the version of the tenth edition.

[90] *US-R* ML96 L814f/3 is inscribed 'The Score of Mr Coperarios Fantazies, / & Galliards of 3 parts to the Organ' in the hand of George Jeffreys. The suites are numbered 1-8 (VdGS Nos. 1-5, 8, 6-7 respectively); suites Nos. 1-3, 5-6 and most of 7-8 were copied by Stephen Bing, and Jeffreys copied suite No. 4 and contributed to the copying of Nos. 7-8. I have been able to examine *US-R* ML96 L814f/3 on microfilm only (available in *Bu*, MF 61), and I am therefore unable to comment on the paper-type for the purpose of dating. It is possible that this fascicle represents another early collaboration between Bing and Jeffreys; the two hands in *US-R* ML96 L814f/3 are very similar to those in *Ob* Mus. Sch. C 204, ff. 46-49^v.

[91] VdGS Nos. 5-8; the opening of the fantasia of No. 5 is lacking. Six folios of the manuscript survive, each ruled with four five-stave systems and with each stave system uniformly divided into eight bars. There are no contemporary titles or ascriptions, but each fantasia-suite is numbered at the beginning (in a seventeenth-century hand). The numbering corresponds to that in *Lbl* R.M. 24.k.3 in which the fifteen suites for violin, bass viol and organ are numbered 1-15 and the eight suites for two violins, bass viol and organ are numbered 16-23. Again, I have been

Coprario was one of the first composers to use the violin in contrapuntal consort music. The violin had first appeared at the English Court in 1540, but until about 1620 it was used almost exclusively for dance music.[92] Once the violin had become established as an instrument for 'serious' contrapuntal chamber music, composers began experimenting with new forms and scorings using mixed groups of violins and viols with keyboard (usually organ) and/or theorbo continuo. Prince Charles formed a violin and viol ensemble in 1622[93] - 'Coperario's Musique' - which consisted of Lupo, Woodington (see above) and Vallet (violins), Ferrabosco II and Coprario (viols) and Orlando Gibbons (keyboard).[94] One of the new forms to emerge was the fantasia-suite,[95] a fixed three-movement sequence of fantasia and two dances (alman and galliard), which was created by Coprario and seems to have remained a court genre until the Civil War, after which it was more widely disseminated. Again we are reminded of the repertoire copied by Bing (and others) in the Sibley Music Library MS ML96 L814f/3, New York Public Library Drexel MS 5624, and Christ Church Mus. 732-4 and Royal Music MS 24.k.3. The latter set also contains Orlando Gibbons' three- and four-part 'Great Dooble Base' fantasias[96] (so-called because they use an instrument a size larger, and tuned a fourth lower, than the normal bass viol); perhaps these pieces were also the result of the experiments with scorings which were taking place in court circles in the 1620s.[97] Another

---

unable to examine the actual manuscript and I am unable to comment on the paper-type for the purpose of dating, but Bing's script corresponds closely with that *US-R* ML96 L814f/3 and has similarities with *Ob* Mus. Sch. C 204, ff. 46-49^v; I suspect that the manuscripts are contemporary. I am very grateful to Dr Christopher Field for drawing *US-NYp* Drexel 5624 to my attention and for providing photocopies and information; the manuscript will be the subject of a forthcoming article by Dr Field.
[92] See P. Holman, 'The English Royal Consort in the Sixteenth Century', *PRMA*, cix (1982-3), 39-59; and ibid. (1993), *passim*.
[93] Dated from Woodington's petition to Charles I (12 May 1625) in which he states that he had been a member of 'Coperario[']s musique 3 yeres' (*Lbl* Add. 64,883, f. 57).
[94] See A. Ashbee, *Records of English Court Music*, iv (Snodland, 1991a), 217-30, *passim*.
[95] The term 'fantasia-suite' is modern (see C.D.S. Field, 'Fantasia-suite', *New Grove*, vi, 392-3).
[96] VdGS Nos. 1-4 (*a* 3) and Nos. 1-2 (*a* 4). Gibbons' four three-part fantasias for the 'Great Dooble Base' in *EIRE-Dm* Z2.1.13 are followed by three anonymous fantasias with the same scoring (treble, bass and 'Great Dooble Base' viols); these three anonymous fantasias had - until recently - been attributed to Gibbons due to their scoring and position in the manuscript (VdGS Nos. 5-7). However, Richard Charteris - 'A Postscript to *John Coprario: A Thematic Catalogue of his Music with a Biographical Introduction* (New York, 1977)', *Chelys*, xi (1982), 16-17 - has recently discovered a fragment of one of the three fantasias (VdGS 'Gibbons' No. 7) attributed to Coprario. This fragment, inserted between the pages of a copy of E. David and M. Lussy, *Histoire de la Notation Musicale* (Paris, 1882) in Case Western Reserve University Library, Cleveland, Ohio, suggests that the three three-part fantasias for the 'Great Dooble Base', VdGS 'Gibbons' Nos. 5-7, are actually by Coprario. See also O. Neighbour, 'Orlando Gibbons (1583-1625): The Consort Music', *EM*, xi (1983), 355-6, where it is argued, on stylistic grounds, that the three anonymous fantasias are by Coprario.
[97] Peter Holman - 'George Jeffries and the *Great Dooble Base*', *Chelys*, v (1973-4), 79-80 - noted that Jeffreys calls for a 'Great Basse' viol in the 'Symphonies' to 'Felice Pastorella' (*Lbl*

feature of many early Stuart music manuscripts is the presence of untexted vocal works intended for instrumental performance. The Great Set contains twenty-three textless five-part madrigals or motets by Lupo, Marenzio, Monteverdi,[98] Pallavicino, Vecchi and Ward. The set also includes all forty-nine of the five-part 'fantasias' attributable to Coprario; forty-seven of these pieces appear in earlier manuscript sources with Italian titles and one - 'Deh cara anima mia' - even appears fully texted.[99] It seems that most, if not all, of Coprario's five part pieces - and indeed a number of the six-part ones (not present in the Great Set) - originated as madrigals 'apt for viols and voyces'.[100]

The repertoire contained in the Hatton, Bing and Great Sets of viol-consort music suggests that they are the product of a court-related circle of scribes working in the mid to late 1630s. This proposed dating is supported by the physical evidence offered by the manuscripts. All three sets of partbooks are made up of the best quality royal paper - the type of paper often used for presentation manuscripts.[101] With the exception of the two bass viol partbooks of the Hatton Set (Mus. 612-13), the paper in the three

---

Add. 10,338, ff. 51^v-56) and, bearing in mind the Hatton family's patronage of Orlando Gibbons, speculated that the Hatton family were the owners of a single example of the 'Great Dooble Base'. He has since withdrawn this suggestion - (1993), 216-17 - in light of the recently discovered references to a 'greate base Vyall' at Court (see Ashbee (1988), 134 & 138; and ibid. (1991a), 215) and the identification of pieces by Coprario which use the instrument (see footnote 96 above). However, given the links between the Hattons, their musicians/copyists and the Court, it is not inconceivable that there was some connection between the Hatton-family's instrument and the Great Bass at Court.

[98] One of the untexted madrigals by Monteverdi, 'Latral' (*recte* 'La tra'l sangue e le morti egro', the second section of a three-section madrigal from *Il Terzo Libro de Madrigali a Cinque Voci* (1592)), is followed by a 'Parte Seconda' by Richard Mico. This textless parody-sequel also appears in *Lbl* Egerton 2485 (Lilly, see below) and *Ob* Mus. Sch. E 415-18. 'Latral' contains a central chromatic fugato on a falling subject and Mico's piece contains a fugato on a rising subject; no other connection between the two is known and no explanation of Mico's contribution can presently be offered.

[99] VdGS Coprario fantasias *a* 5: Nos. 1-49. Nos. 48-9 are untitled in all sources; No. 48 is a parody of Marenzio's 'O voi che sospirate' published in *Il Secondo Libro de Madrigali a Cinque Voci* (1581) (see J. Kerman, *The Elizabethan Madrigal: a Comparative Study* (New York, 1962), 44, note 1); and No. 32 - 'Deh cara anima mia' - is fully texted in *Ob* Tenbury 940-4 and *US-SM* El 25 A 46-51.

[100] For a full examination of the issues concerning Coprario's fantasias of madrigalian origin see: R. Charteris, 'John Coprario's Five- and Six-Part Pieces: Instrumental or Vocal?', *ML*, lvii (1976), 370-8; ibid. (1982), 18-19; and D. Pinto, 'The Fantasy Manner: the Seventeenth-Century Context', *Chelys*, x (1981), 25. The Great Set also contains two five-part fantasias by Lupo (VdGS Nos. 5 & 18) and three by Ward (VdGS Nos. 1, 2 & 14) which have Italian titles in earlier manuscript sources; it is likely that these too are of madrigalian origin (see Charteris (1976), 373).

[101] Music manuscripts were generally copied on good quality paper - paper capable of carrying notation of heavy density (note-heads, etc.) without the ink spreading - but the paper in the Christ Church consort sets is of particularly high quality.

sets comes from the same quartet of moulds;[102] the watermark is the coat of arms of Strasbourg (known as the 'Strasbourg Bend') with an attached monogram 'WR'.[103] Numerous such watermarks have been recorded from the period 1587 to 1651, but the ones most closely resembling our watermark date from 1597 to 1631.[104] The 'WR' monogram most likely refers to Wendelin Riehel, whose family owned a mill at Strasbourg from 1535 to 1639.[105] The two string parts (Mus. 612-13) consist of paper with an encircled-peacock watermark;[106] the mark is very similar to that of British Library Add. MSS 17,816 and 30,829-30 (Part II, MS II), a set which - as we shall see in the following chapter - probably dates from the early 1640s (with later additions). The evidence offered by the paper-types of the Bing and Lilly manuscripts therefore reinforces the mooted copying-date of the mid to late 1630s. This view represents a substantial revision of the accepted datings of the Great Set and related manuscripts. It had, until recently, been argued that the Hatton, Bing and Great Sets were retrospective collections copied after Hatton's return to England in 1656.[107] This can now be challenged in light of (*a*) the identification of the 'Lilly associate' as Stephen Bing and an increased knowledge of his other copying activities; (*b*) the new biographical information concerning John Lilly; (*c*) an examination of the contents of the consort sets in relation to court repertoire of the 1630s (one would surely expect to find Locke, Simpson and late Jenkins represented if

---

[102] A mould consisted of a lattice of fine metal wire supported on top of a wooden frame. It is the mould (which was dipped into a vat of pulp in the first stages of paper making) which gives each sheet of paper its identifiable characteristics: the chain-lines which are visible in paper are left by the vertical wires across the mould, and the watermark (and often a countermark) are produced by a wire design tacked on to the frame. It should be noted that each hand-made mould is unique, and only sheets of paper made in the same mould can properly be described as identical (and these may even change slightly as the mould ages and the wires become distorted). Normally two moulds were used alternately when making a batch of paper; a four mould system indicates that the paper mill probably had two vats. A pair or quartet of moulds would be deliberately made to look alike, but a careful and systematic examination of the watermarks and chain-lines could distinguish between the moulds. See Gaskell (1972), 57-66; and Thompson (1988), 17-30.
[103] Thompson (1988), Watermark L. Dr Thompson notes that eighty-nine folios of Matthew Locke's autograph score, *Lbl* Add. 17,801, have the same paper and rastra rulings as the Christ Church sets: (1988), 524-9, and 'The Sources of Locke's Consort *For Seaverall Friends*', *Chelys*, xix (1990a), 24; he has further suggested (in private correspondence) that Locke may have obtained some 'spare' paper from Bing or Lilly sometime before 1648.
[104] G. Piccard, *Wasserzeichen Lilie* (Stuttgart, 1983), xiii, 147-54.
[105] P. Heitz, *Les Filigranes des Papiers Contenus dans le Archive de la Ville de Strasbourg* (Strasbourg, 1902), 7 & Plates XXI-XXII.
[106] Thompson (1988), Watermark XVI(?). See also E. Heawood, *Watermarks Mainly of the 17th and 18th Centuries* (Hilversum, 1950), Watermark 174 (= Venice, 1628).
[107] For example: Willetts (1967a), 311; Harper (1982), pp. xv-xxix; M. Hobbs, 'Introduction', *Orlando Gibbons: Six Fantasias* (London, 1982), viii; J. Harper, 'The Distribution of the Consort Music of Orlando Gibbons in Seventeenth-Century Sources', *Chelys*, xii (1983a), 3-22, *passim*; and Pinto (1990), 79-80. In her more recent article concerning John Lilly (1992), Pamela Willetts - having filled out the biographical information concerning the copyist's early career - redated the consort sets to the 1630s and suggested a provenance of either Kirby Hall or Cambridge.

the sets were copied post-1650); (*d*) a growing awareness of the early activities and patronage of Christopher Hatton III; and (*e*) the realisation that after 1656, with his court career declining dramatically, Hatton was a spent force as a musical patron.

What part, then, did Hatton play in the compilation of the three collections in the 1630s? Only the Hatton Set (Mus. 432/612-13), with its tell-tale bindings, is of obvious Hatton provenance, but it has always been assumed - due no doubt to the scribal and/or repertorial links between the sets - that the Bing and Great Sets were also the result of Hatton's patronage. The evidence supports this tradition. The fact that the same paper occurs in all the sets, and that the same set of rastra were used for the stave rulings (see Table 16),[108] suggests a common supply and provenance. Hatton, with his court links, was undoubtedly the force behind Lilly and Bing's copying of the Hatton, Bing and Great Sets of viol-consort music. Why the Bing and Great Sets contain so much duplication is a question that cannot yet be answered. Perhaps Hatton was compiling a compendium of the consort music performed at Court for use by his own household musicians, and the Bing Set was designed as a companion set to the already completed Hatton Set? Perhaps the Bing Set was left unfinished because, towards the end of the 1630s when he was becoming more important at Court, Hatton decided to enlarge the project to create a Great Set of all the available consort music from court circles? It is even possible that the Great Set was intended as a presentation set for the King but, at the outbreak of Civil War and the disbandment of the regular court musical establishment,[109] the project floundered and was left unfinished. Whatever the true *raison d'être* of the Christ Church sets of viol-consort music, we should be grateful to Christopher Hatton and his copyists, John Lilly and Stephen Bing, for preserving such a complete record of the instrumental music performed at Court before the 'hostilities'.

Before concluding this section concerning the Christ Church sets of viol-consort music it is necessary to broach the difficult subject of the manuscript sources used by Bing and Lilly when compiling their collections. The Hatton, Bing and Great Sets contain 286 pieces (not counting duplications) for which 2,702 concordances have been noted in ninety-seven separate

---

[108] Our knowledge of rastrological procedures in the seventeenth century is at present very limited, and until a thorough and systematic study of rastra and rastrum rulings is undertaken it will not be possible to ascertain whether the stave ruling was undertaken by the scribes themselves or by a stationer. (Cathie Miserandino-Gaherty of Keble College, Oxford is presently engaged in a project concerning rastrology of music manuscripts from *c*.1575 to *c*.1640; see also J.K. Wolf & E.K. Wolf, 'Rastrology and its Use in Eighteenth-Century Manuscript Studies', *Studies in Musical Sources and Style: Essays in Honor of Jan La Rue*, ed. E.K. Wolf and E.H. Roesner (Madison, 1990), 237-91.)

[109] The court musicians did not move *en masse* to Oxford when the Court moved there in October 1642 (see Ashbee (1988), pp. xii-xiii & 115-29).

Table 16 Rastrum Rulings in Bing's and Lilly's Sets of Viol Consort Music[a]

Manuscript	No. of Staves[b]	Rastrum Span	Individual Staves
Great Set Score (Mus. 2)	2	26.5 mm	9 mm
Great Set Partbooks (Mus. 397-408)	2	40-1 mm	12.5-13 mm
Bing Set Partbooks (Mus. 417-18/1080)	2	38.5 mm	13 mm
Hatton Set Partbooks (Mus. 612-13)	2	39.5 mm	12 mm
Hatton Set Organbook (Mus. 432)	2 (6-line)	40.5 mm	14 mm
Great Set Organbook (Mus. 436)	2 (6-line)	41 mm	14 mm
Great Set Score (Mus. 2)	3	45.5 mm	9 mm

[a] Up to a millimetre should be allowed as a 'variation factor' for the individual staves, and perhaps even more than a millimetre for the total span of a rastrum (particularly for multiple rastra); such variations in the measurements could be the result of differing pressure on the rastrum causing varying amounts of 'spreading', fluctuating viscosity of ink, irregular ink supply, or paper warping. Thus the partbooks (Mus. 397-408, 417-18/1080 & 612-13) were probably ruled with the same two-(five-line-)stave rastrum, and the organbooks (Mus. 432 & 436) were almost certainly ruled with the same two-(six-line-)stave rastrum.
[b] Five-line staves unless stated.

---

sources.[110] It would be well beyond the limits of practicality to compare the readings of all the sources for each piece in an attempt to construct individual stemmata and thence source filiations - this would probably be impossible in any case, as there are undoubtedly a large number of missing sources involved - but a few 'spot checks' have revealed some interesting relationships. For example, the group of textless Italian madrigals which appear in the Great Set represent a common core of oft-transmitted pieces (see Table 17). Not surprisingly, fifteen of the Italian madrigals in the Great Set also appear in British Library Egerton MS 3665: the vast compendium of 1,200 villanelle, madrigals and motets mostly by Italian composers said to have been compiled by Francis Tregian.[111] A substantial number of the Great Set madrigals also appear in two Myriell sources: the single alto partbook British Library Add. MS 29,427, and the organbook Christ Church Mus. 67 (eight and ten concordant madrigals respectively). This should perhaps be expected in light of the comments already made concerning Stephen Bing's links with the St Paul's circle of musicians and copyists; however, the order of the Italian madrigals in the two Myriell sources is different from that in the Great Set, and a direct link between the two is unlikely. After the Tregian

---

[110] For full details of concordant sources see Wainwright (1993), ii, 152-64, 188-91 & 193-4.
[111] For details see B. Schofield & R. Thurston Dart, 'Tregian's Anthology', *ML*, xxxii (1951), 205-16; see also Chapter Six below. For advanced notice of a proposed challenge to the accepted view concerning the prolific copyist see R.R. Thompson, 'The "Tregian" Manuscripts: A Study of their Compilation', *British Library Journal*, xviii (1992), 202-4.

Table 17 Textless Italian Madrigals in the Great Set

Concordant Sources (see below):

	a	b	c	d	e	f	g	h	i	j	k	l	m	n	o	p	q	r
Marenzio: 'Arda pur sempre o mora' (VII *a* 5, 1595)					x			x	x								x	x
Marenzio: 'Rimanti in pace' (VI *a* 5, 1594)				x		x			x									
Marenzio: 'Ond'ei di morte' (VI *a* 5, 1594)			x	x	x	x			x						x			x
Marenzio: 'Caro dolce mio ben' (III *a* 5, 1582)		x				x	x							x				x
Marenzio: 'Che sei tu se'l cor mio' (VI *a* 5, 1594)						x									x			x
Monteverdi: 'La tra'l sangue' (III *a* 5, 1592)				x	x	x		x	x			x			x		x	x
Monteverdi: 'Sovra tenere herbette' (III *a* 5, 1592)				x	x	x			x				x		x			
Monteverdi: 'O com'e gran martire' (III *a* 5, 1592)	x			x	x	x			x				x		x		x	x
Vecchi: 'Clorinda hai vinto' (I *a* 5, 1589)				x	x	x					x				x			
Pallavicino: 'Era l'anima mia' (VI *a* 5, 1600)									x									
Marenzio: 'Ami Tyrsi e me'l nieghi' (VII *a* 5, 1595)										x								
Marenzio: 'Deh poi ch'era' (VII *a* 5, 1595)				x	x	x								x		x		

| | a | b | c | d | e | f | g | h | i | j | k | l | m | n | o | p | q | r |

	a	b	c	d	e	f	g	h	i	j	k	l	m	n	o	p	q	r
Pallavicino: 'Come vivro' (VI a 5, 1600)						x	x									x		x
Marenzio: 'Quell'augellin' (VII a 5, 1595)			x								x							
Marenzio: 'Ma grideran per me' (VII a 5, 1595)									x									
Pallavicino: 'O dolorosa morte' (VII a 5, 1604)									x									
Monteverdi: 'Voi pur da me partite' (IV a 5, 1603)					x				x	x	x							
Monteverdi: 'Luci seren'e chiare' (IV a 5, 1603)				x					x	x	x					x		x
Pallavicino: 'Cor mio deh non languire' (VI a 5, 1600)			x	x					x							x	x	
Pallavicino: 'O come vaneggiate donna' (VI a 5, 1600)			x						x									x

Sources:

a Dublin, Marsh's Library MSS Z3.4.7-12
b London, British Library Add. MSS 29,372-7
c London, British Library Add. MS 29,427
d London, British Library Add. MS 31,440
e London, British Library Add. MSS 37,402-6
f London, British Library Add. MSS 40,657-61
g London, British Library Egerton MS 995
h London, British Library Egerton MS 2485
i London, British Library Egerton MS 3665
j London, Royal College of Music MS 684
k Oxford, Bodleian Library MS Mus. f 1-6
l Oxford, Bodleian Library MS Mus. Sch. E 415-18
m Oxford, Bodleian Library Tenbury MSS 940-4
n Oxford, Bodleian Library Tenbury MS 1016
o Oxford, Christ Church Mus. 44
p Oxford, Christ Church Mus. 67
q Oxford, Christ Church Mus. 527-30/1024
r USA, San Marino, Huntington Library, Ellesmere MSS 25 A 46-51

scorebook (Egerton 3665), the manuscript set which provides the most concordances with the Great Set's Italian madrigals is British Library Add. MSS 40,657-61 (see Part II, MS XII). The so-called 'Shirley Partbooks' contain twelve of the Italian madrigals and, what is more, the ordering of two sequences of pieces is the same as in the Great Set (bracketed in Table 17). This may not be important in itself but it provides a starting point for other checks to be made.

British Library Add. MSS 40,657-61 are a set of five partbooks (lacking the Sextus book) containing viol-consort music for two to six parts (including thirteen untexted five-part Italian madrigals for instrumental performance). Sixty-eight of a total of 116 pieces in the 'Shirley Partbooks' also appear in the Great Set. A detailed comparison of a cross-section of the fantasias with their counterparts in the Great Set reveals that the two collections are almost certainly related in some way;[112] almost all the differences that occur can be explained as either copyists' errors or 'insignificant variants'. The 'Shirley Partbooks' - so-called because the bindings contain the coat of arms of the Shirley family of Staunton Harrold, Leicestershire - are mostly in the hand of William Lawes (copied in two stages), and a second unidentified scribe added nine pieces and copied two parts of four other pieces in conjunction with Lawes (see Part II, MS XII).[113] The sixty-eight pieces concordant with the Great Set are in William Lawes' 'early' hand which David Pinto suggests dates from before 1633 (as Sir Henry Shirley, Second Baronet, died in February 1633 and his heir was only ten years of age).[114] Thus the relevant sections of the 'Shirley Partbooks' appear to pre-date the copying of the Great Set. Could this William Lawes manuscript be one of the sources used by Bing and Lilly when compiling the Great Set? One would perhaps expect to find more of a correlation between the order of the pieces in the two sets, but there can be

---

[112] The following pieces were compared in detail: Coprario, Fantasias *a* 3 (VdGS Nos. 1, 3, 5-6, 9-10); Coprario, Fantasia *a* 4 (No. 2); Coprario, Fantasia *a* 6 (No. 2); Ferrabosco, Fantasias *a* 4 (Nos. 13 & 15); Lupo, Fantasia *a* 6 (No. 1); White, 'Diapente' Fantasia *a* 5 (No. 1); Ward, Fantasias *a* 4 (Nos. 1-6); Ward, Fantasias *a* 5 (Nos. 2 & 4); and White, Fantasias *a* 6 (Nos. 1-6).

[113] The anonymous scribe 'B' also contributed to the copying of *US-SM* EL 25 A 46-51, a set of six partbooks which have the initials 'W H' on their covers (see R. Charteris, 'The Huntington Library Part Books, Ellesmere MSS EL 25 A 46-51', *Huntington Library Quarterly*, 1 (1987), 59-84). Christopher Field - review of John Jenkins, *Consort Music for Viols in Four Parts*, ed. A. Ashbee, and William Lawes, *Consort Sets in Five Parts*, ed. D. Pinto, *ML*, lxii (1981), 101-2 - suggests that the first owner of the partbooks was William Herbert, Third Earl of Pembroke (1580-1630) who was a patron of William Lawes' brother, Henry. *US-SM* EL 25 A 46-51 was later owned by John Egerton, Second Earl of Bridgewater (1622-88) whose father, John Egerton, First Earl of Bridgewater (1575-1626) was also a patron of Henry Lawes (see L. Hamessley, 'The Tenbury and Ellesmere Partbooks: New Findings on Manuscript Compilation and Exchange, and the Reception of the Italian Madrigal in Elizabethan England', *ML*, lxxiii (1992), 177-221). David Pinto - (1995), 15 - suggests the possibility that William Lawes' early caligraphic hand also appears in the Ellesmere partbooks.

[114] D. Pinto, 'William Lawes' Music for Viol Consort', *EM*, vi (1978), 13; and ibid. (1995), 11-15 & 30-33.

no doubt that, even if they are not directly akin, the two collections are very closely related.

Another line of enquiry centred around Jenkins' six five-part fantasias and his single five-part pavan which appear consecutively in the Great Set. These pieces can also be found in the Royal College of Music MS 1145: a composite volume of three partbooks (from an original set of five, lacking Bassus and Quintus) copied by scribes associated with Sir Nicholas Le Strange (1604-55) of Hunstanton (a patron of John Jenkins). The manuscripts copied for Le Strange are particularly remarkable because of their numerous annotations concerning copy-sources.[115] Seven of the eighteen five-part pieces by Jenkins in Royal College MS 1145 contain the annotation 'Barnard score:B[ook]:';[116] these seven compositions by Jenkins happen to be the same seven five-part pieces which appear in the Great Set. This is not surprising given the known connections between Stephen Bing and John Barnard. It is disappointing, then, not to find any significant correspondence between the Great Set and Royal College MS 1145 nor with any of the manuscripts with demonstrable links with Barnard (British Library Add. MS 30,487, Bodleian Library Tenbury MS 302, and Washington D.C., Library of Congress MSS M990.C66F4).[117] It is possible that the incomplete Tenbury scorebook (MS 302) may be Le Strange's 'Barnard score:B[ook]:' (or at least a draft for it), but this cannot be proven as the last section of the manuscript - which perhaps contained the works to which the annotations refer - is missing.[118] Unfortunately the incomplete survival of manuscript sources will continue to hinder further research concerning the identification of Bing and Lilly's copy-sources for the Great Set.

Finally, a note concerning John Lilly's organbook, British Library Egerton 2485 (Part II, MS XIV) which was mentioned in passing above.

---

[115] For full details concerning the Le Strange manuscripts (*Lcm* 921, *Lcm* 1145, *Lbl* Add. 10,444, *Lbl* Add. 23,779, *Lbl* Add. 31,428, *Lbl* Add. 39,550-4, *Och* Mus. 1005 & *US-Cn* Case VM.1.A.18.J.52c) see: P. Willetts, 'Sir Nicholas Le Strange and John Jenkins', *ML* xlii (1961b), 30-43; P. Willetts, 'Sir Nicholas Le Strange's Collection of Masque Music', *The British Museum Quarterly*, xxix (1965), 79-81; A. Ashbee, 'A Further Look at Some of the Le Strange Manuscripts', *Chelys*, v (1973-4), 24-41; A. Ashbee, 'Towards the Chronology and Grouping of Some Airs by John Jenkins', *ML*, lv (1974), 30-44; and Holman (1993), 186-96.
[116] The other contemporary manuscripts mentioned in the Le Strange manuscripts are: 'Bromall', 'Mr: Coleman', 'Mr Collins', 'Couzens Score: B:', 'Mr Derhams Blew Fol. Bookes:', 'Drury', 'Dunn', 'Donne 2d', 'Fakenham-Musick.Num:8', 'Mr Fanshaw Score:b:', 'Fowler', 'Francklin', 'Gibbs', 'Harman', 'Holland', 'Ives', 'Mr Jacobs: Bo:', 'mr Ligons', 'Pettus', 'Pettus: 2d:coppy', 'Rampley', 'Sheppy', 'Staersmoer/Staresmore' and 'Ward'. For suggested identifications see Willetts (1961b), *passim*; Ashbee (1973-4), *passim*; C.D.S. Field, 'Musical Observations from Barbados, 1647-50', *MT*, cxv (1974), 565-7; and I. Payne, 'British Library Add. MSS 30,826-28: A Set of Part-Books from Trinity College Cambridge?', *Chelys*, xvii (1988), 9-10.
[117] See G. Dodd, 'The Coperario-Lupo Five-Part Books at Washington', *Chelys*, i (1969), 36-40; and Willetts (1991).
[118] Willetts (1991), 36.

Superficially this organbook has many similarities with the organbooks of the Hatton and Great Sets (Christ Church Mus. 432 and 436 respectively): a large oblong quarto book made up of royal paper with a 'Strasbourg Bend' watermark, and each page containing eight rastrum-ruled six-line staves. However, the watermark is not exactly the same as that in the Hatton organbook, Bing and Great Sets, and a comparison of the stave measurements reveals that they too are slightly different.[119] The contents of the Egerton organbook are duplicated in the Great Set except for four pieces (see Table 15), but the order of the pieces is completely different. It seems unlikely, therefore, that the Egerton organbook was commissioned by Hatton and dates from the mid to late 1630s; it is more likely to have been copied in the Commonwealth period quite independently of Hatton's patronage. Until more information is available the purpose and date of Lilly's organbook must remain a mystery.

Stephen Bing and the Oxford Court

Stephen Bing's appointment as a Minor Canon at St Paul's Cathedral in 1640/41 coincided with a dramatic increase in the political and religious tensions which had been brewing since the mid 1630s, and which were to culminate in January 1642 with the King's forced withdrawal from London and the start of the Civil War. This period had seen widespread disaffection with the Church of England and the ecclesiastical government under the leadership of the Archbishop of Canterbury, William Laud (1573-1645). Laud's attempts at liturgical reform led to the unjust and eventually fatal accusation of 'popery'. The Puritan paranoia with things popish, fuelled to some extent by the scurrilous Parliamentarian news-sheet *Mercurius Britanicus*, led to the persecution of 'scandalous' ministers and, after the outbreak of open hostilities in the autumn of 1642, to the sequestration of Church incomes. The Parliamentarians needed to raise funds quickly and cathedrals such as St Paul's - a stronghold of 'popish' traditions and Royalists to boot - were quickly targeted for fines and confiscations. An Ordinance of 12 March 1643 set in motion the sequestration of the rents and revenues of St Paul's Cathedral,[120] and from then until 1649[121] the accounts of the Warden of the College of Minor Canons are constantly concerned with payments and petitions to Parliament for the recovery of 'Church-meanes'.[122] These petitions were occasionally successful. For example, in

---

[119] *Lbl* Egerton 2485 was ruled with a two-stave rastrum of 39 mm span and individual six-line staves each measuring 12.5 mm; this should be compared with the measurements for *Och* Mus. 432 & 436 in Table 16.
[120] Firth & Rait (1911), i, 672.
[121] The offices of the Dean and Chapter of St Paul's Cathedral were suppressed in 1649 and were re-established at the Restoration.
[122] See *Lgl* Arch. St P. 25,746, *passim*; and PRO SP 28/355/1 (full details in Willetts (1989), 11-12).

1646 the Minor Canons received a small remuneration to be 'divided apart among nine of us here extant', but the Warden's accounts note that the sequestrators had deducted the monies of 'Mr Bing's and the two dead places'.[123] Stephen Bing had been on the sequestrators' black list as a 'notorious delinquent' (i.e. Royalist) since 19 August 1643 when a warrant had been issued to seize goods from his house in 'Petty Cannons' (to the north of St Paul's).[124] It appears that Bing left St Paul's - presumably to join the King's supporters - sometime after midsummer 1643 and did not return until 1647.[125] Pamela Willetts has noted that a significant number of high-ranking Royalists left London in August 1643 and has suggested that Bing was amongst them.[126] The Royalist stronghold of Oxford, which from October 1642 had been the base for the King's campaigns, was his most likely destination.[127] In Oxford Bing would have been reunited with his sometime musical patron, Sir Christopher Hatton, and his fellow musician and copyist George Jeffreys.

It was suggested earlier that Christopher Hatton assumed some responsibility for the music at the Oxford Court (this hypothesis is examined in detail in Chapter Five), and the evidence suggests that Stephen Bing and George Jeffreys were closely involved. Hatton is known to have purchased Italian music in the late 1630s (see Chapter Two) and it appears that this was put to good use at Oxford. A number of Stephen Bing's surviving manuscripts - copied directly from printed music in the Hatton collection - very probably date from the period 1643-6 (see below). Evidence of the practical use of Hatton's printed music is also to be found in the basso continuo partbook of Valentini's *Secondo Libro de Madrigali* (Venice, 1616) (Christ Church Mus. 255): the pages of the partbook were printed and stitched in the wrong order (page-sequence: 1-15, 32-33, 18-31, 16-17, 34-50) and Bing copied three manuscript slips which were attached to pages 32, 17 and 34 to enable the player to perform the pieces without awkward page turns. Bing's copy of the basso continuo parts to the whole of Dering's *Cantica Sacra* (Antwerp, 1618) - Christ Church Mus. 1023 (see Part II, MS LIX) - is also significant in this context: the Christ Church Library contains two sets of Dering's 1618 publication (Mus. 154-60 and 881-6), the second of which lacks the continuo partbook. Perhaps this set belonged to Hatton, and Bing supplied the missing continuo part so that the music could be

---

[123] *Lgl* Arch. St P. 25,746, f. 26^v.
[124] Willetts (1989), 12.
[125] Stephen Bing signed the accounts of the Warden of the College of Minor Canons (*Lgl* Arch. St P. 25,746) at midsummer 1642 (f. 22^v), 1643 (f. 24), 1647 (f. 29), 1648 (f. 30), 1649 (f. 31^v) and 1661 (f. 33^v), etc.
[126] Willetts (1989), 12.
[127] It should be noted that there is no direct archival evidence to confirm Bing's presence in Oxford. However, the circumstantial evidence outlined above, and the contents and function of his surviving music manuscripts (to be examined in detail below and in Chapter Five), make it highly likely that Bing was in Oxford with Hatton.

performed. Christ Church Mus. 1023 is also notable for the appearance of George Jeffreys' text hand; this is the first of a number of collaborations between the two scribes which probably took place at the Oxford Court.

Stephen Bing's Copies of Italian Music

English musicians, collectors and patrons are known to have been interested in Italian music from the early years of the sixteenth century. Italian musicians appear in the lists of Henry VIII's musicians,[128] and from then onwards Italian music was frequently imported and copied into English manuscripts. The prestige and circulation of the Italian madrigal and its effect on the English madrigalists in Elizabeth I's reign have been thoroughly examined;[129] however, the continued interest in Italian music in England throughout the seventeenth century has been comparatively neglected. The manuscript copies of Italian music made by Christopher Hatton III's musicians, Stephen Bing and George Jeffreys, offer a unique example of the dissemination of Italian music in England in the first half of the seventeenth century - unique because we know precisely which printed sources were used, to whom they belonged, and how and when they came to be in the country.

Five of Stephen Bing's manuscripts contain Italian music copied from printed sources in the Hatton collection: British Library Add. MS 31,434; Christ Church Mus. 880; and Bodleian Library Tenbury MSS 1005, 1009 and 1017. Christ Church Mus. 880 - one of a complex set of four partbooks copied by Bing and a number of other scribes (including Jeffreys) - is examined in detail in Chapter Five and a performance context is suggested for the Italian music. It is my contention that the manuscripts mentioned above, and a number of those in the hand of George Jeffreys (examined in the following chapter), were the product of a school of copyist-musicians working at the Oxford Court under the patronage and supervision of

---

[128] See J. Izon, 'Italian Musicians at the Tudor Court', *MQ*, xliv (1958), 329-37.

[129] The main works are: A. Obertello, *Madrigali Italiani in Inghilterra* (Milan, 1949); A. Einstein, 'The Elizabethan Madrigal and *Musica Transalpina*', *ML*, xxv (1944), 66-77 & ibid., xxvii (1946), 273-4; E.B. Helm, 'Italian Traits in the English Madrigal', *MR*, vii (1946), 26-34; J. Kerman, 'Elizabethan Anthologies of Italian Madrigals', *JAMS*, iv (1951), 122-38; J. Kerman, 'Master Alfonso and the English Madrigal', *MQ*, xxxviii (1952), 222-44; Kerman (1962); L. Hamessley, *The Reception of the Italian Madrigal in England: A Repertorial Study of Manuscript Anthologies ca. 1580-1620* (Ann Arbor, 1990); and Hamessley (1992). (See also J.A. Bernstein, 'Lassus in English Sources: Two Chansons Recovered', *JAMS*, xxvii (1974), 315-25; J.A. Bernstein, 'Philip Van Wilder and the Chanson in Tudor England', *MD*, xxxiii (1979), 55-75; I. Fenlon, 'La Diffusion de la Chanson Continentale dans les Manuscrits Anglais entre 1509-1570', *La Chanson à la Renaissance*, ed. J.-M. Vaccaro (Tours, 1981), 172-89; J.A. Bernstein, 'An Index of Polyphonic Chansons in English Manuscript Sources, c.1530-1640', *RCRMA*, xxi (1988), 21-36; and K. K. Forney, 'Antwerp's Role in the Reception and Dissemination of the Madrigal in the North', *Atti del XIV Congresso della Società Internazionale di Musicologia: Transmissione e Recezione delle Forme di Cultura Musicale* (Bologna, 27 August - 1 September 1987), i, 239-53.)

Christopher Hatton. This claim finds support in the fact that Bing and Jeffreys used a common supply of copy-sources - the Hatton collection - and in the evidence offered by a detailed comparative study of the physical make-up of the manuscripts in question.

Bodleian Library Tenbury MSS 1005, 1009 and 1017 (Part II, MSS XXXII, XXXIII and XL) are scores of madrigals copied stratigraphically across the whole width of unfolded sheets of paper (the blocks of rastrum-ruled staves on the left and right of each sheet had been joined in the middle by freehand). Tenbury MS 1005 contains four madrigals from Monteverdi's fourth book of madrigals, ten madrigals from Bernardi's *Concerti Accademici* Op. 8, and an incomplete anonymous madrigal 'A.2 &. a.4. ad imitazione d'uno del Sig. L.M.';[130] Tenbury MS 1009 contains three madrigals by Gesualdo (one from the third book and two from the fourth), an unpublished Italian madrigal by Richard Dering, three madrigals from Bernardi's second book, and twelve anonymous English madrigals (perhaps unidentified *contrafacta* of Italian madrigals?); and Tenbury MS 1017 contains two madrigals by Merula from his second book. Merula's popular joke-pieces - 'Nominativo hic et haec et hoc' and 'Nominativo quis vel qui quae quod' (grammatical games with declension repetitions) - in Tenbury MS 1017 are fully texted,[131] but a number of the pieces in Tenbury MSS 1005 and 1009 are, in typical English fashion, either textless or partially-texted. Editions of all the printed copy-sources mentioned, except Bernardi's *Concerti Accademici* Op. 8 (1615-16), survive today in Christ Church, Oxford and were most likely originally part of the Hatton collection (see Chapter Two). Furthermore a common provenance for Stephen Bing's manuscripts of Italian music - and those of George Jeffreys - is indicated by the number of correlations between paper types and/or rastrum-rulings in the manuscripts (see Table 18).[132] Thus Tenbury MSS 1005 and 1009 consist of a mix of papers with either a Pelican(?) or Pillars watermark and a single sheet with a Pot lettered IDB (Tenbury MS 1009, f. 7), and Tenbury MS 1017 consists of paper with a Pot lettered ID. This latter mark appears in a number of Hatton-related manuscripts in five very slightly different versions (see Table 18) which Robert Thompson has shown were the result of a

---

[130] 'Luca Marenzio'? The piece bears no resemblance to Marenzio's madrigal-style, and David Pinto - (1990), 94 - has speculated that the anonymous 'imitazione' ('Andianne à gli'horti') may be by George Jeffreys.
[131] Some of the text underlay and the attribution to 'Claudio Merula' was added by Jeffreys.
[132] When comparing rastrum-rulings, up to a millimetre should be allowed as a 'variation factor' for the individual staves, and perhaps even more than a millimetre for the total span of a rastrum (particularly for multiple rastra); as noted in Table 16, such variations in the measurements could be the result of differing pressure on the rastrum causing varying amounts of 'spreading', fluctuating viscosity of ink, irregular ink supply, or paper warping.

Table 18 Stephen Bing's and George Jeffreys' Manuscripts of Italian Music: Watermarks and Rastrum Rulings

Watermark (& mould)	Manuscript	Copyist	No. of staves per page	Stave width mm	No. of staves in rastrum	Rastrum span mm
Cardinals' Hat GR[a]	Lbl Add. 31,479	Jeffreys	10	12	5	108.5
Cardinals' Hat GR	Mad. Soc. G 55-9	Jeffreys	10	12	5	108.5
Pelican(?)	Ob T 1005, ff. 4-16	Bing	12	10.5-11	6	126.5
Pelican(?)	Ob T 1009, ff. 1-3, 5	Bing	12	-	various	-
Pillars DI (ab)[b]	Och Mus. 880: Bing section/2	Bing	10	13	5	117
Pillars	Och Mus. 255[c]	Bing	-	13-14	-	-
Pillars	Ob T 1005, ff. 1-2	Bing	10	13	5	117
Pillars	Ob T 1005, f. 3	Bing	10	12	2(?)	38
Pillars	Ob T 1009, ff. 4, 6, 8-9	Bing	10	-	various	-
Pot GRO [i] (ab)[d]	Lbl Add. 31,434/2	Bing	10	12.5	5	111
Pot GRO [ii]	Lbl Add. 31,434/3	Bing	10	12.5	5	120
Pot GRO [iii]	Ob T 1015	Jeffreys	10	12.5-14	5	118
Pot GRV	Ob T 973-6 & 1273	Jeffreys	10	11.5	5	108
Pot ID (abs)[e]	Lbl Add. 31,434/1	Bing	10	12.5	5	111
Pot ID (abs)	Ob T 1013	Jeffreys	10	12-12.5	5	111
Pot ID (cd)	Ob T 1017	Bing	10	13	5	118.5
Pot ID (cd)	Och Mus. 878/880: Notari section	(Notari)	10	12.5-13	5	119
Pot IDB	Ob T 1009, f. 7	Bing	10	-	various	-
Pot IDB	Ob T 1016	Jeffreys	10	11.5	2	38.5
Pot PB	Ob T 1012	Jeffreys	10	12.5-13.5	5	117
Pot RRO (ab)	Och Mus. 880: Bing section/1	Bing	10	12.5-13	5	117
Pot VI	Ob T 1009, ff. 10-14	Bing	10	-	-	-

[a] Thompson (1988), Watermark XXII. (Lcm 920 iv; see Part II, MS XVII.)
[b] Thompson (1988), Watermark I. (Lbl Add. 10,338 watermark 1; see Part II, MS I.)
[c] The first of three manuscript insertions in the basso continuo partbook of Valentini's *Secondo Libro de Madrigali* (Venice, 1616).
[d] Thompson (1988), Watermark XII.
[e] Thompson (1988), Watermark IX. (Lbl Add. 10,338 watermark 7; see Part II, MS I.)

---

quartet of moulds (a-d) and a single 'spare' mould (s).[133] Bing and Jeffreys appear to have been using the same supply of ruled but unbound paper that was the result not of coincidence but of common provenance.

---

[133] R. Thompson, 'Manuscripts of the Civil War Period?', unpublished paper presented at the Study Day on Music 1550-1650, Oxford, May 1990 (1990b). Watermark 'quartets' were the product of two-vat mills: paper with watermark versions a and b would have been made, alternatively sheet by sheet, using a pair of moulds at one vat, and c and d in the second vat; the fifth watermark 's' could have been the result of a spare or replacement mould used at either vat. Quires of paper from both vats would occasionally have been combined into a single ream, but more usually the paper from the two vats would be kept separate (as is the case with the Pot ID paper: a-b or c-d).

British Library Add. MS 31,434 (Part II, MS VI) is a more varied and complex collection consisting of six partbooks. The misleading ascription on the original front cover to the Cantus I book - 'Composed by and in the Autograph of Henry Lawes', in the hand of Joseph Warren (1804-81) a one-time owner of the manuscript - was accepted without question until quite recently. The entry in the printed catalogue of manuscript music in the British Library follows the ascription and describes the contents of the manuscript as 'Motets, *etc.*, for 5 voices, with a figured bass for harpsichord or organ, in parts, by Henry Lawes. *Autograph.*'[134] However, a comparison with Henry Lawes' autograph song collection, British Library Add. MS 53,723, proves that this is a different hand. The name 'Henry Lawes' is prefixed only to the first piece in Add. MS 31,434 (in Bing's hand) in two of the partbooks (Cantus I, f. 1; and Bassus, f. 50), and there are no other attributions. The first and third pieces are, respectively, settings of paraphrases of Psalms 137 and 104 by Thomas Carew (1595-1640); the second piece is a setting of part of Joseph Hall's paraphrase of Psalm 9 which had been in print since 1607;[135] and the fourth piece is a setting of a nativity text[136] which resembles the carols by Robert Herrick (1591-1674) set by Henry Lawes and known to have been sung in the chapel at Whitehall before the Civil War.[137] David Pinto has pointed out that 'the natural context for these pieces is the Caroline Court of the 1630s or a social setting that imitated its music.'[138] The two Carew paraphrases of Psalms 137 and 104 appear in a printed sheet entitled 'Select PSALMES OF A NEW *TRANSLATION*, To be Sung in VERSE and CHORUS of *five Parts*, with *Symphonies* of *Violins, Organ*, and other Instruments, *Novemb*. 22. 1655. *Composed* by HENRY LAWES, servant to *His late Majesty.*' This printed sheet was found inserted into one of Henry Lawes' publications that once belonged to the library of the Dukes of Bridgewater.[139] The two items (Psalms 137 and 104) also appear - again

---

[134] A. Hughes-Hughes, *Catalogue of Music in the British Museum* (London, 1906-9), i, 288.

[135] J. Hall, *Holy Obseruations Lib. 1. and Some Few of Davids Psalms Metaphrased for a Taste of the Rest* (London, 1607).

[136] 'Harke Shepherd swaynes'; the same text was set for five voices and continuo by George Jeffreys in *Lbl* Add. 10,338, ff. 233^v-238^v.

[137] R. Herrick, *His Noble Numbers or his Pious Pieces* (London, 1647): No. 96, 'What sweeter musick can we bring'; and No. 97, 'Prepare for songs', which were 'sung to the King in the Presence at White Hall' with the 'Musical Part... composed by Master Henry Lawes' (no music is now extant).

[138] Pinto (1981), 20. (The description of 'Sitting by the streames' on p. 19 of this article as 'a dull song', was, I am assured, a misprint for 'a full song'!)

[139] The sole surviving copy(?) is *US-SM* RB 131907. I am very grateful to Professor Ian Spink for sending me a photocopy of the sheet. The description 'new translation' is puzzling as the Carew paraphrases had been in circulation long before 1655; they probably date from the 1620s and are known to have been prepared for publication shortly after Carew's death in 1640. See R. Dunlap, *The Poems of Thomas Carew* (Oxford, 1949), p. lxxi. H.J. Todd, *The Poetical Works of John Milton* (London, 1801), v, 204, describes this single sheet, which was apparently intended for a Cecilian festival, and from it quotes Psalm 137 in Carew's version. Willa McClung Evans - (1941), 211 footnote - also refers to the sheet and quotes the title and the

words only - in James Clifford's *Divine Services and Anthems* (2nd edition, London, 1664) where Henry Lawes is named as the composer.[140] As the first and third pieces in Add. MS 31,434 are by Henry Lawes it seems quite reasonable, therefore, to suggest that the second and fourth pieces are also by him, particularly as the pieces are so similar in style.[141]

The second, third, and fourth pieces belong to the tradition of the verse anthem, but are perhaps closer to the verse anthems written by the Restoration composers than those by Jacobean composers such as Orlando Gibbons. They are, in fact, prototype 'symphony anthems'; the instrumental symphonies are notated in two-part organ score with a violinistic idiom which suggests an original trio texture.[142] However, the third piece, 'My Soule the great Gods prayses singe' may originally have been intended for five string instruments and basso continuo. This suggestion is founded upon David Pinto's discovery that the 'simphonias' of 'My Soule the great Gods prayses singe' correspond to two strains of an alman by William Lawes: the second 'Aire' from his five-part set in C minor.[143] The pieces were most likely intended for private devotional meetings, either at Court or in household chapels. Bing probably copied the four pieces by Lawes from a source closely connected with the composer. It is known that Bing and Henry Lawes were acquainted in the years before the Civil War; Pamela Willetts has shown that Henry Lawes rented the lease of Stephen Bing's incumbent's house[144] which bordered on the hall of the College of Minor Canons at St Paul's.[145] The accounts of the Warden of the College for the year 1640-1 note that 13s 4d was spent on 'Sealing Mr. Bing's lease let to Mr. Lawes for Mr. Nightingale' (it seems that although the lease belonged to Henry Lawes, the house was actually occupied by another of the Minor Canons, Roger Nightingale).[146]

Each of the six partbooks that make up British Library Add. MS 31,434 consists of three distinct sections (see Part II, MS VI). The first sections of

---

opening words of Psalms 137 and 104 in Carew's version (though she ascribes 'My Soule the great Gods prayses singe' to George Sandy).

[140] Only the first item, 'Sitting by the streames', is listed in the first edition of 1663. It is worth noting that both the 1655 sheet and Clifford print all nine verses of Carew's setting of Psalm 137 although only the first and fifth verses are set by Lawes.

[141] Daniel and le Huray (1972) include all four items under Henry Lawes, listing the only source as *Lbl* Add. 31,434. The whole of *Lbl* Add. 31,434 is transcribed and edited in J.P. Wainwright, 'A Study of Five Related Manuscripts Containing Italian Music: British Library Additional Manuscripts 31,434, 31,440 and 31,479; Madrigal Society Manuscripts G.55-9; and Christ Church Manuscripts 877-880' (M.Phil. dissertation, University of Cambridge, 1986), ii; and the four English pieces have been recorded by *The Consort of Musicke* directed by Anthony Rooley (Hyperion A 66135).

[142] I. Spink, *Restoration Cathedral Music 1660-1714* (Oxford, 1995), 106-7.

[143] VdGS: William Lawes, Air No. 77. See Pinto (1981), 19.

[144] Willetts (1989), 13.

[145] *Lgl* Arch. St P. 25,632, ff. 222-3.

[146] *Lgl* Arch. St P. 25,746, f. 20.

each book contain the four English pieces; the second sections contain seven anonymous pieces: three motets, three madrigals and the *Dialogo d'Abram*; and the final sections consist of five motets, three by Aloisi and two by Merula. The complex collation of Add. MS 31,434 is summarised in Table 19.[147] If the three paper-types and the two systems of rastrum-rulings are

Table 19 British Library Add. MS 31,434: Collation

Cantus I		Cantus II		Contratenor		Tenor		Bassus		Basso Cont.		
Folio	Mark	Folio	Mark	Folio	Mark	Folio	Mark	Folio	Mark	Folio	Mark	Rastrum
1	-	14	Ib	26	-	38	Is	50	Ib	62	Is	a
2	Ib			27	Is	39	-	51	-	63	-	a
3	-	15	-	28	Ib	40	-	52	-	64	-	a
4	Ia	16	Is					53	-			a
5	-	17	IIb	29	IIb	41	IIa	54	IIb	65	-	a
						42	IIa					a
6	IIb	18	-	30	IIa	43	-	55	-	66	-	a
7	-	19	IIb	31	-			56	IIa	67	IIa	a
8	IIb	20	IIa	32	-	44	-	57	IIb	68	IIb	a
9	-	21	-	33	IIb	45	IIb	58	-	69	-	a
9a	Ib											a
10	III	22	-	34	III	46	III	59	-	70	-	b
11	-	23	III	35	-	47	-	60	III	71	III	b
12	III	24	-	36	-	48	-	61	-	72	-	b
13	-	25	III	37	III	49	III					b
										73	III	a
13a	Is									74	III	b

Watermark I: Pot ID (a & b: mould pair; s: spare mould)
Watermark II: Pot GRO [i] (a & b: mould pair)
Watermark III: Pot GRO [ii]
Rastrum a: five-stave rastrum of 111 mm span and individual staves measuring 12.5 mm
Rastrum b: five-stave rastrum of 120 mm span and individual staves measuring 12.5 mm

---

[147] Each of the pages of *Lbl* Add. 31,434 were lifted in rebinding and are now individually guarded throughout; however an examination of the watermarks and stave placings enabled an approximate collation to be made; I gratefully acknowledge the assistance of Dr Robert Thompson in this matter.

compared with other manuscripts copied by Bing and George Jeffreys (see Table 18) a number of relationships become apparent. For example, the first paper-type (Pot lettered ID) is from the quartet of moulds mentioned above in relation to Bodleian Library Tenbury MS 1017, paper that was also available to George Jeffreys (see the following chapter); also it is possible that the same rastrum was used to rule the third sections of Add. MS 31,434 and Tenbury MS 1017. The physical evidence offered by Add. MS 31,434 suggests a common provenance and similar date to Bing's other manuscripts containing Italian music.[148]

The pieces in the second sections of the partbooks are all anonymous. It is possible that they were copied from unidentified or lost printed sources, but it is more likely that they were the product of manuscript transmissions.[149] This idea finds some support in the fact that the only noted concordance with a piece in the middle sections of Add. MS 31,434 is with a manuscript and not a printed source. The very fine *Dialogo d'Abram*, 'Splendea qual vivo sole' (which is copied very inaccurately by Bing) is also to be found in Angelo Notari's scorebook British Library Add. MS 31,440 (see Part II, MS VII). Notari (1566-1663), the Italian-born court lutenist and singer, would seem to be a likely candidate for the composer of the *Dialogo d'Abram* and, as we shall see in Chapters Five and Six, he appears to have had links with Hatton and the Oxford Court.[150] One of the two printed copy-sources used by Bing in the final sections of Add. MS 31,434, Aloisi's *Contextus Musicarum Proportionum* (1637), was among the twenty-five prints purchased by Hatton in 1638 (see Table 2), and the copy survives today at Christ Church, Oxford. This gives a *terminus post quem* for the third sections of Add. MS 31,434 - and probably also the first and second

---

[148] Robert Thompson - (1989), 220; and (1990b) - has further noted that paper used in the second sections of *Lbl* Add. 31,434 (Pot GRO [i]) is also the main paper-type of the partbooks *Lbl* Add. 18,940-4. This set of oblong quarto partbooks contains, amongst other music, arrangements of movements from Shirley's monumental masque *The Triumph of Peace* performed at Whitehall in February 1634, and also the only complete sequence of all of Ives' twenty-five four-part ayres. The partbooks appear to have close connections with Simon Ives who was a Vicar Choral at St Paul's Cathedral at the time of Bing's appointment as Minor Canon. Furthermore, an inserted gathering in each partbook of *Lbl* Add. 18,940-4 (added after the original pagination had been completed) consists of paper with a Pillars watermark also found in a letter in the Hatton correspondence dated 1 March 1645 (*Lbl* Add. 29,550, f. 55). Could *Lbl* Add. 18,940-4 perhaps share a common origin with the Bing and Jeffreys manuscripts?

[149] The madrigals do not appear in 'Il Nuovo Vogel' (E. Vogel, A. Einstein, F. Lesure, C. Sartori, *Bibliografia della Musica Italiana Vocale Profana Publicata dal 1500- al 1700* (Pomezia, 1977), 3 vols); nor are there any traces of the three motets in surviving printed sources of Italian motets from the first half of the seventeenth century held in the main British and Italian libraries. I record my thanks to the late Dr Jerome Roche and Dr Graham Dixon for allowing me to consult their index of Italian motets of this period.

[150] It is likely that much of the anonymous music in Notari's scorebook *Lbl* Add. 31,440 is actually by Notari himself; see P.J. Willetts, 'Autographs of Angelo Notari', *ML*, 1 (1969b), 126. It is even possible that Notari was the composer of all the pieces in the second sections of *Lbl* Add. 31,434, but proof for such speculation is unlikely to be forthcoming.

sections - of November 1638. A suitable context for the compilation of a manuscript containing Italian Latin motets is difficult to postulate for the period 1638-42. There are, however, two possibilities: (*a*) could Latin motets have been performed at pre-Civil War Arminian services at Kirby Hall? or (*b*) could the copying-date for British Library Add. MS 31,434 be the period of Bing's residence in Oxford, 1643-6? (The second hypothesis is examined in more detail in Chapter Five.)[151]

Finally it should be noted that the sole-surviving exemplar of the other printed source used by Bing, Merula's *Il Primo Libro de Motetti* (Venice, 1624), is in the Civico Museo Bibliografico Musicale in Bologna. There must have been a copy of the publication in England in the 1630s or 1640s and it is highly likely that it was once a part of the Hatton collection: the publication was listed in Robert Martin's 1633 catalogue and, as both Stephen Bing and George Jeffreys copied music from the print, presumably Hatton purchased a copy which has since gone astray. The Bologna copy of Merula's first book of motets lacks the bass partbook, thus the identification of manuscript copies of pieces from this source has enabled the completion of a number of motets.[152] We return to the subject of Italian music in the context of the Oxford Court in the following two chapters.

Stephen Bing's Later Manuscripts

Oxford yielded to Parliamentarian forces on 20 June 1646 and Bing probably took advantage of the surrender terms to return to his former employment at St Paul's Cathedral. His name reappears in the account book of the Warden of the College of Minor Canons at St Paul's in midsummer 1647 and he signed for his dividend in the two subsequent years.[153] In April 1649 an Act of Parliament, which abolished 'Deans, Deans and Chapters, Canons, Prebends, and other Offices' and ordered the sale of ecclesiastical land and property,[154] deprived Bing of both his job and his home. This must have

---

[151] David Pinto - 'The True Christmas: Carols at the Court of Charles I', *William Lawes (1602-1645): Essays on His Life, Times and Work*, ed. A. Ashbee & L. Hulse (forthcoming) - has suggested a later possible performance circumstance for the Henry Lawes pieces in the high-Anglican services held in the chapel of Exeter House in the Strand, London during the Commonwealth.

[152] The following pieces from Merula's *Il Primo Libro de Motetti* (1624) can now be completed from Bing's *Lbl* Add. 31,434 and/or George Jeffreys' *Lbl* Add. 31,479 & Mad. Soc. G 55-9 (see the following chapter): 'Benedicta tu' CATTBbc: as 'Benedictus tu' in 31,434 & 31,479; 'Benignissime Jesu' CATTBbc: 31,434 & 31,479; 'Cantate Domino' CCBBbc: G 55-9; 'Cum complerentur dies pentecostes' CATBbc: G 55-9; 'Dominus in igne veniet' CBbc: 31,479; 'Fontes et omnia' BBbc: 31,479; 'Jesu dulcissime' CATBbc: G 55-9; 'Magnificate Dominum' CATBbc: G 55-9; 'O bone Jesu' CBbc: 31,479; 'O intemerata' CTBbc: as 'O Immaculate' in 31,479; 'O quam dulcis es tu' TTBbc: 31,479; and 'Sat est Domine' CTBbc: 31,479. (The reasons for the occasional text changes in Bing and Jeffreys' transcriptions are examined in Chapter Five.)

[153] *Lgl* Arch. St P. 25,746, ff. 29, 30 & 31^v.

[154] Firth & Rait (1911), ii, 81-104.

been a difficult period for Bing and his family (we know from his will that he was married, that his wife was called Katharine and that he had three daughters)[155] and he was twice forced to apply to the Committee for the Maintenance of Ministers for 'hardship' grants.[156] Bing found some employment during the Commonwealth as a secretary to the Hatton family and spent at least a short period of time in France with Baron Hatton: British Library Egerton MS 2533, folios 481-2, a letter dated 16/26 March 1649 from Baron Hatton (in exile in Paris) to Edward Nicholas, is in Bing's hand. Two other examples of Bing's secretarial work survive in the Hatton-family correspondence: the transcription of a speech by 'Monsieur du Vain when he delivered the Seales to the King, translated out of French', and a catalogue of manuscripts and printed books in the Hatton collection (not including music); both are undated but most likely derive from the Commonwealth period.[157]

The scarcity of surviving documents in Bing's hand in the Hatton archives indicates that he did not work for the family in a secretarial capacity on a regular basis. His links with the Hattons very likely diminished throughout the 1650s. A source of information concerning Stephen Bing's other activities at this time is John Batchiler's *The Virgin's Pattern: in the Exemplary Life, and Lamented Death of Mrs Susanna Perwich* (London, 1661); Susanna Perwich was a talented and greatly admired viol player who died in July 1661 at the age of twenty-four. We learn from the Epistle Dedicatory and the biographical prose section of Batchiler's eulogistic publication that Susanna Perwich's principal viol teacher at her school in Hackney, 'for the last seven years' (1654-61), had been Stephen Bing.[158] It appears that, like many redundant church and court musicians, Bing had to earn his living as a teacher.[159] A number of Stephen Bing's music manuscripts survive from the Commonwealth and Restoration periods. We cannot be sure that any of them were the direct result of the patronage of Baron Hatton but, if only for the sake of completeness, the manuscripts will be briefly examined in the context of Bing's later career.

The set of partbooks Christ Church Mus. 754-9 (see Part II, MS LVII), which were probably copied by Stephen Bing during the Commonwealth period, demonstrate Bing's continued interest in instrumental consort

---

[155] PRO PROB 11/368/179.
[156] He was awarded £4 on 26 April 1655, and 40s on 6 November 1657; see A.G. Matthews, *Walker Revised* (Oxford, 1948), 11.
[157] *Lbl* Add. 29,587, f. 47; and NRO FH 4025 respectively. It is also possible that it is Bing's handwriting which endorses two bills - NRO FH 2659 & 2661 - from the London stationer William Searle to Hatton for books and bindings, 1657-60.
[158] Extracts from Batchiler's *The Virgin's Pattern* which concern music and musicians are presented in P. Scholes, *The Puritans and Music* (London & New York, 1934), 160-2; and Willetts (1989), 3.
[159] Bing's name appears, alongside the likes of Charles and Edward Coleman, Henry Lawes and Davis Mell, in a list of 'excellent and able masters' for the 'Voyce or Viol' in the prefatory 'rules and directions' to John Playford's *A Musicall Banquet* (London, 1651).

music.[160] These six partbooks contain sixty-six ayres by William Lawes for two violins, two bass viols and two theorbos entitled 'The Royall Consort'. The earliest surviving versions of these pieces (which were possibly composed as early as 1620) are scored for two violins, tenor and bass viol, and continuo consisting of two theorbos and perhaps a bowed bass.[161] In later manuscripts (including Lawes' autograph score: Bodleian Library Mus. Sch. MS B 3) the pieces have been rewritten and the tenor- and bass-viol parts transformed into two 'breakeinge Bases' of identical tessitura which alternate between doubling the bass line of the continuo (provided by the two theorbos) and adding 'divisions'.[162] An explanation for this change is offered in a note on the verso of the first folio of Oxford, Bodleian Library Mus. Sch. MS D 236, in the hand of Edward Lowe:

> The followinge Royall Consorte was first composd for / 2 Trebles a Meane & a Base. but because the Middle / part could not bee performd with equall advantage, to bee / heard as the trebles were. Therefore the Author, involved / the Inner part in two breakeinge Bases: which I / causd to be transcribd for mee in the Tenor & Counter / Tenor Bookes, belonginge to thes. & soe bound. Wher the / two breakinge Bases are to bee found & soe many / figured as agree with thes in Order.[163]

Christ Church Mus. 754-9 contain the latest form of the 'new version' of Lawes' 'Royall Consort', and include two fantasias (Nos. 22 and 32) not found in the 'old version' and two pavans (Nos. 47 and 60) which do not even appear in Lawes' autograph manuscript of the 'new version'.[164] David Pinto has noted that the Pavan in C (No. 47) is notably advanced in its use of fully developed divisions for all six instruments and comments that although 'no corroboration from autograph manuscripts is available, these divisions are wholly in keeping with the style of the fantasias that do occur in the composer's own scores, and they must be among his latest works.'[165] It is

---

[160] The damaged-pot watermark RRO - Pot II/2 in 'Appendix: Watermarks and Paper Types', *VdGS Index of Manuscripts Containing Music for Viols*, ed. A. Ashbee, R. Thompson & J.P. Wainwright (first instalment, forthcoming) - appears in a variety of Commonwealth sources; in *Ob* Mus. Sch. F 568-9 it appears in conjunction with the Cardinals' Hat watermark which can be dated to 1653 (see pp. 126-7 below).
[161] As in *Ob* Mus. Sch. E 431-6 & F 568-9.
[162] See M. Lefkowitz, *William Lawes* (London, 1960), 68-87; and G. Dodd, 'William Lawes - Royall Consort Suite No. 9 in F', *Chelys*, vi (1975-6), 3-9.
[163] For a detailed examination of Lowe's comments relating to the 'Royall Consort', see Pinto (1995), 37-8 & 152-3. *Ob* Mus. Sch. D 233-6 are four partbooks from a set of six which were originally intended as a collection of vocal music (early seventeenth century). Edward Lowe bought the books - which he called 'the parchment books' - on 6 October 1636 (according to a note on the end-paper of D 233, now obscured) and methodically added music to them (including Lawes' 'Royall Consort'). The countertenor (Quintus) and tenor books were lost at an early stage and the remaining volumes were labelled '[No.] 23, 4 Bookes'; *Ob* Mus. Sch. E 451 was adopted as the basso continuo book for a number of the pieces (see Part II, MS XXX).
[164] VdGS Nos. 36 & 40 and 49 & 42 respectively.
[165] Pinto (1990), 82.

likely that William Lawes was present at the Oxford Court for a least some of the time between 1642 and his death at the siege of Chester on 24 September 1645;[166] perhaps Stephen Bing had personal contact with Lawes and may even have received the last version of the 'Royall Consort' directly from the composer? Should this be the case, Bing's Commonwealth (?re-)copying of the 'Royall Consort' gains in importance.

Gresham College Music MSS 469-71 (deposited in the Guildhall Library, London), a set of three instrumental partbooks copied by Bing, also date from the late Commonwealth period. They contain three-part 'Fantazies & Aires' by Jenkins, Locke and Young,[167] and eleven 'Sonata's, Almands, Corants etc' by 'Sieterich Beckron' (presumably the German composer Dietrich Becker) were added at a slightly later date in the back of the treble partbook. Bing's interest in viol-consort music continued into the Restoration period: his handwriting appears, alongside that of John Lilly's and four other unidentified scribes, in a set of five partbooks dated 1674 which contain Jenkins' three-part fantasia-ayre suites and four-part fantasia-ayre-corant suites: British Library Add. MSS 27,550-4 (see Part II, MS III). It is noteworthy that John Lilly (who copied the first thirty pieces in the Treble I partbook) and Stephen Bing (the copyist of the whole of the Treble II book) were still collaborating on projects in the 1670s. Their four fellow copyists in Add. MSS 27,550-4 remain unidentified, although the handwriting of scribe 'F', who copied the first twenty-six pieces in the organ partbook, has been noted in British Library Add. MS 17,784 (a bass partbook from a collection of anthems copied in the 1670s).[168] John Lilly's associations with the North family, patrons of John Jenkins, were discussed above; it is possible that Add. MSS 27,550-4 were the result of North family patronage. In this context mention must be made of Oxford, Bodleian Mus. Sch. MS C 87 (Part II, MS XXVIII) which, in Table 14, I tentatively suggested may include Stephen Bing's handwriting. Mus. Sch. MS C 87, a set of three partbooks containing three-part fantasias by John Jenkins, was copied by two scribes under the supervision of a third who checked and corrected the parts. The handwriting of scribe 'A' could be that of Stephen Bing: many of the details are strikingly similar to those in the other manuscripts listed in Table 14, in particular the numeration and the *custos* marks. It has been suggested that Bodleian Mus. Sch. MS C 87, along with Mus. Sch. MSS C 81-6, C 88-91, C 98-101, E 406-9 and North MS e 37, was copied for Dudley, third Baron North of Kirtling, Cambridgeshire. Five of the sets are bound in old deeds relating to the North family and all contain certain distinctive features common to others, such as a scribal concordance

---

[166] For the known facts concerning William Lawes' whereabouts from 1642 until his death in 1645, see D. Pinto, 'William Lawes at the Siege of York', *MT*, cxxvii (1986), 579-83.
[167] VdGS: Jenkins, Fantasias *a* 3 Nos. 13, 15, 14, 4-6, 1-3, 7, 11-12, 10, 8-9, 16-21; Locke, 'The Flatt Consort' Nos. 1-19, 20b, 21-24; and William Young nine Fantasias, not noted.
[168] Willetts (1967a), 311.

or a uniform annotation. It appears that after the death of Lord North in 1666 these 'sets of choice books of instrumental music' came into the hands of Anthony Wood, and a year later they were bought by Edward Lowe for the Oxford Music School for £22.[169] If Mus. Sch. MS C 87 is in the hand of Stephen Bing it represents another example of his copying activities in the late Commonwealth period. Perhaps Bing was introduced to the North family through his colleague John Lilly or - given that the North and Hatton families were related by marriage (see Figure 2, page 51) - perhaps Christopher Hatton, recently returned from France, was instrumental in introducing him to the Norths?[170]

After the Restoration Bing was appointed Senior Cardinal at St Paul's.[171] During this period Bing assisted in the recovery of lands and revenues lost by St Paul's during the Commonwealth, and his responsibilities, which he promised 'to use ... kindly', included maintenance of choir discipline, noting 'who amongst the singers were idle or negligent in their duty, and [being empowered] to summon the defaulters before the Chapter'.[172] It is not clear whether he was responsible for auditioning singers but, as word spread that places were available in the cathedral choir, letters of application began to arrive, one of which may well have caused him some embarrassment. It came from Baron Hatton on behalf of Henry Frost (possibly the same Frost who was named Gentleman of the Chapel Royal on 8 May 1661), whose 'probity of life and skill in Musick' were emphasised in the testimonial. Hatton declined to concern himself with technical detail, ending 'I shall leave him to declare the part he will best fitt in youre Quire'.[173] But there was no need: the application was unsuccessful. Bing was also appointed Warden of the College of Minor Canons, a post which he held for two years, between Midsummer 1660 and 1662.[174] He seems to have been a diligent member of the College, signing the annual accounts each year until his death (apart from the five years when he lived out of London). So a series of charges made against him and several of his colleagues in October 1662 come as rather a shock. The charges were brought by Bing's successor as Warden, Richard Price (who, incidentally, declined to produce a set of accounts during his

---

[169] P. Willetts, 'Autograph Music by John Jenkins', *ML*, xlviii (1967b) 125-6; and Crum (1972).
[170] There may be more evidence of a link between Hatton and the Norths in the fact that the North manuscripts *Ob* Mus. Sch. C 82-3, 85-6, 88 & 91 include the same paper - watermark of Cardinals' Hat with letters GR - as George Jeffreys' manuscript partbooks of Italian music: *Lbl* Add. 31,479 & Mad. Soc. G 55-9 (see the following chapter), and C 83 & 85 also have the same system of rastrum-rulings. Could it also be significant that the cover of *Ob* Mus. Sch. E 408 contains the hind from the Hatton crest (apparently cut from a printed collection)?
[171] Admitted 14 May 1661: *Lgl* Arch. St P. 25,661, f. 11; and 25,664/1, f. 12^v.
[172] *Lgl* Arch. St P. 25,738/1, p. 15; see W. Sparrow Simpson, *The Chapter and Statutes of the College of the Minor Canons in Saint Paul's Cathedral, London* (London, 1871), 5.
[173] *Lgl* Arch. St P. 25,200/6.
[174] The accounts for 1661 and 1662 are written in Bing's hand: *Lgl* Arch. St P. 25,746, ff. 32-34^v.

term of office), and were laid before a meeting of the Dean and Chapter on Friday 31 October 1662. As a result of this petition the entire College was ordered to appear before the Chapter on the following Monday, immediately after Morning Service. Thirteen allegations were read out and answered verbally, but Bing (who was involved in eight of them) was directed to receive a copy and ordered to submit his answers in writing. Most concerned College property, the rents of which formed part of each Minor Canon's salary. Bing admitted to five charges of sub-letting the lease on College houses, and 'he confesseth he hath some goods of the Colledge in his hands and that the rest are sould'; these he offered to return or repay. Both he and Henry Smyth, the Subdean, admitted that they had been installed 'without any Collation', and Smyth confessed to letting the lease on another College house. The College charter, previously mislaid, was found to be held by William Morris, one of the Vicars Choral. The charges were found to be sufficiently serious to be presented to the Bishop, and a recommendation was made that they be forwarded to the Attorney General.[175] Tantalisingly the outcome is not recorded; but it is a curious episode, particularly since the Minor Canons' accounts record several earlier instances of the leases on College buildings being sub-let, and it appears to show Bing in a new light. Whether the charges arose from a fundamental misunderstanding - possibly concerning stewardship of property during the Commonwealth - cannot be established, but Bing continued to serve the cathedral as Senior Cardinal until his death (and was appointed Sacrist in 1675). He enjoyed the total confidence of the new Dean, William Sancroft,[176] who entrusted him with the keys of his house and the church plate at the time of the plague. He wrote to Bing on 20 September 1665:

> Yours of Sept. 15th came to my hand on Sunday last; & in it an Account of your Disbursements for me: which needed not, for I rely with all confidence upon your fidelity. Yet I cannot but take notice that in one of your Bills you have wrong'd yourself 1s which I pray take of Mr Tillison. The Customary Act of Grace in favour of your widows I know not, but beleeve upon your Report; ...[177]

Unlike the Dean, and several of his colleagues in the choir, Bing remained at the cathedral throughout the plague ministering to the needy, burying the dead (which included two of the Minor Canons) and endeavouring to maintain the worship of the cathedral. A detailed picture of Bing's harrowing time during the plague is given in his surviving correspondence with the Dean of St Paul's, William Sancroft. Bing, acting as the Dean's almoner, nobly distributed his largesse in the neighbouring parishes of St Gregory, St Augustine and St Faith, and dutifully kept the

---

[175] *Lgl* Arch. St P. 25,738/1, pp. 53-61.
[176] John Barwick was Dean of St Paul's from 1661-4, and William Sancroft from 1664-77.
[177] *Ob*Tanner MS 130, f. 106.

absent Sancroft apprised of the situation. The Dean is assured of 'the continuance of the Prayers & Service 3 times a day with the number of 3 Petticanons & allmost 2 vicars' and informed that there was 'a comely congregation, considering the times'; we learn of the death of William Portington, a Minor Canon; that the plague had spread to the area around Bing's house near Sermon Lane; and that 'such a feare possesseth [the people] as it[']s wonderfull to see how they hurry into the Country, as though the same God was not there that is in the city...'[178] Not surprisingly the surviving members of the choir proved rather reluctant to return to their duties, a situation not helped by the example set by their still-absent Dean (staying at the 'Rose & Crowne in Tunbridge'),[179] and choral services seem not to have resumed at the cathedral until the following March.

Against the odds Bing survived the plague but, five months later, in the early hours of Sunday 2 September 1666, the Great Fire began. Having had warning of the fire's advance, the cathedral authorities were able to move their property (including choir music) to safety. After the fire, part of St Paul's was hastily refitted for worship but it was realised that regular choral services could not continue there. As a Minor Canon, Bing continued to qualify for his annual dividend and his name appears in the St Paul's acquittance book from 1671 to 1682 (the year after his death). Following the Great Fire Stephen Bing was 'head-hunted' by the Dean of Lincoln, Michael Honywood who, since 1660, had been attempting to create a choir at the cathedral.[180] In a letter of 24 October 1666 to William Sancroft, Dean of St Paul's, Honywood - who remembered Bing from Cambridge in the 1630s - attempted to entice Bing to Lincoln with the offer of a curateship worth £20 per annum:

---

[178] *Lbl* Harley 3785, ff. 19 (24 July 1665), 20 (27 July 1665), 24 (3 August 1665), 27 (7 August 1665), 29 (10 August 1665) & 47 (9 November 1665). See W.G. Bell, *The Great Plague in London in 1665* (London, rev. 2/1951); and W.R. Matthews & W.M. Atkins, *A History of St Paul's Cathedral* (London, 1957).

[179] *Lbl* Harley 3785, ff. 21^v & 28^v.

[180] Concerning Michael Honywood see footnote 38 above. Honywood's dream of forming a 'good quire' at Lincoln was, at first, somewhat thwarted by the alcoholic tendencies of the organist Thomas Mudd. A letter (now lost) of 16 March 1663 from the Precentor of Lincoln Cathedral to Dean Honywood who was staying 'at a Dutch Barber in the broade sanctuarie in Westminster... Precint' gives a flavour of the problems: 'S[i]r Although I wrote to you on Saturday last: yet I must trouble you with another letter. Yesterday Mr. Mudd shewed the effect of his last weeke's tippling: for when Mr Joyner was in the midst of his sermon, Mudd fell asinging aloud: in so much as Mr. Joyner was compelled to stop; all the auditors gazed, and wonder[e]d what was the matter: at length some neere him stopping his mouth silenced him; and then Mr. Joyner proceeded: but this continued for the space of neerer half a quarter of an hour. So that now wee dare trust him no longer with oure Organ, but request you (if you can) to help us to another; and with what speed may be.' (quoted in A.R. Maddison, 'Lincoln Cathedral Choir, A.D. 1640 to 1700', *Associated Architectural Societies' Reports and Papers*, xx/1 (1889), 41-55). By the time of Bing's arrival in Lincoln in 1667 Mudd had been replaced with an undistinguished Dutch organist, Dr Andreas Hecht; see Watkins Shaw (1991), 160-1.

> I understand from my good friend Mr Thorndike how much I am obliged to you, for your forwardnes to help us, in commending fit persons to us for our Quire ... And I shall take especial care of Mr Bing, for old acquaintance sake, if his name be Stephen. (as I remember it is, if it be he I think of) and a Niece, my now Houskeeper, was his Scholar...[181] And those 3 you named to Mr Thorndyke, Masters, Bing & Jewet, would make us a very good Quire...[182]

The arrangements did not run smoothly; Masters and Jewett had other plans, and Mrs Bing proved reluctant to move. In another letter to Sancroft of 7 November 1666 we learn from Honywood that Bing had still not accepted the offer but 'may yet be prevailed with, since by his letter to us he seemed well enclined'; the letter also informs us that Bing was a countertenor.[183] Honywood's continued optimism was rewarded for on 21 March 1667 Bing was appointed Senior Vicar Choral (that is a vicar in Holy Orders) at Lincoln and given charge of the city church of St Nicholas, Newport.[184] Bing remained at Lincoln until early 1672 when he gained a post of Lay Vicar of Westminster Abbey; he first signed the Precentor's book on 1 April 1672.[185]

It is from this period that we have the first evidence of his Restoration liturgical-copying activities: the set of eight books known as the 'Bing-Gostling Partbooks' which are now in the Library of the Dean and Chapter of York Minster (MSS M.1.S).[186] It is not known how they got to York, but we can be certain that York Minster was not their place of origin. Rather their provenance was Lincoln in the late 1660s, judging from the heading given in the Medius Decani book: 'A Collection of... Anthems... as have bin made at Lincoln... [16]68, 69 & 70', and the distinction between 'Mr' and 'Dr' Rogers made early on in each book (Rogers received his doctorate in July 1669). The majority of pieces, however, appear to have been added in the 1670s following Bing's appointment at Westminster Abbey. On his death the partbooks were acquired by John Gostling (*c*.1650-1733), the renowned *basso profundo*, who added copies of his own on the pages left blank by Bing. It seems that the set was not intended for use in performance;[187] instead the eight partbooks represent the 'file copies' of a professional scribe: a store of the current cathedral repertoire from which he could make fair

---

[181] Could this have been at the ladies' boarding school in Hackney where Bing taught during the Commonwealth? A detailed account of his activities during the Commonwealth period is given in Willetts (1989).
[182] *Ob* Tanner 130, f. 17.
[183] *Ob* Tanner 130, f. 19.
[184] Lincolnshire County Record Office, Lincoln Cathedral Chapter Acts A.3.9, f. 254; his appointment to St Nicholas, Newport, is given on f. 254ᵛ.
[185] *Lwa* Muniments 61,228A, f. 130.
[186] A description and inventory of *Y* M.1.S is given in Watkins Shaw (1986); and Ford (1984), 262-76 gives a more detailed account of the contents.
[187] The page layout and writing is often very cramped, and many pieces appear in only one set of books - that is, either decani or cantoris - and a choir would require both decani and cantoris sets for performance.

copies of anthems, chants and services as required. It is a vast compendium of English cathedral music, containing over 250 pieces composed between c.1570 and 1680: services and anthems from Tallis and Byrd through to Humfrey and Purcell. It also reflects Bing's career, whose earlier connections are seen in the inclusion of music from John Barnard's *The First Book of Selected Church Music* (London, 1641) and six pieces by his old colleague George Jeffreys (whose music was not widely disseminated, see p. 159 below). Bing's Lincoln colleagues Andreas Hecht and John Cutts are also represented by seven and nine pieces respectively. The latter would be virtually unknown but for these partbooks which are the sole source for two of his anthems; five more survive only here and in the Lincoln partbooks.[188] The 'Bing-Gostling Partbooks' are also the sole (music) source for eleven other anthems, including two by Batten, two by Christopher Gibbons and one by Robert Ramsey; and Orlando Gibbons' verse anthem 'O clap your hands' would be known only by the alto line were it not for these books. Bing's London contemporaries are well represented with many pieces by Humfrey, Blow, Purcell and Tucker included. For this more up-to-date repertoire, Bing used manuscripts copied by William Tucker (d.1679) who was a Minor Canon of Westminster Abbey and a Gentleman of the Chapel Royal. Whole sequences of pieces from Tucker's Chapel Royal manuscripts (Royal Music 27.a.1-6) appear in the York partbooks.[189] Stephen Bing's partbooks of Restoration Church music, although not always accurate and reliable, are important because, as a long-lived and experienced singing-man and copyist, Bing would have worked with many of the leading musicians of his day. It is likely that many of his copies of works by composers such as Locke, Christopher Gibbons, Humfrey, Blow, Turner, Wise and of course Purcell, 'derive directly from the composers' holographs or from first-generation copies'.[190] As a Lay Vicar of Westminster Abbey, Bing would certainly have sung some of Henry Purcell's earliest compositions, and it is by virtue of Bing's manuscript copies that we are able to date the following of Purcell's pieces to before November 1681 (Bing's death): 'Blessed be the Lord my strength' (verse anthem, ATB/4vv bc), 'Blow up the trumpet' (full anthem, 10vv), 'Give sentence with me' (verse anthem, TTB/4vv bc), 'I will

---

[188] Lincoln's four partbooks date from 1685, and form the remains of two sets. A Bass Decani book (MS 1, c.April 1685) is the sole survivor of one set. The other consists of the Tenor Decani (MS 2, c.October 1685), Bass Decani/Cantoris (MS 3, c.August 1686; this manuscript changed sides during compilation) and Bass Decani (MS 4, c.October 1685).
[189] For full details see Watkins Shaw (1986), 107-8. See also Watkins Shaw, 'A Contemporary Source of English Music of the Purcellian Period', *AcM*, xxxi (1959), 38-44 (at that time Watkins Shaw had not identified Tucker's handwriting and *Lbl* R.M. 27.a.1-6 were classified as R.M. 23.m.1-6, but a further nine books were discovered and the set was renamed collectively: R.M. 27.a.1-15, see M. Laurie, 'The Chapel Royal Part-Books', *Music and Bibliography: Essays in Honour of Alex Hyatt King*, ed. O. Neighbour (London, 1980), 28-50; only the first six books contain Tucker's handwriting). For more on Tucker see Watkins Shaw, 'A Cambridge Manuscript from the English Chapel Royal', *ML*, xlii (1961), 263-7.
[190] Van Tassel (1977), 381.

sing unto the Lord' (full anthem, 5vv), 'Let God arise' (verse anthem, TT/4vv bc), 'O God, the King of glory' (full anthem, 4vv), 'O Lord our governor' (verse anthem, SSSBB/4vv bc), 'O Praise the Lord, all ye heathen' (TT/4vv bc), and 'Save me O God' (full anthem, 6vv).[191]

Having returned to London by April 1672, Bing renewed his connections with St Paul's[192] and by Midsummer his signatures resume in the Minor Canons' accounts.[193] From now on evidence of his copying activities is more forthcoming, and the following payments are recorded in the Abbey accounts, for the year ending at Michaelmas:[194]

1673 'To Stephen Bing for ruled papyr for a set of Quirebooks... £2-0-0'

1676 'To Mr Bing for Books for the Church for ye last year 1675 then omitted... xxxii*l* 1*s* vi*d*'

1679 'To Mr Bing for writing 29 sheets and 23 staves xxxviij*s*'

To these can be added a further reference from the St Paul's Cathedral records:[195]

22 Jan. 1677 'To Mr Bing in full of his bill for a sett of service books £7-19-7'

Although only one of these entries is unequivocally for copying, they probably represent at least three projects. Evidence of his work for the Abbey can be seen in the remains of two sets of partbooks. The Triforium Set 2 - from which only the Tenor Decani '5' survives - is a composite collection made up of various layers and in which Bing's handwriting makes fairly frequent appearances. Robert Ford has concluded that this was the copying for which Bing was paid in 1676.[196] It must have been a vast project, for the payment was more than double Bing's salary as Senior

---

[191] F.B. Zimmerman, *Henry Purcell (1659-1695): An Analytical Catalogue of his Music* (London, 1963): Z 6, Z 10, Z 12, Z 22, Z 23, Z 34, Z 39, Z 43 & Z 51 respectively. Of these Z 6, Z 10, Z 22, Z 23, Z 34 and Z 39 must be before 28 February 1679, the date of the death of William Tucker, who copied them into two partbooks: *Lwa* Partbooks Triforium Set 1 (which also contain sections in Bing's hand); Van Tassel (1977), 381.

[192] I am most grateful to Sarah Boyer for providing me with information concerning music at St Paul's Cathedral during the Restoration period.

[193] *Lgl* Arch. St P. 25,650/2 & 25,746, *passim*. Sir Jack Westrup - (4/1980) 17, footnote 2 - opposed the idea that Bing could combine the post of Lay Vicar at Westminster Abbey with that of Minor Canon at St Paul's and concluded that there were two men of the same name. This is surely incorrect; a comparison of Bing's signatures in the St Paul's Cathedral and Westminster Abbey accounts books (*Lgl* Arch. St P. 25,650/2 & 25,746, *passim*; and *Lwa* Muniments 61,228A, f. 130) reveals that it is the same person. Furthermore, as Watkins Shaw has shown - (1986), 21 - there are other examples of such dual capacities: Randolph Jewett, a Minor Canon at St Paul's at the time of the Great Fire, became organist of Winchester Cathedral in November 1666 and continued to collect his dividend as a Minor Canon at St Paul's until his death in 1675.

[194] *Lwa* Muniments 33,706 (1673), 33,710 (1676) and 33,714 (1679). The 1679 record of payment is reproduced in Boyer & Wainwright (1995), Illustration 5

[195] *Lgl* Arch. St P. 25,707, p. 100.

[196] Ford (1984), 261-2.

Cardinal at St Paul's. It is hard to tell how many sheets (i.e. bifolia) were involved in this payment. Both St Paul's and the Abbey usually paid their copyists at a flat rate *per* sheet, 1s for each at St Paul's between 1669 and 1674, and the rates appear to have hardly changed by the time of the Abbey payment of 1679. (This method of payment was undoubtedly more equitable than that which existed at the Chapel Royal where canticles and anthems were costed at a flat rate of 10s each.)[197] The 1679 Abbey payment to Stephen Bing was probably for the music he added to the set of books primarily in the hand of William Tucker, who had died on 28 February 1679: Triforium Set 1, of which two books survive: the Alto Cantoris '1A' and Tenor Cantoris '4'. These partbooks must have been regularly available to Stephen Bing for most of the music copied by Tucker also appears in the York partbooks; and, what is more, Bing's handwriting appears on a single leaf inserted at the beginning of each book and on pages following Tucker's last contribution in each book (Tomkins' 'Let my complaint'). As noted above, Bing's handwriting also makes an appearance in the single surviving partbook of Westminster Abbey Triforium Set 2 (Tenor Decani '5'); this is a composite collection made up of various layers and Bing's handwriting appears fairly frequently. All but one of the pieces copied by Bing also appear in the York partbooks, and again a sequence of pieces was derived directly from Barnard's *The First Book of Selected Church Musick* (London, 1641).[198]

Despite being involved with St Paul's for over forty years, Bing appears to have done little copying for the cathedral. This must be due to the fact that in the two decades after the Great Fire - although worship continued in the hastily refitted west end of the cathedral - the services of a full, regular, choir, with an ever-changing repertoire were not required nor indeed practicable (and Bing was, in any case, based in Lincoln from 1667 to 1672). There are, however, a few tantalising references to suggest that there was occasionally a need for choir music at St Paul's.[199] The principal copyist at St Paul's Cathedral after the Restoration appears to have been Thomas Quartermaine, the ninth Minor Canon, who received occasional payments, between 1664 and his death in 1674, for copying and purchasing paper.[200] It is possible, therefore, that the 1677 payment to Bing (see above) represents the first (and only?) copying that he undertook for the cathedral. Indeed, there are remnants of a set of service books largely in Bing's hand at St

---

[197] The Cathedral rate for copying is given in an undated payment to Thomas Quartermaine (d. 1674) (see note 200 below). That for the Chapel Royal is implied in a list of music copied between 1670 and Midsummer 1676; see Ashbee (1986), 162-4.

[198] For a detailed discussion of *Lwa* Triforium Sets 1 & 2, see Watkins Shaw (1986), 107-11.

[199] Occasions such as when Dean Sancroft preached before the King at the west end of the cathedral (10 October 1667), and Edward Stillingfleet's installation as Dean (16 January 1678) would presumably have been enhanced by music.

[200] For example, *Lgl* Arch. St P. 25,643/1 (no foliation nor pagination): undated payment to Quartermaine for 'pricking of Chore Books 264 sheets & 1 page, at 1s per sheet - 13*l*-4*s*-3*d*'.

Paul's: Partbooks A 1 (Contratenor Cantoris and Tenor Decani only).[201] Bing's surviving contribution to these partbooks is thirteen services and, although they contain later additions and cross-references, it is likely that these are the books for which he was paid in 1677.[202] Whether charges for paper and binding were included in this bill is impossible to tell. But if the payment was solely for copying it suggests that about twenty sheets had been used for each of a set of eight books (i.e. six pages for each service), and that, despite the presence of some incomplete canticles, traces of all the services copied have survived.

What was possibly Bing's final copying project came to light in May 1988, when a book containing a printed Psalter and the bass parts to various chants and services was presented to St Paul's Cathedral (now shelved as MS 43.D).[203] The music was copied by several seventeenth-century scribes, possibly including Bing.[204] Largely unknown to scholars and not mentioned in the literature, the volume is unusual in its function and method of service selection, provides significant evidence of a cathedral repertory, and gives a more precise date for the Purcell Service in B Flat. It measures 17.5 x 11.75 cm, and is bound in what appear to be its original, tooled leather, covers. The spine is lettered 'Sacred Music' and the book is in good condition, showing little sign of wear. The section containing services is foliated, in a contemporary hand, and the music is written on pages of eight rastrum-ruled staves. No watermarks have been found. Although the printed Psalter lacks a title-page it probably formed part of the octavo edition of *The Book of Common Prayer* printed by John Bill and Christopher Barker in 1676. (A similar copy is held by the British Library, C.64.c.7.) Nothing is known of the volume's history; the donors - the Parish Church of St Mary and St Eanswythe, Folkestone - believe it to have been purchased at auction, but have no details of the sale. The opening leaves have been inscribed by one of the anonymous copyists:

> For Mr Short Twenty Morning & Evening Services of the Best
> now performd in the Cathedrall. church of Pauls. London

A 'Jonas Short' was living about 500 yards from the cathedral between 1674 and 1681. He is the only person of that name in the area,[205] and the dates

---

[201] John Gostling's hand appears towards the end of the books, imitating Bing's hand closely.
[202] The existence of this set of services may explain why the next known payment for copying (to John Gostling in September 1699; *Lgl* Arch. St P. 25,473/34, p. 70) is solely for anthems.
[203] The partbook was separately and independently identified as 'possibly containing the hand of Stephen Bing' by the present writer and Sarah Boyer soon after the presentation of the partbook to St Paul's. Ms Boyer's study of the partbook was incorporated into our collaborative article (1995) and the present section is heavily reliant on Ms Boyer's work.
[204] *Lsp* 43.D, ff. 33^v-34, (?)Bing's copy of the bass part of Purcell's Nunc Dimittis, Z 230/E(8), is reproduced in Boyer & Wainwright (1995), Illustration 6.
[205] Sixteen rolls of tithe rents from eleven nearby parishes (recorded between c.1661 and 1686), comprising about 1600 names, revealed two people by the name of Short. One was 'Widow

would seem to fit in well with the music of the book. This was also a time when great interest was being shown in music of the service.[206] The evidence suggests that the book was compiled for Mr Short in order for him to follow the sung services.[207] The inscription is in one of the music hands and the formality of the title 'Mr' Short is in keeping for the time. The implications of the contents having been selected for quality, representing current cathedral repertoire, and copied for a layman are significant and the book provides further evidence that choral services were being held at the cathedral following the fire. Furthermore it suggests that not all surviving 'singleton' manuscripts should now be considered as part of an incomplete set.[208]

The service music in MS 43.D was probably copied between c.1677 and c.1681, to judge from the title of 'Dr' Blow and the possible presence of Bing's hand (as the fourth copyist). A comparison with the repertory of the (January) 1677 set (Partbooks A 1) would suggest that Mr Short's book was copied later. The latter gives services by Humfrey, Tucker, Rogers and Purcell, in addition to two others by Child and Blow. The balance of full and verse settings is almost equal (which was not so in the other set), and a pre-1687 St Paul's repertoire can be discerned in the absence of younger composers such as Wise and Turner, who were soon to be associated with the cathedral and whose compositions then appear in the sources. If this book does give 'Twenty ... Services of the Best', from the 1677 repertoire, there are some notable omissions: the settings by Byrd, Bevin, Portman and

---

Short' of the parish of St Faith under Paul's; the other was Jonas, of the parish of St Andrew by the Wardrobe (*Lgl* 980/1).

[206] As can be seen from the various wordbooks of anthems published at this time. These include Stephen Bulkley's book of anthem texts, published for use in York Minster (no copy of which is known to survive), and *Anthems to be Sung at the Celebration of Divine Service, in the Cathedral Church of the Holy and Undivided Trinity in Dublin* (Dublin, Trinity College R.f.53); both volumes were published in 1662. James Clifford published two wordbooks of *The Divine Services and Anthems* in 1663 and 1664; and two Playford advertisements offer the copying of anthems and services: the first was issued in 1679 ('Whereas some years since I made a large collection of Full Service and Anthems (with the organ parts) of Four Parts for Sides which I intended to have printed but not finding incouragement thereto, have them still by me. If any gentleman shall desire part or all of them I shall be willing to prick them out fairly for them at a reasonable rate'; see F. Kidson, 'John Playford, and 17th Century Music Publishing', *MQ*, iv (1918), 525), and the second appears at the end of Henry Playford's *General Catalogue* of 1697 ('Anthems and Services, in all their Parts, being a very choice Collection, may be had, fairly Prick'd, here'; *Lbl* Harley 5936).

[207] That the volume was originally copied for the cathedral choir and subsequently acquired by Mr Short can probably be discounted on the grounds that the size and format is radically different from the other Restoration sources. It is also unlikely to have been a commonplace book, since the copyists share the work (there are several changes of hand mid-canticle) and two hands reappear.

[208] The partbook *Lsp* 43.D is examined in detail and an inventory given in Boyer & Wainwright (1995), 635-8.

Farrant are not found here.[209] Among Bing's contributions to the partbook was the Magnificat and Nunc Dimittis to Purcell's Service in B Flat which he copied jointly with an unidentified scribe.[210] We should remember that, as a colleague of Purcell's at the Abbey, Bing's copy-source was most likely close to the composer. Purcell must have composed the service by Michaelmas 1682 when it was apparently copied into the Westminster Abbey books,[211] but its (partial) presence here in Bing's hand dates the B Flat Service to before 26 November 1681, the date of Bing's death, a little earlier than hitherto believed.[212]

Bing remained at Westminster Abbey until his death on 26 November 1681.[213] In his will, dated 12 February 1681 and proved 16 December 1681, Bing requested to be buried in the church yard of St George the Martyr, Canterbury near his father and mother, and we learn, in the many bequests to his family, that he owned land in Grantchester, Cambridge.[214] Before concluding this survey of Bing's copying activities it must be put on record that Stephen Bing was, to some extent, an uncritical copyist whose texts were apt to be careless and sometimes debased (for example, his Italian text for the *Dialogo d'Abram* in British Library Add. MS 31,434 is risibly poor). He was at his best, it seems, when he was closely supervised; in this case his work was thoroughly professional and resulted in such beautiful sources as the 'Great Set' scorebook and organbook which are as pleasant to the eye as, in realisation, to the ear. Despite his variability, Stephen Bing is undoubtedly one of the most important seventeenth-century English music copyists yet identified. The sheer chronological range of his activities is impressive: his close associations with the country's best musicians and most influential musical patrons lasted for over fifty years and, although it is likely that we have lost many of the details of his numerous contacts, influences, performance situations and contexts for his copying activities, the

---

[209] It is impossible to tell whether the 1677 set provided a copy-source, since the bass books do not survive.

[210] Bing's copying begins on f. 32^v with the majority of the 'Gloria Patri' from the Benedictus; further down on the same page he begins the Magnificat.

[211] *Lwa* Muniments 33,717, f. 5^v, records a payment of 30s 'for writing Mr. Purcells Service and Anthem'; the amount of money involved implies that this refers to Purcell's largest service setting, that in B flat, and 'this suggestion is strengthened by the additional reference to an anthem, which was probably the five-part work 'O God, Thou art my God'' (see F.B. Zimmerman, 'Purcell's "Service Anthem", *O God, Thou Art my God* and the B-flat Major Service', *MQ*, 1 (1964), 207).

[212] We should note that Bing did not add the service to the 'Bing-Gostling' books (*Y* M.1.S), although Gostling did copy the service into the partbooks at a later date.

[213] Bing's death is recorded in the unofficial Register of the Abbey: 26 November 1681 'Mr Stephen Bing dyed and buried the 1st day of December att Canterbury'; see J.L. Chester ed., *The Marriage, Baptismal, and Burial Registers of the Collegiate Church or Abbey of St Peter, Westminster*, Publications of the Harleian Society, x (London, 1876), 203-4. The appearances of Bing's name in the Abbey accounts at Michaelmas 1682 and 1683 were due to a clerk erroneously copying the previous years' lists; see Watkins Shaw (1986), 21-2.

[214] PRO PROB 11/368/179.

information which does survive does help us to construct a picture of musical activity in England in the seventeenth century. This chapter has attempted to construct a chronology for Bing's surviving manuscripts and to place the music they contain in a historical context. These ideas are further developed in the following chapters when we examine the activities of Stephen Bing's colleague, George Jeffreys. Table 20 offers a summary of the suggested chronology of Stephen Bing's copying activities.

Table 20 A Proposed Chronology of the Surviving Manuscripts Copied by Stephen Bing

Manuscript	Date	Patron	Provenance	Contents
Pre-Civil War				
(?) Oxford, Bodleian Library Mus. Sch. C 204, ff. 46-49^v	c.1634	Hatton	Cambridge	Antonelli motets
Oxford, Christ Church Mus. 1215, fascicle 3	1630s	Hatton	London	Organ part to verse anthems *a* 3 by Ward
New York, Public Library Drexel 5624	1630s?	Hatton	London	Coprario fantasia-suites (incomplete)
Rochester, NY, Eastman School of Music ML96 L814f, fascicle 3	1630s?	Hatton	Court	Coprario fantasia-suites
Oxford, Christ Church Mus. 732-5	early to mid 1630s	Hatton	Court	2 fantasias *a* 4 by O. Gibbons
Oxford, Christ Church Mus. 2/436	mid to late 1630s	Hatton	Court	Score & organbook to consort music *a* 3-6
Oxford, Christ Church Mus. 417-18/1080	mid to late 1630s	Hatton	Court	Parts to consort music *a* 3-4
Oxford, Christ Church Mus. 432, ff. 109-3 rev.	mid to late 1630s	Hatton	Court	Organ-score to Mico *a* 3
Civil War				
London, British Library Add. 31,434	c.1643-6	Hatton	Court	H. Lawes & Italian music
Oxford, Bodleian Library Tenbury1005	c.1643-6	Hatton	Court	Madrigal scores
Oxford, Bodleian Library Tenbury1009	c.1643-6	Hatton	Court	Madrigal scores
Oxford, Bodleian Library Tenbury1017	c.1643-6	Hatton	Court	Scores to Merula madrigals
Oxford, Christ Church Mus. 255	c.1643-6	Hatton	Court	Valentini MSS insertions
Oxford, Christ Church Mus. 878-880, 1st sections	c.1643-6	Hatton	Court	Motets *a* 2-3 by Dering, etc.
Oxford, Christ Church Mus. 880, last section, 2nd part	c.1643-6	Hatton	Court	Basso continuo to Gesualdo Bks 1, 2 & 4
Oxford, Christ Church Mus. 1023	c.1643-6	Hatton	Court	Bc to Dering *Cantica Sacra* (1618)

Commonwealth

Oxford, Christ Church Mus. 754-9	c.1653	?	London	W. Lawes 'The Royall Consort'
Oxford, Christ Church Mus. 880, last section, 1st part	1650s	?	London	Bc to Italian music
Oxford, Christ Church Mus. 1185	1650s	?	London	Coprario Fantasia-Suites
London, Gresham College Mus. 469-71	late 1650s	?	London	Jenkins, Locke & Young *a* 3
(?) Oxford, Bodleain Library Mus. Sch. C 87	c.1654-64	North family		Jenkins *a* 3

Restoration

London, British Library Add. 27,551	1674	North family?	Jenkins consort music *a* 3-4
York, Minster Library M.1.S	c.1668-80	File copies	Partbooks of English cathedral music
(?) London, St Paul's Cathedral, Partbook 43.D	c.1672-80	Presentation copy	Bass partbook of English chants and services
London, St Paul's Cathedral Partbooks A 1	by 22.i. 1677	St Paul's Cathedral	English services
London, Westminster Abbey Partbooks: Triforium Set 1 & 2	c.1672-80	Westminster Abbey	English services and anthems

CHAPTER FOUR

GEORGE JEFFREYS (c.1610-1685): STEWARD TO THE HATTON FAMILY

George Jeffreys: Biography

Christopher Hatton's longest serving musician and secretary was the composer and organist George Jeffreys. Jeffreys was one of the first English composers to show a wholehearted commitment to the most up-to-date Italianate style and, as such, has been the subject of a number of thorough studies.[1] His career, compositions and copying activities have not, however, been examined in relation to the patronage of Christopher Hatton or in light of the Hatton music collection. George Jeffreys' surviving output is listed in Table 21 and the manuscripts are examined in detail below.

No information is presently available concerning Jeffreys' life before 1631. The Oxford historian Anthony Wood, in his 'Notes on the Lives of Musicians' (c.1688 with later additions),[2] states that he was descended from the family of Matthew Jeffries (fl. c.1590) a Vicar Choral at Wells Cathedral, but in a marginal note adds 'Dr Rogers thinks he was born in Northamptonshire about Weldon'.[3] George Jeffreys is known to have been associated with the village of Weldon throughout his life and therefore Rogers' suggestion would seem to be very likely.[4] Jeffreys appears to have had connections with the Hatton family from at least 1631 when he set verses by Richard - later Sir Richard - Hatton, a cousin of Christopher Hatton's from the Cambridge branch of the family. Both Richard and Christopher Hatton were students at Cambridge, but there is no record that

---

[1] See P. le Huray, *Music and the Reformation in England 1549-1660* (2/Cambridge, 1978), 350-3; P. Aston, 'George Jeffreys', *MT*, cx (1969), 772-6; P. Aston, 'George Jeffreys and the English Baroque' (D.Phil. dissertation, University of York, 1970); P. Aston, 'Tradition and Experiment in the Devotional Music of George Jeffreys', *PRMA*, xcix (1972-3), 105-15; K. Bergdolt, 'The Sacred Music of George Jeffreys' (Ph.D. dissertation, University of Cincinnati, 1976); and P. Aston, 'Jeffreys, George', *New Grove*, ix, 583-6.
[2] See H. Watkins Shaw, 'Extracts from Anthony à Wood's *Notes on the Lives of Musicians* Hitherto Unpublished', *ML*, xv (1934), 157-62; and J.D. Shute, 'Anthony à Wood and his MSS Wood D.19(4) at the Bodleian' (Ph.D. dissertation, International Institute of Advanced Studies, Clayton, Missouri, 1979) (microfilm in *Ob*: Diss FILMS 817).
[3] *Ob* Wood D.19(4), f. 72^{r-v}; ff. 111-12 are a letter to Wood from Benjamin Rogers (dated 9 April 1695) which includes information about Jeffreys.
[4] The Weldon Parish records are incomplete for the period c.1610. Peter Aston has speculated that Jeffreys was descended from the Jefferies of Holme Castle, Worcestershire who had connections with another distinguished Worcestershire family, the Salweys of Stanford. Aston further notes that George Jeffreys' wife was the daughter of one Elizabeth Salwey and that Elizabeth's brother, Thomas Salwey, left a substantial amount of property to Jeffreys describing him in his will as 'my cousin'; see Aston (1970), iv, 57-8, and *New Grove*, ix, 583.

Jeffreys attended the University himself; he did however compose some of the music for Peter Hausted's comedy *The Rival Friends* that was performed at Cambridge in March 1632 in the presence of the King and Queen (see pages 8-9 above). Jeffreys was certainly working for Christopher Hatton in some capacity by 1633, as a manuscript in the Northamptonshire Record Office, in Jeffreys' hand, is headed 'A Cattalogue of some Manuscripts of my Masters taken at Moulton Parke Aprill 15th. 1633' (Moulton Park was one of the Hatton estates).[5] Jeffreys worked for the Hatton family for the rest of his life, and correspondence exists, preserved in either the Northamptonshire Record Office or the British Library, between Jeffreys and various members of the Hatton family until the 1680s. As usual there is no mention of musical matters; the letters are primarily concerned with the administration of the Hatton estates (see Table 21b for more details).

It is very likely that George Jeffreys met Stephen Bing in Cambridge some time in the early 1630s. This would explain the appearance of Jeffreys' hand (annotations, clefs and time signatures?) in Bodleian Mus. Sch. MS C 204, folios 46-49^v, a manuscript dating from the mid 1630s which contains the parts to two three-voice motets by Abundio Antonelli. It was suggested in the previous chapter that the main hand may be that of Stephen Bing (see page 60 above) and, if this is so, that the manuscript represents the first of many collaborations between Jeffreys and Bing. The short-score to Coprario's eight fantasia-suites for two violins, bass viol and organ (Rochester U.S.A., Eastman School of Music, Sibley Music Library MS ML96 L8 14f, fascicle 3) may represent the two copyists' next collaboration and was probably the result of Hatton's court links in the 1630s.[6] Despite the fact that Jeffreys was employed by Hatton primarily as a secretary/steward and not as a musician, he maintained a passionate interest in music throughout his life and music manuscripts in his hand survive from the 1630s through to the 1680s. His latest surviving manuscript is Oxford, Bodleian Library Tenbury MS 1011 (see Part II, MS XXXV), a copy of three of Purcell's *Sonnata's of III. Parts* published in 1683; Jeffreys must therefore have copied the sonatas during the last two years of his life.[7] His copies of Italian music also show his fascination with the most up-to-date compositional styles and his own works show an assimilation of these techniques and a willingness to experiment still further (see below).

During the Civil War Jeffreys, no doubt due to the patronage of Hatton, became Charles I's organist at Oxford; this was Jeffreys' only professional

---

[5] NRO FH 4016.
[6] See Chapter Three, footnote 90.
[7] A comparison of the readings indicates that the manuscript was copied from the printed source (albeit carelessly).

Table 21   George Jeffreys

a. Manuscripts copied by Jeffreys

Lbl Add. 10,338: scorebook of Jeffreys' own compositions: instrumental music; masque songs *a* 2-5; Italian madrigals *a* 3; Latin motets *a* 1-6; services, English anthems and devotional songs *a* 1-5.

Lbl Add. 17,816 & 30,829-30: incomplete set of parts containing Latin motets and English anthems *a* 4-6 by Jeffreys.

Lbl Add. 29,282: set of partbooks containing Latin motets *a* 2-3 by Jeffreys.

Lbl Add. 31,479 & Madrigal Society G 55-9: parts to motets *a* 1-5 by Aloisi (1628, 1637 Op. 4 & 5), Anon., Carissimi, Cifra (1612), Facchi (1635), Gallerano (in Aloisi 1628), Grandi (1610, 1613, 1616, 1619, 1629, 1630), Gregori (1635), Hayne (1646), F.M. Marini (1637), Merula (1624, 1628), Pecci (1629), Pio (1622-4), Reggio, Rovetta (1635 arr.), Sances (1638), Tomasi (1635), Trabattone (1629).

Lcm 920: set of partbooks containing English anthems and Latin motets *a* 1-3 by Jeffreys.

Lcm 920A: set of partbooks containing canticles, mass movements, anthems and motets *a* 4 by Jeffreys.

NRO FH 3431C: a Gigue (incomplete) and Courant in tablature.

Ob Tenbury 973-6 & 1273: parts to madrigals *a* 2-4 by Arrigoni (1635), Grandi (1615), Merula (1633), Rovetta (1629), Turini (1621).

Ob Tenbury 1010: score of 'With notes that are both loud and sweet' *a* 2 by Jeffreys.

Ob Tenbury 1011: score to three *Sonnata's* by Purcell (1683).

Ob Tenbury 1012: score to madrigals *a* 4 by Rovetta (1629).

Ob Tenbury 1013: score to Grandi's 'Messa a 4 voci' (1610).

Ob Tenbury 1015: score to Nenna's *Il Settimo Libro de Madrigali a Cinque Voci* (1608) with English words.

Ob Tenbury 1016: score to madrigals *a* 1-3 by Dering.

Ob Tenbury 1285b: score of 'In the midst of life' *a* 4 and 'What praise can reach thy clemency' *a* 4 by Jeffreys.

EIRE-Dm Z3.4.13, ff. 47-59^v: score to 'Fantasies of Three Parts' by Jeffreys.

US-R ML96 L8 14f, fascicle 3: short score to Coprario's eight fantasia-suites for two violins, bass viol and organ. Copied by Jeffreys and Bing in collaboration.

Table 21 continued

b. Other examples of Jeffreys' hand

Lbl Add. 29,548-96, *passim*: Jeffreys' letters to Christopher Hatton and others, 1648-85 (see Bibliography for more details).

NRO FH 1407, 3921 & 4180: letters from Jeffreys to Lady Hatton.

NRO FH 2409: Italian verse 'Mane vado, a la guerra o soigniora' [*sic*] (fragment).

NRO FH 2652: Robert Martin's 1638 bill to Hatton; annotated by Jeffreys 'Mr Martins byll paid 9 Novemb^r. 1641'.

NRO FH 4016: 'A Cattalogue of some Manuscripts of my Masters taken at Moulton Parke April 15th. 1633'.

Ob Mus. Sch. C 204, ff. 46-49^v: a few annotations added by Jeffreys.

Och Mus. 878-880, 1st sections: parts to motets *a* 2-3 by Dering and anonymous (also Dering?): mixture of three layers: (*a*) anonymous scribe; (*b*) another anonymous scribe provided the music but with text underlay by Jeffreys and with occasional text alternatives added by Bing; and (*c*) Bing's music with underlay by Jeffreys.

Och Mus. 1023: Jeffreys added text headings to Bing's copies of the basso continuo parts to Dering's *Cantica Sacra* (1618).

PRO SP 23/200, pp. 115 (14 December 1648), 117 (9 February 1648), 119 (15 December 1648), 121 (30 November 1647), 126 (26 June 1646), 137 (8 May 1646), 140 (20 March 1646), 141 (5 December 1646): representations to the Committee for Compounding made by George Jeffreys on behalf of Christopher Hatton III (pp. 126 & 141 are signed by Hatton).

PRO SP 23/233, f. 87^v: representation to the Committee for Compounding made by George Jeffreys on behalf of Christopher Hatton III (4 May 1649).

Ob Tenbury 1017: Jeffreys added some of the text underlay to Bing's copies of Merula's 'Nominativo hic' and 'Nominativo quis' (1633).

Cover annotations in Jeffreys' hand (see Table 5c).

---

musical appointment.[8] One suspects that, rather as Hatton had made the best of the circumstances of the Civil War to advance his own position, Jeffreys –

---

[8] Both Anthony Wood and Sir John Hawkins report that Jeffreys was Charles I's 'organist at Oxford' (Clark ed. (1891), i, 274; A. Wood, *Athenae Oxonienses* (London, 1691; 3rd edn, with additions by Philip Bliss (London, 1813-21), repr. New York & London, 1967), i, pp. xxxiv-xxxv; and Hawkins (1776), iv, 56, 64 & 323). Jeffreys confirms that his presence in Oxford was due to Hatton in a letter of 1665 to Lady Hatton (*Lbl* Add. 29,550, f. 236^v): he reports that, when asked if he had been at the Oxford Court, he replied 'I was, being sent for by my Lord and Master [i.e. Hatton]'.

a musician with no previous record as a Court musician[9] - also took advantage of the unique situation to gain an appointment which in peace time would have been inconceivable.[10] We should note, however, that during the war-time court, with the normal system of court appointments and payments in disarray, any musical post or title would probably be regarded as temporary and somewhat unofficial. This confused state of affairs is reflected in Hawkins' comment that Jeffreys 'was succeeded in the king's chapel by Edward Low'.[11] When did Lowe replace Jeffreys as the King's organist? Lowe had been organist at Christ Church since 1631 and, as far as is known, was present in Oxford throughout the Civil War and Commonwealth periods.[12] It is possible that Lowe and Jeffreys both played the organ in Christ Church when the Court was based there; perhaps Lowe played for the public services in the cathedral and Jeffreys for the King's private devotions in his chambers? The thorny question of music in Civil War Oxford is examined in the following chapter.

Jeffreys' duties in Oxford were not solely musical; he continued to work for Baron Hatton in a secretarial capacity[13] and he was one of eleven servants who attended him in his office of joint commissioner for the King at the Uxbridge conference in 1645.[14] After the capitulation of Oxford and Baron Hatton's move to France in November 1646, Jeffreys returned to his family in the village of Weldon near Kirby Hall, and continued to serve Lady Hatton who had remained in England. It seems that he spent most of his time in Northamptonshire and only occasionally visited London, where the Hattons maintained a house, in Ely Place, Holborn. In 1637 Jeffreys had married Mary Peirs, the widowed daughter of Elizabeth (née Salwey) and Thomas Mainwaring (the rector of Weldon and Dene from 1614 to 1663).[15] By this marriage Jeffreys had two children: Christopher and Mary. Christopher (b. c.1642) was educated at Westminster School and Christ Church, Oxford (B.A. 1663, M.A. 1666)[16] and obviously inherited his father's gift for music as he was described by Anthony Wood as having 'an Excellent hand on the Organ'.[17] Christopher Jeffreys married Anna Brydges,

---

[9] Hawkins' claim that Jeffreys had been one of 'the gentlemen of king Charles the First's chapel' - (1776), iv, 56 - is almost certainly erroneous; Jeffreys' name does not appear in any of the surviving court records concerning music; see Ashbee (1988).

[10] Jeffreys did, however, have some reputation as a musician before the outbreak of war: he is listed as ninth out of the ten 'most excellent Artists in musicke in our dayes sub anno 1640' in Sir Peter Leycester's 'Booke of Miscellany Collections', dated 1659; see H. Abbey, 'Sir Peter Leycester's Book on Music', *Journal of the Viola da Gamba Society of America*, xx (1984), 28-44.

[11] Hawkins (1776), iv, 64.

[12] P. le Huray, 'Lowe, Edward', *New Grove*, xi, 287-8.

[13] Jeffreys often recopied Hatton's draft letters; e.g. *Lbl* Add. 29,570, ff. 37-8 is a letter dated 14-15 August 1645 recopied from Hatton's draft: ff. 34-5.

[14] See Firth & Raith (1911), i, 609 & 612; and Pinto (1990), 86.

[15] Foster (1891-2), iii, 960.

[16] Ibid., ii, 805; and *DNB*, x, 714.

[17] *Ob* Wood D.19(4), f. 72^v. (See also Clark ed. (1891), i, 274.)

the sister of James, Lord Chandos, and one of their four children was the poet George Jeffreys (1678-1755) an associate of Pope and Handel.[18] Mary Jeffreys' marriage was not so propitious: to the distress of her father she secretly married a local Weldon man, William Goode.[19] George Jeffreys strongly disapproved of Goode but nevertheless used his influence to gain him employment at Kirby Hall.[20] Jeffreys spent the rest of his life serving the Hatton family, not as a musician but as an administrator and secretary. David Pinto has pointed out that after 1646 Jeffreys dealt mostly with Lady Hatton and Christopher Hatton IV and notes that in the 1660s, as Baron Hatton became more irresponsible and temperamental, there was alienation between Jeffreys and his patron.[21] By the time of the Restoration Jeffreys had acquired some land of his own in Weldon, and he was obviously no longer dependent solely on the employment and patronage of Baron Hatton. Nevertheless he continued to serve Christopher Hatton IV after the death of the First Baron in July 1670 and, as part of the attempts to repair the family's finances, Jeffreys may even have been involved in the negotiations concerning the dispersal of the Hatton music collection.[22]

George Jeffreys died at Weldon on 1 July 1685 and his music manuscripts presumably passed to his immediate descendants before being gradually dispersed.[23] The majority of his manuscripts eventually found their way to the British Library, the Royal College of Music, or the Library of St Michael's College, Tenbury (now in the Bodleian Library, Oxford). Jeffreys' scorebook (now British Library Add. MS 10,338) became part of the collection of Edmund Warren (later Warren-Horne, *c*.1730-1794) and subsequently belonged to Thomas Oliphant (1799-1873) who presented the manuscript to the British Library. Oliphant also presented a bass partbook, now Add. MS 17,816, to the British Library 'as proof that the handwriting in Add. MS 10,338 is that of George Jeffreys' (see Part II, MS II); Oliphant was also the owner of two more of Jeffreys' sets of partbooks: Royal College of Music MSS 920 and 920A (Part II, MSS XVII and XVIII). Part of Jeffreys' collection of Italian motets (now British Library Add. MS 31,479, see below), along with Stephen Bing's manuscript British Library Add. 31,434 and many others, was offered to the then British

---

[18] *DNB*, x, 721.
[19] *Lbl* Add. 29,552, f. 213.
[20] *Lbl* Add. 29,552, f. 223.
[21] Examples of the antagonism between Jeffreys and Hatton III can be found in the following letters from Jeffreys to Hatton IV: *Lbl* Add. 29,551, f. 35, Jeffreys states that if he does not receive payment from Hatton III he will be arrested (13 April 1663); *Lbl* Add. 29,552, f. 7, Jeffreys complains of 'their usage of me at Kirby' (10 January 1669); and *Lbl* 29,552, f. 302, Jeffreys mentions an unexpected visit from Hatton III and states the he 'was resolved not to stirr a foot towards him'. See also Pinto (1990), 86-7 & notes 37-8.
[22] See Chapter Two, footnote 40.
[23] Jeffreys' manuscripts are not mentioned in his will which survives in NRO. (For a transcription of the will see Aston (1970), iv, 224-8.)

Museum in 1879 by the collector Julian Marshall (1836-1903).[24] Marshall had obtained a number of manuscripts - including Add. MS 31,434 - from the collection of Joseph Warren (1804-81).[25] A number of Warren's other manuscripts had passed to Sir Frederick Ouseley, the son of Sir Frederick Arthur Gore Ouseley, the founder of St Michael's College, Tenbury and this reveals an intriguing possibility. Amongst Joseph Warren's manuscripts were a number that once belonged to William Gostling (c.1695-1777), a Minor Canon of Canterbury Cathedral, and the son of John Gostling (c.1650-1733) the famous *basso profundo*. It was noted at the end of the previous chapter that John Gostling obtained some of Stephen Bing's manuscripts (such as the Bing-Gostling Partbooks now at York); perhaps John Gostling received a large number of manuscripts from Bing including all those in Bing's hand that are now in the Tenbury collection? The line of transmission would therefore be as follows: Bing—John Gostling—William Gostling—?—Joseph Warren—Julian Marshall—Frederick Ouseley and St Michael's, Tenbury (now in the Bodleian Library, Oxford) *or* British Museum (now British Library). Perhaps it is not too fanciful to suggest that a number of Jeffreys' manuscripts that are now in the Tenbury Collection, particularly those of Italian music copied during the Civil War (examined below), remained with Bing and thus followed the line of transmission outlined above?[26]

George Jeffreys' Copies of Italian Music

Jeffreys' copies of Italian music survive today as British Library Add. MS 31,479 and Madrigal Society MSS G 55-9 (housed in the British Library) and Oxford, Bodleian Library Tenbury MSS 973-6/1273, 1012, 1013 and 1015. (Tenbury MS 1016, Italian madrigals by the English composer Richard Dering, will also be covered in this section.) Apparently the manuscripts were not originally bound, which explains why sections have become separated: British Library Add. MS 31,479 and Madrigal Society MSS G 55-9 are so similar in format and repertoire that they must originally have been intended to form a single collection (see Part II, MS IX), and Tenbury MS 1273 is the basso continuo book to the vocal partbooks

---

[24] The Marshall collection was classified as *Lbl* Add. 31,384-31,823; see A. Searle, 'Julian Marshall and the British Museum: Music Collecting in the Late Nineteenth Century', *British Library Journal*, xi (1985), 67-87.
[25] Concerning Joseph Warren see A.H. King, *Some British Collectors of Music c.1600-1960* (Cambridge, 1963), 56-8 & *passim*.
[26] David Pinto has further suggested that 'Some printed items used by Jeffreys could have followed the paths taken by his manuscripts without leaving trace of their former ownership', and cites Arrigoni's *Concerti da Camera* (Venice, 1635) as an example: The only surviving copy of this print in England is in the British Library (D.29); the print is listed in Martin's book catalogues of 1635 and 1639; and the print was used by Jeffreys when copying *Ob* Tenbury 973-6/1273 and by Bing when copying *Och* Mus. 880, last section. It seems likely, therefore, that the print was once part of the Hatton collection. See Pinto (1990), 89 & note 60.

Tenbury MSS 973-6 (see Part II, MS XXXI). Most of the music in these collections was derived - some perhaps indirectly (see below) - from printed sources; Jeffreys' copy-sources are listed in Table 22. Of the twenty-seven identified sources, seven were definitely owned by Sir Christopher Hatton (Martin 1638 bill, see Chapter Two) and are now in the Christ Church Library, Oxford;[27] twenty appear in Robert Martin's printed booklists and were most likely also part of the Hatton collection (of which seventeen are now in Christ Church);[28] and four are today in Christ Church, were bound by Aldrich with 'Hatton prints', and therefore may originally be from Hatton's library - the fact that Jeffreys used them seems to add weight to the hypothesis. The only three sources which do not appear in Martin's list and are not today part of the Christ Church collection are Hayne's *Motetti Sacri* Op. 4 (Antwerp, 1646), Merula's *Libro Secondo de Concerti Spirituali* (Venice, 1628) and Pio's *Liber Primus Motectorum* (Venice, 1622-4). However, given Jeffreys' almost total reliance upon his patron's music library for copy-texts, it is very likely that these three publications once also came within the ambit of the Hatton collection.[29]

George Jeffreys' manuscripts of Italian music in the Tenbury collection (MSS 972-6/1273, 1012-13 and 1015 - now in the Bodleian Library,

---

[27] The Christ Church copy of Facchi's *Motetti* (Venice, 1635) is unique; and the Christ Church prints of F.M. Marini's *Concerti Spirituali* (Venice, 1637) and Tomasi's *Motecta* Op. 6 (Venice, 1635) are the only complete copies in existence.

[28] The Christ Church copies of Pecci's *Sacri Modulatus* Op. 3 (Venice, 1629) and Trabattone's *Concerti... Libro Secondo* Op. 4 (Venice, 1629) are *unica*. The three prints listed by Martin but not today in Christ Church are Arrigoni's *Concerti di Camera* (Venice, 1635), Gregori's *Sacrarum Cantionum* (Venice, 1635) and Tarquinio Merula's *Il Primo Libro de Motetti* (Venice, 1624). There is an incomplete copy of the Arrigoni print in the British Library, and a unique Cantus I partbook of the Gregori print survives in the Euing Collection in the library of Glasgow University. It is likely that there were copies of both these prints in Hatton's collection at one time, and it may be that the British Library copy of Arrigoni's *Concerti* is the actual Hatton copy (see footnote 26 above), but it is unlikely that the Gregori *Sacrarum Cantionum* in Glasgow is the Hatton copy (see Chapter Two, footnote 22). The only existing copy of Merula's *Il Primo Libro de Motetti* - a source also used by Stephen Bing - is in the Civico Museo Bibliografico Musicale, Bologna (lacking the bass partbook). There must have been a copy of this publication in England in the 1630s or 1640s and it is likely that it was once part of the Hatton collection. The fact that Jeffreys copied from this now lost copy means that a number of motets (incomplete in the surviving print) can now be completed (see Chapter Three, footnote 152)

[29] The sole-surviving exemplar of Hayne's *Motetti Sacri* (1646) in Paris, Bibliothèque Ste Geneviève lacks the first partbook; the following pieces can be completed from Jeffreys' manuscript copies in *Lbl* Add. 31,479: 'Quid mihi est in caelo' (TTBbc) and 'O Domine Deus' (ATBbc). As there is no other indication that there was ever a copy of the Hayne publication in England, one is tempted to speculate on a link between the Ste Geneviève copy and the presence of Hatton in Paris during his exile 1646-56. A basso continuo partbook to Merula's *Libro Secondo* (1628) survives in *Lbl* (D.159a); it is possible that this copy was once part of the Hatton collection. The only surviving copy - lacking the Cantus partbook - of Pio's *Liber Primus Motectorum* (1622-4) is in the Murharsche Bibliothek der Stadt und Landesbibliothek, Kassel, Germany; it is likely that there was a copy of this publication in England in the 1630s or 1640s and it may have been part of the Hatton collection. I am grateful to Dr Gunter Morche for drawing my attention to the two pieces by Pio in *Lbl* Add. 31,479.

Oxford) are very similar in contents and physical make up to Stephen Bing's manuscripts of Italian music examined in Chapter Three. Jeffreys and Bing used the same supply of copy-sources - the Hatton collection - and the number of correlations between paper-types and/or rastrum-rulings in Jeffreys and Bing's manuscripts (see Table 18) suggests a common paper-supply and therefore a uniform provenance. Tenbury MS 1013 (Part II, MS XXXVII), Jeffreys' score of Alessandro Grandi's *Messa a 4 voci* from the first book of motets,[30] is copied stratigraphically across the whole width of sheets of paper with a watermark of a Pot lettered ID.[31] This paper came from the same quartet of moulds (plus a spare mould) as did paper in Bing's British Library Add. MS 31,434 (first sections of the partbooks) and Tenbury MS 1017;[32] and the stave rulings of Tenbury MS 1013 are the same as those in the first two sections of the partbooks of Add. MS 31,434 (see Table 18). Tenbury MS 1015 (Part II, MS XXXVIII) is a score (copied strati-graphically across the whole width of the sheets, like most of Jeffreys' and Bing's other Tenbury manuscripts) of all but two of the pieces from Pomponio Nenna's seventh book of madrigals for five voices;[33] the Italian texts have, however, been replaced with rather poor English verse. The watermark found in Tenbury MS 1015 is a version of the Pot GRO mark not found elsewhere in the Jeffreys and Bing manuscripts, but the system of rastrum rulings is common to a number of manuscripts (see Table 18). The same applies to Tenbury MS 1012 (Part II, MS XXXVI), a stratigraphically copied score of three four-voice madrigals from Giovanni Rovetta's *Madrigali Concertati.... Libro Primo* Op. 2 (Venice, 1629):[34] the Pot PB watermark does not occur elsewhere but the system of stave-rulings can be found in a number of other manuscripts.[35] Parts to the three Rovetta madrigals appear, along with other madrigals by Rovetta, Arrigoni, Grandi, Merula and Turini, in Tenbury MSS 973-6/1273 (Part II, MS XXXI). All

---

[30] Grandi's *Il Primo Libro de Motetti* was first published in Venice in 1610; an unspecified edition was advertised in Martin's 1633 booklist and there is a copy of the fifth edition (1628) in the Christ Church library. It is highly likely that this edition was Jeffreys' copy-source.

[31] The blocks of rastrum-ruled staves on the left and right of each sheet are joined in the middle by freehand.

[32] The sections of *Och* Mus. 878 & 880 copied by Angelo Notari also consist of Pot ID paper; see Chapter Five.

[33] The fourth edition (1624) is listed in Martin's catalogues, and a copy of this edition is today in Christ Church (very likely from the Hatton collection). Only 'Scherzava Amor, e Clori' and 'Ove stavi avvolto' from the 1624 edition do not appear in *Ob* Tenbury 1015; the first edition has one more madrigal than the fourth edition, 'Amorosetto neo, che tra le perle', and this does not appear in Tenbury 1015.

[34] Listed in Martin's catalogues of 1633 and 1635; the copy at Christ Church, Oxford was probably from the Hatton collection.

[35] For example *Och* Mus. 880, second manuscript sequence (see Chapter Five) and, given the variation factor of approximately 1-2 mm for a multiple-stave rastrum, perhaps also *Och* Mus. 878 & 880 Notari sections, *Ob* Tenbury 1005 ff. 1-2, Tenbury 1015, Tenbury 1017, and possibly even *Lbl* Add. 31,434, third sections of the partbooks.

Table 22 George Jeffreys' Copy-Sources of Italian Music

† Copy at Christ Church (†¹: *unicum*; †²: only complete copy in existence)
‡ Listed in Robert Martin's printed catalogues
* Copy bought by Sir Christopher Hatton in 1638 from Robert Martin

G.B. Aloisi, *Coelestis Parnasus* Op. 1 (B. Magni, Venice, 1628)†¹
G.B. Aloisi, *Contextus Musicarum Proportionum* Op. 4 (B. Magni, Venice, 1637)†‡*
G.B. Aloisi, *Corona Stellarum* Op. 5 (B. Magni, Venice, 1637)†² ‡*
G.G. Arrigoni, *Concerti di Camera* (B. Magni, Venice, 1635)‡
A. Cifra, *Motecta* Bk 5, Op. 11 (G.B. Robletti, Rome, 1612; 2/ G. Vincenti, 1616†)
A. Facchi, *Motetti* Bk 2 (B. Magni, Venice, 1635)†¹ ‡*
A. Grandi, *Il Primo Libro de Motetti* (G. Vincenti, Venice, 1610; 5/1628†)‡
A. Grandi, *Il Secondo Libro de Motetti* (G. Vincenti, Venice, 1613; 5/1628†)‡
A. Grandi, *Madrigali Concertati* (G. Vincenti, Venice, 1615; 6/1626†)
A. Grandi, *Il Quarto Libro de Motetti* (G. Vincenti, Venice, 1616; 5/1628†)‡
A. Grandi, *Celesti Fiori* Bk 5 (B. Magni, Venice, 1619; 3/1625†‡, 4/1638†‡)
A. Grandi, *Motetti... con Sinfonie* Bk 3 (A. Vincenti, Venice, 1629)†
A. Grandi, *Il Sesto Libro de Motetti* (A. Vincenti, Venice, 1630)†‡
A. Gregori, *Sacrarum Cantionum* Bk 3, Op. 8 (B. Magni, Venice, 1635)‡
G. Hayne (E. Hennio), *Motetti Sacri* Op. 4 (M. Phalèse, Antwerp, 1646)
F.M. Marini, *Concerti Spirituali* Bk 1 (B. Magni, Venice, 1637)†² ‡*
T. Merula, *Il Primo Libro de Motetti* Op. 6 (A. Vincenti, Venice, 1624)‡
T. Merula, *Libro Secondo de Concerti Spirituali* (A. Vincenti, Venice, 1628)
T. Merula, *Madrigali et Altre Musiche Concertate... Libro Secondo* Op. 10 (B. Magni,
　　　　　　Venice, 1633; 2/1635†‡* as *Musiche Concertate*)
P. Nenna, *Il Settimo Libro de Madrigali a Cinque Voci* (G.B. Sottile, Naples, 1608;
　　　　　　5/ B. Magni, Venice, 1624†‡)
D. Pecci, *Sacri Modulatus* Op. 3 (B. Magni, Venice, 1629)†¹ ‡
F. Pio, *Liber Primus Motectorum* (A. Vincenti, Venice, 1622-4)
G. Rovetta, *Madrigali Concertati* Bk 1, Op. 2 (B. Magni, Venice, 1629)†‡; 4/H. de
　　　　　　Bruyn, Rotterdam, 1660†)
G.F. Sances, *Motetti* (B. Magni, Venice, 1638)†‡*
B. Tomasi, *Motecta* Op. 6 (B. Magni, Venice, 1635)†² ‡*
E. Trabattone, *Concerti* Bk 2, Op. 4 (B, Magni, Venice, 1629)†¹ ‡
F. Turini, *Madrigali... Libro Primo* (B. Magni, Venice, 1621; 2/1624†‡)

---

the copy-sources except Arrigoni's *Concerti di Camera* (B. Magni, Venice, 1635)[36] are in the library of Christ Church, Oxford and were most likely once part of the Hatton collection.

The latest copy-sources used by Jeffreys for Tenbury MSS 973-6/1273, 1012-13 and 1015 are dated 1635: Arrigoni's *Concerti di Camera* and Merula's *Musiche Concertate*; the second of these publications was bought by Hatton in November 1638 from the London bookseller Robert Martin

---

[36] See footnote 28 above.

(see Chapter Two).³⁷ November 1638 therefore seems to have been the earliest date that Jeffreys could have started his manuscript copies. Thus it seems likely that the Tenbury manuscripts mentioned above were all copied between November 1638 and the summer of 1646 (which saw the fall of Oxford, Hatton's departure to Paris and Jeffreys' removal to Weldon in Northamptonshire). The theory that Jeffreys' Tenbury manuscripts and Stephen Bing's copies of Italian music (examined in Chapter Three) were the product of a school of copyist-musicians working at the Oxford Court under the patronage and supervision of Christopher Hatton is further examined in the following chapter, and a performance context is suggested for the Italian music. This hypothesis fits well with what we know about Jeffreys' own development as a composer. A sustained period of copying, studying, and no doubt performing Italian music explains the change from the composition of old-fashioned English secular pieces (pre-*c*.1640) to Latin motets and English devotional music in the most up-to-date Italianate style (post-*c*.1640) (see below).

What then of the sets of partbooks British Library Add. MS 31,479 and the Madrigal Society MSS G 55-9 (Part II, MS IX)? This vast collection of 159 Latin motets for one to five voices and basso continuo by Italian composers has been the subject of much debate.³⁸ In an article in 1990 I suggested that, like Jeffreys' Tenbury manuscripts, the partbooks dated from *circa* 1638-46 with six pieces added in the 1670s.³⁹ At that time two concordances with Hayne's *Motetti Sacri* Op. 4 (Antwerp, 1646) had not

---

[37] Hatton's 1638 purchases probably represent his last transaction with Martin due to the imminence of war and his financial difficulties (FH 4106 indicates that he was in debt to the tune of £18,600).

[38] I have been unable to identify sixteen of the 159 Italian motets copied by Jeffreys despite examining a large number of printed sources in both British and Italian libraries. I record my thanks to the late Dr Jerome Roche and Dr Graham Dixon for allowing me to consult their index of Italian motets of the period as a final check for possible sources. It is very tempting to speculate that these few remaining anonymous piece may have been copied from the now lost (or not yet discovered) sources which are listed in Martin's catalogues. The following are Martin's catalogue entries for unlocated motet publications: 'Arigoni [sic] Motetti a voce sola con la partitura per l'Organo & c.' (1633 catalogue); 'Florani [Cristoforo Floriani] motecta a 2.3.4. voci cum basso 4. Ven. 1623.' (1633 & 1635); 'Giuliano [Francesco?] Concerti a voce sola con basso continuo per L'Organo. 4. 1632.' (1633); 'Gratiani Motetti concertati a 2 voce. 4. Ven. 1630.' (1633) [N.B. *Y* M.5.S, dated 1688, contains a piece by a Tomaso Gratiani - 'Cantate Domino' for ABbc - which is inscribed 'Venetia 1630']; 'Monteverdi Motetti a 2.3.4. & 6 voci. 4. Venet. 1620' (1633); 'Gab. de Pultis [Gabriello Puliti] motecta [1635: 'Sacrae Modulationes'] a una voce. 4. Ven. 1629.' (1633, 1635, 1639 & 1640); 'Sarti [Giovanni Vincenzo?] Concerti a 2.3. & 4. voci. 4. Venetia. 1629.' (1633); 'Torre lib. 1° a 2.3.4. & 5 voci con Basso continuo 4. Veneti. 1623' (1633), 'Girolamo Torre Sacra Girlanda a 2.3.4. & 5. voci con Basso Contin.' (1625); 'Concerti ecclesiastici a una & due voce. fol. Venet. 1627.'; and 'Giardino primo... lib. a voce sola. 4. Ven. 1634.' (1633 & 1635). (See Wainwright (1993), i, Appendix III for a complete transcription of the Martin Catalogues and for identifications and locations of the prints.)

[39] J.P. Wainwright, 'George Jeffreys' Copies of Italian Music', *RCRMA*, xxiii (1990), 109-24.

been noted[40] and - with the exception of the six pieces obviously added at a later date (see below) - the latest identified copy-source was Sances' *Motetti* which was published in Venice in 1638 (the same year that Hatton purchased a copy from Robert Martin). The discovery of a concordant printed source of 1646 has necessitated a revision of the previously proposed date for British Library Add. MS 31,479 and Madrigal Society MSS G 55-9. Dr Robert Thompson's work concerning the paper-type of the partbooks has been invaluable in reaching a correct date for the manuscripts.[41] He notes that, whilst the rastrum ruling of the partbooks is the same as in manuscripts dating from the 1640s (such as Tenbury MSS 973-6/1273) through to the 1660s,[42] the watermark - a Cardinals' Hat lettered GR - appears only in sources of the 1650s or later. Dr Thompson notes the appearance of the Cardinals' Hat GR watermark in the following manuscript sources:[43]

(*a*) *Ruled with a 5-stave rastrum of 108-9 mm span and individual staves measuring approx. 12 mm*

>British Library Add. MS 31479 and Madrigal Society MSS G 55-9
>Royal College of Music MS 920, basso continuo part
>Oxford, Bodleian Library Mus. Sch. MS C 53
>Oxford, Bodleian Library Mus. Sch. MS C 83, final gathering of each part
>Oxford, Bodleian Library Mus. Sch. MS C 85, Treble and Bass parts
>Oxford, Bodleian Library Mus. Sch. MSS F 568-9, first section of each
>
>partbook

(*b*) *Ruled with a 5-stave rastrum of 118.5 mm span and individual staves measuring approx. 13 mm*

>Oxford, Bodleian Library Mus. Sch. MS C 82
>Oxford, Bodleian Library Mus. Sch. MS C 86
>Oxford, Bodleian Library Mus. Sch. MS C 88
>Oxford, Bodleian Library Mus. Sch. MS C 91

The Royal College of Music MS 920 (Part II, MS XVII), a set of four partbooks containing Jeffreys' copies of his own music, dates from the late 1650s or early 1660s (see below);[44] Bodleian Mus. Sch. MS C 53 is Christopher Gibbons' autograph set of parts to three-part instrumental music dated '[16]53'; Bodleian Mus. Sch. MSS F 568-9 (two partbooks from an

---

[40] 'Quid mihi est in caelo' (TTBbc) and 'O Domine Deus' (ATBbc): *Lbl* Add. 31,479, *a* 3 section: Nos. 21 and 27. See footnote 29 above.
[41] Thompson (1988), 394-430; and ibid. (1990b).
[42] See also *Lbl* Add. 10,338 paper with the following watermarks: Pots lettered GPO, POO, RDP and ID (see Part II, MS I).
[43] Four slightly different versions of the Cardinals' Hat GR watermark appear, i.e. two pairs produced at a two-vat mill. For full details see Thompson (1988), 413-30 (the distribution of the quartet of watermarks is given for *Lbl* Add. 31,479: Table III; *Ob* Mus. Sch. C 83 final gathering of each of the six parts: Table IV; and *Ob* Mus. Sch. C 85 Tr & B: Table V).
[44] Only the basso continuo book contains paper with the Cardinals' Hat watermark.

original set of five) are in two sections: the first sections of each partbook, containing ayres by William Lawes and Christopher Simpson, are made up of Cardinals' Hat paper and probably date from the 1650s; and Bodleian Mus. Sch. MSS C 82-3, 85-6, 88 and 91 are part of the North collection of consort music mentioned in Chapter Three in connection with Stephen Bing (see pages 102-3 above) and probably date from the mid to late 1650s.[45] Added to this, Robert Spencer discovered the Cardinals' Hat GR paper in two publications of 1653: John Playford, *Select Musicall Ayres and Dialogues* (T. Harper for J. Playford, London, 1653) and Henry Lawes, *Ayres and Dialogues* (T. H[arper] for J. Playford, London, 1653).[46] This is incontrovertible evidence that the Cardinals' Hat paper dates from the early 1650s. It appears that the stationer John Playford acquired a consignment of the Cardinals' Hat GR paper from Italy in the early 1650s and issued his printer, Thomas Harper, with the poor quality outer quires and kept the thicker inner quires of reams for 'pricking' paper. This paper was ruled by Playford using two five-stave rastra (one of 108-9 mm span with individual staves measuring approximately 12 mm, and another of 118.5 mm span with individual staves measuring approximately 13 mm). George Jeffreys, Christopher Gibbons and the North-family scribes presumably purchased this paper from Playford's shop in London for use in the manuscripts described above.[47]

Thus it can now be stated that George Jeffreys' partbooks of Italian motets for one to five voices and basso continuo were copied in the mid to late 1650s and not *circa* 1638-46 as had been suggested. In the examination of the manuscripts of Jeffreys' own compositions (in the last section of this chapter) it will be demonstrated that the period around 1657 was one of intense musical activity for Jeffreys, one which coincided with Baron Hatton's return from France. It is likely that the partbooks of Italian motets - British Library Add. MS 31,479 and Madrigal Society MSS G 55-9 - are (ignoring the six additional pieces for the moment) a product of this industrious period. However, the following facts still remain: (*a*) the greater majority of the pieces copied by Jeffreys date from before 1638 (see Table 22); (*b*) George Jeffreys is known to have been interested in Italian music from as early as *circa* 1634 (see his annotations in Bodleian Mus. Sch. MS C 204, ff. 46-9ᵛ: Part II, MS XXIX); (*c*) it will be demonstrated in the

---

[45] See Crum (1972).
[46] Reported by Robert Thompson (1990b).
[47] The presence of the two systems of rastrum-ruling in manuscripts probably copied at the Oxford Court in the early 1640s (such as *Ob* Tenbury 973-6/1273 and sections of *Lbl* Add. 10,338, see below) is not necessarily problematic despite the fact that Playford's tenancy of the Middle Temple shop dated from 1646 (see M. Dean-Smith, 'John Playford i', *New Grove*, xv, 1). Playford could not have been responsible for these early rastrum rulings but, as Robert Thompson has noted (1990b) it is possible that Playford 'acquired the stave-ruling equipment from another stationer, perhaps his master John Benson, who had been using it earlier, and that the ruled sheets had been taken from London to Oxford by someone such as Stephen Bing.'

following chapter that Civil War Oxford (1642-6) was the ideal and receptive environment for small-scale Italian *concertato* motets such as those copied by Jeffreys; and (*d*) it is shown below that many of Jeffreys' own Italianate compositions - no doubt inspired by the study and performance of Italian motets - were written during the early 1640s.[48] It seems inconceivable that British Library Add. MS 31,479 and Madrigal Society MSS G 55-9 represent Jeffreys' first copies of Italian motets from his patron's printed music collection. The partbooks do not, in any case, show signs of having been copied directly from the printed copy-sources, but rather from a number of separate intermediary manuscripts (now lost). This hypothesis finds some support in the fact that the order of motets in British Library Add. MS 31,479 and Madrigal Society MSS G 55-9 bears little resemblance to the sequence of pieces in the printed sources, and there are never more than four motets in sequence from any one print. Moreover, certain texts in the manuscript partbooks are different from the original printed texts; it appears that some texts were considered unacceptably Marian in reference and were therefore changed. For example, Alessandro Grandi's two-voice motets 'Ave sanctissima Maria' and 'Tu pulchra es Maria' have become 'Ave sanctissime Messia' and 'Tu dulcis es, Messia'. Even so the two manuscripts still contain five settings of the 'Salve Regina', three of the 'Ave Regina', one setting of the Litany of Our Lady, and other settings of blatantly Marian texts. I suggest that Civil War Oxford (1642-6) would provide the circumstances for performances of both the openly Marian pieces and those pieces with their texts modified to suit a more Protestant-taste (this hypothesis is examined in the following chapter)

The evidence, then, seems to indicate that British Library Add. MS 31,479 and Madrigal Society MSS G 55-9 were copied from manuscript sources that are now lost. These sources were probably roughly copied performing parts or scores (like the Tenbury manuscripts mentioned above) copied in the early to mid 1640s. Jeffreys refers to 'my other Score book' in a note on folio 154 of British Library Add. MS 10,338; could this lost book have included some of the original copies of Italian motets which he recopied in the late 1650s? The final section of Christ Church Mus. 880 needs mention here as it appears to have very close links with Jeffreys' Madrigal Society MSS G 55-9. Christ Church Mus. 880 is examined in detail in the following chapter, but for present purposes it should be noted that the last section of the partbook, copied by Stephen Bing in the late 1650s, contains the basso continuo parts for forty-six Italian four-voice pieces of which thirty-four also appear in Jeffreys' Madrigal Society MSS G 55-9. This would seem to indicate that there was a common core of popular pieces

---

[48] It is worth noting that Jeffreys himself set nine of the Latin texts of motets in *Lbl* Add. 31,479 and Mad. Soc. G 55-9: 'Audite caeli', 'Caro mea vere est cibus', 'Ego sum panis vitae', 'O bone Jesu', 'O Domine Deus', 'O quam dulcis es tu', 'O quam iucundum', 'O quam suave est nomen' and 'Quid mihi est in caelo'.

which had been copied from 'Hatton-prints'. The recopying in the late 1650s of Italian music probably first copied and performed at the Oxford Court may have been the result merely of fastidious and careful copyists wishing to preserve what they perceived as a lost Royalist repertoire. Alternatively, with their patron Baron Hatton recently returned, and with renewed Royalist fervour at the prospect of the end of the Commonwealth and the restoration of the King, Jeffreys and Bing may have been inspired to recopy their manuscripts of Italian motets in preparation for the new Royalist age. Unfortunately the Restoration did not bring for Hatton - or his musicians - the expected return to the glory-days of the Oxford Court.

A number of pieces copied in Jeffreys' manuscripts of Italian music did, however, become popular and were transmitted in a number of Restoration manuscripts - perhaps via his son's musical associates in Oxford in the 1660s as much as by Jeffreys' own connections (see Excursus II below). Despite Jeffreys' relative isolation from the country's main musical establishments, he did manage to keep in touch with the most up-to-date Italian music. This is demonstrated by the six pieces added to British Library Add. MS 31,479 at a later date than the main copying: Giacomo Carissimi's 'Lucifer cælestis olim' (not published until Playford's 1693 edition), 'Insurrexerunt in nos', 'Desiderata nobis' and 'Audite sancti' (first published in 1642, 1667, and 1645 respectively),[49] Pietro Reggio's 'Miserere mei', and the arrangement of Giovanni Rovetta's 'Quam pulchra es' which is misattributed to 'Charissimi' by Jeffreys. The four partbooks of British Library Add. MS 31,479 are divided into three sections: pieces for one, two or three voices and basso continuo, with blank pages of manuscript between each section (see Part II, MS IX). The six pieces in question all appear at the end of a section: 'Lucifer cælestis olim' at the end of the one-voice sections, and the remainder at the end of the three-voice sections of the partbooks. The handwriting in Reggio's 'Miserere mei' in particular - although definitely still that of Jeffreys - is very uneven compared with the earlier sections (signs of old age?). We know that Jeffreys continued his copying activities in his later years,[50] and I have suggested that these six pieces were added to his earlier copies of Italian music after about 1670.[51]

It is unlikely that Carissimi's 'Desiderata nobis' and 'Audite sancti' were copied directly from printed sources. A comparison of the Add. MS 31,479 versions of these two pieces with their printed versions reveals a number of discrepancies, and it would have been very difficult for Jeffreys to have noticed, and thereby correct, the few errors that appear in the printed sources, particularly as he would have been copying from partbooks into

---

[49] L. Grignani ed., *Sacrarum Modulationum* (Rome, 1642); A. Belmonte ed., *Scelta de'Motetti... Parte Seconda* (Rome, 1667); and Florido de Silvestri ed., *Sacras Cantiones* (Rome, 1645).
[50] See *Ob* Tenbury 1011: Jeffreys' copies of three of Purcell's *Sonnata's* of 1683.
[51] Wainwright (1990), 109-11.

partbooks.⁵² It is therefore likely that Jeffreys' copy-sources for Carissimi's 'Desiderata nobis' and 'Audite Sancti' were manuscript scores of the works which were already in circulation in England in the 1660s and 1670s. However, Carissimi's 'Insurrexerunt in nos' does appear to have been copied directly from a printed source. The Add. MS 31,479 version of the piece is scored for ATBbc and is a fourth lower than in the three printed versions where it is scored for CATbc.⁵³ In the second (enlarged) edition of Giorgio Rolla's anthology *Teatro Musicale* (Milan, 1653), although the piece is scored for CATbc, a possible alternative scoring for ATBbc is specified; the designation 'alla quarta' suggests the possibility of a downward transposition of a fourth. Taking this transposition into account, Jeffreys' version of 'Insurrexerunt in nos' and that in the second edition of *Teatro musicale* correspond in all but very minor and insignificant details. This seems to indicate a direct line of transmission from the 1653 *Teatro Musicale* to the Jeffreys' transcription, a suggestion made even more plausible by the fact that a copy of the 1653 print is extant in the British Library (Royal Music Library 15.g.15).

Between the final two Carissimi pieces in British Library Add. MS 31,479 is a setting of 'Quam pulchra es'. Jeffreys, in one of his few attributions, states that the piece is by Carissimi. The piece is actually an arrangement for CCBbc of a motet by Giovanni Rovetta, which was originally scored for CCbc. The two versions are very different; not only does Jeffreys' version have an added bass voice part (either based on the original basso continuo or newly composed), but also parts are swapped round (with octave transpositions where necessary), and the last section of the Jeffreys' version bears little resemblance to the original - there are just hints of the original, but nothing corresponds exactly.⁵⁴ Rovetta's motet also has a repeat of the first eleven bars followed by an 'Alleluia' final section; these do not appear in the British Library Add. MS 31,479 version. Rovetta's 'Quam pulchra es' was first published in Venice in 1635 in his collection *Motetti Concertati* Op. 3 which was reprinted in 1640. The two-voice pieces of the collection were then published separately as *Bicinia Sacra* in 1648, and this duet 'off-print' was itself reprinted in 1668.⁵⁵ The motet could therefore have been known in England by the early 1640s, and possibly Jeffreys had heard performances of it, and later reconstructed the piece (freely) from memory, and in doing so confused the original

---

⁵² The pieces are transcribed from the printed sources in Jones (1982), ii, 299-307 & 260-8 respectively.
⁵³ L. Grignani ed., *Sacrarum Modulationum* (Rome, 1642); G. Rolla ed., *Teatro Musicale de Concerti Ecclesiastici* (Milan, 1649; enlarged 2/1653); and Florido de Silvestri ed., *Sacras Cantiones... Pars Prima* (Rome, 1651).
⁵⁴ The two versions are transcribed and compared in detail in Wainwright (1986), i, Example 5 & pp. 45-7.
⁵⁵ Three partbooks (CAT) of the 1640 edition of *Motetti Concertati* Op. 3 are preserved in *Lbl*, and there are complete copies of *Bicinia Sacra* in *DRc* (1648) and *Och* (1668).

composer. If Jeffreys actually had Rovetta's music in front of him, and deliberately made the various alterations (for whatever reason), it is unlikely that he would make a false attribution in two partbooks due to a simple slip of the pen. One possible reason for the alterations could be that Jeffreys was practising writing in the style of the Italians, and used the themes from Rovetta's motet in an exercise of pastiche, finally producing a strange mixture of Rovetta and Jeffreys.[56] This, however, still does not explain how the piece came to be attributed to Carissimi. So far, it has been taken it for granted that the arranger was Jeffreys; but it is possible that this was not the case, and Jeffreys was only the copyist of someone else's arrangement. Possibly the arrangement was made by Carissimi and the attribution is therefore technically correct? Andrew Jones considers that 'This hypothesis would presuppose the existence of an additional manuscript source (either no longer extant or simply undiscovered) from which Jeffreys was transcribing; but the musical style of the alterations makes the hypothesis unlikely. Much more probable is that Jeffreys himself was responsible for the changes in Rovetta's original.'[57]

The sixth piece which appears to have been added to British Library Add. MS 31,479 at a later date is 'Miserere mei', the final unnumbered three-voice motet in the manuscript. This piece is attributed to Pietro Reggio in the three other known sources of the piece: Oxford, Christ Church Mus. 43 and 48 (late seventeenth-century manuscripts connected with Dean Aldrich of Christ Church; see Part II, MSS XLVI and XLVII), and Oxford, Bodleian Library Tenbury MS 335 (an early eighteenth-century source).[58] Pietro Reggio (*c*.1632-85) was an Italian musician who travelled widely and eventually settled in England.[59] The earliest reference to him in England is 1664, which leads to the suggestion that Jeffreys copied 'Miserere mei' (and perhaps also the other five 'additional' pieces) in the early 1670s.

Finally mention must be made of Tenbury MS 1016 (Part II, MS XXXIX), a score of eighteen Italian madrigals by the English composer Richard Dering (*c*.1580-1630) for one to three voices and basso continuo. This manuscript was copied stratigraphically across the whole width of sheets of paper with a watermark of a small Pot lettered IDB. The same watermark appears in a single sheet in Stephen Bing's madrigal score:

---

[56] We know from an annotation in *Lbl* Add. 17,816 that Jeffreys was capable of subconscious plagiarism; Jeffreys supplied a revised beginning for his four-voice 'Jubilate' and noted 'I designe this begin[n]ing for ye next Song, having since I Made it heard som[e]thing to[o] neer it' (see Part II, MS II).
[57] Jones (1982), i, 74.
[58] The various attributions of other pieces in *Lbl* Add. 31,479 to Reggio in the British Library catalogue - Hughes-Hughes (1906-9) - are incorrect. They stem from the erroneous idea that all the anonymous pieces in *Lbl* Add. 31,440 were by Reggio, and thus all concordant pieces in *Lbl* Add. 31,479 were also considered to be by Reggio. See Willetts (1962) & (1969b), and Chapter Six below.
[59] For details of Reggio's life see G. Rose, 'Pietro Reggio: A Wandering Musician', *ML*, xlvi (1965), 207-16.

Tenbury MS 1009 folio 7, and the rastrum used to rule Tenbury MS 1016 (a two-stave rastrum of 38.5 mm span and individual staves each measuring 11.5 mm) was probably also used to rule a single folio in another of Bing's madrigal scores: Tenbury MS 1005 folio 3. This could lead to the suggestion that Tenbury MS 1016, like the other Jeffreys and Bing manuscripts in the Tenbury collection, dates from the period *circa* 1638-46. However, the Pot IDB watermark is rather smaller than the other Pot watermarks in Jeffreys' and Bing's other manuscripts (see Table 18) and so, following the general rule for Pot watermarks that the smaller the pot the earlier the paper,[60] it is possible that Tenbury MS 1016 is slightly earlier than the other Tenbury manuscripts (mid 1630s?). Tenbury MS 1016 is an important manuscript as it is the only complete source for Dering's eighteen Italian madrigals. The same sequence of pieces appear in a single Cantus and Tenor I partbook, Christ Church Mus. 435, which must be roughly contemporary with, and closely related to Jeffreys' score; the only other source to contain a substantial number of Dering's madrigals is Yale University, Music Library, Filmer MS 5, a single Tenor II partbook. Dering's music - both secular and sacred - continued to be popular long after his death in 1630; his sacred music is examined in the following chapter and in Excursus I.

Manuscripts of George Jeffreys' Compositions

George Jeffreys' surviving compositions consist of seven instrumental fantasias, thirteen Italian madrigals, sixteen English songs, sixty-three Latin motets, six Latin canticles, two Latin mass movements, twenty-eight English anthems or devotional pieces, and four settings of texts from the English Communion Service: an impressive output for someone employed for most of his life not as a musician but as steward. Jeffreys' compositions are listed in Table 23. Only one of his works was published during his lifetime - the two-voice motet 'Erit gloria Domini', which appeared in John Playford's *Cantica Sacra.... The Second Sett* (London, 1674) - although his name appears twice in James Clifford's text anthology of *The Divine Services and Anthems Usually Sung in the Cathedrals and Collegiate Choires in the Church of England* (London, 1663).[61] George Jeffreys' compositions are preserved in the following autograph manuscripts: British Library Add. MSS 10,338, 17,816/30,829-30 and 29,282; Royal College of Music MSS 920 and 920A; Bodleian Library Tenbury MSS 1010 and 1285b; and Dublin, Archbishop Marsh's Library MS Z3.4.13, folios 47-59ᵛ. Various

---

[60] See R. Thompson, 'George Jeffreys and the *Stile Nuovo* in English Sacred Music: a New Date for his Autograph Score, British Library Add. MS 10338', *ML*, lxx (1989), 325.

[61] Jeffreys is listed as a composer of the Communion service texts: 'Glory to God on high' (Anthem CXIX) and 'Holy, holy, holy Lord' (Anthem CXX); his name appears against the same two texts in Clifford's *The Divine Services and Anthems Usually Sung in His Majesties Chappell and in the Cathedrals and Collegiate Choires in England and Ireland The Second Edition, with Large Additions* (London, 1664).

dates and annotations in the manuscripts reveal that Jeffreys was active as a composer throughout his career,[62] and this information, combined with a detailed study of the physical make up of the collections, enables us to reconstruct a fairly precise chronology of his activities as a composer.

The scorebook British Library Add. MS 10,338 (Part II, MS I) is of seminal importance to any study of George Jeffreys' compositions. The manuscript, which contains 126 pieces (all but thirteen of Jeffreys' total number of works), has been described as 'a well organized, retrospective, fair-copy collection'.[63] This is true to some extent. The manuscript was certainly well organised in that it was divided up into sections of different types of music: instrumental pieces, Italian madrigals, English secular songs, and sacred music for one, two, three, four and five parts, but the system faltered due to insufficient space having been allowed for the three- and four- part music; certain pieces in the scorebook were copied retrospectively some years after composition, but others were added in chronological order as they were composed; and some were indeed 'fair copies', but others are obviously 'working-copies' as they contain various alterations and marginal notes. A detailed examination of the scorebook's contents, dates, annotations, paper-types, rastrum-rulings and gatherings, in relation to events in Jeffreys' life, has gone some way towards revealing the complex history of the manuscript.[64]

British Library Add. MS 10,338 consists of thirty-five gatherings of thirteen different types of paper (see Part II, MS I). The great variety of paper used by Jeffreys indicates that the collection did not start life as a single volume but was collected together at a later date. A system of binder's marks is present in the manuscript which appear to relate to a binding during

---

[62] The following pieces are dated in the manuscript sources: *Songs made for some Comedyes by Sir Richard Hatton* (1631): 'Cupid blushes to behold' 4vv bc, 'Fond Maydes take warninge while you may' 4vv bc, 'Hymen hath together tyed ye lusty bridegroome' 4vv bc, and 'You that have been this Evenings light' 4vv bc; *The Rivall Friends* (Peter Hausted) (1631, NS 1632): 'But why do ye wing'd minutes fly so fast away' 5vv bc, 'Cruell but once againe' 1v bc, 'Cupid if a God thou art' 5vv bc, 'Drowsy Phœbus com[e] away' 5vv bc, 'Have pity greefe 1v bc, 'Have you a desyre to see the glorious heavens' 5vv bc, and 'To the ladyes joy delight' 5vv bc; 'Turne thee againe' 4vv bc (1648); 'Te Deum laudamus' 4vv bc (1649); 'Gloria Patri qui creavit nos' 4vv bc (1651); 'O quam iucundum' 4vv bc (1651); 'Glory to God on high' 3vv bc (May 1652); 'Turn thou us good Lord' 4vv bc (1655); 'In the midst of life' 4vv bc (October 1657); 'Paratum cor meum' 3vv bc (November 1657); 'Quando natus est' 3vv bc (December 1657); 'O quam iucundum' 3vv bc (August 1658); 'Gloria tua manet in aeternum' 3vv bc (1658/1659); 'Florete flores' 3vv bc (1660); 'Quid mihi est in caelo' 3vv bc (October 1661); 'A musick strange' 5vv inst bc (1662); 'See, see the Word is incarnate' (2nd pt 'The paschall lambe', 3rd pt 'Glory be to the lambe') 3vv bc (March-April 1662); and 'He beheld the citty' 4vv bc (December 1675).

[63] Holman (1973-4), 79. Until recently *Lbl* Add. 10,338 was assumed to have originated as a single bound volume into which Jeffreys copied his works. Thomas Oliphant (a one-time owner of the manuscript) read the last date in the score as 1669 (*recte* 1662) and this date was accepted as the date of copying by subsequent commentators without question.

[64] The following studies of the manuscripts of Jeffreys' compositions are indebted to the work of Dr Robert Thompson: (1988), 172-220; and (1989).

Table 23 George Jeffreys' Compositions

Sources:
1. Dublin, Marsh's Library MS Z3.4.13
2. Durham, Cathedral Library MS B.1
3. London, British Library Add. MS 10,338
4. London, British Library Add. MSS 17,816 & 30,829-30
5. London, British Library Add. MS 29, 282
6. London, Royal College of Music MS 920
7. London, Royal College of Music MS 920A
8. London, Royal College of Music MS 2033
9. London, Royal College of Music MS 2039
10. Oxford, Bodleian Library Mus. MS d 10
11. Oxford, Bodleian Library Mus. Sch. MS C 11
12. Oxford, Bodleian Library Mus. Sch. MS E 451
13. Oxford, Bodleian Library Tenbury MS 892
14. Oxford, Bodleian Library Tenbury MS 1010
15. Oxford, Bodleian Library Tenbury MS 1285b
16. Oxford, Christ Church Mus. 17
17. Oxford, Christ Church Mus. 18
18. Oxford, Christ Church Mus. 417-18 & 1080
19. Oxford, Christ Church Mus. 459-62
20. Oxford, Christ Church Mus. 468-72
21. Oxford, Christ Church Mus. 747-9
22. York, Minster Library MS M.1.S
23. York, Minster Library MS M.5.S
24. J. Playford ed., *Cantica Sacra* (London, 1674)

Title	Scoring	Source	Date
a. Instrumental works			
Fantasia	vln b.vl org	3	[1630s]
Fantasia 1	tr tr b.vl	1, 3, 18, 19, 20	[1630s]
Fantasia 2	tr tr b.vl	1, 3, 18, 19, 20	[1630s]
Fantasia 3	tr tr b.vl	1, 3, 18, 19, 20	[1630s]
Fantasia 4	tr tr b.vl	1, 3, 18, 19, 20	[1630s]
Fantasia 5	tr tenor b.vl	1, 3, 18, 20	[1630s]
Fantasia 6	tr tenor b.vl	1, 3, 18, 20	[1630s]

Table 23 continued

b. Italian madrigals

All'ombra de gli'allori viddi mesta	CCB	3	[late 1630s?]
Che nove'arti son queste per catena mi	TTBbc	3	[late 1630s?]
Crudel tu per fugire	CCB	3	[late 1630s?]
Donna Crudell	CCB	3	[late 1630s?]
Donna s'io miro voi giaccio divengo	CCB	3	[late 1630s?]
Felice Pastorella	CCATBbc & inst	3	[late 1630s?]
Felice pastorelle ch'in compagnia	CCBbc	3	[late 1630s?]
Le parole soavi hor aspre	CCB	3	[late 1630s?]
Occhi stelle mortali ministri	CCB	3, 16 for SSBbc	[late 1630s?]
O vaghe O O care stelle	CCB	3	[late 1630s?]
Provate la mia fiamma	CCBbc	3	[late 1630s?]
Quand'io miro le rose	CCB	3	[late 1630s?]
Si miro il tuo bel viso	CCB	3	[late 1630s?]

c. English secular music

But why do ye wing'd minutes fly so fast away	CCATBbc	3	March 1632
Coy Caelia dost thou see	TTBbc	3	[early 1630s?]
Cruell but once againe	Cbc	3	March 1632
Cupid blushes to behold	CATBbc	3	1631
Cupid if a God thou art	CCATBbc	3	March 1632
Drowsy Phoebus come away	CCATBbc	3	March 1632
Fond maydes take warninge while you may	CMABbc	3	1631
Have pity greefe	Cbc	3	March 1632
Have you a desyre to see the glorious heavens	CCATBbc	3	March 1632
Hymen hath together tyed ye lusty bridegroome	CATBbc	3	1631
Lovely sheaphard (*Dialogue Febisse Endimion*)	CBbc	3	[early 1630s?]
Musicke thou Queen of soules	TTBbc	3	[early 1630s?]
Say daunce how shall wee go (*The Maskque of Vices*)	CCbc	3	[early 1630s?]
To the ladyes joy delight	CCATBbc	3	March 1632

136 *Musical Patronage in Seventeenth-Century England*

Table 23c continued

You that have been this Evenings light	CMABbc	3	1631
Why sigh you swayne (*Dialogue Nymphe and Sheaphard*)	CBbc	3	[early 1630s?]

d. Latin sacred music

Amor Jesu dulcis amor	CATBbc	3, 4	[before 1648]
Audite caeli	MATBbc	3, 4	[before 1648]
Audite gentes	ATBbc	3, 6	[1658-9]
Audivi vocem de caelo	TTbc	3, 6	[before 1648]
Beatus auctor saeculi	TTBbc	3, 6, 21 for AABbc	[before 1648]
Bone Jesu verbum Patris	CCATBbc	3, 4	[before 1648]
Caro mea vere est cibus	MABbc	3, 6 for AABbc	[before 1648]
Christo Jesu debes omnem vitam tuam	TTBbc	3, 6, 21	[before 1648]
Credo in unum Deum	AATBbc	4, 7	[*c.*1657-62]
Domine Deus salutis meae	TTbc	3, 6	[before 1648]
Domine Dominus noster	MABbc	3, 6 for AABbc	[before 1648]
Domine Jesu dilexisti me	TTBbc	3, 6	[before 1648]
Ecce dilectus meus	TTBbc	3, 6, 8, 9, 11, 12, 21	[before 1648]
Ego sum panis	CMTBbc	3, 4	[before 1648]
Erit gloria Domini in saeculum	TTbc	3, 6, 10 for CCbc, 13 for CCbc, 17 for STbc, 24 for CCbc	[before 1648]
Et ingrediar ad altare Dei (*Ps 43*)	TTbc	3, 6, 17 for STbc	[before 1648]
Et recordatus est Petrus verborum Jesus	TTBbc	3, 6	[before 1648]
Exurge quare obdormis Domine	TTBbc	3, 6, 21 for AABbc	[before 1648]
Florete flores	ATBbc	3, 5, 6	1660
Gloria in excelsis Deo	CCATBbc	3, 4	[before 1648]
Gloria Patri et Filio	ATBbc	3, 5, 6, 11	[1659-60]
Gloria Patri et Filio	AATBbc	3, 4, 7	[*c.*1649-51]
Gloria Patri qui creavit nos	ATTBbc	3, 4, 7	1651
Gloria tua manet in aeternum	ATBbc	3, 5, 6	1658/1659
Heu me miseram (*Dialogue Maria et Angelis*)	CBbc	3, 5, 6, 17 for SBbc	[before 1648]
Heu mihi Domine miserere mei	TTBbc	3, 6	[before 1648]
Hosanna filio David	TTBbc	3, 6	[before 1648]

Table 23d continued

Hosanna filio David	CCMATBbc	3, 4	[c.1660?]
Invocavi nomen tuum Domine	CCBbc	3, 5, 6	[before 1648]
Jerusalem quae occidis prophetas	CCBbc	3, 6	[before 1648]
Jesu dulcedo cordium	CATBbc	3, 4	[before 1648]
Jesu mi Dulcissime	TTBbc	3, 6	[before 1648]
Jesu rex admirabilis	ABbc	3, 5, 6	[before 1648]
Jubilate Deo	CATBbc	3, 4	[before 1648]
Jubilate Deo	AATBbc	4, 7	[c.1657-62]
Lapidabant Stephanum	TTBbc	3, 6, 21 for AABbc	[before 1648]
Magnificat	AATBbc	7	[late 1660s?]
Nescio quid amore maius	TTBbc	3, 6	[before 1648]
Nil canitur suavius	TTBbc	3, 6, 11, 12, 23	[before 1648]
Nunc dimittis	AATBbc	7	[late 1660s?]
O bone Jesu	CATBbc	3, 4	[before 1648]
O Deus meus	ATBbc	3, 6	[early-mid 1658]
O Deus meus [Pt 2 of O Domine Deus]	ATTBbc	7, 22 for MATB	[late 1660s?]
O Domine Deus (2 pts)	ATTBbc	3, 4, 22 for MATB	[c.1651-5]
O nomen Jesu	ABbc	3, 6	[before 1648]
O panis angelorum	TBbc	3, 6	[before 1648]
O piissime Domine Jesu	ATBbc	3, 6	[c.1660]
O pretiosum et admirandum convivium	ABbc	3, 6	[before 1648]
O quam dulcis	CBbc	3, 5, 6	[before 1648]
O quam gloriosum est regnum	AABbc	3, 6 for TTBbc, 21	[before 1648]
O quam iucundum	ATBbc	3, 6	August 1658
O quam iucundum	ATTBbc	3, 4, 7	1651
O quam suave	Bbc	3, 6	[before 1648]
O tu unus Deus Pater [Pt 3 of Pater de caelis]	TTBbc	3, 6	[c.1662]
Paratum cor meum	ATBbc	3, 6	November 1657
Pater bone [Pt 2 of Pater de caelis]	TTBbc	6	[c.1662]
Pater de caelis Deus [3 pts]	TTBbc	6	[c.1662]
Prior Christus dilexit nos	TTBbc	3, 6, 8 for CCBbc, 9 for CCBbc, 11, 12, 21	[before 1648]
Quando natus est	ATBbc	3, 5, 6	December 1657
Quid commisisti Jesu	CATBbc	3, 4	[before 1648]
Quid mihi est in caelo	ATBbc	3, 5, 6	October 1661

Table 23d continued

Salve caelestis curia triumphale decus	ATBbc	3, 5, 6	[c.1660]
Si diligitis me	TTbc	3, 6	[before 1648]
Sive vigilem sive dormiam	TTbc	3, 6	[before 1648]
Speciosus forma	Bbc	3, 6	[before 1648]
Te Deum laudamus (*Canticum Sanctorum Ambrosii et Augustine*)	ATTBbc	3, 4, 7	1649
Timor et tremor	TTbc	3, 6	[before 1648]
Utinam concessa mihi peccatorum venia	TTBbc	3, 6	[before 1648]
Venite exultemus	AATBbc	7	[late 1660s?]
Vere languores nostros ipse tulit	TTBbc	3, 6	[before 1648]
Visa urbe flevit super ea	TTBbc	3, 6	[before 1648]

e. English sacred music and devotional songs

Almighty God who mad'st thy blessed sonne	CCATBbc	4	[after 1662]
A musick strange	CCATBbc & insts	3, 4	1662
Awake my soule	CATBbc	4, 7, 22	[c.1657-62]
Brightest of dayes	CMATBbc	3, 4	[before 1648]
Brightest sunne how was thy light	TTBbc	3, 6	[before 1648]
Bussie tyme this day	CCATBbc	3, 4	[before 1648]
Glory be to the Lambe [*Pt 3 of* See the word]	ATBbc	3, 6	(March-April 1662)
Glory to God on high (*Morning Hymne*)	ATBbc	3, 6	May 1652
Glory to God on high	CATBbc	3, 7	[c.1651-5]
Great and marvelous are thy workes	CATBbc	7, 22	[late 1660s?]
Harke sheapard swaynes	CCATBbc	3, 4	[before 1648]
Hear my prayer (*Psalme 39*)	TTBbc	3, 6	[before 1648]
He beheld the citty	CATBbc	7	December 1675
Holy, holy, holy Lord	CATBbc	3, 7	[c.1651-5]
How wretched is the state you all are in	CATBbc	4, 7, 22	[c.1657-62]
In the midst of life	AATBbc	3, 4, 7, 15	October 1657
Looke upp all eyes	CCATBbc	3, 4	[before 1648]
Prayse the Lord O my soule (*104 Ps*)	Bbc	3, 6	[late 1650s?]

George Jeffreys 139

Table 23e continued

Prayse the Lord O my soule (*Psalme 104*)	CCBbc	3, 6	[before 1648]
Responses [Communion Service]	CATB	3	[*c*.1651-5]
Ryse hart thy Lord is rysen	CCATBbc	3, 4	[before 1648]
See, see the word is incarnate [*3 pts*]	ATBbc	3, 6	March-April 1662
Shew me thy wayes O Lord [*Pt 2* of Unto thee]	TTBbc	3, 6	[before 1648]
Singe unto the Lord	TTBbc	3, 6, 8, 11, 12, 21	[before 1648]
The Lord in thy adversity regard thy cry (*Psalme 20*)	CMATBbc	3, 4	[before 1648]
The pascall lambe [*Pt 2* of See the word]	ATBbc	3, 6	(March-April 1662)
Turne thee againe O Lord God of hosts	MATBbc	3, 4, 7 for AATB, 22	1648
Turn thou us good Lord	ATTBbc	3, 4, 7, 22 for MATB	1655
Unto thee O Lord (*Psalme 25*) [*2 pts*]	TTBbc	3, 6, 21 for AABbc	[before 1648]
What praise can reach thy clemency	AATBbc	3, 4, 15	[Oct. 1657-Aug. 1658]
Whisper it easily	CCATBbc	3, 4	[before 1648]
With notes that are both loud and sweet	BBbc	2, 3, 14, 17	[late 1650s?]

f. Doubtful works

Euge serve bone (CTBbc): anonymous in *Ob* Mus. Sch. C 11 and *Och* Mus. 749-9, but apparently attributed - to 'Mr Geofryes' - in *Ob* Mus. Sch. E 451, p. 79 (bc only; see Part II, MS XXX). The implied attribution must, however, be questioned in light of the fact that the motet does not appear in any of Jeffreys' autograph manuscripts.

My song shall be always (8vv): attributed to 'Jeffries' in *Lcm* 1045-51. This is most likely Matthew Jeffreys (*fl. c.*1590): the contrapuntal writing compares well with Matthew Jeffreys' anthems in *Lbl* Add. 29,372-7 (Myriell's *Tristitiae Remedium*), *Och* Mus. 56-60 ('Fanshawe' partbooks) and *Och* Mus. 1220-4 (Oxford, Christ Church Cathedral partbooks).

Table 23f concluded

We knowledge thee (Te Deum in F): 'Mr Jeffreys in fa ut', pp. 76-8 in *Och* Mus. 1246, the sole surviving partbook (Second Tenor) from a set copied by various Christ Church musicians in the late seventeenth century (including Goodson, Lowe, Estwick, Husbands, Aldrich, Withey, Hull and Kelway); the Te Deum was copied by the main anonymous scribe. 'Mr Jeffreys' is unlikely to be George Jeffreys as the piece does not appear in any of his autograph manuscripts; possibly by Christopher Jeffreys?

The following two-voice pieces, misattributed to Jeffreys in *Lcm* 660 (an 18th-century manuscript), are by Richard Dering: 'Ardens est cor meum', 'Conceptio tua Dei', 'Gaudent in caelis', 'Gratias tibi Deus', 'Justus cor suum tradidit', 'O Domine Jesu Christe', 'O donna troppo' and 'Sancta et immaculata virginitas'; the pieces were apparently copied from *Och* Mus. 878-80 which is annotated 'A Collection of Songs by Jeffries' (see Chapter Five).

Jeffreys' lifetime rather than subsequent ones (the present binding probably dates from about 1849 when Thomas Oliphant presented the manuscript to the British Museum). The seventeenth-century binder numbered the first and last folios of each gathering (1-2, 3-4, etc.) to ensure the correct ordering of the pieces;[65] that the binder felt that this was necessary probably indicates that a considerable amount of music had already been copied. Jeffreys also appears to have instructed the binder to incorporate gatherings of unused ruled paper in certain places so that further copies could be added in a systematic way.[66] Only one gathering in the manuscript (the one beginning on f. 171 and extending to f. 176b) does not contain the binder's marks. This gathering, which consists of paper with a Pot GRO watermark,[67] was inserted between the binder's marks 43 and 44 and provides evidence of the date of the original binding. The gathering contains the four-voice anthem 'Turn thou us good Lord' (ff. 172-6) which is dated 1655; if the manuscript had been bound after this date the gathering would have been incorporated into the binder's scheme. The paper used in this added gathering was not the

---

[65] There is an error in the binder's markings at the gathering 11-[12] as the final number is also marked 11: the sequence of odd and even numbers thereafter is reversed (12-13, 14-15, etc.).

[66] It is noteworthy that, with the exception of 'Mottects of 2. pts' (f. 73^v), the section-headings of the sacred music are on the first folio of a gathering: 'Mottects a 1 voc' (f. 60), 'Mottects of 3 parts English and Lattyn' (f. 106^v), 'Songs of 4. Parts For the Church' (f. 177), and 'Songs Mottects of 5. Parts' (f. 226). Perhaps there were four separate volumes of pieces for one and two voices, three voices, four voices, and five and six voices before they were all bound together to form the present scorebook.

[67] Watermark No. 9; see Part II, MS I. Watermark No. 9, along with Nos. 1, 3-8 and 11, is represented by a pair of marks (a & b): the product of the paper-maker's system of using two moulds at each vat.

usual ready-ruled paper: the stave lines were ruled individually by hand and, as Robert Thompson has noted, the same paper appears in Jeffreys' letters to Lady Hatton of 1649.[68] Therefore the score was probably bound around 1650.[69]

Jeffreys appears to have copied the four-part music in British Library Add. MS 10,338 in the following order: having filled up the manuscript's section allocated for 'Songs of 4. Parts For the Church' (beginning on f. 177 with 'Turne thee againe', dated 1648, and extending to the Communion Service responses on f. 225), he then began copying the four-voice motet 'O Domine Deus' on blank paper at the end of the three-voice section (f. 165^v). Unfortunately he misjudged how much space he would require and was forced to add a gathering of paper from his supply of ordinary writing paper; the final two pages of 'O Domine Deus' and the whole of 'Turn thou us O good Lord' were copied on this added gathering of Pot GRO paper. After this Jeffreys returned to the blank pages at the end of the three-voice section and, after leaving some space for more three-part pieces, copied the four-voice anthem 'In the midst of life' composed 'in the tyme of [Jeffreys'] sicknes[s] Octob. 1657' (ff. 160^v-4^v). Finally he copied 'What praise can reach thy clemency' (ff. 153^v-9^v), again using some of the remaining blank pages after the three-part music; this anthem was copied between October 1657, the date of 'In the midst of life', and August 1658, the date of the last motet in the original three-voice section of the manuscript (see below). The order of the copying of the four-part pieces in Jeffreys' scorebook is summarised in Table 24.

It should be noted at this point that the last mentioned anthem, 'What praise can reach thy clemency', is annotated 'This song being blotted & Altered, I have transposed into my other Score Book 1665' (f. 154), and likewise 'In the midst of life' is followed by the note 'This Song being blotted I have transposed to my other booke' (f. 160^v). Oxford, Bodleian Library Tenbury MS 1285 (see Part II, MS XLI) contains scores to both 'In the midst of life' and 'What praise can reach thy clemency'; this would appear to be all that remains of Jeffreys' 'other Score Book' (it was certainly once part of a larger manuscript as there are remnants of a pagination system: 111-128). The proposed chronology of the copying of the four-part pieces in Add. MS 10,338 is confirmed by an examination of another set of manuscripts copied by George Jeffreys: British Library Add. MSS 17,816 and 30,829-30 (see Part II, MS II). This incomplete set of three partbooks contains sacred music in English and Latin by Jeffreys for four to six voices and basso continuo (the Cantus I, Cantus II and Basso

---

[68] *Lbl* Add. 29,550, ff. 91-3^v (see Thompson (1988), 206; and (1989), 324).
[69] Jeffreys' copies of pieces dated 1651 and after are more untidy than those copied before binding; this was perhaps due to the difficulties of writing in a large newly (and tightly?) bound volume.

Table 24 A Proposed Chronology of the Copying of the Four-Part Pieces in British Library Add. MS 10,338

Title	Scoring	Folios in Add. 10,338	Date	Order in Add. 17,816/ 30,829-30
Turne thee againe	MATBbc	177-80^v	1648	12
Quid com[m]isisti Jesu	CATBbc	181-2^v	[before 1648]*	1
Ego sum panis	CMTBbc	183-5^v	[before 1648]	4
Jubilate Deo	CATBbc	187-90	[before 1648]	5
Amor Jesu dulcis amor	CATBbc	190^v-2^v	[before 1648]	3
O bone Jesu	CATBbc	193-6	[before 1648]	2
Audite caeli	MATBbc	196^v-9	[before 1648]	6
Jesu dulcedo cordium	CATBbc	199^v-203	[before 1648]	7
Te Deum laudamus	ATTBbc	204-15	1649	8
Gloria Patri et Filio	AATBbc	215^v-16^v	[c.1649-51]	9
O quam iucundum	ATTBbc	217-21	1651	10
Gloria Patri qui creavit nos	ATTBbc	221^v-23	1651	11
Glory be to God on high	CATB	223^v-4^v	[c.1651-5]	
Holy, holy, holy Lord	CATB	225	[c.1651-5]	
Communion service responses	CATB	225	[c.1651-5]	
O domine Deus	ATTBbc	165^v-71^v	[c.1651-5]	13
Turn thou us good Lord	ATTBbc	172-6	1655	14
In the midst of life	AATBbc	160-4^v	October 1657	15
What praise can reach thy clemency	AATBbc	153^v-9^v	[Oct. 1657- Aug. 1658]	16

* See below for an explanation of the dating.

Continuo partbooks are lacking). The surviving partbooks are the only Jeffreys autographs which have retained their original bindings, gilded white leather, and the paper is of superior quality to the scorebook.[70] The physical evidence offered by the partbooks is entirely consistent with a date of origin in the early 1640s. (Jeffreys' annotation on the front cover of Add. MS 17,816 reads 'Bassus 38 [or 30?]'; one is tempted to speculate that it is a date: '[16]38'.) All except five of the thirty-two pieces in the partbooks also appear in the scorebook Add. MS 10,338 and, as we shall see, the order of

---

[70] The watermark is an encircled peacock; see Thompson (1988), Watermark XVI(?); and Heawood (1950), Watermark 174 (Venice 1628). A very similar watermark appears in *Och* Mus. 612-13, the partbooks of the 'Hatton Set' of consort music copied by John Lilly (see Chapter Three).

the pieces in the partbooks is significant for an understanding of the structure of the score. Robert Thompson has noted that most of Jeffreys' music dated between 1648 and 1662 avoids using the treble voice; the fact that some music in the partbooks Add. MSS 17,816 and 30,829-30 calls for one or even two trebles suggests a pre-1648 date for these pieces: 'Probably not only the undated four-voice motets but also the undated five-voice works were composed well before 1648 and included in these fine partbooks at a time when such music might have been performable, perhaps during the early years of the Civil War when Jeffreys was at Oxford.'[71] Dr Thompson further suggests that the new pieces, dated 1649 to 1657 in the score, were added to the partbooks in chronological order culminating with the six-voice 'Hosanna filio David' (perhaps celebrating the Restoration) and 'A musick strange' (dated 1662 in Add. MS 10,338).[72]

To return to the earlier pieces in the partbooks Add. MSS 17,816 and 30,829-30: the order of pieces 6-11 and 13-16 in the partbooks coincides with the chronological order of copying in the scorebook as outlined in Table 24. It was suggested above that the first seven pieces in the partbooks were copied before 1648; why, then, does this same group of pieces (in a slightly different order) appear in the score following 'Turne thee againe' which is dated 1648? 'Turne thee againe' would appear to be out of chronological sequence in Add. MS 10,338. Robert Thompson has offered a convincing explanation. He notes that the seventh piece in the partbook Add. MS 17,816 ('Jesu dulcedo') is annotated 'Finis Geo: Jeffreys' implying that the first seven motets were copied as a series; he also points out that all except one of these seven pieces employs the treble voice, whereas the pieces copied after 1648 conspicuously avoid the treble voice (see above).[73] Dr Thompson has shown that the partbook versions of a number of the motets and anthems differ in certain respects from the score. A detailed comparison of the readings indicates that the first seven motets in the partbooks were the copy-sources for the same seven pieces in the score (starting on f. 181 with 'Quid comisisti Jesu'); but the remainder of the concordant four-part pieces ('Turne thee againe', 'Te Deum' and the subsequent dated and undated compositions) were copied from the score into the partbooks. It appears that in 1648, when Jeffreys decided to bring together his complete works, he not only incorporated various earlier scores, but also decided to recopy a number of pieces composed earlier in his career (presumably because the manuscripts - now lost - were worn or damaged). The newly composed anthem 'Turne thee againe' was placed first in his section of 'Songs of 4. Parts For the Church' (for the reason outlined below), and he then recopied seven motets from his Civil War partbooks (Add. MSS 17,816 and 30,829-30). Jeffreys left some provision for later additions to his scorebook but, as

---

[71] Thompson (1989), 329.
[72] Ibid.
[73] Thompson (1988), 208-14; and ibid. (1989), 326-30.

we have seen, he finished up composing far more than he had anticipated and was forced to compromise his originally intended order. It seems that around 1650, when the manuscript was bound, he was not expecting to have to compose much music in the future. We should remember that the King had recently been executed and that the Anglican Rite had been discontinued. In this context it is not surprising that a Royalist composer should set part of Psalm 80, 'Turne thee againe', and give it pride of place in his manuscript. In the words of Robert Thompson: 'the text of the anthem... reflects the personal, political and religious misfortunes suffered by Jeffreys and other Anglicans after the Civil War':[74]

> Turne thee againe, O Lord God of Hosts: shew the light of thy countenance upon us, and we shall be whole.
> O Lord God of Hosts: how long wilt thou be angry with thy people that prayeth? Thou givest them plenteousness of tears to drink.
> Turne thee againe...
> Thou hast brought a vine out of Egypt: thou hast cast out the heathen, and planted it.
> Thou madest room for it: and when it had taken root, it filled the land.
> The hills were covered with the shadow of it: and the boughs thereof were like the goodly cedar-trees.
> Why hast thou broken down her hedge: that all they that go by pluck off her grapes?
> Turne thee againe...

The period 1648-56 must have been a deeply depressing time for an ardent Royalist such as Jeffreys. By 1657 things seemed to have improved for Jeffreys (due either to a resigned acceptance of the Puritan rule, or the first hints of the possible end of the Commonwealth and the restoration of the King?) and there followed a period of intense musical activity. It was noted in the previous section that this coincided with Baron Hatton's return from France; it also coincided with Jeffreys' recovery from a serious illness (mentioned in his scorebook on folio 164). Twenty-eight of Jeffreys' compositions date from the years 1657-62 (see Table 23), soon after the period of Jeffreys' copying - or recopying - of much of the Italian music in British Library Add. MS 31,479 and Madrigal Society MSS G 55-9 (see pages 125-31 above). Jeffreys' renewed interest in composition post-1657 is reflected in the three-voice section of his scorebook, British Library Add. MS 10,338: sixteen three-part works were added to the scorebook between November 1657 and about 1662. The first four of these pieces ('Paratum cor meum' through to 'O quam iucundum', ff. 142ᵛ-52) were copied after a long sequence of twenty-seven three-voice anthems and motets dating from before 1648 (see below); at the end of 'O quam iucundum' (f. 152) Jeffreys

---

[74] Thompson (1989), 330.

had just two blank pages before the start of the last copied four-voice anthem 'What praise can reach thy clemency' (ff. 153^v-9^v), which must date from between October 1657 (the date of the previous four-voice anthem 'In the midst of life') and August 1658 (the date of the three-voice 'O quam iucundum'). The final folio of 'O quam iucundum' is annotated 'Mind that some of these last Threes are placed before at ye beginning & some before the 2 pt songs' (f. 152) which is reinforced in a marginal note: 'M[i]nd That some of these later 3 parts are placed at ye beginning of ye 3 parts. And others of these 3s. are placed next the songs of one voice, for want of roome.' Sure enough, seven three-part pieces can be found after the two-voice section, starting with 'Audite gentes' on folio 91^v (long before the 'official' beginning of the 'Mottects of 3 parts English and Lattyn' at f. 106^v); four three-part pieces appear after the solo-voice section, starting with 'Quid mihi est in cælo' on folio 64^v; and finally the incomplete 'O tu unus Deus Pater' (ff. 57^v-9) was copied on spare paper before the start of 'Mottects a 1 voc'. The chronology of the copying of the three-part pieces is summarised in Table 25.

The one piece that appears to be out of chronological sequence is 'Glory to God on high', a setting of the Communion service text, which is annotated 'Composed at Mr Gunning[']s motion May 1652'; the piece, however, appears after motets copied in 1660 or thereabouts. It must be assumed that Jeffreys' annotation refers to the date of composition and that he decided to recopy the piece into his scorebook between 1660 and October 1661 (the date of 'Quid mihi est in cælo', the next three-part piece to be copied). 'Mr Gunning' is presumably Peter Gunning (1614-84), the prominent Royalist divine, who was mentioned in Chapter One in relation to Christopher Hatton's religious circle; a possible context for the performance of Jeffreys' 'Glory to God on high', following Gunning's commission in May 1652, is examined below.

The ten five-voice pieces (one with instruments) and the single six-voice motet in British Library Add. MS 10,338 were mentioned above in the discussion concerning their single concordant source: the partbooks British Library Add. MSS 17,816 and 30,829-30. It was suggested that the six-voice 'Hosanna filio David' (ff. 266^v-70) was written to celebrate the Restoration (it is certainly a late addition to the scorebook as it is in Jeffreys' 'late hand': the slightly scruffier handwriting of the post-binding copies) and 'A musick strange', for five voices, instruments and basso continuo (ff. 270^v-4^v, the last piece in the manuscript), is dated 1662. The other nine five-voice works (beginning with 'Gloria in excelsis Deo' on f. 226) are all pre-1648 pieces. There remain three solo-voice pieces and fourteen two-voice pieces to consider. Only two of these pieces are in Jeffreys' 'late hand': 'Prayse the Lord O my soule' (ff. 62-3^v) for solo bass and basso continuo, and 'With notes that are both loud and sweet' for two

Table 25 A Proposed Chronology of the Copying of the Three-Part Pieces in British Library Add. MS 10,338

Title	Scoring	Folios	Date
Unto thee O Lord *Pt 1*	TTBbc	106^v-7	[before 1648]
Shew me thy wayes O Lord *Pt 2*	TTBbc	107^v-8	[before 1648]
Hear my prayer	TTBbc	108^v-9^v	[before 1648]
Singe unto the Lord	TTBbc	110-11	[before 1648]
Prayse the Lord O my soule	CCBbc	111^v-12	[before 1648]
Brightest sunne how was thy light	TTBbc	112^v-14	[before 1648]
Exurge quare obdormis Domine	TTBbc	114^v-15^v	[before 1648]
O quam gloriosum est Regnum	AABbc	116-17	[before 1648]
Lapidabant Stephanum	TTBbc	117^v-18^v	[before 1648]
Et recordatus est Petrus	TTBbc	119^{r-v}	[before 1648]
Beatus auctor seculi	TTBbc	120-1	[before 1648]
Jesu mi dulcissime	TTBbc	121^v-3	[before 1648]
Vere languores nostros ipse tulit	TTBbc	123^v-4	[before 1648]
Nescio quid amore maius	TTBbc	124^v-5	[before 1648]
Utinam concessa mihi peccatorum	TTBbc	125^v-6	[before 1648]
Nil canitur suavius	TTBbc	126^v-7	[before 1648]
Ecce dilectus meus	TTBbc	127^v-8	[before 1648]
Prior Christus dilexit nos	TTBbc	128^v-9	[before 1648]
Domine Jesu dilexisti me	TTBbc	129^v	[before 1648]
Christo Jesu debes omnem vitam tuam	TTBbc	131^{r-v}	[before 1648]
Hosanna filio David	TTBbc	132-3	[before 1648]
Heu mihi Domine miserere mei	TTBbc	133^v-4	[before 1648]
Visa urbe flevit super ea	TTBbc	134^v-5	[before 1648]
Invocavi nomen tuum domine	CCBbc	135^v-7^v	[before 1648]
Jerusalem quae occidis prophetas	CCBbc	138^{r-v}	[before 1648]
Domine dominus noster	MABb	139-40^v	[before 1648]
Caro mea vere est cibus	MABb	141-2	[before 1648]
Paratum cor meum	ATBbc	142^v-5	November 1657
Quando natus est	ATBbc	145^v-7^v	December 1657
O Deus meus Deus et omnia	ATBbc	148-50	[early-mid 1658]
O quam iucundum	ATBbc	150^v-2	August 1658
Audite gentes	ATBbc	91^v-3^v	[1658-9]
Gloria tua manet in aeternum	ATBbc	94-8	1658/1659
Gloria Patri et Filio	ATB	96^v	[1659-60]
Florete flores	ATBbc	97-9	1660
O piissime domine Jesu	ATBbc	99^v-101	[*c.*1660]
Salve cælestis curia	ATBbc	101^v-3a^v	[*c.*1660]
Glory to God on high	ATBbc	104^v-6	May 1652
Quid mihi est in cælo	ATBbc	64^v-7	October 1661
See see the word is incarnate *Pt 1*	ATBbc	67^v-8^v	March-April 1662
The pascall lambe *Pt 2*	ATBbc	69-71	(March-April 1662)
Glory be to the lambe *Pt 3*	ATBbc	71^v-3	(March-April 1662)
O tu unus Deus Pater	TTBbc	57^v-9	[*c.*1662]

basses and basso continuo (ff. 89-91), the last pieces of the sections for 'Mottects a 1 voc' and 'Mottects of 2. pts' respectively. These two pieces probably date from the late 1650s; this proposed date finds some support in a possible identification of 'Mr Pett' who is named at the head of 'With notes that are both loud and sweet' (f. 89): according to Anthony Wood, a lawyer called Peter Pett entertained the violinist Davis Mell at Oxford in 1657.[75] Robert Thompson has speculated that this Peter Pett was the second bass singer available to Jeffreys in the late 1650s, for whom Jeffreys composed 'With notes that are both loud and sweet', and was also possibly the reason for the copying (recopying?) of Tarquinio Merula's 'Fontes et omnia' (also for two basses and basso continuo)[76] as the last motet in the two-voice section of British Library Add. MS 31,479 (see Part II, MS IX).[77] The first two solo-voice motets and the first thirteen two-voice pieces in the scorebook Add. 10,338 were all probably composed before 1648; add to this the twenty-seven three-voice, seven four-voice, and nine five-voice pieces and we have a total of forty-eight Italianate *concertato* anthems and motets composed by Jeffreys before 1648.

The evidence offered by the paper-types in British Library Add. MS 10,338 supports the suggested chronology of copying of Jeffreys' sacred music. Here, again, Robert Thompson must be acknowledged as the authority on paper-types and watermarks in Jeffreys' manuscripts.[78] The majority of the paper in the scorebook Add. MS 10,338 contains one of three watermarks: Pots lettered GPO, PI or POO (see Part II, MS I: Watermarks 3-5, Pots 1-3); twenty-three of the total thirty-five gatherings are made up of this paper (ignoring the occasional added sheet). All the pieces which have been labelled as 'before 1648' were copied on this Pot paper, and the only dated works found in these sections are later additions: the four-voice pieces copied back into the three-part section (ff. 153^v-64^v) and the 'later 3 parts' (ff. 142^v-52, 91^v-106 and 64^v-73) dated 1657-62. The paper with watermarks of Pots lettered GPO and POO are related by a common system of stave-rulings; gatherings of Pot PI paper alternate with gatherings of Pots GPO and POO paper within the same sequence of music (see, for example, the 'Mottects of 3 parts' section, ff. 106^v-53); and in one instance a sheet of Pot PI paper appears as the outer sheet of a gathering otherwise consisting of Pot POO paper (ff. [29d]-[32d]). This indicates that the Pots GPO, PI and POO papers are roughly contemporary; the watermark evidence therefore supports the suggestion that the sections of sacred music for one and two voices, three voices, and for five and six voices existed as separate - but contemporary - entities before the addition of extra paper and

---

[75] Clark ed. (1891), i, 241-2. Pett, a Fellow of All Souls' College from 1648, was admitted to Gray's Inn in 1658; see Foster (1889), 285.
[76] From T. Merula, *Il Primo Libro de Motetti* Op. 6 (Venice, 1624).
[77] See Thompson (1988), 424 & 428-9.
[78] Ibid., *passim*; and Thompson (1989).

binding in about 1650. This is further clarified by an examination of the section of 'Songs of 4. Parts For the Church' (ff. 177-225ᵛ) which, it was postulated, was copied after 1648: the paper here is entirely different from that in the 'original' sections described above.

The gatherings in the four-part section of the manuscript consist primarily of three types of paper with the following watermarks: Posthorn lettered G DVRAND (Part II, MS I: Watermark 11),[79] Pot lettered DO (Watermark 8, Pot 6), and Pot lettered RDP (Watermark 6, Pot 4).[80] Paper with watermarks of Pots DO and RDP does not appear within gatherings of the earlier papers (those with watermarks of Pots GPO, PI and POO), and the Posthorn paper only appears amongst the early Pot papers as later additions: folios 72 and 157 are singletons (half sheets) added to Pot PI and POO gatherings respectively.[81] The Posthorn G DVRAND and Pot DO papers are linked by a common system of stave-rulings and are thus probably contemporary. The watermark Pot DO is very similar to, and therefore probably contemporary with, that of the Pot lettered GRO in folios 171-[176b]ᵛ - the gathering added after binding which consisted of ordinary writing paper also used in letters dated 1649 (see above). The other paper-type found in the four-part section of British Library Add. MS 10,338 has the watermark of a large Pot lettered RDP. This mark appears at the end of the pages originally allotted to four-voice music which includes pieces dated 1649 and 1651;[82] the watermark has all the characteristics of Pot watermarks of the 1650s and compares well with those in dated manuscripts of the period (such as Oxford, Bodleian Library Mus. Sch. MS D 220 which is dated 1654, and British Library Add. MS 10,337 first section, dated 1657).[83] The evidence indicates that the Posthorn G DVRAND, Pot DO, Pot GRO and Pot RDP papers are all roughly contemporary and date from between 1648 and the early 1650s.[84]

---

[79] The Durand mill was near Maisoncelles-le-Jourdain in Normandy; see C.M. Briquet, *Les Filigranes*, ed. A.H. Stevenson (Amsterdam, 1968), supplementary material, 35.

[80] A single sheet with a Pillars watermark (Part II, MS I: Watermark 2, Pillars 2) makes an appearance as the outer folios of the first gathering of the four-part section (ff. 177 & 184). Pillars watermarks do not tend to appear in manuscript dating from after 1648; the single sheet of Pillars 2 paper in *Lbl* Add. 10,338 was therefore probably taken from a residual supply of older spare paper which Jeffreys had lying around. Also a singleton (half sheet), added to the second gathering of the four-part section (f. 186), has a Foolscap watermark (Watermark 12, Foolscap 1), which most likely dates from the 1660s (see Thompson (1989), 325); this sheet was therefore a later addition to the four-part section of the manuscript.

[81] Folio 157 does not contain a watermark but the stave-ruling suggest that it is a half-sheet of the Posthorn paper (see Thompson (1988), 195; and (1989), 324).

[82] 'Te Deum laudamus': 1649 (ff. 204-15); and 'Gloria Patri qui creavit nos': 1651 (ff. 221ᵛ-3).

[83] See Thompson (1988), 221-6, 230-50 & Watermarks XIII-XIV. *Ob* Mus. Sch. D 220 is the bass partbook of a large anthology of two-part instrumental music, and *Lbl* Add. 10,337 first section: 'Elizabeth Roger hir virginall booke'.

[84] The following two watermarks also appear on extension slips pasted to ff. 246 and 264 respectively: Foolscap (Part II, MS I: Watermark 13, Foolscap 2); and Pot lettered DI (Watermark 10, Pot 8). Both watermarks are likely to date from the 1660s; see Thompson (1989), 324-5.

The pot watermarks of the original gatherings of the scorebook (Pots lettered GPO, PI and POO) are slightly smaller than those lettered DO, GRO and RDP, and, following the general rule that the smaller the pot, the earlier the paper,[85] it can safely be assumed that the Pots GPO, PI and POO watermarks are all pre-1648. A further clue to the date of the 'early' pot watermarks comes in the eighth gathering of the scorebook (ff. 53-59a^v) where paper with a Pot lettered POO (Part II, MS I: Watermark 5, Pot 3) is combined with two sheets of paper with a Pot ID watermark (Watermark 7, Pot 5). The Pot ID paper appears in the first sections of the partbooks Add. MS 31,434 copied by Stephen Bing (see Part II, MS VI); it was shown in the last chapter that this manuscript probably dates from the years 1643-6. It seems likely that the paper with watermarks of Pots GPO, PI and POO also date from this period. In this case Jeffreys' forty-eight Italianate *concertato* anthems and motets (described cautiously in Table 23 only as 'before 1648') could have been written for performance at the Oxford Court in 1642-6, and may even date back earlier to the period around 1638 when Hatton was purchasing Italian music from Robert Martin. The significance of such an early date for so many of Jeffreys' compositions is considered below, and a possible context for the performance of such music at Oxford is suggested in the following chapter. A *raison d'être* for Jeffreys' post-1648 sacred music is more difficult to find. Perhaps some of the anthems and motets were written for private devotional services at Kirby Hall (the distinction between liturgical and non-liturgical devotional music is certainly not made apparent in Jeffreys' manuscripts). It was noted in Chapter Two that, although there was no chapel, there was an organ at Kirby Hall: Jeffreys' small-scale *concertato* music (most of which - by the 1650s - avoided the treble voice) would have been most suitable for performance with only a handful of voices and a chamber organ. It is equally possible that Jeffreys' music was performed in London. Hatton House, Holborn had been commandeered by Parliamentarian soldiers in early 1649, and it is therefore unlikely that any Anglican worship took place in the chapel there;[86] however, despite the fact that High Church worship was officially banned, we know that Peter Gunning did manage to maintain such services in the chapel of Exeter House on the north side of the Strand. (Lady Hatton's arrest at the 1657 Christmas Day service at the Exeter House Chapel was described in Chapter One; see pages 18-19 above.) Perhaps Jeffreys' post-1648 music was written for performance at the Exeter House services? It was noted above that, according to an annotation on folio 106 of British Library Add. MS 10,338, Jeffreys was asked by Gunning, in May 1652, to compose the music for the

---

[85] Ibid., 325.

[86] Hatton House was inherited by Baron Hatton in 1646 on the death of Elizabeth Newport-Hatton (see Figure 1). Two of Jeffreys' letters to Lady Hatton of 5 and 8 February 1649 (*Lbl* Add. 29,550, ff. 91-3) describe his negotiations with Colonel Barkstead, the commander of soldiers billeted at Hatton House; see Thompson (1989), 330.

Communion text 'Glory to God'. Both Gunning and Jeffreys were employed by the Hatton family and both had a common background of Royalist service at Oxford: a collaboration between the two at the unofficial High Church services in the Exeter House Chapel would therefore seem likely.[87]

Before leaving Add. MS 10,338, the first section of the scorebook must be examined. The first fifty-six folios of the manuscript contain Jeffreys' earliest surviving compositions: his seven instrumental fantasias, thirteen Italian madrigals, and songs for stage plays (such as Thomas Randolph's *The Maskque of Vices* and Peter Hausted's *The Rivall Friends*). The fantasias and the English songs, which most likely date from the 1630s, show that Jeffreys was well versed in the native English musical tradition; and his earliest experiments with an Italianate style of writing are revealed in the madrigals. The first two gatherings of the scorebook, which contain the six 'Fantasies of 3. Parts for ye Violls and the Virginall', the 'Fantazia of 2 pts to the Organ For the violin', and nine three-part Italian madrigals (without basso continuo), are made up of paper with a watermark of Pillars lettered DI (Part II, MS I: Watermark 1, Pillars 1); this paper can also be found in the last section of Christ Church Mus. 880: basso continuo parts to Gesualdo's Madrigal Books I, II and IV copied by Stephen Bing (see the following chapter). Robert Thompson noted that the two gatherings probably once formed a separate volume as a worm bore passes through the gatherings from folio 4 to 18, but does not extend into the paper on either side;[88] he has also demonstrated that the Pillars ID watermark is probably contemporary with the Pot GPO, PI and POO paper described above, and can be dated as *circa* 1640.[89]

The three-part fantasias in British Library Add. MS 10,338 are concordant with a number of other manuscripts. The first four fantasias also appear, as later additions, in Christ Church Mus. 459-62, a set of four books copied in part by Thomas Myriell (see pages 64-6 above). The first stage of copying in these partbooks must have taken place between 1616 and 1625,[90] and the four Jeffreys fantasias were probably added in the early 1630s (by an unidentified scribe using an old-fashioned heavy black

---

[87] It is just possible that, until 1663, Jeffreys' liturgical music was performed in his local church in Weldon, Northamptonshire where the rector was Jeffreys' father-in-law, Thomas Mainwaring (rector from 1614 to his death in 1663). We can be certain, however, that Jeffreys' music was not performed at Weldon after 1663 for Thomas Mainwaring was replaced by John Elkin (rector 1663-81) who, according to a letter of 11 December 1679 from Jeffreys to Christopher Hatton IV, 'has still the Presbyterian itch' (*Lbl* Add. 29,557, f. 309); the animosity between Jeffreys and Elkin is apparent in a number of Jeffreys' letters of the 1670s.
[88] Thompson (1989), 319.
[89] Thompson (1988), 220; Dr Thompson notes that similar Pot and Pillars watermarks appear in *Lbl* Add. 18,940-44 which contain music for Shirley's masque *The Triumph of Time* performed in 1634.
[90] See Willetts (1968) 36-42; Willets (1972), 431-3; Monson (1977), 419-65; and Monson (1982), 5-69 *passim*.

diamond-shaped notation).[91] Robert Thompson has noted that the readings of the four three-part fantasias in the Myriell partbooks differ in a number of details from those in the autograph scorebook. The Christ Church partbooks appear to contain the earliest versions and the British Library scorebook copies represent later revisions.[92] Perhaps in the late 1630s, when his colleagues Stephen Bing and John Lilly were engaged in copying the sets of viol consort music examined in Chapter Three, Jeffreys had a renewed burst of interest in instrumental music and revised his four existing three-part fantasias, composed two more plus one for violin, bass viol and organ (an instrumental combination closely associated with the Court), and then copied them all into his manuscript reserved for consort music (which was later to become ff. 4-18^v of his composite scorebook). The instrumental pieces in British Library Add. MS 10,338 are followed by a number of blank pages which probably indicate that Jeffreys intended to compose more fantasias. That this was not realised was perhaps a result of his patron's changing interests, in the late 1630s, from court-oriented instrumental music (hence the various sets of consort music described in Chapter Three) towards Italianate vocal music (which was to be of practical use at the Oxford Court). Jeffreys' nine three-part Italian madrigals, copied at the end of the instrumental gatherings (ff. 14^v-18^v), are perhaps the first examples of his Italianate compositions. Two other facts should be noted which further link Jeffreys with the court-related instrumental repertoire of the 1630s, and demonstrate his working relationship with Stephen Bing: (*a*) Bing and Jeffreys collaborated in copying Coprario's eight fantasia-suites for two violins, bass viol and organ (Rochester, Eastman School of Music, Sibley Music Library MS ML96 L814f, fascicle 3; see page 80 above); and (*b*) Stephen Bing copied Jeffreys' six three-part fantasias in Christ Church Mus. 417-18 and 1080.

Two other manuscript sources contain Jeffreys' six three-part fantasias: Dublin, Archbishop Marsh's Library MS Z3.4.13, folios 47-59^v (see Part II, MS LXV), and Christ Church Mus. 468-72. The Marsh's Library fascicle is an autograph score bound with miscellaneous other fascicles and loose papers.[93] Its presence in Ireland is undoubtedly due to Narcissus Marsh (1638-1713), Archbishop of Armagh, who founded his library in 1704.[94] Marsh lived in Oxford from 1655-78 and we know, from his diary, that he was keenly interested in consort music and, from 1666, organised

---

[91] The appearance of music by Jeffreys in a set of partbooks connected with Thomas Myriell (albeit added at a slightly later date) is another piece of evidence to support the tentative suggestion, postulated in Chapter Three, that there is a link between the presence of Myriell manuscripts in Christ Church and Stephen Bing and/or Christopher Hatton.
[92] Thompson (1990b).
[93] See R. Charteris, 'Consort Music Manuscripts in Archbishop Marsh's Library, Dublin', *RCRMA*, xiii (1976), 31-2, 38 & 40-1; and ibid., *A Catalogue of the Printed Books on Music and Music Manuscripts in Archbishop Marsh's Library, Dublin* (Clifden, 1982), 112-18.
[94] *DNB*, xii, 1102-3.

weekly music meetings.[95] Many of the manuscripts of consort music in Dublin were collected by Marsh during his Oxford years for use at his musical gatherings. MS Z3.4.13, folios 47-59^v could have been obtained through Christopher Jeffreys, who was a student at Christ Church from about 1658 to 1666,[96] and is therefore likely to have known Marsh and may even have participated in his earliest music meetings. Jeffreys copied his fantasias stratigraphically across the inside openings of MS Z3.4.13, folios 47-59^v on paper with a grapes watermark. The paper is consistent with a copying date of 'pre-1648' and thus may be contemporary with the first section of British Library Add. MS 10,338; unfortunately a comparison of readings does not offer any further information concerning the chronology or links between the two scores.[97] The other manuscript source which contains Jeffreys' six three-part fantasias, Christ Church Mus. 468-72, appears to date from about 1660.[98] The first folio of the second partbook (Mus. 469) contains the perplexing annotation 'Geore Jeffreys 1729' [*sic*] and this has led to the unlikely dating of Jeffreys' fantasias to 1629;[99] no explanation can presently be offered for the annotation.[100]

Gatherings C to E of British Library Add. MS 10,338 (ff. 19-[32d]) contain three Italian madrigals for three voices and basso continuo, and five English secular songs or dialogues; they are copied on the same type of paper as that found in the 'early' sacred sections (Pots GPO, PI and POO) and the copying could therefore date from the early 1640s (the pieces were, however, most likely composed in the 1630s). The music contained in gatherings F and G (ff. 33-52^v) was definitely copied retrospectively: the Pot RDP paper also appears in the post-1649 four-voice section of the manuscript (ff. 194-225^v) but the annotations on folios 33, 43 and 51 (see Part II, MS I) refer to performances in 1631-2 (see pages 7-9 above).[101] The description of Richard Hatton as 'Sir' (knighted 1645),[102] and Peter Hausted

---

[95] See p. 9 of Marsh's diary (*EIRE-Dm* Z2.2.3a; Z2.2.3b is a typescript transcription); cited in Charteris (1976), 33 & 35.

[96] Christopher Jeffreys matriculated at Christ Church on 9 December 1659 - Foster (1891-2), ii, 805 - although Anthony Wood described him as the fifteenth new member of William Ellis' music meetings in Oxford in 1658: Wood (1691), i, pp. xxxiv-xxxv.

[97] *EIRE-Dm* Z3.4.13, ff. 47-59^v have a few 'ornaments' squeezed in - in Jeffreys' handwriting - at a later date than the original copying.

[98] The paper contains the watermark of a fleur-de-lys with a countermark IHS and is typical of Angoumois papers of the period *c*.1657-62; see Thompson (1988), 260-5 & 276-7. A comparison of readings suggests that *Och* Mus. 468-72 may have been copied from *EIRE-Dm* Z3.4.13, ff. 47-59^v.

[99] Aston: (1969), 772 & 775; (1972-3), 107; and *New Grove*, ix, 584 & 586.

[100] Jeffreys' grandson, the poet George Jeffreys (1678-1755), could possibly have been responsible for the annotation but, as David Pinto has noted (in correspondence with the present writer), he was educated at Trinity College, Cambridge and had no connections with Oxford.

[101] Hausted's *The Rivall Friends* was performed on 19 March 1632.

[102] Metcalfe (1885), 202.

as 'Dr' (created Doctor of Divinity in 1642),[103] is confirmation that these are retrospective copies and that '1631' records the date of composition. The last three pages of gathering G (ff. 51^v-2^v) contain the beginning of Jeffreys' madrigal (or secular cantata) 'Felice pastorella' for five voices with instrumental 'Symphonies'. Gathering H contains the conclusion to 'Felice pastorella' (ff. 53-6) and, after a number of blank folios,[104] an incomplete copy of a late three-voice motet: 'O tu unus Deus Pater' (ff. 57^v-9). This last 'secular' gathering of the scorebook (the sacred section begins on f. 60) consists of two sheets of Pot ID paper and two sheets of Pot POO paper (ignoring the unruled ff. [56a]-[56f] which are probably later additions). Both these papers are 'pre-1648' types: the Pot POO paper appears in various 'early' sacred sections of Add. 10,338, and the Pot ID paper is also found in the first sections of the partbooks that make up British Library Add. 31,434 (see Part II, MS VI). The fact that 'Felice pastorella' was begun on 'post-1648' paper and completed on 'pre-1648' paper indicates that Jeffreys had a supply of residual paper which he could dip into when required; it is possible that 'Felice pastorella' was, like the other Italian secular works, composed in the 1630s and therefore is also a retrospective copy.

Finally mention must be made of Jeffreys' other autograph manuscripts: British Library Add. MS 29,282, Royal College of Music MSS 920 and 920A, and Oxford, Bodleian Library Tenbury MS 1010. The earliest of these is probably the Royal College of Music MS 920 (Part II, MS XVII), a set of four partbooks. The manuscript contains a selection of forty-five of Jeffreys' sacred works for one to three voices and basso continuo; all but two pieces also appear in the scorebook British Library Add. MS 10,338. An annotation in the scorebook gives a clue to the date of the partbooks: on folio 142^v at the head of the three-voice motet 'Paratum cor meum' is the annotation: 'Some small things altered in this song since it was transcribed into my Bookes'. The annotation appears to refer to the Royal College of Music MS 920 and, as 'Paratum cor meum' is dated 'Nov: [16]57' on folio 145 of the scorebook, the Royal College partbooks can therefore be dated as after November 1657. The physical evidence offered by the partbooks supports this proposed dating: no watermark is visible in the three vocal partbooks but the basso continuo book is made up of paper with the watermark of a Cardinals' Hat lettered GR. It was demonstrated above (see pages 126-7) that this paper, which is also found in Jeffreys' manuscript partbooks of Italian music, dates from the 1650s.[105] The Royal College of

---

[103] Venn & Venn (1922), Part 1, ii, 332.
[104] Folios 56^v & 57 are ruled but no music has been entered. Folios [56a]-[56f]^v are blank and unruled, and - as the paper is unlike any other in the manuscript - may be later additions (they do contain Warren's original ink pagination).
[105] That the basso continuo book consists of different paper from the vocal partbooks is perplexing. It is just possible that sections of the partbooks are earlier than has been suggested, and that the two-voice pieces and the first six three-voice pieces in the vocal partbooks were copied in the 1640s (it is unfortunate that the binding is too tight to allow for a detailed

Music partbooks appear to be the product of Jeffreys' period of great musical activity towards the end of the 1650s, and the transcribing of his music into partbooks indicates that there was a practical purpose to his copying: perhaps Christopher Hatton's return from France heralded a renewed interest in performance either at Kirby Hall or in London?

The partbooks which make up British Library Add. MS 29,282 (Part II, MS IV) are probably roughly contemporary with the Royal College of Music MS 920. This manuscript (four partbooks bound together as a single volume) contains motets for two or three voices and basso continuo. The partbooks are made up of paper with a foolscap watermark and countermark GB which is consistent with a date of copying sometime in the 1660s;[106] at present it is not possible to be more precise. No such problems exist for Oxford, Bodleian Library Tenbury MS 1010 (Part II, MS XXXIV), a single-leaf rough score of Jeffreys' Ascension anthem 'With notes that are both loud and sweet' for two basses and basso continuo, for which the date of copying is given as '[16]69'. Jeffreys' latest surviving manuscript of his own compositions is the Royal College of Music MS 920A (Part II, MS XVIII), a set of four partbooks containing a selection of his four-voice music (ten of the pieces do not appear in the scorebook Add. 10,338). The partbooks were probably begun in the late 1660s, but were not completed until December 1675 - the date of 'He beheld the citty', Jeffreys' last known composition. A summary chronology of all Jeffreys' surviving manuscripts is given in Table 26.

George Jeffreys' Compositions: An Historical Perspective

The most significant fact to emerge from the detailed examination of the autograph manuscripts of Jeffreys' compositions is that forty-eight of his small-scale Italianate *concertato* pieces date from before 1648, and that some could have been composed as early as 1638. This is not the place for a detailed analysis or critical appraisal of George Jeffreys' compositions - for this the reader is referred to Peter Aston's admirably thorough studies[107] - but, in light of the 'new date for his autograph score'[108] and the findings concerning the Hatton music collection, a few comments on Jeffreys' work in the wider context of seventeenth-century English music will help to

---

collation of the partbooks). In this case the basso continuo book would represent a recopy of a lost part.
[106] Thompson (1988), Watermark XXVIII & *passim*.
[107] See footnote 1 above. Aston was not aware at the time of the importance of the Hatton collection as a formative influence on Jeffreys, nor that many of the anthems and motets in *Lbl* Add. 10,338 dated from before 1648.
[108] From the title of Robert Thompson's *Music and Letters* article (1989); this study was the first to assess the significance of the earlier datings of much of Jeffreys' music.

Table 26 A Proposed Chronology of the Surviving Manuscripts Copied by George Jeffreys

Manuscript	Date	Provenance	Contents
Pre-Civil War			
Oxford, Bodleian Library Mus. Sch. C 204, ff. 46-49^v	c.1634	Cambridge	Antonelli motets (parts copied by Bing with annotations by Jeffreys)
Rochester, NY, Eastman School of Music ML96 L8 14f, fascicle 3	1630s?	Court/London?	Short-score to Coprario fantasia-suites (with Bing)
Oxford, Bodleian Library Tenbury 1016	mid 1630s?	Court/London?	Score to madrigals *a* 1-3 by Dering
Dublin, Marsh Library Z3.4.13, ff. 47^v-59	c.1640	?	Score to Jeffreys fantasias *a* 3
Civil War			
London, British Library Add. 10,338 in part	c.1638-48	Oxford Court	Score to Jeffreys motets and anthems *a* 1-5
Oxford, Bodleian Library Tenbury 973-6 & 1273	c.1638-46	Oxford Court	Parts to Italian madrigals *a* 2-4
Oxford, Bodleian Library Tenbury 1012	c.1638-46	Oxford Court	Score to madrigals *a* 4 by Rovetta
Oxford, Bodleian Library Tenbury 1013	c.1638-46	Oxford Court	Score to Grandi 'Messa a 4 voci'
Oxford, Bodleian Library Tenbury 1015	c.1638-46	Oxford Court	Score to Nenna Madrigals Book VII with English words
London, British Library Add. 17,816 & 30,829-30 in part	early 1640s	Oxford Court	Parts to Jeffreys anthems and motets *a* 4-5
Oxford, Christ Church Mus. 878-880, 1st sections	c.1643-6	Oxford Court	Parts to Dering motets *a* 2-3 (Bing, etc., some text underlay by Jeffreys)
Oxford, Christ Church Mus. 1023	c.1643-6	Oxford Court	Bc to Dering 1618 (Bing with text headings added by Jeffreys)
Oxford, Bodleian Library Tenbury 1017	c.1638-46	Oxford Court	Score to Merula 2 madrigals (Bing with some text underlay by Jeffreys)
Commonwealth			
London, British Library Add. 10,338 in part	c.1648-62	File copies	Score to Jeffreys instrumental music, masque songs, madrigals, motets, canticles, anthems and devotional songs
London, British Library Add. 17,816 & 30,829-30 in part	c.1648-65	London/ Kirby Hall	Jeffreys motets and anthems *a* 4-6
London, British Library Add. 31,479 & Mad. Soc. G 55-9	mid to late 1650s	(Preservation)	Parts to Italian motets *a* 1-5
London, Royal College 920	late 1650s- early 1660s	London/ Kirby Hall	Parts to Jeffreys anthems and motets *a* 1-3

Table 26 concluded

		Restoration	
London, British Library Add. 29,282	1660s?	London/ Kirby Hall	Parts to Jeffreys Latin motets *a* 2-3
Oxford, Bodleian Library Tenbury 1285b	*c*.1665	London/ Kirby Hall	Score to 2 anthems *a* 4 by Jeffreys
Oxford, Bodleian Library Tenbury 1010	1669	London/ Kirby Hall	Score to Jeffreys 'With notes that are both loud and sweet' *a* 2
London, British Library Add. 31,479 additions	1670s	(Personal copies)	Carissimi, Reggio, Rovetta arr.
London, Royal College 920A	late 1660s?- 1675	London/ Kirby Hall	Parts to Jeffreys canticles, mass movements, anthems & motets *a* 4
Oxford, Bodleian Library Tenbury 1011	1683-5	(Personal copies)	Score to three *Sonnatas* by Purcell
Northampton, Record Office FH 3431C	?	Kirby Hall	Gigue & Corant in tablature

provide a perspective for a realistic assessment to be made of his achievements.

Central to any examination of English music in the seventeenth century is the question of foreign - and particularly Italian - influence. The fact that English musicians, collectors and patrons had been interested in Italian music from the early years of the sixteenth century has already been mentioned, and the manuscripts of Italian music copied by Stephen Bing and George Jeffreys are symptomatic of the continued interest in such music in the seventeenth century. But what effect did the importation, copying and - presumably - performance of Italian music have on native compositional style? The question of foreign influences on English musicians at this time is a thorny one; awkward questions have to be asked, such as: when do foreign influences end and personal style begin, and when do foreign elements become assimilated into the native English idiom? Nor can the issue of influence be divorced from that of the dissemination of foreign music in England in the seventeenth century. Before useful comment can be made on this issue it is necessary to establish precisely what Italian music was available in England, to which composers, and when. Here the case of George Jeffreys is perhaps unique, for we know exactly what music was available to him (the Venetian printed music in the Hatton collection) and how and when it came to be in the country (bought by Hatton from Robert Martin around 1638).

But what of Italian influence before 1638? Italian monodies had been available in England from about 1610 onwards through publications such as Robert Dowland's *Musicall Banquet* (London, 1610) and Angelo Notari's

Prime Musiche Nuove (London, c.1613)[109] and, although the precise relationship between Italian monody and the English declamatory style is difficult to assess due to the different characteristics of the Italian and English languages, it must have provided the underlying principles for the development of an English recitative.[110] Sacred and devotional music in England, however, remained fundamentally conservative in approach and showed little or no awareness of the so-called *stile nuovo*. Robert Thompson noted that the only publications to contain *stile nuovo* sacred compositions before the Commonwealth period were Walter Porter's *Madrigales and Ayres* (London, 1632)[111] - a single sacred work, 'Praise the Lord' - and William Child's *The First Set of Psalmes of III. Voyces Fitt for Private Chappels or Other Private Meetings with a Continued Base either for the Organ or Theorbo Newly Composed after the Italian Way* (London, 1639).[112] It is noteworthy that as late as 1639 Child is describing his psalms as 'after the Italian Way' as if it was something unusual. The title of Child's publication also emphasises the private nature of his music as if 'modern' Italianate music was considered best suited to private devotional meetings rather than public liturgy. With just a few exceptions the Anglican liturgical repertoire, as performed in cathedrals and the Chapel Royal, was extremely conservative.[113] This is reflected in the contents of John Barnard's *First Book of Selected Church Musick* (London, 1641): of the twenty-one composers represented in the publication, nine were born before 1550 and none was born after 1600.[114] The same traditional repertoire appears in James Clifford's word-book of *Divine Services and Anthems Usually Sung in the Cathedrals and Collegiate Choires in the Church of England* (London, 1663), although a year later, in the enlarged second edition, Clifford did include a number of more progressive works by composers such as Henry Lawes (1596-1662), Henry Cooke (c.1615-72) and Pelham Humfrey (1647-74).[115] In the words of Robert Thompson, 'any composer who wrote

---

[109] See I. Spink, 'Angelo Notari and his *Prime Musiche Nuove*', *MMR*, lxxxvii (1957), 168-77; and see Chapter Six.
[110] For a full examination of this issue see P. Walls, 'The Origins of English Recitative', *PRMA*, cx (1983-4), 25-40.
[111] See I. Spink, 'Walter Porter and the Last Book of English Madrigals', *AcM*, xxvi (1954), 18-36; and ibid., 'An Early English Strophic Cantata (Porter's *Farewell*)', *AcM*, xxvii (1955), 138-40. Spink stresses the progressive Italianate elements of the madrigals and cantata in Porter's *Madrigales and Ayres*.
[112] Thompson (1989), 318.
[113] The exceptions include William Child's anthems 'Bow down thine ear' (4vv), 'O God, wherefore art thou absent' (4vv), 'Turn thou us' (verse anthem) and 'Woe is me' (4vv) which are 'successful essays in the *stile nuovo*'; and Child's Te Deum and Jubilate 'for Dr. Cosin' include *stile concitato* choral writing (see le Huray (2/1978), 360-3).
[114] It should be noted that Barnard purposely excluded works by living composers, but even so the conservative nature of the Anglican liturgical repertoire is revealed; see R. Shay, 'Henry Purcell and "Ancient" Music in Restoration England' (Ph.D. dissertation, University of North Carolina, Chapel Hill, 1991), 18-26 & 48-54.
[115] For full details see le Huray (2/1978), 367-8; and Shay (1991), 48-54.

liturgical works in the modern style before the Interregnum was swimming against a strong conservative tide.'[116]

Before returning to George Jeffreys' Italianate anthems and motets, mention must be made of another English composer who contributed to the genre of the small-scale *concertato* motet: Richard Dering (c.1580-1630), organist to Queen Henrietta Maria 1625-30. Dering's Latin motets for two and three voices and basso continuo were most likely written for performance at the Queen's Roman Catholic services, and probably had only limited circulation during the composer's lifetime. However, the motets appear to have remained in the repertoire throughout the 1630s and 1640s and, surprisingly, were even popular during the Commonwealth; their appeal was such that John Playford published a substantial number of the motets in two publications entitled *Cantica Sacra* in 1662 and 1674 (see Chapter Five and Excursus I). Dering spent time in both Venice and Rome in the second decade of the century and the influence of the most up-to-date Italian music is apparent in his motets.[117] It seems, then, that the interest in Italian music (which had perhaps reached its zenith in Elizabeth I's reign) did, in certain - Court related? - circles, continue in the first half of the seventeenth century. This is further indicated by the fact that the London bookseller Robert Martin thought it worthwhile to publish five catalogues of Venetian music between 1633 and 1650 (see pages 28-30 above).[118] It has been demonstrated that one of Martin's main customers was Sir Christopher Hatton III and that the musician who benefited most from Hatton's purchases was George Jeffreys.

It was undoubtedly Jeffreys' exposure to the Italian music in the Hatton collection - particularly the small-scale *concertato* motets written by contemporaries of Monteverdi such as Alessandro Grandi - which led to Jeffreys' most successful compositions; his anthems, devotional songs and motets show a complete assimilation of the Italian *seconda prattica* style, especially with regard to melodic shape and the expressive use of dissonance. Other Italianate features appearing in Jeffreys' works include: the use of contrasting triple-time sections, contrasting homophonic sections in a pervading imitative texture, affective declamation, virtuoso solo writing, musical imagery, melodic and harmonic chromaticism, and unexpected harmonic progressions (for example, C major - E major) to draw attention to words such as 'dulcissime'.[119] Jeffreys' compositional style has many

---

[116] Thompson (1989), 318.

[117] For full details see P. Platt: 'Richard Dering: An Account of his Life and Work' (B.Litt. dissertation, University of Oxford, 1951-2); 'Dering's Life and Training', *ML*, xxxiii (1952), 41-9; 'Perspectives of Richard Dering's Vocal Music', *Studies in Music* i, University of Western Australia (1967), 56-66; and 'Dering, Richard', *New Grove*, v, 382-3.

[118] See also Krummel (1980); and Wainwright (1993), i, Appendix III.

[119] These techniques are not - of course - in themselves inherently 'Italian'; it is the context and combination of the many elements which justify the description 'Italianate'. For examples of many of these features in Jeffreys' compositions see Aston (1970), *passim*.

similarities with that of Richard Dering, but his melodies are far bolder and wide ranging and he was also harmonically more adventurous. Indeed, in his later works Jeffreys went beyond his Italian models and experimented - not always successfully - with extreme chromatic writing for expressive purposes.[120] Peter Aston notes that in his later works Jeffreys arrived 'at a balance between tradition and experiment by bringing together English and Italian styles in a highly individual way.'[121]

The realisation that forty-eight of Jeffreys' *concertato* anthems and motets date from the period 1638-48 necessitates a reassessment of the composer's position in the history of seventeenth-century English music. No other pre-Commonwealth composer showed such a wholehearted commitment to the *stile nuovo* and, as such, George Jeffreys must be recognised as the main pioneer of Italianate sacred music in England. Why then did Jeffreys have so little influence on either his contemporaries or on the succeeding generation of English composers? His compositions were not widely disseminated (see Table 23)[122] and only one piece appeared in print during his life (the two-voice motet 'Erit gloria Domini').[123] Jeffreys was unfortunate: his short professional musical career came to an end in 1646 with the fall of Oxford, and thereafter he was employed primarily as a steward and not as a musician. As a result Jeffreys' pioneering achievements of the 1640s were soon forgotten. We are now in the position to acknowledge fully Jeffreys' remarkable contribution to English seventeenth-century music.

---

[120] See for example the Whitsunday anthem 'A musick strange' 5vv bc (1662); quoted in Aston (1969), 776.
[121] Aston (1972-3), 109.
[122] Jeffreys' vocal pieces in *Ob* Mus. Sch. C 11 (Part II, MS XXIV), *Ob* Mus. Sch. E 451 (Part II, MS XXX), *Och* Mus. 17 (Aldrich *c*.1670-80s), and *Och* Mus. 18 (Part II, MS XLIV) were most likely transmitted via Christopher Jeffreys who was a student at Christ Church from 1658 to 1666. The concordant sources for Jeffreys' instrumental music were described above (see pp. 150-2); concerning the concordant pieces in *Y* M.1.S see p. 107 above; and for *Lcm* 2033 (Part II, MS XIX), *Lcm* 2039 (Part II, MS XXI) and *Och* Mus. 747-9 (Part II, MS LVI) see Excursus I. No information is currently available concerning the transmission of the pieces by Jeffreys to *Y* M.5.S (partbooks dated 1688) or *DRc* B.1 (organbook, 1660s).
[123] The motet, published in Playford's *Cantica Sacra.... The Second Sett* (London, 1674), is one of Jeffreys' less adventurous pieces (being similar in style to the motets of Dering) and is not representative of Jeffreys' mature *concertato* style of composition.

CHAPTER FIVE

CHRIST CHURCH, OXFORD MUS. 877-880: 'A STRANGE MEDDLEY'

The Composite Partbooks Christ Church Mus. 877-880

Christ Church Mus. 877-80 (see Part II, MS LVIII) are a complex set of four partbooks containing both printed and manuscript music. The manuscript sections of the partbooks consist of various layers copied, at different times, by five scribes (including Stephen Bing and George Jeffreys). As we shall see, the partbooks have many links with Christopher Hatton and his musicians, and thus offer the opportunity to draw together a number of the important themes that have emerged in the preceding chapters.

'M^r. Jeffreys Coll: of songs - verry / imperfect - on the first page of one / of the books... it appears / that he was organist of Christ Church. / M.S. / Dr Wilsons Psalterium Carolinum printed / Mr Walter Porters Motetts - printed / Thorough Bass to the Prince of / Venosa 5 parts & c. M.S. / a strange meddley.' This description of the contents of Christ Church Mus. 877-80 (copied from the inscription on the flyleaf of Mus. 880) is found in a catalogue of Richard Goodson's and Henry Aldrich's music collections compiled in July 1787 by Johann Baptist Malchair (1730-1812).[1] The designation 'M^r. Jeffreys Coll[ection] of songs' has led to the suggestion that George Jeffreys copied substantial sections of the partbooks.[2] Jeffreys' actual contribution to the copying of the manuscripts was small; he did, however, supervise the work of two of the other copyists: by organising the layout of the pages (by writing the clefs) and adding the text underlay to the music copied by the second anonymous scribe ('B') and Stephen Bing. The inscription 'M^r. Jeffreys Coll[ection]' would therefore appear only to indicate that Jeffreys once owned the partbooks (or certain sections of the partbooks). The handwriting of two other copyists is present in the partbooks: that of another unidentified scribe ('A') and that of Angelo Notari. Jeffreys' 'supervisory' hand is not present in the sections of the partbooks copied by these two scribes.

---

[1] *Lcm* 2125, Aldrich section, f. 36.
[2] Willetts (1962), 331-2, considered that 'the handwriting of much of the manuscript sections of Christ Church 878-80 is in Jeffries' autograph'. Arkwright (1915-23), ii, 94, stated that *Och* Mus. 878-80 are 'in Dean Aldrich's hand-writing', apparently not having noticed the fact that there are five hands in the manuscripts. Arkwright probably compared the hand of the final section of *Och* Mus. 880 (Bing) with that of *Och* Mus. 2, a manuscript also copied by Bing but to which Aldrich added the titles (see page 67 above, and Plate 8).

The first sections of Mus. 878-80,[3] which contain motets and one madrigal by Richard Dering (c.1580-1630) and other anonymous motets, were copied either by Anonymous A alone, by Anonymous B under the supervision of Jeffreys (who added the clefs and text), or by Stephen Bing (also supervised by Jeffreys).[4] A number of the pieces copied jointly by Anonymous B and Jeffreys, and by Bing and Jeffreys also include text alternatives (sometimes only occasional words) added by Bing above the original script. For example, 'Conceptio tua' has the alternative 'Nativitas tua', 'Beatus laurentius' could be performed as 'O fælix Ecclesia', and 'O crux ave' could become 'Jesu salve'.[5] It seems that certain texts were considered unacceptably Marian in reference, or too supine towards the saints, and thus the words were moderated; the significance of this is examined below.

An examination of the physical make-up of the partbooks reveals that the first pieces to be copied were the ten Dering motets transcribed by Anonymous A (numbered 1-8 and followed by two unnumbered motets). The original layer of each partbook, into which these ten pieces were copied, consisted of three bifolios (single folded sheets); the three sheets in the two vocal partbooks (Mus. 878 and 879) have the watermark of a small pot lettered DIV, and those in the basso continuo part (Mus. 880) have that of a shield. It appears that these fascicles then came into the possession of Jeffreys and his circle of copyists. Two '6s' gatherings of Pot CAB paper were inserted between the fourth and fifth Dering motets (that is after the second folio) in each book; these gatherings contained music for one or two voices and basso continuo copied by Anonymous B and Jeffreys, or by Bing and Jeffreys. These scribes also added more three-voice motets after the last of the 'original' three-voice pieces ('Qualis est dilectus'); they started by filling up the remaining folios of Pot DIV paper then added gatherings of paper with a Grapes watermark. The three types of paper appearing in the 'Dering' sections of the partbooks (Pot DIV, Pot CAB and Grapes) are all consistent with a copying date in the early 1640s.[6]

---

[3] *Och* Mus. 877 contains the Cantus I part of John Wilson's *Psalterium Carolinum* (London, 1657) and eighteen folios of blank (but ruled) paper with a coat of arms watermark. This paper is later than that in the other partbooks and was presumably added by Aldrich when he had the partbooks bound in the late seventeenth century.

[4] It should be noted that many of the pieces are incomplete: those copied by Bing lack the basso continuo parts, and the third vocal partbook is missing (and was apparently missing when the parts were bound).

[5] None of the pieces copied by Anonymous A include text expurgations by Bing. This suggests that Bing had access only to the work of Anonymous B and not to the original layers of the partbooks copied by Anonymous A. This is perplexing because Anonymous B copied pieces on the last folios of gatherings containing the work of Anonymous A. It may, of course, have been pure coincidence that Bing did not feel he needed to add to, or change, the texts of those pieces copied by Anonymous A.

[6] I am grateful to Dr Robert Thompson for advice concerning the watermarks in *Och* Mus. 877-880.

The music in the manuscript sections of the partbooks Christ Church Mus. 878-80 is all unattributed; the composers of many pieces can, however, be identified from concordant printed or manuscript sources. All the identifiable pieces in the first sections of the partbooks appear to be by Richard Dering, the majority of which are easily identified from John Playford's *Cantica Sacra* (London, 1662). A few other motets can also be attributed to Dering from ascriptions in concordant manuscript sources. The manuscript transmissions of Dering's motets are examined in Excursus I, and a case is made for attributing a number of anonymous motets (found only in manuscript sources) to Dering. It will be tentatively suggested that some, or all, of the anonymous motets in the first sections of Christ Church Mus. 878-80 are by Dering.

The only secular piece in the first sections of the Christ Church partbooks is 'O donna troppo cruda', for two voices and basso continuo; this Italian madrigal is attributed to Dering in Oxford, Bodleian Library Tenbury MS 1016 which was copied by George Jeffreys (see Part II, MS XXXIX, and pages 130-2 above).[7] In two of the Christ Church partbooks (Mus. 878 and 880) the 'Dering' fascicles are followed by a series of primarily secular pieces copied by the Italian-born composer, singer and lutenist Angelo Notari (1566-1663).[8] Both Notari sections appear originally to have consisted of a single gathering of twenty-four folios of Pot ID paper (ten 'spare' folios were, however, removed from Mus. 880; see Part II, MS LVIII); the two gatherings must originally have been part of a separate set of performing parts from which at least one partbook is missing. The paper used by Notari has the same watermark (Pot lettered ID), and contains the same system of rastrum-rulings, as a number of manuscripts copied by Stephen Bing (the first sections of the partbooks of British Library Add. MS 31,434 and Bodleian Library Tenbury MS 1017) and by George Jeffreys (Tenbury MS 1013) (see Table 18). The fact that Notari had access to this paper must immediately raise the possibility that he was connected with Hatton and his circle of copyists.[9] It has been shown that the Pot ID paper most likely dates from the early 1640s, and it was suggested that the Bing and Jeffreys manuscripts were copied at the Oxford Court between 1642/3 and 1646 (see pages 92-9 and 121-5 above). We know from court records that Notari arrived in England in about 1610 and entered the household of

---

[7] The Cantus part of 'O donna troppo cruda' also appears, unattributed, in *Och* Mus. 435, a single Cantus/Tenor I partbook. The madrigal also appears in *Lcm* 660 attributed to Jeffreys; the copy-text for this eighteenth-century manuscript was *Och* Mus. 878-80 and the scribe was misled by the inscription 'Mr Jeffrey's [sic] Collection of Songs'.

[8] Notari's handwriting was identified from an autograph letter found in papers relating to the Harington family of Bath, now *Lbl* Add. 46,378 B, f. 3. Full details, including the text and a reproduction of the letter, can be found in Willetts (1969b), 124-7; see also Willetts (1962).

[9] The fact that the Notari sections were bound - albeit in the late seventeenth century - with manuscript fascicles copied by Hatton scribes is in itself suggestive of a common provenance (see below).

Prince Henry,[10] and that, with the exception of the Commonwealth years, he remained in Royal service as a singer and lutenist until 1663 (under Prince Charles c.1618-25, King Charles I 1625-49, and, nominally, Charles II 1660-3).[11] As one of Charles I's musicians, it is quite possible that he was present at the Oxford Court for at least some of the period 1642-6, and he would therefore have encountered Hatton, Jeffreys and Bing. The implications of this are further explored in Chapter Six in relation to Notari's scorebook British Library Add. MS 31,440.

The only pieces so far identified in the Notari fascicles are by Monteverdi or Notari himself. Three of the four Monteverdi pieces, like a number of those in Notari's scorebook British Library Add. MS 31,440 (see Chapter Six), are arrangements (presumably by Notari) of five-part madrigals for two high voices and bass. These arrangements are skilful reworkings of the original five-part madrigals which involved a certain amount of recomposition to ensure that the voice-leading was satisfactory and the harmonies were complete.[12] John Whenham cites various precedents for Notari's arrangements, and gives a number of examples where sixteenth-century madrigals or canzonettas were arranged as duets or trios.[13] For example Emanuel Adriaenssen's *Pratum Musicum* (Antwerp, 1584) contains arrangements of madrigals and chansons by Lassus, Striggio, Ferretti and others, for two or three vocal parts (usually cantus and bassus), each with an intabulation for one or more lutes. Whenham notes that a number of similar arrangements were published in Italy, such as the collections of lute intabulations by Giovanni Antonio Terzi published in Venice in 1593 and 1599,[14] and suggests that Notari's arrangements are a seventeenth-century

---

[10] According to a contemporary biography and astrological scheme of his nativity (*Lbl* Sloane 1707, f. 2 in the hand of Francis Bernard, astrologer to James II), Notari was born in Padua on 14 (N.S. 24) January 1566; see Spink (1957); ibid., 'Notari, Angelo', *New Grove*, xiii, 333; and C. Egerton, 'The Horoscope of Signor Angelo Notari (1566-1663)', *The Lute*, xxviii (1988), 13-18. Peter Holman, however, has noted that the portrait of the composer in his *Prime Musiche Nuove*, dated 24 November 1613, gives his age as 'Di Anni 40', thereby giving an alternative birth-date of c.1573 (it is possible, however, that the engraving was taken from a dated portrait of c.1606); Holman (1993), 201. Whatever the case, he was certainly a mature composer when he entered Prince Henry's service in 1610. His only identified composition dating from before 1610 is a single canzonet, 'Io ardo e gl'occhi miei', published in N. Legname ed., *Amilla Libro Secondo di Canzonette a Tre Voci* (Venice, 1608). Notari was a member of the 'Accademia degli Sprovisti' in Venice, and it is therefore possible that there are manuscripts of his works yet to be discovered in Venetian libraries. (*Ob* Mus. Sch. D 237, ff. 41^v-42 contain an incomplete Italian song, '... dolor te partita[?]', by 'Angelo Padoana' for tenor and lute (in tablature); this may be a composition by Notari.)
[11] See Ashbee (1988), (1991a) & (1991b), *passim*.
[12] Notari's task was made easier by the fact that many of the five-voice madrigals in Monteverdi's fifth book of madrigals (1605) include trio sections within the five-voice texture.
[13] J. Whenham, *Duet and Dialogue in the Age of Monteverdi* (Ann Arbor, 1982), i, 71.
[14] G.A. Terzi, *Intavolatura di Liutto, Accomodata con Diversi Passaggi per Suonar in Concerti a Duoi Liutti, et Solo, Libro Primo* (Venice, 1593); and ibid., *Il Secondo Libro de Intavolatura di Liuto* (Venice, 1599).

remnant of this practice.[15] Notari's main reason for making the arrangements would, however, have been a practical one: to suit particular performance circumstances where singers were in short supply (such as the wartime Court at Oxford?).

The other attributable pieces in these fascicles are by Notari himself and were published in his *Prime Musiche Nuove* (London, [1613]).[16] This collection (the only volume of the period to be entirely devoted to Italian music) is important as it is, along with the undated keyboard collection *Parthenia*, the earliest engraved music in England.[17] The collection is also something of a showpiece of Notari's compositional skills in a variety of styles: chamber duets and trios, two- and three-voice canzonettas, strophic variations on a 'Romanesca' bass, and monodies.[18] Only a few copies of the collection appear to have been produced,[19] and its influence and effect are

---

[15] Whenham (1982), i, 72.

[16] See Spink (1957); and Holman (1993), 201-3. The fact that Notari entitled his collection 'Prime' may indicate that he intended to publish subsequent books; no such publications exist. A collection of notes made for a projected history of music, 1708-11, by Thomas Ford, one-time Chaplain of Christ Church, Oxford (*Ob* Mus. e 17), mentions a publication of Notari's dated 1616, but the full description: 'Prime Musiche Nove *a* 1, 2, 3v. con tiorbo. fol. Lond. 1616.' makes it clear that this is a misdated reference to the 1613 publication. The two pieces in *Och* Mus. 878 and 880 concordant with *Prime Musiche Nuove* differ in a number of details from the print. The partbook versions were probably copied from now-lost performing parts in which a number of variant readings had become established since the publication of *Prime Musiche Nuove* in 1613. Moreover, the basso continuo parts in *Och* Mus. 880 are extensively figured; figures were not deemed necessary in the publication, as the pieces were in score format.

[17] See Krummel (1975), 143-7.

[18] The contents of Notari's *Prime Musiche Nuove* are as follows: 1. 'Intenerite voi' (text: Rinuccini) CCbc; 2. 'Occhi miei' (Guarini) CCbc; 3. 'Su la riva del Tebro' (anonymous) CCbc; 4. 'Piangono al pianger mio' (Rinuccini) CCbc; 5. 'Occhi un tempo mia vita' (Guarini) TTbc; 6. 'Girate occhi girate' (Chiabrera) CCbc; 7. 'Ahi, che s'acresce' (anonymous) Cbc; 8. 'Che farai Meliseo? (Sannazzaro) Bbc; 9. Musa, Amor porta novella (anonymous) CCBbc; 10. 'Si da me pur mi desviano' (Chiabrera) CCBbc; 11. 'Ecco ch'un'altra volta' (Sannazzaro) CCTbc; 12. 'Se nasce in cielo' (anonymous) CBbc; 13. 'O bella Clori' (anonymous) CBbc; 14. 'Mesta ti scorgo' (anonymous) ATBbc; 15. 'Anima eletta' (Sannazzaro) Bbc; 16. 'Con esperanças espero' (anonymous) CCBbc; 17. 'Cosi di ben amar' (Petrarca) CCB 2vln bc; and 18. 'Ben qui si mostra' (anonymous) Bbc. Concerning the sixteenth piece, 'Con esperanças espero', Notari writes in the introduction to the publication: 'There came lately to my handes a Spanish songe of two partes, which seeminge to me very delightfull and pleasant, I have for my owne particular gust added to it a third part, altering only in some sort the Bassus'. *Lbl* Add. 36,877, f. 53 is a copy of 'Con esperanças', among many Spanish songs described as 'VILLANELLE Di piu sorte con l'Intra volatura per sonare, et cantare su la Chittara alla Spagnola di Giovanni Casolotti'. The cantus part is missing, but the guitar tablature shows it to be a version very similar to Notari's. This manuscript also contains the words of 'Occhi un tempo' (f. 36) and 'Piangono al pianger mio' (f. 119^v) which are Nos. 5 and 4 respectively in Notari's collection. The final piece of Notari's *Prime Musiche Nuove*, 'Ben qui si mostra', is based on a four-part madrigal by Cipriano de Rore which was published in C. de Rore & A. Padovano, *Madrigali a Quattro Voci... Libro Quinto* (Venice, 1561).

[19] Only two exemplars of Notari's publication survive today, one in the British Library and the other in the Royal Library, Copenhagen. The Danish copy was probably the result of the visit to England in 1611-14 of four Danish musicians of the Royal Chapel of Christian IV. The musicians, Hans Brachrogge, Jacob Ørn, Martinus Otto and Morgens Pedersøn, were sent by Christian IV to serve his sister Anne, who was James I's queen. They would undoubtedly have

difficult to assess, but that it was published at all must indicate that in certain circles, at least, Italian music was appreciated and performed. The Notari fascicles in Christ Church reflect a continued interest in such music almost three decades later. Two anonymous pieces in the partbooks are also found in Notari's scorebook British Library Add. MS 31,440 (see Chapter Six, and Part II, MS VII). It is likely that many of the anonymous pieces in the Notari sections of the partbooks (and indeed in the scorebook) are actually by the copyist himself; confirmation of this is, however, unlikely to be forthcoming.

The Notari fascicles in the partbooks Mus. 878 and 880, and the 'Dering' fascicles in Mus. 879, are followed by two sections of printed material: John Wilson's *Psalterium Carolinum* and Walter Porter's *Mottets for Two Voyces* (both printed in London in 1657). John Wilson (1595-1674), who was one of Charles I's musicians and subsequently Professor of Music at Oxford, subtitled his *Psalterium Carolinum*: 'The Devotions of his Sacred Majestie in his Solitudes and Sufferings',[20] and the dedication showed that Wilson deliberately intended to fly his colours as a Royalist and an Anglican: 'To the Glory of God, the Sacred Memory of His Late Maiestie, and to the Right Reverend Clergy of the Church of England, *John Wilson*, Dr. in Musick, dedicates this his last of labours.' Such an openly Royalist declaration could, at that time, easily have caused arrest, trial, and severe punishment for the author. In the words of Peter le Huray: 'That Wilson dared to publish such a work at that time is a tribute to his royalist loyalties if not to his common sense. He seems, nevertheless, to have escaped serious trouble with the authorities, though there is some evidence that he was quickly forced to withdraw the book from circulation.'[21] The Wilson publication is followed in the partbooks by Walter Porter's *Mottets* 'for Treble or Tenor and Bass. With the Continued Bass or Score: To be performed to an Organ, Harpspycon [sic], Lute or Bass-Viol'. The 'mottets' are actually seventeen settings of metrical psalms, all but two of which were published in 1636 by George Sandys.[22] Two copies of Porter's *Mottets*

---

come into contact with the musicians of Prince Henry's household and it seems likely that Notari presented one of them with a copy of his recently published *Prime Musiche Nuove* just before they returned to Denmark. See J. Bergsagel, 'Danish Musicians in England 1611-14: Newly-Discovered Instrumental Music', *Dansk Aarbog for Musikforskning*, vii (1973-6), 9-20.

[20] The subtitle is taken from the title of *Eikon Basilike: the Portraicture of his Sacred Majestie in his Solitudes and Sufferings*, a book which appeared shortly after Charles I's execution on 30 January 1649. The work was published, in London, as the work of Charles I, but it was in fact by the cleric John Gauden who seems to have had access to some of the King's private papers. See F. Madan, *A New Bibliography of the Eikon Basilike of King Charles the First with a Note on the Authorship*, Oxford Bibliographical Society Publication, New Series, iii (1950). The texts set by Wilson in *Psalterium Carolinum* are verses by Thomas Stanley rendered from *Eikon Basilike*.

[21] le Huray (2/1978), 399.

[22] G. Sandys, *Paraphrase upon the Psalmes of David* (London, 1636).

survive in the library of Christ Church, Oxford: Mus. 878-80 and 818-23.[23] Both these sets have, in the prefaces, the annotation 'Monteverde' added in Porter's handwriting after the words 'my good Friend and Maestro'.[24] This has been taken as proof that Porter studied with Monteverdi,[25] and Ian Spink notes that the style of his *Madrigales and Ayres* (London, 1632) 'certainly supports Porter's claim. They are virtually the only English madrigals in concertato style.'[26] Whilst it is, of course, feasible that Porter was a pupil of Monteverdi's, it should be noted that it would have been possible for Porter to have been well acquainted with the works of Monteverdi without having left England.

The two publications were bound with the manuscript fascicles by Henry Aldrich, towards the end of the seventeenth century, in the common Oxford brown leather binding (see page 36 above). One can only speculate why these particular prints and manuscripts were combined. Perhaps they were considered to be related and representative of Royalist music: Notari, Wilson and Porter were all musicians to Charles I; Dering had been employed by Queen Henrietta Maria; and Dering's motets were apparently popular in Royalist circles. Or perhaps the link in Aldrich's mind was with Italian music: Dering's motets are Italianate; Notari was, of course, an Italian; Porter was the self-styled pupil of Monteverdi; and, according to Henry Lawes' dedicatory verse in *Psalterium Carolinum*, Wilson was one of the foremost exponents of the Italian style. Perhaps it was these links which appealed to Aldrich when he combined the manuscripts and prints? The 'Dering' and Notari fascicles appear to be the remnants of performing parts from the time of the Oxford Court, and the presence of Bing and Jeffreys' handwriting in the partbooks suggests Hatton provenance. It has been noted that, when organising bindings, Aldrich appears to have kept together any prints and manuscripts which had a common origin (see pages 36-9 above); it is not inconceivable, therefore, that the Wilson and Porter publications were once also part of the Hatton collection (perhaps purchased in the late 1650s soon after Hatton's return from exile).

In Christ Church Mus. 880 (the basso continuo partbook) the printed material is followed by two more manuscript sections, both copied by Stephen Bing.[27] The first of these contains the basso continuo parts to forty-

---

[23] The *Och* Mus. 878-80 copy of Porter's *Mottets* is omitted in A. Hiff, *Catalogue of Printed Music Published Prior to 1801 now in the Library of Christ Church Oxford* (Oxford, 1919).
[24] Porter's handwriting can be identified from the autograph dedications added to the following exemplars of the *Mottets*: *Och* Mus. 819, and *Ob* Mus. Sch. D 349.
[25] For example, G.E.P. Arkwright, 'An English Pupil of Monteverdi', *The Musical Antiquary*, iv (1913), 236; and C.W. Hughes, 'Porter, Pupil of Monteverdi', *MQ*, xx (1934), 278-88.
[26] I. Spink, 'Porter, Walter', *New Grove*, xv, 137. See also ibid. (1954) & (1955); and S. Boorman, 'Notari, Porter and the Lute', *Lute Society Journal*, xiii (1971), 28-32.
[27] It is possible that the last two manuscript sections of *Och* Mus. 880 are the only remaining parts of otherwise lost sets. But it is equally possible that vocal parts never existed, and that the fascicles were a continuo player's personal anthology of popular pieces.

six unattributed four-voice pieces (forty motets and six madrigals) by Italian composers. The section was originally a single gathering of twenty-four folios (lacking the eighth folio) with the pieces numbered continuously 1-46 (by Bing). In binding, however, the single fascicle was divided into four gatherings: A^8(A8 removed) B^4 $C-D^6$; the sequence of pieces is therefore now numbered: 1-9, 42-46, 10-13, 38-41, 14-19, 32-37, 20-31 (see Part II, MS LVIII). All except two of the forty-six pieces are concordant with printed sources which were once most likely part of the Hatton collection (see Chapter Two);[28] the two pieces without concordances in the Hatton printed music are 'Nigra sum' by Virgilio Mazzocchi (published in Florido de Silvestri's anthology *Concentus Sacras* (Rome, 1643))[29] and 'Fuerunt mihi [lacrimae]' by the elder Alfonso Ferrabosco (which has only manuscript concordances).[30] The repertorial evidence, then, suggests that this section is contemporary with the 'Dering' and Notari fascicles. However, as in the case of George Jeffreys' partbooks of Italian sacred music (British Library Add. MS 31,479 and Madrigal Society MSS G 55-9), the facts are rather more complex.

Bing's forty-six basso continuo parts must date from after 1643 (the publication date of the anthology containing Mazzocchi's 'Nigra sum'). It is therefore just possible that the section, like the previous manuscript fascicles in the partbook, is a product of the Civil War years, 1643-6. However, it is more likely that it was copied in the mid to late 1650s at the same time as

---

[28] All but three of these printed sources survive today in Christ Church, Oxford. There are incomplete copies of both Arrigoni's *Concerti di Camera* (Venice, 1635) and Merula's *Libro Secondo de Concerti Spirituali* (Venice, 1628) in the British Library; the Arrigoni print is listed in Martin's book catalogues of 1635 and 1639; and both prints were copy-sources for Jeffreys (see pp. 121-5 above). It is therefore very likely that both publications were once part of the Hatton collection, and it is possible that the British Library prints (D.29 and D.159a respectively) are the actual copies. The only existing exemplar of Merula's *Il Primo Libro de Motetti* (Venice, 1624) is in the Civico Museo Bibliografico Musicale, Bologna. This publication is listed in Martin's 1633 book catalogue and, as both Jeffreys and Bing used the print - directly or indirectly - as a copy-source, there must have been a copy in England in the 1630s or 1640s; it is highly likely that it was once part of the Hatton collection.
[29] There are no copies of Florido de Silvestri ed., *Concentus Sacras* (Rome, 1643) in Great Britain today. However, Mazzocchi's 'Nigra sum' can also be found in Florido de Silvestri ed., *Sacras Cantiones... Pars Secunda* (Rome, 1652); although no copies of this publication survive in British Libraries today, the fact that the manuscript *Ob* Mus. c 57 contains a complete transcription of the publication suggests that there was once a copy in the country. As we shall see, it is possible that this lost copy of *Sacras Cantiones* (1652) was Bing's copy-source. (*Ob* Mus. c 57 also contains a complete transcription of Florido de Silvestri ed., *Sacras Cantiones* (Rome, 1650); the scribe of *Ob* Mus. c 57 also copied *Lbl* R.M. 24.c.10 and *Lcm* 1076.)
[30] 'Fuerunt mihi lacrimae' is sometimes attributed to Ferrabosco II (e.g. J.V. Cockshoot, 'Alfonso Ferrabosco (ii)', *New Grove*, vi, 482) on dubious stylistic grounds; however, the piece is ascribed to Ferrabosco I in *Lbl* Egerton 3665 by the copyist who was always careful to distinguish between the two Ferrabuscos. It is therefore probably correct to ascribe the piece to the elder Ferrabosco. See R. Charteris, '*Fuerunt mihi lacrymae*: Alfonso Ferrabosco the Elder or the Younger?', *Altro Polo: Essays on Italian Music in the Cinquecento*, ed. R. Charteris (Sydney, 1989), 113-30.

Jeffreys' partbooks of Italian music,[31] and was therefore also a product of the period of renewed musical activity which coincided with Baron Hatton's return from exile. A date in the mid to late 1650s is supported by the watermark evidence. The twelve bifolio sheets - actually twenty-three folios: one removed - which make up this section of the partbook each contain one of a watermark-pair of Pots lettered RRO. This watermark also appears in a number of manuscripts associated with the North family of Kirtling, Cambridgeshire, which have been shown to date from the mid to late 1650s (see pages 102-3 above).[32] It must, however, be significant that all but one of the pieces in this section of the partbook date from before 1638. I suggest that the basso continuo parts are primarily recopies of pieces which had originally been transcribed for use at the Oxford Court 1643-6. Perhaps the copy-sources for Bing's continuo parts were the same hypothetical lost manuscripts which, it was suggested, were used by Jeffreys when copying his partbooks of Italian music (see pages 127-8 above).[33] The presence of this 1650's fascicle in 'Mr Jeffrey's Coll[ection]' is evidence that Bing maintained some links, at least, with Jeffreys and the Hattons during the Commonwealth.

The final section of the basso continuo partbook (Mus. 880) consists of three gatherings which each contain six folios of paper with a watermark of Pillars lettered DI. The same watermark appears in the first two gatherings of George Jeffreys' scorebook (British Library Add. MS 10,338) which contain his instrumental pieces and three-voice Italian madrigals; it was demonstrated above that these sections of the scorebook were probably copied in the 1640s (see pages 150-3 above). The final section of the partbook Mus. 880 would appear, then, to be contemporary with the 'Dering' and Notari sections of the partbooks. The contents of these last gatherings of the continuo book offer a fascinating glimpse of the sort of music that was performed in Hatton/Court circles of the 1640s. Stephen Bing provided basso continuo parts for the first, second and fourth books of Carlo Gesualdo's five-part madrigals. These parts were most likely made, from printed sources in the Hatton collection, for a keyboard or theorbo player to provide support for the singers (a common practice throughout

---

[31] It should be noted that thirty-four of the forty-six pieces in this section of *Och* Mus. 880 also appear in Jeffreys' partbooks Mad. Soc. G 55-9 (see pages 125-9 above, and Part II, MS IX).

[32] Pot RRO paper appears in the following North manuscripts: *Ob* Mus. Sch. C 85, Partbook iii; *Ob* Mus. Sch. C 87 *passim*; *Ob* Mus. Sch. C 88, Partbook iii; and *Ob* Mus. Sch. F 568-9, *passim*. The RRO paper is often found combined with, or alongside, Cardinals' Hat paper which has been shown to date from *c*.1653 (see pp. 126-7 above).

[33] This theory finds some support in the fact that a number of the text incipits in this section of *Och* Mus. 880 show that the copy-source had an expurgated text which differed from the original printed version: Sances' 'Salve ò Christe' (No. 45) is 'Salve Regina' in the original printed source, Facchi's 'O Jesu clementissime' (No. 40) was originally 'O virgo prudentissima', and Aloisi's 'Dulcissime [Jesu Christe]' (No. 22) was 'Dulcissima Christi Mater'. All three pieces also appear in Mad. Soc. G 55-9 but only the Aloisi has the altered text.

Europe).³⁴ That the copy-sources were - directly or indirectly³⁵ - from the Hatton collection is confirmed by the order of which Bing copied Gesualdo's first and second books of madrigals. According to today's accepted nomenclature of Gesualdo's first and second books, Bing copied the two books in reverse order: the second book (ff. 24-9) followed by the first book (ff. 29-34). It should be noted, however, that the second and fifth editions of Gesualdo's 'first' book of madrigals (1603 and 1617) were published as *Libro Secondo*, and the second and fourth editions of the 'second' book (1603 and 1616) were published as *Libro Primo*.³⁶ Copies of all four of these editions survive in Christ Church (Mus. 908-12), and it is likely that at least one edition of each book was once part of the Hatton collection.³⁷ As Bing's basso continuo parts for Gesualdo's first and second books are copied in reverse order (the beginning of 'Book I' on folio 29 is annotated 'A.5. lib.2'), it seems likely that his copy-sources - either directly or indirectly - were the Christ Church prints.

Music in Civil War Oxford

It has been shown in the preceding sections that a number of manuscripts copied by Hatton's musicians date from the period before 1648; furthermore, it has been suggested that these manuscripts may have been copied for use at the Oxford Court 1642-6. Is this really a tenable hypothesis? What evidence is there of music at the Oxford Court? It must be admitted immediately that there is not an overabundance of evidence. But this is surely to be expected: the Oxford Court was, after all, a wartime Court and it is not surprising that the chroniclers felt they had more important things to report. Archival evidence concerning music - both sacred and secular - at the Oxford Court is almost non-existent.³⁸ The official Court records for the period 1642-6 are deficient; they do, however, indicate that the payment of musicians continued for a short time after the move from

---

³⁴ See A. Newcomb, 'Secular Polphony in the 16th Century', *Performance Practice: Music Before 1600*, New Grove Handbook in Music (London, 1989), 229.
³⁵ It is possible that the basso continuo parts were constructed from now-lost scores of the madrigals. It should be noted that *Ob* Tenbury 1009, a collection of Italian madrigals copied by Bing (see Part II, MS XXXIII), contains scores to the two six-voice madrigals from Gesualdo's fourth book.
³⁶ The works-list given in L. Bianconi, 'Gesualdo, Carlo', *New Grove*, vii, 322, does not note the reversed nomenclature for the 1603 editions, and the entries in *RISM* do not take into account these contradictory numberings and are therefore totally confused.
³⁷ Mus. 908-12 also contains two editions of Gesualdo's fourth book of madrigals (1604 and 1616); it is likely that one or both of these editions were also once part of the Hatton collection.
³⁸ Official information concerning the Court between 1642 and 1646 is scarce due to the Royalists' decision, in June 1646, to destroy all their papers before surrendering; see Larkin (1983), p. vi. As a result, only a small number of Royalist records survive, such as the Bankes papers and the those of the Royal secretaries Nicholas and Walker; see Chapter One, footnote 75.

London (in January 1642), and that this appears to have stopped once the Court was established in Oxford (November 1642).[39] Money would, of course, have been scarce due to the lack of traditional revenues and the immense cost of the Royalist campaign, and it appears that the only fees paid to musicians were those awarded for performing at the ceremonies associated with the conferring of noble dignities.[40] It is not surprising, therefore, that a substantial number of court musicians chose not to join the King in Oxford.[41] Many of the records of Oxford Colleges for the period are incomplete (political expediency would have dictated that any incriminating reference to Royalist collaboration was destroyed after the fall of the city in July 1646). The disbursement books at Christ Church (lacking from 1645-57), which (as the Court was based there) one would perhaps expect to supply some information concerning musicians, contain only the standard college records and offer nothing about the Court. Likewise the Register of Merton College (where Queen Henrietta Maria lodged from 14 July 1643 to 17 April 1644)[42] is conspicuously lacking in detailed reference to the period.

Even so, there are a few clues to suggest that music played a part at the Oxford Court. The fact that Jeffreys was Charles I's 'organist at Oxford in 1643' (according to both Wood and Hawkins)[43] indicates that there was at least some music. Hawkins, however, gives a more detailed account of music in Oxford during the Civil War:[44]

> It will easily be conceived that the prohibition of Cathedral service left a great number of musicians, as namely, organists, minor canons, lay-clerks and other persons attendant on choirs, without employment; and the gloomy and sullen temper of the times, together with the frequent hostilities that were carried on in different parts of the kingdom, during usurpation, had driven music to a great degree out of private families. The only place which these men could, as to an asylum, resort, was to Oxford, whither the King had retired; there went with him thither, Dr. Wilson, one of the gentlemen of his chapel, and he had an organist with him named George Jeffries; these and a few others, with the assistance

---

[39] See Ashbee (1988), pp. xii-xiii, 114-21, 158-60, & 241-3.

[40] *Ob* Rawlinson B 121 is a list of fees paid to musicians for performing at such ceremonies; see Ashbee (1988), 119-21.

[41] There are, however, a few references to Court musicians at Oxford: William King (1624-80) who was to become Organist of New College, Oxford in 1664, 'was one of the musicians who gathered in Oxford round the court of Charles I' (M. Tilmouth, *New Grove*, x, 67; see also J. Pulver, *A Biographical Dictionary of Old English Music* (London, 1927; rev. 1968), 277-8). Petitions to King Charles II at the Restoration indicate that three musician were in Oxford for at least part of the Civil War: John Wilson (PRO SP 29/2, No. 58), the violinist Simon Hopper (PRO SP 29/33. No. 85), and Thomas Lanier (PRO SP 29/45, No.54); see Ashbee (1995), 137, 139 & 147.

[42] See Varley (1932), 6, 8, & 56-63.

[43] Clark ed. (1891), i, 274; Wood (1691; 3/1813-21), i, pp. xxxiv-xxxv; and Hawkins (1776), iv, 56, 64 & 323.

[44] Hawkins (1776), iv, 323.

of the University people, made a stand against the persecution of the times; choral services were performed there after a very homely fashion, and concerts of vocal and instrumental music were sometimes had in the rooms of Gentlemen of the University for the entertainment of each other. But this lasted only till the surrender of the garrison in 1646, when the King was obliged to leave the place; however, the spirit that had been excited in favour of music during his residence there, and the continuance of Dr. Wilson in the University, who was professor, and a man of chearful disposition, contributed to an association of Gentlemen of the University, with the musicians of the place, and these together established a weekly concert.

This would seem to indicate - if Hawkins' account can be trusted - that the Oxford Court was something of a musical centre. Perhaps Bing and Jeffreys copied their manuscripts - supervised by Baron Hatton - for these 'homely' choral services and concerts of vocal and instrumental music? Another reference to music at the Oxford Court appears in the *Declaration* published in London in 1644 by the turncoat Sir Edward Dering (1598-1644) shortly after he had abandoned Oxford.[45] One of the reasons he gave for his defection was his dislike of the form of Church services and the music that they contained. He complained of 'a parasiting part of the Clergie' who led 'lazie performances' in which 'Organs, Sackbutts, Recorders, Cornets, &c., and Voices are mingled together', and then quoted a Catholic writer (in Latin) who attacked the use of polyphonic music in the liturgy.[46]

Dering's comments, which presumably referred to the High Church services in Christ Church which the King would have attended, reveal the puritanical attitudes to liturgy and ceremony which existed in the minds of many Protestants. The sort of High Church worship found primarily in cathedrals and collegiate churches and chapels - which revelled in candles, coloured vestments, stained glass, statues and ornaments, and the music of organs and choirs (perhaps even singing in Latin) - was anathema to many Protestants who preferred to worship in the austere surroundings of a whitewashed church, with the focus on the pulpit rather than the altar (which was a simple wooden table in the nave). Charles I was a sincere Protestant whose theological and liturgical concept of worship - as defined by

---

[45] Dering had originally defected from the Parliamentarian cause in 1641. Like Hatton, Dering was an avid collector of charters and documents and, as an antiquary, worked alongside Hatton and Dugdale; see *DNB* v, 845-6.

[46] In his *Discourse of Proper Sacrifice* published soon after the *Declaration* (but written in the summer of 1640), Dering attributed the quotation to Henry Cornelius Agrippa. In 1660, when attitudes had changed somewhat, the Reverend Joseph Brooksbank, in his defence of church music, quoted this section of Dering's text in a refutation of his argument; [J. Brooksbank], *The Well-Tuned Organ, or, an Exercitation; Wherein, this* Question *is Fully and Largely Discussed,* Whether or No *Instrumental, and Organical* Musick be Lawful in Holy Publick *Assemblies?* (London, 1660), 51-2. Joseph Brooksbank was married to Stephen Bing's daughter Elizabeth; see Willetts (1989), 14.

Archbishop William Laud (1573-1645) - acknowledged the possibility of an evocative and emotive response to human artistic creations in the context of the Divine Office.[47] It was unfortunate that the more puritanical elements of the Church regarded the Laudian movement - quite unfairly - as subversively Roman Catholic, and generally fuelled the popish paranoia which helped kindle the Civil War. Charles I's image in all this was severely tarnished by the fact that his Queen, Henrietta Maria (the youngest daughter of King Henry IV of France and the Florentine Marie de Medici, and sister of Louis XIII), was a Catholic, and many of his subjects were convinced that Charles had strong leanings towards, or at least a weakness for, Rome.[48] One of the principal articles of Queen Henrietta Maria's marriage treaty was that she could have her own Chapel in which she was free to exercise her Roman Catholic faith. Her private chapel, at Somerset House (see below), was staffed by an entourage of Capuchin friars, and the music was provided by French musicians and an English organist: first Richard Dering (1625-30) and then Richard Mico (1630-*c*.1642).[49] By the time of the Oxford Court, Queen Henrietta Maria's musical establishment - like the 'King's Musick' - had dispersed, but the possibility must be raised that there was at least some music at the Queen's private services during her nine-month stay in Merton. Again there is no archival evidence to support this suggestion (nor should we expect there to be, given the political situation),[50] but we should note that when the Queen left Oxford in April 1644 she took with her the organist of Magdalen College and Professor of Music at the University ('Choragus'), Arthur Phillips (1605-95), who had 'changed his religion for that of Rome, and become Organist to Henrietta Maria, Queen of England'.[51] This hints that there was some association between Henrietta Maria and musicians at the Oxford Court.

David Pinto has discovered one further piece of evidence concerning music-making at the Oxford Court.[52] He notes that three of William Cartwright's poems, published in his posthumous *Comedies, Tragi-*

---

[47] See, *inter alia*, K. Sharpe, *The Personal Rule of Charles I* (New Haven & London, 1992), 328-33.
[48] See J.P. Kenyon, 'The Church Question', *Stuart England*, The Pelican History of England vi (London, 2/1985), 27-36; and K. Sharpe, 'Archbishop William Laud and the University of Oxford', *Politics and Ideas in Early Stuart England: Essays and Studies* (London, 1989), 123-46.
[49] For details of Queen Henrietta Maria's musical establishment see I. Spink, 'The Musicians of Queen Henrietta-Maria: Some Notes and References in English State Papers', *AcM*, xxxvi (1964), 177-82; Bennett & Willetts (1977), 35-40 & 46; and Ashbee (1988), 244-52. It seems that the French musicians left England in 1642-3.
[50] The Merton College Register contains a transcript of a letter from Charles I dated 28 December 1645, in the hand of Secretary Edward Nicholas, which mentions 'enjoining the regular performance of divine service, and appointing a special form for Wednesdays & Fridays'; but the Queen had left Oxford by that date.
[51] J.R. Bloxam, 'Chaplains, Clerks and Organists', *The Magdalen College Register*, (Oxford, 1857), ii, 191-2. See also J. Caldwell, 'Phillips, Arthur', *New Grove*, xiv, 659.
[52] D. Pinto, 'The True Christmas: Carols at the Court of Charles I' (forthcoming).

Comedies, with other Poems (London, 1651), were written 'For the King's Musick' on the occasions of the Nativity, Circumcision and Epiphany:

'Heark, 'Tis the Nuptiall Day of Heav'n and Earth' - 'On the Nativity a3 *voc* and chorus'

'Gently, o Gently, Father, do not bruise' - 'On the Circumcision a2 Levites and chorus'

'See this is He, whose Star Did becken us from far' - 'On the Epiphany a3 Magi and chorus'

Pinto has suggested that these 'court carols' were performed at the Oxford Court at Christmas 1642, for Cartwright, a Fellow of Christ Church with no connections with Court before its arrival in Oxford, died of 'camp fever' on 29 November 1643. Seasonal verses for subsequent Christmas celebrations at the Oxford Court were supplied by Martin Lluelyn (chaplain to the Royal forces). Lluelyn's *Men-Miracles. With other Poems* ([Oxford], 1646) includes the following 'Carolls':

'Harke! harke! the *Spheares* inticeing notes' - 'Sung to His Majesty on Christmas Day, 1644.'

'Great *Copie* of this *Solemne* Day' - 'Sung to his Majesty on Christmas day, 1645.'

'*Moses chaire* had long obtain'd' - 'Sung to his Majesty on New-yeares day, being the Circumcision. 1643.'

'First Magus. What bright and unaccustomed shine' - 'Sung to his Majesty on Twelfe day, being the Epiphany. 1644.'

'From Arabia's fragrant wombe' - 'Sung to his Majesty on Twelfe day, being the Epiphany, 1645.'

No music survives for these carols but Henry Lawes and George Jeffreys must be likely candidates for composers: Lawes because he had set carols by Robert Herrick 'Sung to the King in the Presence at White-Hall' probably in 1640-2;[53] and Jeffreys because we know him to have been in the right place at the right time. We should also note that Martin Lluelyn was known to Christopher Hatton, and when the Baron arrived in Calais, at the beginning of his exile (November 1646), he was greeted with welcoming verses by Lluelyn[54] 'who must have reckoned from previous acquaintance that Hatton's attentions were still worth a modest outlay of effort to retain.'[55]

---

[53] The text were published as Nos. 96-7 in [R. Herrick], *His Noble Numbers or his Pious Pieces* (London, 1647): 'What sweeter musick can we bring' - 'A Christmas Caroll a4 *voc* and chorus The Musical Part was composed by M[r] Henry Lawes'; and 'Prepare for Songs' - 'The New-Yeeres Gift, or Circumcision Song a5 *voc* and chorus Composed by M[r] Henry Lawes'.

[54] The poem survives only in manuscript: *Ob* Rawlinson Poet 62, f. 14^{r-v}.

[55] D. Pinto, 'Musical Settings in Civil-War Oxford', paper given at the Fourth Biennial Conference on Baroque Music (Egham, July 1990); to be published as 'The True Christmas', see footnote 52 above.

The primary evidence for music in Civil War Oxford is, however, offered by the manuscripts copied by George Jeffreys and Stephen Bing, musicians to Baron Hatton, Comptroller of the King's Household. These manuscripts, which have all been described in detail in the preceding chapters, are listed in Table 27. The preponderance of small-scale pieces - both sacred and secular - should be noted, as should the large number of Italian or Italianate works. This varied repertoire could be performed with only a handful of singers and a continuo player - perhaps all that was available at the wartime Court - and the most up-to-date Italian pieces would be most suitable for the educated tastes of noblemen (and a welcome distraction from the worries of war). But it is the manuscripts of sacred music - Jeffreys' British Library Add. MS 31,479 and Madrigal Society MSS G 55-9 (Part II, MS IX), and Bing's Christ Church Mus. 880, second sequence ff. 1-23^v (Part II, MS LVIII) - which offer the best hint that we are dealing with a Royalist repertoire from the time of the Oxford Court. It has been suggested that these two collections of Italian motets were recopies of lost Civil War manuscripts, and this suggestion is supported by an examination of the repertoire.

Both collections contain a substantial number of motets with Marian texts (such as Marian antiphons, Song of Songs texts, and Litanies of our Lady). The Song of Songs, in particular, was one of the most popular sources of Marian imagery for the Roman Catholic cult of the Virgin, and many of the motet texts seem especially pertinent to the wartime Court and to Henrietta Maria in particular. For example, Alessandro Grandi's four-voice setting of 'Obaudite me' - 'Hear me my devout sons said Ignatius to his companions, and blossom like a rose planted by a stream; spread your fragrance like incense and bloom like a lilly' - is a text which refers to Saint Ignatius Loyola, the soldier who founded the Roman Catholic Jesuit order in 1534. This was surely significant for a Roman Catholic Queen surrounded by soldiers at a wartime Court. The manuscripts also contain five settings of the 'Salve Regina', three of the 'Ave Regina', one setting of the Litany of Our Lady, and many other settings of openly Marian texts. Indeed, with such Roman Catholic music in mind, it is necessary to consider the imagery surrounding Queen Henrietta Maria in relation to the cult of the Virgin Mary.

Queen Henrietta Maria had been at the height of her power and influence in England in the 1630s. She had, on 14 September 1632, laid the foundation stone for her chapel at Somerset House which was designed by Inigo Jones and dedicated to the Virgin. The chapel was opened with conspicuous ceremony on 8 December 1636 and thereafter became an embarrassingly public magnet for Roman Catholics and a large number of

Table 27 Music Manuscripts from Civil War Oxford?

a. Manuscripts copied by George Jeffreys

Lbl Add. 10,338 in part: anthems and motets *a* 1-5 by Jeffreys
Lbl Add. 17,816/30,829-30 in part: anthems and motets *a* 4-5 by Jeffreys
Ob Tenbury 973-6/1273: Italian madrigals *a* 2-4
Ob Tenbury 1012: madrigals *a* 4 by Rovetta
Ob Tenbury 1013: mass *a* 4 by Grandi
Ob Tenbury 1015: Nenna madrigals Book VII 'englished'
Ob Tenbury 1017: two madrigals *a* 4 by Merula; with Bing
Och Mus. 878-80, 1st sections: Dering motets *a* 2-3; with Bing, etc.
Och Mus. 1023: basso continuo parts to Dering 1618; with Bing
[?Lost scores of Italian motets later recopied in *Lbl* Add. 31,479 and Mad. Soc. G 55-9]

b. Manuscripts copied by Stephen Bing

Lbl Add. 31,434: H. Lawes and Italian music
Ob Tenbury 1005: Italian madrigal *a* 4-6
Ob Tenbury 1009: English and Italian madrigals *a* 5-6
Ob Tenbury 1017: two madrigals *a* 4 by Merula; with Jeffreys
Och Mus. 255: Valentini manuscript insertions
Och Mus. 878-80, 1st sections: Dering motets *a* 2-3; with Jeffreys, etc.
Och Mus. 880, last section: basso continuo to Gesualdo Books I, II, & IV
Och Mus. 1023: basso continuo parts to Dering 1618; with Jeffreys
[?Lost scores of Gesualdo madrigals used to create the basso continuo parts in *Och* Mus. 880, last section]

---

converts.[56] The discomfiture of the Anglican establishment was such that Archbishop Laud was forced to issue a proclamation against the resorting to Mass. The Queen promptly held a Midnight Mass at the Somerset House chapel for all recent converts in defiance of Laud. This was also the period, too, when statues to the Virgin, which had been broken or defaced after the Reformation, began to return to public prominence.[57] In 1635 a discourse, 'wherein... the *B. Virgin Mary* Mother of God, is defended, and vindicated', was published under the title *Maria Triumphans*. The

---

[56] The chapel had been planned as early as 1623 as part of Charles' madcap scheme to entice the Spanish Infanta into marriage. See [C. de Gamaches], *Mémoires de la Mission des Capucins*, ed. A. de Valence (Paris, 1881), 29 & 34-7; and T. Birch, *The Court and Times of Charles I*, (London, 1848), ii, 176 & 310-12.

[57] An example is the statue of the Virgin Mary and baby Jesus which adorns the porch of the University Church in Oxford (the 'baroque' porch was added to the church by Nicholas Stone in 1637).

anonymous author dedicated the book to Queen Henrietta Maria and in the dedication he explicitly associated the Queen's name with that of the Virgin:

> She, whom [the book] cheefely concernes, will a new become your Patronesse: And thus will *Mary*, the Queene of Heauen for a great Queene vpon earth; the Mother of our *Celestiall King*, for the mother of our future terrene King. And finally, by your protecting and pleading for it, the Immaculate Virgin will (in a more full manner) become an Aduocate for you, her *Aduocate*.

There can be little doubt from the dedication the author was intending the 'Maria' in his title to be dually interpreted as the Blessed Virgin Mary in Heaven and Queen Henrietta Maria, the Virgin's champion and representative on earth. (Incidentally Maria was the King's preferred name for his Queen.) Indeed the association of the name of the Queen with that of the Virgin would have seemed quite natural to contemporaries; Catholics would have seen parallels between the Virgin Mary and Henrietta Maria: the piety of a mother and bride who protected and interceded for her followers. We have returned here to the Song of Song imagery which imbues many of the motet texts in Jeffreys' and Bing's manuscripts, and in light of this I suggest that the presence of so many Marian pieces in the manuscripts demonstrates that we have here the remnants of the musical repertoire of Henrietta Maria's Roman Catholic Chapel - a repertoire which was a symbolic representation of not only the Virgin Mary but of the Queen herself.[58]

We should, however, remember that a number of motets in the manuscript collections have had alternative texts added (see pages 128 and 161 above). I suggest that Civil War Oxford (1642-6) would provide the circumstances for performances of both the openly Marian pieces and those pieces with their texts modified to suit a more Protestant taste. Perhaps the Marian pieces were performed in the Queen's private chapel (in Merton College?) away from the public, and the pieces with adapted texts were used in more public performances (the King's devotions in Christ Church?). When one considers the size and contents of Hatton's music collection, his patronage of High Church Anglicans (see pages 13-15 above), and the activities of his musicians and copyists, it seems inconceivable that, as Comptroller of the King's Household, Hatton did not have some responsibility for music. Perhaps, with the majority of the regular court musicians absent, Hatton's musicians acted as replacements and as a result the Court was treated to performances of the most up-to-date Italian or Italianate music. It seems that the manuscripts copied by Christopher Hatton's musicians are representative of a Royalist repertoire from the

---

[58] See E. Veevers, *Images of Love and Religion: Queen Henrietta Maria and Court Entertainments* (Cambridge, 1989), 75-109.

wartime Court at Oxford, and they provide an indication of the music which was performed to 'his Sacred Majestie in his Solitudes and Sufferings'.[59]

---

[59] From the subtitle to John Wilson's *Psalterium Carolinum* of 1657, which was, in turn, taken from the title of John Gauden's recasting of Charles I's record of his sufferings and religious meditations: *Eikon Basilike, The Pourtraicture of his Sacred Majestie in his Solitudes and Sufferings* [London, 1649]; see footnote 20 above.

EXCURSUS I

NEWLY-IDENTIFIED MOTETS BY RICHARD DERING

The popularity of Richard Dering's two- and three-voice Latin motets in Protestant England is a strange phenomenon. Dering (c.1580-1630) was a Roman Catholic composer who - following study at Oxford (Christ Church, B.Mus., 1610) - decided to live abroad (like so many English Catholic musicians).[1] He travelled in Italy (c.1612),[2] and by 1617 was organist to the English nuns of the Convent of the Blessed Virgin Mary at Brussels. While he was in the Low Countries he published two sets of motets: *Cantiones Sacrae Quinque Vocum* and *Cantica Sacra... Senis Vocibus* (P. Phalèse, Antwerp, 1617 and 1618 respectively), and two sets of canzonettas: *Canzonette a Tre Voci* and *Canzonette a Quattro Voci* (both P. Phalèse, Antwerp, 1620). In 1625 Dering returned to England to become organist to Queen Henrietta Maria; he died in 1630 and his post was taken immediately by Richard Mico.[3]

Dering's two- and three-voice motets show a complete assimilation of the techniques of contemporary Italian *concertato* music (which he probably studied during his travels in Italy or from printed Italian music circulating in the Low Countries). A number of his small-scale motets may have been written during his time in Brussels, but most were probably composed in England specifically for Queen Henrietta Maria's Roman Catholic services in her private chapel. The motets remained popular after Dering's death in 1630[4] and, as we shall see, they appear in manuscripts throughout the Civil War, Commonwealth and Restoration periods. Anthony Wood reports that

---

[1] Foster (1891-2), i, 398. For full details of Dering's life and work see P. Platt: 'Richard Dering: an Account of his Life and Work' (B.Litt. dissertation, University of Oxford, 1951-2); 'Dering's Life and Training', *ML*, xxxiii (1952), 41-9; 'Perspectives of Richard Dering's Vocal Music', *Studies in Music* i, University of Western Australia (1967), 56-66; and 'Dering [Deering, Dearing, Diringus etc], Richard', *New Grove*, v, 382-3. Platt corrects many erroneous statements made in previous biographies of Dering which were too reliant upon Anthony Wood's rather fanciful account of the composer in his 'Notes on the Lives of Musicians' (*Ob* D.19(4), ff. 41ᵛ-42).
[2] A 'Mʳ Dearing' - very likely the composer - is noted as being present in Rome, having visited Venice and 'now gone to see more of Italy', in a letter from Sir Dudley Carleton (the King's envoy in Venice) to Sir John Harryngton; PRO SP 99/10, p. 62: 26 June 1612.
[3] See Ashbee (1988), 244-52; and Bennett & Willetts (1977), 35-40.
[4] Thomas Mace - *Musick's Monument* (London, 1676), 235 - reports that, in the days before the Civil War, after he and his friends had finished playing consort music they 'did *Conclude All*, with some *Vocal Musick*, to the *Organ*, or (for want of *That*) to the *Theorboe*... viz. *Mr Deering's Gloria Patri* and other of *His Latin Songs... Wonderfully Rare, Sublime* and *Divine*, beyond all Expression.'

the motets were popular with Oliver Cromwell,[5] and their appeal was such that John Playford published a substantial number of them in his two books of *Cantica Sacra* (1662 and 1674). These two publications have been regarded as the primary sources for Dering's two- and three-part motets (despite the fact they were published three or four decades after the death of the composer), and the numerous manuscript sources of the motets have been totally ignored.[6] A number of the manuscript transmissions of the motets offer slightly different readings to the Playford prints[7] and, what is more, also contain a number of motets attributed to Dering which are not found in the publications. Table 28 offers a summary of the sources of Dering's two- and three-voice Latin motets.

It should be noted that Playford himself was aware of some of the problems surrounding the attributions of Dering's motets, for in his second book of *Cantica Sacra* (1674) he notes that the second to eighth pieces, although 'much of Mr *Deering's* Way', were not considered authentic by everyone. The eighth piece, 'O Rex [*or* crux] ave spes unica', appears in a pre-1674 manuscript source amongst many other Dering motets (Christ Church Mus. 878-80) and so is possibly authentic (see below), but the only identified manuscripts with concordances for motets Nos. 2-7 were actually copied from *Cantica Sacra* II, and so are no help in ascertaining the authenticity of the attribution to Dering (see Table 28b).[8] All the motets published in the 1662 *Cantica Sacra* are likely to be authentic, as all but one ('O lux et decus Hispaniæ') appear with attributions in pre-1662 manuscript sources (see Table 28a). The primary early manuscript sources are: British Library Evelyn MS 189, Royal College of Music MSS 2033, 2034 and 2039, and Christ Church Mus. 747-9 and 878-80.[9] The recently discovered

---

[5] *Ob* Wood D.19(4) *sub* 'Hingston' (appended note in the hand of Benjamin Rogers): '*Hingston*, John, an able Composer, and Organist; He was Org[a]n[ist] to Oliver Protector, who had the Organ of Magd[alen] College in the Palace Hall of Hampton Court: till his ma[jes]ties Restauration: he bred up two Boyes to sing with Himselfe (Mr. Dearings) printed latin songs for 3 voices: which Oliver was most taken with: tho[ugh] he did not allow singing, or Organ in Churches. He had them sung at the Cokepit at White Hall, where he had an Organ: and did allow this John Hingston 100^l per Annum during his usurpation.'

[6] For example, Peter Platt's statement - (1952), 44, footnote 5 - that the 'MSS all appear to be copies of the actual publications', can now be shown to be untenable.

[7] For example, there are occasional differences in note-values, reversal of voices, and scoring for tenor rather than cantus or *vice versa*.

[8] *Ob* Mus. d 10 is an early eighteenth-century copy, and *Ob* Tenbury 892 a mid-eighteenth century copy, of Playford's *Cantica Sacra* II (1674).

[9] The other manuscripts containing concordances with Playford's *Cantica Sacra* (1662) are: *Ckc* 321 & *US-LAuc* C 6968 M4: copied c.1639 (see R. Charteris, 'Four Caroline Part-Books', *ML*, lix (1978), 49-51); *CAR* 'Bishop Smith's Part-Song Books' (housed in the Cumbria Record Office): two partbooks, Cantus and Bassus, annotated 'Thomas Smith Jan: 8. Ani 1637' (see J.P. Cutts, *Roger Smith, his Book: Bishop Smith's Part-Song Books in Carlisle Cathedral Library*, American Insititute of Musicology (Stuttgart, 1972)); *Gu* R.d. 58-61: copied by John Playford in the 1650s (see I. Spink, 'The Old Jewry *Musick-Society*: A Seventeenth Century Catch Club', *Musicology*, ii (1967), 35-41); *Lbl* Add. 11,587: copied by Charles Burney before

Table 28 Motets for Two- and Three Voice and Basso Continuo by Richard Dering

Sources:
1. Cambridge, King's College Rowe MS 321 & USA, University of California, Los Angeles, William Andrews Clark Memorial Library MSS C 6968 M4
2. Carlisle Cathedral 'Bishop Smith's Part-Song Books' (deposited in the Cumbria Record Office)
3. Glasgow, University Library MSS Rd 58-61
4. London, British Library Add. MS 11,587
5. London, British Library Add. MS 11,608
6. London, British Library Add. MS 30,382
7. London, British Library Egerton MS 2013
8. London, British Library Evelyn MS 189
9. London, Royal College of Music MS 660
10. London, Royal College of Music MS 2033
11. London, Royal College of Music MS 2034
12. London, Royal College of Music MS 2039
13. Madrigal Society MSS G 33-6 (housed in the British Library)
14. Oxford, Bodleian Library Mus. MS d. 10
15. Oxford, Bodleian Library Mus. MSS f 17 & 19
16. Oxford, Bodleian Library Mus. Sch. MS C 11
17. Oxford, Bodleian Library Mus. Sch. MSS D 233-6
18. Oxford, Bodleian Library Mus. Sch. MS E 451
19. Oxford, Bodleian Library Tenbury MS 892
20. Oxford, Christ Church Mus. 747-9
21. Oxford, Christ Church Mus. 878-80
22. Christ Church Mus. 1013-15
23. York, Minster Library MSS M.5.S
24. C. Burney, *A General History of Music* (London, 1776-89), iii, 479
25. J. Hilton ed., *Catch that Catch Can* (London, 1652)
26. J. Playford ed., *Cantica Sacra* (London, 1662)
27. J. Playford ed., *Cantica Sacra.... The Second Sett* (London, 1674)

1782; *Lbl* Add. 11,608: copied by John Hilton 1656-9 (see M. Chan, 'John Hilton's Manuscript British Library Add. MS 11,608', *ML*, lx (1979), 440-9; and ibid., 'A Mid-Seventeenth-Century Music Meeting and Playford's Publishing', *The Well Enchanting Skill: Music, Poetry, and Drama in the Culture of the Renaissance: Essays in Honour of F.W. Sternfeld*, ed. J. Caldwell, E. Olleson & S. Wollenberg (Oxford, 1990), 231-44); *Lbl* Add. 30,382: copied by Henry Bowman c.1678-85 (see Part II, MS V); *Lbl* Egerton 2013: copied 1650-60s (see Chan (1990)); *Lcm* 660: copied in the eighteenth century (mostly from *Och* Mus. 878-80); Mad. Soc. G 33-6: copied in the 1630s(?) (same hand as *Och* Mus. 430 & *Ob* Tenbury 1162-7); *Ob* Mus. f 17-19: copied by Thomas Hamond, finished 1655/6 (see M. Crum, 'A Seventeenth-Century Collection of Music Belonging to Thomas Hamond, a Suffolk Landowner', *Bodleian Library Record*, vi (1957), 373-86); *Ob* Mus. Sch. C 11: copied by Edward Lowe in the late 1660s(?) (see Part II, MS XXIV); *Ob* Mus. Sch. D 233-6: copied by Edward Lowe in the 1670s(?); *Ob* Mus. Sch. E 451: Edward Lowe's continuo book, the Dering pieces were added in the mid-seventeenth century(?) (see Part II, MS XXX); *Och* Mus. 1013-15: copied in the 1650s(?); and *Y* M.5.S: dated 1688 (see Griffiths, (1981), 42-65).

Table 28 continued

Title	Scoring	Source
a. Motets published in J. Playford ed., *Cantica Sacra* (London, 1662)		
Ardens est cor meum No. 1	CBbc	1, 5, 7-9, 11, 12, 16, 17, 20, 21, 23
Beatus vir qui inventus est No. 3	TTbc	11, 20
Canite Jehovae No. 2	CBbc	11, 20, 23
Cantate Domino No. 18	CCBbc	1, 10, 20, 21
Conceptio tua No. 12	CBbc	9, 11, 17, 18, 21
Duo seraphin clamabant No. 5	TTbc	11, 21
Ego dormio No. 14	BBbc	9, 11, 20, 21
Gaudent in cœlis No. 7	CCbc	1, 9, 11, 17, 18, 20, 21, 23
Gloria Patri et Filio No. 24	ATBbc	1-6, 8, 10, 13, 16, 20, 22-25
Gratias tibi Deus No. 8	CBbc	5, 9, 11, 12, 20, 21
Isti sunt sancti No. 20	CCBbc	1, 8, 10, 12, 16-18, 20, 21, 23
Justus cor suum tradidit No. 6	TBbc	1, 8, 10, 17, 18, 20, 21
Justus germinabit No. 21	TTBbc	1, 10, 20, 21
Lætamini cum Maria No. 17	CTBbc	1, 8, 10, 17, 18, 20, 21
Miserere mei Deus No. 13	CBbc	11
O bone Jesu, O dulcis Jesu No. 4	TTbc	11, 12, 17, 18, 20-22
O Domine Jesu Christe No. 11	CBbc	1, 9, 11, 14 (down a tone), 16-18, 19 (down a tone), 20, 21, 27 (down a tone)
O lux et decus Hispaniæ No. 23	CTBbc	
O quam suavis est Domine No. 19	CTBbc	10, 20, 21
Panis angelicus No. 16	CCBbc	8, 17, 18, 20, 21
Qualis est dilectus tuus No. 22	CTBbc	1, 10, 12, 17, 18, 20, 21
Sancta et immaculata virginitas No. 10	TTbc	9, 11, 17, 18, 21
Veni electa mea Cicilia No. 9	CBbc	1, 9, 11, 20, 21
Vulnerasti cor meum No. 15	TTBbc	10, 20, 21

b. Motets published in J. Playford ed., *Cantica Sacra*.... The Second Sett (London, 1674)

Playford states in the Preface: 'Those at the beginning (from the Second to the Eighth) are much of M*r* *Deering's* Way, yet by some believed not to be his, but all that have heard them conclude them Excellently Good.'

Table 28b continued

Duo seraphin clamabant No. 2	CBbc	14, 19
Ego sum resurrectio No. 5	CBbc	14, 19
Hierusalem quae edificatur No. 7	CBbc	14, 19
Laetatus sum No. 6	CBbc	14, 19
O Rex/crux ave spes unica No. 8	CBbc	9, 14, 19, 21
O Domine Jesu Christe No. 1	CBbc	1, 9, 11 (up a tone), 14; 16-18 (up a tone), 19; 20, 21, 26 (up a tone)
O sacrum convivium No. 3	CBbc	14, 19
Tres sunt qui testimonium No. 4	CBbc	14, 19

c. Motets in manuscripts with firm attributions to Dering

Alleluia gaudeamus	CCBbc	8 (anon.), 10 (attrib.), 12 (attrib.)
Anima Christi	CBbc	1 (anon.), 9 (attrib.), 21 (anon.)
Hei mihi Domine	CBbc	9 (attrib.), 21 (anon.)
O Domine Jesu Christe	ATBbc	12 (anon.), 15 (attrib.)
O nomen Jesu	CCBbc	8 (anon.), 10 (attrib.)
O sacrum convivium	CBbc*	9 (attrib.), 21 (anon.)
Tibi laus	CTBbc	10 (anon.), 12 (attrib.), 20 (anon.), 21 (anon.)
Veni sponsa Christi	CC[B]bc	10 (attrib.), 12 (anon.)

* Not the 1674 setting

d. Anonymous motets found amongst attributable Dering motets

Angelus ad pastores ait	C-bc	11
Augustine	-TBbc	21
Beatus laurentius	CB[bc]	21
Confitemini	BB[B]bc	21
Dulcissime Jesu Christe	C-bc	11
Exultate justi	CC-[bc]	8
Exultavit cor meum	CCBbc	10, 12, 21
Gloria tibi trinitas	T[bc]	21
Jesu auctor	B[bc]	21
O dulcissime Jesu	AB-[bc]	8
O Maria	C-Bbc	21
Paratum cor meum	C-Bbc	21
Propitius esto	CT[bc]	21
Protector noster	CC[bc]	21
Quemadmodum	C-B[bc]	21

Table 28d concluded

Si diligis me Simon Petre	CB-[bc]	8
Te gloriosus Apostolorum	CB-[bc]	8
Tua Jesu dilectio	T[bc]	21

e. Motets with questionable attributions to Dering

The attributions by the second scribe in Royal College of Music MS 2034 are questionable as the copyist also ascribes pieces to Dering that are actually by Finetti (see Part II, MS XX).

Domine Deus gratia	C-bc	11 (Italian?)
Gloria tibi Domine	C-bc	11 (Italian?)

Evelyn MS 189 (Part II, MS XVI) consists of two partbooks from an original set of four (lacking Cantus and Basso Continuo).[10] The partbooks contain twelve three-voice motets, six of which can be found in Playford's *Cantica Sacra* I (1662). Two of the other motets appear, attributed to Dering, in manuscripts in the Royal College of Music: 'Alleluia gaudeamus' is in MSS 2033 and 2039, and 'O nomen Jesu' is in MS 2033; both motets lack the bass part in the Royal College manuscripts, and the discovery of the Evelyn MS enables the completion of the two motets.[11] The manuscript is possibly one of the earliest surviving sources of Dering motets, and may even date from the late 1620s (the common Grapes watermark in the Altus partbook is, at present, no help in assigning a precise date to the manuscript).

The three Royal College of Music MSS 2033, 2034 and 2039 (Part II, MSS XIX, XX and XXI respectively) may also be relatively early. MSS 2033 and 2034 are closely related: they appear to consist of the same paper-type (although no watermarks are visible in either manuscript); were both ruled with the same rastrum; and the manuscripts have two scribes in common. Unfortunately the lack of a watermark makes a precise dating impossible, but a date in the 1640s does not seem unreasonable (the three compositions by George Jeffreys in MS 2033 are all 'pre 1648' pieces).[12] Royal College of Music MS 2039 may be contemporary with MSS 2033 and 2034: it has the watermark of a small pot lettered AB which is consistent

---

[10] The two partbooks were discovered by Dr John Milsom amongst papers relating to the Evelyn family (now in the British Library).

[11] It should be noted, however, that *Lbl* Evelyn 189 and *Lcm* 2033 & 2039 come from different lines of filiation for they differ in many aspects (bars missing/added, different underlay, different accidentals, etc.).

[12] Five of the six pieces copied by scribe 'B' in *Lcm* 2034 are attributed to 'Richard deering'; two of them, however, are actually by Finetti, which must call into question scribe B's other three attributions.

with a date in the fourth decade of the seventeenth century. The contents of MS 2039 are, however, more varied than those of MSS 2033 and 2034: as well as motets by Dering and Jeffreys, MS 2039 includes instrumental music and English devotional songs. Seven unidentified scribes contributed to the copying of the manuscript, which may therefore have taken place over a number of years, but again the 1640s would seem to be the most likely date of origin.

The partbooks Christ Church Mus. 747-9 (Part II, MS LVI) also contain music by Dering and Jeffreys (all 'pre-1648')[13] and probably date from the 1640s. A comparison of the readings of the Dering motets in the partbooks with those in Playford's *Cantica Sacra* (1662) indicates that the two sources are closely related, for they agree in all but very minor and insignificant details. The usual interpretation of this has been that the Christ Church partbooks were copied from the printed source sometime in the mid 1660s;[14] but as the manuscripts contain a Pillars watermark (which is not found in manuscripts after 1648)[15] it is far more likely that the partbooks pre-date the print and were closely related to Playford's lost manuscript copy-source.[16] A close relationship between the partbooks and the print is confirmed by the presence of Alessandro Grandi's motet 'O bone Jesu' in both sources. The motet, originally from Grandi's second book of motets of 1613, seems out of place in both the manuscript and the print, for it is the only composition by an Italian, and the only four-part piece, in both sources.[17] It is therefore possible that the three Royal College of Music manuscripts and the Christ Church partbooks Mus. 747-9, together with the various sections of the Christ Church partbooks Mus. 878-80 (examined in the previous chapter), are surviving performing parts dating from the time of the Oxford Court.

Table 28c lists eight motets which are attributed to Dering in manuscript sources but do not appear in Playford's publications; these motets (and particularly those contained in the manuscripts examined above)[18] should be added to the list of authentic motets by Dering. It should also be noted that the primary manuscript sources of Dering's motets - Evelyn MS 189, Royal

---

[13] Locke's 'Agnosce O Christiane' and Child's 'Come Hymen come' were later additions to the partbooks.
[14] See, for example, Platt (1952), 44, footnote 5.
[15] Thompson (1988), 220, & *passim*.
[16] *Och* Mus. 747-9 is unlikely to be Playford's actual copy-source as the order of the motets in the partbooks differs from that in the print, and the print contains four motets which are not found in the manuscripts; the two must, however, be closely related.
[17] Indeed Grandi's motet is the only piece in *Cantica Sacra* (1662) which is not by Dering. It also appears, anonymously, in Mad. Soc. G 33-6, a set of parts which also contains Dering's 'Gloria Patri et Filio'; and in Lowe's basso continuo partbook *Ob* Mus. Sch. E 451, attributed to Dering in the body of the manuscript and to Legrand in the index.
[18] The attributions in *Lcm* 660 may be questionable: the manuscript was copied in the eighteenth century, and the primary copy-source appears to have been *Och* Mus. 878-80 where all the pieces are anonymous. The copyist may, however, have had access to other information concerning the attributions which is now lost.

College of Music MSS 2033, 2034 and 2039, and Christ Church Mus. 747-9 and 878-80 - also contain a number of anonymous motets; these pieces, which appear amongst authentic Dering motets, are listed in Table 28d. Unfortunately many of these motets are incomplete, but - from the parts that survive - they appear to be stylistically akin to the 'authentic' Dering motets. For these reasons it is tentatively suggested that these eighteen pieces are also by Richard Dering.

CHAPTER SIX

HATTON-RELATED MANUSCRIPTS

More Manuscripts from the Hatton Collection?

Having examined the activities of Christopher Hatton III's musicians and scribes we are now in the position to explore links and relationships between the Hatton collection and various other manuscripts. Here a word of warning is necessary: the evidence we are dealing with is incomplete, and therefore any attempt at uncovering the complex web of relationships between manuscripts, scribes and patrons is fraught with difficulties. The main danger is one of over-simplification: the temptation to try to assign a Hatton provenance to all the pre-1646 manuscripts and prints in Christ Church must be avoided. The Hatton collection was undoubtedly of primary importance in the formation of the Christ Church music library, but we should remember that there are also present the remnants of a number of other music collections from the first half of the seventeenth century.[1] It is even possible that, due to the presence of Court in Oxford between 1642 and 1646, the library of Christ Church, Oxford became a *de facto* depository for Royalist music collections. Future work on the large number of manuscripts of unknown provenance in Christ Church will, hopefully, reveal evidence of other collectors and patrons' music libraries.

With the above warning in mind, it is my intention to explore a number of scribal and repertorial links that exist between Hatton sources and a number of other manuscripts. The following comments are not offered as definitive statements; the intention is rather to present ideas for testing by other scholars as more research is undertaken and new evidence unearthed. The first three manuscript sets to be considered in this section - Christ Church Mus. 372-6, 463-7 and 1155-61 - have already been proposed as part of the Hatton collection in Chapter Two, due to the fact that their bindings contain annotations in the handwriting of Hatton's scribes (see

---

[1] For example, the collection belonging to Hatton's fellow Northamptonshire resident, John Browne (1608-91), Clerk of the Parliaments. The following manuscripts in Christ Church are considered to be from his collection: partbooks of consort music: *Och* Mus. 367-70, 379-81, 423-8, 473-8 and (probably) 716-20; and organbooks: *Och* Mus. 430 and (probably) 1004. See A. Ashbee, 'Instrumental Music from the Library of John Browne (1608-91), Clerk of the Parliaments', *ML*, lviii (1977), 43-59; Pinto (1978), 12-24; and N. Fortune with I. Fenlon, 'Music Manuscripts of John Browne (1608-91) and from Stanford Hall, Leicestershire', *Source Materials and the Interpretation of Music: a Memorial Volume to Thurston Dart*, ed. I. Bent (London, 1981), 155-68. The various Browne manuscripts, which were probably copied *c*.1630-42, appear to have been part of Dean Aldrich's bequest to Christ Church in 1710 (see J.B. Malchair's 1787 catalogue: *Lcm* 2125); it is not known how Aldrich came to own the manuscripts.

pages 32-5 above). It was pointed out that the annotations do not prove that Hatton was the original owner of the manuscripts, but merely that they were connected with the Hatton family at some stage. These manuscripts are earlier in origin than those copied by Baron Hatton's scribes - Bing, Lilly and Jeffreys - and are probably roughly contemporary with the various annotated prints which are listed in Table 5. David Pinto has suggested that these printed sources came from the library of Christopher Hatton II and were purchased before 1619.[2] (For alternative hypotheses concerning the annotated prints and manuscripts see page 35-6 above.) The partbooks Christ Church Mus. 372-6 (see Part II, MS XLIX) contain four- and five-part instrumental music (some perhaps of vocal origin) and a three-section five-voice madrigal by 'Signior Diomede' Cato (*c.*1570-*c.*1607), and were probably copied in the early seventeenth century. The presence of music by Cato, a Venetian-born lutenist who worked at the Court of King Sigismund III of Poland, can perhaps be explained by the fact that, in May 1597, there was a Polish deputation to England led by Paweł Działńyski, secretary to Sigismund III.[3] The five partbooks Christ Church Mus. 463-7 probably also date from the early years of the seventeenth century and contain twenty motets, fifteen madrigals and two instrumental pieces, all by Ferrabosco I, one motet by Clemens non Papa, one motet by Ferrabosco II, and one anonymous motet. The partbooks are related, by repertoire and scribal concordance, to another set of Christ Church partbooks, Mus. 78-82, which together represent the primary sources for vocal works by the elder Ferrabosco.[4] The unidentified scribe who contributed to both Mus. 78-82 and 463-7 was also the copyist of the variant version of Alessandro Striggio's *Il Cicalamento delle Donne al Bucato* found in Christ Church Mus. 1155-61 (see Part II, MS LXI).

Another Christ Church manuscript which may have connections with the Hatton family is Mus. 21 (see Part II, MS XLV). This is an important early source for the music of Orlando Gibbons (1583-1625) who was employed by Christopher Hatton II (see page 6 above). The authoritative annotations added by the first anonymous scribe ('A') appear to indicate that the manuscript was closely connected with Gibbons or his circle.[5] This evidence alone is enough to hint that the manuscript may have some connection with

---

[2] Pinto (1990), 85.

[3] Ibid., 105, note 27.

[4] *Och* Mus. 78-82 contains a number of motets by Ferrabosco I which are concordant with *Och* Mus. 463-7, and also the whole of the contents of Ferrabosco's first book of madrigals of 1587; see Kerman (1962), 89-90.

[5] The inscription pasted to p. 1 in the hand of Benjamin Rogers (1614-98) (a later owned of the manuscript), which includes the words: 'This Score booke was done formerly, by that rare Musition, M^r. Orlando Gibbons...', gave rise to the idea that the manuscript was copied by Orlando Gibbons; see Fellows (rev. 2/1970), 63-4. This cannot be substantiated from the available evidence, but Scribe A's inscriptions do indicate that the manuscript was, at least, closely connected with the composer's circle.

the Hattons,[6] but - as David Pinto has noted[7] - this becomes even more likely when it is realised that the printed copy-sources of the Italian madrigals in Mus. 21 (copied by Scribe B) have all been nominated as part of the Hatton collection (see Chapter Two); namely:

C. Gesualdo, *Madrigali* Bk 6 (Venice, 2/1616)	*Och* Mus. 908-12
T. Merula, *Motetti* Bk 1, Op. 6 (Venice, 1624)	-
G.L. Missino, *Tirsi Doglioso* Bk 1 (Venice, 1615)	*Och* Mus. 442-6
C. Monteverdi, *Madrigali* Bk 4 (Venice, 7/1622)	*Och* Mus. 881-6
P. Nenna, *Madrigali* Bk 4 (Venice, 1617)	*Och* Mus. 908-12
P. Nenna, *Madrigali* Bk 5 (Venice, 1612)	*Och* Mus. 908-12

If this manuscript was, as the evidence appears to suggest, once part of the Hatton collection, it found its way to Christ Church via a different route to that described on pages 41-3 above: an annotation on the first page of Christ Church Mus. 21, in the hand of a one-time owner, Benjamin Rogers, informs us that the manuscript was given to him by the stationer John Playford on 18 August 1673; what is more, the score was part of Richard Goodson's bequest, not that of Henry Aldrich.[8] If this manuscript was part of the Hatton collection it must, at some stage (perhaps in 1670 following Hatton's death), have become separated from the rest of the collection and was bought by Playford in the belief that it was a Gibbons autograph; it then passed from Playford to Rogers in August 1673; on Rogers' death in 1698 it came into the possession of Richard Goodson; and finally, with Goodson's bequest to Christ Church in 1718, was reunited with the rest of the Hatton collection.

In Chapter Three various links were explored between the Hatton scribe Stephen Bing, the composer John Ward, and the cleric-copyist Thomas Myriell (see pages 64-6 above). It was noted that John Ward, who was closely connected with Myriell, was patronised by Sir Henry Fanshawe, the Remembrancer of the Exchequer, whose half-sister Alice was married to Sir Christopher Hatton II.[9] On this basis it was tentatively suggested that a number of the Myriell manuscripts (Christ Church Mus. 44, 61-7 and 459-62) may have come to Christ Church via the Hatton collection.[10] Another set

---

[6] On such evidence one could further speculate that the incomplete Christ Church copy of Orlando Gibbons' *Fantazies of III Parts* [London, *c*.1620] may be of Hatton provenance; *Och* Mus. 105-6, lacking Tenor book, first impression: see Thurston Dart, 'The Printed Fantasies of Orlando Gibbons', *ML*, xxxvii (1956), 342-9.

[7] Pinto (1990), 91-2.

[8] See J.B. Malchair's 1787 catalogue (*Lcm* 2125: Goodson section, f. 3).

[9] It is worth noting at this point that, as well as their main estate at Ware Park, Hertfordshire, the Fanshawes had a London residence in Warwick Lane near to St Paul's Cathedral. This places the Fanshawe family in close proximity to the 'St Paul's circle' of musicians and copyist (which included Myriell and Barnard; see pp. 64-6 above).

[10] David Pinto - (1990), 90-1 - has noted a further link between Myriell and the Hatton collection concerning *Lbl* Add. 29,427 (a single Altus partbook copied by Myriell and his associate scribes). He notes that the partbook includes two four-part instrumental pieces from

of Jacobean partbooks in the Christ Church library appear to be connected with the Fanshawe family: Mus. 56-60. This set, which lacks the Bassus partbook, includes twelve compositions by John Ward, one of which - the six-part 'If heaven's just wrath' - is a lament on the death of Sir Henry Fanshawe.[11] This set of parts would seem to be another prime candidate for the following line of transmission: Sir Henry Fanshawe—Lady Alice Hatton (née Fanshawe)—Baron Hatton—Henry Aldrich—Christ Church. Another possible line of transmission from the Fanshawes to the Hattons is raised by the intriguing fact that, in 1642 when the Fanshawes' Ware Park estate was sequestrated and sold by Parliament (because Royalist troops had been harboured there), it was Lady Elizabeth Newport-Hatton (see pages 3-5 above) who purchased the property.[12] Perhaps she also bought the Fanshawe's music manuscripts when the contents of Ware Park were auctioned? When Lady Elizabeth Newport-Hatton died in 1646 her estate (which included Hatton House, Holborn) was inherited by Baron Hatton. In this case the line of transmission for Christ Church Mus. 56-60 (and perhaps the Myriell manuscripts) would be: Sir Henry Fanshawe—Lady Elizabeth Newport-Hatton—Baron Hatton—Henry Aldrich—Christ Church.

It is possible that these attempts at bringing various other Christ Church manuscripts under the Hatton 'umbrella' may be flawed, that the various links and relationships are no more than coincidences, and that the lack of surviving evidence has disguised what is actually a far more complex picture. However, it is equally possible that, hidden amongst the vast number of manuscripts of unknown provenance in Christ Church (and perhaps other libraries), there are other items that were once part of the Hatton collection. This chapter concludes with an examination of the work of two scribes whose copy-sources included printed music from the Hatton collection.[13]

Giuseppe Guami's *Canzonette Francese* (Antwerp, 1612), a copy of which survives in Christ Church in Aldrich's composite partbooks *MAD*[rigal] E (now Mus. 502-7), and asks 'Was this another print that passed through Hatton hands?'

[11] John Aplin - 'Sir Henry Fanshawe and Two Sets of Early Seventeenth Century Part-Books at Christ Church, Oxford', *ML*, lvii (1976), 11-24 - has suggested that John Ward was the compiler of the manuscripts. The partbooks, however, contain at least three hands, none of which can be identified with the handwriting of Ward; see Payne (1984), 176-88. Craig Monson has noted the appearance of the handwriting of one of the subsidiary scribes in *Cfm* Mu 734 (*olim* Mus. 24 E 13-17), Mad. Soc. G 37-42, & *US-LAuc* F 1995 M4; see (1982), 61 (the hand, however, does not appear in *Och* Mus. 397-400 (Lilly) as Monson states). David Pinto considers the main hand of *Och* Mus. 56-60 to have 'some affinities with a hand found in [*Och*] Mus. 878-80', (1990), 90; the present writer cannot agree.

[12] See John Loftis' introduction to *The Memoirs of Anne, Lady Halkett and Ann, Lady Fanshawe* (Oxford, 1979); and H.C. Fanshawe, *The History of the Fanshawe Family* (Newcastle-upon-Tyne, 1927), *passim*.

[13] There is no suggestion, however, that the resultant manuscripts were ever part of the Hatton collection.

The 'Tregian' Manuscripts

The main copyist of three vast manuscript anthologies, the Fitzwilliam Virginal Book (Cambridge, Fitzwilliam Museum MS Mu 168, *olim* Mus. 32 G 29) and two scorebooks of vocal and instrumental music (British Library Egerton MS 3665 and the 'Sambrooke Manuscript' in New York Public Library, Drexel MS 4302), is thought to be Francis Tregian (1574-1619?).[14] Tregian, a staunch Roman Catholic, is said to have compiled the manuscripts whilst he was incarcerated in the Fleet prison between 1609 and 1619 having been convicted for recusancy. This traditional view is in need of revision: it can now be shown that Tregian was at liberty until 1616, that the copying is unlikely to have taken place in prison (prisoners could, in return for payment, leave the Fleet for periods, under surveillance), it is no longer certain that Tregian died in 1619,[15] and - what is more - the very identity of the copyist has recently been called into question.[16] But, whatever the true facts concerning the copyist, there are undoubtedly some intriguing links between the 'Tregian' manuscripts and the Hatton collection.

The Egerton and Sambrooke manuscripts together contain approximately 1,550 pieces copied from a large number of printed and manuscript sources. Thurston Dart was the first to note that a number of the scribe's copy-sources appear to have found their way to Christ Church, Oxford;[17] these include the following rare publications:[18]

O. Bartolini, *Madrigali* Bk 1 (Venice, 1606)	*Och* Mus. 442-6
E. du Caurroy, *Fantasies* (Paris, 1610)	*Och* Mus. 592-7
A. Cifra, *Madrigali* Bk 3 (Venice, 1615)	*Och* Mus. 484-8
T. Pecci, *Madrigali* Bk 1 (Venice, 3/1609)	*Och* Mus. 442-6

---

[14] See J.A. Fuller Maitland & W. Barclay Squire, 'Introduction', *The Fitzwilliam Virginal Book Edited from the Original Manuscript* (London and Leipzig, 1894-9), i, pp. v-xi; Schofield & Dart (1951); E. Cole, 'In Search of Francis Tregian', *ML*, xxxiii (1952), 28-32; E. Cole, 'Seven Problems of the Fitzwilliam Virginal Book', *PRMA*, lxxix (1952-3), 51-64; and Thurston Dart & R. Marlow, 'Tregian, Francis', *New Grove*, xix, 126-7.

[15] A. Cuneo, 'Francis Tregian the Younger: Musician, Collector and Humanist?', *ML*, lxxvi (1995), 401-2.

[16] Ruby Reid Thompson (1992) has recently challenged the accepted view that Tregian was the compiler of the manuscript anthologies. Based on a close examination of all the manuscripts attributed to Tregian (paper, watermarks, inks, margin-rulings, alterations, etc.), she has given advanced notice that she proposes to prove that the 'Tregian' manuscripts were the work of several copyists. The present writer is prepared to accept that there are subsidiary hands at work in certain sections of the manuscripts, but is not yet prepared to dismiss Tregian as the main copyist. I reserve my final judgement until Ms Thompson's complete study is available. (For a challenge to Thompson (1992), see Cuneo (1995), 398-404.)

[17] R. Thurston Dart, 'Tregian, Francis', *Grove's Dictionary of Music and Musicians* (5th edition, London, 1954), viii, 539. See also Pinto (1990), 91.

[18] The Christ Church copies of O. Bartolini, *Madrigali* Bk 1 (Venice, 1606) (Mus. 442-6), and E. du Caurroy, *Fantasies* (Paris, 1610) (Mus. 592-7) are the only complete copies in existence. The annotation on the cover of *Och* Mus. 129-34 (Philips, *Madrigali a* 6 Bks 1 & 2) may be in the hand of one of the subsidiary scribes who contributed to the copying of *Och* Mus. 56-60.

P. Philips, *Madrigali a 6* Bk 1 (Antwerp, 2/1604)   *Och* Mus. 129-34, 586-91
P. Philips, *Madrigali a 6* Bk 2 (Antwerp, 1603)   *Och* Mus. 129-34, 538-43
P. Rimonte, *Parnaso Español* (Antwerp, 1614)   *Och* Mus. 592-7

The Bartolini, du Caurroy, Cifra and Pecci prints have already been cited, in Chapter Two, as being 'of possible Hatton provenance'. It is possible, then, that at some stage the Hatton family acquired a number of the 'Tregian' scribe's printed copy-sources. If Francis Tregian was the main copyist of the manuscript anthologies - and until evidence to the contrary is presented I am quite happy to believe this - an interesting possibility is raised. It is known that on his death Tregian's books, 'whereof there were many hundreds', passed to a fellow prisoner in the Fleet, Sir Francis Englefield, and were presumably then dispersed.[19] The fact that Hatton House was just round the corner from the Fleet[20] leads one to venture the speculation that it was Lady Elizabeth Newport-Hatton who procured some of Tregian's music, which then passed to Baron Hatton and, via Aldrich, finally to Christ Church in the manner outlined above. This is pure speculation, but it does seem very likely that there was some link between the 'Tregian' copyist and the Hattons. This is further indicated by the presence in Christ Church of a set of five partbooks in the 'Tregian' hand: Christ Church Mus. 510-14 (see Part II, MS LII).[21] This set of forty-five Italian five-voice madrigals by Fontanelli, Gagliano, Gesualdo,[22] Pecci and Quintiani, was bound by Henry Aldrich (together with four English pieces he copied himself) in his usual brown leather bindings and labelled 'Z V B[ooks]'.[23] Presumably the partbooks came into Aldrich's possession in the same way as the prints listed above.

Angelo Notari's Scorebook: British Library Add. MS 31,440

A link between Angelo Notari (1566-1663)[24] and Hatton's scribes was proposed in Chapter Five (see pages 162-5 above) due to the presence of Notari's handwriting in 'M^r. Jeffreys Coll: of songs' (Christ Church Mus.

---

[19] See *New Grove*, xix, 127.
[20] It should be noted that Lady Elizabeth herself spent a short time in the Fleet prison in 1638 when, during a dispute with the Bishop of Ely over Hatton House, she ignored a Royal injunction; see Marryat & Broadbent (1930).
[21] See P. Willetts, 'Tregian's Part-Books', *MT*, civ (1963), 334-5.
[22] It should be noted that pieces from Gesualdo's first book of madrigals were copied after pieces from Gesualdo's second book of madrigals. This would seem to suggest that the copyist - as with Bing in the last section of *Och* Mus. 880 - was using copy-sources which have the numeration reversed, i.e. Book I is numbered Book II and *vice versa*, as in the Christ Church Mus. 908-12 (see p. 169 above).
[23] Aldrich presumably excluded the partbooks from either the *MOT*[et] or *MAD*[rigal] series because they contained both sacred and secular music, and were also manuscript copies.
[24] For a brief description of Notari's life and work see pp. 162-5 above.

877-880); it was noted too that the paper which Notari used for his partbooks (with the watermark of a Pot lettered ID) was also available to Stephen Bing and George Jeffreys (see Table 18). On this evidence it was suggested that Notari was present at the Oxford Court for at least part of the period of 1642-6. Notari's scorebook of Italian music, British Library Add. MS 31,440 (see Part II, MS VII), offers further evidence of a link between Notari and Hatton. This important collection is described in the British Library catalogue as 'Motets with a bass... for harpsichord or organ, in score, by Pietro Reggio (d. 1685). *Autograph*; signed by the composer on f. 157....' and, in another reference, a little more cautiously as 'Songs, with a bass for harpsichord, in score, by P. Reggio. *Autograph* (?)'.[25] These two completely unfounded statements were accepted without question until Pamela Willetts' important article on the manuscript.[26] Miss Willetts demonstrated that none of the original contents is by Reggio, and that his hand does not appear in the manuscript. The misunderstanding was due to the piece on folios 156^v-7, 'As water fluid is', which is ascribed to 'P. Reggio'. The item is in a different hand to the rest of the manuscript and is obviously a later addition. Nowhere else in the manuscript does the handwriting occur, nor does the name 'Reggio' appear again. On this evidence the whole contents of the manuscript were considered to be by Reggio.[27] As was noted in Chapter Five, the discovery of an autograph letter of Notari's proved beyond doubt that he was the copyist of Add. MS 31,440 and the middle sections of Christ Church Mus. 878 and 880.[28]

Notari's scorebook appears to be a personal collection of music by Italian composers written between *circa* 1600 and 1643; however, the manuscript, which includes much of Notari's own music, appears to have been copied in the 1640s (see below). A number of the pieces are arrangements, or substantial reworkings, of pieces by other composers. For example, 'Ferma Caronte. Chi è colui, che grida?' (ff. 63^v-5) is an ornamented version of Bartolomeo Barbarino's madrigal printed in his *Secondo Libro de Madrigali* (Venice, 1607).[29] Other pieces are substantial reworkings of the original, for example, 'Occhi soli d'amore' (ff. 32^v-3)

---

[25] Hughes-Hughes (1906-9), i, 287, & ii, 486.
[26] Willetts (1962).
[27] It followed that concordant pieces in other manuscripts (e.g. *Lbl* Add. 31,479) were erroneously attributed to Reggio in Hughes-Hughes (1906-9), and these misattributions were then frequently quoted. Even the handwriting of the later addition in *Lbl* Add. 31,440 is not Reggio's: *Lbl* Harley 1501 has written on the final folio, 'Scritto a richesta [sic] di Monsieur Didie In Londra. Anno Domini 1681. Pietro Reggio'; this manuscript therefore appears to be Reggio's autograph, and the handwriting is not the same as either the original or the additional handwriting of *Lbl* Add. 31,440.
[28] Full details, and the text and a reproduction of the letter (*Lbl* Add. 46,378 B, f. 3), can be found in Willetts (1969b), 124-7. (In her 1962 article, Willetts had tentatively suggested that the hand of *Lbl* Add. 31,440 was that of Walter Porter.)
[29] A copy of the second edition of this publication (1611) survives in *Och* (Mus. 798, annotated by Stephen Bing).

which is a very free arrangement of Caccini's monody; and in 'Parlo miser'ò taccio?' Caccini's original is presented in an ornamented form with two newly composed sections.[30] Presumably these arrangements are the work of Notari himself who had access to the originals in manuscript form (or perhaps he 'reconstructed' the pieces from memory?). Among the most interesting pieces in the collection are the arrangements of various of Monteverdi's five-part madrigals for two high voices and basso continuo. These were described in detail on pages 162-3 above, where it was suggested that the arrangements were the result of a shortage of singers at the Oxford Court.

British Library Add. MS 31,440 was possibly copied around 1643 - the publication date of the anthology which contains Virgilio Mazzocchi's 'Nigra sum' (ff. 150^v-2).[31] After this anthology the latest identified copy-source is Tarquinio Merula's *Madrigali et Altre Musiche Concertate.... Libro Secondo* (Venice, 1633),[32] indeed the great majority of Notari's sources are from the 1620s, and one is therefore tempted to speculate that Notari had access to an earlier, now lost, printed version of the Mazzocchi piece from the 1620s or 1630s. A number of Notari's other printed copy-sources survive in Christ Church, Oxford and were probably once part of the Hatton collection (see Chapter Two):

B. Barbarino, *Madrigali* Bk 2 (Venice, 2/1611)	*Och* Mus. 798
A. Grandi, *Motetti* Bk 2 (Venice, 5/1628)	*Och* Mus. 926-30
C. Monteverdi, *Madrigali* Bk 4 (Venice, 7/1622)	*Och* Mus. 881-6
C. Monteverdi, *Madrigali* Bk 5 (Venice, 9/1620)	*Och* Mus. 881-6
C. Monteverdi, *Concerto* Bk 7 (Venice, 4/1628)	*Och* Mus. 881-6

Given that Notari appears to have been connected with Hatton's scribes in Oxford in the 1640s (see page 163 above) it seems very likely that these prints were - either directly or indirectly - Notari's actual copy-sources.

However, the case is not as clear cut as with Jeffreys' manuscripts of Italian music, for there are a number of printed sources used by Notari which cannot be shown to have had any connection with Hatton or Oxford. For example, copies of Raffaello Rontani's fifth and sixth books of *Varie Musiche* (Rome, 1620 and 1622) survive in the British Library and are of unknown provenance. The basso continuo partbook of another source used by Notari, Tarquinio Merula's *Libro Secondo de Concerti Spirituali* (Venice, 1628), also survives in the British Library, but it seems likely that a copy of

---

[30] Caccini's original monodic version appears in *B-Bc* 704, ff. 190^v-1; I record my thanks to Mr Clifford Bartlett for providing me with a transcription. The piece also appears, arranged for four voices and basso continuo, in P.M. Marsolo, *Secondo Libro di Madrigali a quattro voci, Opera X* (1614), No. 3: 'Aria di Guilio Romano'; this is the only ascribed source.
[31] Florido de Silvestri ed., *Concentus Sacras* (Rome, 1643); also found in Bing's basso continuo manuscript: *Och* Mus. 880 (see Chapter Five).
[32] The second edition, *Musiche Concertate* (Venice, 1635) was bought by Hatton for 4s 0d in November 1638 (see Table 2), and survives in *Och* (Mus. 484-8).

this print - perhaps even the British Library copy - was once part of the Hatton collection for both Stephen Bing and George Jeffreys used it as a copy-source.[33] Notari's collection also contains concordant pieces with the following publications:[34]

F. Caccini, *Musiche* Bk 1 (Florence, 1618), copies in *F-Pc*, *I-Fn* and *I-MOe*
P.A. Giramo, *Arie* (Naples, 1630), only copy in *I-Fn*
S. Landi, *Arie Musiche* Bk 2 (Rome, 1627), only copy in *I-Bc*
T. Merula, *Motetti* Bk 1 (Venice, 1624), only copy in *I-Bc* (lacking B)
P. Possenti, *Canora Sampogna* (Venice, 1623), only copy in *I-Bc* (lacking CII & TII)
F. Rasi, *Vaghezze di musica* (Venice, 1608), only copy in *I-Gu*

With the exception of the Merula and Possenti publications there is no evidence that these prints were ever in this country. Perhaps Notari got to know the pieces through various manuscripts (now lost)? This could account for the fact that there are a number of differences between the printed and the manuscript versions in both Landi's 'Chiudete l'orecchi' and Rasi's 'Ò che felice giorno'. (It has not been possible to compare the printed and manuscript versions of Francesca Caccini's 'Ecco ch'io verso il sangue' or Giramo's 'Tra doglie e dispetto'.) It appears, however, that copies of Merula's *Il Primo Libro de Motetti* and Possenti's *Canora Sampogna* were once in the country. Both prints are listed in Robert Martin's printed catalogues, and both Bing and Jeffreys used Merula's *Motetti* as a copy-source for their manuscripts (which suggests that it was once part of the Hatton collection).

To return to the question of the date of British Library Add. MS 31,440: it is, of course, possible that a collection of this size was compiled over a number of years; but there is nothing in the source to suggest this, and the hand is remarkably consistent throughout, with no changes in the firmness or steadiness. It is possible that Notari's scorebook was the product of the Civil War years 1643-6. This idea finds support in the fact that there are concordances between British Library Add. MS 31,440 and a number of Hatton prints. Perhaps Notari, based at the doomed Oxford Court, decided to recopy his old and damaged scores (some perhaps twenty or thirty years old) into a scorebook for preservation; and alongside this more old-fashioned music he copied his favourite pieces from the Oxford Court repertoire (Hatton's Italian music).

---

[33] The only other surviving copy is in *I-Bc* (complete).
[34] I record my thanks to Professor Lorenzo Bianconi for his help in checking concordances in *I-Bc*, and also to the music librarians of *I-Fn* and *I-Gu*. The concordances with Giramo (1630) and Possenti (1623) are noted in Whenham (1982), ii, 153 & 154 respectively.

EXCURSUS II

THE DISSEMINATION AND INFLUENCE OF ITALIAN MUSIC IN RESTORATION ENGLAND

Charles II's return to England in May 1660 created a mood of euphoria and expectation amongst a populace who were weary of Puritan rule.[1] Charles had spent much of the interregnum at the French Court of Louis XIV where he had witnessed a stable monarchy which patronised the finest artists, writers and musicians in Europe. It is not surprising that on his return to England Charles sought to emulate the French Court both politically and culturally. He quickly became the acknowledged arbiter of taste and fashion in a society which, after eleven years of Puritanical restraint, sought every kind of entertainment - from the sophisticated to the lewd.[2] The theatres, which had officially been closed since the beginning of the Civil War, were authorised to reopen, and the King surrounded himself with music, both sacred and secular, in emulation of the magnificent French Court. One of the most important records of Restoration musical taste is the diary of Samuel Pepys. As well as his daily reports on women, fashion, food and drink, Pepys vividly describes musical gatherings, theatre-going, and church services enlivened by the most up-to-date music.[3] On 23 April 1661 Pepys reported that, at Charles II's coronation festivities, he 'took a great deal of pleasure to go up and down and look upon the ladies - and to hear the Musique of all sorts; but above all, the 24 viollins.'[4] The King's violin band (in reality a string orchestra) had been reformed in emulation of the 'grande bande des vingt-quatre violons de la Chambre du roi' to play when the King dined in state and at court balls.[5] By September 1662 violinists were being

---

[1] It is perhaps not too fanciful to suggest that the intense musical activity in the late 1650s amongst Hatton's musical associates (Jeffreys and Bing), as noted in the preceding chapters, was an early example of Royalist euphoria.
[2] It should be stressed that the Puritans were not opposed to music *per se*; see Scholes (1934). It is true that the musical profession suffered great hardships during the Commonwealth due to the disbandment of the main musical establishments - i.e. Court, Church of England, and theatres - but the Puritans did not object to domestic or devotional music. As was noted in Excursus I, Cromwell had an organ at Hampton Court (removed from the chapel of Magdalen College, Oxford), employed the organist John Hingeston, and apparently enjoyed listening to Richard Dering's Latin motets. In fact Puritan rule positively aided the cultivation of domestic music and created a market which the publisher and bookseller John Playford successfully exploited.
[3] For a commentary on the musical references in Pepys' diary see R. Luckett, 'Music', *The Diary of Samuel Pepys*, ed. R. Latham and W. Matthews (London, 1970-83), x, 258-82.
[4] Latham & Matthews ed. (1970-83), ii, 86.
[5] It should be noted that the violin band was not a new concept in England. The violin had been brought to the English Court as early as 1540, although until the early 1620s it was used only for dance music; for full details see Holman (1993).

used in Chapel Royal services whenever the King was present, and in 1664 they were used in the theatres. In fact the full complement of instrumentalists were rarely used together, even at Court, for in May 1662 John Banister the elder had been asked to form a select group of twelve players from the twenty-four. This was probably a direct result of Banister's visit(s) to France the previous year where he would have heard the 'Petits Violons' directed by Jean-Baptiste Lully.

At the Restoration the music of the re-established Chapel Royal[6] was entrusted to Captain Henry Cooke (c.1615-72), who had himself been a chorister in the Chapel Royal of Charles I before his war service - firstly as a lieutenant and then a captain - on the Royalists' side.[7] Cooke's task in rebuilding the Chapel Royal choir was not an easy one; although he could ensure a degree of continuity with the past by re-appointing a number of Gentlemen who had been members of Charles I's Chapel, the sixteen-year break meant that the boys' section of the choir had to be rebuilt from scratch. Cooke went about his task with a vengeance and revived the 'pressing system' whereby a promising chorister could be removed from a provincial cathedral for service in the Chapel Royal. By the end of 1660 Cooke had a full complement of twelve boys, and over the next ten years - due no doubt to Cooke's ear for natural talent - many of the best musicians of the next generation were trained in the Chapel: Pelham Humfrey, John Blow, Michael Wise, William Turner, Thomas Tudway and Henry Purcell were all Children of the Chapel Royal in the 1660s.

The most precociously talented of Cooke's first batch of choirboys was Pelham Humfrey (1647-74),[8] who was a chorister during the early 1660s until his voice broke and he was forced to leave the choir on Christmas Day 1664. By this time a number of his anthems had been performed by the Chapel Royal choir - the texts of five of these works were published in the second edition of James Clifford's *The Divine Services and Anthems* (London, 1664) - and he had collaborated on the 'Club Anthem', 'I will always give thanks', with two fellow choristers, William Turner and John Blow. Humfrey's talent was such that between 1664 and 1666 he was granted £450 from the secret service fund 'to defray the charge of his journey into France and Italy'.[9] Presumably the trip was undertaken in order to study the latest musical styles of composers such as Lully and Carissimi,

---

[6] It should be remembered that the Chapel Royal is not a single building but a body of persons within the Royal Household responsible for the ordering and performance of divine service in the sovereign's presence.

[7] See R. McGrady, 'Captain Cooke: A Tercentenary Tribute', *MT*, cxiii (1972), 659-60; I. Cheverton, 'Captain Henry Cooke (c.1616-72): The Beginnings of a Reappraisal', *Soundings*, ix (1982), 74-86; Dennison (1986), 13-17; and Spink (1995), 107-9.

[8] Humfrey's life and works are examined in detail in Dennison (1986).

[9] Cited in E.F. Rimbault, *The Old Cheque-Book or Book of Remembrance of the Chapel Royal from 1561 to 1744* (London, 1872), 213, but the location of the original manuscript is unknown; see Ashbee (1991b), v, 270-1.

and it is therefore unfortunate that no details survive concerning Humfrey's experiences abroad. He certainly came back an 'absolute Monsieur' according to Pepys,[10] but just how much he learnt abroad is difficult to assess.

Although much has been made of the French influence on musical life at the Restoration Court, it was not the only, nor even the chief influence on English music. Underpinning English - and indeed French[11] - 'Baroque' music are Italian methods. The dissemination and influence of Italian music in England in the seventeenth century has been a recurring theme in the preceding chapters (see pages 92-9, 121-32 and 156-9 above). We have seen that, in certain (probably Court-related) circles, the phenomenal interest in Italian music shown by Elizabethan patrons and musicians continued unabated into the seventeenth century; that the most up-to-date Italian music of the 1620s and 1630s was readily available in Robert Martin's London bookshop; and that Christopher Hatton III was the owner of a substantial library of Italian music, from which manuscript copies were made (probably for performances at the Oxford Court). It has also been shown how one English composer, George Jeffreys, through exposure to the Italian music in the Hatton collection (particularly the small-scale *concertato* motets written by contemporaries of Monteverdi such as Alessandro Grandi) was able to assimilate many of the features of the Italian *seconda prattica* styles and produce his own - often quite successful - *concertato* pieces. Unfortunately for Jeffreys, the political situation (Civil War and Commonwealth) assured that his music was not widely disseminated and that he had little influence on either his contemporaries or on the succeeding generation of English composers. It is ironic, therefore, that some of the Italian music which Jeffreys copied from the Hatton collection was - in the long run - rather more influential; as we shall see, certain pieces by Tarquinio Merula, Giovanni Felice Sances and Egidio Trabattone, in particular, were widely disseminated and were frequently copied into Restoration manuscripts.

Another English composer who is known to have been interested in Italian music in the mid-seventeenth century is the composer Matthew Locke (1621/2-1677). Towards the end of the 1640s Locke visited the Netherlands (perhaps as part of Queen Henrietta Maria's and Prince Charles' exiled retinue) and while he was there he copied various Latin motets by Francesco Costanzo, Giovanni Rovetta and Galeazzo Sabbatini.[12] It seems that while

---

[10] 15 November 1667; Latham & Matthews ed. (1970-83), viii, 529.

[11] We should remember that Jean-Baptiste Lully (1632-87) - the leading composer in France in the mid-seventeenth century - was actually born in Florence and did not move to France until 1646, and that this was the period when Cardinal Mazarin was striving to promote Italian entertainments at the French Court; see J.R. Anthony, *French Baroque Music from Beaujoyeulx to Rameau* (London, rev. 2/1978), 40-53.

[12] *Lbl* Add. 31,437, ff. 29-43: 'Collection of Songs [made] when / I was in the Low / Countreys 1648'. The contents are as follows: f. 29^V 'Jesu Domine Jesu' (CBbc), f. 30^V 'O verum Christi corpus' (CBbc), f. 30^V 'Domine Jesus in qua nocte tradebatur' (CABbc), f. 32 'O nomen Jesu'

he was in the Low Countries Locke converted to Catholicism, and his own Latin motets, which were clearly influenced by Italianate idioms, may have been written for the Roman Catholic chapel of Charles II's Queen, Catherine of Braganza.[13] His English anthems and instrumental pieces, however, are rather more conservative in style and, in these works, Locke must be regarded as a standard bearer of an 'English style' in the face of ever-increasing foreign influence.[14]

Perhaps the greatest advocate of 'the Italian way' was the aforementioned Captain Henry Cooke. The diarist John Evelyn described him as 'the best singer after the *Italian* manner of any in *England*',[15] and in the 1664 edition of *A Brief Introduction to the Skill of Musick* - which includes an abridged translation of Caccini's treatise on Italian vocal practice[16] - John Playford considered that the Italian manner of singing 'is now come to the Excellency and Perfection..., by the Skill and furtherance of that Orpheus of our time Henry Cook'. Sir Jack Westrup suggested that Cooke's knowledge of 'the Italian manner' implied 'residence in Italy or at least study with Italian masters';[17] while this is a possibility, it seems more likely that Cooke's experience of Italian music was gained at home from imported publications.[18] During the Commonwealth, like many Royalist musicians, Cooke earned his living as a teacher[19] and, as was mentioned in

---

(ATBbc), and f. 32ᵛ 'O clementissime Domine' from G. Sabbatini's *Sacrae Laudes Musicis Concentibus* Bk 1, Op. 3 (Venice, 1626); f. 34ᵛ 'Salve meum salutare' (CBbc) from Sabbatini's *Sacrarum Laudum Musicis Conceptibus* Bk 2, Op. 7 (Venice, 1637); f. 35ᵛ 'Dulcis Christe ad te venio' (ATBbc) from G. Rovetta, *Gemma Musicalis* (Antwerp, 1649); 36ᵛ 'Domine Deus meus peccavi graviter coram te' (TTBbc) from G. Rovetta, *Motetti Concertati* Op. 5 (Venice, 1639); f. 38 'Ecce Dominus posuit mensam' (ATBbc) by Rovetta ('Ex manipulo ejusdem Authoris', print not identified); f. 38ᵛ 'Salve Regina (TTBbc), anonymous; f. 39ᵛ 'Anima mea liquefacta est' (TTBbc) from F. Costanzo de Cosena's lost second book of motets; f. 40ᵛ 'O Jesu mi dulcissime' (ATBbc) and f. 40ᵛ *Seconda pars* 'Amor Jesu' (TTBbc), anonymous (perhaps also from Costanzo's lost second book?); f. 41ᵛ 'Congregavit Dominus' (Cbc) from G. Sabbatini's *Sacre Lodi Concerto a Voce Sola* Op. 9 (Venice, 1640); and f. 41ᵛ 'O bone Jesu fili Mariæ' (Abc) and f. 42ᵛ 'Jesu quæram in lectulo clauso' (Abc), anonymous (perhaps also from Sabbatini's Op. 9?). For full details see Thompson (1988), 387-92.

[13] Locke was organist to Catherine of Braganza's chapel in St James's Palace from 1662 to 1671, and then at Somerset House from 1671 to his death in 1677 (the King's mother, Queen Henrietta Maria, had occupied Somerset House until her death in 1669). Alternatively, Locke's Latin motets may have been written for Oxford Music Meetings as most of the works survive in manuscripts connected with the University Music School.

[14] See P. Dennison, 'The Sacred Music of Matthew Locke', *ML*, lx (1979), 60-75.

[15] 28 October 1654; de Beer ed. (1955), iii, 144.

[16] Originally the preface to *Le Nuove Musiche* (Florence, 1601/2).

[17] Westrup (rev. 4/1980), 20.

[18] Cooke's first exposure to Italian music may have been as a chorister in the Chapel Royal in the late 1620s at the time when Walter Porter - the self-styled pupil of Monteverdi - was a Gentleman.

[19] Cooke's name occurs - with that of Stephen Bing - in a list of 'excellent and able masters' in the Rules and Directions prefixed to John Playford's *A Musicall Banquet* (London, 1651); his name is given under the heading for 'Voyce or Viol'.

Chapter Two, he appears to have been employed by Lady Hatton to teach her children.[20] Given that the Hatton family owned a substantial amount of Italian music, it is not unreasonable to suggest that it was at a Hatton residence, in the 1650s, that Cooke learned 'the Italian manner'.

One of the most popular Italian composers in England in the mid-seventeenth century was Giacomo Carissimi (1605-74). His motets and cantatas were widely disseminated, and at least one of the former was known in England as early as 1645/6.[21] Carissimi's music was certainly popular after the Restoration; in 1664 Pepys wrote of an evening spent 'singing the best piece of musique, counted of all hands in the world, made by Seignor Charissimi the famous master in Rome'.[22] The presence of Italian musicians (such as Vicenzo Albrici, a pupil of Carissimi's) in London in the 1660s undoubtedly contributed to the dissemination of his motets and cantatas,[23] and over the next four decades George Jeffreys, Henry Aldrich, Henry Bowman, Charles Morgan and Richard Goodson the elder all included music by Carissimi in their manuscripts.[24] He was so popular that pieces by other Italian composers - such as Cazzati, Graziani, F.M. Marini, Monferrato, Trabattone and Rovetta - were often incorrectly attributed to Carissimi by English copyists.[25] A thorough examination of the manuscripts reveals that Carissimi was just one of many Italian composers whose music was readily available in England. Part II includes a representative selection of manuscripts from the second half of the seventeenth century which contain Italian music; comprehensive descriptions and inventories are given for the following:[26]

---

[20] This is indicated in a letter dated 11 December 1656 from George Jeffreys to Lady Hatton (*Lbl* Add. 29,550, f. 275); see page 25 above.
[21] *Lbl* Evelyn 211, a copy - in an Italian hand - of Carissimi's motet 'Si linguis hominum', bears Evelyn's annotation: 'Coll: Evelynus: Romæ Aprilis: 11 : 1645'; for details of Evelyn's visit to Rome, 7 February - 4 May 1645, see de Beer ed. (1955), ii, 355-91.
[22] 22 July 1664; Latham & Matthews ed. (1970-83), v, 217. Pepys was a bass and one is therefore tempted to speculate that this 'best piece of musique' was Carissimi's solo-bass motet, 'Lucifer caelestis olim'. The piece was later transcribed for Pepys by Cesare Morelli, who was his household musician between 1675 and 1693; the manuscript is preserved in the Pepys Library (*Cmc* 2803, ff. 80^v-87^v).
[23] See J.A. Westrup, 'Foreign Musicians in Stuart England', *MQ*, xxvii (1941), 70-89; M. Mabbett, 'Italian Musicians in Restoration England (1660-90), *ML*, lxvii (1986), 237-47; and G. Dixon, 'Purcell's Italianate Circle', *The Purcell Companion*, ed. M. Burden (London, 1995), 38-51.
[24] For details see Jones (1982), *passim*.
[25] For full details of Latin motets attributed (both correctly and incorrectly) to Carissimi in English manuscripts, see Jones (1982), *passim*.
[26] Henry Aldrich (1648-1710): composer, collector and architect, Dean of Christ Church, Oxford 1689-1710, bequeathed his music library to Christ Church (see Hiscock (1960); and Watkins Shaw, *New Grove*, i, 234-6). John Blow (1649-1708): composer, organist of Westminster Abbey 1668-79 & 1695-1708, Master of the Children of the Chapel Royal 1674, Almoner and Master of the Choristers at St Paul's Cathedral 1687-1703 (see H. Watkins Shaw: 'John Blow', *MT*, xcix (1958), 542-4; 'The Autographs of John Blow', *MR*, xxv (1964), 85-95; ibid. (1991), 9; and *New Grove*, ii, 805-12). Henry Bowman (*fl. c.*1670-85): Oxford composer (see P. Dennison, *New Grove*, iii, 136-7). Richard Goodson I (*c.*1655-1718): Oxford

Manuscript	Copyist	Part II, MS No.
London, British Library Add. 30,382	Bowman	V
London, British Library Add. 31,460	Bowman, etc.	VIII
London, British Library Add. 33,234	Morgan	X
London, British Library Add. 33,235	W. Husbands/Goodson I	XI
London, British Library Egerton 2960	Bowman	XV
Oxford, Bodleian Library Mus. Sch. C 9	Goodson II, etc.	XXII
Oxford, Bodleian Library Mus. Sch. C 10	C. Husbands	XXIII
Oxford, Bodleian Library Mus. Sch. C 11	Lowe	XXIV
Oxford, Bodleian Library Mus. Sch. C 12-19	Lowe/Goodson I & II	XXV
Oxford, Bodleian Library Mus. Sch. C 24-7	Lowe, etc.	XVI
Oxford, Bodleian Library Mus. Sch. E 451	Lowe	XXX
Oxford, Christ Church Mus. 14	Blow	XLIII
Oxford, Christ Church Mus. 18	Aldrich	XLIV
Oxford, Christ Church Mus. 43	Bowman/Aldrich	XLVI
Oxford, Christ Church Mus. 48	Aldrich/Goodson I, etc.	XLVII
Oxford, Christ Church Mus. 49	Lowe/F. Withey, etc.	XLVIII
Oxford, Christ Church Mus. 621	Lowe/Bowman, etc.	LIII
Oxford, Christ Church Mus. 623-6	Bowman	LIV
Oxford, Christ Church Mus. 1151	Lowe/ ?	LX
Oxford, Christ Church Mus. 1178	Lowe/ ?	LXII

A detailed examination of each manuscript would be out of place in the present study,[27] but the following points should be noted: The most remarkable feature of these Restoration manuscripts is the frequent appearance, amongst the current music of the day (both English and Italian), of a number of Italian pieces which had originally been copied from 'Hatton prints'. The most popular pre-1638 Italian pieces in the Restoration repertoire are listed in Table 29. With the exception of the manuscripts

---

musician, organist of New College 1682-92, organist of Christ Church 1692-1718, praelector (professor) of music 1682-1718 (see Watkins Shaw: (1991), 211; and *New Grove*, vii, 531). Richard Goodson II (*c*.1685-1741): Oxford musician, succeeded his father as organist of Christ Church and professor of music (1718-41) (see Watkins Shaw: (1991), 211; and *New Grove*, vii, 531). Charles Husbands, the elder (d. 1678): professional copyist, clerk of St George's Chapel, Windsor and Gentleman of the Chapel Royal (see Ashbee (1986), 109, 136, 143; ibid. (1991b), 73). William Husbands (1664-1701, son of the elder Charles Husbands): Oxford singer and composer, singing-man at Christ Church 1673-84 & 1692-4, 'Organista' and 'Inform: Gram: & Mus:' at Christ Church 1684-92 (see Christ Church Disbursement Books 1673-92; and Watkins Shaw (1991), 211). Edward Lowe (*c*.1610-82): cathedral musician, copyist and composer, organist of Christ Church *c*.1631-49 & 1660-82, co-organist of the Chapel Royal 1660-82 (see Watkins Shaw (1991), 210-11; and le Huray, *New Grove*, xi, 287-8). Charles Morgan (*fl. c*.1682): Oxford musician and copyist. Francis Withey (d. 1727), copyist and singing-man at Christ Church, Oxford 1680-1713 (see R. Thompson, '"Francis Withie of Oxon" and his Commonplace Book, Christ Church, Oxford, MS 337', *Chelys*, xx (1991), 3-27).

[27] The reader is, however, referred to the descriptions and inventories of the manuscripts in Part II.

Table 29 Popular pre-1638 Italian Pieces in English Restoration Manuscripts

Manuscript sources:
1. Birmingham, University, Barber Institute of Fine Arts MS 5002
2. London, British Library Add. MS 11,585
3. London, British Library Add. MS 17,835
4. London, British Library Add. MS 24,293
5. London, British Library Add. MS 30,382
6. London, British Library Add. MS 31,399
7. London, British Library Add. MS 31,460
8. London, British Library Add. MS 31,479
9. London, British Library Add. MS 33,234
10. London, British Library Add. MS 33,235
11. London, British Library Egerton MS 2960
12. London, Royal Academy of Music MS 42
13. London, Royal Academy of Music MS 107
14. London, Royal College of Music MS 660
15. London, Westminster Abbey Library MS CG 63
16. Madrigal Society MSS G 33-6 (housed in the British Library)
17. Madrigal Society MSS G 55-9 (housed in the British Library)
18. Oxford, Bodleian Library MS Mus. c 27
19. Oxford, Bodleian Library Mus. Sch. MS C 9
20. Oxford, Bodleian Library Mus. Sch. MS C 10
21. Oxford, Bodleian Library Mus. Sch. MS C 11
22. Oxford, Bodleian Library Mus. Sch. MSS C 12-19
23. Oxford, Bodleian Library Mus. Sch. MSS C 24-7
24. Oxford, Bodleian Library Mus. Sch. MSS D 217
25. Oxford, Bodleian Library Mus. Sch. MS E 451
26. Oxford, Bodleian Library Tenbury MS 335
27. Oxford, Bodleian Library Tenbury MS 713
28. Oxford, Bodleian Library Tenbury MS 720
29. Oxford, Bodleian Library Tenbury MS 926
30. Oxford, Bodleian Library Tenbury MS 1017
31. Oxford, Christ Church Mus. 14
32. Oxford, Christ Church Mus. 43
33. Oxford, Christ Church Mus. 48
34. Oxford, Christ Church Mus. 49
35. Oxford, Christ Church Mus. 621
36. Oxford, Christ Church Mus. 623-6
37. Oxford, Christ Church Mus. 747-9
38. Oxford, Christ Church Mus. 880
39. Oxford, Christ Church Mus. 1078
40. Oxford, Christ Church Mus. 1151
41. Oxford, Christ Church Mus. 1178
42. York, Minster Library MSS M.93.S
43. France, Paris, Bibliothèque Nationale MS Rés F 934a
44. Japan, Tokyo, Nanki Music Library MS N-4/39

Table 29 continued

Composer	Title	Scoring	Sources
G.B. Aloisi:	Quid mihi est in cælo	ATBbc	*Contextus Musicarum* (1637), 8, 22, 23, 36
A. Facchi:	Audite cæli	CCBbc	*Motetti* Bk 2 (1635), 8, 22, 23, 36
A. Facchi:	Exurgat Deus	CCBbc	*Motetti* Bk 2 (1635), 8, 22, 23, 26, 36
A. Grandi:	O bone Jesu	ATTBbc	*Motetti* Bk 2 (1613), Playford ed. (1662), 16, 17, 25 attrib. Legrand & Dering, 37, 38
F.M. Marini:	Anima mea liquefacta est	CABbc	*Concerti Spirituali* (1637), 1 attrib. Joh: Baptista, 5, 8, 9, 12 attrib. Carissimi, 15 attrib. Jo: Baptista, 19 attrib. Joha. Baptista, 22, 23 attrib. Jo: Bap:, 26, 36
F.M. Marini:	O vos omnes	ATBbc	*Concerti Spirituali* (1637), 5, 8, 22, 23 attrib. Johannes Baptista, 26, 36
T. Merula:	Nominativo hic	CATBbc	*Madrigali* Bk 2 (1633), 2, 9, 14, 15, 22, 28, 30, 38, 39, 43 attrib. on cover to Carissimi
T. Merula:	Nominativo quis	CATBbc	*Madrigali* Bk 2 (1633), 2, 9, 14, 15, 22, 28, 30, 38, 39, 43 attrib. on cover to Carissimi
C. Monteverdi:	Al lume delle stelle	CCTBbc	*Concerto* Bk 7 (1619), 1, 6, 19, 31
C. Monteverdi:	Parlo misero	CCBbc	*Concerto* Bk 7 (1619), 1, 4, 10, 19, 22, 31
C. Monteverdi:	Tu dormi?	CATBbc	*Concerto* Bk 7 (1619), 1, 6, 15, 19, 31
G. Rovetta:	Io mi sento morir	CCbc	*Madrigali Concertati* (1629), 4, 5, 9, 10, 15, 21, 22, 25, 31, 35
F. Sances:	Ardet cor meum	Cbc	*Motetti* (1638), 7, 11, 20, 22, 32, 33, 34
F. Sances:	Audite me divini fructus	Bbc	*Motetti* (1638), 7, 8, 11, 20, 22, 32, 33, 40

Table 29 concluded

F. Sances: Conditor cæli	Tbc	*Motetti* (1638), 7, 11, 20, 22, 34
F. Sances: Deus in ajutorium	CBbc	*Motetti* (1638), 8, 20, 22, 32, 34, 36, 41,
F. Sances: Domine ne memineris	CCbc	*Motetti* (1638), 20, 22, 34, 36, 41
F. Sances: Dulcis amor Jesu	Bbc	*Motetti* (1638), 7, 8, 11, 20, 22, 32, 33, 40
F. Sances: Judica me Deus	CCbc	*Motetti* (1638), 5, 20, 22, 34, 36, 41
F. Sances: Lætamini in Domino	Cbc	*Motetti* (1638), 7, 11, 20, 22, 32, 33, 34
F. Sances: Laudemus viros gloriosos	TTbc	*Motetti* (1638), 20, 22, 25, 34, 41
F. Sances: O crux benedicta	ATBbc	*Motetti* (1638), 8, 20, 22, 23, 36, 26
F. Sances: O Domine guttae	ATBbc	*Motetti* (1638), 1, 5 attrib. Monferrato, 8, 9, 19, 20, 22, 23, 24, 26, 29, 36, 42
F. Sances: O Jesu mi dulcissime	CCABbc	*Motetti* (1638), 17, 20, 36, 38
F. Sances: O quam speciosa	Abc	*Motetti* (1638), 7, 11, 20, 22, 34
F. Sances: Plagæ tuæ Domine	ATBbc	*Motetti* (1638), 1, 5, 8, 9, 10, 13, 15, 18, 19, 20, 22, 23, 24, 26, 27 attrib. Carissimi, 29, 36, 42 as 'Plaga luce', 44
F. Sances: Quemadmodum desiderat	Abc	*Motetti* (1638), 7, 11, 20, 22, 34
F. Sances: Solvatur lingua mea	Tbc	*Motetti* (1638), 7, 11, 20, 22, 34
F. Sances: Tota pulchra es	ATbc	*Motetti* (1638), 5, 8, 20, 22, 34, 36, 41
E. Trabattone: Anima mea in æterna	CBbc	*Concerti* Bk 2 (1629), 8, 10, 22; 3, 5, 9, 21, 32, 35, 36, 41 & 44: attrib. Carissimi

copied by Hatton's scribes, the majority of the listed manuscripts were copied after 1670 - by which time the Hatton collection had passed to Henry Aldrich (see pages 41-3 above). It is no surprise, therefore, that a number of the Oxford copyists appear to have used the actual Hatton prints (which were, by then, probably on Dean Aldrich's shelves) as copy-sources. Some scribes, however, copied not from the prints but from other manuscripts. Henry Aldrich himself provides an example in Christ Church Mus. 18 (Part II, MS XLIV). This scorebook contains two motets by Alessandro Grandi ('Oh quam gloriosus' and 'Tu dulcis es Messia') which have different texts to the concordant printed sources (the sixth and fifth books of motets respectively) which were once part of the Hatton collection;[28] the altered texts are the ones which appear in George Jeffreys' partbooks British Library Add. MS 31,479 (see Part II, MS IX). Perhaps Aldrich copied the pieces from Jeffreys' manuscripts or from related transcriptions (possibly even the hypothetical lost manuscripts mentioned on page 128 above)? The fact that Aldrich used manuscripts as his copy-sources rather than prints for these pre-1638 Italian pieces perhaps indicates that he had not yet purchased the Hatton collection; in that case Christ Church Mus. 18 must date from before *circa* 1670. A possible line of transmission of these pieces from Jeffreys to Aldrich would be via his son, Christopher Jeffreys, who was a student at Christ Church from 1658 to 1666; this would also explain the presence of three motets by George Jeffreys in Mus. 18.[29]

Another example of a piece which was disseminated primarily by manuscript transmissions is the two-voice motet 'Anima mea in æterna dulcedine' by Egidio Trabattone. The motet was originally published in 1629 in *Concerti... Libro Secondo*,[30] was copied by Jeffreys in British Library Add. MS 31,479, and also appears in eleven other music manuscripts which date from the late seventeenth or early eighteenth centuries (see Table 29). In nine of the eleven manuscripts the motet is attributed to Carissimi. It is not possible at present to ascertain which of the manuscripts was the first to misattribute the piece, but it appears that once the error had been made it was repeated, without a second thought, by subsequent copyists.[31] The frequent misattribution of Italian pieces to Carissimi in manuscripts of the period is

---

[28] The Hatton copies of A. Grandi, *Il Sesto Libro de Motetti* (Venice, 1630) and *Celesti Fiori... Libro Quinto* (Venice, 3/1625) were bound by Aldrich in the five composite partbooks 'MOT[et] C', now *Och* Mus. 926-30.

[29] Aldrich's copy of Jeffreys' dialogue between Mary and an Angel, 'Heu me miseram' in *Och* Mus. 18, alters the dramatic interruption of the word 'eum' at bar 14 by adding a note in place of the rest. This destroys Jeffreys' intended effect which was obviously inspired by the final few bars of the motet 'Plorabo die ac nocte' (one of the motets Jeffreys copied in *Lbl* Add. 31,479) from Alessandro Grandi's fourth book of motets of 1616, which concludes with an unfinished sob halfway through the word 'Jesu'.

[30] The only surviving copy is in Christ Church and was probably once part of the Hatton collection (see pp. 30-2 above).

[31] The misattribution to Carissimi was repeated in Roger North's writings; see Wilson ed. (1959), 113-14.

indicative of the high esteem in which the composer was held by English musicians.[32] But we should note that, although Carissimi was the most popular Italian composer in England in the second half of the seventeenth century, a large amount of music by his Italian contemporaries was also copied (alongside the pre-1638 'Hatton pieces'). The following publications, in particular, were favourite copy-sources for the scribes:

G.B. Caifabri ed., *Scelta de'Motetti* Parts 1-3 (Rome, 1665, 1667 & 1675)
G. Casati, *Motetti Concertati* Bk 1, Op. 1 (Venice, 1643)
G. Casati, *Amoenum Rosarium* Op. 5 (Antwerp, 1649)
M. Cazzati, *Motetti a Due Voci* Op. 10 (Venice, 1648)
Florido de Silvestri ed., *Sacras Cantiones* Parts 1 & 2 (Rome, 1659 & 1663)
J. van Geertsom ed., *Scelta di Motetti* (Rotterdam, 1656)
B. Graziani, *Motetti a Voce Sola* [Bk 1] Op. 3 (Rome, 1652)
B. Graziani, *Motetti a Voce Sola* Bk 4, Op. 10 (Rome, 1665)
N. Monferrato, *Motetti Concertati* Op. 3 (Venice, 1655; 3/Antwerp, 1660)
P. Phalèse ed., *Florida Verba* (Antwerp, 1661)
A. Poggioli ed., *Delectus Sacrarum Cantionum* (Antwerp, 1652)

Two of the foremost English Restoration composers, John Blow (1649-1708) and Henry Purcell (1659-95), also copied music by Italian composers and must - to some extent - have been influenced by the 'Italian manner'. A detailed examination of Italianate features in their music would be out of place in this study. Were this to be attempted, a number of awkward questions would have to be asked: such as, by the time of Blow and Purcell, to what extent had Italianate elements become assimilated into the native English idiom, and when do foreign influences end and personal style begin? An examination of the contents of John Blow's early scorebook, Christ Church Mus. 14 (Part II, MS XLIII), is of interest in relation to these points. Mus. 14, which was probably copied in the mid 1670s,[33] is a folio album of miscellaneous English and Italian vocal music. Madrigals and cantatas by Carissimi, Crivelli, Monteverdi, Pesenti and Rovetta appear alongside English anthems by Blow himself, Cooke, Christopher Gibbons, Locke and Wise. The scorebook also contains nine Latin motets by Blow: seven are for two voices and basso continuo, and two are for five voices and basso continuo. These are his most Italianate works and, in the tradition of Dering and Jeffreys, include affective declamation, virtuoso solo writing, expressive dissonance, melodic and harmonic chromaticism, contrasting triple-time sections, and a number of examples of ground basses in the duet motets. Blow appears to have been consciously imitating the sort of Italian

---

[32] See footnote 25 above.
[33] *Och* Mus. 14 includes the duet motet 'In lectulo meo' which also appears in *Lbl* Add. 33,234 ascribed to '*Mr*. Blow'; Blow received his doctorate in 1677. Certain features of Blow's handwriting in *Och* Mus. 14 also suggest that the manuscript may have been copied before 1677; see Watkins Shaw (1964), 88-9.

concertato music he had copied elsewhere in his scorebook. But, as Watkins Shaw has noted, the direct Italianate style of these motets is not typical of Blow's other music,[34] and in his English Church music, songs, odes and the opera *Venus and Adonis*, Italianate elements have been assimilated into an eclectic personal style.

The two surviving examples of Italian pieces copied by Henry Purcell are an indication of the chronological range of his interest in Italian music: an autograph score of Purcell's Benedicite in B flat (Z 230M/3)[35] contains a correction slip on the reverse of which, in Purcell's handwriting, is a fragment of a score of Monteverdi's five-voice madrigal 'Cruda Amarilli',[36] and another of his autograph manuscripts[37] includes a copy of a two-voice motet, 'Crucior in hac flamma', by Maurizio Cazzati.[38] Purcell's interest in Italian music is further demonstrated in his contribution to the twelfth edition of Playford's *Introduction to the Skill of Music* (London, 1694) in which he quotes a few bars from a trio sonata by 'the famous Lelio Colista' (although the piece is actually by Carlo Ambrogio Lonati).[39] By the early 1680s the most up-to-date Italian instrumental music was available in London, and Purcell very probably knew sonatas by Bassani, Cazzati, Colista (or Lonati), Legrenzi, Vitali, and possibly even Corelli's *Sonate a Tre* Op. 1 (Rome, 1681).[40] It is not surprising that Purcell - who was keenly aware of the latest market trends - stated in the preface of his *Sonnata's of III Parts* (London, 1683) that 'he has faithfully endeavour'd a just imitation of the fam'd Italian Masters'; he was less flattering about the French and warned that his 'Country-men... should begin to loath the levity, and balladry of our neighbours'. Purcell, then, like his teacher John Blow, was keenly aware of the latest Italian styles, but equally important to him was the indigenous musical tradition. Purcell's Fantasias and In Nomines and his full anthems can be cited as the most obvious examples of his reverence for the older English traditions, and we should remember that, according to Roger North, even Purcell's fashionable trio sonatas were 'clog'd with somewhat of an English vein'.[41] English musical style of the second half of the seventeenth

---

[34] *New Grove*, ii, 808.
[35] *Ob* Mus. a.1. The manuscript fragment is reproduced in I. Holst ed., *Henry Purcell 1659-1695: Essays on his Music* (London, 1959), Plate II; Zimmerman (2/1983), 53; and M. Burden ed., *The Purcell Companion* (London, 1995), Plate 3.
[36] From *Il Quinto Libro de Madrigali a Cinque Voci* (Venice, 1605).
[37] *Lbl* R.M. 20.H.8, ff. 127-125^v rev.
[38] From *Tributo di Sagri Concerti* Op. 23 (Bologna, 1660). The motet is unattributed in the manuscript.
[39] See P. Allsop, 'Problems of Ascription in the Roman *Simfonia* of the late Seventeenth Century: Colista and Lonati', *MR*, 1 (1989), 34-44; and ibid., *The Italian 'Trio' Sonata: From its Origins Until Corelli* (Oxford, 1992), 197.
[40] See, for example, *Lbl* Add. 31,431 (dated 1680), and *Lbl* Add. 33,236 (early 1680s); these and other instrumental manuscripts of the period are discussed in Thompson (1988), 431-67. See also P. Walls, 'The Influence of the Italian Violin School in 17th-Century England', *EM*, xviii (1990), 575-87.
[41] 'An Essay of Musicall Ayre', *Lbl* Add. 32,536, f. 78^v.

century was, in fact, a synthesis of English, French and Italian elements and, in the words of Lorenzo Bianconi, was 'voraciously heterogeneous and versatile, to the point at which the strength of the composer's own personal imprint of melodic and harmonic invention becomes the only truly recognizable factor.'[42]

---

[42] *Music in the Seventeenth Century* (Cambridge, 1987), 252.

CONCLUSION

Is Christopher, First Baron Hatton of any real importance in our understanding of seventeenth-century English music? If he is important, how come he is not mentioned in any of the text books of music history? Sir Christopher Hatton II, as the patron of Orlando Gibbons, occasionally gets a mention, but nothing is heard of the illustrious Lord Hatton. He was, it seems, a victim of the unique political circumstances which existed in England during the mid-seventeenth century. In a period which saw a Civil War, the execution of the King, the creation of the Commonwealth, and the Restoration of the monarchy, it is not surprising that there is little obvious evidence concerning music. This is undoubtedly the reason why, until recently, Baron Hatton has been ignored by music historians. It can now be argued that Christopher Hatton III is one of the most important and influential musical patrons of the seventeenth century. The following comments are intended to offer a realistic summary of his musical achievements without repeating the arguments and conclusions of the preceding chapters.

It has been shown that Baron Hatton owned a substantial music library, that he was supplied with Venetian printed music by the London bookseller Robert Martin, and that much of the collection survives today in the library of Christ Church, Oxford. This alone would be sufficient to mark Hatton as an important patron, particularly in light of the fact that, preserved amongst the 'Hatton prints' in Christ Church, there are at least thirty-four unique publications and another twenty-five sources which are now the only complete copies in existence (see Table 30). We have also seen how important the Hatton collections is to the question of the dissemination and influence of Italian music in England. But what does the collection tell us about Hatton's musical taste? If we take the 1638 purchases (see Table 2) as a representative example of his musical interests - and here we can be absolutely sure that these prints were part of the Hatton collection - it is possible to argue that he was an extremely erudite musical connoisseur with wide ranging and adventurous tastes (from the slightly old-fashioned large-scale motet publications of Aloisi, Costantini and Facchi, to the up-to-date continuo madrigals by Merula, monodies by Saracini, and other virtuoso solo vocal music). However, we must beware of reading too much into this apparent choice of music. The evidence of the 1638 purchases suggests that Hatton's collection was largely the result of random and indiscriminate buying. If one puts the 1638 prints into alphabetical order, as has been done in Table 2, it will be noted that there is a preponderance of prints whose

Table 30 A Provisional List of Unique Music Publications in the Library of Christ Church, Oxford

a. *Unica*

G.B. Aloisi, *Coelestis Parnasus* Op.1 (Venice, 1628)
B. Barbarino, *Il Quarto Libro de Madrigali* (Venice, 1614)
B. Barbarino, *Canzonette a Una e Due Voci* (Venice, 1616)
B. Barbarino, *Madrigali a Tre voci* (Venice, 1617)
S. Bonini, *Serena Celeste* Op.8 (Venice, 1615)
G. Carrone, *Il Primo Libro delli Motetti* Op.1 (Venice, 1629)
J. de Castro, *Chant Musicale* (Cologne, 1597)
F. Cauda, *Catena Sacrarum Cantionum* Op.3 (Venice, 1626)
T. Cecchino, *Amorosi Concetti* (Venice, 1616)
G.M. Cesare, *Concerti Ecclesiastici... Libro Primo* (Venice, 1614)
F. Costantini ed., *Motetti... Libro Quarto* Op.12 (Venice, 1634)
A. Cremonese, *Madrigali Concertati* Op.1 (Venice, 1636)
A. Facchi, *Motetti... Libro Sec.* (Venice, 1635)
B. Ferrari, *Musiche Varie e Voce Sola* (Venice, 1633)
N. Fontei, *Bizzarrie Poetiche* (Venice, 1635)
N. Fontei, *Bizzarrie Poetiche... Libro Secondo* (Venice, 1636)
L. Gallerano, *Ecclesiastica Armonica Concerti* Op.6 (Venice, 1624)
J. van Geertsom, *XIV Motetta... Liber Secundus* (Rotterdam, 1661)[1]
A. Gualtieri, *Motetti... Libro Terzo* Op.10 (Venice, 1630)
G. Guami, *Canzonette Francese* (Antwerp, 1612)
S. d'India, *Le Musiche e Balli a Quattro Voci* (Venice, 1621)
S. d'India, *Le Musiche... Libro Quarto* (Venice, 1621)
S. d'India, *Le Musiche... Libro Quinto* (Venice, 1623)
B. Marini, *Per le Musiche di Camera Concerti* Op.7 (Venice, 1634)
B. Marini, *Madrigaletti... Libro Quinto* Op.9 (Venice, 1635)
T. Merula, *Curtio Precipitato et Altri Capricii* Op.13 (Venice, 1638)
G. da Monte dell'Olmo, *Sacri Affetti... Libro Secondo* (Venice, 1637)
C. Orlandi, *Arie* Op.2 (Venice, 1616)
B. Pallavicino, *L'Ottavo Libro de Madrigali* (Venice, 1612)
D. Pecci, *Sacri Modulatus* Op.3 (Venice, 1629)
A. de Pisticci, *Motetti... Libro Quarto* Op.7 (Venice, 1637)
A. Poggioli ed., *Delectus Sacrarum Cantionum* (Antwerp, 1652)[1]
E. Trabattone, *Concerti... libro Secondo* Op.4 (Venice, 1629)
L. Valvasensi, *Secondo Giardino d'Amorosi Fiori* Op.8 (Venice, 1634)

---

[1] Not in *RISM*: only copy?

Table 30 concluded
b. Sole surviving complete copies
G.B. Aloisi, *Corona Stellarum* Op. 5 (Venice, 1637)
A. Aux-Cousteaux, *Meslanges de Chanson* (Paris, 1644)
O. Bartolini, *Il Primo Libro de Madrigali* (Venice, 1606)
D. Bellante, *Concerti Accademici* Op.1 (Venice, 1629)
C. Burgh, *Hortus Marianus* (Antwerp, 1630)
E. du Caurroy, *Fantasies* (Paris, 1610)
A. della Ciaia, *Madrigali* Op.1 (Venice, 1636)
M. Delipari, *I Baci Madrigali... Libro Primo* (Venice, 1630)
A. Facchi, *Madrigali... Libro Secondo* (Venice, 1636)[2]
G. Filippi, *Concerti Ecclesiastici* (Venice, 1637)
G. Finetti, *Concerti Ecclesiastici* (Antwerp, 1621)
Florido de Silvestri ed., *Cantiones Sacras...* (Rotterdam, 1657)[3]
N. Fontei, *Melodiae Sacrae* Op.3 (Venice, 1638)
S. d'India, *Libro Secondo de Madrigali* (Venice, 1611)
S. d'India, *Il Terzo Libro de Madrigali* (Venice, 1615)
S. d'India, *Il Quarto Libro de Madrigali* (Venice, 1616)
S. d'India, *Liber Primus Motectorum Quatuor Vocibus* (Venice, 1627)
L. Marenzio, *Il Sesto [-] Nono Libro... de Madrigali* (Antwerp, 1609)[4]
F.M. Marini, *Concerti Spirituali* (Venice, 1637)
F. de Monte, *Musica Sopra il Pastor Fido... Libro Secondo* (Venice, 1600)
G. da Monte dell'Olmo, *Applaudi Ecclesiastici... Libro Primo* (Venice, 1636)
P. Nenna, *Il Primo Libro de Madrigali a 4* (Venice, 1621)
B. Tomasi, *Motecta* Op.6 (Venice, 1635)
R. Trofeo & G.D. Rognoni Taeggio, *Canzonette Leggiade* (Milan, 1600)
R. Vecoli, *Il Secondo Libro de Madrigali* (Paris, 1586)

---

composers begin with certain letters of the alphabet. Could it be that the buyer merely picked prints from the nearest shelves, those shelves being - in this case - stocked with prints whose composers began with A, C, F, M, P and S? This rather cynical interpretation may be unfair to Hatton, who was undoubtedly an educated man, but we should bear in mind that the collector's acquisitive urge was not always guided by musically selective criteria.

A far safer indication of taste and influence is provided by the manuscripts copied by Hatton's scribes from his prints. The surviving

---

[2] CI in *Ge*.
[3] Not in *RISM*. A and bc in *B-Br*.
[4] Only complete copy of this edition.

manuscripts actually give us an idea of the music which was performed, and are perhaps, therefore, more valuable than the prints when it comes, for example, to examining the dissemination and influence of Italian music in England in the seventeenth century. Here we are in the privileged position of knowing exactly how, and when, a substantial number of Italian prints came to be in England: brought from Venice by the London bookseller Robert Martin, bought by Baron Hatton, and then used as copy-sources by his scribes - perhaps in preparing performing parts for use at the Oxford Court. The disbandment of the Court and the general restraints of the Commonwealth period, however, staunched the dissemination (and therefore the influence) of Hatton's Italian music. It is ironic that only after Hatton's death, when his music collection had passed to Henry Aldrich, did certain Italian pieces of 'Hatton origins' become really popular. At the Restoration the rewards which Baron Hatton could justifiably have expected were not forthcoming, and the mood of euphoria, which was apparent amongst his musicians at the time of his return from exile, was unfortunately premature. This should not, however, be allowed to disguise the fact that in his day - particularly when he was Comptroller of the King's Household at the Oxford Court - Hatton was an important and influential patron who, in the words of Michael East's dedication to his *Seventh Set of Bookes*, was a 'truely noble lover of learning, and patron of the arts'.

PART II

MANUSCRIPT SOURCES: INTRODUCTION

The following descriptive form is used for each manuscript:

Brief descriptive sentence.

Detailed description using the following formula:[1]

Approximate date.

Number of leaves: roman numerals are used to indicate flyleaves; modern flyleaves are not noted unless there is some reason to do so (for example, they contain an interesting later inscription); pastedowns are noted only if they have been lifted to become, in effect, flyleaves.

Foliation and/or pagination.

Page details: dimensions given in millimetres, height first and width second (these figures are often approximations, since the size of the leaves usually varies slightly).[2] Number of staves per page and rastra details. Blank pages.

Watermarks: not described in detail due to the limitations of space.[3]

Collation: given where possible (although the tightness of bindings often precludes a detailed examination of the gatherings) using the formula A-Z (no I, U or W) and thereafter Aa-Zz and Aaa-Zzz, with the number of leaves in a gathering indicated by a superscript number;[4] end-papers are not included in the collations; signatures are editorial unless stated.

---

[1] The order in which the information is presented is occasionally altered in the interests of clarity.

[2] Up to a millimetre should be allowed as a 'variation factor' for the individual staves, and perhaps even more than a millimetre for the total span of a rastrum (particularly for multiple rastra). Such variations in the measurements could be the result of differing pressure on the rastrum causing varying amounts of 'spreading', fluctuating viscosity of ink, irregular ink supply, or paper warping.

[3] The author is aware that brief watermark descriptions are of limited use. Ideally each watermark, including 'twins' and all variants, would be reproduced (entailing tracing and, in some cases, beta-radiography) and detailed measurements of chain lines given. Such an undertaking, however, would not be practical for the purposes of the present study, particularly in light of the fact that much of this ground will be covered by Robert Thompson in 'Appendix: Watermarks and Paper Types', *VdGS Index of Manuscripts Containing Music for Viols*, ed. A. Ashbee, R. Thompson & J.P. Wainwright (forthcoming). Frequent reference is made to Dr Thompson's work in the following manuscript descriptions and I record my thanks for his help on a number of matters.

[4] A singleton is indicated as superscript '1' - thus breaking with the bibliographical convention that 'the superior figure must always be an even number' - unless it is obvious which leaf of the bifolio has been removed; e.g. a bifolio with the first leaf removed would be indicated: 'A^2(A1 removed)'.

Script: the division of scribal labour is detailed.

Inscriptions: unless stated, in round brackets at the end of the inscription, the hand is unidentified; line ends are indicated thus: / . (Other inscriptions are given at the relevant point in the inventory, see below.)

Binding and decorations.

Manuscript inventory giving the following information:

- Composers as given in the source;[5] square brackets are used when the composer is ascribed from another source, and for comments on the ascription.

- Original numbering systems (where they exist).

- First line or title;[6] original capitalisation (or non-capitalisation) and orthography are retained.

- Inscriptions are given in inverted commas; unless stated, in round brackets at the end of the inscription, the hand is that of the main scribe; line ends are indicated thus: / .

- Scoring.

- Folios and/or pages; a folio number alone indicates recto.

- Catalogue or Thematic Index references.

- Concordances with printed sources, identified by *RISM* number.[7]

---

[5] In the inventories of partbooks, the composer and title are taken from the first book in numerical sequence to contain the piece in question (usually the Cantus book).
[6] See note 5 above.
[7] For full concordance listings (both printed and manuscript) see Wainwright (1993), ii.

MANUSCRIPT I

LONDON, BRITISH LIBRARY ADD. MS 10,338

A large scorebook containing both vocal and instrumental compositions by George Jeffreys.

Various layers copied *c*.1640-62.
ff. iii + 300.
Modern pencil foliation: ff. 1-275. The flyleaves are foliated, but blank folios are not foliated; thus f. 11 is followed by one unnumbered folio [11a], f. 13 by two unnumbered folios [13a]-[13b], f. 29 by six unnumbered folios [29a]-[29f], f. 32 by four unnumbered folios [32a]-[32d], f. 56 by six unnumbered folios [56a]-[56f], f. 59 by one unnumbered folio [59a], f. 63 by two unnumbered folios [63a]-[63b], f. 103 by one unnumbered folio [103a], and f. 176 by two unnumbered folios [176a]-[176b]. Ink pagination (hand of E.T. Warren): pp. 1-580 beginning on f. 4; unpaginated pages as follows: two between pp. 130 and 131, two between pp. 174 and 175, two between pp. 236 and 237, two between pp. 344 and 345; pp. 477 and 478 are omitted, and pp. 555-6 occurs twice.

Paper: 305 x 195 mm. Marginal rulings on left and right. Unruled pages: ff. 1-3^v (f. 1^r: inscriptions; ff. 2^r and 3^r: index in hand of E.T. Warren); 39^{r-v} and 42^{r-v} (inserted notes, Warren); [56a]-[56f]^v; 176^v-[176b]^v; 234^{r-v} (inserted note, Warren). No music entered on ff. 11^v-12, [13a]-14, 19, 24, [29a]-[29f]^v, [32a]-[32d]^v, 56^v, 57, 59^v-[59a]^v, [63a]-64, 103^v-[103a], 104, 152^v-153, 157, 160, 203^v, 225^v, 262^v, 275^{r-v}. f. 72 is a folded bifolio with the staves joined, by hand, in the middle to enable the scribe to copy stratigraphically across the whole width of the paper. Slips of paper have been stuck to the following folios for corrections or completions: ff. 91, 100^v, 147, 207 (whole leaf), 223, 226, 246 (whole leaf), 264.

Collation: iii A^{10} B-C^8 D^6 E^{10} F^{12} G^8 H^{14} J^8 K^8(singleton added between K6 & K7) L-V^8 X^8(singleton added between X3 & X4) Y-Aa^8 Bb^8(singleton added between Bb1 & Bb2) Cc-Gg^8 i Hh-Kk^8 Ll^8(singleton added between Ll3 & Ll4) Mm^8. The recto of the first folio and the verso of the last folio of each gathering are marked with a binder's mark; e.g. f. 4 is marked '1' and f. 12 is marked '2', the second gathering therefore begins on f. 13. There is an error in the markings at the gathering 11-12 as the final number is also 11: the alteration of odd and even numbers thereafter is reversed; one gathering is omitted between the binder's marks 43 and 44 (ff. 171-[176b]).

Scribe: George Jeffreys.

Watermarks and stave rulings:[a]

No.	Watermark[b]	No. of staves	Stave width mm	No. of staves in rastrum	Rastrum span mm
1	Pillars 1: lettered DI	12	10	4	75
2	Pillars 2	10	13	5	115
3	Pot 1: lettered GPO	10	12	5	110
4	Pot 2: lettered PI	10	13	5	119
5	Pot 3: lettered POO	10	12	5	110
6	Pot 4: lettered RDP	10	12	5	109
7	Pot 5: lettered ID	10	12	5	110
8	Pot 6: lettered DO	10	13	5	118
9	Pot 7: lettered GRO	Supplied as unruled paper: lines drawn individually			
10	Pot 8: lettered DI	9[c]	11.5	5	117
11	Posthorn: lettered G DVRAND	10	13	5	118
12	Foolscap 1	12	11	4	81
13	Foolscap 2	10	11	5	106

Inscriptions: f. ii^v: 'This book is in the handwriting of one / person, and he evidently the composer of so / many of the pieces contained therein, that the / whole may be fairly attributed to him. / From a Bass Part-book in the same handwriting / ( ) [sic] his name appears to be George Jeffreys[d] / who according to Anthony Wood was "Steward to / the Lord Hatton of Kirbie in Northamptonshire / and Organist to King Charles the 1st at Oxford." / Tho. Oliphant. / X These remarks [i.e. those on f. 1] and the Index are in the handwriting of E.T. Warren, / the Secretary of the Catch Club, and Publisher of / Warren's collection of Glees, &c - T. Oliphant / 1669[e] / see last page' (pencil inscription: Thomas Oliphant). f. 1^v: 'Upon a careful examination of this book, it appears to be the hand writing / of one or two authors, being ... [illegible (displays?)] in every kind of Composition, and shews / by many Memorandums & Dates to be found therein, that it was compos'd / between the years 1630 & 1662, some may have been earlier. / The Contents are / Fancies in 3 p[art]s for Violls & Virginall / Songs and Dialogues for 2.3 & 4 Voices for several Comedies and / Masques perform'd before the King. Charles the first. / Motetts and Anthems for 2.3.4 & 5 Voices / Psalms, Hymns and Te Deums in English / and Latin for 2,3,4,5 & 6 Voices / All in Score. / N.B. W^m. & Henry Lawes were then

---

[a] I am indebted to Dr Robert Thompson for the information concerning the watermarks and stave rulings; see Thompson (1988), 165-220, and ibid. (1989).
[b] Watermarks 1, 3-9 & 11 are each represented by a pair of marks (a & b); for full details see Thompson, ibid.
[c] Trimmed; originally 10 staves.
[d] Oliphant is referring to *Lbl* Add. 17,816 which he presented to the British Museum 'as proof that the handwriting in Add. MS 10,338 is that of George Jeffreys'; see MS II below.
[e] *Recte* 1662.

favrite [sic] / Composers. W^m. was kill'd in 1645 and / Henry Dy'd in 1662. / Math. Locke, Dr Coleman, & Dr Wilson were in favor / early in Charles the Second's reign. / The former quitted his service by ... [illegible] & Dy'd a Papist 1677 / The book is perfected by the authors own Correcctions [sic]. / - [illegible ('Lanier'?)] was living & a favorite / at this day / and Alphonso Ferabosco jun.' (E.T. Warren). (For George Jeffreys' inscriptions see the inventory below.)

Binding: modern.

Contents of *Lbl* Add. MS 10,338:

Music by George Jeffreys

Page	Folio	Binder's mark	Title Inscription	Scoring	Watermark No.
-	1		'The Italian use 4. words in their vocall / Musick to express their Fancy / Presto speed to hasten the Time / Adagio Slow to prolong / Fortis Strong to sing it louder / Piano To sing softlier'		
-	1^v		[Unruled & blank]		
-	2		[E.T. Warren's Index]		9b
-	2^v		[Unruled & blank]		
-	3		[E.T. Warren's Index]		
-	3^v		[Unruled & blank]		
1	4	1	Fantasies of 3. Parts for ye Violls and the Virginall		
2	4^v				
3	5		Fantazia the 2 of 3 pts		
4	5^v				
5	6		3 Fantazia		1b
6	6^v				1b
7	7				
8	7^v		Fantasia 4th 3pts		
9	8				
10	8^v		Fantazia 5^t A 3		
11	9				1b
12	9^v				1b
13	10		Fantazia 6^t A.3		1b
14	10^v				1b
15	11				
16	11^v		[No music entered]		
17	[11a]		[No music entered]		1a
18	[11a]^v		[No music entered]		1a
19	12		[No music entered]		1a
20	12^v	2	Fantazia of 2 pts to the Organ For the violin	vln b.vl org	1a
21	13	3			1b
22	13^v				1b
23	[13a]		[No music entered]		
24	[13a]^v		[No music entered]		
25	[13b]		[No music entered]		1b

26	[13b]ᵛ		[No music entered]			1b
27	14		[No music entered]			1b
28	14ᵛ		Le parole soavi hor aspre	1	CCB	1b
29	15		O vaghe O O care stelle	2	CCB	
30	15ᵛ		Donna Crudell	3	CCB	
31	16		Quand'io miro le rose	4	CCB	
32	16ᵛ		All'ombra de gli'allori viddi mesta	5	CCB	
33	17		Si miro il tuo bel viso	6	CCB	1b
34	17ᵛ		Occhi stelle mortali ministri	7	CCB	1b
35	18		Crudel tu per fugire	8	CCB	
36	18ᵛ	4	Donna s'io miro voi giaccio divengo	9	CCB	
37	19	5	[No music entered]			3a
38	19ᵛ		Felice Pastorelle ch'in compagnia		CCBbc	3a
39	20					
40	20ᵛ		Provate la mia fiamma		CCBbc	
41	21					
42	21ᵛ					
43	22		Che nove'Arti son queste per catena mi		TTBbc	3b
44	22ᵛ					3b
45	23					
46	23ᵛ					
47	24		[No music entered]			3a
48	24ᵛ		Musicke thou Queen of Soules[f]		TTBbc	3a
49	25					3b
50	25ᵛ					3b
51	26					
52	26ᵛ	6	Coy Cælia dost thou see		TTBbc	
53	27	7				
54	27ᵛ					
55	28					
56	28ᵛ		Say Daunce how shall wee go 'Or for 2 Tenores'		CCbc	
57	29					4a
58	29ᵛ		'The Maskque of Vices'			4a
59	[29a]		[No music entered]			
60	[29a]ᵛ		[No music entered]			
61	[29b]		[No music entered]			4a
62	[29b]ᵛ		[No music entered]			4a
63	[29c]		[No music entered]			4a
64	[29c]ᵛ	8	[No music entered]			4a
65	[29d]	9	[No music entered]			4b
66	[29d]ᵛ		[No music entered]			4b
67	[29e]		[No music entered]			5b
68	[29e]ᵛ		[No music entered]			5b
69	[29f]		[No music entered]			
70	[29f]ᵛ		[No music entered]			
71	30		[2 bar insert for X on p. 73]			5b

---

[f] T. Randolph, *Poems, with Muses' Looking-Glass and Amyntas* (London, 1638); 'Say Daunce how shall wee go' (*The Maskque of Vices*) is part of *The Muses' Looking-Glass*, 'Musicke thou Queene of Soules', 'Coy Cælia dost thou see' and 'Why sigh you swayne' (Dialogue Nymphe & Sheaphard) are from the poems. See Hazlitt ed. (1875), i, 587, 586, 193 & 585 respectively.

72	30ᵛ		Why sigh you swayne	CBbc	5b
			'Dialogue Nymphe & Sheaphard'		
73	31				5b
74	31ᵛ		Lovely Sheaphardᵍ 'Dialogue'	CBbc	
			'Febisse Endimion' [in margin]		
75	32		[No music entered]		
76	32ᵛ		[No music entered]		
77	[32a]		[No music entered]		
78	[32a]ᵛ		[No music entered]		
79	[32b]		[No music entered]		5a
80	[32b]ᵛ		[No music entered]		5a
81	[32c]		[No music entered]		
82	[32c]ᵛ		[No music entered]		
83	[32d]		[No music entered]		
84	[32d]ᵛ	10	[No music entered]		
85	33	11	You that have been this Evenings light	CMABbc	6b
			'Songs made for some Comedyes / A 4 voc: 1631 / Sʳ R. Hatton'		
86	33ᵛ				6b
87	34				
88	34ᵛ		Fond Maydes, take warninge while you may	CMABbc	
89	35				6b
90	35ᵛ				6b
91	36				
92	36ᵛ		Cupid blushes to behold	CATBbc	
93	37				6a
94	37ᵛ				6a
95	38				
96	38ᵛ		Hymen hath together tyed ye lusty bridegroome	CATBbc	
-	39		[Note in hand of E.T. Warren]		
-	39ᵛ		[Unruled & blank]		
97	40				6b
98	40ᵛ				6b
99	41				
100	41ᵛ				
-	42		[Note in hand of E.T. Warren]		
-	42ᵛ		[Unruled & blank]		
101	43		Drowsy Phœbus com[e] away 'Dialogue'	CCATBbc	6a
			'Songs made for Dʳ Hausteds / Comedy called ye Rivall friends / Acted before ye Kinge / & Queene An. 1631. / 19. March.'		
102	43ᵛ				6a
103	44				
104	44ᵛ	11ʰ			
105	45	12			6b
106	45ᵛ		Have pity greefe '2. Song'	Cbc	6b
107	46		Cruell but once againe	Cbc	
			'This song was made for the / Comedie but I thinke not sunge'		

ᵍ The text to the pastoral dialogue 'Lovely Sheaphard' may also be by Randolph; see Moore Smith (1925), 244-57.

ʰ *Sic*: error in the binder's marking.

108	46ᵛ		Cupid if a God thou art	CCATBbc	
109	47				
110	47ᵛ		To the Ladyes Joy, delight	CCATBbc	
111	48				
112	48ᵛ		But why do ye wing'd minutes fly so fast away	CCATBbc	
113	49				6a
114	49ᵛ		Have you a desyre to see the glorious Heavens	CCATBbc	6a
115	50				6a
116	50ᵛ				6a
117	51		'The Dialogue / Drowsy hebus & / ye rest to this place were / made to and sung in Dr / Hausteds unfortunate / Comedy at Cambridge / before the King / and Queene called ye / Rivall Friends. [16]31.'		
118	51ᵛ		Felice Pastorella 'A 5 voc to Symphonies'	CCATBbc & inst	6a
119	52				
120	52ᵛ	13			
121	53	14			7b
122	53ᵛ				7b
123	54				
124	54ᵛ				
125	55				5b
126	55ᵛ				5b
127	56				5b
128	56ᵛ		[No music entered]		5b
129	[56a]		[Unruled & blank]		
130	[56a]ᵛ		[Unruled & blank]		
-	[56b]		[Unruled & blank]		
-	[56b]ᵛ		[Unruled & blank]		
131	[56c]		[Unruled & blank]		
132	[56c]ᵛ		[Unruled & blank]		
132	[56d]		[Unruled & blank]		
133	[56d]ᵛ		[Unruled & blank]		
135	[56e]		[Unruled & blank]		
136	[56e]ᵛ		[Unruled & blank]		
137	[56f]		[Unruled & blank]		
138	[56f]ᵛ		[Unruled & blank]		
139	57		[No music entered]		
140	57ᵛ		O tu unus Deus Pater[i]	TTBbc	
141	58				
142	58ᵛ				
143	59				7a
144	59ᵛ		[No music entered]		7a
145	[59a]		[No music entered]		
146	[59a]ᵛ	15	[No music entered]		
147	60	16	O quam suave 'Mottects a 1 voc'	Bbc	5a
148	60ᵛ				5a
149	61		[Includes revision of section of 'Speciosus forma' below]		
150	61ᵛ		Speciosus forma	Bbc	

[i] Incomplete

London, British Library Add. MS 10,338   223

151	62		Prayse the Lord O my soule '104 Ps'	Bbc	5a
152	62ᵛ				5a
153	63				
154	63ᵛ				
155	[63a]		[No music entered]		5b
156	[63a]ᵛ		[No music entered]		5b
157	[63b]		[No music entered]		
158	[63b]ᵛ		[No music entered]		
159	64		[No music entered]		5a
160	64ᵛ		Quid mihi est in cælo	ATBbc	5a
161	65				
162	65ᵛ	17			
163	66	18			4a
164	66ᵛ				4a
165	67		'Finis Octob. [16]61'		
166	67ᵛ		See see the word is incarnate '1°. pars' 'This Altered in my other Booke' 'Composed March / & Apr: 1662'	ATBbc	
167	68				4a
168	68ᵛ				4a
169	69		The Pascall lambe '2° pars'	ATBbc	4a
170	69ᵛ				4a
171	70				
172	70ᵛ				
173	71				
174	71ᵛ		Glory be to the Lambe '3.° pars'	ATBbc	
-	72				11a
-	72ᵛ				11a
175	73				4b
176	73ᵛ		Timor et Tremor 'Mottects of 2. pts'	TTbc	4b
177	74				
178	74ᵛ	19	Audivi vocem de Cælo	TTbc	
179	75	20			
180	75ᵛ		Si diligitis me	TTbc	
181	76				5a
182	76ᵛ		Sive vigilem sive dormiam	TTbc	5a
183	77				
184	77ᵛ		Erit gloria Domini in Seculum	TTbc	
185	78				5a
186	78ᵛ		Domine Deus salutis meæ	TTbc	5a
187	79				
188	79ᵛ		Et ingrediar ad Altare Dei	TTbc	
189	80				5b
190	80ᵛ		Heu me misera[m] 'Dialogue Maria & Angelis'	CBbc	5b
191	81				
192	81ᵛ				
193	82				5a
194	82ᵛ	21			5a
195	83	22	O quam dulcis	CBbc	
196	83ᵛ				
197	84				

198	84ᵛ		O Panis Angelorum	TBbc	
199	85				5b
200	85ᵛ		O Nomen Jesu	ABbc	5b
201	86				
202	86ᵛ		O Pretiosum et admirandum convivium	ABbc	
203	87				5b
204	87ᵛ		Jesu Rex admirabilis	ABbc	5b
205	88				
206	88ᵛ				
207	89		With notes that are both loud and sweet ʲ 'For the Ascension of oʳ Bˡᵈ Saviour' 'Mr Pett'ᵏ	BBbc	5b
208	89ᵛ				5b
209	90				5b
210	90ᵛ	23			5b
211	91	24			
212	91ᵛ		Audite gentes	ATBbc	
213	92				3b
214	92ᵛ				3b
215	93				
216	93ᵛ				
217	94		Gloria tua manet in [a]eternum	ATBbc	3b
218	94ᵛ				3b
219	95				
220	95ᵛ				
221	96		'1658 / 1659'		3b
222	96ᵛ		Gloria Patri et Filio	ATB[bc]	3b
223	97		Florete flores	ATBbc	
224	97ᵛ				
225	98				3b
226	98ᵛ	25			3b
227	99	26	'[16]60'		5b
228	99ᵛ		O Piissime domine Jesu	ATBbc	5b
229	100				
230	100ᵛ				
231	101				
232	101ᵛ		Salve Cælestis curia triumphale Decus	ATBbc	
233	102				5b
234	102ᵛ				5b
235	103				
236	103ᵛ		[No music entered]		
-	[103a]		[No music entered]		5a
-	[103a]ᵛ		[Conclusion to 'Salve Cælestis' above]		5a
237	104		[No music entered]		5a
238	104ᵛ		Glory to God on high 'Morning Hymne'	ATBbc	5a
239	105				
240	105ᵛ	27			

ʲ Dated '[16]69' in *T* 1010; see MS XXXIV below.
ᵏ According to Anthony Wood (Clark ed. (1891), i, 241-2) a lawyer called Peter Pett entertained the violinist Davis Mell at Oxford in 1657; see Thompson (1988), 424 & 428-9.

241	106	28	'Composed at Mr / Peter Gunnings motion / May 1652'[1]		
242	106ᵛ		Unto thee O Lord [Pt 1] 'Psalme 25'	TTBbc	4a
			'Mottects of 3 parts / English and Lattyn'		
243	107				
244	107ᵛ		Shew me thy wayes O Lord 'Second part'	TTBbc	
245	108				4a
246	108ᵛ		Hear my Prayer 'Psalme 39'	TTBbc	4a
247	109				
248	109ᵛ				
249	110		Singe unto the Lord	TTBbc	4a
250	110ᵛ				4a
251	111				
252	111ᵛ		Prayse the Lord O my Soule 'Psalme 104'	CCBbc	
253	112				4b
254	112ᵛ		[Alleluia to 'Brightest Sunne' below]		4b
255	113		Brightest Sunne how was thy light 'Epiphany'	TTBbc	
256	113ᵛ	29			
257	114	30			
258	114ᵛ		Exurge Quare obdormis Domine	TTBbc	
259	115				4a
260	115ᵛ				4a
261	116		O Quam gloriosum est Regnum	AABbc	4a
262	116ᵛ				4a
263	117				4a
264	117ᵛ		Lapidabant Stephanum	TTBbc	4a
265	118				
266	118ᵛ				
267	119		Et Recordatus est Petrus verborum Jesus	TTBbc	
268	119ᵛ				
269	120		Beatus Author [recte auctor] S[a]eculi	TTBbc	
270	120ᵛ				
271	121				4b
272	121ᵛ	31	Jesu mi Dulcissime	TTBbc	4b
273	122	32			
274	122ᵛ				
275	123				5a
276	123ᵛ		Vere languores nostros ipse tulit	TTBbc	5a
277	124				
278	124ᵛ		Nescio quid Amore maius	TTBbc	
279	125				
280	125ᵛ		Utinam concessa mihi peccatorum Venia	TTBbc	
281	126				5a
282	126ᵛ		Nil Canitur Suavius	TTBbc	5a
283	127				5a
284	127ᵛ		Ecce Dilectus meus	TTBbc	5a
285	128				
286	128ᵛ		Prior Christus dilexit nos	TTBbc	
287	129				4b
288	129ᵛ	33	Domine Jesu dilexisti me	TBbc	4b

---

[1] Peter Gunning, the prominent Royalist divine, was closely connected with the Hatton family; see pp. 14-15, 18 & 149-50 above.

289	130	34	[No music entered]		4a
290	130ᵛ		[No music entered]		4a
291	131		Christo Jesu debes omnem vitam tuam	TTBbc	
292	131ᵛ				
293	132		Hosanna filio David	TTBbc	4a
294	132ᵛ				4a
295	133				4a
296	133ᵛ		Heu mihi Domine Miserere mei	TTBbc	4a
297	134				
298	134ᵛ		Visa urbe flevit super ea	TTBbc	
299	135				
300	135ᵛ		Invocavi nomen tuum domine	CCBbc	
301	136				4b
302	136ᵛ				4b
303	137				
304	137ᵛ	35			
305	138	36	Jerusalem quae occidis prophetas	CCBbc	
306	138ᵛ				
307	139		Domine Dominus Noster	MABbc	
308	139ᵛ				
309	140				4a
310	140ᵛ				4a
311	141		Caro mea vere est Cibus	MABbc	4a
312	141ᵛ				4a
313	142				4a
314	142ᵛ		Paratum cor meum 'Some small things altered in this song since it was transcribed into my Bookes'ᵐ	ATBbc	4a
315	143				
316	143ᵛ				
317	144				4b
318	144ᵛ				4b
319	145		'Nov: [16]57'		4a
320	145ᵛ	37	Quando natus est	ATBbc	4a
321	146	38			
322	146ᵛ				
323	147				
324	147ᵛ		'Dec: 1657'		
325	148		O Deus meus Deus et Omnia 'See at the end for an / other begin[n]ing'	ATBbc	
326	148ᵛ				
327	149				5b
328	149ᵛ				5b
329	150				
330	150ᵛ		O quam iucundum	ATBbc	
331	151				5a
332	151ᵛ				5a

ᵐ i.e. *Lcm* 920; see MS XVII below.

London, British Library Add. MS 10,338   227

333	152		'Mnd That some of these later 3 parts are placed at ye beginning of ye 3 parts. / And others of these 3^s. are placed next the songs of one voice, for want of roome.' [in margin] 'Mind that some of these last Threes are placed before at ye beginning & some / before the 2 pt songs.' 'Finis Aug: [16]58'		
334	152^v		[No music entered]		5a
335	153		[No music entered]		5b
336	153^v	39	What praise can reach thy Clemency 'Es[s]ay 38'^{n}	AATBbc	5b
337	154	40	'This song being blotted & Altered, I have transposed / into my other Score Book 1665'^{o}		
338	154^v				
339	155				5a
340	155^v				5a
341	156				
342	156^v				
343	157		[No music entered]		
344	157^v		['What praise' continued]		
-	158				5a
-	158^v				5a
345	159				
346	159^v				
347	160		[No music entered]		5b
348	160^v		In the midst of life 'This Song being blotted I have transposed / to my other booke'^{p}	AATBbc	5b
349	161				
350	161^v				
351	162				5b
352	162^v	41			5b
353	163	42			
354	163^v				
355	164		'The Alleluia is altered as on / the other side of this leafe' 'Finis. Made in the tyme / of my sicknes Octob. 1657'		8b
356	164^v				8b
357	165		[Alteration] 'This alteration belongs to the following Song / 5 Leaves forward'		
358	165^v		O Domine Deus	ATTBbc	
359	166				11b
360	166^v				11b
361	167				
362	167^v				
363	168				11a
364	168^v				11a
365	169				

^{n} G. Sandys, 'A Paraphrase upon the Songs Collected out of the Old and New Testaments', *A Paraphrase upon the Divine Poems* (London, 1638), Es[s]ay XXXVIII, Part 2.
^{o} *Ob* Tenbury 1285b appears to be a remnant of this 'Score Book'; see MS XLI below.
^{p} See note o above.

366	169ᵛ				
367	170				8a
368	170ᵛ	43			8a
369	171				9a
370	171ᵛ				9a
371	172		Turn thou us Good Lord	ATTBbc	9b
372	172ᵛ				9b
373	173				
374	173ᵛ				
375	174				
376	174ᵛ				
377	175				9a
378	175ᵛ				9a
379	176		'[16]55'		9a
380	176ᵛ		[Unruled & blank]		9a
381	[176a]		[Unruled & blank]		
382	[176a]ᵛ		[Unruled & blank]		
383	[176b]		[Unruled & blank]		
384	[176b]ᵛ		[Unruled & blank]		
385	177	44	Turne thee againe O Lord God of Hosts '1648' 'Songs of 4. Parts For the Church'	MATBbc	
386	177ᵛ				
387	178				
388	178ᵛ				
389	179				
390	179ᵛ				
391	180				
392	180ᵛ				
393	181		Quid com[m]isisti Jesu	CATBbc	11b
394	181ᵛ				11b
395	182				11b
396	182ᵛ				11b
397	183		Ego Sum Panis	CMTBbc	8a
398	183ᵛ				8a
399	184				2
400	184ᵛ	45			2
401	185	46			
402	185ᵛ				
403	186		[Textless fragment]		12
404	186ᵛ		Jubilate Deo [altered beginning] 'Altered / the first pt / Booke'	CATBbc	12
405	187		Jubilate Deo 'I have heard something too neer this since I made it / have made some Alteration according to ye begin[n]ing of this Paper'	CATBbc	8b
406	187ᵛ				8b
407	188				11b
408	188ᵛ				11b
409	189				
410	189ᵛ				
411	190				11a

412	190ᵛ		Amor Jesu Dulcis Amor	CATBbc	11a
413	191				
414	191ᵛ				
415	192				
416	192ᵛ				
417	193		O Bone Jesu	CATBbc	8b
418	193ᵛ	47			8b
419	194	48			6b
420	194ᵛ				6b
421	195				6b
422	195ᵛ				6b
423	196				6b
424	196ᵛ		Audite C[a]eli	MATBbc	6b
425	197				6b
426	197ᵛ				6b
427	198				
428	198ᵛ				
429	199				
430	199ᵛ		Jesu Dulcedo Cordium	CATBbc	
431	200				
432	200ᵛ				
433	201				
434	201ᵛ	49			
435	202	50			6b
436	202ᵛ				6b
437	203				6b
438	203ᵛ		[No music entered]		6b
439	204		Te Deum laudamus	ATTBbc	6b
440	204ᵛ				6b
441	205				6b
442	205ᵛ				6b
443	206				
444	206ᵛ				
445	207				
446	207ᵛ				
447	208				
448	208ᵛ				
449	209				
450	209ᵛ	51			
451	210	52			
452	210ᵛ				
453	211				6b
454	211ᵛ				6b
455	212				6b
456	212ᵛ				6b
457	213				6b
458	213ᵛ				6b
459	214				
460	214ᵛ				
461	215		'1649'		

462	215^{v}		Gloria Patri et Filio	AATBbc	
463	216				
464	216^{v}				
465	217		O quam iucundum	ATTBbc	6a
466	217^{v}	53			6a
467	218	54			
468	218^{v}				
469	219				
470	219^{v}				
471	220				
472	220^{v}				
473	221		'1651'		
474	221^{v}		Gloria Patri qui creavit nos	ATTBbc	
475	222				6a
476	222^{v}				6a
479[q]	223		'1651'		6b
480	223^{v}		Glory be to God on high	CATB	6b
481	224				6a
482	224^{v}				6a
483	225		Holy, holy, holy Lord	CATB	6a
			Responses (Communion service)	CATB	
484	225^{v}	55	[No music entered]		6a
485	226	56	Gloria in Excelsis Deo	CCATBbc	3b
			'Songs Mottects of 5. Parts.'		
486	226^{v}				3b
487	227				
488	227^{v}				
489	228				3b
490	228^{v}				3b
491	229				3a
492	229^{v}				3a
493	230				
494	230^{v}		Bone Jesu verbum Patris	CCATBbc	
495	231				
496	231^{v}				
497	232				3a
498	232^{v}				3a
499	233				
500	233^{v}	57	Harke Sheapard swaynes	CCATBbc	
			'For ye Nativity of our most blessed Saviour'		
-	234^{r-v}		[Note in hand of E.T. Warren]		
501	235	58			
502	235^{v}				
503	236				
504	236^{v}				
505	237				
506	237^{v}				
507	238				
508	238^{v}				

[q] Lacks pp. 477 & 478: error in pagination.

509	239		Bussie tyme this day		CCATBbc	3b
			'For the B^ld Innocents Day'			
510	239^v					3b
511	240					3b
512	240^v					3b
513	241					3b
514	241^v					3b
515	242					3a
516	242^v	59	Brightest of dayes 'For the Epiphany'		CMATBbc	3a
517	243	60				
518	243^v					
519	244					3a
520	244^v					3a
521	245					3b
522	245^v					3b
523	246					
			[Extension-leaf adding 'Alleluia]			13
524	246^v		Whisper it easily		CCATBbc	
			'On the Passion of our B. Saviour'			
525	247					3a
526	247^v					3a
527	248					
528	248^v					
529	249					
530	249^v					
531	250					3b
532	250^v	61	Ryse Hart thy Lord is rysen^r		CCATBbc	3b
			'For the Resurrestion of our B. Saviour'			
533	251	62				3b
534	251^v					3b
535	252					3a
536	252^v					3a
537	253					
538	253^v					
539	254					3a
540	254^v					3a
541	255					
542	255^v		Looke upp all Eyes		CCATBbc	
			'For the Ascension of o^r B. Saviour'			
543	256					3b
544	256^v					3b
545	257					
546	257^v					
547	258					
548	258^v	63				
549	259	64				

---

[r] G. Herbert, 'Easter', *The Temple. Sacred Poems and Private Ejaculations* (Cambridge, 1633).

550	259ᵛ		The Lord, in thy adversity regard thy Cry 'Psalme 20'	CMATBbc	
551	260				
552	260ᵛ				
553	261				
554	261ᵛ				
555[i]	262		[Inserted leaf]		
-	262ᵛ		[No music entered]		
555[ii]	263				
556	263ᵛ				
557	264				3b
			[Extension slip]		10
558	264ᵛ				3b
559	265				3a
560	265ᵛ				3a
561	266				3a
562	266ᵛ		Hosanna filio David	CCMATBbc	3a
563	267				3b
564	267ᵛ	65			3b
565	268	66			3b
566	268ᵛ				3b
567	269				
568	269ᵛ				
569	270				
570	270ᵛ		A musick strange 'For Whitsunday'	CCATBbc & insts	
571	271				
572	271ᵛ				
573	272				5b
574	272ᵛ				5b
575	273				5a
576	273ᵛ				5a
577	274				5b
578	274ᵛ		'1662'		5b
579	275		[No music entered]		
580	275ᵛ	67	[No music entered]		

MANUSCRIPT II

LONDON, BRITISH LIBRARY ADD. MSS 17,816 & 30,829-30

An incomplete set of three partbooks containing sacred music in English and Latin for four, five or six voices and basso continuo by George Jeffreys.

The first seven four-voice pieces and possibly the first nine five-voice pieces were copied in the early 1640s and the remaining pieces appear to have been added in roughly chronological order c.1648-65.

Add. MS 30,829 *Altus*: ff. i + 48 + i. Pencil foliation: ff. 1-35, followed by thirteen unnumbered folios [36]-[48]. No music entered on ff. 4, [36]-[48]^v. Collation: A-H^6. Inscriptions: front cover: 'Altus' (Jeffreys); f. i: 'Purch[ase]d at Sotheby's / 27 May 1878'.

Add. MS 30,830 *Tenore*: ff. i + 48 + i. Pencil foliation: ff. 1-38, followed by ten unnumbered folios [39]-[48]. No music entered on ff. 4, 28, 35, 38^v-[48]^v. Collation: A-H^6. Inscription: front cover: 'Tenore' (Jeffreys).

Add. MS 17,816 *Bassus*: ff. i + 48 + i. Pencil foliation: ff. 1-40, followed by nine unnumbered folios [41]-[49] (the front flyleaf is numbered). No music entered on ff. 6, 37, [41]-[49]^v. Collation: A-H^6. Inscriptions: front cover: 'Bassus / 38 [or 30?]' (Jeffreys); f. 1^v: 'Presented to the Trustees of the British Museum, as proof that the handwriting / in Add. MS 10,338 is that of George Jeffreys / who was Organist to King Charles the First / at Oxford. A perfect set of Part-Books / by the same (at present in my possession) / bears the date of December. 1675^a / Tho. Oliphant / B.Mus, 2nd July 1849' (Thomas Oliphant); f. 8: 'Finis Geo: Jeffreys' (autograph).

The Cantus I, Cantus II and Basso Continuo partbooks are lacking.
Paper: 250 x 193 mm. Marginal rulings on left and right. Eight rastrum-ruled staves per page (ruled with a two-stave rastrum of 37 mm span and individual staves each measuring 12.5 mm).
Watermark: peacock; Thompson (1988), Watermark XVI.
Scribe: George Jeffreys.
Bindings: original gilded white leather.
Contents of *Lbl* Add. MSS 17,816 & 30,829-30:

---
^{a} Now *Lcm* 920A; see MS XVIII below.

Music by George Jeffreys

Title	Scoring	Folios 30829	30830	17816
Quid Com[m]isisti Jesu	[C]ATB[bc]	1	1	2
O Bone Jesu	[C]ATB[bc]	1^v	1^v	2^v
Amor Jesu Dulcis Amor	[C]ATB[bc]	2^v	2^v	3^v
Ego sum Panis	[C]MTB[bc]	3	3	4
Jubilate Deo^b	[C]ATB[bc]	4^v	4^v	4^v
Audite C[a]eli	[M]ATB[bc]	5^v	5^v	6^v
Jesu Dulcedo Cordium	[C]ATB[bc]	6^v	6^v	7^v
Te Deum Laudamus^c 'Canticum Sanctorum Ambrosii & / Augustine'	[A]ATB[bc]	7^v	7^v	8^v
Gloria Patri	[A]ATB[bc]	10^v	10^v	11^v
O Quam iucundum	[A]TTB[bc]	11	11	12
Gloria Patri qui Creavit nos^d	[A]TTB[bc]	12	12	13
Turne thee againe^e 'For the Church'	[M]ATB[bc]	12^v	12^v	13^v
O Domine Deus	[A]TTB[bc]	14	14	15
Turne thou us O good Lord^f	[A]TTB[bc]	15^v	15^v	16^v
In the midst of life^g 'Liturgy'	[A]ATB[bc]	16^v	16^v	17^v
What Praise can reach thy clemency?^{h} 'Es[s]ay 38 / Sands'^{i}	[A]ATB[bc]	18	17^v	18^v
Credo in unum Deum	[A]ATB[bc]	19^v	19	20^v
Jubilate Deo	[A]ATB[bc]	21^v	21	22^v
How wretched is the State you all are in	[C]ATB[bc]	22^v	22^v	23^v
Awake my Soule	[C]ATB[bc]	23^v	23^v	24^v
Gloria in Excelsis Deo	[CC]ATB[bc]	24^v	24^v	25^v
Bone Jesu	[CC]ATB[bc]	25	25^v	26^v
The Lord in thy aduersity 'Psal: 20'	[CM]ATB[bc]	25^v	26^v	27^v
Harke Sheaphard Swaynes 'For the Nativity of our blessed Saviour'	[CC]ATB[bc]	26^v	28^v	29^v

---

^{b} A revised beginning is given in each partbook, and in Add. 17,816, f. 4^v, Jeffreys notes: 'I designe this begin[n]ing for ye next Song, / having since I Made it heard som[e]thing / to[o] neer it'.
^{c} Dated 1649 in *Lbl* Add. 10,338; see MS I above.
^{d} Dated 1651 in *Lbl* Add. 10,338; see MS I above.
^{e} Dated 1648 in *Lbl* Add. 10,338; see MS I above.
^{f} Dated 1655 in *Lbl* Add. 10,338; see MS I above.
^{g} Dated October 1657 in *Lbl* Add. 10,338; see MS I above.
^{h} Dated 1665 in *Lbl* Add. 10,338; see MS I above.
^{i} Sandys (1638), Es[s]ay XXXVIII, Part 2.

Bussie tyme this day 'For Innocents Day'	[CC]ATB[bc]	28	29ᵛ	31
Brightest of dayes 'For th'Epiphanie'	[CM]ATB[bc]	29	30ᵛ	32
Whisper it easily 'For the Passion of our Bl[essed] Saviour'	[CC]ATB[bc]	30ᵛ	31ᵛ	33ᵛ
Ryse hart thy Lord is risen [j] 'For the Resurrection of our Bl[essed] Saviour'	[CC]ATB[bc]	31ᵛ	32ᵛ	34ᵛ
Looke up all Eyes 'For the Ascension of our Bl[essed] Saviour'	[CC]ATB[bc]	32ᵛ	34	36
Hosanna filio David	[CC]MATB[bc]	33ᵛ	35ᵛ [k]	37ᵛ
A Musick Strange 'For Whitsunday'	[CC]ATB[bc]	34	36ᵛ	38ᵛ
Almighty God who mad'st thy blessed sonne 'For the Circumcision of our Bl[essed] Saviour'	[CC]ATB[bc]	35	37ᵛ	40

MANUSCRIPT III

LONDON, BRITISH LIBRARY ADD. MSS 27,550-4

A set of five partbooks containing Fantasia-Ayre Suites for two treble viols, bass viol and basso continuo, and Fantasia-Ayre-Corant Suites for two treble viols, two bass viols and basso continuo by John Jenkins.

> Dated 1674.
> Scribes: A: John Lilly
>   B: unidentified
>   C: Stephen Bing
>   D: unidentified
>   E: unidentified
>   F: unidentified[a]

Add. MS 27,550 *1st Treble*: ff. 69. Modern pencil foliation: ff. 1-15, one unnumbered folio [15a], 16-26, followed by forty-two unnumbered folios. Collation: not possible due to tightness of binding (originally gatherings of twelve?); ff. 19 and 23 are inserted slips of paper. No music entered on ff. 15ᵛ-[15a]ᵛ, 16, nor on any of the unnumbered folios. Script: ff. 1-14: A;

---

[j] Herbert (1633), 'Easter'.
[k] f. 35ᵛ: alto part; f. 36: tenor part.
[a] Scribe F also copied the majority of the Windsor bass partbook: *Lbl* Add. 17,784.

ff. 14ᵛ-26ᵛ: B. Inscription on front cover: 'Mr Jenkins / 3 & 4. Parts. / First Treble. [in red] / I 53'; f. 1: '1674'.

Add. MS 27,551 *2nd Treble*: ff. 70. Modern pencil foliation: ff. 1-11, one unnumbered folio [11a], 12-19, followed by fifty unnumbered folios. No music entered on ff. 11ᵛ-[11a]ᵛ, 12, 19ᵛ, nor on any of the unnumbered folios. Collation: not possible due to tightness of binding (originally gatherings of twelve?). Script: C throughout. Inscription on front cover: 'Mr Jenkins / 3 & 4 Parts / Second Treble.'

Add. MS 27,552 *First Base*: ff. 68. Modern pencil foliation: ff. 1-15, one unnumbered folio [15a], 16-24, followed by forty-three unnumbered folios. No music entered on ff. 15ᵛ-[15a]ᵛ, 16, 24ᵛ, nor on any of the unnumbered folios. Collation: not possible due to tightness of binding (originally gatherings of twelve?). Script: ff. 1-15: D; ff. 16ᵛ-24: B. Inscription on front cover: 'Mr Jenkins / 3 & 4 Parts. / First Base.'

Add. MS 27,553 *Second Base*: ff. 72. Modern pencil foliation: ff. 1-8, followed by sixty-four unnumbered folios. No music entered on the unnumbered folios. Collation: A-F^{12}. Script: E throughout. Inscription on front cover: 'Mr Jenkins / 3 & 4 Parts / Second Base.'

Add. MS 27,554 *Organ* (figured bass): ff. 60. Original ink foliation: ff. 1-7, modern pencil foliation: ff. 8-13, one unnumbered folio [13a], modern pencil foliation: ff. 14-18, followed by forty-one unnumbered folios. No music entered on ff. 9ᵛ-10, [13a]ʳ⁻ᵛ, 18ᵛ-end. Collation: A^{14}(A1 removed) B^{12} C^{10} D^{14}(D14 removed) E^{12}. Script: ff. 1-7: F; ff. 7-18: E.[b] Inscription on front cover: 'Mr Jenkins. / 3 & 4. Parts. / Organ'.

Paper: 310 x 205 mm. Red marginal rulings on left and right. Twelve rastrum-ruled staves per page (ruled with a four-stave rastrum of 80 mm span and individual staves each measuring 11 mm); Add 27,554, ff. 1-11ᵛ have had an extra line added by hand to each of the staves.

Watermarks: foolscap.

Bindings: modern, but the original vellum front cover survives.

Contents of *Lbl* Add. MSS 27,550-4:

---

[b] The hand changes half-way through f. 7.

London, British Library Add. MSS 27,550-4   237

Three-Part Fantasia-Ayre Suites by John Jenkins

No.	Title	Folios				
		27550	27551	27552	27553	27554
1	Ayre	1	1	1	-	1
2	Ayre	1	1	1	-	1
3	Fantasie *or* Fancy	1	1	1v	-	1
4	Ayre	1v	1v	2	-	1v
5	Fantasia *or* Phansy *or* Fancy	2	1v	2v	-	1v
6	Ayre	2v	2	2v	-	1v
7	Fantasie *or* Phansy *or* Fancy	2v	2v	3	-	2
8	Ayre	3	3v	3v	-	2
9	Fancy	3v	3 c	4	-	2v
10	Ayre	4	3v	4v	-	2v
11	Fansie *or* Fansy *or* Fancy	4v	3v	4v	-	3
12	Ayre	5	4	5	-	3
13	Fantasie *or* Fancy	5v	4v	5v	-	3v
14	Ayre	6	4v	6	-	3v
15	Fancy	7	5	6v	-	4
16	Ayre	7v	5v	7	-	4
17	Fancie *or* Fancy	8	5v	7v	-	4v
18	Ayre	8v	6	8	-	4v
19	Fancy	8v	6	8v	-	5
20	Ayre	9	6v	9	-	5
21	Phansi *or* Phansy	9v	7	9v	-	5v
22	Ayre	10	7v	10	-	5v
23	Fancy *or* Phansy	10v	7v	10v	-	6
24	Ayre	11	8	11	-	6v
25	Phansi *or* Phansy	11v	8v	11v	-	6v
26	Ayre	12	9	12	-	7
27	Phansi *or* Phansie	12v	9	12v	-	7v
28	Ayre	13	9v	13	-	7v
29	Fancie *or* Phansy	13v	9v	13v	-	8
30	Ayre	14	10	14	-	8v
31	Fancy	14v	10v	14v	-	8v
32	Ayre d	15	11	15	-	9

c *Sic*: out of sequence.
d 'Almain' in Add. 27,552.

Four-Part Fantasia-Ayre-Corant Suites by John Jenkins

1	Fancy	16ᵛ	12ᵛ	16ᵛ	1	10ᵛ
2	Ayre	17	12ᵛ	17	1ᵛ	11
3	Coranto	17ᵛ	13	17	1ᵛ	11
4	Fancy	17ᵛ	13ᵛ	17ᵛ	2	11ᵛ
5	Ayre	18	14	18	2ᵛ	12
6	Coranto	18ᵛ	14ᵛ	18	2ᵛ	12
7	Fancy	18ᵛ	14ᵛ	18ᵛ	3	12ᵛ
8	Alman *or* Almaine	20	15	19	3ᵛ	13
9	Corant *or* Coranto	20ᵛ	15ᵛ	19	3ᵛ	13
10	Fancy	20ᵛ	15ᵛ	19ᵛ	4	13ᵛ
11	Ayre	21	15ᵛ	20	4ᵛ	14
12	Coranto	21ᵛ	16	20	4ᵛ	14
13	Fancy	21ᵛ	16	20ᵛ	5	14ᵛ
14	Ayre[e]	22ᵛ	16ᵛ	21	5ᵛ	15
15	Coranto	22ᵛ	16ᵛ	21	5ᵛ	15
16	Fancy *or* Fantasy	24	17	21ᵛ	6	15ᵛ
17	Ayre	24ᵛ	17ᵛ	22	6ᵛ	16
18	Coranto	24ᵛ	17ᵛ	22ᵛ	6ᵛ	16
19	Fancy *or* Fantasy	25	18	22ᵛ	7	16ᵛ
20	Ayre	25ᵛ	18	23	7ᵛ	17
21	Coranto	25ᵛ	18ᵛ	23	7ᵛ	17
22	Fancy *or* Fantasy	26	18ᵛ	23ᵛ	8	17ᵛ
23	Ayre	26ᵛ	19	24	8ᵛ	18
24	Coranto *or* Corant	26ᵛ	19	24	8ᵛ	18

MANUSCRIPT IV

LONDON, BRITISH LIBRARY ADD. MS 29,282

A set of four partbooks containing Latin motets for two or three voices and basso continuo by George Jeffreys.

>Copied in the 1660s?
>Four partbooks bound together: ff. i + 46. Modern pencil foliation:
>partbook i: ff. 1-8 and four unnumbered folios [8a-d];
>partbook ii: ff. 9-16 and four unnumbered folios [16a-d];
>partbook iii: ff. 17-23 and five unnumbered folios [23a-e];
>partbook iv: ff. 24-29 and four unnumbered folios [29a-d].

---

[e] 'Alman' in Add. 27,552.

Paper: 310 x 195 mm. Red marginal rulings on left and right. Ten rastrum-ruled staves per page (ruled with five-stave rastrum of 120 mm span and individual staves each measuring 12.5 mm). No music entered on ff. 8^v-[8d]^v, 9^v, 16^v-[16d]^v, 17^v, 23^v-[23e]^v, 27, [29a]-[29d]^v.
Collation: A-C^{12} D^{10} (i.e. one gathering per partbook).
Watermark: foolscap with countermark GB; Thompson (1988), Watermark XXVIII.
Scribe: George Jeffreys.
Inscription on f. i: 'Purchased at ... [illegible] Puttick's / 28 Oct 1872.'.
Binding: modern.
Contents of *Lbl* Add. MS 29,282:

Motets by George Jeffreys

Title	Scoring	Folios			
		ii	iii	i	iv
O Quam Dulcis	CBbc	9	-	1	24
Jesu Rex admirabilis	ABbc	-	17	1^v	24^v
Heu me misera[m] 'Dialogue Maria & Angelis'	CBbc	14^v	-	2	25
Florete Flores	ATBbc	10	18	3	25^v
Gloria Patri	ATBbc	10^v	18^v	3^v	26
Gloria tua	ATBbc	11	19	4	26^v
Invocaui Nomen	CCBbc	11^v	19^v	4^v	27^v
Salve Cælestis	TABbc	12^v	20^v	5^v	28^v
Quid mihi est in Cælo	TABbc	13^v	21^v	6^v	29
Quando natus es	ATBbc	15^v	22^v	7^v	29^v

MANUSCRIPT V

LONDON, BRITISH LIBRARY ADD. MS 30,382

Henry Bowman's scorebook of sacred and secular music by English and Italian composers.[a]

Copied *c*.1678-85.
ff. ii (modern) + 91 + i (index).
Original (irregular) pagination: nine unnumbered, 4, 25-9, one unnumbered, 24, 22, one unnumbered, 24-46, 53-64, 67-74, four

---
[a] See *New Grove*, iii, 136-7.

unnumbered, 75-84, two unnumbered, 91-4, 101-6, four unnumbered, 107-56, two unnumbered, 161-86, and twelve unnumbered. Modern pencil foliation: ff. 2-93 (the endpaper/index is foliated).

Paper: 305 x 200 mm. Marginal rulings on left and right. ff. 6-10^v: twelve rastrum-ruled staves per page (ruled with four-stave rastrum of 73 mm span and individual staves each measuring 10 mm); the remaining folios were ruled by hand (ff. 29-30 and 48^v-49 in red ink); f. 40^r: unruled and blank; f. 93^r: Bowman's index (including a list of 'Songs composed by me').

Collation: not possible as the pages were lifted in rebinding and are now individually guarded throughout.

Watermarks: f. 3: coat of arms (Amsterdam); ff. 7-8, 10, 12, 14, 16, 18, 20, 22, 24-5, 28-9, 31, 35, 38-9, 42-3, 48-9, 51-2, 54, 57-8, 62-3, 65-6, 68, 70, 73-4, 76, 80, 82-3, 86: foolscap; ff. 40, 47: posthorn.

Scribe: Henry Bowman (see f. 23 and 83^v: 'by me H[enry] B[owman]').

Inscription on f. 90^v: 'For / Mrs Gray at hur [sic] house in the Collidg[e] / off Dorhan [Durham?]' (Bowman). f. ii contains the coat of arms of 'Katherine Sedley sole daughter and / heyre of S^r. Charles Sedley of South / fleet in Kent Baronet.'[b] (The printed armorial shield is pasted to the recto of the second modern flyleaf).

Binding: modern.

Contents of *Lbl* Add. MS 30,382:

Folio	Composer	Title	Scoring	Printed Concordances
2		... to ye heavens[c]	SABbc	
2^v	Felice Sances	Plagæ tuæ Domine	ATBbc	S768
5	[Bowman?]	While vulger [sic] beauty	Sbc	
5^v		[Scribbles]		
6		[While vulger beauty *cont.*][d]		
6^v	Sig^r. Monferrato [*recte* Sances]	O Domine guttæ	ATBbc	S768
10	H[enry] B[owman]	In te Domine speravi	CTBbc	
13	Richard Dering	Gloria Patri	ATBbc	1652[10]; 1662[4]
13^v	Sig: Charissimi	Audite Sancti	CCBbc	C1221; 1645[2]; 1656[2]
16	Maria Marini	Anima mea liquefacta est	CABbc	M672
18	Maria Marini	O vos omnes	ATBbc	M672

[b] Catherine Sedley, Countess of Dorchester (1657-1717).
[c] Fragment only.
[d] Incomplete

19ᵛ	[Bowman]	Tribularer ego[e]	CCBbc	
23	H[enry] B[owman]	Miserere mei Deus[e]	SSBbc	
29	[Carissimi]	[Amanti che dite][f]	CCBbc	
29ᵛ	Casatj	Omnes gentes plaudite	CCbc	C1411
31ᵛ	Dʳ: Blow	Go perjur'd man[g]	SB 2vln bc	B2985; B2987-91
33	Bowman[h]	The thirsty earth[e]	CCB	
35	H[enry] B[owman]	In some kind dream	SSBbc	
36	Mʳ: Pursell	Go tell Aminta	SBbc	P6039
38	H[enry] B[owman]	For the few houres of life	SSB	
39	H[enry] B[owman]	Fill the Bowle	SSB	
40ᵛ	Bowman[g]	Yee Cats [that] at midnight[e]	SSB	
41	H[enry] B[owman]	[Drink on til night][i]	SSB	
41ᵛ	H[enry] B[owman]	Gaze not on Swannes	SSB	B4036
42ᵛ	H[enry] B[owman]	Come all noble souls[e]	SSB	
43	H[enry] B[owman]	[When I a parting kiss][i]	SSB	
43ᵛ	H[enry] B[owman]	Wake sleeping ones 'A Dialogue between the Angel & the Soul at ye Judgement Day'	SS/SATBbc	
46	H[enry] B[owman]	Usquequo Domine	SSBbc	
48ᵛ	Monfer[r]a[to]	Regina cæli lætare	TTbc	M3037
49ᵛ	[Cesti?][j]	Amanti sentite Amor	CAbc	
50ᵛ	Rovetta	Io mi sento morir	CCbc	R2981
52ᵛ	Cassati	Exultate justi	CCbc	C1411
54ᵛ	Cassati	Alleluja Jubilat Ecclesia	CBbc	C1411
56ᵛ	Cassati	Cantemus Deo	CBbc	C1411
59	Cassati	Bone Jesu verbum Patris	CCbc	C1411
62ᵛ	Sigʳ: Charissimi [*recte* Trabattone][k]	Anima mea in æterna dulcedine	CBbc	T1070
64ᵛ	[Sances]	Tota pulchra es	ATbc	S768
66	[Sances]	Judica me Deus	CCbc	S768
68	Cassati	Magnificate cæli	CCbc	C1411
70ᵛ	Natal Monferratto	Lætentur Cæli	CCbc	M3037

[e] Incomplete.

[f] Incomplete; concluding sixteen bars of the last movement of the cantata *I Naviganti* ('Sciolto hauean'). Roger North records an occasion when the final trio 'Amanti che dite' was performed before Charles II; described in both 'The Musicall Grammarian' (c.1726) and 'Memoires of Musick' (1728): see Wilson ed. (1959), 120-2, 300 & 350.

[g] An Act song written for the Oxford Encænia of 1680; text from R. Herrick, *Hesperides: or, The Works both Humane & Divine* (London, 1648), 53.

[h] Attributed in the index only.

[i] Lacks opening

[j] Attributed to 'Sigʳ. Marco [Cesti]' in *Och* Mus. 996, to 'Marco Marazzolli in *I-Bc* Q 50, to 'Luigi' [Rossi?] in *I-Fc* f.I.25, and anonymous in all other concordant sources.

[k] Also misattributed to Carissimi in *Lbl* Add. 17,835, 33,234, 33,235; *Ob* Mus. Sch. C 11; *Och* Mus. 43, 621, 623-6, 1178; and *J-Tn* N-4/39

71ᵛ	Cassati [*recte* Martinengo]	Congratulamini mihi	CCbc	C1411
72ᵛ	[Monferrato]	[Lætentur cæli *concluded*]		
73ᵛ	[Martinengo]	[Congratulamini mihi *concluded*]		
73ᵛ	Cassati	Jesu amor dulcissime	CBbc	C1411
75ᵛ	Cassati	Quam suavis es	ABbc	C1411
77	Cassatj	Dulcis Christe ad te venio	ATbc	C1411
78ᵛ	Monferrato	O cæli gloria	ACbc	M3037
80ᵛ	Sigʳ. Silvestro [Durante]	Cantate Domino	CCbc	1661[1]
82ᵛ	Cassati	O Jesu mea vita	TTbc	C1411
83ᵛ	H[enry] B[owman]	Sing unto the Lord 'Funerall / Anthem / by me / HB: / Psal 30. / v: 4'	SS/SATBbc	
87	H[enry] B[owman]	Hark! how he groans	ATbc	
87	H[enry] B[owman]	Close thine eyes 'This a note higher'	CCbc	
89	Mʳ: Wise	How are the mighty fal'n '2. Sam: 1.c. 19.v:'	CTB/ CATB[bc]	
90ᵛ	H. Lawes [*recte* William Lawes]	The Lord is my light 'Psal: 90:'	ATB/CATBbc	

MANUSCRIPT VI

LONDON, BRITISH LIBRARY ADD. MS 31,434

A set of six partbooks containing four English sacred songs, nine Latin motets, two Italian madrigals, and an Italian dialogue.

Copied 1643-6. Six partbooks bound together: ff. i + 76 (i being the original front cover of the *Cantus I* partbook).

Modern pencil foliation: *Cantus I*: ff. 1-13, *Cantus II*: ff. 14-25, *Contratenor*: ff. 26-37, *Tenor*: ff. 38-49, *Bassus*: ff. 50-61, *Basso Continuo*: ff. 62-72. Unnumbered folios between ff. 9 and 10 [= 9a], and ff. 13 and 14 [13a], and two at the end: [73]-[74].

Paper: 310 x 120 mm. Marginal rulings on left and right. Ten staves per page (ruled with five-stave rastra as follows: ff. 1-9ᵛ,[9a]ʳ⁻ᵛ, [13a]ʳ⁻ᵛ, 14-21ᵛ, 26-33ᵛ, 38-45ᵛ, 50-8ᵛ, 62-9ᵛ: rastrum of 111 mm span and individual staves each measuring 12.5 mm; ff. 10-13ᵛ, 22-5ᵛ, 34-7ᵛ, 46-9ᵛ, 59-61ᵛ, 70-72ᵛ, [73]-[74]ᵛ: rastrum of 120 mm span and individual staves each measuring 12.5 mm). No music entered on ff. 4ᵛ, 9ᵛ, [9a]ʳ⁻ᵛ, 13ᵛ, [13a]ʳ⁻ᵛ, 16ᵛ, 25ᵛ, 28ᵛ, 33ᵛ, 37ᵛ, 40ᵛ, 45ᵛ, 49ᵛ, 53ᵛ, 58ᵛ, 72ᵛ, [73]-[74]ᵛ.

Collation: the pages were lifted in rebinding and are now individually guarded throughout, however it is possible to reconstruct an approximate collation through an examination of the watermarks and stave placings:[a]
Cantus I: A-B^2 C^1 D-E^2 F^1 G-H^2 J^1; *Cantus II*: A^1 B^2 C^1 D-G^2; *Contratenor*: A^2 B^1 C^1 D-G^2; *Tenor*: A^2 B^1 C^4(C^1 removed) D-F^2; *Bassus*: A-B^2 C^1 D-F^2 G^1; *Basso Continuo*: A^2 B^1 C^1 D-F^2 G^1 H^1 J^1.

Watermarks: ff. 2, 4, [9a], [13a], 14, 16, 27, 28, 38, 50, 53, 62: pot with letters ID; ff. 5, 6, 8, 17, 19, 20, 29, 30, 33, 41, 42, 45, 54, 56, 57, 67, 68: pot with letters GRO (i); ff. 10, 12, 23, 25, 34, 37, 46, 49, 60, 71, [73], [74]: pot with letters GRO (ii).

Scribe: Stephen Bing.

Inscriptions: f. i: 'Sacred / Songs Ayres / and / Dialogues [plural: sic] / in / Five Parts / In MS. / Composed by and / in the Autograph of / Henry Lawes / A very curious ... [illegible]/ set of parts. / Joseph Warren. / All the Six parts are here.' (Joseph Warren); 'The Bassus part is signed' (pencil inscription); f. 4^v rev.: 'John Sweet Jussin' (not the main hand?); f. 13^v: 'Thomas' (pencil inscription).

ff. 1, 13^v, 14, 25^v, 26, 37^v, 38, 49^v, 50 and [74]^v are discoloured (from acting as outer covers?). f. 26, below 2nd and 3rd staves: text corrections made by pasting slips of paper over the original text. f. [73]: a slip of paper with the three-bar 'solo' missing from f. 18^v, 7th stave, is pasted here. (The scribe was obviously leaning on f. 18^v when he copied these missing bars, as the lower half of the text - 'O Padre, ò Padre mio' - appears there, and the top half on the slip.)

Binding: modern.

Contents of *Lbl* Add. MS 31,434:

Composer	Title	Scoring	Folios					Concordances
			CI	CII	A	T	B	bc
Henry Lawes	Sitting by the streames[b] 'Full Song'	CCATBbc	1	14	26	38	50	62
[H. Lawes][c]	Thee and thy wondrous deeds[d]	CCATBbc	1	14^v	26^v	38^v	50^v	62
[H. Lawes][e]	My Soule the great Gods prayses singe[f]	CCATBbc	2	15	27	39	51	62^v
[H. Lawes][c]	Harke Shepherd swaynes	CCATBbc	3	16	27^v	40	52^v	64

[a] See Table 19 above.
[b] T. Carew, adaptation of Psalm 137; *Ob* Ashmole MS 38, p. 98c. See Dunlap (1949), 149-50.
[c] Attributed to Henry Lawes by virtue of its position in the manuscript and on stylistic grounds.
[d] Hall (1607), 'Psalm 9'.
[e] Attributed to Henry Lawes in Clifford (2/1664), text only; 'Sitting by the streames' appears, attributed to Henry Lawes, in both the first edition (1663) and the second edition of Clifford's wordbook.
[f] T. Carew, adaptation of Psalm 104; manuscript text-sources include *Ob* MS Don. b. 9, f. 9^v (the 'Wybard' Manuscript) and *Ob* Ashmole MS 38, p. 98e. See R. Dunlap (1949), 139-42.

	Angelus ad pastores	CCATBbc	5	17	29	41	54	65	
	Ave O gloriosa virgo	CCATBbc	5ᵛ	17ᵛ	29ᵛ	41ᵛ	54ᵛ	65ᵛ	
	En morior	CCATBbc	6	18	30	42	55	66	
	Splendea qual vivo sole 'Dialogo d'Abram'	CCATBbc	6ᵛ	18ᵛ	30ᵛ	42	55ᵛ	66ᵛ	
	Negatemi pur cruda	CCMTBbc	8	20ᵛ	32	44	57	68ᵛ	
	Donna mentr'io vi miro	CCMTBbc	8ᵛ	20ᵛ	32ᵛ	44ᵛ	57ᵛ	69	
	O Vergine felice	CCATBbc	9	21ᵛ	33	45	58	69ᵛ	
[Aloisi]	Exurgat Deus	CCATBbc	10	22	34	46	59	70	A876
[Aloisi]	O dulcis virgo	CCATBbc	10ᵛ	22ᵛ	35ᵛ	46ᵛ	59ᵛ	70ᵛ	A876
[Aloisi]	Vocem iocunditatis	CCATBbc	11ᵛ	23ᵛ	35ᵛ	47ᵛ	60	71	A876
[Merula]	Benedictus tu	CATTBbc	12ᵛ	24ᵛ	36ᵛ	48ᵛ	61	71ᵛ	M2338ᵍ
[Merula]	Benignissime Jesu	CATTBbc	13	25	37	49	61ᵛ	72	M2338

MANUSCRIPT VII

LONDON, BRITISH LIBRARY ADD. MS 31,440

A large manuscript score of madrigals, motets, and monodies copied by the Italian-born composer Angelo Notari.

Copied in the mid 1640s?
Score; copied stratigraphically across the double opening: ff. 195 + i.
Modern pencil foliation: ff. 1-195. Original pagination in four sections: ff. 1ᵛ-47ᵛ: pp. 1-95 (pp. 22-3 missing); ff. 50ᵛ-97ᵛ: pp. 1-95; 100ᵛ-147ᵛ: pp. 1-95; 149ᵛ-180: pp. 1-62. Original indexes: f. 48ᵛ: 'A una Voce'; f. 49: 'A due voci'; f. 98: 'A 5 Voci' (misplaced: index for ff. 149-195ᵛ); f. 99: untitled index of *a* 2 items; f. 148: untitled index of *a* 3 items.
Paper: 320 x 208 mm. Twelve staves per page: ff. 1-47ᵛ (ruled with a four-stave rastrum of 79 mm span and individual staves each measuring 10 mm), ff. 50-97ᵛ (ruled with a three-stave rastrum of 56 mm span and individual staves each measuring 10-11 mm), and ff. 100-147ᵛ (ruled with a four-stave rastrum of 78 mm span and individual staves each measuring 11 mm); fifteen rastrum-ruled staves per page: ff. 149-195ᵛ (ruled with a five-stave rastrum of 76 mm span and individual staves each measuring 8 mm). No music entered on ff. 50, 97ᵛ, 100, 147ᵛ, 149. ff. 48ᵛ-49ᵛ, 98-99ᵛ and 148ʳ⁻ᵛ are unruled, being for the indices; ff. 48, 49ᵛ, 98ᵛ, 99ᵛ and 148ᵛ are completely blank. One unnumbered and unruled folio between ff. 99 and 100.

ᵍ 'Benedicta tu' in printed source.

Collation: the manuscript has been repaired and rebound, but fortunately the middle-of-gathering bifolios remained intact; the following are bifolios (superscript numbers indicate the number of folios between these doubles): 6^v-7^{10} (pp. 22-3 of original pagination missing, i.e. between ff. 11^v & 12), 17^v-18^{12}, 29^v-30^{12}, 41^v-42^{14}, 55^v-56^{12}, 67^v-68^{12}, 79^v-80^{12}, 91^v-92^{15} (three added), 105^v-106^{12}, 117^v-118^{12}, 129^v-130^{12}, 141^v-42^6, 148^6, (index folio between change from twelve- to fifteen-stave paper), 154^v-55^{10} (two removed before original pagination), 165^v-66^{12}, 177^v-78^{17} (no more doubles; volume ends imperfectly). The basic gatherings were therefore in twelves.

Watermarks: coat of arms of Berne, Switzerland; J. Lindt, *The Paper-Mills of Berne and their Watermarks* (Hilversum, 1964), no. 190: Zeendel and Tribolet mill, dated 1630-5. The basic watermark can be seen on ff. 155, 172, 185, 188 and 189, and its twin on ff. 10, 52 and 153; a damaged version of the same watermark appears on ff. 50, 133 and 164, with its twin on ff. 23 and 65. (A different coat of arms watermark appears on the added slip of paper on f.85^v.)[a]

Scribe: Angelo Notari, with the following additions: ff. 1, 20 and 111: fragments (late 17th-century hand?); f. 11^v: first line only of an alternative English text written out below the two already existing texts in Italian and Latin (18th-century hand?); f. 45: an 18th-century hand(?) has added the title 'Lamento di Olimpia nell'Orlando Furioso'; ff. 53^v-54: same hand has added 'Nello Pastor Fido de Guarini'; f. 98 index: unidentified 18th-century hand has added references to the single Reggio item; ff. 156^v-57: Reggio's 'As water fluid is' copied in a different hand from the rest of the volume.

Inscription on f. 1^v: '[I]n Nomine D[omi]ni' (Notari). Pencil remarks (18th century?): 100^v: 'Eccellent' (sic); 142^v: 'Excellent. Luca Marenzio or in his style'; f. 149^v: 'admirable'; f.153^v: 'Great science and contrivances'; f. 157^v: 'True Madrigal Style'; and 172^v: 'Ingenious and learned'. ff. 63, 85 and 113: additional slips pasted-in for final bars.

Binding: modern.

Contents of *Lbl* Add. MS 31,440:

Folio	Composer	Title	Scoring	Printed Concordancs
1		[Fragments of music]		
1^v-2		Lasciatemi qui solo, Tornato Augelli al nido	Cbc	
2^v-3		La gran Balena [Pt 1] Bella Marina [Pt 2]	Cbc	
2^v-3		Faretrato arcier	Cbc	
3^v-4		Non vò più seguire	Cbc	

---

[a] I am grateful to Mr Robert Spencer for advice concerning the watermarks.

4v-5		Se mille tormenti	Cbc	
4v-5		Non andarà cosi	Cbc	
5v-6		Che soffri ò mio core	Cbc	
5v-6		Tempo già fu, ch'io vissi amante	Cbc	
6v-7		O schiere d'amanti	Cbc	
6v-7		Voi vedet'il mio mal	Cbc	
7v-8	[F. Caccini]	Ecco ch'io verso il sangue	Cbc	C2
7v-8		Aure placid'e volanti	Cbc	
8v-9		Ascoltate i miei crucci 'Sonetto' [Pt 1] O Tartaree spelonche [Pt 2] Udite e da l'accese arene [Pt 3] Direte poi, che non hà fiamme Averno [Pt 4]		
9v-10		Più non sento del tuo dardo	Cbc	
9v-10		Doppò un lungo servire 'Villanella recitativa'	Cbc	
10v-11		Non vi dolete amanti	Cbc	
11v		Mi convien di partir[b]	Cbc	
11v		Non sei più bella[bc]	Cbc	
12		Begins imperfectly: 'gioite del mio pianto'; 2nd verse: 'So ben, che col mio piangere'; 3rd verse: 'Qual atra nube'[b]	Cbc	
12		Begins imperfectly: 'sperar da lui mercè'; 3rd verse: 'Nacque la nott'el dì'[bd]	Cbc	
12v-13		Cor mio se questa fera	Cbc	
12v-13		Perche mio tesoro	Cbc	
12v-13		In bel seno[e]	Cbc	
13v-14		Qu[a]esivi quem diligit anima mea	Cbc	
13v-14	[Rontani]	Fuggi crudele Dove mi lasci tu?	Cbc	R2470
14v-17		Ardo misero, e sento [Pt 1] E tu fatta ver me cruda [Pt 2] Ma dim[m]i anima cara [Pt 3] Soavissimi lumi [Pt 4] Emula chioma [Pt 5]	Cbc	

[b] Incomplete.
[c] Also includes Latin text 'O quam tu pulchra es', and a later hand has added the first line of an English text 'You are no more charming'.
[d] A later hand has added the text 'From it so hope'.
[e] Another copy appears on ff. 17v-18.

17	[S. Landi]	Chiudete l'orecchi[f]	Cbc	L532
17v-18	[Rontani]	Augelletti canori	Cbc	R2471
17v-18		In bel seno	Cbc	
18v-19		Io vò penar, Io vò morir	Cbc	
18v19		Fiumi, e fonti, Boschi, e Monti	Cbc	
19v-20		Seguir piu non voglio	Cbc	
19v-20		Non voglio amare	Cbc	
20v-1		Udite Amanti	Cbc	
20v-1		Alle gioie ò pastori	Cbc	
			with *sinfonia* in tablature	
21v-3		[10 *modi* on a repeated bass]	[vln] bc	
23v-6		[12 *modi* on a different bass]	[vln] bc	
25v-8		[10 *modi* on a different bass]	[vln] bc	
28v-9		Fuggite gli ingan[n]i d'Amore	Cbc	1669[5]
28v-9		Senti Tirsi crudel	Cbc	
29v-30		Cruda signora 'Ciaconna'[g] [Pt 1]	Cbc	
		Sol per tuo amore [Pt 2]		
		Di me ti ridi [Pt 3]		
		Ben son mi accorto [Pt 4]		
		Hor fa, che vuoi [Pt 5]		
30v-1		Questa crudel [Pt 1]	Cbc	
		Deh mira Amor [Pt 2]		
		Rompi lo smalto [Pt 3]		
		Ma date (lasso) [sic] in darnoa [Pt 4]		
31v-2		Bella Filli crudele	Cbc	
31v-2		Fillide mia se di beltà	Cbc	
32v-3	[G. Caccini]	Occhi soli d'Amore[h]	Cbc	M756 (for 4vv)
33v-4		Crud'Amarilli	Cbc	
34v-7		'La medesima canzone passaggiata'[i]	vln bc	
36v-7		Intenerite voi lagrime	Cbc	1669[5]
37v-8		Soccorso oimè ben mio	Cbc	
38v-9		Sciogli ardito [Pt 1]	Cbc	
		Ecco d'onda spumosa [Pt 2]		
39v-40		O dolce anima mia	Cbc	
40v-1		Fill'il bel volto tuo	Cbc	

---

[f] Variant of piece in S. Landi, *Il Secondo Libro d'Arie Musicali* (Rome, 1627).
[g] The five sections are called 'modi'.
[h] Free reworking of Caccini's piece.
[i] Two versions: plain and elaborated.

Folio	Composer	Title	Scoring	Ref
41v-2		Bel Rusignuol che si soavi fai Suonare 'Sonetto'	Cbc	
42v-3		Ò del silençio figlio 'Sonetto' [Pt 1] Hor, ch'in grembo [Pt 2] E vien col dolce tuo tranquill'oblio [Pt 3] Che se'n te la sembianza [Pt 4]	Cbc	
43v-4	[G. Caccini]	Parlo miser'ò taccio? [j]	Cbc	M756 (for 4vv)
44v-5	[Rasi]	Ò che felice giorno	Cbc	R290
44v-7		Voglio morir[k]	Cbc	
47v		Non più strali pungenti	Cbc	
50v-3		D'Amor altri si lagni [Pt 1] Nel bel Regno [Pt 2] Il dimandar pietà [Pt 3]	Cbc & [2vln][l]	
53v-9	[Monteverdi]	Ecco Silvio [Pt 1] Ma se con la pietà [Pt 2] Dorinda ah dirò [Pt 3] Ecco piegando [Pt 4] Ferir quel petto Silvio? [Pt 5]	CCbc[m]	M3475
59v-60		[Instrumental]	[2vln] bc	
60v-3	[Monteverdi]	Ch'io t'ami [Pt 1] Deh bella, e cara [Pt 2] Ma tu più, che mai dura [Pt 3]	CCbc[mn]	M3475
63v-5	[Barbarino]	Ferma Caronte. Chi è colui, che grida?[o]	CBbc	B870
65v-7		Che fai alma? Languisco 'Dialogo. Core, et Alma'	CBbc	
67v-9	[Merula]	Domine inclina c[a]elos tuos	ABbc	M2339
69v-70		À la caccia Pastori	Cbc with tablature accomp. and *sinfonia*	
70v-2	[Merula]	Hodie nobis de c[a]elo	CCbc	M2339
71v-3	[Merula]	Quasi cedrus exaltata sum	ATbc	M2339
73v-5	[Merula]	Fontes et omnia	BBbc	M2338

---

[j] Free reworking of Caccini's piece.
[k] 'Voglio morir' - the *Lamento d'Olimpia* - is 'incautiously ascribed to Monteverdi in a contemporary hand' in *Lbl* Add 30,491; it is 'so flagrantly derived (in music as in words!) from *Arianna* as to render quite unlikely any attribution to Monteverdi'; Bianconi (1987), 210-13. The *Lamento d'Olimpia* is published as by Monteverdi in W. Osthoff ed., *Composizioni vocali profane e sacre (inedite)* (Milan, 1958), 10.
[l] Two-part *sinfonia* repeated after each section.
[m] An arrangement of the five-part madrigal for two voices and basso continuo.
[n] The original five-part madrigal appears on ff. 191v-4.
[o] Ornamented version of the piece in B. Barbarino, *Il Secondo Libro de Madrigali* (Venice, 1607).

75ᵛ-6	[Possenti]	O stelle omicide	CCbc	P5247
76ᵛ-8	[Monteverdi]	Ò come sei gentile	CCbc	M3494
78ᵛ-80	[Monteverdi]	Io son pur vezzosetta Pastorella	CCbc	M3494
80ᵛ-1	[Giramo]	Tra doglie, e dispetto	ATBbc	G2503
81ᵛ-3	[Monteverdi]	Ò viva fiam[m]a	CCbc	M3494
83ᵛ-5	[Monteverdi]	Vorrei baciartiᵖ	AAbc	M3494
85ᵛ-7	[Monteverdi]	Dice la mia bellissima licori	TTbc	M3494
87ᵛ-9	[Monteverdi]	Non vedrò mai le stelle	TTbc	M3494
89ᵛ-9	[Monteverdi]	Soave libertate	TTbc	M3494
90ᵛ-2	[Monteverdi]	Ah che non si conviene	TTbc	M3494
92ᵛ-4	[Monteverdi]	Ecco vicine ò bella Tigre	TTbc	M3494
94ᵛ-5	[Monteverdi]	Interrote speranze	TTbc	M3494
95ᵛ-7	[Monteverdi]	Perche fuggi	TTbc	M3494
100ᵛ-3	[Merula]	Sempre terrò memoria Del di sesto d'Aprile	CTBbc	M2348
102ᵛ-5	[Antonelli]ᑫ	Dulcis Jesu pie Deus	CCBbc	
104ᵛ-7		Tollite iugu[m]	CCCbc	
106ᵛ-9		Surgamus eamus, et descendamus	CCTbc	
109ᵛ-11	[Antonelli]ᑫ	Ave Jesu quem vocavi	TTBbc	
111ᵛ-13		Jesu Rex admirabilis et triumphator	CCAbc	
113ᵛ-18		Il crudo amore assale attera 'Battaglia amorosa à 3. Voci'	CCBbc	
117ᵛ-19		Canite tuba in Sion	CCAbc	
119ᵛ-20		Ò Domine Jesu Christe	CCBbc	
120ᵛ-2		Deus canticum novum cantebo tibi	CCMbc	
122ᵛ-4	[Merula]	Sat est Domine	CTBbc	M2338
124ᵛ-6	[Merula]	Ò quam dulcis es tu	TTBbc	M2338
126ᵛ-8	[Grandi]	E cosi pur languendo	CTBbc	G3469
128ᵛ-30		Ò panis mellifluus	CCCbc	
130ᵛ-40ᵛ		Splendea q[ua]l vivo sole 'Dialogo à cinque Voci'	CCATBbc	
140ᵛ-2	[Rore arr.]	Ancor, che col partireʳ	B vln bc	R2500-1
142ᵛ-4		Io rido amanti	CCBbc	
144ᵛ-6	[Monteverdi]	Taci Armelin	ATBbc	1624[11]; M3501

ᵖ The last few bars of this madrigal are copied onto a slip of paper attached to f. 85; the verso of the slip contains, in Notari's hand, a fragment of Monteverdi's 'Ohimè se tanto amate' - from *Il Quarto Libro de Madrigali* (Venice, 1603) - beginning imperfectly: '...-so, e doloros'oimè sentire'.

ᑫ Attributed in *Ob* Mus.Sch. C 204; no printed source identified.

ʳ Divisions on Rore's 4vv madrigal from *Il Primo Libro de Madrigali a Quatro Voci* (Ferrara, 1550; Venice, 1551).

145v-7		Da le piume amorosetta	CCBbc	
149v-51		Son si avvezzo alle pene	CCATB	
150v-2	[Mazzocchi]	Nigra sum sed formosa	CCBBbc	1643¹, 1652¹
152v-4		Anima mea Angelorum pane saturata est	CCATbc	
153v-5	[Merula]	Cum complerentur dies	CATBbc	M2338
155v-7	[Merula]	Jesu dulcissime	CATBbc	M2338
156v-7	Reggio	As water fluid is[s]	CB[bc]	
157v-9		Ò don[n]a un solo amante	CCATB	
159v-61		Io ti disfido ài baci	CMATB	
161v-2		Ò pretiosum [*leading to:*] Surgite esurientes	CCbc CCATB[bc]	
162v-5		Sancta, et venerabilis	CC [2vln] bc	
165v-8		Venio ad te O bone Jesu	CCT [vln] bc	
168v-72		Apollinaris incliti	CC [2vln] bc with *sinfonia*	
172v-4		Crudelissima Dori se tal'hor mesta piangi	CATBbc	
174v-6		Ò sguardo incauto ladro	CATBbc	
175v-7		Cara, e soave bocca	CTBbc	
177v-9		Vedo la don[n]a mia	CABbc	
179v-81		Hoc tegitur sacro	CCTbc	
181		Non nobis Domine	*a* 120	
		'Canon a 120 parti in unisono, et ogni parte resta unaminima l'una doppo l'altera'		
181v-2	[Monteverdi]	Voi pur da me partite[t]	CCATB	M3467
182v-3	[Monteverdi]	Cor mio mentre vi mi[ro][t]	CMATB	M3467, 1606⁵
182v-3v	[Monteverdi]	Cor mio no[n] mori[t]	CMTTB	M3467
183v-4v	[Monteverdi]	Luci seren'e chiare[t]	CCATB	M3467
184v-6	[Monteverdi]	O[h]imè se tanto amate[u]	CCATB	M3467
185v-7	[Monteverdi]	Si ch'io [vorrei morire][u]	CMATB	M3467
186v-7	[Monteverdi]	Era [l'anima mia][u]	CCATB	M3475
187v-8	[Monteverdi]	Ahi [com'a un vago sol][u]	CCTTB(bc)	M3475
188v-90	[Monteverdi]	Troppo [ben può][v]	CMATB(bc)	M3475

---

[s] Later addition to the manuscript.
[t] First line only of Cantus [I] part is underlaid.
[u] Occasional text incipits only.
[v] Cantus part is underlaid sporadically.

189ᵛ-90ᵛ	[Monteverdi]	T'amo mia vitaʷ	CCATBbc	M3475
190ᵛ-2	[Monteverdi]	Ah dolente partitaʷˣ	CCMAB	M3467, 1605[7]
191ᵛ-4	[Monteverdi]	Ch'io t'ami [Pt 1]ʷ Dhe [*recte* Deh bella] [Pt 2]ʷ Ma tu [piu che mai dura] [Pt 3]ʷ	CCATBʸ	M3475
193ᵛ-5	[Monteverdi]	Ah dolente partitaʷ	CCMAB	M3467, 1605[7]
194ᵛ-5ᵛ	[Monteverdi]	Crud'Amarilliʷᶻ	CCAAB(bc)	M3475, 1606[5]

MANUSCRIPT VIII

LONDON, BRITISH LIBRARY ADD. MS 31,460

A scorebook of solo-voice music by English and Italian composers.

Copied *c*.1670-90.
ff. iv + 94 + i.
Original pagination: pp. 1-145, 150-92 (146-9 omitted in error). Modern pencil foliation: ff. 1-98 (the opening flyleaves are numbered).
Paper: 220 x 285 mm. Red marginal rulings on left and right. Eight rastrum-ruled staves per page (ruled with a four-stave rastrum of 80 mm span and individual staves measuring 11/11.5/11.5/11 mm). No music entered on ff. 78ᵛ and 82. Flyleaves: f. 1: various inscriptions (see below); ff. 1ᵛ-2: biography of Simon Child; ff. 2ᵛ-3: blank; ff. 3ᵛ-4ᵛ: alphabetical index.
Collation: not possible due to tightness of binding.
Watermark: fleur-de-lys with countermark VI.
Script: ff. 5-71: Henry Bowman; ff. 71ᵛ-81ᵛ, 83ᵛ-84: unidentified scribe A; ff. 82ᵛ-83: unidentified scribe B; ff. 84ᵛ-85: unidentified scribe C; ff. 85ᵛ-86ᵛ: unidentified scribe D; ff. 87-89ᵛ: unidentified scribe E; ff. 90-98ᵛ: unidentified scribe F. (A later eighteenth/nineteenth-century hand has added figures in red ink to the basso continuo of many pieces.)
Inscriptions on f. 1: 'Mottetts, Anthems by Blow, Lock, Purcell / Gratiani, Orland[o] Gibbons, Henry Aldrich / &c / (Valuable)'; 'Mr Child his Book' (autograph, three times); 'Mr Simon Child was Organist / of

---

ʷ Occasional text incipits only.
ˣ Another copy appears on ff. 193ᵛ-5.
ʸ A three-part arrangement of the madrigaal appears on ff. 60ᵛ-63.
ᶻ Incomplete.

Christ Church College Oxon / Before Mr Richard Goodson, who / was succeeded by Mr Richard Church / who was succeeded by Mr Thomas Norris / who was succeeded by Mr Crotch, / about 1792 / who was when a Child prodigy in / Music, [sic] An Account of Him was sent / to the Royal Society by Dr Burney / Author of the History of Music, [illegible sentence ending:] ... succeeds me as Proffessor [sic] Ph. Hayes [crossed through]' (Philip Hayes); 'This book / was in the possession of / Dr William Hayes. / Dr Philip Hayes. / Purchased with many / more books of the Ex of the late / D^r. P.H. at Oxford. Rd'. ff. 1^v-2: biography of 'William Child Mus. Doc. Oxon. MDCLXIII'.[a]

Binding: modern.

Contents of *Lbl* Add. MS 31,460:[b]

Composer	Title	Scoring	Folio	Page	Printed Concordances
[Carissimi]	Lucifer, cælestis olim	Bbc	5	1	1693[1]
[Casati]	Sic ergo, bone Jesu	Cbc	8	7	C1424
[Casati]	Benedicam Dominum	Cbc	11^v	14	C1411
[Sances]	Lætamini in Domino	Cbc	14^v	20	S768
[Sances]	Ardet Cor meum	Cbc	18	27	S768
[Sances]	Conditor Cæli	Tbc	21^v	34	S768
[Sances]	Audite me divini fructus	Bbc	24^v	40	S768
[Sances]	Dulcis amor Jesu	Bbc	28	47	S768
[Sances]	Solvatur lingua mea	Tbc	30	51	S768
[Sances]	O quam speciosa	Abc	32	55	S768
[Sances]	Quemadmodum desiderat	Abc[c]	34^v	60	S768
	Anima mea suspira	Sbc	36^v	64	
Bonifacio Gratiani	O dulcis Jesu	Cbc	40^v	72	G3674
Bonifacio Gratiani	Per asperos mundi errores	Sbc	44	79	G3674
Desgranges	Usquequo Domine	Sbc	47^v	86	
[Graziani]	Velut palma velut Rosa	Sbc	49^v	90	1693[1]
Mr: Blow	Turn thee unto me O Lord	Sbc[d]	54^v	100	
Mr: Orlando Gibbons	Behold thou hast made my dayes	Abc[de]	56^v	104	1641[5]
Mr: Henry Aldrich	I waited patiently for ye Lord	Cbc	58^v	108	
Mr: Henry Aldrich	O God thou art my God	Tbc[e]	62^v	116	
M^r: Michael Wise	I charge you O Daughters of Jerusalem	Sbc[f]	67	125	1674[2]
M^r: William Lawes	Let God arise	Bbc	68	127	
Mr: Blow	Peaceful is he & most secure	Sbc	70	131	1688[1]

[a] See Watkin Shaw (1990), 390. Perhaps *Lbl* Add. 31,460 was one of the books which Philip Hayes 'purchased of Mr Simon Child's widdow, at Oxford'? (note on f. 2 of *Lbl* Add. 33,235; see MS XI below).
[b] The first eleven pieces appear in exactly the same sequence in another scorebook copied by Bowman: *Lbl* Egerton 2960; see MS XV below.
[c] Most of the basso continuo part is lacking.
[d] Lacking the chorus parts found in most other sources.
[e] The organ part is occasionally written out in full.
[f] Chorus parts in short score (SB).

[Purcell]	Awake and with attention hear '34 chap. of Isajah. by Mr. Cowley.'[g]	Bbc	71[v]	134	1688[1]
H. P[urcell]	How long great God[h] 'The Aspiration'	Sbc	77	145	1688[1]
H. P[urcell]	Let the night perish 'Jobes curse'	Sbc[i]	79	153	1688[1]
[Blow]	Arise my darkn'd melancholy Soul	Tbc[j]	80[v]	156	
....
[Cooke][k]	Sleep downy Sleep[l]	Sbc	82[v]	160	
....
[Cooke]	Awake my soul	Sbc	83[v]	162	
....
[Cooke]	Sleep downy Sleep	Sbc	84[v]	164	
D[r] John Blow	Arise my darkn'd melancholy Soul	Sbc	85[v]	166	
....
[Ramsey]	In guilty night[m]	STbc	87	169	
....
D[r] John Blow	Hear God's Almighty Voice	Bbc	90	175	
M[r] Matthew Locke	Then from a Whirlwind Oracle	Bbc	91	177	1688[1]
[J. Jackson][n]	There's no disturbance 'The Words made by a lady' '1 or 2 voices'	S[B]bc	93	181	1688[1]
M[r] Henry Purcell	Now that the Sun 'An Evening Hymn: words by D[r] William Fuller, late Lord-Bishop of Lincoln.'	Sbc	93[v]	182	1688[1]
M[r]. Henry Purcell	Thou wakeful Shepherd 'A Morning Hymn: Words by D[r]. William Fuller. late Lord Bishop of Lincoln.'	Sbc	95[v]	186	1688[1]
M[r] Matthew Lock	Come, honest Sexton 'The Passing-Bell'	Sbc	96[v]	188	1688[1]
M[r] Henry Purcell	In the black dismal Dungeon of Dispair [sic] 'Words by D[r]. William Fuller, late Lord Bishop of Lincoln'.	Sbc	97[v]	190	1688[1]

---

[g] A. Cowley, *Poems ... III. Pindarique Odes* (London, 1656), 48.
[h] Text by John Norris, *Collection of Miscellanies* (London, 1687).
[i] Chorus parts in short score (SB).
[j] Another version for Sbc (an octave higher) was copied on ff. 85[v]-86[v]; see below.
[k] Later pencil misattribution to Locke.
[l] Another version a tone lower was copied on ff. 84[v]-85.
[m] See B. Smallman, 'Endor Revisited: English Biblical Dialogues of the Seventeenth Century, *ML*, xlvi (1965), 142-3; and M. Chan, 'The Witch of Endor and Seventeenth-Century Propaganda', *MD*, xxxiv (1980), 205-14.
[n] Either John Jackson (d.1688) or Jeffrey Jackson (fl.1662-79).

MANUSCRIPT IX

LONDON, BRITISH LIBRARY ADD. MS 31,479 AND MADRIGAL SOCIETY MSS G 55-9

Two sets of partbooks containing Latin motets for one to five voices and basso continuo by Italian composers, copied by George Jeffreys. The two sets complement each other and are so similar in format that they must originally have formed a single collection.

a) British Library Add. MS 31,479

Copied in the mid to late 1650s (from earlier manuscripts?) and include a few additions made in the 1670s.
Four partbooks:

Cantus: ff. 69. Modern pencil foliation: ff. 1-58. Unnumbered folios: four between ff. 4 and 5, six between ff. 33 and 34, and one final unnumbered folio. No music entered on ff. 4^v, 5, 33^v, 53^v, 56^v, 57, nor on any of the unnumbered folios.

Alto: ff. 56. Modern pencil foliation: ff. 1-52. Unnumbered folios: one between ff. 20 and 21, and three between ff. 28 and 29. No music entered on ff. 20^v, 21, 28^v, nor on any of the unnumbered folios.

Bassus: ff. 57. Modern pencil foliation: ff. 1-46. Unnumbered folios: three between ff. 8 and 9, seven between ff. 24 and 25, and one final unnumbered folio. No music entered on ff. 8^v, 24^v, nor on any of the unnumbered folios.

Basso Continuo: ff. i + 48. Modern pencil foliation: ff. 1-44 (the flyleaf is numbered). Unnumbered folios: two between ff. 20 and 21, two between ff. 31 and 32. and one final unnumbered folio. No music entered on f. 31^v, nor on any of the unnumbered folios.

The pieces are numbered in the partbooks as follows: one voice and basso continuo: 1-13; two voices and basso continuo: 1-62 (no number 49); and three voices and basso continuo: 1-35 and one unnumbered piece.

Paper: 305 x 200 mm. Ten staves per page (ruled with a five-stave rastrum of 108.5 mm span and individual staves each measuring 12 mm).

Collations: not possible due to tightness of the bindings, but the gatherings appear to be large (only one per partbook?).

Watermark: Cardinals' hat with letters GR; Thompson (1988), Watermark XXII.

Scribe: George Jeffreys. (A later hand has added the attributions, in pencil, to *Cantus*: ff. 39ᵛ, 52ᵛ, 54 and 54ᵛ; and *Basso continuo*: ff. 42 and 43.)

Inscription: *Basso continuo* f. 1: 'N.B. The paper made in Italy. T[he] mark being a Cardinals Hat. The Musick not copyd by an Italian' (18th-century hand?).

Bindings: modern.

Contents of *Lbl* Add. MS 31,479:

No.	Composer	Title	Scoring	Folios C	A	B	bc	Concordances
1	[Sances]	Dulcis amor Jesu	Bbc	-	-	1	2	S768
2		Jubilate Deo	Bbc	-	-	1ᵛ	2ᵛ	
3	[Grandi]	Salvum me fac Deus	Bbc	-	-	2ᵛ	3	G3450
4	[Sances]	Audite me divini fructus	Bbc	-	-	3ᵛ	3ᵛ	S768
5		Exultate Deo	Bbc	-	-	4ᵛ	4	
6		Anima mea desiderat te	Bbc	-	-	5ᵛ	4ᵛ	
7		Gaudeamus omnes in Domino	Cbc	1	-	-	.5	
8		Cantate Domino	Cbc	1ᵛ	-	-	5ᵛ	
9		Salvator mundi	Cbc	2ᵛ	-	-	6	
10		O Maria quam pulchra es	Cbc	3	-	-	6	
11		Ave maris stel[l]a	Cbc	3ᵛ	-	-	6ᵛ	
12	[Merula]	Dominus illuminatio mea	B 2vln bc	-	-	6ᵛ	7ᵃ	M2339
13	Carissimo	Lucifer cælestis olim	Bbc	-	-	7	8ᵛᵇ	1693¹
1	[Grandi]	Hodie nobis de cælo	CCbc	5ᵛ	1	-	10	G3417
2	[Grandi]	Jesu noster Dignissimus	CCbc	6	1ᵛ	-	10ᵛ	G3431
			as 'Haec est arbor dignissimus'					
3	[Grandi]	Venite filii	CCbc	6ᵛ	2	-	11	G3422
4	[Facchi]	Bonum est confiteri Domino	CCbc	7	2ᵛ	-	11	F44
5	[Facchi]	Quid timidi estis?	CCbc	7ᵛ	3	-	11ᵛ	F44
6	[Grandi]	O dulce numen numinum	CCbc	8ᵛ	4	-	12	G3455
			as 'O dulcis virgo'					
7	[Grandi]	Salvum me fac Domine	CCbc	9	4ᵛ	-	12ᵛ	G3431
8	[Grandi]	O quam gloriosus	CCbc	9ᵛ	5	-	12ᵛ	G3455
			as 'O quam gloriosa'					
9	[Grandi]	O quam suave est nomen	CCbc	10	5ᵛ	-	13	G3422
10	[Merula]	Hodie nobis de cælo	CCbc	10ᵛ	6	-	13ᵛ	M2339
11	[Merula]	O magnum misterium	CCbc	11	6ᵛ	-	13ᵛ	M2339
12	[Merula]	O nomen Jesu	CCbc	11ᵛ	7	-	14	M2339
13	[Facchi]	Jesu dulcis memoria	CCbc	12	7ᵛ	-	14	F44
14	[Tomasi]	Fulcite me floribus	CCbc	12ᵛ	8	-	14ᵛ	T922
15	[Facchi]	Omni die dic Mariæ	CCbc	13	8ᵛ	-	14ᵛ	F44
16		Qui laudes tuas cantat	CCbc	13ᵛ	9	-	15	
17	[Trabattone]	O beatum virum	CCbc	14	9ᵛ	-	15ᵛ	T1070
18	[Trabattone]	O admirabile com[m]ercium	CCbc	14ᵛ	10	-	15ᵛ	T1070
19	[Trabattone]	Indica mihi quem diligit	CCbc	15	10ᵛ	-	16	T1070

ᵃ Score with full text.
ᵇ Score with text incipits.

b) **Madrigal Society MSS G 55-9** (housed in the British Library)

Copied in the late 1650s (possibly from earlier manuscripts).

Five partbooks from a set of six:

G 55 *Cantus*: ff. i + 54 + i. Modern pencil foliation: ff. 1-43, followed by eleven unnumbered folios. No music entered on ff. 5^v-6^v, 26^v-39, 43^{r-v}, nor on the eleven unnumbered folios. (f. 7 contains only the title 'Dulcissime Jesu A 4', a C clef (c1), and B flat signature; the piece is written out in full on f. 7^v.) Collation: one gathering of fifty-six. Pieces 1-9 only are numbered by the scribe. f. 41 includes extra hand-drawn stave for the final bars of the piece.

G 56 *Altus*: ff. i + 54 + i. No foliation or pagination. Pieces not numbered. No music entered on the four pages between pieces [9] and [10], on the twenty-eight pages between pieces [42] and [43], nor on the final twenty-two pages. Collation: one gathering of fifty-six.

G 57 *Tenore*: ff. i + 54 + i. No foliation or pagination. Pieces not numbered. No music entered on the four pages between pieces [9] and [10], on the thirty pages between pieces [42] and [43], nor on the final twenty-two pages. Collation: one gathering of fifty-six.

G 58 *Bassus*: ff. i + 52 + i. No foliation or pagination. Pieces not numbered. No music entered on the four pages between pieces [9] and [10], on the twenty-six pages between pieces [42] and [43], nor on the final twenty-three pages. Collation: one gathering of fifty-four.

G 59 *Basso Continuo*: ff. i + 48 + i. No foliation or pagination. Pieces not numbered. No music entered on the two pages between pieces [9] and [10], on the twenty-seven pages between pieces [42] and [43], nor on the final twenty-five pages. Collation: one gathering of fifty.

Paper: 305 x 200 mm. Ten staves per page (ruled with a five-stave rastrum of 108.5 mm span and individual staves each measuring 12 mm).

Watermark: same mark and paper as *Lbl* Add. MS 31,479.

Scribe: George Jeffreys.

No bindings.

Contents of Mad. Soc. MSS G 55-9:

No.	Composer	Title	Scoring	Folio in G 55	Printed Source
1	[Grandi]	Benedictus Dominus	ATTBbc	1	G3417
2	[Grandi]	Hic est vere Martyr	ATTBbc	1^v	G3417
3	[Grandi]	Cantabo Domino	ATTBbc	2	G3417
4	[Grandi]	Heu mihi	ATTBbc	2^v	G3422
5	[Grandi]	Caro mea vere est cibus	CATBbc	3	G3417
6	[Grandi]	Magnum hereditatis	TTBBbc	3^v	G3422

Scribe: George Jeffreys. (A later hand has added the attributions, in pencil, to *Cantus*: ff. 39^v, 52^v, 54 and 54^v; and *Basso continuo*: ff. 42 and 43.)

Inscription: *Basso continuo* f. 1: 'N.B. The paper made in Italy. T[he] mark being a Cardinals Hat. The Musick not copyd by an Italian' (18th-century hand?).

Bindings: modern.

Contents of *Lbl* Add. MS 31,479:

No.	Composer	Title	Scoring	C	A	B	bc	Concordances
1	[Sances]	Dulcis amor Jesu	Bbc	-	-	1	2	S768
2		Jubilate Deo	Bbc	-	-	1^v	2^v	
3	[Grandi]	Salvum me fac Deus	Bbc	-	-	2^v	3	G3450
4	[Sances]	Audite me divini fructus	Bbc	-	-	3^v	3^v	S768
5		Exultate Deo	Bbc	-	-	4^v	4	
6		Anima mea desiderat te	Bbc	-	-	5^v	4^v	
7		Gaudeamus omnes in Domino	Cbc	1	-	-	.5	
8		Cantate Domino	Cbc	1^v	-	-	5^v	
9		Salvator mundi	Cbc	2^v	-	-	6	
10		O Maria quam pulchra es	Cbc	3	-	-	6	
11		Ave maris stel[l]a	Cbc	3^v	-	-	6^v	
12	[Merula]	Dominus illuminatio mea	B 2vln bc	-	-	6^v	7^a	M2339
13	Carissimo	Lucifer cælestis olim	Bbc	-	-	7	8vb	1693^1
1	[Grandi]	Hodie nobis de cælo	CCbc	5^v	1	-	10	G3417
2	[Grandi]	Jesu noster Dignissimus	CCbc	6	1^v	-	10^v	G3431
		as 'Haec est arbor dignissimus'						
3	[Grandi]	Venite filii	CCbc	6^v	2	-	11	G3422
4	[Facchi]	Bonum est confiteri Domino	CCbc	7	2^v	-	11	F44
5	[Facchi]	Quid timidi estis?	CCbc	7^v	3	-	11^v	F44
6	[Grandi]	O dulce numen numinum	CCbc	8^v	4	-	12	G3455
		as 'O dulcis virgo'						
7	[Grandi]	Salvum me fac Domine	CCbc	9	4^v	-	12^v	G3431
8	[Grandi]	O quam gloriosus	CCbc	9^v	5	-	12^v	G3455
		as 'O quam gloriosa'						
9	[Grandi]	O quam suave est nomen	CCbc	10	5^v	-	13	G3422
10	[Merula]	Hodie nobis de cælo	CCbc	10^v	6	-	13^v	M2339
11	[Merula]	O magnum misterium	CCbc	11	6^v	-	13^v	M2339
12	[Merula]	O nomen Jesu	CCbc	11^v	7	-	14	M2339
13	[Facchi]	Jesu dulcis memoria	CCbc	12	7^v	-	14	F44
14	[Tomasi]	Fulcite me floribus	CCbc	12^v	8	-	14^v	T922
15	[Facchi]	Omni die dic Mariæ	CCbc	13	8^v	-	14^v	F44
16		Qui laudes tuas cantat	CCbc	13^v	9	-	15	
17	[Trabattone]	O beatum virum	CCbc	14	9^v	-	15^v	T1070
18	[Trabattone]	O admirabile com[m]ercium	CCbc	14^v	10	-	15^v	T1070
19	[Trabattone]	Indica mihi quem diligit	CCbc	15	10^v	-	16	T1070

^{a} Score with full text.
^{b} Score with text incipits.

20	[Grandi]	Ave sanctissime Messia	CCbc	15ᵛ	11	-	16	G3455
		as 'Ave sanctissima Maria'						
21	[Trabattone]	Ecce fideles	TTbc	16ᵛ	12	-	16ᵛ	T1070
22	[Sances]	Salvum me fac	TTbc	17	12ᵛ	-	16ᵛ	S768
23	[Sances]	Jubilent in c[a]elis	TTbc	17ᵛ	13	-	17	S768
24	[Trabattone]	Egredimini charissimi	TTbc	18ᵛ	14	-	17ᵛ	T1070
25	[Grandi]	O Im[m]aculate	CAbc	19	14ᵛ	-	17ᵛ	G3422
		as 'O intemerata'						
26		Amore langueo	CAbc	19ᵛ	15	-	18	
27	[Trabattone]	Veni O Sanctissima	CAbc	20	15ᵛ	-	18	T1070
28	[Grandi]	Tu dulcis es Messia	CTbc	20ᵛ	16	-	18ᵛ	G3439
		as 'Tu pulchra es Maria'						
29	[Trabattone]	Luce serena lucent	CTbc	21	16ᵛ	-	18ᵛ	T1070
30	[Merula]	Misericordias Domini	CAbc	21ᵛ	17	-	19	M2338
31	[Tomasi]	Ave Maria gratia plena	CAbc	22	17ᵛ	-	19ᵛ	T922
32	[Facchi]	Quem terra pontus	ATbc	23	18ᵛ	-	20	F44
33	[Sances]	Tota pulchra es	ATbc	23ᵛ	19	-	20	S768
34	[Trabattone]	Gaudete omnes	ATbc	24ᵛ	19ᵛ	-	20ᵛ	T1070
35	[Merula]	Domine inclyna cælos	ABbc	-	21ᵛ	9	21	M2339
36	[Trabattone]	Domine Dominus noster	CBbc	-	22	9ᵛ	21	T1070
37	[Tomasi]	Trahe me post te	CBbc	-	22ᵛ	10	21ᵛ	T922
38	[Grandi]	Exulta et lætare	CBbc	-	23	10ᵛ	21ᵛ	G3431
39	[D. Pecci]	Sub tuum pr[a]esidium	CBbc	-	23ᵛ	11	22	P1100
40		Anima Christi	CBbc	-	24	11ᵛ	22	
41	[Trabattone]	Deus meus ad te	ABbc	-	24ᵛ	12	22ᵛ	T1070
42	[Tomasi]	Tota pulchra es	CBbc	-	25	12ᵛ	22ᵛ	T922
43	[Sances]	Deus in adiutorium	CBbc	-	25ᵛ	13	23ᵛ	S768
44		O dulcis Jesu	CBbc	-	26ᵛ	14	24	
45	[Aloisi]	Salve Regina	CBbc	-	27	14ᵛ	24ᵛ	A877
46	[Aloisi]	Inclyna Domine aurem	TBbc	-	28	15	24ᵛ	A876
47	[F.M.Marini]	Sicut lilium inter spinas	CBbc	25	-	16	25	M672
48	[Pio]	Peccavi super numerum	CBbc	25ᵛ	-	16ᵛ	25ᵛ	P2411
50ᶜ	[Pio]	Et introeuntes	CBbc	26	-	17	25ᵛ	P2411
51		Consolare O Mater 'Dialogue'	CBbc	26ᵛ	-	17ᵛ	26	
52		O Jesu vita mea	CBbc	27	-	18	26ᵛ	
53	[Grandi]	Quemadmodum desiderat 'Dialogue'	CBbc	27ᵛ	-	18ᵛ	26ᵛ	G3455
54	[Trabattone]	Confitemini Domino	CBbc	28	-	19ᵛ	27ᵛ	T1070
55	[Merula]	Dominus in igne veniet	CBbc	28ᵛ	-	20	28	M2338
56	[Merula]	Salvum me fac Deus	CBbc	29ᵛ	-	20ᵛ	28ᵛ	M2339
57	[Trabattone]	O pulcher[r]ima 'Dialogue'	CBbc	30	-	21ᵛ	29	T1070
58	[Trabattone]	Sancti tui Domine	CBbc	30	-	22	29ᵛ	T1070
59	[Trabattone]	In convertendo Dominus	CBbc	31	-	22ᵛ	29ᵛ	T1070
60	[Trabattone]	Anima mea in æterna dulcedine	CBbc	31ᵛ	-	23	30	T1070
61	[Merula]	O bone Jesu	CBbc	32ᵛ	-	23ᵛ	30ᵛ	M2338
62	[Merula]	Fontes & omnia	BBbc	33	-	24	30ᵛ	M2338
1	[Grandi]	Sicut oculi servorum	ATBbc	34	29	25	32	G3417
2	[Grandi]	O quam tu pulchra es	TTBbc	34ᵛ	29ᵛ	25ᵛ	32	G3417
3	[Grandi]	Salve mundi gloria	ATBbc	35	30	26	32ᵛ	G3422
		as 'Salve radix sancta'						

ᶜ *Sic*: error in numbering.

#	Composer	Title	Voices					RISM/Source
4	[Grandi]	O magnum sacramentum	CTBbc	35ᵛ	30ᵛ	26ᵛ	32ᵛ	G3439
5	[Grandi]	O lux splendidior	CTBbc	36	31	27	33	G3455
								as 'O crux splendidior'
6	[Grandi]	Hymnum cantemus Domino	ATBbc	36ᵛ	31ᵛ	27ᵛ	33	G3431
7	[Grandi]	Hæc est vera Ecclesia	TTBbc	37	32	28	33ᵛ	G3431
								as 'Haec est virgo sapiens'
8	[Grandi]	Benedicta sit Sancta Trinitas	ATBbc	37ᵛ	32ᵛ	28ᵛ	33ᵛ	G3439
9	[Tomasi]	Tota pulchra es	CCBbc	38	32ᵛ	29	34	T922
10	[Facchi]	Exurgat Deus	CCBbc	38ᵛ	33ᵛ	29ᵛ	34	F44
11	[Tomasi]	O gloriosa Domina	CCBbc	39	34	30	34ᵛ	T922
12	[Sances][d]	O Domine gutt[a]e	ATBbc	39ᵛ	34ᵛ	30ᵛ	35	S768
13	[Aloisi]	Salve Regina	CTBbc	40ᵛ	35ᵛ	31ᵛ	35ᵛ	A877
14	[Sances]	Plag[a]e tu[a]e Domine	ATBbc	41	36ᵛ	32ᵛ	35ᵛ	S768
15	[Sances]	O crux benedicta	ATBbc	42ᵛ	37ᵛ	33ᵛ	36	S768
16	[Merula]	O Immaculate	CTBbc	43	38	34	36ᵛ	M2338
								as 'O intemerata'
17	[Merula]	O quam dulcis es tu	TTBbc	43ᵛ	38ᵛ	34ᵛ	37	M2338
18	[Sances]	Ave Regina	ATBbc	44	39	35	37	S768
19	[Aloisi]	Quid mihi est in c[a]elo	ATBbc	44ᵛ	39ᵛ	35ᵛ	37ᵛ	A876
20	[Facchi]	O sacrum convivium	CABbc	45	40	36	37ᵛ	F44
21	Hennio [= Hayne]	Quid mihi est in caelo	TTBbc	45ᵛ	40ᵛ	36ᵛ	38	H4924
22	[F.M.Marini]	Anima mea liquefacta est	CABbc	46ᵛ	41ᵛ	37ᵛ	38ᵛ	M672
23	[F.M.Marini]	Magnum hereditatis	CABbc	47	42	38ᵛ	38ᵛ	M672
24	[F.M.Marini]	O vos omnes	ATBbc	47ᵛ	43	39	39	M672
25	[Aloisi]	Benignissime Jesu	TTBbc	48	43ᵛ	39ᵛ	39ᵛ	A876
26	[Trabattone]	O quam iucundum	CCBbc	49	44	40	39ᵛ	T1070
27	[Hayne]	O Domine Deus	ATBbc	49ᵛ	44ᵛ	40ᵛ	40	H4924
28	[Facchi]	Audite c[a]eli	CCBbc	50ᵛ	45ᵛ	41ᵛ	40ᵛ	F44
29	[Aloisi]	Ave Regina	CCBbc	51	46	42	40ᵛ	A877
30	[Merula]	Sat est Domine	CTBbc	51ᵛ	46ᵛ	42ᵛ	41	M2338
31	[Aloisi]	Dulcissima Maria	CABbc	52	47	43	41ᵛ	A876
32	Carissimi	Insurrexerunt in nos	ATBbc	52ᵛ	47ᵛ	43ᵛ	42	1642[1], 1649[1], 1651[e]
33	Charissimi	Desiderata nobis	ATBbc	54	48ᵛ	44ᵛ	42ᵛ	1667[1]
34	Charissimi [recte Rovetta arr. Jeffreys?][f]	Quam pulchra es	CCBbc	54ᵛ	49ᵛ	45ᵛ	43	R2964, R2975
35	Charissimi	Audite sancti	CCBbc	55ᵛ	50	46	43ᵛ	C1221, 1645[2], 1651,[e] 1656[2], 1693[1]
-	[Reggio]	Miserere mei	CCBbc	57ᵛ	51	46ᵛ	44	

---

[d] Later pencil misattribution to Carissimi.
[e] Florido de Silvestri ed., *Sacras Cantiones... Pars Prima* (V. Mascardi, Rome, 1651): not in *RISM*.
[f] A free arrangement of Rovetta's two-voice motet.

b) **Madrigal Society MSS G 55-9** (housed in the British Library)

Copied in the late 1650s (possibly from earlier manuscripts).
　Five partbooks from a set of six:

G 55 *Cantus*: ff. i + 54 + i. Modern pencil foliation: ff. 1-43, followed by eleven unnumbered folios. No music entered on ff. 5^v-6^v, 26^v-39, 43^{r-v}, nor on the eleven unnumbered folios. (f. 7 contains only the title 'Dulcissime Jesu A 4', a C clef (*c*1), and B flat signature; the piece is written out in full on f. 7^v.) Collation: one gathering of fifty-six. Pieces 1-9 only are numbered by the scribe. f. 41 includes extra hand-drawn stave for the final bars of the piece.

G 56 *Altus*: ff. i + 54 + i. No foliation or pagination. Pieces not numbered. No music entered on the four pages between pieces [9] and [10], on the twenty-eight pages between pieces [42] and [43], nor on the final twenty-two pages. Collation: one gathering of fifty-six.

G 57 *Tenore*: ff. i + 54 + i. No foliation or pagination. Pieces not numbered. No music entered on the four pages between pieces [9] and [10], on the thirty pages between pieces [42] and [43], nor on the final twenty-two pages. Collation: one gathering of fifty-six.

G 58 *Bassus*: ff. i + 52 + i. No foliation or pagination. Pieces not numbered. No music entered on the four pages between pieces [9] and [10], on the twenty-six pages between pieces [42] and [43], nor on the final twenty-three pages. Collation: one gathering of fifty-four.

G 59 *Basso Continuo*: ff. i + 48 + i. No foliation or pagination. Pieces not numbered. No music entered on the two pages between pieces [9] and [10], on the twenty-seven pages between pieces [42] and [43], nor on the final twenty-five pages. Collation: one gathering of fifty.

　Paper: 305 x 200 mm. Ten staves per page (ruled with a five-stave rastrum of 108.5 mm span and individual staves each measuring 12 mm).
　Watermark: same mark and paper as *Lbl* Add. MS 31,479.
　Scribe: George Jeffreys.
　No bindings.
　Contents of Mad. Soc. MSS G 55-9:

No.	Composer	Title	Scoring	Folio in G 55	Printed Source
1	[Grandi]	Benedictus Dominus	ATTBbc	1	G3417
2	[Grandi]	Hic est vere Martyr	ATTBbc	1^v	G3417
3	[Grandi]	Cantabo Domino	ATTBbc	2	G3417
4	[Grandi]	Heu mihi	ATTBbc	2^v	G3422
5	[Grandi]	Caro mea vere est cibus	CATBbc	3	G3417
6	[Grandi]	Magnum hereditatis	TTBBbc	3^v	G3422

7	[Grandi]	Vidi spetiosam	ATTBbc	4	G3417
8	[Grandi]	Obaudite me	ATTBbc	4^v	G3417
9	[Grandi]	O bone Jesu	ATTBbc	5	G3422, 1662[4]
[10]	[Aloisi]	Dulcissime Jesu Christe	CATBbc	7^v	A872 as 'Dulcissima Christi Mater'
[11]	[Trabattone]	In cælis hodie	CATBbc	8	T1070
[12]	[Trabattone]	Kyrie eleison [Litaniæ BVM]	CATBbc	9	T1070
[13]	[Aloisi]	Impetum inimicorum	CATBbc	10	A872
[14]	[Aloisi]	Cantate Domino	CATBbc	10^v	A872
[15]	[Grandi]	Congratulamini omnes	CATBbc	11	G3417
[16]	[Grandi]	Inter vestibulum	CTTBbc	11^v	G3422
[17]	[Grandi]	Domine ne in furore	CATBbc	12	G3455
[18]	[Grandi]	Deus qui nos in tantis	CATBbc	12^v	G3431
[19]	[Grandi]	Diligam te Domine	CCBBbc	13	G3431
[20]	[Aloisi]	Attollite portas	CTTBbc	13^v	A872
[21]	[Gallerano]	In Domino confido	CCTBbc	14	A872
[22]	[Sances]	O Jesu mi dulcissime	CCABbc	14^v	S768
[23]	[Sances]	Salve Regina	CATBbc	15^v	S768
[24]	[Merula]	Cum complerentur	CATBbc	16^v	M2338
[25]	[Merula]	Magnificate Dominum	CATBbc	17	M2338
[26]	[Merula]	Ego sum panis vitæ	CATBbc	17^v	M2339
[27]	[Merula]	Panis angelicus	CATBbc	18	M2339
[28]	[Facchi]	O virgo prudentissima	CCABbc	18^v	F44
[29]	[Tomasi]	O Maria sanctissima	CATBbc	19	T922
[30]	[Trabattone]	Lætis nunc mentibus	CATBbc	19^v	T1070
[31]	[Aloisi]	Regina c[a]eli	CATBbc	20	A877
[32]	[Gregori]	O Jesu O bone Jesu	CATBbc	20^v	G3813
[33]	[Gregori]	Ave Regina	CATBbc	21	G3813
[34]	[Cifra]	O quam pulchra	CCABbc	21^v	C2190
[35]	[Grandi]	Plorabo die ac nocte	CATBbc	22	G3431
[36]	[Trabattone]	Dicite nobis	CATBbc	22^v	T1070
[37]	[Trabattone]	Laudate Dominum	CATBbc	23	T1070
[38]	[Trabattone]	Qui habitatis	CATBbc	23^v	T1070
[39]	[Merula]	Jesu dulcissime	CATBbc	24	M2338
[40]	[Facchi]	Ave saluber[r]ima	CCABbc	24^v	F44
[41]	[Aloisi]	Salve Regina	CATBbc	25	A877
[42]	[Merula]	Cantate Domino	CCBBbc	25^v	M2338
[43]	[Merula]	Benignissima Jesu [sic]	C[A]TTBbc[g]	39^v	M2338 as 'Benignissime Jesu'

---

[g] Lacks alto part.

[44]	[Merula]	Benedictus tu	C[A]TTBbc[h]	40	M2338 as 'Benedicta tu'
[45]	[Facchi]	Salve Regina	C[C]ATBbc[i]	40[v]	F44
[46]	[Aloisi]	Exurgat Deus	C[C]ATBbc[i]	41	A876
[47]	[Aloisi]	O dulcis virgo virginum	C[C]ATBbc[i]	41[v]	A876
[48]		Tibi laus	-CATBbc[j]	42	
[49]		Ascendo ad Patrem	-CATBbc[j]	42[v]	

MANUSCRIPT X

LONDON, BRITISH LIBRARY ADD. MS 33,234

Charles Morgan's scorebook of sacred and secular music by English and Italian composers.

Copied $c.1682$-92.
ff. ii + 188 + i.
Modern pencil foliation: ff. 1-190 (the flyleaves/index folios are foliated). Original pagination: pp. 1-344 (200-1 were numbered 220-1 in error) followed by thirty-two unnumbered pages [345-76] (the flyleaves/index pages are not numbered).
Paper: 325 x 205 mm. Red marginal rulings on left and right. Twelve rastrum-ruled staves per page (ff. 3-34^v, 37-72^v, 79-102^v, 119-30^v ruled with six-stave rastrum of 138 mm span and individual staves each measuring 12-12.5 mm; ff. 35-6^v, 73-8^v, 103-18^v, 131-90^v ruled with six-stave rastrum of 130 mm span and individual staves each measuring 11.5-12 mm). No music entered on ff. 169, 175, 190^v. ff. i-ii: index (Morgan).
Collation: A-F^6 G^4 H-R^6 S-T^8 U-GG^6 (the first twenty-four gatherings contain binder's marks: A-Z).[a]
Watermarks: ff. 3-34, 37-72, 79-102, 119-30: foolscap with the initials A[braham] J[anssen] beneath and countermark PB; ff. 35-6, 73-8, 131-90: foolscap with countermark I[ean] M[onédière]; ff. 103-18: foolscap. See Thompson (1988), 292-4 and Watermarks XXIX-XXXI.
Scribe: Charles Morgan (with the exception of the mass on ff. 175^v-90 which was added by an unidentified scribe $c.1700$?).

---

[h] Lacks alto part.
[i] Lacks second cantus part.
[j] Lacks one voice (CII?).
[a] Robert Thompson (1988), 294, has suggested that the incomplete sequence of binder's marks probably dates from a rebinding in the late 1680s, when there were still approximately forty folios of unused paper at the end of the volume.

Inscriptions on front cover: 'Liber Caroli Morgan / è Coll. Magd: / Dec:mo 6:to Die 7:bris / Anno Domini / 1682' (Morgan); 'Vincent Novello / The gift of his kind friend / Wm. Patten.'

Binding: modern (the original cardboard front cover is preserved inside).
Contents of *Lbl* Add. MS 33,234:

Composer	Title	Scoring	Page	Folio	Concordances
	Un jour le berger Tirsis	Sbc	1	3	
Mr: Joh[n] Blow	Tho our Town be destroy[']d	SSMBbc	2	3v	1688[6]
Mr: Hen[ry] Aldrich	I come into my Garden	SBbc	4	4v	
Sigr: Pietro Reggio	Underneath this Mirtle shade	Bbc	8	6v	
	Here[']s a health to the King 'A: Ballad'	SSBbc	10	7v	
Merula	Nominativo Hic [Pt 1]	CATB[bc]	11	8	M2348
Merula	Nominativo Quis [Pt 2]	CATB[bc]	16	10v	M2348
Sgr: Charissimi	Lucifer cælestis olim	Bbc	21	13	1692[1]
Pietro Reggio	Wake Sleeping ones	CTBbc	25	15	
Pietro Reggio	The big limb[']d Babe 'Hercules in the Cradle'	Bbc	29	17	
Pietro Reggio	I'le sing of Heros	Sbc	33	19	R724
Pietro Reggio	Awake my Lyre	Cbc	35	20	R724
Mr John Blow	Awake my lyre[b]	SSTBbc [& 2vln b.vl]	37	21	1681[4]
	O Time thy wings are wet	SSBbc	48	26v	
Mr: John Banister	The bread is all bak'd	Sbc	52	28v	
Mr: John Banister	From lasting and unclouded Day	Sbc	56	30v	
Captain Cooke	Awake my soul 'The Morning Song'	Sbc	59	32	
Captain Cooke	Sleep downy sleep 'The Evening Song'	Sbc	61	33	
Mr John White	Yee Cats that at Midnight spit love	Sbc	63	34	
Mr [William] Turner	Beneath a Shady Willow 'A song in Madam Fickle'[c]	Sbc	64	34v	
M. Locke	All things their certain periods have 'A New Year[']s Song'	ATTB[bc]	65	35	
Pietro Reggio	Arise yee Subterranian winds	Sbc	71	38	R724
Pietro Reggio	Often I am by the Women told	Sbc	73	39	
Sgr: Pietro Reggio	You Solitary deserts	Sbc	75	40	
Cassati	Alleluja Jubilate Ecclesia	CBbc	77	41	C1411
Maria Marini	Anima mea liquefacta est	CABbc	83	44	M672
Mr: Hen[ry] Hall	All the follys of Love	SABbc	87	46	
Mr: Loosemore	Oh that mine eyes	Sbc	89	47	
Mr: Hen[ry] Hall	All the follys of Love	SABbc	87	46	
Mr: Loosemore	Oh that mine eyes	Sbc	89	47	

---

[b] An Act Song written for the Oxford Encænia of 1678; text: Cowley (1656), iii, §57, 101.
[c] Thomas D'Urfey's play *Madam Fickle: or the Witty False One*, first produced at the Dorset Garden Theatre in November 1676.

Composer	Title	Scoring	p.	f.	RISM
M^r: Wise	Justly now let's tribute pay	SSBbc	91	48	
D^r: John Blow	Goe perjurd man^d	SB [2vln] bc	93	49	B2985, B2987-91, 1683^5, 1687^5, 1695^{17}
M^r: S:^{som} Eswich	An amorous sigh	Sbc	97	51	
Rovetta	Io mi sento morir	CCbc	100	52^v	R2981
H. Purcell^e	Hast[e] gentle Charon	BBbc	105	55	
H. Purcell^e	Has yet your breast no pitty learn'd	SBbc	109	57	1688^6
Hart	Cure Nymph oh! cure	Sbc	113	59	1679^7
Purcell^e	Hark Damon hark	SSBbc	114	59^v	
M^r: H. Bowman	Miserere mei Deus	SSBbc	117	61	
Sg^r: Charissimi [recte Trabattone]^f	Anima mea in æterna Dulcedine	CBbc	135	70	T1070
Mr John Blow	Turn thee unto me O L[or]d	SATBbc	140	72^v	
Mr Aldrich	I waited patiently for the L[or]d	SATBbc	144	74^v	
Mr Hen[ry] Aldrich	Give the king thy judgements	CATBbc	153	79	
Mr Hen[ry] Purcell	Alas how Barbarous are wee	SBbc	159	82	
D^r: Blow	Come Poetry	SSBbc	161	83	1688^7
Felice Sances	Plagæ tua[e] Domine	ATBbc	165	85	S768
Sg^r: Monferratto	Salve Regina	ATBbc	174	89^v	M3037
Felice Sances	O Domine guttæ	ATBbc	180	92^v	S768
Cassati	Bone Jesu Verbum Patris	CCbc	187	96	C1411
Cassati	Magnificate Cæli	CCbc	195	100	C1411
Cassati	Exultate Justi	CCbc	[201]	103	C1411
Caspari Cassati	O Dulce nomen Jesu	CCbc	205	105	C1411
[Casati]	Tota pulchra es	CCbc	210	107^v	C1411
Monferratto	Regina Cæli lætare	TTbc	215	110	M3037
S:^{gr} Charissimi	Audite Sancti	CCBbc	219	112	C1221, 1645^2, 1651,^{g} 1656^2, 1692^1
[Stradella?]^h	Lontani del core	CCBbc	226	115^v	
Sig:^{r} Stradella	Sopra'un ecclesa ['Il Nerone']	Bbc	232	118^v	
D^r: Blow	Lovely Silena	Sbc	242	123^v	1682,^{i} 1683^5, 1695^{17}
M^r: Hen[ry] Purcell	She loves and she confesses too	Sbc	244	124^v	P5979, 1683^5, 1695^{17}
M^r: Hen[ry] Purcell	From Silent shades ['Bess of Bedlam']	Sbc	246	125^v	P5978-9, P6011-14, 1683^5, 1695^{17}

---

^{d} An Act song written for the Oxford Encænia of 1680; text from Herrick (1648), 53.

^{e} Attributed in the index only.

^{f} Also misattributed to Carissimi in *Lbl* Add. 17,835, 30,382, 33,235; *Ob* Mus. Sch. C 11; *Och* Mus. 43, 621, 623-6, 1178; and *J-Tn* N-4/39.

^{g} Florido de Silvestri ed., *Sacras Cantiones... Pars Prima* (V. Mascardi, Rome, 1651): not in *RISM*.

^{h} Attributed to Stradella in *Lbl* Add. 33,235; not listed in O. Jander, *A Catalogue of Manuscripts of Compositions by Alessandro Stradella*, The Wellesley Edition Cantata Index Series, iv (1960; rev. 2/1962), and considered 'doubtful' in C. Gianturco & E. McCrickard, *Alessandro Stradella (1639-1682): A Thematic Catalogue of his Compositions*, Thematic Catalogue Series 16 (New York, 1991).

^{i} D. Brown & T. Benskin ed., *The Newest Collection of the Choicest Songs* (T. Haly, London, 1682): not in *RISM*.

Composer	Title	Scoring	p.	f.	Source
D^r: Blow	In vain brisk God of love	SBbc	250	127^v	1683[5], 1695[17]
M^r: Hen[ry] Purcell [*recte* Blow]	Why do[e]s the morn in blushes rise	Sbc	251	128	1683[5], 1695[17], 1700[4]
Mr James Hart	Whilst our flocks feed	Sbc	253	129	1683[5]
M^r: H[enry] Hall	Hast[e] Charon hast[e]	SABbc	254	129^v	1685[6], 1695[17]
Sig:^{r} Silvestro [Durante]	Cantate Domino Canticum novum	CCbc	260	132^v	1661[1]
S^r: Carissimi ^{j}	Amanti che dite^k	CCBbc	265	135	
M^r: John Blow	Post haec audivi	ABbc	268	136^v	
M^r: John Blow	In lectulo meo	ATbc	273	139	
M^r: S:^{son} Estwich	What art thou loves	Sbc	276	140^v	
[Bowman]	When I a parting kiss did take	SSBbc	279	142	
Dr John Blow	As on Septimia[']s panting breast	SSBbc	281	143	B2985, 1685[5], 1695[17]
M^r: Purcell	Urge me no more	Sbc	286	145^v	
M^r: Blow	Peacefull is he	Sbc	289	147	1688[1]
M^r: Wise	Old Chiron thus preacht	SBbc	292	148^v	W1688 & P6057, 1685[4], 1686[4]
S^{gr} Batteist [Draghi]	Where art thou God of Dreams	C 2vln bc	294	149^v	1686[3]
M^r: H[enry] Purcell	When on my Sick bed I languished	TTBbc	297	151	
M^r: H[enry] Purcell	Plung'd in the Confines	TTBbc	303	154	
M^r: Henry Purcell	O all yee people clap your hands	SSTBbc	308	156^v	
D^r. Blow	Alexis dear Alexis 'Mr Flatman on the death of his son'	Sbc	318	161^v	1684[3], 1695[17]
Gratiana [*recte* Graziani]	Velut Palma velut Rosa	Cbc	321	163	1692[1]
[Lully] ^{l}	Sciocca pur	Sbc	327	166	
Banister ^{j}	'The clear Cavelier'	vln bc	329	167	
	Lovely Clarinda	Sbc	330	167^v	
[W. Turner]	Cheer up my friends^m	Abc	332	168^v	1681[4]
[Purcell]	A Grasshopper and a fly	SB[bc]^n	334	169^v	1686[3]
D^r: Blow	O Nigrocella 'The fair lover and his black Mistress'	Sbc	336	170^v	B2985, 1691[6]
M^r: Purcell	How happy[']s the lover ^{o}	SBbc	338	171^v	
M^r: Purcell	Let Cæsar and Urania live ^{p}	AAbc	340	172^v	P5979, P6047

---

^{j} Attributed in the index only.
^{k} Last movement of the cantata *I Naviganti* ('Sciolto hauean').
^{l} See R. Klakowich, '*Scocca pur*: Genesis of an English Ground', *JRMA*, cxvi (1991), 63-77; & F.W. Sternfeld, 'Cavalli and Purcell', Correspondence, ibid., 324-5.
^{m} Fragment only.
^{n} The basso continuo part was not copied.
^{o} From *King Arthur* (1691).
^{p} From *Sound the Trumpet* (1687).

[Carissimi]	Tronchi si pensier il vuo[q] [*recte* Tronchisi pensieri]		CBbc 343	174
Jacobo Carissimi[?] [r]	Kyrie - Gloria[q] 'Missa a quinque et a novum... Anno M.DC.LXVI'	CAATTB [B 2vln] bc	[346]	175[v]

MANUSCRIPT XI

LONDON, BRITISH LIBRARY ADD. MS 33,235

A scorebook of sacred and secular music by English and Italian composers.

Copied in the 1690s?[a]
ff. ii + 144 + i.
Modern pencil foliation: ff. 1-146 (the opening flyleaves are numbered). Original pagination: pp. 1-234, 225-290 (225-34 appear twice).
Paper: 293 x 235 mm. Red marginal rulings on left and right. Twelve rastrum-ruled staves per page ruled with a four-stave rastrum of 98 mm span and individual staves each measuring 14 mm. f. 2[v]: index.
Collation: A-Aa[6].
Watermark: fleur-de-lys with countermark VI.
Script: ff. 3-4: William Husbands;[b] ff. 4[v]-145[v]: Richard Goodson I.[c]
Inscriptions on f. 1[v]: 'Phil Hayes / 1757' (autograph); 'The Gifft of / M[r] Cave';[d] and various notes in the hand of Vincent Novello who donated the manuscript to the British Museum on 21 March 1887. f. 2: page of text in the hand of Philip Hayes beginning: 'This is one of the Books I purchased of / Mr Simon Child's Widdow, at Oxford...'[e] Philip Hayes added many comments and inscriptions to the manuscript; see the inventory below.
Binding: modern.
Contents of *Lbl* Add. MS 33,235:

---

[q] Incomplete.
[r] Later addition to the manuscript. The attribution is highly unlikely to be authentic, see G. Massenkeil, Über die Messen Giacomo Carissimi', *AnMc*, i (1963), 28-37; ibid., 'Carissimi, Giacomo', *New Grove*, iii, 786 & 791; and G. Dixon, *Carissimi* (Oxford, 1986), 15-17.
[a] The manuscript must have been copied after 1688 as both Playford's *Harmonia Sacra* (1688[1]) and *The Banquet of Music* II (1688[7]) appear to have been amongst the copyist's sources.
[b] William Husbands: Oxford, Christ Church musician (see Excursaus II, footnote 26); copied *Och* Mus. 10, and sections of *Och* Mus. 1220-4 & 1246. I am grateful to Robert Thompson for this identification.
[c] Goodson took over the copying midway through the second piece; for Goodson I, see Excursus II, footnote 26.
[d] Walter Cave, precentor of Christ Church, Oxford?
[e] Simon Child was a choirister at Christ Church, Oxford (1689-90), and organist of New College, Oxford (1702-31); see Watkin Shaw (1990), 390.

Composer	Title	Scoring	Folio	Page	Concordances
	W[he]n David heard 'David's Song upon Absalon'	SSB	3	1	
Charissime	Militia est vita hominis	CCBbc	4	3	C1220, 1643[1], 1652[1]
Henry Purcell	Since God so tender 'Upon a Ground' 'Corrected from Hen Purcell's original'[f] [P. Hayes]	TTBbc	7[v]	10	
Henry Purcell[g]	Early O Lord my fainting soul thy mercy does implore 'Corrected from Henry Purcell's / own copy in my Possesion P. Hayes'[f]	CCABbc	10[v]	16	
M[r]: Henery [sic] Purcell	When on my sick bed I languish 'Written by Tho[mas] / Flatman / & Printed / in his Book / of Poems'[h] 'Corrected from Hen. Purcell's / original copy.'[f] [Hayes]	TTBbc	14[v]	24	
Hen. Purcell	O All yee people Clap y[ou]r hands 'Corrected from the / original copy of / Henery Purcell'[f] [Hayes]	SSTBbc	17[v]	30	
P. Humphreys[g]	O Lord my God 'Printed in / Boyces 2[d] vol Cathedral / Music' [Hayes]	CATBbc & strings	21[v]	38	Boyce 1768
[Sances]	Plag[a]e tu[a]e domine	ATBbc	26[v]	48	S768
Charissime	Suscitavit Dominus	ATBbc	30[v]	56	C1220, 1665[1]
Charissime	Surgamus eamus	ATBbc	33	61	C1220, 1649[2], 1652[1], 1656[2]
[Casati]	Tota pulchra es	CCbc	36[v]	68	C1411
Gratiani[i]	Velut palma velut rosa	Sbc	39[v]	74	1693[1]
[Graziani]	O Dulcis jesu	Cbc	42	79	G3674
[Graziani]	Per asperos mundi errores	C[j] bc	44	83	G3674
[Rossi]	Dite O cieli 'This Song is Printed in the 2[d] Book of the Banquet of Music / page 20 with a continued Bass under the voice parts' [Hayes]	SB[bc]	46[v]	88	1688[7]
[Lully][k]	Sciocca pur	Sbc	47	89	
M[r] Purcell[l] [recte Blow]	Arise my darkned malancholy soul	Sbc	47[v]	90	
H. P[urcell]	Let the night perish 'Jobs Curse' 'Page 10. 1st Book / of Harmonia Sacra' [Hayes]	SBbc	48[v]	92	1688[1]
Dr. Blow	Alexis Dear Alexis	Sbc	50	97	1684[3], 1695[17]
M[r]: Henery Purcell	How long great God 'The Aspiration' 'Page 33. 1st Book / 3d edition Harmonia / Sacra' 'Written by Mr Norris / of Wadham Coll: Oxford' [Hayes]	Sbc	51[v]	98	1688[1]

---

[f] Now *Lbl* Add. 30,930.
[g] Attribution added by Philip Hayes.
[h] T. Flatman, 'A Thought of Death', *Poems and Songs* (London, 1674), 41-2.
[i] Attributed in the index only.
[j] The clef changes from C1 to G2 midway through the piece.
[k] See Klakowich (1991).
[l] Misattributed to Purcell by both Goodson and Hayes.

Composer	Title	Scoring	Folio	Page	RISM/Date
[W. Turner]	Chear up my friends	Abc	53	101	1681[4]
Mr: Henery Purcell	Above ye tumults of a busy State	CBbc	54	103	
	Shall all the buds	SBbc	55v	106	
H. P[urcell]	In a deep vision's intelectual scene 'Mr Cowley's Complaint'	SSBbc	57v	110	
Mr: Henery Purcell	How pleasant is thy flowry plain [2vln b.vl] 'This is printed in the 1st Book of / The Banquet of Musick Page 41' [Hayes]	STbc	63v	122	P5979, 1688[6]
Dr Blow	Go Perjurd man[m] 2vln b.vl	SBbc	67v	130	B2985, B2987-91, 1683[5], 1687[5], 1695[17]
Dr Blow	Paratum cor meum Deus	SSbc	70	135	
	Correte amante	CCBbc	74	143	
	Sospiri Che fate	CCBbc	75v	146	
[Rovetta]	Io mi sento morir	CCbc	77	149	R2981
[Pesenti]	Vano e il desio	CCbc	79	153	P1549
Stradella[?][n]	Lontani del core	CCBbc	82	159	
[Monteverdi]	Parlo misero	CCBbc	84v	164	M3494
[Casati]	Bone Jesu verbum patris	CCbc	87v	170	C1411
Bassani [recte Casati][o]	Omnes Gentes plaudite	CCbc	89v	174	C1411
[Trabattone][p]	Anima mea in æterna dulcedine	ABbc	92	180	T1070
Bassani [recte Monferrato][o]	Regina Caeli laetare	TTbc	94	184	M3037
[Monferrato]	Salve regina	ATBbc	96	188	M3037
Carissime	Amanti che Dite 'The last chorus of a Serenata composed by Carissime'[q] [Hayes]	CCBbc	99	194	
Dr Child	O Bone Jesu	CATBbc	100v	197	
	Mortali che fate 'A bad copy' [Hayes]	ATB[bc]	102	200	1686[4]
[Carissimi]	Lucifer cælestis olim	Bbc	103	202	1693[1]
Dr Blow	Jesus seeing ye multitudes	AATBorg	104v	205	
[C.] Gibbons	Sing unto ye Lord	SSATBbc	109v	215	1674[2]
Dr. Blow	Sing we merrily	SSATTBbc	112v	221	
Pelham Humphreys[r]	Have mercy upon me O God[s]	CATBbc	116	228[i]	
Dr. Blow	I said in ye cutting off of my dayes	ATTbc & 4 inst	120v	227[ii]	

---

[m] An Act song written for the Oxford Encænia of 1680; text from Herrick (1648), 53.

[n] Not listed in Jander (2/1962), and considered 'doubtful' in Gianturco & McCrickard (1991).

[o] The misattribution to Bassani was added by Philip Hayes.

[p] A pencil misattribution (at the end of the piece) to Bassani is crossed out and 'Charissime' inserted; also misattributed to Carissimi in *Lbl* Add. 17,835, 30,382, 33,234; *Ob* Mus. Sch. C 11; *Och* Mus. 43, 621, 623-6, 1178; and *J-Tn* N-4/39.

[q] Last movement of the cantata *I Naviganti* ('Sciolto hauean').

[r] Attribution added by Philip Hayes.

[s] This is the second working of this text by Humfrey; see Dennison (1986), 56-63. Robert Ford's claim - 'Henman, Humfrey and *Have mercy*', *MT*, cxxvii (1986), 463-6 - that the 'first version' of the anthem is not a childhood composition by Humfrey but one modelled on Humfrey's 'second version' by Richard Henman, is refuted by Dennison, ibid., 117.

D^r. Blow	How doth ye Sity [sic] sitt solitary	ATBbc	125^v	247	
[Locke]^t	How doth ye citty sit solitary	CCATBorg	129	254	
Blow	As on Euphrates Shady banks 'A paraphrase upon ps[al]m written by Sandys'^{u} [Hayes]	SSBbc	132	260	
[Blow]	Post hæc audivi	ABbc	135^v	268	
Dr Blow^v	And I heard a great voice	SATBbc & 4 inst	138	273	
Dr Blow	Peacefull is he & most secure 'Written by Mr Tho[ma]s Flatman. set by Dr Blow'^{w} [Hayes]	Sbc	144	285	1688^1
M^r· Purcell	Oh, Solitude my Sweetest choice	Bbc	145	287	P5979, 1687^4, 1687^5, 1695^{17}

MANUSCRIPT XII

LONDON, BRITISH LIBRARY ADD. MSS 40,657-61

The 'Shirley Partbooks'^{a} of consort music of two to six parts which include a number of untexted five-part Italian madrigals.

Copied *c*.1630-45.
Five partbooks from a set of six (lacking *Sextus*: first bass):

Add. MS 40,657 *Cantus*: ff. iv + 109 + i. Modern pencil foliation: ff. 1-50 (the first flyleaf is numbered); unnumbered folios: two between ff. 15 and 16, ten between ff. 30 and 31, twenty-three between ff. 44 and 45, and twenty-five after f. 50. No music entered on ff. 15^v, 29^v, 44^v, nor on any of the unnumbered folios. Inscription on front cover and f. 1 (flyleaf): 'Cantus'.

Add. MS 40,658 *Altus*: ff. iv + 100 + iii. Modern pencil foliation: ff. 1-50 (the first flyleaf is numbered); unnumbered folios: one between ff. 15 and 16, eleven between ff. 30 and 31, twenty-two between ff. 44 and 45, and seventeen after f. 50. No music entered on ff. 15^v, 44^v, nor on any of the unnumbered folios. Inscription on front cover and f. 1 (flyleaf): 'Altus'.

---

^{t} A note in pencil at the end of the piece reads: 'Suppos'd to be Mathew Lock's [crossed out] Dr Blow'.
^{u} Psalm CXXXVII, Sandys (1636), 219-20.
^{v} Attribution added by Philip Hayes with the following note: 'By Dr Blow. as originally composed without / The words conjoind viz: "I was in the spirit upon the Lords / Day." / which were added by / Dr Aldrich'; an unidentified scribe added: 'A curious anecdote' (in red crayon).
^{w} Flatman, 'The Happy Man', (1674), 50-1.
^{a} So-called because the bindings contain the coat of arms of the Shirley family; no other link between Lawes and the Shirley family is known. See pp. 88-9 above; see also Pinto (1978), and ibid. (1995), 11-15 & 30-33.

Add. MS 40,659 *Tenor*: ff. iii + 68. Modern pencil foliation: ff. 1-35 (the first flyleaf is numbered); unnumbered folios: ten between ff. 16 and 17, twenty-four between ff. 30 and 31. No music entered on f. 30ᵛ, nor on any of the unnumbered folios. Inscription on front cover and f. 1 (flyleaf): 'Tenor'.

Add. MS 40,660 *Bassus*: ff. iii + 103. Modern pencil foliation: ff. 1-50 (the first flyleaf is numbered); unnumbered folios: two between ff. 15 and 16, eight between ff. 30 and 31, twenty-one between ff. 44 and 45, and twenty-three after f. 50. No music entered on ff. 15ᵛ, 44ᵛ, nor on any of the unnumbered folios. Inscription on front cover and f. 1 (flyleaf): 'Bassus'.

Add. MS 40,661 *Quintus*: ff. iv + 64 + iii. Modern pencil foliation: ff. 1-35 (the first flyleaf is numbered); unnumbered folios: one between ff. 21 and 22, seven between ff. 24 and 25, and twenty-two between ff. 30 and 31. No music entered on ff. 15ᵛ-16, 21ᵛ, 22, 24ᵛ, 31ᵛ, nor on any of the unnumbered folios. Inscription on front cover and f. 1 (flyleaf): 'Quintus'.

Paper: 295 x 195-200 mm. Marginal rulings on left and right. Ten rastrum-ruled staves per page (ruled with a five-stave rastrum of 119 mm span and individual staves each measuring 13.5 mm).

Watermark: coat of arms.

Collations: not possible due to tightness of bindings.

Scribes: (see inventory below)

    A¹: William Lawes (early hand)[b]
    A²: William Lawes (later hand)
    B: unidentified (also contributed to *US-SM* EL 25 A 46-51)
    C: unidentified (18th-century addition)

Bindings: brown calf with ties; gold tooling with central coat of arms of the Shirley family of Staunton Harrold, Leicestershire.

Contents of *Lbl* Add. MSS 40,657-61:

---

[b] Pinto (1995), 11-14 suggests that Lawes' earliest copies pre-date the death of Sir Henry Shirley, second baronet, in February 1633.

Composer	No.	Title	Scoring	Hand	Folios -57	-58	-59	-60	-61	VdGS No.	Concordances
Tho: Lupo	1	[Fantasia]	A 3 voc:	A¹	2	2	-	2	-	2	
[Lupo]	2	[Fantasia]	A 3	A¹	2ᵛ	2ᵛ	-	2ᵛ	-	3	
[Lupo]	3	[Fantasia]	A 3	A¹	3	3	-	3	-	10	
[Lupo]	4	[Fantasia]	A 3	A¹	3ᵛ	3ᵛ	-	3ᵛ	-	13	
Mr Chetwoode	5	[Fantasia]	A 3 voc:	A¹	4	4	-	4	-	1	
[Chetwoode]	6	[Fantasia]	A 3	A¹	4ᵛ	4ᵛ	-	4ᵛ	-	2	
[Chetwoode]	7	[Fantasia]	A 3	A¹	4ᵛ	4ᵛ	-	4ᵛ	-	3	
[Chetwoode]	8	[Fantasia]	A 3	A¹	5	5	-	5	-	4	
Will: Lawes	9	Ayres	A 3	A¹	5ᵛ	5ᵛ	-	5ᵛ	-	320	
[W. Lawes]	10	[Ayre]	A 3	A¹	5ᵛ	5ᵛ	-	5ᵛ	-	321	
[W. Lawes]	11	[Ayre]	A 3	A¹	6	6	-	6	-	75	
[W. Lawes]	12	[Ayre]	A 3	A¹	6ᵛ	6ᵛ	-	6ᵛ	-	83	
[W. Lawes]	14	[Ayre]	A 3	A¹	7	7	-	7	-	206	
Tho: Holmes	15	Ayres	A 3 voc:	A¹	7ᵛ	7ᵛ	-	7ᵛ	-	1	
[Holmes]	16	[Ayre]	A 3	A¹	8	8	-	8	-	2	
[Holmes]	17	[Ayre]	A 3	A¹	8	8	-	8	-	3	
Jo: Coprario	18	[Fantasia]	A 3 voc:	A¹	8ᵛ	8ᵛ	-	8ᵛ	-	1	
[Coprario]	19	[Fantasia]	A 3	A¹	9	9	-	9	-	2	
[Coprario]	20	[Fantasia]	A 3	A¹	9ᵛ	9ᵛ	-	9ᵛ	-	3	
[Coprario]	21	[Fantasia]	A 3	A¹	10	10	-	10	-	4	
[Coprario]	22	[Fantasia]	A 3	A¹	10ᵛ	10ᵛ	-	10ᵛ	-	5	
[Coprario]	23	[Fantasia]	A 3	A¹	11	11	-	11	-	6	
[Coprario]	24	[Fantasia]	A 3	A¹	11ᵛ	11ᵛ	-	11ᵛ	-	7	

[Coprario]	[Fantasia]	25	A³	12	-	12	12ᵛ	-	8
[Coprario]	[Fantasia]	26	A³	12ᵛ	-	12ᵛ	12ᵛ	-	9
[Coprario]	[Fantasia]	27	A³	13	-	13	13	-	10
Tho: Holmes	Pavan	28	A³	13ᵛ	-	13ᵛ	13ᵛ	-	4
Tho: Holmes	Almaine	29	A³	13ᵛ	-	13ᵛ	13ᵛ	-	5
Nich: Guy	[Fantasia]	30	A³	14	-	14	14	-	-
W. Lawes	[Ayre]	-	A³	14ᵛ	-	14ᵛ	14ᵛ	-	227
W. Lawes	[Ayre]	-	A³	14ᵛ	-	14ᵛ	14ᵛ	-	207
[W. Lawes]	[Ayre]	-	[a3]	15	-	15	15	-	342
Wj. Lawes	[Ayre]	-	[a3]	15	-	15	15	-	208
John Warde	[Fantasia]	1	A 4 voc:	16	2	16	16ᵛ	-	1
[Ward]	[Fantasia]	2	A4	16ᵛ	2ᵛ	16ᵛ	16ᵛ	-	2
[Ward]	[Fantasia]	3	A4	17	3	17	17	-	4
[Ward]	[Fantasia]	4	A4	17ᵛ	3ᵛ	17ᵛ	17ᵛ	-	5
[Ward]	[Fantasia]	5	A4	18	4	18	18	-	3
[Ward]	[Fantasia]	6	A4	18ᵛ	4ᵛ	18ᵛ	18ᵛ	-	6
Tho: Lupo	[Fantasia]	7	A4 Voc:	19	5	19	19	-	8
Tho: Ford	[Fantasia]	8	A4 Voc:	19ᵛ	5ᵛ	19ᵛ	19ᵛ	-	-
[Sandrin]	Dulcis Memoriæᶜ	9	A4:	20	6	20	20	-	-
Sym: Ive[s]:	[Fantasia]	10	A4:	20ᵛ	6ᵛ ᵈ	20ᵛ	20ᵛ	-	4
[Ives]	[Fantasia]	11	A4	21ᵛ	7ᵛ	21ᵛ	21ᵛ	-	3
Jo: Coperario	[Fantasia]	12	A4:	22ᵛ	8ᵛ	22ᵛ	22ᵛ	-	1

ᶜ Textless chanson by Sandrin *alias* Pierre Regnault; see F. Dobbins, '"Doulce Mémoire": A Study of the Parody Chanson', *PRMA*, xcvi (1969-70), 85-102.
ᵈ The bass part of the first of William Lawes' four-part Ayres was copied in error at the foot of f. 7 of Add. 40,659 and was then crossed out.

Composer	Title							
[Coprario]	[Fantasia]	A 4:	A¹	23	23	9	23	-	2
[Coprario]	[Fantasia]	[a 4]	A¹	23v	23v	9v	23v	-	3
[Coprario]	[Fantasia]	[a 4]	A¹	24	24	10	24	-	4
[Coprario]	[Fantasia]	[a 4]	A¹	24v	24v	10v	24v	-	5
[Coprario]	[Fantasia]	[a 4]	A¹	25	25	11	25	-	6
Alfonso: [Ferrabosco II]	[Fantasia]	A 4	A¹	25v	25v	11v	25v	-	13
[Ferrabosco II]	[Fantasia]	[a 4]	A¹	26	26	12	26	-	15
Doc: Bull	[Fantasia]	[a 4]	B	26v	26v	12v	26v	-	-
Wi: Lawes	Aire	a.4	A²	27	27	13	27	-	110
Wi: Lawes	Aires	A 4	A²	27v	27v	13v	27v	-	306
Wi: Lawes	Aire	A 4	A²	28	28	14	28	-	336
Wj: Lawes	Aire	A 4	A²	28v	28v	14v	28v	-	109
W. Lawes	Aire	A 4	A²	29	29	15	29	-	318
Wj. Lawes	Aire	A 4	A²	-	29v	15v	29v	-	319
-	[Ayre]	[a 4]	A²	30	30	16	30	-	337
-	[Ayre]	[a 4]	A²	30	30	16	30	-	103
-	[Corant]	[a 4]	A²	30v	30v	16v	30v	-	339
[W.Lawes]	[Fantasia]	A 5	B	31	31	17	31	2	11
Tho: Lupo	[Fantasia: 'Il vago']ᶠ	[a 5]	B	31v	31v	17v	31v	2v	5
[Lupo]	[Fantasia]	[a 5]	B	32	32	18	32	3	12
[Lupo]	[Fantasia]	[a 5]	B	32v	32v	18v	32v	3v	13

ᵉ *Sic.*
ᶠ Fantasia of madrigalian origin; title from *Lbl* Egerton 3665.

[Lupo]	5	[Fantasia]	[a 5]	B	33	33	19	33	4	1	
[Lupo]	6	[Fantasia]	[a 5]	B	33v	33v	19v	33v	4v	2	
Cla: Monteverdie	7	[O com'e gran martire][g]	[a 5]	A[1]	34	34	20	34	5	-	M3459
[Monteverdi]	8	[La tra'l sangue e le morti egro][g]	[a 5]	A[1]	34	34	20	34	5	-	M3459
Jo: Coprario	9	[Dove il liquido argento or Fuggendo mi strugge][hi]	A 5	A[1]	34v	34v	20v	34v	5v	45	
[Coprario]	10	[Occhi miei con viva speme][h]	[a 5]	A[1]	35	35	21	35	6	46	
[Coprario]	11	[Io piango][h]	[a 5]	A[1]	35v	35v	21v	35v	6v	5	
[Coprario]	12	[Ohime la gioia e breve][h]	[a 5]	A[1]	36	36	22	36	7	35	
[Coprario]	13	[Fantasia][j]	[a 5]	A[1]	36v	36v	22v	36v	7v	49	
[Coprario]	14	[O voi che sospirate][hk]	[a 5]	A[1]	37	37	23	37	8	48	
Jo: Ward	15	[Fantasia]	A 5	A[1]	37v	37v	23v	37v	8v	2	
[Ward]	16	[Fantasia]	[a 5]	A[1]	38	38	24	38	9	4	
[Ward]	17	[Fantasia]	[a 5]	B	38v	38v	24v	38v	9v	-	
Will: White	18	[Fantasia]	A 5	B	39	39	25	39	10	1	
Luca Marenzio	19	Arda pur: [sempre o mora][g]	A 5	A[1]	39v	39v	25v	39v	10v	-	M560
[Marenzio]	20	Rimanti in pace[g]	A 5	A[1]	39v	39v	25v	39v	10v	-	M557
[Marenzio]	21	Ond'ei di mortie[g] [recte morte]	A 5	A[1]	40	40	26	40	11	-	M557
[Marenzio]	22	Caro dolce [mio ben][g]	A 5	A[1]	40	40	26	40	11	-	M546

[g] Textless madrigal.
[h] Fantasia of madrigalian origin. See Charteris (1976); ibid. (1982b), 18-19; and Pinto (1981), 25.
[i] Entitled 'Dove il liquido argento' in *Lbl* Egerton 3665 and *EIRE-Dm* Z3.4.13; and 'Fuggendo mi strugge' in *US-SM* EL 25 A 46-51.
[j] Untitled in all sources.
[k] A parody of Marenzio's 'O voi che sospirate' published in *Il Secondo Libro de Madrigalia Cinque Voci* (Venice, 1581); see Kerman (1962), 44, note 1.

Composer	Title	#										
[Marenzio]	Che se[']tu [se'l cor mio][1]	23	A 5	A[1]	40v	40v	40v	26v	40v	11v	-	M557
Horatio Vecchi	Clorind'hai vinto[1]	24	A 5	A[1]	40v	40v	40v	26v	40v	11v	-	V1043
Monteverdio	Saura [*recte* Sovra] tenere herbette[1]	25	A 5	A[1]	41	41	41	27	41	12	-	M3459
[Marenzio]	Deh poi ch'era[1]	26	A 5	A[1]	41v	41v	41v	27v	41v	12v	-	M560
Be: Pallavicino	Com'viuro[1]	27	A 5	A[1]	41v	41v	41v	27v	41v	12v	-	P793
Luca Marenzio	Quell[']augellin[1]	28	A 5	A[1]	42	42	42	28	42	13	-	M560
-	[Textless]	-	[m]	A[1]	42	-	-	-	-	-	-	-
Alfonso Ferobosco [II]	Paven	29	A 5	A[1]	42v	42v	42v	28v	42v	13v	1	
Luca Marenzio	[Solo e pensoso][1]	-	A 5	A[1]	43	43	43	29	43	14	-	M567
Wj. Lawes	[Fantasia]	-	A 5	A[1]	43v	43v	43v	29v	43v	14v	68	
Wj. Lawes	In nomine	-	A 5	A[1]	44	44	44	30	44	15	69	
-	[Primo & Secondo violin parts to dances, songs, and psalms]	-		C	-	-	-	-	-	16v	-	
Tho. Lupo	[Fantasia]	1	A 6	A[1]	45	45	45	31	45	25	1	
Alfonso: [Ferrabosco II]	[Fantasia]	2	A 6	A[1]	45v	45v	45v	31v	45v	25v	2	
Will: White	[Fantasia]	3	A 6	A[1]	46	46	46	32	46	26	3	
[W. White]	[Fantasia]	4	[*a* 6]	A[1]	46v	46v	46v	32v	46v	26v	4	
Jo: Warde	In nomine	5	A 6	A[1]	47	47	47	33	47	27	2	

[1] Textless madrigal.
[m] Textless cantus part only.

Composer	№	Title	Scoring						
Alfonso [Ferrabosco II]	6	[Fantasia]	A 6	A^1/B^n	47^v	33^v	47^v	27^v	3
Alfonso [Ferrabosco II]	7	In nomine	A 6	A^1/B^n	48	34	48	28	1
Will. White	8	[Fantasia]	A 6	A^1/B^n	48^v	34^v	48^v	28^v	1
[W. White]	9	[Fantasia]	[a 6]	A^1/B^n	49	35	49	29	2
[W. White]	10	[Fantasia]	[a 6]	A^1	49^v	35^v	49^v	29^v	6
[W. White]	11	[Fantasia]	[a 6]	A^1	50	–	50	30	5
Jo Coperario	12	[Fantasia]	A 6	A^1	50^v	–	50^v	30^v	2
–	–	[Fragment]	°	C	–	–	–	31 rev	–
[Coprario]	–	[Fantasia]	[a 2]	A^1	–	–	–	32 rev	8
[Coprario]	–	[Fantasia]	[a 2]	A^1	–	–	–	32^v rev	7
[Coprario]	–	[Fantasia]	[a 2]	A^1	–	–	–	33 rev	3
[Coprario]	–	[Fantasia]	[a 2]	A^1	–	–	–	33^v rev	4
[Coprario]	–	[Fantasia]	[a 2]	A^1	–	–	–	34 rev	6
[Coprario]	3	[Fantasia]	A 2	A^1	–	–	–	34^v rev	2
[Coprario]	2	[Fantasia]	A 2	A^1	–	–	–	35 rev	1
Jo: Coprario	1	Duo	[a 2]	A^1	–	–	–	35^v rev	5

---

[n] Copied by Scribe A^1 in Add. MSS 40,657 & 40,660-1; and by Scribe B in Add. MSS 40,658-9.
° Melody instrument: fragment only.

MANUSCRIPT XIII

LONDON, BRITISH LIBRARY ADD. MS 59,869

'The Cartwright Lyra Viol Manuscript': a manuscript section added to the back (reversed) of Christopher Simpson's *The Division-Violist: / OR / AN INTRODUCTION / To the PLAYING upon a GROUND: / Divided into Two PARTS* (W. Godbid, London, 1659).

Copied *c*.1659?
ff. ii + 46 + 39 (printed matter) + iii.
Modern pencil foliation: ff. 1-34, eight unnumbered folios [34a-h], 35-77.
Paper: 303 x 198 mm. Red marginal rulings on left and right. Twelve rastrum-ruled staves per page (ruled with a four-stave rastrum of 84 mm span and individual staves measuring 11-11.5 mm); an extra line has been added by hand to each stave of ff. 1^v-34^v. No music entered on ff. [34a]-[34h]^v, 35, 38^v.
Watermarks: f. i: countermark 'I [?] DLO'; f. ii: grapes; ff. 1-77: coat of arms (Amsterdam).
Collation: A-G^6 H^4 (manuscript section).
Script: ff. 1-34^v: unidentified scribe (Cartwright?); ff. 35^v rev - 38 rev: John Lilly.
Inscriptions: f. i: 'Wm[?] Cartwright', 'J.E. Cartwright' (two signatures crossed out) followed by a table of ornaments, and: 'Mutatâ, mutantur, & mores. / Dictum Socratis à Plutone & Cicerone laudatum'; inscription on slip pasted to f. ii^v (with modern folliation iii): 'Mr Jo. Wray of Brant Broughton / Violist'.
Binding: brown leather with gold tooling; spine inscription: 'SIMPSON'S / VIOLIST'.
Contents of *Lbl* Add. MS 59,869:

Music for Lyra Viol

Folio	No.	Title	Composer	VdGS No.
1		[Bass part]	Jo Banister	
1		[Fragment of bass part]		
1^v		A Prelude [in D]		8510
1^v		Almain [in D]	Mr Jenkins	322
2		A division to the precedent Almain		
2^v	1.	Alphonso way [in a]		9124

2ᵛ	2.	[Alman in A]		9125
3	3.	Allmane		
3		Another Almane [in A]		9127
3ᵛ		An Almane		
3ᵛ		Coranto [in A]		9195
4		Corant [in a]		9129
4		Coranto [in a]		9130
4ᵛ-5		[Prelude in G]	[Ives]	32
5		A Mock Eccho [in G]	[Ives]ᵃ	57
5ᵛ		An Almane [in G]	[Ives]	33
6		Ayre [Corant in G]	[Ives]	47
6		[Saraband in G]	[Ives]	48
6		[Saraband in G]	[Ives]	44
6ᵛ		[Alman in G]		7301
6ᵛ		Corant [in G]		7302
6ᵛ		Sarabrand [in G]		7303
7		An Aire [in G]		7304
7		A Corant [in G]	[Hudson]	117
7		A Sarabrand [in G]		7305
7ᵛ		Almaine [in G]		7306
7ᵛ		Sarabrand [in G]		7307
7ᵛ		Sarabrand [in G]		7308
8		An Aire [in G]	Mʳ Lawes [*recte* Ives]	50
8		Corant [in G]	Mʳ Lawes	429
8ᵛ		Almaine [in G]	Mʳ Lawes	430
9		Corant [in G]	Mʳ Lawes	431
9ᵛ		[Saraband in G]	[W. Lawes]ᵃ	432
9ᵛ		Sarabrand [in G]	Mʳ Lawes	433
10		Almaine [in G]	Jo: Lilly	1
10		Corant [in G]	J: Lilly	2
10ᵛ		Sarabrand [in G]	J: Lillie	3
10ᵛ		A Jigge [in G]		7309
11		Prelude [in G]		7310
11		Prelude [in G]	J: Grome	1
11ᵛ		[Prelude in G]		7311
11ᵛ		[Alman in G]	Mʳ Mace	6
12		[Alman in G]	[Mace]ᵃ	7
12ᵛ		[Corant in G]	Mʳ Mace	8
12ᵛ		[Alman in G]		7312, 7332, 7435
13		[Corant in G]		7313
13		[Saraband in G]	[Ives]	31
13ᵛ		[Ayre in G]		7314

ᵃ Attributed by virtue of its position in the manuscript.

London, British Library Add. MS 59,869   277

13ᵛ		The Duke of Loraines March [in G]		7315
13ᵛ		The Apes Dance at the 2ᵈ Opera [in G]		7037
14		Bone jure [set] by R[obert] W[adham]	Sir Ed. Golding	7
14		The Glory of the Vale. Set by Mʳ Wadham	Sir Edw. Golding	8
14ᵛ		[Toll, toll, gentle bell in G]		7029
14ᵛ		Jigg [in G]		7207
14ᵛ		Jigg [in G]		7316
15		Scotch-Tune [in G]		7053
15		O the bonny Christ Church Bells [in G]		7042
15ᵛ-16		The Canaries [in G]		7411
16		Sawmy was tal etc. [in G]		7041
16		A Scottish Tune [in G]		7317
16		[Jig in G]		7221
16ᵛ		The Ground to Sweet Jane [in G]		7318
16ᵛ		Sweet Jane [in G]		7054
17	1.	A Prelude Flat harp Tuning	J: G[rome]	2
17	2.	An Almane [in g]	[Young]	72
17ᵛ	3.	[Alman in g]	[Esto]	22
17ᵛ	4.	[Saraband in g]	[Esto]	23
18	5.	An Almane [in g]	Mʳ John Esato	38
18	6.	Corant [in g]	Mʳ J. E[sto]	39
18	7.	Sarabrand [in g]	Mʳ J: Easto	40
18ᵛ	8.	[Alman in g]	Mʳ Lilly	8
18ᵛ	9.	Sarabrand [in g]		
19	10.	[Alman in g]		7921
19ᵛ	11.	[Alman in g]	Mʳ. W. Lawes	462
19ᵛ	12.	[Alman in g]		7922
20	13.	[Alman in g]	[Esto]	21
20	14.	[Prelude in g]		7923
20ᵛ	15.	[Prelude in g]		7924
20ᵛ	16.	[Corant in g]		7925
20ᵛ	17.	[Corant in g]	[Esto]	19
21	18.	[Alman]	[Coleman]	462
21	19.	[Saraband]	[Coleman]	464
21ᵛ	20.	Coranto	Coleman	474
21ᵛ	21.	Almain [in g]		7926
22	22.	Sarabrand [in g]		7927
22	23.	The Queenes Sarabrand [in g]		7928
22	24.	[Saraband in g]	[Lilly]	9
22ᵛ	25.	The Eccho [in g]	Mʳ John Jenkins	250
23	26.	[Alman in g]		7929
23	27.	Terwet Gibsons wife	Sir Edw. Golding	9

23	28.	Stantons Jig [in g]	7930
23ᵛ	29.	[Alman in g]	Mʳ Wᵐ Lawes 463
23ᵛ	30.	Almane	Mr Rob. Wadham
24	31.	[The clean contrary way in g]	7895
24		A Health to Bety [in g]	7931
24ᵛ		Almain	[Steffkens] 8
24ᵛ		Corant [in d]	8835
25		Saraband	[Steffkens] 102
25		[Alman]	[Steffkens] 56
25		[Saraband]	Mʳ Steofkins 58
25ᵛ		Almain	Mʳ Steoffkins 107
25ᵛ		Almain	[Steffkens]ᵇ 108
25ᵛ		Corant	Mʳ Steoffkins 109
26		Almain	Mʳ Steofkins 94
26		Saraband	[Steffkens] 96
26ᵛ		Præludium [in B flat]	[Jenkins] 491
26ᵛ-27		Almain	[Steffkens] 121
27		Corant	[Steffkens] 122
27		Saraband [in B flat]	9691
27		Prelude [in D]	Mʳ W: Young [recte Lilly]
27ᵛ		Almain	Mʳ W: Young [or Steffkens 54]
27ᵛ		Coranto	Mʳ Drue [or Steffkens 57]
28		Corant [in D]	J: Lilly 17
28ᵛ-29		[Saraband in D]	[Lilly]ᵇ 18
29ᵛ		[Corant in D]	[Lilly]ᶜ 19
29ᵛ-30		[Corant in D]	[Lilly]ᵇ 20
30		[Corant in D]	[Lilly]ᵇ 21
30ᵛ		Almaine [in D]	Jo: Lilly 22
31		Sarabrand [in D]	Jo: Lilly 23
31ᵛ		Hunsdon house [in C]	6535
31ᵛ		Oxford [in C]	6536
31ᵛ		New Mutarre [in G]	7065
32		Queens Country dance [in g]	6537
32		Bellony [in g]	6538
32		Petite Boree [in d]	6539
32		Grand Boree [in g]	6540, 6296
32ᵛ		Galliard Artois [in d]	6541
32ᵛ		Sir Rich. Haughtons Rant [in G]	6542
32ᵛ		The Sword tune [in d]	6543
32ᵛ		Little boy go with me [in G]	6544
33		Bone jure	Sir Ed. Golding 4

ᵇ Attributed by virtue of its position in the manuscript.
ᶜ Attributed to Lilly in *Ob* Mus. Sch. F 575, f. 82ᵛ rev.

33	The Sarabrand to my Lady Williams her bonjure	[Golding][d]	5
33	A Jig	Sr Edw. Golding	3
33	Lanes Country Dance [in e]		6545
33^v	The new Vagary [in B flat]		7809
33^v	[Corant in g]		6546
33^v	The Cricket [in G]		6547
34	Mr Byrons Hornpipe [in C]		6548
34	Duke of Monmouths Jig [in G]		6549
34	Hum, Drum [in F]		6550
34^v	Mack beth [sic; in G]		7022
34^v	Hearts ease [in F]		6551
34^v	Mardike [in G]		7059
38-37^v rev	[Divisions for bass viol]	[Polewheele]	4
37-35^v rev	[Divisions for bass viol]		58

MANUSCRIPT XIV

LONDON, BRITISH LIBRARY EGERTON MS 2485

An organ score containing accompaniments to five-part consort music by Coprario, Ferrabosco II, Orlando Gibbons, Lupo, Mico, Ward and William White, and madrigals by Marenzio and Monteverdi.

Copied in the late-1640s or 1650s?
ff. 45 + i.
Modern pencil foliation: one unnumbered folio [a], ff. 1-43, followed by an unnumbered folio.
Paper: 280 x 415 mm. Marginal rulings on left and right. Eight six-line staves per page (ruled with a two-stave rastrum of 39 mm span and individual six-line staves each measuring 12.5 mm). No music entered on ff. [a]$^{r-v}$, [44]$^{r-v}$.
Collation: each folio consists of half a sheet of paper (probably cut before binding and each folio sewn individually) with horizontal chain lines stiched along what was originally the top or bottom of a sheet; there are therefore no gatherings in the normal sense.[a]

---

[d] Attributed by virtue of its position in the manuscript.
[a] I am grateful to Dr Robert Thompson for this information.

Watermark: coat of arms of Strasbourg (the 'Strasbourg Bend') with countermark 'MC'.
Scribe: John Lilly.
Inscription on f. 1: 'Heare begins Mr Coperario his Fanceys of 5 parts' (Lilly).
Binding: modern.
Contents of *Lbl* Egerton MS 2485:

Folio	Composer	Title	VdGS No.
1	[Coprario]	Io son feritta [*recte* ferito] amore^b	2
1^v	Giova[n]ni Coprario	Occhi [miei con viva speme]	46
2	Giova[n]ni Coprario	Per far una [leggiadre vendetta]	31
2^v	Giova[n]ni Coprario	Crudel perchi [*recte* perche]^c	1
3^v	Giova[n]ni Coprario	Lucretia mia	12
4^v	Giova[n]ni Coprario	Lume tuo fugace	4
5^v	Giova[n]ni Coprario	Rapina l'alma	3
6^v	Giova[n]ni Coprario	Luci beate [e care]	9
7^v	Giova[n]ni Coprario	Dolci [*recte* Dolce] mia vita	14
8	Giova[n]ni Coprario	Ohime [la gioia e breve]	35
8^v	Giova[n]ni Coprario	Ninnfa crudeli [*recte* crudele]	29
9	Giova[n]ni Coprario	Passa madon[n]a	15
9^v	Giovan[n]i Coprario	Quall vaghezza^d	23
10^v	[Coprario]	[Fantasia]^e	49
11	[Coprario]	Cresce in voy	16
11^v	Mr Richard Mico	Paven	2
12	Mr Richard Mico	Paven	1
12^v	Giovan[n]i Coprario	Gittene Ninfe^b	34
13^v	[Coprario]	[O sonno, della mia morte *or* Deh preg'Amore]^f	21
14	[Coprario]	[Deh cara anima mia]^g	32
14^v	[Coprario]	[Io piango]	5
15^v	[Coprario]	[In voi moro]	8

^{b} Fantasies of madrigalian origin; see Charteris (1976); ibid. (1982b), 18-19; and Pinto (1981), 25.
^{c} Entitled 'Crudel perche' in *Lbl* Egerton 3665, *Och* Mus. 61-6 and *US-Wc* M990 C66F4; 'Corsea' or 'Corisca' in *Och* Mus. 527-30 & 1024; and both titles are included in *Lbl* Add. 39,550-4.
^{d} Incomplete.
^{e} Untitled in all sources.
^{f} Entitled 'O sonno' in *Lbl* Egerton 3665, *Och* Mus. 61-6 and *US-Wc* M990 C66F4; and 'Deh preg'Amore' in *EIRE-Dm* Z3.4.1-6.
^{g} Another copy appears on f. 37^v. (Fully texted in *Ob* Tenbury 940-4 and *US-SM* EL 25 A 46-51.)

16ᵛ	[Coprario]	[In te mio novo sole]	6
17ᵛ	[Coprario]	[Del mio cibo amoroso]	7
18ᵛ	[Coprario]	[Al primo giorno *or* In un boschetto][h]	10
19ᵛ	[Coprario]	[Chi pue miravi *or* Non posso piu soffrire][i]	11
20ᵛ	[Ferrabosco II]	[In Nomine]	3
21ᵛ	[Ferrabosco II]	[In Nomine]	1
22ᵛ	[Ferrabosco II]	[In Nomine]	2
23ᵛ	[Mico]	[In Nomine]	-
24ᵛ	[Ferrabosco II]	[Pavan]	3
25	[Ferrabosco II]	[Pavan][j]	4
25ᵛ	[Ferrabosco II]	[Pavan][k]	9
26	[Ferrabosco II]	[Alman][k]	4
26ᵛ	[O. Gibbons]	[In Nomine]	2
27ᵛ	[Ferrabosco II]	[Pavan][l]	1
28	[Coprario]	[Leno]	47
28ᵛ	[Monteverdi]	[Voi pur da me partite][m]	-
29	[Monteverdi]	[Luci seren'e chiare][m]	-
29ᵛ	[Lupo]	[Fantasia]	4
30ᵛ	[Lupo]	[Fantasia]	2
31ᵛ	[Lupo]	[Fantasia]	1
32ᵛ	[Lupo]	[Fantasia]	3
33ᵛ	[Lupo]	[Fantasia]	11
34ᵛ	[Lupo]	[Fantasia]	12
35ᵛ	[Lupo]	[Fantasia]	13
36ᵛ	[Lupo]	[Fantasia]	14
37ᵛ	[Coprario]	[Deh cara anima mia][n]	32
37ᵛ		[Fantasia]	-
38ᵛ	[Lupo]	[Alte parole][o]	9
39ᵛ	[W. White]	['Diapente' Fantasia]	1
40ᵛ	[Ward]	[Leggiadre sei]	13

[h] Entitled 'Al primo giorno' in *Lbl* Egerton 3665 and *US-Wc* M990 C66F4; and 'In un boschetto' in Mad. Soc. G 37-42.

[i] Entitled 'Chi pue mirarvi' in *Lbl* Egerton 3665 and *US-Wc* M990 C66F4; and 'Non posso piu soffrire' in Mad. Soc. G 37-42 (although it is possible that this is the text of the entry at the 44th semibreve).

[j] The so-called 'Four Notes Pavan' is underlaid with Ben Jonson's text 'Hear me, O God' in the following sources: *Lbl* Add. 29,372-7, *Lbl* Egerton 2013, *Lbl* Egerton 3665, *Ob* Tenbury 1018 and *Och* Mus. 423-8.

[k] Begins imperfectly.

[l] The 'Dovehouse Pavan'; begins imperfectly.

[m] Textless madrigal, first published in *Il Quarto Libro de Madrigali a Cinque Voci* (Venice, 1603).

[n] Another copy appears on f. 14.

[o] Fantasia of madrigalian origin; title from *Lbl* Egerton 3665.

41ᵛ	[Ward]	[Dolce languir]	1
42ᵛ	[Monteverdi]	[Latral Parte Prima]ᵖ	-
43	[Mico]	[Parte Seconda]	-
43ᵛ	[Marenzio]	[Arda pur sempre o mora]ᑫ	-

MANUSCRIPT XV

LONDON, BRITISH LIBRARY EGERTON MS 2960

A scorebook of sacred and secular music by English and Italian composers.

The first layer was copied by Henry Bowman $c.1670$-90; the second layer was copied by an unidentified scribe and must be roughly contemporary with the first layer.

ff. i + 98.

Modern pencil foliation: ff. 1-65, one unnumbered folio [65a], 66-99 (f. 1 is the original paper cover). Original pagination: pp. 1-104; later pencil pagination: 105-28; two unnumbered pages; later pencil pagination: 67-1 (volume reversed).

Paper: ff. 2-53: 370 x 235 mm; ff. 54-99: 380 x 235 mm. Red marginal rulings on left and right. ff. 2-53ᵛ: twelve rastrum-ruled staves per page (ruled with a three-stave rastrum of 64 mm span and individual staves each measuring 12 mm); ff. 54-99ᵛ: sixteen rastrum-ruled staves per page (ruled with a four-stave rastrum of 71 mm span and individual staves each measuring 9.5-10 mm). No music entered on ff. 57ᵛ-58. 64, 65ᵛ, [65a]ʳ⁻ᵛ, 66.

Collation: not possible due to tightness of binding.

Watermark: ff. 2-53: fleur-de-lys with countermark VI; ff. 54-99: indistinguishable.

Script: ff. 2-53: Henry Bowman; ff. 54-99: unidentified; f. 99ᵛ: fragment in another unidentified hand.

Binding: modern (the original paper front cover survives as f. 1).

ᵖ 'Latral' is a textless version of 'La tra'l sangue e le morti egro', the second section of a three-section madrigal from Monteverdi's *Il Terzo Libro de Madrigali a Cinque Voci* (Venice, 1592) ('Vattene pur crudel', 'La tra'l sangue' and 'Poi ch'ella', text by Tasso). Mico's 'Parte Seconda' is attached in two other sources (*Ob* Mus. Sch. E 415-18, and *Och* Mus. 2, 404-8 & 436). 'Latral' contains a central chromatic fugato on a falling subject and Mico's piece contains a fugato on a rising subject; no other connection between the two is known and no explanation of Mico's contribution can presently be offered.

ᑫ Textless madrigal, first published in *Il Settimo Libro de Madrigali a Cinque Voci* (Venice, 1595).

Contents of *Lbl* Egerton MS 2960:[a]

Composer	Title	Scoring	Folio	Page	Printed Concordances
[Carissimi]	Lucifer, cælestis olim	Bbc	2	1	1693[1]
[Casati]	Sic ergo bone Jesu	Cbc	4^v	6	C1424
[Casati]	Benedicam Dominum	Cbc	7	11	C1411
[Sances]	Lætamini in Domino	Cbc	9^v	16	S768
[Sances]	Ardet cor meum	Cbc	12	21	S768
[Sances]	Conditor Cæli	Tbc	15	27	S768
[Sances]	Audite me, divini fructus	Bbc	17^v	32	S768
Gio: Felice Sances	Dulcis amor Jesu	Bbc	20	37	S768
[Sances]	Solvatur lingua mea	Tbc	21^v	40	S768
[Sances]	O quam speciosa	Abc	23	43	S768
[Sances]	Quemadmodum desiderat	Abc	25	47	S768
Caspari Cassati	Pater noster	Cbc	27	51	C1411
Cassati	Domine ad adjuvandum me	Cbc	28^v	54	C1411
Cassati	O bone Jesu	Cbc	29^v	56	C1411
Cassati	Fuge anima mea	Abc	31^v	60	C1411
[Casati]	Quam suavis es Domine	Cbc	33^v	64	C1424
Caspari Cassati	Veni amor Jesu	Cbc	35^v	68	C1424
Cassati	Assurgite de Vineis	Cbc	37^v	72	C1424
[Casati]	Quo fugiam miser	Cbc	39^v	76	C1424
Cassati	O Amor amantissime	Cbc	42	81	C1424
Sig^r. Pietro Reggio	Ye meaner beauties	Sbc	44^v	86	
Mr H[enry] A[ldrich]	Give ye king thy judgem[en]ts	Bbc	45	87	
Mr H[enry] A[ldrich]	I waited patiently for ye Lord	Cbc	47	91	
	Falalaleero[b]	A	50^v	98	
Signior Pietro Reggio	Happy Insect 'The Grasshopper'	Sbc	51	99	R724
Signiori Pietro Reggio	Foolish Prater what dost Thou see 'The Swallow'	Sbc	51^v	100	R724
[Reggio]	Arise yee subterranean Winds	Sbc	52^v	102	R724
Signior Pietro Reggio	I'll sing of Heroes 'Love'	Sbc	53	103	R724
M^r: Purcell	Ah mee! Too many Deaths 'Song written by M^r [John] Crowne'	Sbc	54	105	P5979, P6001
M^r: Purcell	Young Thirsis 'An Elegy upon M^r: Thomas Farmer'	SBbc	54^v	106	P5983
	Be wise and live fast	SSS	56	109	
[Purcell]	Fair Cloe my breast so alarms	SBbc	56^v	110	P5979, P6028-30, 1692[8]
M^r: Purcell	Fain Iris & her Swain 'A Dialogue M^r: Dryden'	SBbc	58^v	113	P5826, P5983, P6031
M^r: Purcell	Young Collin cleaving 'A Catch'	SSS	60	116	1691[6]

[a] The first eleven pieces appear in exactly the same sequence in another scorebook copied by Bowman: *Lbl* Add. 31,460; see MS VIII above.
[b] Fragment.

M^r. Purcell	Lost is my quiet for ere	SBbc	60^v	117	P5978-9, P6050-1, 1691[6]
D^r: Blow	O Nigrocella	Sbc	61^v	119	B2985, 1691[6]
	'A Fair Lover to his Black Mistress'				
M^r. Hen: Purcell	Why my Daphne	SBbc	62^v	121	P5983, 1691[6]
	'A Dialogue'				
[Courtville]	Vertumnus Flora	Sbc	64^v	125	1696[10]

Volume reversed:

	[Textless fragment]	SSB	99^v	1 rev
M^r: Ramsey	In guilty night[c]	SSBbc	99	2 rev
	'Saul and the Witch of Endor Mr Cowley'			
M^r: Purcell	High on a Throne	SBbc	97^v	5 rev
	'Ode on ye Queen. 1690. M^r: Durfey'[d]			
M^r: H[enry] Purcell	Praise ye Lord O my Soul	AB 2vln bc	95	9 rev
	'Anthem. Part of the 104th Psalm'			
D^r: Blow	The Angell Gabr'el	TBbc	90	20 rev
	'The Vision M^r: Cowley David: Lib: 2nd at ye Conclusion'[e]			
D^r: Blow	Alas poor death	SBbc	89	22 rev
	'A Dialogue Between Death and a Christian'			
M^r: Pel. Humphreys	Hear my prayer	SATB 2vln bc	88^v	23 rev
	'Part of the .55. Psalm'			
D^r: Blow	As on Euphrates Shady banks	SBbc	85^v	29 rev
	'A Paraphrase on ye 137.th Psalm Mr Sandys'[f]			
M^r: Lock	Blessed is he that considereth the poor 'Psalm .41. the .1. & 2. verses'	SATBbc	83	34 rev
D^r: [C.] Gibbons	Ah my soul why so dismay'd	SSBbc	82	36 rev
M^r: Hen: Cooke	Adjuro vos Filiae Jerusalem	CBbc	81	38 rev
[Carissimi]	Hodie Simon Petrus	TTbc	80	40 rev
Mr: Purcell	O Praise ye Lord O yee Heathens 'The .117. Psalm'	SATTBbc	79	42 rev
Mr: Purcell	O Praise God in his holiness 'Anthem / & strings & chorus Being the .150. Psalm'	ATBBbc	77^v	45 rev
Mr: Purcell	Why do ye Heathen 'Anthem / The second Psalm' & strings	ATBbc	71^v	56 rev
	[Textless fragment]	SSTTBBbc	67	66 rev

---

[c] See Smallman (1965), 142-3; and Chan (1980).
[d] D'Urfey, 'An Ode to the Queen', *New Poems, Consisting of Satyrs, Elegies, and Odes: Together with a Choice Collection of the Newest Court Songs* (London, 1690), 19-21.
[e] Cowley (1656), Pt. IV.
[f] Sandys (1636), 219-20.

MANUSCRIPT XVI

LONDON, BRITISH LIBRARY EVELYN MS 189[a]

Two of a set of four partbooks containing eight motets by Dering (all unattributed) and four anonymous motets (possibly also by Dering).

Copied 1625-40?
Two partbooks:

a *Bassus*: ff. 8. Original pagination: pp. 1-16. Paper: 199 x 158 mm. Six hand-ruled staves per page. Marginal rulings on left and right. No watermark visible. Collation: A-B^4.

b *Altus*: ff. 8. Original pagination: pp. 1-16. Paper: 199 x 158 mm. Six hand-ruled staves per page. Marginal rulings on left and right. Watermark: ff. [1] & [4] and [5] & [8]: grapes. Collation: A-B^4.

Scribe: unidentified.
No bindings.
Contents of *Lbl* Evelyn MS 189 a & b:

Composer	Title	Scoring	Pages a:Bassus b:Altus		Concordances[b]
[Dering]	Lætamini cum Maria	[C]TB[bc]	1	1	1662^4
[Dering]	Justus cor suum tradidit	[C/T]B[bc]	2	-	1662^4
[Dering]	Ardens est cor meu[m] 'a 2'	[C]B[bc]	3	-	1662^4
[Dering][c]	Alleluia gaudeamus	[C]CB[bc]	4	2	
[Dering]	Isti sunt sancti	[C]CB[bc]	5	3	1662^4
[Dering]	Gloria patri 'A 3'	A[T]B[bc]	6	5	1652^{10}, 1662^4
	Exultate justi	CC	7	6	
	Te gloriosus Apostoloru[m]	CB	9	8	
[Dering][d]	O nomen Jesu	[C]CB[bc]	10	10	
[Dering]	Panis angelicus	[C]CB[bc]	12	12	1662^4
	Si diligis me Simon Petre	CB	14	13	
	O dulcissime Jesu	AB	16	15	

---

[a] The Evelyn family papers have recently been purchased by the British Library and the manuscripts have not yet been catalogued; it is possible that the manuscripts will be assigned new call numbers. The call number cited in the present study is that used when the papers were on deposit in the library of Christ Church, Oxford.

[b] For manuscript concordances see Table 28c & d above.

[c] Not in Playford ed. 1662^4, but is attributed to Dering in *Lcm* 2033 & 2039 (both lack B). The discovery of Evelyn MS 189 means that the piece can now be completed.

[d] Not in Playford ed. 1662^4, but is attributed to Dering in *Lcm* 2033 (lacking B). The discovery of Evelyn MS 189 means that the piece can now be completed.

MANUSCRIPT XVII

LONDON, ROYAL COLLEGE OF MUSIC MS 920

Four partbooks containing English anthems and Latin motets for one to three voices and basso continuo by George Jeffreys.

Copied in the late 1650s or early 1660s.
Four partbooks bound together: ff. i + 191 + i.
Modern pencil foliation: partbook i: ff. 1-54^v; partbook ii: ff. 55-90^v; extra paper: ff. 91-8^v; partbook iii: ff. 99-159^v; partbook iv (basso continuo): ff. 160-91^v.
Paper: ff. 1-54^v, 91-8^v, 107-59^v: 290 x 215 mm; ff. 55-90^v: 280 x 215 mm; ff. 99-106^v: 280-5 x 215 mm; ff. 160-91^v: 290 x 195 mm (the bottom section of f. 181 is folded up revealing the measurements before trimming as 298 x 195 mm). Marginal rulings on left and right. ff. 1-159^v: eight rastrum-ruled staves per page (ruled with a two-stave rastrum of 39-40 mm span and individual staves each measuring 12 mm); ff. 160-91: ten rastrum-ruled staves per page (ruled with a five-stave rastrum of 109 mm span and individual staves each measuring 11.5-12 mm). No music entered on ff. 32, 40, 46^v-54^v, 84, 90^v-99, 102^v-6^v, 145, 151^v-9^v, 161^v, 190.
Collation: not possible due to tightness of binding.
Watermarks: ff. 1-159: not visible. ff. 160-91: Cardinals' hat with letters GR; Thompson (1988), Watermark XXII.
Scribe: George Jeffreys.
Inscription in pencil on f. i^v: 'all the parts complete. / These sacred Songs in one two and three / parts are the composition and in the handwriting of George Jefferies / an Organist of some celebrity, in the / middle of the seventeenth century / he was alive in 1675' (Thomas Oliphant).
Binding: modern.
Contents of *Lcm* MS 920:

Anthems and Motets by George Jeffreys

No.	Title	*Folios*				Scoring
		i	ii	iii	iv	
[1]	Prayse the Lord	-	-	99^v	160	Bbc
[2]	O Quam Suave	-	-	100^v	160^v	Bbc
[3]	Spetiosus forma	-	-	101^v	161	Bbc
[1]	Timor et Tremor 'Psalme 55'	1	-	107	162	TTbc
2	Audivi vocem de Cælo	1^v	-	107^v	162^v	TTbc
3	Domine Deus	2	-	108	163	TTbc

4	Si Diligitis me	2ᵛ	-	108ᵛ	163ᵛ	TTbc
5	Sive vigilem	3	-	109	164	TTbc
6	Erit gloria Domini 'Ps.' [sic]	3ᵛ	-	109ᵛ	164ᵛ	TTbc
7	Et ingrediar 'Ps 43'	4	-	110	165	TTbc
8	Heu me misera[m] 'Dialogue Maria & Angelis'	4ᵛ	-	110ᵛ	165ᵛ	CBbc
9	O Quam Dulcis	5ᵛ	-	111ᵛ	166ᵛ	CBbc
10	O Pretiosum	6ᵛ	-	112ᵛ	167	ABbc
11	O Panis Angelorum	7ᵛ	-	113ᵛ	167ᵛ	TBbc
12	O Nomen Jesu	8	-	114	168	ABbc
13	Jesu Rex Admirabilis	9	-	115	168ᵛ	ABbc
1	Unto thee O Lord [Pt 1]	10	55	116	169	TTBbc
2	Shew me thy wayes O Lord 2. pars	10ᵛ	55ᵛ	116ᵛ	169ᵛ	TTBbc
3	Heare my Prayer O Lord	11	56	117	170	TTBbc
4	Singe unto the Lord	11ᵛ	56ᵛ	117ᵛ	170ᵛ	TTBbc
5	Prayse the Lord O my soule	12	57	118	171	CCBbc
6	Brightest Sunne	12ᵛ	57ᵛ	118ᵛ	171ᵛ	TTBbc
7	Glory to God[a]	13ᵛ	58ᵛ	119ᵛ	172	ATBbc
8	Exurge [quare obdormis Domine]	14ᵛ	59ᵛ	120ᵛ	172ᵛ	TTBbc
9	O Quam Gloriosum[b]	15ᵛ	60ᵛ	121ᵛ	173	TTBbc
10	Lapidabant Stephanum	16ᵛ	61ᵛ	122ᵛ	173ᵛ	TTBbc
11	Et Recordatus	17ᵛ	62ᵛ	123ᵛ	174	TTBbc
12	Beatus [auctor saeculi]	18	63	124	174ᵛ	TTBbc
13	Jesu mi Dulcissime	18ᵛ	63ᵛ	124ᵛ	175	TTBbc
14	Vere languores	19ᵛ	64ᵛ	125ᵛ	175ᵛ	TTBbc
15	Nescio quid Amore	20	65	126	176	TTBbc
16	Utinam Concessa	20ᵛ	65ᵛ	126ᵛ	176ᵛ	TTBbc
17	Nil Canitar Suavius	21	66	127	177	TTBbc
18	Ecce dilectus meus	21ᵛ	66ᵛ	127ᵛ	177ᵛ	TTBbc
19	Prior Christus	22	67	128	178	TTBbc
20	Domine Jesu	22ᵛ	67ᵛ	128ᵛ	178ᵛ	TTBbc
21	Christo Jesu	23	68	129	179	TTBbc
22	Hosanna filio David	23ᵛ	68ᵛ	129ᵛ	179ᵛ	TTBbc
23	Heu mihi Domine	24ᵛ	69ᵛ	130	180	TTBbc
24	Visa Urbe	25	70	130ᵛ	180ᵛ	TTBbc
25	Invocavi Nomen	25ᵛ	70ᵛ	131	181	CCBbc
26	Jerusalem [quae occidis prophetas]	26ᵛ	71ᵛ	132	181ᵛ	CCBbc
27	Domine Dominus Noster	27	72	132ᵛ	182	AABbc
28	Caro mea	28	73	133ᵛ	182ᵛ	AABbc
29	O Deus meus	29	74	134ᵛ	183	ATBbc

[a] Dated May 1652 in *Lbl* Add. 10,338; see MS I above.
[b] 'Gloriosus' on f. 173.

30	Paratum cor meum[c]	30	75	135^v	183^v	ATBbc
31	O Quam iucundum[d]	31	75^v	136^v	184	ATBbc
32	Quando natus es[e]	32^v	76^v	137^v	184^v	ATBbc
33	Audite gentes	33^v	77^v	138^v	185	ATBbc
34	Gloria tua[f]	34^v	78^v	139^v	185^v	ATBbc
35	Gloria Patri	35^v	79^v	140^v	186	ATBbc
36	Florete Flores[g]	36	80	141	186^v	ATBbc
37	O Piissime domine Jesu	37	81	142	187	ATBbc
38	Salve Cælestis	38	82	143	187^v	ATBbc
39	Quid mihi est in Cælo[h]	39	83	144	188	ATBbc
40	See see the word is incarnate[i] 1º pars	40^v	84^v	145^v	188^v	ATBbc
41	The Paschall Lambe is offred 2º Pars	41^v	85^v	146^v	189	ATBbc
42	Glory be to the Lambe 3º pars	42^v	86^v	147^v	189^v	ATBbc
43	Pater de Cælis Deus [Pt 1] 'To the B[lesse]d Trinity'	43^v	87^v	148^v	190^v	TTBbc
44	Pater Bone [Pt 2] 'To the Bl[essed] Trinity'	44^v	88^v	149^v	191	TTBbc
45	O tu unus Deus Pater [Pt 3] 'To the Bl[essed] Trinity'	45^v	89^v	150^v	191^v	TTBbc

MANUSCRIPT XVIII

LONDON, ROYAL COLLEGE OF MUSIC MS 920A

Four partbooks containing canticles, mass movements, anthems and motets for four voices and basso continuo by George Jeffreys.

Copied late 1660s(?)-1675.
Five partbooks bound together: ff. i + 86 + i.
Modern pencil foliation: partbook i: ff. 1-18^v; partbook ii: ff. 19-35^v; partbook iii: ff. 36-52^v; partbook iv: ff. 53-69^v; partbook v (basso continuo): ff. 70-86^v.

---

[c] Dated November 1657 in *Lbl* Add. 10,338.
[d] Dated August 1658 in *Lbl* Add. 10,338.
[e] Dated December 1657 in *Lbl* Add. 10,338.
[f] Dated 1658/1659 in *Lbl* Add. 10,338.
[g] Dated 1660 in *Lbl* Add. 10,338.
[h] Dated October 1661 in *Lbl* Add. 10,338.
[i] Dated March-April 1662 in *Lbl* Add. 10,338.

Paper: 315-20 x 200 mm. Red marginal rulings on left and right. Ten rastrum-ruled staves per page (ruled with a five-stave rastrum of 121 mm span and individual staves each measuring 12.5-13.5 mm). The following folios are not ruled and act as 'endpapers' to each partbook: ff. 1, 18, 35, 52, 69, 86. No music entered on ff. 46^{r-v}, 78-81^v.

Collation: not possible due to tightness of binding (one gathering per partbook?).

Watermark: coat of arms (Amsterdam).

Scribe: George Jeffreys.

Inscriptions: f. i^v (pencil): 'The music in four Parts (all complete) / contained in theis volume is composed / by and in the handwriting of George / Jefferies. There is a date: Dec 1675 at the end of "He beheld the city".' (Thomas Oliphant); f. 63: 'Finis / [16]75' (Jeffreys); f. 77^v: 'Finis / Dec: [16]75' (Jeffreys).

Binding: modern.

Contents of *Lcm* MS 920A:

Music by George Jeffreys

No.	Title	Folios					Scoring
		i	ii	iii	iv	v	
2	Te Deum Laudamus[a][b]	2	19	36	53	70	AATBbc
3	Jubilate Deo[a]	4	21	37^v	55	71^v	AATBbc
4	Credo in unum Deum[a]	5	22	38^v	56	72	AATBbc
5	Magnificat[a]	6^v	23^v	40	57^v	73^v	AATBbc
6	Nunc dimittis[a]	7^v	24^v	41	58^v	74	AATBbc
1	Venite exultemus[a]	8	25	41^v	59	74^v	AATBbc
	Holy, holy, holy Lord 'At the Office Bl[essed] Sacrament'	9	26^v	43	60^v	75^v	CATBbc
	Glory be to God on high[c]	9	26	42^v	60	75^v	CATBbc
	Great and Marvelous 'Hymne'	10	26^v	43^v	61	76	CATBbc
	How wretched is the state	10^v	27^v	44^v	61^v	76^v	CATBbc
	Awake my Soule	11^v	28^v	45	62^v	77	CATBbc
	He beheld the Citty 'Luc: 19'	12	28^{vd}	45^v	63	77^v	CATBbc

---

[a] In Latin.
[b] Dated 1649 in *Lbl* Add. 10,338; see MS I above.
[c] Dated May 1652 in *Lbl* Add. 10,338.
[d] Folio 28^v contains the tenor part to 'He beheld' with a note stating that 'This Tenor part was misplaced'; the alto part is copied on f. 29 and the tenor was copied again in its proper place in partbook iii, f. 45^v.

Volume reversed:

1	O Domine Deus [Pt 1]	17ᵛ	34ᵛ	51ᵛ	68ᵛ	85ᵛ	ATTBbc
2	O Deus meus 2º Pars	17	34	51	68	85	ATTBbc
3	O Quam iucundumᵉ	16ᵛ	33ᵛ	50ᵛ	67ᵛ	84ᵛ	ATTBbc
4	In the Midst of Lifeᶠ	15ᵛ	33	50	67	84	AATBbc
5	Turne thee againeᵍ	15	32	49	66	83ᵛ	AATBbc
6	Turn thou usʰ	14	31	48	65	83	ATTBbc
	Gloria Patri	13	30	47ᵛ	64	82ᵛ	AATBbc
	Gloria Patri qui Creavit nosⁱ	12ᵛ	29ᵛ	47	63ᵛ	82	ATTBbc

MANUSCRIPT XIX

LONDON, ROYAL COLLEGE OF MUSIC MS 2033

Three of a set of four partbooks containing motets and a single anthem for three voices and basso continuo by Richard Dering and George Jeffreys (the bass part is lacking).

Copied in the 1640s?

i (Cantus I): ff. 24 + ii. Modern pencil foliation: ff. 1-17, followed by seven unnumbered folios [18]-[24]. Collation: A-C⁸. No music entered on ff. 1, 17-[24]ᵛ. Script: three unidentified scribes A-C (ff. 1-14: A (music & text); ff. 14ᵛ-17: B (music and ascriptions) and C (text)).ᵃ Inscription on f. 1: '1 / Motetts for Three Voices / No. 13 bears the name of Mr [George] Jefferies / Organist to Charles I at Oxford during the troubles / The last there / also no. 1, 6, 8, 10, 11 and 12 / are by Rich Deering, who was / Organist to Queen Henrietta during the same period / and died in 1657 - Probably the whole are by the / two masters. / [circa 1650]' (Thomas Oliphant).ᵇ

ii (Cantus II): ff. 24 + ii. Modern pencil foliation: ff. 1-16, followed by eight unnumbered folios [17]-[24]. Collation: A-C⁸. No music entered on ff. 1, [17]-[24]ᵛ. Script: three unidentified scribes (ff. 1-14: A (music & text);

ᵉ Dated 1651 in *Lbl* Add. 10,338.
ᶠ Dated October 1657 in *Lbl* Add. 10,338.
ᵍ Dated 1648 in *Lbl* Add. 10,338.
ʰ Dated 1655 in *Lbl* Add. 10,338.
ⁱ Dated 1651 in *Lbl* Add. 10,338
ᵃ Scribes A and B also copied *Lcm* 2034; see MS XX below.
ᵇ Oliphant is inaccurate concerning the date of Dering's death: he died in 1630; see *New Grove*, v, 382. (The square brackets within the inscriptions are Oliphant's.)

ff. 14ᵛ-[16]ᵛ: B (music and ascriptions) and C (text)). Inscription on f. 1: '2 / Motetts for Three Voices / [circa 1650]' (Oliphant).

iii (Basso Continuo): ff. 24 + ii. Modern pencil foliation: ff. 1-17, followed by seven unnumbered folios [18]-[24]. Collation: A-C⁸. No music entered on ff. 1, 17ᵛ-[24]ᵛ. Script: three unidentified scribes (ff. 1-14: A (music & text); ff. 14ᵛ-[17]: B (music and ascriptions) and C (text)). Inscription on f. 1: '3 / Motetts for Three Voices / [circa 1650]' (Oliphant).

Paper: 137 x 210-15 mm. Marginal rulings on left and right. Five rastrum-ruled staves per page (ruled with a five-stave rastrum of 119 mm span and individual staves each measuring 12.5-13 mm).
Watermark: not visible.
Bindings: modern.
Contents of *Lcm* MS 2033:ᶜ

No.	Composer	Title	Scoring	Folios i	ii	iii
1	[Dering]	Qualis est dilectus tuus	CT[B]bc	1ᵛ	1ᵛ	1ᵛ
2	[Dering]	Panis Angelicus	CC[B]bc	2ᵛ	2ᵛ	2ᵛ
3	[Dering]	Vulnerasti cor meum	TT[B]bc	3ᵛ	3ᵛ	3ᵛ
4	[Dering]	Lætamini cum Maria	TC[B]bc	4ᵛ	4ᵛ	4ᵛ
5	[Dering]	Gloria Patri	AT[B]bc	5ᵛ	5ᵛ	5ᵛ
6	[Jeffreys]ᵈ	Ecce dilectus meus	TT[B]bc	6	6	6
7	[Dering]	Justus germinabit	TT[B]bc	6ᵛ	6ᵛ	6ᵛ
8	[Dering]	Isti sunt sancti	CC[B]bc	7ᵛ	7ᵛ	7ᵛ
9	[Dering]	O quam suavis est Domine	CC[B]bc	8ᵛ	8ᵛ	8ᵛ
10	[Dering]	Tibi laus	CT[B]bc	9ᵛ	9ᵛ	9ᵛ
11	[Dering?]ᵉ	Exultavit cor meum	CC[B]bc	10ᵛ	10ᵛ	10ᵛ
12	[Jeffreys]	Prior Christus	CC[B]bc	11ᵛ	11ᵛ	11ᵛ
13	Mʳ. Jefferies	Sing unto the Lord	TT[B]bc	12ᵛ	12ᵛ	12ᵛ
14	[Dering]	Cantate Domino	CC[B]bc	13ᵛ	13ᵛ	13ᵛ
	Rich dering	Alleluia gaudeamus	CC[B]bc	14ᵛ	14ᵛ	14ᵛ
	Rich dering	O Nomen Jesu	CC[B]bc	15ᵛ	15ᵛ	15ᵛ
	Rich dering	Veni sponsa Christi	CC[B]bc	16ᵛ	16ᵛ	16ᵛ

ᶜ For the concordant sources (printed and manuscript) of the Dering motets see Table 28, and for the Jeffreys pieces see Table 23.
ᵈ Later pencil misattribution to Dering in i.
ᵉ A later pencil annotation in *Och* Mus. 877-80 attributes the piece to Dering (on uncertain grounds); see also Excursus I.

MANUSCRIPT XX

LONDON, ROYAL COLLEGE OF MUSIC MS 2034

Two of a set of three partbooks containing motets for two voices and basso continuo by Richard Dering and Giacomo Finetti (misattributed to Dering).

Copied in the 1640s?

i (Cantus I): ff. i + 21. Modern pencil foliation: ff. 1-21. No music entered on ff. 1, 21^v. Collation: not possible due to tightness of binding. Script: two unidentified scribes (A: ff. 1-17; B: ff. 17^v-21).[a] Inscription on f. i: '1 / Motetts for two voices / No / 2, 5, 9, 11, 17 to 21 / and probably the whole / are composed by Rich^d. Deering / who was Organist to Queen Henrietta / until the troubles of the times obliged him to / leave the country. / [circa 1650]' (Thomas Oliphant).[b]

ii (Basso Continuo): ff. 21. Modern pencil foliation: ff. 1-21. No music entered on ff. 1, 21^v. Collation: A-B^8 C^6(C2 removed). Script: two unidentified scribes (A: ff. 1-17; B: ff. 17^v-21). Inscription on f. 1: '2 / Motetts for Two voices' (Oliphant).

Paper: 137 x 210 mm. Marginal rulings on left and right. Five rastrum-ruled staves per page (ruled with a five-stave rastrum of 119 mm span and individual staves each measuring 12.5-13 mm).
Watermark: not visible.
Bindings: modern.
Contents of *Lcm* MS 2034:[c]

No.	Composer	Title	Scoring	Folios i	ii
1	[Dering]	Canite Jehovæ	C[B]bc	1^v	1^v
2	[Dering]	Ardens est cor meum	C[B]bc	2^v	2^v [d]
3		Angelus ad Pastores	C-bc	3^v	3^v
4	[Dering]	Beatus vir	T[T]bc	4^v	4^v
5	[Dering]	O bone Jesu	T[T]bc	5^v	5^v
6	[Dering]	Duo seraphim	T[T]bc	6^v	6^v
7	[Dering]	Veni electa mea	C[B]bc	7^v	7^v

---

[a] The same two scribes also contributed to the copying of *Lcm* 2033; see MS XIX above.
[b] Oliphant is inaccurate concerning Dering's biographical details: he died in 1630; see *New Grove*, v, 382. (The square brackets within the inscriptions are Oliphant's.)
[c] For the concordant sources (printed and manuscript) of the Dering motets see Table 28.
[d] Short score; a later hand has added the full text.

8	[Dering]	Sancta et immaculata	T[T]bc	8ᵛ	8ᵛ
9	[Dering]	Justus cor suum tradidit	T[B]bc	9ᵛ	9ᵛ ᵉ
10	[Dering]	Gaudent in cælis	T[T]bc	10ᵛ	10ᵛ ᵉ
11	[Dering]	Gratias tibi Deus	C[B]bc	11ᵛ	11ᵛ
12	[Dering]	Miserere mei Deus	S[B]bc	12ᵛ	12ᵛ
13	[Dering]	O Domine Jesu Christe	S[B]bc	13ᵛ	13ᵛ
14	[Dering]	Ego dormio	B[B]bc	14ᵛ	14ᵛ
15		Dulcissime Jesu Christe	C-bc	15ᵛ	15ᵛ
16	[Dering]	Conceptio tua	S[B]bc	16ᵛ	16ᵛ
17	[Finetti]ᶠ	Quam dilecta	C[B]bc	17ᵛ	17ᵛ
18	Richard deering [*recte* Finetti]ᶠ	Vox dilecti mei	C[T]bc	18ᵛ	18ᵛ
19	Richard deering [*recte* Finetti]ᶠ	Sit nomen domini	T[T]bc	19ᵛ	19ᵛ
20	Richard deering[?]ᵍ	domine deus gratia	S-bc	20ᵛ	20ᵛ
21	Richard deering[?]ᵍ	Gloria tibi Domine	S-bc	20ᵛ	21
22	Richard deering[?]ᵍ	Sanctum et terribile	S-bc	21	21ᵛ

MANUSCRIPT XXI

LONDON, ROYAL COLLEGE OF MUSIC MS 2039

Three of a set of five partbooks containing consort music, devotional songs and motets by English composers.

Copied in the 1640s?

i: ff. i + 53. Modern pencil foliation: ff. 1-42 followed by eleven unnumbered folios [43]-[53]. No music entered on ff. [43]-[53]ᵛ. Collation: not possible due to tightness of binding (various pages removed: stubs remain). Script: six unidentified scribes (A: ff. 1-5; B: ff. 5ᵛ-9; C: ff. 9ᵛ-31; D: ff. 31ᵛ-34ᵛ; E: 35ᵛ-39; F: 39ᵛ-[42]ᵛ). Inscription on f. i: 'Treble: 3 Parts / Mʳ Sandly. / Mr Deerings / 2 and 3 parts' (hand E); and f. iᵛ: 'Canto' (in red ink).

ᵉ A later hand has added text to the basso continuo part.
ᶠ Printed sources: G. Finetti, *Motecta Binis Vocibus Concinenda... Libro Secundus* (A. Gardano, Venice, 1611) [*RISM* F815]; and ibid., *Cantiones Binis Vocibus Concinendae... Liber Tertius* (B. Magni, Venice, 1613) [*RISM* F820].
ᵍ These attributions must be treated with caution in light of the preceding misattributions to Dering.

ii: ff. i + 63. Modern pencil foliation: ff. 1-48 followed by fifteen unnumbered folios [49]-[63]. No music entered on ff. 48^v-[63]^v. Collation: not possible due to tightness of binding. Script: seven unidentified scribes (A: ff. 1-5; B: ff. 5^v-9; C: ff. 9^v-32; D: ff. 32^v-35^v; E: ff. 36-38^v, 39^v-42; F: 39, 42^v-44^v; G: 45-8). Inscription on f. i: 'Tenor: 3 parts / Mr Sandly. / Mr Deerings / 2 and 3 parts: Bassus Continuus' (hand E); and f. i^v: 'Alto' (in red ink).

iii: ff. ii + 59. Modern pencil foliation: ff. 1-32 followed by twenty-seven unnumbered folios [33]-[59]. No music entered on ff. 32^v-[59]^v. Collation: not possible due to tightness of binding. Script: five unidentified scribes (A: ff. 1-5; B: ff. 5^v-9; C: ff. 9^v-27; E: ff. 27^v, 30^v-31; F: 28-30, 32).[a] Inscription on f. i: 'Mr Deerings / 2 and 3 parts' (hand E); and f. ii^v: 'Tenor' (in red ink).

Paper: 140 x 190 mm. Marginal rulings on left and right. Five rastrum-ruled staves per page (ruled with a five-stave rastrum of 112-13 mm span and individual staves each measuring 12 mm).

Watermark: pot with letters AB.

Bindings: brown leather with gold tooling: initials RB and coat of arms of the Prince of Wales.

Contents of *Lcm* MS 2039:[b]

No.	Composer	Title	Scoring	Folios i	ii	iii
1		[Pavan *a* 5]	CAT--vl	1	1	1
2		[Pavan *a* 5]	CAT--vl	1^v	1^v	1^v
3		[Pavan *a* 5]	SAT--vl	2	2	2
4		[Alman *a* 5]	SAT--vl	2^v	2^v	2^v
5	[Tomkins][c]	[Pavan *a* 5]	CAT--vl	3	3	3
6	[Weelkes][d]	[Pavan *a* 5]	SAT--vl	3^v	3^v	3^v
7		[Galliard *a* 5]	SAT--vl	4	4	4
8	Mr. Reade[e]	[Pavan *a* 5?]	SAT--vl	4^v	4^v	4^v
9	Mr. Reade[e]	[Galliard *a* 5?]	SAT--vl	5	5	5
10		[Pavan *a* 5]	SAT--vl	5^v	5^v	5^v
		[Galliard *a* 5]	SAT--vl	6	6	6
		[Pavan *a* 5]	SAT--vl	6^v	6^v	6^v

[a] Scribes E and F appear to have worked in conjunction: F often supplied the text to E's music.
[b] For the concordant sources (printed and manuscript) of the Dering and Jeffreys motets see Tables 28 and 23 respectively.
[c] G. Dodd ed., *Thematic Index of Music for Viols*, The Viola da Gamba Society (London, 1980-), TOMKINS-3 Pavan No. 6.
[d] *Lbl* Add. 30,826-8, no. 16: 'Mr Weelkes his 3 pavin'.
[e] Richard Reade (*fl*.1570-1616) singing-man at Christ Church, Oxford?

London, Royal College of Music MS 2039   295

	[Alman a 5]	SAT--vl	7	7	7
	[Pavan a 5]	SAT--vl	7ᵛ	7ᵛ	7ᵛ
	[Pavan a 5]	SAT--vl	8	8	8
	[Pavan a 5]	SAT--vl	8ᵛ	8ᵛ	8ᵛ
	[Galliard a 5]	SAT--vl	9	9	9
1	Confirme the thinge O god 'Psa: 80 / ver: 5o'	CC[B]	9ᵛ	9ᵛ	-
2	Thou shalt find us	CC[B]	10ᵛ	10ᵛ	-
3	O lord god bow ye heavens 'Psalm,. 144, ver: 5ᵗʰ'	CB-	11ᵛ	11ᵛ	-
4	O sacred communion	CC[B]	12ᵛ	12ᵛ	-
5	I will magnifie thee 'Psalm,. 33. Exultabo. &c.'	CC[B]	13	13	-
6	In that very tyme	CC[B]	14	14	-
7	Sanctifie thou O lord	CC[B]	15	15	-
8	Behould the bread of Angells	CC[B]	16	15ᵛ	-
9	The bread of Angells	SS[B]	16ᵛ	16ᵛ	-
10	As I came by the liuing father	CC[B]	17	17ᵛ	-
11	When the day of pentecoste	SS[B]	18	18ᵛ	-
12	O thou eternall trinitye	SS[B]	19	20	-
13	O comfortable sacrifice	CCBᶠ	19ᵛ	20ᵛ	9ᵛ
14	Rise up speedilye	CC[B]	20	21	-
15	Come [an]d rejoyce	CC[B]	21	22	-
16	Come my joye my chosen	SS[B]	21ᵛ	23	-
17	That childe whoe is borne	SS[B]	22ᵛ	23ᵛ	-
18	Here is the beloued	CC[B]	23ᵛ	24ᵛ	-
19	Ther[e] was a man sent downe	CC[B]	24ᵛ	25ᵛ	-
20	Gabriell the Angell	SS[B]	25ᵛ	27	-
21	Thou are [that] shepherd	SS[B]	26ᵛ	27ᵛ	-
22	On this day Symon Peter	SC[B]	27	28ᵛ	-
23	In that tyme thus spake	CC[B]	28	29ᵛ	-
24	Hee's truly a martyr	CC[B]	28ᵛ	30	-
	Joye is in heaven	CC[B]	29ᵛ	30ᵛ	-
25 [sic]	Come thou spouse of christ	SS[B]	30ᵛ	31ᵛ	-
	All haile comfortable sacrifice	-B	-	-	10
	All haile thou true body	-B	-	-	10ᵛ
	I am that true bread	-B	-	-	11
	O world[']s sauiour	-B	-	-	11ᵛ
	O Lord my god	-B	-	-	12
	Remember now o lord	-B	-	-	12ᵛ
	O holy bread of life	-B	-	-	13

ᶠ iii f. 9ᵛ incorrectly states: 'A.2.'

		A certaine man did make	-B	-	-	13v
		O bread delicious	-T	-	-	14v
		Whoe more to many	-T	-	-	15
		Behould where he cometh	-B	-	-	16
		To thee be praise	-T	-	-	16v
		The righteous called	-B	-	-	17v
		If the Lord himselfe	-B	-	-	18v
		The wise men seeing	-B	-	-	19v
		O singe unto the Lord	-B	-	-	20v
		Maruellous glad tidings	-C	-	-	21v
		Come my joye my chosen	-C	-	-	22v
		I have not put my trust	-B	-	-	23v
		Betweene the vesterye	-B	-	-	24v
		O lord god of all consolation	-B	-	-	25
		As on this daye	-B	-	-	26v
1	Mr Sandly[g]	Prelud[e]	SA[B] vl	31v	32v	-
2	[Sandley]	Almaine	SA[B] vl	31v	32v	-
3	[Sandley]	Corant	SA[B] vl	32	33	-
4	[Sandley]	Sarabrand	SA[B] vl	32	33	-
5	[Sandley]	Prelud[e]	SA[B] vl	32v	33v	-
6	[Sandley]	Almaine	SA[B] vl	32v	33v	-
7	[Sandley]	Corant	SA[B] vl	33	34	-
8	[Sandley]	Sarab[and]	SA[B] vl	33	34	-
9	[Sandley]	Prelud[e]	SA[B] vl	33v	34v	-
10	[Sandley]	Almaine	SA[B] vl	34	35	-
12	[Sandley]	Corant	SA[B] vl	34v	35	-
13	[Sandley]	Sarabrand	SA[B] vl	35	35v	-
	Mr Deering	Tibi laus	CT[B]bc	38v	38	27v
	[Dering]	O Domine Jesu Christe	CTBbc	39v	38v [h]	28
	Mr Deeringe	Halleluiah, Gaudeamus	CC[B]bc	40	39v	28v
	R: Deereing	Qualis est dilectus tuus	CC[B]bc	41	40v	29v
	Mr Deering	Justus cor su[u]m tradidit	CBbc	35v	36 [h]	-
	Mr Deering	Gratias tibi Deus	CBbc	36v	36v [h]	-
	Mr Deering	O bone Jesu	TTbc	37	37	30v
	Mr Deering	Ardens est cor meum	C[B]bc	37v	37v	-
	[Jeffreys]	Ecce dilectus meus	[TT]Bbc	-	39 [h]	-
	R: Deering	Isti sunt sancti	CC[B]bc	42	41v	31v

[g] Presumably Ben Sandley, whose two-part ayres were published in J. Playford ed., *Court-Ayres* (London, 1655); the dances by 'Mr Sandly' in *Lcm* 2039 are not listed in Dodd ed. (1980-).
[h] Both the bass-voice part and the basso continuo combined.

[Dering?][i]	Exultavit cor meum	[CCB]bc	-	42v	-
[Jeffreys]	Prior Christus	[CCB]bc	-	43v	-
[Dering]	Veni sponsa Christi	[CCB]bc	-	44v	-
Dr Rogers	Laudate Dominum	-A--[bc]	-	45	-
	Gloria Patri	-A-?[bc]	-	46	-
	Canite Jehovæ	-A-?[bc]	-	46v	-
Dr Rogers	Quem vidistis	-A-?[bc]	-	47	-

MANUSCRIPT XXII

OXFORD, BODLEIAN LIBRARY MUSIC SCHOOL MS C 9

A score of sacred and secular music mostly by Italian composers, collected by Richard Goodson II who incorporated leaves from earlier books with his own copies.

Compiled in the early eighteenth century.
ff. i + 153 + i.[a]
Original pagination: two unnumbered pages [a]-[b], pp. 1-252, 254-305 (253 was omitted in error).
Paper: 350 x 235 mm. Red marginal rulings on left and right. Twelve rastrum-ruled staves per page (pp. 1-24, 87-94, 119-26, 169-208, 217-85 ruled with a four-stave rastrum of 94.5 mm span and individual staves each measuring 13-13.5 mm; pp. 25-44 ruled with a three-stave rastrum of 64 mm span and individual staves each measuring 11.5 mm; pp. 79-86, 95-118, 127-68, 209-16 ruled with a four-stave rastrum of 95.5 mm span and individual staves each measuring 12-12.5 mm; pp. 45-78, 286-99 ruled with a four-stave rastrum of 93-93.5 mm span and individual staves each measuring 12-12.5 mm; pp. 300-5 ruled with a four-stave rastrum of 96 mm span and individual staves each measuring 12.5-13.5 mm). No music entered on pp. [a], [b], 15, 20-4, 45, 127, 169, 215-16, 240-1, 300. Index by Philip Hayes inside front cover. The following pages preserve their original page numbers (bottom right-hand corner, reversed): pp. 25-32 (= 136-129), 33-40 (= 94-87), and 41-5 (= 144-141).

---

[i] A later pencil annotation in *Och* Mus. 877-80 attributes the piece to Dering (on uncertain grounds); see also Excursus I.
[a] A loose-leaf index has recently been removed from the front of *Ob* Mus. Sch. C 9 and is now enclosed in the folder *Ob* Mus. Sch. A 641; the index is in Lowe's hand and lists various loose papers, at least some of which can now be found in *Ob* Mus. Sch. C 204 (see MS XXIX below).

Watermark: pp. [a] & [b], 1-24, 87-94, 119-26, 169-208, 217-85: fleur-de-lys with countermark DS; pp. 25-44, 79-86, 95-118, 127-68: fleur-de-lys with countermark IHS / IC (Thompson (1988), Watermark XXXVIII); pp. 45-78: fleur-de-lys with countermark HG; pp. 209-16: fleur-de-lys with countermark IHS / ET (Thompson (1988), Watermark XLII); pp. 286-99: fleur-de-lys with countermark P; pp. 300-5: fleur-de-lys with countermark GP.

Collation: not possible due to tightness of binding (numerous pages have been removed - stubs remain - and a number of singletons have been added).

Script: pp. 1-14, 16-19, 87-94, 150-68, 170-214, 217-39, 242-52, 254-99, 301-5: Richard Goodson II (the basso continuo part on pp. 204-11 was copied by an unidentified scribe); pp. 25-44, 95-118: Francis Smith;[b] pp. 46-86, 119-26, 128-50: Edward Lowe (the text on pp. 148-9 was copied by an unidentified scribe); pp. 203-11: unidentified.

Inscriptions: f. i[r]: 'Richard' (Goodson II); p. 55: 'See this Piece printed in ye 2[d] Book / of Harmonia Sacra' (Goodson II); verso of endpage: '3 Singing parts / square books 7 & ye blew schore [sic] - as pants with / Blow / Crofts act Musick / Acis & Galatea' (Goodson II, referring to *Och* Mus. 68-75 and 615); inside back cover: 'Richard Goodson. Christ Church Coll / This Book was bequeath'd / to the Music School / by Richard Goodson Jun[r]. Bac. Mus. / and / Professor of Music / in this University / Oxford.'

Binding: brown calf with blind tooling.

Contents of *Ob* Mus. Sch. MS C 9:

Page	Composer	Title	Scoring	Printed Sources
1	Sig[r]: Alessandro Stradella	Benedictus Dominus Deus	CAbc	
16	D Ellis	Date jam modulos 'Cho.'	SCATBbc	
25	Carissime	Sicut mater consolatur filios suos	CCbc	C1221
31	Carissime	O Quam mirabilia sunt	CCbc	1675[3]
37	Carissime	Anima nostra sustinet Dominum	CCbc	C1221
46	[Monferrato][c]	Salve Regina	ATBbc	M3037
51	Sig: Carissimo	Audite Sancti	CCBbc	C1221, 1645[2], 1656[2], 1693[1]

---

[b] Francis Smith (1672-98) was a singing man at Christ Church, Oxford *c*.1692-6, and also worked as an artist and engraver (he was Peter de Walpergen's partner in the publication of *Musica Oxoniensis* (Oxford, 1698) for which he designed the moveable typeface). Smith was paid three times for copying music at Christ Church between 1693 and 1696; these copies survive in *Och* Mus. 1220-4 and 1246. I am grateful to Dr Robert Thompson for this information.

[c] Misattributed to 'Carissime' in Philip Hayes' index; also misattributed to Carissimi in *Lbl* Add. 31,476, *Lbl* Add. 31,477, & *Lcm* 1064.

Oxford, Bodleian Library Music School MS C 9   299

56	Joha. Baptista [*recte* F.M. Marini]	Anima mea liquefacta est	CABbc	M672
60	Felice Sances	Plag[a]e tu[a]e Domine	ATBbc	S768
66	Felice Sances	O Domine gutt[a]e	ATBbc	S768
72	[Monteverdi]^d	Tu dormi Ah crudo core	AATbc	M3494
75	[Monteverdi]^d	Allume del[l]e stelle	CCTbc	M3497
78	[Monteverdi]^d	Parlo misero	CCBbc	M3497
82	Carissimi^e	Amante che dite^f	CCBbc	
86	Carissimi^e [*recte* Locke]	Gloria patri 'Canon 4 in 2'	SSTB	
87	Bassani [*or* Carissimi?]^g	O quam suave	CCCbc	
95	Charissimi	Cum vocasset in prœlium 'Jephtha'	CCCATBbc	
119	Carissime^e	E pur v[u]ole il Cielo	CCbc	
128	Charissime	Exultabunt justi	CCCbc	
137	Charissime	A solis ortu^h 'Judicium Salomonis'	CCTBbc	
148	Sig^r: Carissime	Annuntiate gentes^i	CCATBbc	C1222
156	Sign: Carissime	Confitebor Tibi Domine	CCBbc	1646^2, 1662^2
170	Carissime	Exulta gaude filia Sion	CCbc	C1222
175	Carissimi	Cantabo Domino	CCbc	C1222
180	Carissimi	Quo tam lætus	CCbc	C1221-2
187	Carissimi	Laudemus virum gloriosum	CCbc	C1222, 1656^2
192	Carissimi	Cum reverteretur David	CCCbc	C1222
198	G Carissimi	Egredimini cælestis curiæ	CCCbc	1657^j
203	Carissimi	A pie d'un verde'alloro 'Duetto [Democritus et Heraclitus]'	CCbc	
212	J.P. Prænestini [Palestrina]	Manus tuæ Domine^k	CATTBbc	P728
217	[Palestrina]	[Tui] sunt cœli^l	SMAAT	P746-7
220	[Palestrina]	Elegerunt Apostoli	SMAAT	P746-7

---

^{d} Attributed to 'Felice Sances' in Philip Hayes' index.
^{e} Attribution added by Philip Hayes.
^{f} Last movement of the cantata *I Naviganti* ('Sciolto hauean').
^{g} Attributed to Carissimi in *Lbl* Add. 31,477, *Ob* Tenbury 926, and *Och* Mus. 83; to Bassani in *Lbl* Add. 31,399, *Ob* Mus. d 16, *Ob* Mus. Sch. C 9 & *Ob* Tenbury 335; anonymous in *Lcm* 995.
^{h} The English text 'O pr[ais]e ye name of ye L[or]d' has been added in pencil to the final chorus 'Plaudite Regi'.
^{i} The copying of 'Annuntiate gentes' was begun by Lowe (pp. 148-50) and completed by Goodson II (pp. 150-5); the text was copied by an unidentified scribe.
^{j} A. Poggioli ed., *Delectus Sacrarum Cantionum* (P. Phalèse, Antwerp, 1652): not in *RISM*.
^{k} Part 2 of 'Paucitas dierum' from *Motettorum Quinque Vocibus Liber Quintus* (Rome, 1584).
^{l} Lacks beginning.

223	[Palestrina]	Justus ut palma	SMAAT	P746-7
226	[Palestrina]	Anima nostra sicut passer	SMAAT	P746-7
230	[Palestrina]	Posuisti Domine	SMATB	P746-7
233	[Palestrina]	Deus enim firmavit orbem	SMAAT	P746-7
236	[Palestrina]	Inveni David	SMAAT	P746-7
242	[Bassani]	Pulchra es amica mea	CCbc	
251	[Bassani]	Advolate fideles populi[m]	CCbc	
258	[Casati]	Exultate Justi	CCbc	C1411
263	Casatus	Magnificate cæli	CCbc	C1411
269	Bassani	Lætare filia Principes	CCbc	B1191
277	Stradella	La ragion m'assicura[n]	CBbc & inst	
284	[Locke]	Agnosce O Christiane	CBbc	1674[2]
287	Dr Chris. Gibbons	Celebrate dominum	CBbc	1674[2]
290	Bassani	Gaude Alma dilecta	CCAbc	B1191
299		'Aria'[o]	SSSbc	
301	Bononcini	Impara a non dar fede 'Cantata'	Cbc	

MANUSCRIPT XXIII

OXFORD, BODLEIAN LIBRARY MUSIC SCHOOL MS C 10

A manuscript copy of Giovanni Felice Sances' *Motetti* (Venice, 1638).[a]

Copied in the 1670s?
Five partbooks:

i *Canto*: ff. ii + 31 + ii. Modern pencil foliation: ff. 1-35 (the flyleaves are numbered). Original pagination: pp. 1-61, followed by one unnumbered page. Collation: A^6(A3 removed) B^6 C^8(C1 removed) $D-E^6$ F^1. f. 33^v contains a copy of the 'Tavola' (Husbands). Inscription on front cover: 'Felice Sances / Canto:' (Husbands).

ii *Alto*: ff. ii + 20 + ii. Modern pencil foliation: ff. 36-59 (the flyleaves are numbered). Original pagination: pp. 1-39, followed by one unnumbered

---

[m] Incomplete.
[n] From the cantata 'Vola, vola in altri petti'; see Gianturco & McCrickard (1991), 103-5.
[o] Textless fragment.
[a] The parts are described in the 1682 catalogue of the Music School manuscripts (*Ob* Mus. Sch. C 204* [R]) as 'A set of Latine Songs for 3 & 4 Voices composed by Felice Sances'; see M. Crum, 'Early Lists of the Oxford Music School Collection', *ML*, xlviii (1967), 23-34.

Plate 1 Oxford, Christ Church Mus. 708

Plate 2 Oxford, Christ Church Mus. 432

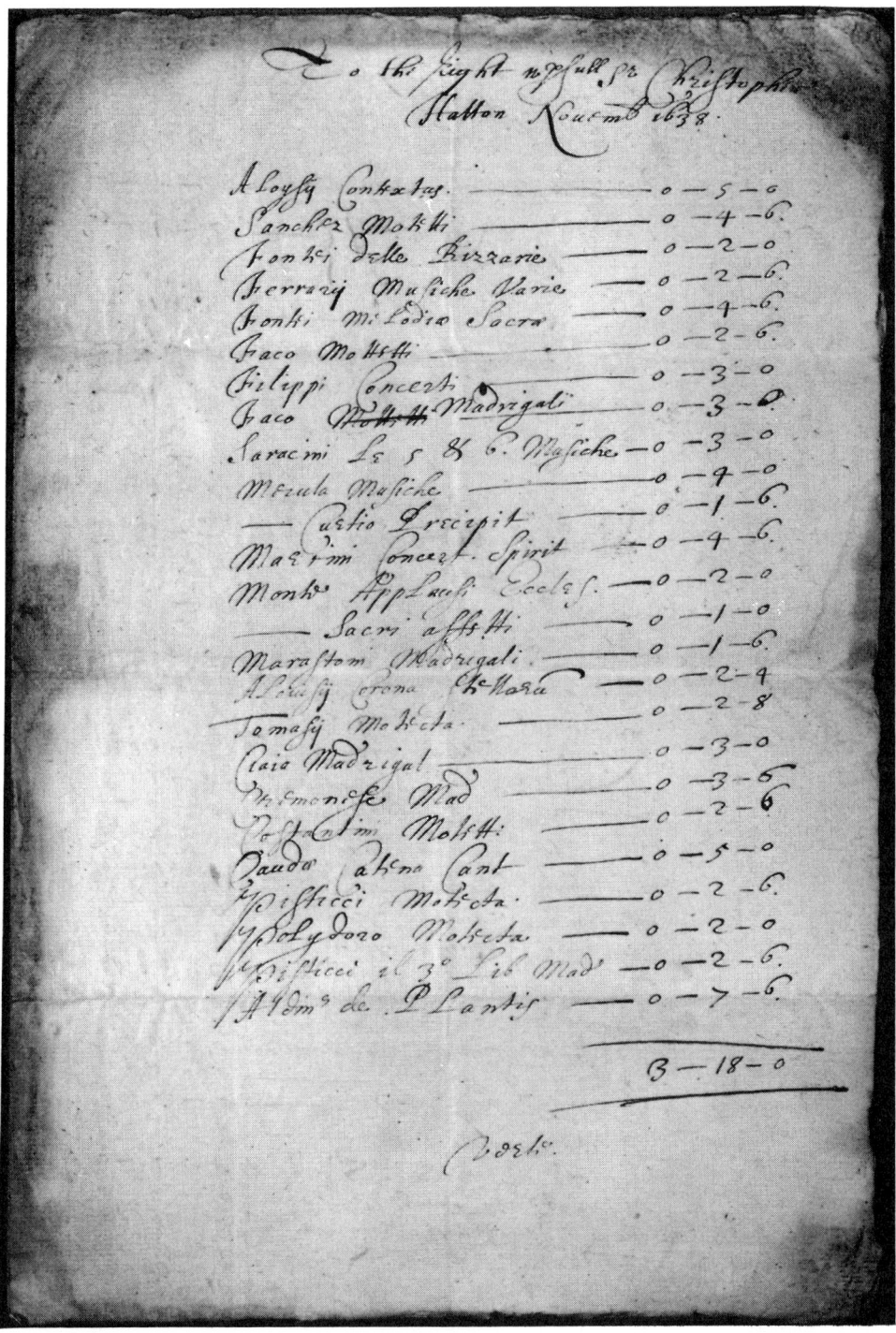

To the right worshipfull Sr Christopher Hatton Nouemb 1638.

Aloysij Contextus	0 – 5 – 0
Sanchez Motetti	0 – 4 – 6
Fonei delle Bizzarie	0 – 2 – 0
Ferrarij Musiche Varie	0 – 2 – 6
Fonchi Melodia Sacra	0 – 4 – 6
Graco Motetti	0 – 2 – 6
Filippi Concerti	0 – 3 – 0
Graco Madrigali	0 – 3 – 0
Saracini L 5 & 6. Musiche	0 – 3 – 0
Merula Musiche	0 – 4 – 0
Curtio Precipit	0 – 1 – 6
Martini Concert. Spirit	0 – 4 – 6
Monte Applaus Eccles	0 – 2 – 0
Sacri affetti	0 – 1 – 0
Marastoni Madrigali	0 – 1 – 6
Alouysij corona Chethara	0 – 2 – 4
Tomasi Motecta	0 – 2 – 8
Ciaio Madrigal	0 – 3 – 0
Mesmonichi Mad	0 – 3 – 6
Rossi m Motetti	0 – 2 – 6
Daudo Catena Cant	0 – 5 – 0
Pisticci Motecta	0 – 2 – 6
Polydoro Motecta	0 – 2 – 0
Pisticci il 3º Lib Mad	0 – 2 – 6
Aldmi de Plantis	0 – 7 – 6
	3 – 18 – 0

Boste

Plate 4　Oxford, Christ Church Mus. 317

Plate 5 Oxford, Christ Church Mus. 880, f. 1 second sequence

Plate 6 York Minster MS M.1.S, Medius Cantoris, f. 14ᵛ

Plate 7 London, British Library Add. MS 31,434, f. 1

Plate 8　Oxford, Christ Church Mus. 436, f. 53v

page. Collation: not possible due to tightness of binding. f. 57ᵛ: 'Tavola'. Inscription on front cover: 'Felice Sances / Alto:'.

iii *Tenore*: ff. ii + 39 + ii. Modern pencil foliation: ff. 60-102 (the flyleaves are numbered). Original pagination: pp. 1-77, followed by one unnumbered page. Collation: not possible due to tightness of binding. f. 100ᵛ: 'Tavola'. Inscription on front cover: 'Felice Sances / Tenore:'.

iv *Basso*: ff. ii + 22 + ii. Modern pencil foliation: ff. 119-44 (the flyleaves are numbered). Original pagination: pp. 1-43, followed by one unnumbered page. Collation: A^6(A6 removed) B-C^6 D^6(D1 removed). f. 142ᵛ: 'Tavola'. Inscription on front cover: 'Felice Sances / Basso:'.

v *Basso Continuo*: ff. ii + 14 + ii. Modern pencil foliation: ff. 103-18 (the flyleaves are numbered). No original pagination. No music entered on f. 109ᵛ. Collation: A^6 B^8. Inscription on front cover: '39 / Basso Continuo / Basso Continuo'.

Paper: 315 x 200 mm. Red marginal rulings on left and right. Ten rastrum-ruled staves per page (ruled with a five-stave rastrum of 120 mm span and individual staves each measuring 12.5-13 mm).

Watermark: coat of arms (Amsterdam).

Scribe: Charles Husbands the elder.[b]

Bindings: early seventeenth-century vellum documents listing names and places; **v** is signed 'Roger Goode'.

Contents of *Ob* Mus. Sch. MS C 10:

Latine Songes... by Felice Sances[c]

Title	Scoring	Folios				
		i	*ii*	*iii*	*iv*	*v*
Ardet cor meum	Cbc	3[d]	-	-	-	-
L[a]ettamini in Domino	Cbc	5ᵛ [d]	-	-	-	-
O quam speciosa	Abc	-	38[d]	-	-	-
Quemadmodum desiderat	Abc	-	40[d]	-	-	-
Soluatur lingua mea	Tbc	-	-	62 [d]	-	-
Conditor c[a]eli	Tbc	-	-	63ᵛ [d]	-	-
Audite me diuina fructus	Bbc	-	-	-	121[d]	-
Dulcis amor Jesu	Bbc	-	-	-	124[d]	-

---

[b] The hand can be identified from a note in *Och* Mus. 1151 (f. 1: '... 2 [motets] for a meane alone in ye Duos. prickt by Mʳ Husband'; see MS LX below) which appears to refer to *Och* Mus. 49, ff. 152-89 (see MS XLVIII below). Charles Husbands, a professional copyist, was a clerk of St George's Chapel, Windsor and a Gentleman of the Chapel Royal. See Ashbee (1986), 109, 136, 143; and ibid., (1991b), 73.

[c] G. F. Sances, *Motetti* (Venice, 1638); *RISM* S768.

[d] Score.

Iudica me Deus	CCbc	8	-	66	-	104
Domine ne memineris	CCbc	10ᵛ	-	68ᵛ	-	104ᵛ
Tota pulcra es	ATbc	14ᵛ	-	72ᵛ	-	105
Saluum me fac	TTbc	19ᵛ	-	77ᵛ	-	106
Psalite Domino	CCbc	12ᵛ	-	70ᵛ	-	106ᵛ
Laudemus uiros gloriosos	TTbc	17	-	75	-	107
Iubilent in c[a]elis	TTbc	21ᵛ	-	79ᵛ	-	107ᵛ
Vulnerasti cor meum	CTbc	23ᵛ	-	81ᵛ	-	108ᵛ
Deus in adjutorium	CBbc	25ᵛ	-	83ᵛ	-	109
Plag[a]e tu[a]e Domine	ATBbc	-	42	85	126	110
O Crux benedicta	ATBbc	-	44ᵛ	87	128	110ᵛ
O Domine gutt[a]e	ATBbc	-	46	88ᵛ	129ᵛ	111ᵛ
Aue Regina C[a]elorum	ATBbc	-	48	90ᵛ	131ᵛ	112ᵛ
O Jesu mi dulcis amor meus	CTTbc	-	49ᵛ	92	133	113ᵛ
Magnificemus in cantico	CCBbc	-	51	93ᵛ	134ᵛ	114
O Jesu mi dulcissime	CCABbc	27	53	95ᵛ	136ᵛ	114ᵛ
Salve Regina	CATBbc	28ᵛ	54ᵛ	97	138	115ᵛ
Iste Confessor	CC 2vln bc	30ᵛ	56ᵛ	99	139ᵛ	116ᵛ
Ave Maris Stella	CC 2vln bc	32	57	99ᵛ	141	117

MANUSCRIPT XXIV

OXFORD, BODLEIAN LIBRARY MUSIC SCHOOL MS C 11

A score of sacred and secular music by English and Italian composers.[a]

Copied in the late 1660s?
ff. ii + 97 + ii.
Modern pencil pagination: pp. 1-198 (the endpapers are paginated).
Paper: 345 x 215 mm. Marginal rulings on left and right. Ten rastrum-ruled staves per page (ruled with a two-stave rastrum of 45.5 mm span and individual staves each measuring 12.5 mm). No music entered on pp. 1, 8-13, 20-5, 43-5, 51, 68-73, 86-141, 194.
Watermark: coat of arms lettered CIB.
Collation: not possible due to tightness of the binding.

---

[a] The score is described in the 1682 catalogue of the Music School manuscripts (*Ob* Mus. Sch. C 204* [R]) as 'A score book of Italian & Latine Songs & some English, in Folio with black covers & purple strings'; see Crum (1967).

Script: Edward Lowe; the Italian text on pp. 46-67 and 74-81 was copied first by an unidentified scribe.

Inscription on p. 82: 'This songe & another was sent his ma[jes]t[ye] by the Author: Jan: 10. 1665.' (Lowe).

Binding: brown calf with gold fillets, the remnants of purple ties and initials 'G.S.' on front and back.

Contents of *Ob* Mus. Sch. MS C 11:

Page	Composer	Title	Scoring	Printed Sources[b]
2	M[r] Deeringe	Ardens est cor meum	CBbc	1662[4]
4	M[r] Deeringe	Justus cor suum tradidit	CBbc	1662[4]
6	M[r] Deeringe	O domine Jesu Christe	SBbc	1662[4], 1674[2]
14	E[dward] L[owe]	When Israell left th'Egiptian land	Sbc	
16	E[dward] L[owe]	Behold in sin was I conceived	Sbc	
18	M[r]: Nich: Lanier	O Amantissime Domine	Cbc	
26	[Jeffreys]	Prior Christus	[T]TBbc[c]	
28	[Jeffreys]	Ecce dilectus meus	[T]TBbc[c]	
30	[Jeffreys]	Nil Canitur suavis	[T]TBbc[c]	
32	[Jeffreys?][d]	Euge serve bone	[C]TBbc[c]	
34	M[r] Geo: Jeffryes	Sing unto the Lord	[T]TBbc[c]	
36	Alphonso Fer[r]abosco ye yonger	Rorate caeli	AB[bc]	
38	[Dering]	Isti sunt sancti	[C]CBbc[c]	1662[4]
40	[Dering]	Panis Angelicus	[C]CBbc[c]	1662[4]
42	M[r] Deeringe	Gloria patri	A[T]Bbc[c]	1652[10], 1662[4]
46		Non si creda[e]	Cbc	
52		O se mai d'un bel crin d'oro	Cbc	
56		E chi non dirà prigione	Cbc	
62		À me queste cose?	Cbc	
74		Rispondere si ò nò	Cbc	
78		Pensier che vuoi dà me?	Cbc	
82	B. Albrici	Su su mio cor	Cbc	

---

[b] For a full list of concordant sources (printed and manuscript) for the Dering and Jeffreys pieces see Tables 28 and 23 respectively.
[c] Short score.
[d] Attributed to Jeffreys in *Ob* Mus. Sch. E 451 (basso continuo only) but not included in any of Jeffreys' autograph manuscripts (e.g. *Lbl* Add. 10,338, *Lcm* 920).
[e] Music incomplete.

Volume reversed:

193 rev	Cazzatti	Veni veni Maria	ABbc	C1589
188 rev	Cazzatti	O crux nobilitata	ATbc	C1589
182 rev	Cazzatti	O vere, & Care Jesu	ATbc	C1589
175 rev	Supposd Charissime [*recte* Trabattone][f]	Anima mea in æterne dulcedine	CBbc	T1070
169 rev	[Jeffreys]	Gloria patri	ATB[bc]	
167 rev	[Rovetta]	Io mi sento morir	CCbc	R2981
161 rev	Merula	Non un bacio vorrei	CCbc	M2348
155 rev	[Merula]	Egli è pur trop[p]o vero	CCbc	M2348
149 rev	[Merula]	Sempre terro memoria	CTBbc	M2348

MANUSCRIPT XXV

OXFORD, BODLEIAN LIBRARY MUSIC SCHOOL MSS C 12-19

A set of eight partbooks containing sacred and secular music by English and Italian composers.[a]

Copied by Edward Lowe *c.*1660-82, and then additional music was added by Richard Goodson I and II (late seventeenth/early eighteenth century).
　　　　Watermarks: No. 1: foolscap with countermark CDG
　　　　　　　　　　No. 2: coat of arms (Amsterdam) countermark PG
　　　　　　　　　　No. 3: coat of arms (Amsterdam) countermark LM
　　　　　　　　　　No. 4: foolscap lettered HC (no countermark)
　　　　　　　　　　No. 5: foolscap with countermark PR
　　　　Eight partbooks:

MS C 12

First Treble: ff. iv + 71.

Original pagination: pp. 1-95 (71 misnumbered 81; lacking 96-9), 100-33, 234-5 (sic: misnumbered [134]-[135]), followed by eleven unnumbered pages [136]-[146]. ff. ii^v-iii^v: index (Lowe).

Paper: 320 x 205 mm. Red marginal rulings on left and right. Ten rastrum-ruled staves per page (pp. 1-72, 101-[146] ruled with a five-stave

---

[f] Also misattributed to Carissimi in *Lbl* Add. 17,835, 30,382, 33,234, 33,235; *Och* Mus. 43, 621, 623-6, 1178; and *J-Tn* N-4/39.

[a] The partbooks are listed in the 1682 catalogue of the Music School manuscripts (*Ob* Mus. Sch. C 204* [R]); see Crum (1967).

rastrum of 128 mm span and individual staves each measuring 12.5-13.5 mm; pp. 73-100 (lacking 96-9) ruled with a five-stave rastrum of 120 mm span and individual staves each measuring 12-13 mm). No music entered on pp. 76, 86-7, [142]-[146].

Collation: A-M^4 N-P^6 Q^6(Q6 removed). Watermarks: pp. 1-72, 101-[146]: No. 1; pp. 73-96, 99-100: No. 2.

Script: pp. 1-75, 77-85, 88-96, 99-[137]: Edward Lowe; pp. [138]-[141]: Richard Goodson I.

Binding: marbled board inscribed: 'First Treble / Latin songes for 1.2.3 / voices' (Lowe).

MS C 13

Second Treble: ff. iv + 76.

Original pagination: pp. 1-140 (56 *bis*: 56[a] and 56[b]), followed by eleven unnumbered pages [141-[151]. f. iii^{r-v}: index (Lowe).

Paper: 320 x 205 mm. Red marginal rulings on left and right. Ten rastrum-ruled staves per page (pp. 1-71 ruled with a five-stave rastrum of 128 mm span and individual staves each measuring 12.5-13.5 mm; pp. 72-[151] ruled with a five-stave rastrum of 120 mm span and individual staves each measuring 12-13 mm). No music entered on pp. 28, 72, 75-6, 80-8, 117, [143]-[151].

Collation: A-N^4 O-R^6. Watermarks: pp. 1-71: No. 1; pp. 72-95: No. 2; pp. 96-[151]: No. 3 with occasional appearances of No. 2.

Script: pp. 1-27, 29-71, 73-4, 77-9, 89-116, 118-34: Lowe; pp. 135-[142]: Goodson I.

Binding: marbled board inscribed: 'Second Treble / Latin songes for 1.2.3 / voices' (Lowe).

MS C 14

ff. iv + 60 + i.

Original pagination: pp. 1-91, followed by twenty-nine unnumbered pages [92]-[120]. ff. iii^{r-v} & endpaper verso rev: index (Lowe).

Paper: 320 x 205 mm. Red marginal rulings on left and right. Ten rastrum-ruled staves per page (pp. 1-56, 59-62, 65-[120] ruled with a five-stave rastrum of 128 mm span and individual staves each measuring 12.5-13.5 mm; pp. 57-8, 63-4 ruled with a five-stave rastrum of 120 mm span and individual staves each measuring 12-13 mm). No music entered on pp. 7, 32-9, [98]-[112].

Collation: A-J^4 K-N^6. Watermarks: pp. 1-56, 59-62, 73-[120]: No. 1; pp. 57-8, 63-4: No. 2; pp. 65-72: No. 3.

Script: pp. 1-6, 8-31, 40-83, 88-9, [113]-[120]: Lowe; pp. 84-7, 90-[97]: Goodson I.

Binding: marbled board.

MS C 15

Tenor: ff. iv + 53 + i

Original pagination: pp. 1-85[a], two unnumbered pages [85b]-[85c], 86-7, followed by seventeen unnumbered pages [88-104]. f. iii^{r-v}: index (Lowe).

Paper: 320 x 205 mm. Red marginal rulings on left and right. Ten rastrum-ruled staves per page (pp. 1-50, 55-6, 73-[104] ruled with a five-stave rastrum of 128mm span and individual staves each measuring 12.5-13.5 mm; pp. 51-4, 57-72 ruled with a five-stave rastrum of 120 mm span and individual staves each measuring 12-13 mm). No music entered on pp. 29-39, [88]-[104].

Collation: A-J^4 K-L^6 M^2(M2 removed). Watermarks: pp. 1-50, 55-6, 73-[104]: No. 1; pp. 51-4, 57-8, 63-4: No. 2; pp. 59-62, 65-72: No. 3.

Script: pp. 1-28, 40-81: Lowe; pp. 82-7: Goodson I.

Binding: marbled board inscribed: 'Tenor / Latin songes for 1.2.3 / voices' (Lowe).

MS C 16

Singeing Base: ff. iv + 82.

Original pagination: pp. 1-111 ([30] and [31] mis-numbered as 40 and 41), followed by fifty-three unnumbered pages [112]-[164]. f. iii^{r-v}: index (Lowe).

Paper: 320 x 205 mm. Red marginal rulings on left and right. Ten rastrum-ruled staves per page (pp. 1-42, 47-8, 73-[120] ruled with a five-stave rastrum of 128 mm span and individual staves each measuring 12.5-13.5 mm; pp. 43-6, 49-72 ruled with a five-stave rastrum of 120 mm span and individual staves each measuring 12-13 mm; pp. [121]-[164] ruled with a five-stave rastrum of 128 mm span and individual staves each measuring 13.5 mm). No music entered on pp. [31], [132]-[164].

Collation: A-K^4 L-O^6 P-Q^8 R^6. Watermarks: pp. 1-42, 47-8, 73-[120]: No. 1; pp. 43-6, 49-56: No. 2; pp. 57-72; No. 4: pp. [121]-[164]: No. 3.

Script: pp. 1-[30], 32-[115]: Lowe; pp. [116]-[131]: Goodson I.

Binding: marbled board inscribed: 'Singeing Base / Latin songes for 1.2.3 / voices' (Lowe).

MS C 17

ff. ii + 48 + i.

Modern pencil foliation: ff. 1-51 (the original flyleaves are numbered); ff. 3-8 contain original pagination: pp. 1-11. f. 2: index (Lowe).

Paper: 320 x 205 mm. Red marginal rulings on left and right. Ten rastrum-ruled staves per page (ff. 3-50^v ruled with a five-stave rastrum of

128-9 mm span and individual staves each measuring 12.5-14 mm). No music entered on ff. 12, 17-50^v (ff. 1-2 & 51 are flyleaves).

Collation: A-H^6. Watermarks: ff. 3-50^v: No. 5.

Script: ff. 3-9, 11^v, 12^v-13: Lowe; ff. 9^v-11: Goodson I; ff. 13^v-16^v: Goodson II.

Binding: marbled board.

MS C 18

8° Booke: ff. ii + 47 + ii.

Original pagination: pp. 1-45, followed by forty-nine unnumbered pages [46]-[94]. f. ii: index (Lowe).

Paper: 320 x 205 mm. Red marginal rulings on left and right. Ten rastrum-ruled staves per page (pp. 1-[94] ruled with a five-stave rastrum of 128-9 mm span and individual staves each measuring 12.5-14 mm). No music entered on pp. 19, 21, 31-3, 42-[94].

Collation: A-G^6 H^6(H6 removed). Watermarks: pp. 1-[94]: No. 5.

Script: pp. 1-13, 18, 20, 34-41: Lowe; pp. 14-17: Goodson I; pp. 22-30: Goodson II.

Inscription on f. 1^v: '8 Books' (Goodson II).

Binding: marbled board inscribed: '8° Booke' (Lowe).

MS C 19

Basso Continuo: ff. iv + 60 + ii.

Original pagination: pp. 1-33 (33 is numbered both 33 and 34), 35-113 (42 *bis*: 42[a] and 42[b]), followed by seven unnumbered pages [114]-[120]. f. ii^v-iv: index (Lowe).

Paper: 320 x 205 mm. Red marginal rulings on left and right. Ten rastrum-ruled staves per page (pp. 1-64, 73-[120] ruled with a five-stave rastrum of 128 mm span and individual staves each measuring 12.5-13.5 mm; pp. 65-72 ruled with a five-stave rastrum of 120 mm span and individual staves each measuring 12-13 mm). No music entered on pp. 71, 87, 100-1, 105, [114]-[120].

Collation: A-J^4 K-N^6. Watermarks: pp. 1-64, 73-[120]: No. 1; pp. 65-72: No. 2.

Script: pp. 1-70, 72-86, 88-99, 106-7: Lowe; pp. 102-4: Goodson I; pp. 108-13: Goodson II.

Binding: marbled board inscribed: 'Basso Continuo / Latin Songes for 1.2.3 / voices' (Lowe).

Contents of *Ob* Mus. Sch. MSS C 12-19:

Composer	Title	Scoring[b]	C12 p.	C13 p.	C14 p.	C15 p.	C16 p.	C17 f.	C18 p.	C19 p.	Printed Concordances
[Casati]	Domine ad adjuvandum me	Cbc	-	1	-	-	-	-	-	1	C1411
[Casati]	Benedicam Dominum	Cbc	-	3	-	-	-	-	-	2	C1411
Felice Sances	Ardet cor meum	Cbc	-	7	-	-	-	-	-	4	S768
Felice Sances	L[a]etamini in Domino	Cbc	-	12	-	-	-	-	-	6	S768
Felice Sances	O Quam speciosa	Abc	-	-	1	-	-	-	-	8	S768
[Sances]	Quemadmodum desiderat	Abc	-	-	4	-	-	-	-	10	S768
[Sances]	Conditor c[a]elj	Tbc	-	-	-	1	-	-	-	11	S768
[Sances]	Solvatur lingua mea[c]	Tbc	-	-	-	5	-	-	-	12	S768
[Sances]	Audite me divini fructus	Bbc	-	-	-	-	1	-	-	13	S768
[Sances]	Dulcis amor Jesu	Bbc	-	-	-	-	6	-	-	15	S768
M[r] Math: Locke	Agnosce O Christiane	CBbc	1	-	-	-	9	-	-	16	1674[2]
D[r] Christopher Gibbons	Celebrate dominum	SBbc	3	-	-	-	11	-	-	17	1674[2]
[Trabattone]	Anima mea in æternæ dulcedine	CBbc	6	-	-	-	14	-	-	18	T1070
D[r] Wilson	Donec gratus eram tibj	SBbc	9	-	-	-	17	-	-	19	
Felice Sances	Deus in adjutorium	CBbc	11	-	-	-	19	-	-	20	S768
Felice Sances	Judica me Deus	CCbc	14	17	-	-	-	-	-	21	S768
Felice Sances	Domine ne memineris	CCbc	18	21	-	-	-	-	-	23	S768
Felice Sances	Tota pulcra es	ATbc	-	-	8	8	-	-	-	24	S768

[b] The vocal partbooks (C 12-16) also include a copy of the basso continuo part below the voice part.
[c] 'Salvatur' in C 19.

Felice Sances	Laudemus viros gloriosos	TTbc	–	–	12	12	–	26	S768
[Monferrato]	Regina cœlj l[a]etare[d]	TTbc	–	–	16	16	–	28	M3037
Cassatus	O Jesu mea vita	TTbc	–	–	19	19	–	29	C1411
Cazzatti	Venj Maria	ABbc	–	–	22	–	22	30	C1589
Cazzatti	O Crux nobilitata palma[e]	TTbc	–	–	25	22	–	31	C1589
Cazzatti	O vere et care Jesu	ATbc	–	–	29	26	–	32	C1589
Cassatus	Omnes gentes	CCbc	22	25	–	–	–	33/34	C1411
Cassatus	Bone Jesu verbum patris	CCbc	25	29	–	–	–	35	C1411
Cassatus	O dulce nomen Jesu	CCbc	29	33	–	–	–	37	C1411
Cassatus	Tota pulchra es	CCbc	32	36	–	–	–	38	C1411
[Casati]	Regina cœli lætare	CCbc	36	40	–	–	–	39	C1411
[Casati]	Exultate justj	CCbc	39	43	–	–	–	40	C1411
Cassatus	Magnificate cœli	CCbc	43	46	–	–	–	41	C1411
[Martinengo]	Adoro te laudo te	CCbc	47	50	–	–	–	42[b]	C1411
[Martinengo]	Congratulamini mihj	CCbc	50	53	–	–	–	43	C1411
[F.M. Marini]	Venite gentes	CCbc	53	56[a]	–	–	–	44	M672
[F.M. Marini]	Euge serve bone	CCbc	56	58	–	–	–	45	M672
[Filippi]	Canite tuba	CCbc	59	61	–	–	–	46	F733
[Fontei]	Laudamus Dominum	CCbc	61	63	–	–	–	47	F1487
[Fontei]	Felix victoria	CCbc	65	67	–	–	–	48	F1487
[Rovetta]	Io mi sento morir	CCbc	67	69	–	–	–	49	R2981

[d] Alternative text 'Laudate dominum' given in C 15.
[e] 'O Crux noblita' in C 15 & 19.

Composer	Title	Scoring					
[Stradella?][f]	Lontanj del core[g]	CCBbc	107	102	–	–	50	–
[Carissimi]	Amanti che dite[h]	CCBbc	114	109	–	–	51	–
M[r] Blow	Paratum cor meum Deus	SSbc	116	73	–	72	52	–
Seig[r]. Alessandro Vincenti [recte Pesenti][i]	Vano è il desio	CCbc	70	77	–	80	53	P1549
	O misera Dorinda	C/A Bbc [j]	73	–	84	–	54	–
	In lectulo meo	SBbc	81	–	–	[116]	55	–
[Fontei]	Et ecce sonuit vox	ATBbc	–	–	–	26[k]		–
[Filippi]	Intuens in cælum	ATBbc	–	40	40	32	56	F1487
[Filippi]	Vidi turbam magnum	BBBbc	–	43	43	35	57	F733
[Aloisi]	Quid mihj est in cælo	ATBbc	–	45	45	37	58	F733
[Facchi]	Exurgat Deus	CCBbc	88	49	47	39	59	A876
[Facchi]	Audite c[a]elj	CCBbc	91	89	–	41	60	F44
[F.M. Marini]	Anima mea liquefacta est	CABbc	–	91	–	44	61	F44
[Sances]	Plag[a]e tu[a]e Domine[l]	ATBbc	–	93	52	46	62	M672
[Sances]	O Domine gutt[a]e	ATBbc	–	–	55	49	63	S768
Charissime	Audite sanctj	CCBbc	93	96	59	53	65	S768
					–	57	67	C1221, 1645[2], 1656[2], 1693[1]

[f] Attributed to Stradella in *Lbl* Add. 33,235; not listed in Jander (2/1962).
[g] 'Lontane,' in C 12.
[h] Last movement of the cantata *I Naviganti* ('Sciolto hauean').
[i] The misattribution to 'Alessandro Vincenti', the publisher, is also found in *Och* Mus. 14 and *Lwa* CG 63.
[j] Lowe copied the cantus and basso continuo parts (C 12 & 19); the elder Goodson recopied the cantus part an octave lower (C 14) and also copied the Bass part (C 16).
[k] False start on p. 25.
[l] 'Plage tui' in C 15.

Composer	Title	Scoring										Catalog
[Monferrato]	Salve Regina[m]	ATBbc	-	-	63	59	60	-	-	68		M3037
[F.M. Marini]	O vos omnes	ATBbc	-	-	66	63	63	-	-	69		M672
[Sances]	O crux benedicta	ATBbc	-	-	68	65	65	-	-	69		S768
Merula	Nominativo hic [Pt 1]	CATBbc	100	-	70	67	67	-	-	72		M2348
Merula	Nominativo quis vel qui [Pt 2]	CATBbc	102	-	73	69	68	-	-	72		M2348
[Lowe?]	Quam dulcis es[n]	CCATB 2vln bc	105	100	76	72	70	3	1	74		-
[Monteverdi]	Parlo misero	CCBbc	109	104	-	-	75	-	-	76		M3494
	Sospiri che fate[o]	CCBbc	112	107	-	-	78	-	-	77		-
M[r] Hen: Bowman	Tribularer ego[p]	CCBbc	118	111	-	-	82	-	-	78		-
Henry Bowman	Cantate [Jehovah][q]	-bc	-	-	-	-	-	-	-	80		-
[Cazzati?][r]	O quam pulchra es	CCBbc	77	-	-	-	88	-	-	82		-
	O æternæ misericors Deus	Cbc	-	118	-	-	-	-	34	84		-
	Domine non secu[n]dum peccata	Cbc	-	-	-	-	-	-	38	85		-
	O fideles misereremini	Sbc	-	-	-	-	-	-	40	86		-
M[r] Hen: Bowman	Miserere mej Deus	CCBbc	124	122	-	-	92	-	-	88		1686[4]
	Mortale che fate[s]	ATBbc	-	-	78	74	101	-	-	92		-
Casatj	Cantemus Deo[t]	CBbc	[134]	-	-	-	103	-	-	93		C1411

[m] C 14-16 include the alternative text 'Salve beate Jesu, salve Messia'.
[n] 'Quam dulces es' in C 12 & 15.
[o] 'Sospire' in C 16.
[p] Dated '15 Novem[ber] 1676' in C 19.
[q] Incomplete; basso continuo only.
[r] Attributed to Cazzati in *Ob* Tenbury 926 on unknown grounds (no printed source identified).
[s] 'Mortali que fata' in C 19.
[t] 'Cantamus Deo' in C 12 and 'Cantemus Domino' in C 19.

Cassatj	Alleluja Jubilat Ecclesiæ	CBbc	-	131	107	-	94	C1411
	Ad te levavi oculos meos[u]	- bc	-	-	-	-	96	
[Carissimi]	Turbabuntur impii[v]	ATBbc	75	79	111	-	98	C1220, C1222
Dr Blow	Go perjurd man[w]	SB 2vln b.vl bc	-	[118] rev[x]	29	5[v] & 16[y]	6 & 29[y]	B2985, B2987-91, 1683[5], 1687[5], 1695[17]
Mr John Blow	Awake my Lyre[z]	[SSTB] 2vln b.vl [bc]	-	[120] rev	-	4	3	1681[4]
Charissime	In te Domine speravi[a]	[ATB] 2vln b.vl [bc]	-	[117] rev	-	6	7	C1220
[Carissimi]	Suscitavit Dominus[a]	[ATB] 2vln b.vl [bc]	-	[115] rev	-	7	9	C1220, 1665[1]
Charissime	Surgamus eamus[a]	[ATB] 2vln b.vl [bc]	-	[115] rev	-	7[v]	10	C1220, 1649[2], 1652[1], 1656[2]
Carissime	Militia est[a]	[ATB] 2vln b.vl [bc]	-	[114] rev	-	8	11	C1220, 1643[1], 1652[1]

---

[u] Incomplete; basso continuo only.
[v] Originally the opening of the motet/oratorio *Damnatorum Lamentatio*.
[w] An Act song written for the Oxford Encenia of 1680; text: Herrick (1648), 53.
[x] Annotated: 'playinge Base in the Base of the new consort Bookes page 1' (Lowe); i.e. *Ob* Mus. Sch. E 443-6 which Lowe acquired in 1677.
[y] Goodson II copied the basso continuo part (C 19) and also recopied Lowe's violin parts in C 17 & 18.
[z] An Act Song written for the Oxford Encænia of 1678; text: Cowley (1656), iii, 57, 101.
[a] Vocal parts in *Ob* Mus. Sch. C 20-3 (copied by Lowe).

Attribution	Title	Scoring									Source
	Deus misereatur[b]	[ATB] 2vln b.vl [bc]	–	[113] rev[c]	–	–	–	8v	12[c]	–	1646[2], 1662[2]
	Sanctum redemptoris nomen	[C]A[B]bc	–	–	47	–	–	–	–	–	
	Laudate Dominum	-AT[bc]	–	–	80	–	–	–	–	–	
d	Kyrie[e]	TTB 2vln bc	–	–	88	[120]	–	9v	14	102	
d	Gloria[e]	TTB 2vln bc	–	–	90	[122]	–	10	15	103	
					92						
					84						
[Carissimi]	Sicut erat [from Confitebor tibi Domine]	[SSB] 2vln [bc][f]	–	–	–	–	–	11v	18	–	
[Carissimi]	Annuntiate gentes	[SSATB] 2vln bc[f]	–	–	–	–	–	12v	20	106	C1222
Sig[r] Silvestro [Durante]	Cantate Domino[e]	CCbc	[138]	135	–	–	–	–	–	–	1661[1]
[Carissimi]	Tronchisi pensier[i][e]	CBbc	–	139	–	[128]	–	–	–	108	
[Carissimi]	[A solis ortu 'Judicium Salomonis'][h]	[SSTB]2vln bc[g]	–	–	–	–	–	13v	22	–	
	Integer vitae[h]	- 2vln -	–	–	–	–	–	14v	24	–	

[b] Vocal parts in *Ob* Mus. Sch. C 20-3, and violin and basso continuo parts in *Ob* Mus. Sch. E 450 (copied by Lowe).
[c] Incomplete.
[d] Attributed to Carissimi in *Lbl* Add. 33,234 but this is highly unlikely to be authentic. See Massenkeil (1963); ibid, *New Grove*, iii, 786 & 791; and Dixon (1986), 15-17.
[e] Copied by Richard Goodson I.
[f] The violin parts are not by Carissimi.
[g] The violin parts are not by Carissimi; according to *Och* Mus. 13 'The symphonies being not Carissimi's but some musty Dutchman's.'
[h] Copied by Richard Goodson II.

MANUSCRIPT XXVI

OXFORD, BODLEIAN LIBRARY MUSIC SCHOOL MSS C 24-7

A set of four partbooks containing sacred music by Italian composers.[a]

The first sections were copied by Charles Husbands[b] (1670s?) before the partbooks came into the possession of Edward Lowe. Additional music was added by Matthew Hutton[c] and Lowe working in conjunction with an unidentified scribe (before 1679),[d] and two pieces were appended by Richard Goodson I (late seventeenth/early eighteenth century).
Four partbooks:

MS C 24 *Altus*: ff. i + 18 + i. Modern pencil foliation: ff. 1-20 (the flyleaves are numbered). f. 1: index (Lowe). No music entered on ff. 10, 17^v-19^v. Collation: single gathering of eighteen. Script: ff. 2-9^v, 10^v-11: Charles Husbands the elder; f. 11^v: Matthew Hutton;[e] ff. 12-15^v: Edward Lowe and an unidentified scribe (who provided most of the text underlay); ff. 16-17: Richard Goodson I. Inscription on cover: '4 Bookes: / Latin songes / For 3 voices / Altus. / Ed. Lowe' (Lowe).

MS C 25 *Tenor*: ff. i + 16 + i. Modern pencil foliation: ff. 1-18 (the flyleaves are numbered). f. 1: index (Lowe). No music entered on f. 17^{r-v}. Collation: single gathering of sixteen. Script: ff. 2-11: Husbands; ff. 11^v-12: Hutton; ff. 12^v-15: Lowe and 'text-assistant'; ff. 15^v-16: Goodson I. Inscription on cover: '4 Bookes: / Tenor. / Latin songes. / for 3 voices / Ed. Lowe'.

MS C 26 *Bassus*: ff. i + 16 + i. Modern pencil foliation: ff. 1-18 (the flyleaves are numbered). f. 1: index (Lowe). No music entered on ff. 12^v, 16^v-17^v. Collation: single gathering of sixteen. Script: ff. 2-11: Husbands; ff. 11^v-12: Hutton; ff. 13-15^v: Lowe (the 'text-assistant' provided the words

---

[a] The partbooks are listed in the 1682 catalogue of the Music School manuscripts (*Ob* Mus. Sch. C 204* [R]) as 'A set in Folio Covered with Blew Paper of Latine Songs for 4 voices by several Italian Authors'; see Crum (1967).

[b] The hand can be identified from a note in *Och* Mus. 1151 (f. 1: '... 2 [motets] for a meane alone in ye Duos. prickt by Mr Husband'; see MS LX below) which appears to refer to *Och* Mus. 49, ff. 152-89 (see MS XLVIII below). Charles Husbands, a professional copyist, was a clerk of St George's Chapel, Windsor and a Gentleman of the Chapel Royal. See Ashbee (1986), 109, 136, 143; and ibid., (1991b), 73.

[c] See J.A. Irving, 'Matthew Hutton and York Minster MSS M 3/1-4 (S)', *MR*, xliv (1983), 163-77.

[d] Hutton left Oxford in 1679 to become Rector of Aynho in Northamptonshire; see Irving (1983).

[e] Piece no. 11 was begun by Hutton (f. 11^v) and completed by Lowe (f. 12).

for piece no. 14); f. 16: Goodson I. Inscription on cover: '4 Bookes. / Bassus. / Latin songes / for 3 voices / Ed. Lowe'.

MS C 27 *Basso Continuo*: ff. i + 12 + i. Modern pencil foliation: ff. 1-14 (the flyleaves are numbered). f. 1: index (Lowe). No music entered on ff. 10, 13^v. Collation: single gathering of twelve. Script: ff. 2-9^v: Husbands; ff. 10^v-13: Lowe. Inscription on cover: '4 Bookes. / Latin Songes. / for 3 voices / Basso Continuo. / Ed. Lowe'.

Paper: 335 x 210 mm. Red marginal rulings on left and right. Ten rastrum-ruled staves per page (ruled with a five-stave rastrum of 120 mm span and individual staves each measuring 13.5-14 mm).
Watermark: coat of arms (Amsterdam).
Bindings: dark blue paper covers.
Contents of *Ob* Mus. Sch. MSS C 24-7:

No.	Composer	Title	Scoring	Folios C24	C25	C26	C27	Concordances
1	Aug: Faccho^f	Exurgat Deus	CCBbc	2	2	2	2	F44
2	Augustino Faccho^f	O Sacrum Convivium	CABbc	2^v	2^v	3	2^v	F44
3	Aug: Faccho^f	Audite c[a]eli	CCBbc	3^v	3^v	3^v	3	F44
4	Johannes Baptista^f [*recte* Aloisi]	Quid mihi est in c[a]elo	ATBbc	4	4	4^v	3^v	A876
5	Joha: Bap:^{f} [F.M. Marini]	Anima mea liquefacta est	CABbc	4^v	5	5^v	4^v	M672
6	Jo: Bap:^{f} [F.M. Marini]	Magnum h[a]ereditatis	CABbc	5^v	5^v	6^v	5^v	M672
7	Jo: Bap:^{f} [F.M. Marini]	O Vos Omnes^g	ATBbc	6^v	6^v	7^v	6^v	M672
8	Felice Sances^f	Plag[a]e tu[a]e Domine	ATBbc	7	7^v	8	7	S768
9	Fe: Sances^f	O Domine gutt[a]e	ATBbc	8^v	9	9^v	8^v	S768
10	Gaspare Phillippi	O Sacrum Convivium	ATBbc	10^v	10^v	10^v	9^v	
11	Felice Sances	Magnificemus in cantico	CCBbc	11^v	11^v	11^v	10^v	S768
12	[Sances]	O Crux benedicta	ATBbc	12^v	12^v	13	^{h}	S768
13	Charissime	Audite Sanctj	CCB[bc]	13	13	13^v	-	C1221, 1645^2, 1656^2, 1693^1
14	[Monferrato]	Salve Regina	ATBbc	15	14^v	15	11^v	M3037
15		Sanctum redemptoris nomen	[CAB]bc	-	-	-	12	
16	[Fontei]	Et ecce sonuit	[ATB]bc^i	-	-	-	12^v	F1487
17	[F.M. Marini]	O vos omnes	ATB[bc]	16	15^v	16	-	M672
18	[Scarani]	Transfige mi Domine	CT[Bbc]	16^v	16	-	-	S1168

^{f} Attribution from the index in C 27.
^{g} A duplicate copy appears as no. 17.
^{h} C 27, f. 11: 'Through base in my great folio' (possibly *Ob* Mus. Sch. C 10; see MS XXIII above).
^{i} Voice parts in *Ob* Mus. Sch. C 12-19 (see MS XXV above).

MANUSCRIPT XXVII

OXFORD, BODLEIAN LIBRARY MUSIC SCHOOL MSS C 54-7

A set of four partbooks containing Christopher Simpson's 'Months and Seasons' for treble viol, two bass viols and basso continuo.[a]

Dated 1668.
Four partbooks:

MS C 54

Treble Part: ff. 4 + i + 38 + i(half of which is pasted to the back board).
Modern pencil foliation: ff. 1-42 (11 *bis*: 11[a] and 11[b]).
Paper: ff. 1-4: 330 x 210 mm; ff. 5-42: 354 x 235 mm. Red marginal rulings on left and right. ff. 1-4^v: ten rastrum-ruled staves per page (ruled with a five-stave rastrum of 121-2 mm span and individual staves each measuring 12 mm); f. 5^{r-v}: unruled (originally a flyleaf); ff. 6-42^v: twelve rastrum-ruled staves per page (ruled with a four-stave rastrum of 92.5 mm span and individual staves each measuring 13 mm). No music entered on ff. 3^v-4^v, (5^{r-v}), 11[b], 23^v-42^v. f. 42: section of paper 49 x 111 mm cut from bottom right-hand corner.
Collation: A^4 i B^6 C^2 D^{10} E-F^6 G^8.
Watermarks: ff. 1-4: foolscap with countermark DI; ff. 6-42: Angoumois fleur-de-lys with countermark IHS (Thompson (1988), Watermark XXXVII); f. 5 and endpaper: fleur-de-lys with countermark AI.
Scribes: ff. 1-4: unidentified; ff. 6-23: John Lilly.
Binding: vellum; front cover inscribed: 'Mr Simpsons Months & Seasons / for 2 Bases & a Treble / 4 Bookes. / Treble Part' (Edward Lowe); and in the top left-hand corner of the front cover: 'Numb 20 4 B' (John Lilly?).

MS C 55

Bassus Primus: ff. i + 40 + i(half of which is pasted to the back board).
Modern pencil foliation: ff. 1-42 (the flyleaves are numbered).
Paper: 354 x 235 mm. Red marginal rulings on left and right. ff. 1 & 42: flyleaves (unruled); ff. 2-41^v: twelve rastrum-ruled staves per page (ruled

---

[a] The partbooks are listed in the 1682 catalogue of the Music School manuscripts (*Ob* Mus. Sch. C 204* [R]); see Crum (1967).

with a four-stave rastrum of 92.5 mm span and individual staves each measuring 13 mm). No music entered on ff. (1^{r-v}), 3^v-4, 21^v-41^v, (42^{r-v}).
   Collation: A^8 B^6 C-D^8 E^6 F^4.
   Watermarks: ff. 2-41: Angoumois fleur-de-lys with countermark IHS; ff. 1 & 42: fleur-de-lys with countermark AI.
   Script: John Lilly.
   Binding: vellum; front cover inscribed: 'Mr Simpsons Months & Seasons / for 2 Bases, & a Treble / 4 Bookes. / Bassus Primus:' (Lowe).

MS C 56

Bassus Secundus: ff. i + 34 + i.
   Modern pencil foliation: ff. 1-36 (the flyleaves are numbered).
   Paper: 354 x 235 mm. Red marginal rulings on left and right. ff. 1 & 36: flyleaves (unruled); ff. 2-35^v: twelve rastrum-ruled staves per page (ruled with a four-stave rastrum of 92.5 mm span and individual staves each measuring 13 mm). No music entered on ff. (1^{r-v}), 8, 20^v-35^v, (36^{r-v}).
   Collation: A^6 B^4 C-F^6.
   Watermarks: ff. 2-35: Angoumois fleur-de-lys with countermark IHS; ff. 1 & 36: fleur-de-lys with countermark AI.
   Script: John Lilly.
   Binding: vellum; front cover inscribed: 'Mr Simpsons Months & Seasons / for 2 Bases, & a Treble. / 4 Bookes. / Bassus Secundus.' (Lowe).

MS C 57

Basso Continuo: ff. i + 24 + i.
   Modern pencil foliation: ff. 1-25 (12 *bis*: 12[a] and 12[b]; the flyleaves are numbered).
   Paper: 354 x 235 mm. Red marginal rulings on left and right. ff. 1 & 25: flyleaves (unruled); ff. 2-24^v: twelve rastrum-ruled staves per page (ruled with a four-stave rastrum of 92.5 mm span and individual staves each measuring 13 mm). No music entered on ff. (1^{r-v}), 8, 12[b]^v-24^v, (25^{r-v}).
   Collation: A^6 B^2 C-D^6 E^4.
   Watermarks: ff. 2-24: Angoumois fleur-de-lys with countermark IHS; ff. 1 & 25: fleur-de-lys with countermark AI.
   Script: John Lilly.
   Inscriptions: f. 1^v: 'Thes 4 Bookes were prickt by Mr John Lillye, who had of mee $5^£$ for the prickinge them 29th of December. 1668: besides my Charge of paper & bindeinge. Ed. Lowe' (Lowe); and below: 'Richard Goodso[n]' signature of Richard Goodson I?
   Binding: vellum; front cover inscribed: 'Mr Simpson's Months, & Seasons / for 2 Bases & a Treble / 4 Bookes / Bass: Continuo.' (Lowe).

   Contents of *Ob* Mus. Sch. MSS C 54-7:

Simpson's 'Months & Seasons'

No.	Title			Folios			
				C 54	C 55	C 56	C 57
-	[April][b]			1	-	-	-
-	[May]			1v	-	-	-
-	[June]			2v	-	-	-
1	January			6	2	2	2
2	February			6v	2v	2v	2v
3	March			7	3	3	3
4	April			7v	4v	3v	3v
5	May			8	5	4	4
6	June			8v	5v	4v	4v
7	July			9	6	5	5
8	August			9v	6v	5v	5v
9	September			10	7	6	6
10	October			10v	7v	6v	6v
11	November			11[a]	8	7	7
12	December			11[a]v	8v	7v	7v
13	Spring	[i]	Fancy	11[b]v	9v	8v	8v
14		[ii]	Ayre	12v	10v	9v	9v
15		[iii]	Galliard	13v	11v	10v	9
16	Summer	[i]	Fancy	14v	12v	11v	9v
17		[ii]	Ayre	15v	13v	12v	10
18		[iii]	Galliard	16v	14v	13v	10
19	Autumne	[i]	Fancy	17v	15v	14v	10v
20		[ii]	Aire	18v	16v	15v	11
21		[iii]	Galliard	19v	17v	16v	11
22	Winter	[i]	Fancy	20v	18v	17v	11v
23		[ii]	Aire	21v	19v	18v	12[a]
24		[iii]	Galliard	22v	20v	19v	12[a]

---

[b] Incomplete: final section only.

MANUSCRIPT XXVIII

OXFORD, BODLEIAN LIBRARY MUSIC SCHOOL MS C 87

A set of three partbooks containing fantasies for two trebles and a bass viol by John Jenkins.[a]

Copied c.1654-64.[b]
Three partbooks bound together: **i** first treble viol; **ii** second treble viol; **iii** bass viol.
ff. 72 (ff. 1 and 26, 27 and 52, and 53 and 72 are the original front and back blue-paper covers to the three partbooks).
Pencil foliation: ff. 1-5, 7-15, 6, 16-72.
Paper: 280 x 175-85 mm. Marginal rulings on left and right. Ten or eleven staves per page, ruled with a five-stave rastrum in two blocks with a gap in between; the gap was then filled with a hand-ruled stave and the bottom rastrum-ruled stave trimmed away (remnants are visible). (ff. 4-5^v, 7-15^v, 28-29^v, 32^{r-v}, 34-36^v and 41-45^v are ruled with a five-stave rastrum of 106 mm span and individual staves each measuring 10.5/10.5/10/10/10.5 mm; ff. 23^{r-v}, 6^{r-v}, 16-17^v, 30-31^v, 33^{r-v}, 37-40^v, 54-55^v and 57-69^v are ruled with a five-stave rastrum of 109 mm span and individual staves each measuring 11/11.5/11/11.5/11.5 mm; and ff. 18-25^v, 46-51^v, 56^{r-v} and 70-71^v are ruled with a five-stave rastrum of 118 mm span and individual staves each measuring 12/12.5/12.5/13.5/13 mm.) No music entered on ff. (1^{r-v}), 2^v, 3^v, 5^v, 7^v, 8, 9^v, 10, 11^v, 12^v, 13, 14^v, 15, 6^v (sic), 17^v, 18, 19^v, 21^v, 22^v, 23^v, 24^v, 25^v, (26-7^v), 28^v, 29^v, 30, 31^v, 32^v, 33^v, 34, 35^v, 36, 37, 38^v, 39, 40^v, 41, 42, 43^v, 44^v, 48^v, 49^v, 51^v, (52-3^v), 54^v, 55^v, 56, 57^v, 58^v, 59, 60^v, 61, 62, 63^v, 64^v, 66^v, 71^v, (72^{r-v}).
Collation: originally there appears to have been one gathering per partbook (16, 16 and 18 folios respectively?) consisting of two types of paper with pot watermarks, and the second copyist added the paper with a foolscap watermark (see below).
Watermarks: ff. 4, 5, 9, 13, 15, 32, 34, 35, 42, 44: pot with letters RRO; ff. 3, 6, 17, 30, 37, 39, 54, 55, 60, 61, 63, 66, 67, 68: pot with letters IB; ff. 18, 21, 23, 24, 48, 49, 51, 70, 71: foolscap.
Scribes: A: Stephen Bing (?); B: unidentified; C: unidentified supervisor.
A: ff. 2-15^v, 16^v-17, 28-45^v, 54-64; B: 16, 18^v-25, 46-51, 65-71 and

---

[a] The partbooks are listed in the 1682 catalogue of the Music School manuscripts (*Ob* Mus. Sch. C 204* [R]); see Crum (1967).

[b] It has been suggested that this set, together with *Ob* Mus. Sch. C 81-6, 88-91, 98-101, Mus. Sch. E 406-9, and North e 37, was copied for Dudley, third Baron North at Kirtling, Cambridgeshire; see Willetts (1967b), 124-6, and Crum (1972).

added *custos* marks to f. 54; C: added corrections to ff. 22, 28, 38, 45, 47^v, 51, 58, 59^v, 60, 61^v and 70^v.[c] (Scribe A originally copied pieces nos. 1-14 in **i**, pieces 1-14 in **ii**, and pieces 1-10 in **iii**; subsequently piece no. 9 was moved to become no. 3, the old nos. 3-8 being changed to 4-9. Scribe B then copied pieces nos. 15-21 in **i** and **ii**, and nos. 11-21 in **iii**; he recopied no. 12 in **i**, removed the original copy and pasted his copy to the blank recto of f. 16.)

Inscriptions: the original covers (ff. 1, 27 and 53) were inscribed: 'First Treble' [**ii**: 'Second Treble', **iii**: 'Bass'] Fantazies of three parts By Mr Jenkins' by an unidentified scribe, and were also labelled '10. 3 Bookes' in the top left-hand corner by Edward Lowe.

Binding: modern.

Contents of *Ob* Mus. Sch. MS C 87:

Three-Part Fantasies by Jenkins

No.	Title	VdGS No.	Folios i	ii	iii
1	[Fantasia *a* 3 in C minor]	13	2	28	54
2	[Fantasia *a* 3 in C minor]	14	3	29	55
3	[Fantasia *a* 3 in C minor]	15	4^v	30^v	56^v
4	[Fantasia *a* 3 in D minor]	4	6	32	57
5	[Fantasia *a* 3 in D minor]	5	7	33	58
6	[Fantasia *a* 3 in D minor]	6	8^v	34^v	59^v
7	[Fantasia *a* 3 in G minor]	1	10^v	36^v	61^v
8	[Fantasia *a* 3 in G minor]	2	11	37^v	62^v
9	[Fantasia *a* 3 in G minor]	3	12	38	63
10	[Fantasia *a* 3 in A minor]	7	13^v	39^v	64
11	[Fantasia *a* 3 in A minor]	8	15^v	41^v	65
12	[Fantasia *a* 3 in A minor]	9	16	42^v	65^v
13	[Fantasia *a* 3 in E minor]	11	16^v	44	66
14	[Fantasia *a* 3 in E minor]	12	17	45	67
15	[Fantasia *a* 3 in E minor]	10	18^v	46	67^v
16	[Fantasia *a* 3 in F]	17	20	46^v	68
17	[Fantasia *a* 3 in F]	18	20^v	47^v	68^v
18	[Fantasia *a* 3 in F]	16	22	49	69^v
19	[Fantasia *a* 3 in B flat]	20	23	50	70
20	[Fantasia *a* 3 in B flat]	21	24	50^v	70^v
21	[Fantasia *a* 3 in B flat]	19	25	51	71

[c] The annotations 'Exam' or 'ex' added to the first twelve pieces in all three partbooks are in the hand of Scribe A and not that of 'J.J.' as claimed by C. Coxon, 'A Handlist of the Sources of John Jenkins' Vocal and Instrumental Music', *RCRMA*, ix (1971), 74. The annotation 'J:J: Exam' on f. 2 is also in the hand of Scribe A (Stephen Bing's italic hand?); it is possible that this refers to John Jenkins (see Crum (1972), 9).

MANUSCRIPT XXIX

OXFORD, BODLEIAN LIBRARY MUSIC SCHOOL MS C 204

Miscellaneous sets of parts.[a]

Eighteen sections [**A-R**] continuously foliated (modern pencil ff. 1-68) and bound (modern) as follows:

A ff. 1-3^v. Paper: 330 x 210 mm. Ten rastrum-ruled staves per page with marginal rulings on left and right. Collation: three single leaves. Watermark: coat of arms. Scribe: Henry Bowman. Copied: *c*.1669?

f. 1^{r-v}	[Bowman]	Usquequo Domine	Cantus primus
f. 2^{r-v}	[Bowman]	Usquequo Domine	Bassus
f. 3^{r-v}	[Bowman]	Usquequo Domine	Bassus Continuus

---

[a] The original cover to *Ob* Mus. Sch. C 204 survives in the folder *Ob* Mus. Sch. A 641; the cover is inscribed as follows: recto 'My score song [crossed out] / Latin Songe; English / all for that time / Dialogue & ayres for saturday / Except papers of Monk'; verso '... use at ye / Theatre in the Act / Act [sic] Saturday. 9th July / 1669', and below reversed: 'Mye papers of my song in ye Theatre: & ye Dialougs. [sic] of Dr Wilsons', all in the hand of Edward Lowe. Also enclosed in the folder *Ob* Mus. Sch. A 641 is a loose-leaf index found in *Ob* Mus. Sch. C 9 which is also in Lowe's hand and lists various loose papers, some of which can now be found in *Ob* Mus. Sch. C 204; the list is transcribed below:

> Loose papers in this Cubberd. vocall.
> 5 papers, all the parts of Dr Childs O bone Jesu 4 parts
> A score paper of Matt Locks Anthem for 2 Bases. And a voice came out of the Throne
> 3 papers of Amante Sentite for 2 voices
> O quam pulchra es for two Meanes with a thorough base/.
> Cantate in papers for 2 (or 3) of Mr Bowmans
> Usque quo - Mr Bowmans.
> His Miserere with a through base in loose papers
> His Tribularer alsoe in loose papers
>
> Instrumental
> 4 severall sheets of Mr Halls Ayres: folio
> 4 more papers in 4to of the same
> 3 papers of 6 Ayres of Mr Rich: Cobb in A
> Song & Ayres of Mr Blundevills of Windsor/
> Mr Goodsons Ayres in loose papers
> Two loose papers relatinge to Mr Baptist Sett of Ayres.
>
> 3 severall sortes of Instrumentall Ayres of Mr Kellers. his owne prickinge.
> loose papers of Mr Oldis Ayres
>
> 4 papers of an Italians Latin Songe O dulcis Jesu. wch I had of Mr Jeffreys.
> Loose papers all ye partes of Mortale qui fate

B ff. 4-9^v. Paper: 330 x 210 mm. Ten rastrum-ruled staves per page with red marginal rulings on left and right. Collation: A-C^2. Watermark: foolscap with countermark IM; Thompson (1988), Watermark XXX. Scribe: unidentified. Copied: *c*.1669?

f. 4^{r-v}	[Cazzati?]^b	O quam pulcra es	[Cantus I]
f. 5^{r-v}		no music entered	
ff. 6-7	[Cazzati?]^b	O quam pulcra es	[Cantus I]
f. 7^v		no music entered	
f. 8^{r-v}	[Cazzati?]^b	O quam pulcra [es]	[Basso Continuo]
f. 9^{r-v}		no music entered	

C ff. 10-11^v. Paper: 300 x 190 mm. Ten rastrum-ruled staves per page with red marginal rulings on left and right. Collation: two leaves. Watermark: not visible. Scribe: Bowman. Copied: *c*.1669?

ff. 10-11	[Lowe?]^c	Quam dulcis es a 7.	Canto Primo
f. 11^v		no music entered	

D ff. 12-13^v. Paper: 370 x 245 mm. Twelve rastrum-ruled staves per page with red marginal rulings on left and right. Collation: two leaves. Watermark: fleur-de-lys with countermark VI. Scribe: Edward Lowe. Copied: *c*.1669?

ff. 12^{r-v}	[Lowe?]^c	Quam dulces [sic] es	[Cantus I] (as **C** above)
ff. 13^{r-v}	[Lowe?]	Quam dulcis es	[Cantus II]

E ff. 14-15^v. Same paper as **C** above. Collation: a single bifolio. Scribe: Bowman. Copied: *c*.1669?

ff. 14-15	[Lowe?]^c	Quam dulcis es a 7	Canto 2.do. (as **D** above)
f. 15^v		no music entered	

F f. 16^{r-v}. Same paper as **D** above. Collation: a single leaf. Scribe: Lowe. Copied: *c*.1669?

f. 16	[Lowe?]^c	Quam dulcis es	Alto a 7.
f. 16^v		no music entered	

G ff. 17-18^v. Same paper as **C** and **E** above. Collation: two leaves. Scribe: Bowman. Copied: *c*.1669?

f. 17^{r-v}	[Lowe?]^c	Quam dulcis es	Alto a 7 (as **F** above)
f. 18^{r-v}	[Lowe?]	Quam dulcis es	Tenore a 7

---

^{b} Attributed to Cazzati in *Ob* Tenbury 926 on unknown grounds (no printed source identified). Also in *Ob* Mus. Sch. C 12-19; see MS XXV above.
^{c} Also in *Ob* Mus. Sch. C 12-19; see MS XXV above.

H ff. 19-24^v. Paper: ff. 19-20, 22 & 24: 370 x 245 mm, twelve rastrum-ruled staves per page with red marginal rulings on left and right; ff. 21 & 23: 185-90 x 230 mm, six rastrum-ruled staves per page with red marginal rulings on left and right. Remnants of an original pagination: f. 20^{r-v} = 137-8; f. 21^{r-v} = 141-2. Collation: five leaves. Watermark: fleur-de-lys with countermark VI. Scribes: ff. 19^{r-v}, 22 & 24: Lowe; ff. 20-21^v & 23^{r-v}: Richard Goodson I. Lowe's parts copied c.1669?; Goodson's in the 1680s? Inscription on f. 24^v: 'Quam dulcis es all ye Papers' (Lowe).

f. 19^{r-v}	[Lowe?]^d	Quam dulces es	[Tenor]
f. 20^{r-v}	[Lowe?]	Quam dulces es	[Bass]
f. 21^{r-v}	[Lowe?]	Quam dulces es	Violino primo
f. 22	[Lowe?]	Quam dulces es	Violino primo
f. 22^v		no music entered	
f. 23^{r-v}	[Lowe?]	Quam dulces es	Violino 2do
f. 24	[Lowe?]	Quam dulces es	Vionino 2do
f. 24^v		no music entered	

I ff. 25-29^v. Same paper as **B** above. Collation: two bifolios (f. 28 being a slip of paper pasted to f. 29). Scribe: Lowe. Copied: c.1669?

f. 25		no music entered	
ff. 25^v-26	[Lowe?]^d	Quam dulcis es	[Basso Continuo]
f. 27		no music entered	
ff. 27^v-29	[Lowe?]	Quam dulcis es	[Basso Continuo]
f. 29^v		no music entered	

J f. 30^{r-v}. Same paper as **C, E & G** above. Collation: a single leaf. Scribe: Bowman. Copied: c.1669?

f. 30^{r-v}:	[Lowe?]^d	Quam dulcis es.	A.7. Basso Continuo

K ff. 31-35^v. Paper: f. 31^{r-v}: 300 x 190 mm, ten rastrum-ruled staves per page with red marginal rulings on left and right; ff. 32-35^v: 330 x 210 mm, ten rastrum-ruled staves per page with marginal-rulings on left and right. Collation: five leaves. Watermark: foolscap. Scribe: unidentified. Copied: c.1660-80?

f. 31	Dr W. Child	O bone Jesu	[Cantus]
f. 31^v		no music entered	
f. 32	Dr W. Child	O bone Jesu	[Alto]
f. 32^v		no music entered	
f. 33	Dr W. Child	O bone Jesu	[Tenor]
f. 33^v		no music entered	
f. 34	Dr W. Child	O bone Jesu	[Bass]

^{d} Also in *Ob* Mus. Sch. C 12-19; see MS XXV above.

f. 34ᵛ				no music entered
f. 35		Dr W. Child	O bone Jesu		[Basso Continuo]
f. 35ᵛ				no music entered

L ff. 36-[36a]ᵛ. Paper: 330 x 210 mm. Twelve rastrum-ruled staves per page with red marginal rulings (the staves on ff. 36ᵛ-[36a] have been joined by hand in the middle to enable the scribe to copy stratigraphically across the whole width of the paper). Collation: a single bifolio. Watermark: foolscap with countermark PC. Scribe: Lowe. Copied: *c*.1660-80?

f. 36					no music entered
ff. 36ᵛ-[36a]	[Wilson]	Surge amica mea	[SSbc] in score
f. 36					no music entered

M ff. 37-40ᵛ. Paper: 300 x 200 mm. Ten rastrum-ruled staves per page with marginal rulings on left and right (the staves on ff. 37ᵛ-38 and 39ᵛ-40 have been joined by hand in the middle to enable the scribe to copy stratigraphically across the whole width of the paper). Collation: two bifolios. Watermark: cardinal's hat with letters DVI. Scribe: Lowe. Copied: *c*.1660-80?

f. 37				no music entered
ff. 37ᵛ-38	[Anon.]	Laudate dominum	[SSbc] in score
ff. 38ᵛ-39			no music entered
ff. 39ᵛ-40	[Anon.]	Paratum cor meum	[SSbc] in score
f. 40ᵛ				no music entered

N ff. 41-44ᵛ. Paper: 325 x 210 mm. Ten rastrum-ruled staves per page with marginal rulings on left and right. Collation: two bifolios (the second bifolio was not intended to have been folded). Watermark: foolscap. Scribe: Lowe. Copied: *c*.1660-80?

f. 41		[Anon.]		Laudate Dominum	in short score (SII & bc) (see **M**)
f. 41ᵛ		[Anon.]		Cantate Cœli		?in short score (S & bc)
f. 42		[Wilson]	Surge amica mea	in short score (SII & bc) (see **L**)
f. 42ᵛ		[Wilson]	Surge amica mea	fragment of SI part (see **L**)
ff. 44ᵛ/43	[Anon.]		Paratum cor meum	in short score (SII & bc) (see **M**)
ff. 43ᵛ-44	[Anon.]		Ecce Pulchra es		?in short score (S & bc)
				amica mea

f. 45: lacking (error in foliation)

O ff. 46-49ᵛ. Paper: 275 x 180 mm. Marginal rulings on left and right. Ten rastrum-ruled staves per page (ruled with a five stave rastrum of 118 mm span and individual staves each measuring 12.5-13 mm). Collation: four leaves. Watermark: pillars (as in *Ob* Tenbury 1005, ff. 1-3). Scribes:

Stephen Bing(?) with annotations by George Jeffreys(?). Inscription on f. 47: 'I received this songe [and] ye other from Rome the 11 of Novem^b 1634 wth directions to sing them [in] a slow tyme' (Bing?). Copied: *c*.1634.

f. 46	Abundis Antonelli	Dulcis Jesu^e	a 3	ad organa
f. 46^v	[Abundis Antonelli]	Ave Jesu^f	a 3	pro Organo
f. 47	[Abundis Antonelli]	Dulcis Jesu	a 3	[Bass]
f. 47^v	[Abundis Antonelli]	Ave Jesu	a 3	Bassus
f. 48	Abundis Antonelli	Dulcis Jesu	a 3	[Cantus II]
f. 48^v	A[bundis] A[ntonelli]	Ave Jesu	a 3	Cant. 2dus
f. 49	[Abundis Antonelli]	Dulcis Jesu	a 3	[Cantus I]
f. 49^v	A[bundis Antonelli]	Ave Jesu	a 3	Can: Primo

P ff. 50-63^v. Paper: 350 x 235 mm. Twelve rastrum-ruled staves per page with red marginal rulings on left and right. Collation: A^{12} B^2. Watermark: fleur-de-lys. Scribe: Bowman. Copied: 1670s?

ff. 50-52^v	[Carissimi *Jephte*]	Canto primo
ff. 53-53^v	no music entered	
ff. 54-55	[Carissimi *Jephte*]	Canto Secunda
f. 55^v	no music entered	
ff. 56-57	[Carissimi *Jephte*]	Canto Tertia
f. 57^v	no music entered	
ff. 58-59	[Carissimi *Jephte*]	Alto
f. 59^v	no music entered	
ff. 60-61	[Carissimi *Jephte*]	Tenore
f. 61^v	no music entered	
ff. 62-63	[Carissimi *Jephte*]	Basso
f. 63^v	no music entered	

Q ff. 64-66^v. Paper: ff. 64-5^v: 165 x 215 mm, six rastrum-ruled staves per page; f. 66^{r-v}: 325 x 207 mm, twelve rastrum-ruled staves per page. Red marginal rulings on left and right. Collation: three leaves. Watermark: coat of arms (Amsterdam). Scribe: Bowman. Copied: 1670s?

f. 64	[Carissimi 'Plorate filii Israel', final chorus from *Jephte*] [Violin I]
f. 64^v	no music entered
f. 65	[Carissimi 'Plorate filii Israel', final chorus from *Jephte*] [Violin II]
f. 65^v	no music entered
f. 66	[Carissimi 'Plorate filii Israel', final chorus from *Jephte*] [String bass]
f. 66^v	no music entered

---

^{e} Also in Lbl Add. 31,440 (see MS VII above), and *Ob* Mus. Sch. E 451 (see MS XXX below).

^{f} Also in Lbl Add. 31,440 (see MS VII above).

R ff. 67-68ᵛ. Paper 335 x 237 mm. Twelve rastrum-ruled staves per page with red marginal rulings on left and right. Collation: a single bifolio. Watermark: not visible. Scribe: Bowman. Copied: 1670s?

ff. 67-68 [Carissimi] Dialogum Jesse a 6 [Basso Continuo to *Jephte*]

MANUSCRIPT XXX

OXFORD, BODLEIAN LIBRARY MUSIC SCHOOL MS E 451

Edward Lowe's copies of vocal and instrumental music by English and Italian composers.

Copied by Edward Lowe over a long period (*c.*1636-82): the singing parts of music by William and Henry Lawes (pp. 1-2, 26-72 and 219-20) were probably copied soon after the book's acquisition in 1636 and spaced throughout the book according to a partly-completed plan; the scores of music by Richard Dering, William Lawes and Lowe (pp. 253-85, 297-300 and 335-6) were probably added next; and finally, probably after *c.*1674, the book was adopted as the basso continuo book for Lowe's partbooks (now *Ob* Mus. Sch. MSS D 233-6 and D 241-4) when the remaining spaces between earlier entries were filled.

ff. i + 191 + i. Original pagination: pp. 1-46[a], 46[b]-161, 164-206[a], 206[b]-207, 209-384 (i.e. 46 *bis*, 162-3 were removed, 206 *bis*, and 208 was omitted in error). f. iʳ⁻ᵛ: index in Lowe's hand.

Paper: 180 x 225 mm. Marginal rulings on left and right. Six rastrum-ruled staves per page (ruled with a three-stave rastrum of 66 mm span and individual staves each measuring 12.5-13 mm). No music entered on pp. 6-25, 73-8, 85, 85, 87, 89, 91, 93, 95, 97-102, 105, 107, 109-10, 113-18, 121-2, 125-6, 130, 133, 135-9, 151, (162-3 removed), 164, 183-6, 189, 191, 193, 195, 207, (208 omitted), 209-12, 214-18, 221-36, 245, 247, 251-2, 291-2, 295-6, 301-2, 313-14, 317, 337-9, 349-55, 361-2, 364, 366, 368, 370, 372, 374, 376, 378, 380, 382.

Collation: A-K⁸ L⁸(L2 removed) M-Aa⁸.

Watermark: coat of arms (details indistinguishable due to page trimming).

Scribe: Edward Lowe (copied over a long period and therefore includes different styles of handwriting).

Binding: vellum with white leather ties.

Inscriptions: front cover: 'This Book belongs to the two / sets of Books bound in Vellum / those of D^r. Rogers & Mr Jenkins / Workes [*Ob* Mus. Sch. MSS D 241-4] & the others of Mr Locks / and Severall other Authors [*Ob* Mus. Sch. MSS D 233-6]' (Lowe); inside front cover: '[Bought] Of M^r. Davis. price 3^6. May. 28: 1636' (Lowe); (for other inscriptions see the inventory below).

Contents of *Ob* Mus. Sch. MS E 451:

Page	Composer	No.	Title/Inscription	Scoring	VdGS No.	Printed Sources
1	W. Lawes		She weepeth sore in the night [A Canon of 4. Voc. in the Unison]	4vv		1648[4]
1	W. Lawes		Happy Sonnes of Israell 'Canon in / the 4th & 8th below:'	3vv		1648[4]
2	W. Lawes		Lord thou has bin favorable 'Canon in / the unison'	3vv		1648[4]

'Thes[e] 6 new ayres a la mode were made & given mee in May. 1674'[a]

Page	Composer	No.	Title/Inscription	Scoring	VdGS No.	Printed Sources
3			Prelude	[TrTrB vl] bc		
3			Corant	[TrTrB vl] bc		
4			Saraband	[TrTrB vl] bc		
4			Jig	[TrTrB vl] bc		
4			Saraband	[TrTrB vl] bc		
5			Jig	[TrTrB vl] bc		
26	M^r: H[enry] L[awes][b]		How are the gentiles 'Psal: 2^d'	CCB		1648[4]
28	Mr Henry Lawes		To heare mee Lord 'Psal / 5th'	CCB		1648[4]
30	W[illiam] L[awes]		Lord thy deserved wrath 'Psall: 6'	SSB		1648[4]
30	W[illiam] L[awes]		To thee I cry 'psal: 141.'	SSB		1648[4]
32	H[enry] L[awes]		Lord Judge my Cause 'psal: 26'	CCB		1648[4]
32	H[enry] L[awes]		With Sighs & Cryes 'psal: 142'	CCB		1648[4]
34	W[illiam] L[awes]		Oft from my early youth 'psal: 129'	SCB		1648[4]
36	W[illiam] L[awes]		I am wearye 'psal: 6'	SCB		1648[4]
38	Henry Lawes]		Who trusts in thee 'psall: 31'	CCB		1648[4]
38	H[enry] L[awes]		O thou from whom all mercy springs 'psa: 57.'	CCB		1648[4]
40	H[enry] L[awes]		Not in thy wrath 'psal: 38'	CCB		1648[4]
40	H[enry] L[awes]		Cast of[f] & scatter[e]d	CCB		1648[4]
42	H[enry] L[awes]		Lord showre on us 'Psal: 67'	CCB		1648[4]
43	H[enry] L[awes]		Accept my praires	SSB		1648[4]
44	[Henry Lawes]		The bountye of Jehovah praise 'psal: 136'	SSB		1648[4]
46[a]	[William Lawes]		Let all in sweet accord 'psal: 48'	SSB		1648[4]

[a] Parts in *Ob* Mus. Sch. G 612: four pocket partbooks in a leather case given to Lowe by the composer of the original contents, Valentine Oldis, on '24th March 1659. at ye Legg in Kings Street / Westminster'.

[b] The three-part settings of Psalms by Henry and William Lawes on pp. 26-72 - texts mostly from Sandys (1636) - are copied in tablebook format (i.e. the top two voice parts are reversed).

46[a]	W[illiam] L[awes]	Thou that art inthrond	SSB	1648[4]
47	W[illiam] L[awes]	You Nations of the earth 'psal: 100'	SSB	1648[4]
49	W[illiam] L[awes]	To thee O god 'psal. 63'	SSB	1648[4]
51	W[illiam] L[awes]	To the God whom wee adore 'psal: 149'	SSB	1648[4]
53	[William Lawes]	Come singe the great Jehovahs praise 'psal: 95.'	SSB	1648[4]
55	W[illiam] L[awes]	Thou mover of the Rolling spheares 'psal: 123'	SSB	1648[4]
57	W[illiam] L[awes]	How longe wilt thou forget mee 'psal: 6'	SSB	1648[4]
59	W[illiam] L[awes]	Praise the lord inthroand 'psal. 150'	SCB	1648[4]
61	W[illiam] L[awes]	They who the Lord their fortress make 'psal: 125'	SCB	1648[4]
63	W[illiam] L[awes]	My god, O why hast thou forsooke 'psal. 22'	SCB	1648[4]
63	W[illiam] L[awes]	Sing to the King of Kings 'psal: 98'	SCB	1648[4]
65	W[illiam] L[awes]	Out of the Horror 'psal: 130'	SCB	1648[4]
65	W[illiam] L[awes]	In the substraction of my yeares 'Es[s]ay: 38'[c]	SCB	1648[4]
67	W[illiam] L[awes]	Lord as the hart 'Psal: 42'	SCB	1648[4]
67	W[illiam] L[awes]	Let god the god of battaile rise 'Psal: 68'	SCB	1648[4]
69	H[enry] L[awes]	Lord for thy promise sake defend 'psal: 54'	CCB	1648[4]
70[d]	H[enry] L[awes]	Woe is mee	CCB	1648[4]

....

	'Mottets. of 3 voc: By M[r] Geofryes [George Jeffreys]'[e]			
79	[Jeffreys]	Prior Christus	[TTB] bc	
80	[Jeffreys]	Nil Canitur	[TTB] bc	
81	[Jeffreys]	Ecce dilectus [meus]	[TTB] bc	
82	[Jeffreys?][f]	Euge [serve] bone	[CTB] bc	
83	M[r] Sy[mon] Ive[s]	He that in heaven	- bc	
84	M[r] Ives	Singe praises	- bc	

	'Basso Continuo to M[r] Rich[ard] Cookes'				
86		[1]	Pavan [in D]	[TrTrBB vl] bc	21
86		2	Aire [in D]	[TrTrBB vl] bc	22
88		3	Eccho [in D]	[TrTrBB vl] bc	23
90		4	Eccho Corant [in D]	[TrTrBB vl] bc	24
90		5	Sarabrand [in D]	[TrTrBB vl] bc	25
92		6	Pavan [in E minor]	[TrTrBB vl] bc	26
92		7	Ayre [in E minor]	[TrTrBB vl] bc	27
94		8	Almaine [in E minor]	[TrTrBB vl] bc	28

[c] Sandys (1636), 263.
[d] Words only copied on p. 70; complete on pp. 71-2 (later copy?).
[e] Duplicated on pp. 241-4. For concordant manuscript sources for the Jeffreys motets see Table 23.
[f] 'Euge serve bone' is not to be found in any of Jeffreys' autograph manuscripts (e.g. *Lbl* Add. 10,338, *Lcm* 920); the implied attribution on p. 79 is therefore questionable.

Oxford, Bodleian Library Music School MSS E 451   329

94	[Cooke]	9	Corant [in E minor]	[TrTrBB vl] bc	29
94		10	Sarabrand [in E minor]	[TrTrBB vl] bc	30
96			[Pavan in D]g	- bc	
103	W[illiam] Child		O bone Jesu	[CATB] bc	
104	Mr Christopher Gibbons		O bone Jesu	[SAAB] bc	
106	Mr Heardsonh		Gloria patri	[CTB] bc	
108	W[illiam] Kinge		O blest estate 'Ecce quam bonum. Sand's Translation.'i	[2vv] bc	
111	Mr. Rogersh		Laudate Dominum [omnes gentes]	[4vv] bc	
	Mr. Math[ew] Lock[e]		[The 'Broken Consort' Part 2] j		
119		6k	Galliard [in C]	[TrTrB vl] bc	6
120		7	Pavan [in D minor]	[TrTrB vl] bc	7
123		8	Ayre [in D minor]	[TrTrB vl] bc	8
123		9	Galliard [in D minor]	[TrTrB vl] bc	9
124		10	Ayre [in D]	[TrTrB vl] bc	10
124		11	Sarab[and in D]	[TrTrB vl] bc	11
127		12	Pavan [in E minor]	[TrTrB vl] bc	12
128		13	Ayre [in E minor]	[TrTrB vl] bc	13
128		14	Corant [in E minor]	[TrTrB vl] bc	14
129		15	Chiconæ [in E minor]	[TrTrB vl] bc	15
131		16	Pavan [in F]	[TrTrB vl] bc	16
132		17	Galliard [in F]	[TrTrB vl] bc	17
132		18	Ayre [in F]	[TrTrB vl] bc	18
134		19	Corant [in F]	[TrTrB vl] bc	19
134		20	Jigg [in F]	[TrTrB vl] bc	20
	'Mr. Baltzar consort for 3 violins' [in C] l				
140		1	Pavan	[3vln] bc	61
141		2	Galliard	[3vln] bc	62
142		3	Almaine	[3vln] bc	63
142		4	Almaine	[3vln] bc	64
142		5	Almaine	[3vln] bc	65
142		6	[Alman]	[3vln] bc	66
143		7	Corant	[3vln] bc	67
144		8	Corant	[3vln] bc	68
144		9	Saraband	[3vln] bc	69
144		10	Saraband	[3vln] bc	70
	'The 3 thinges I brought from Court in B [flat]' m				
145		1	[Untitled]	- bc	
145		2	[Untitled]	- bc	
146		3d	[Untitled]	- bc	

---

g Unfinished. Perhaps also by Richard Cooke?
h Attribution from the index f. iv.
i Sandys, 'Psalm CXXXIII', (1636).
j Parts in Ob Mus. Sch. D 233-6.
k Nos. 1-5 of the second part of the 'Broken Consort' appear on pp. 194-8.
l Parts in Ob Mus. Sch. D 241-4.
m According to the index on f. i.

	['Rogers 9 Muses in A. #3 4 pts'][n]				
147		1	Prelude	[TrTrTB vl] bc	81
147		2	Aire	[TrTrTB vl] bc	82
147		3	Aire	[TrTrTB vl] bc	83
148		4	Corant	[TrTrTB vl] bc	84
148		5	Saraband	[TrTrTB vl] bc	85
149		6	Jigg	[TrTrTB vl] bc	86
149		7	Coranto	[TrTrTB vl] bc	87
150		8	Aire	[TrTrTB vl] bc	88
150		9	Jigg	[TrTrTB vl] bc	89
	'Roger's Retrograde Ayres'[n]				
152			Ayre [in G]	[TrTrB vl] bc	77
152			Corant [in G]	[TrTrB vl] bc	78
152			Sarabrand [in G]	[TrTrB vl] bc	79
152			Aire [in D minor]	[TrTrB vl] bc	71
152			Corant [in D minor]	[TrTrB vl] bc	72
152			Sarabrand [in D minor]	[TrTrB vl] bc	73
153			Jiggue [in D minor]	[TrTrB vl] bc	74

'Thes[e] 15 followinge Ayres were compos[e]d by Mr Bowman & first perform[e]d in the schooles / the 5 of Feb: 1673/4'[n]

154		1	[Prelude in G minor]	[TrTrBB vl] bc	1
154		2	[Allem[an in G minor]	[TrTrBB vl] bc	2
154		3	Corant [in G minor]	[TrTrBB vl] bc	3
155		4	Gavot[te in G minor]	[TrTrBB vl] bc	4
155		5	Sarabrand [in G minor]	[TrTrBB vl] bc	5
155		6	Prelude [in A minor]	[TrTrBB vl] bc	6
156		7	Allem[an in A minor]	[TrTrBB vl] bc	7
156		8	Corant [in A minor]	[TrTrBB vl] bc	8
157		9	Gavot[te in A minor]	[TrTrBB vl] bc	9
157		10	Sarabrand [in A minor]	[TrTrBB vl] bc	10
157		11	Allm[an in D]	[TrTrBB vl] bc	11
158		12	Ayre [in D]	[TrTrBB vl] bc	12
159		13	Gavot[te in D]	[TrTrBB vl] bc	13
159		14	Ayre [in D]	[TrTrBB vl] bc	14
160		15	Sarab[and in D]	[TrTrBB vl] bc	15
	'M^r. Rogers 2^d Sett in E la me'[o]				
161			Prelude [in E minor]	[TrTrBB vl] bc	161
	Mr Jenkins		[Suite in G minor][n]		1
165			Fancy	[TrTrBB vl] bc	
167			Ayre	[TrTrBB vl] bc	
168			Corant	[TrTrBB vl] bc	
	[Jenkins]		[Suite in A minor][n]		2
169			Fancy	[TrTrBB vl] bc	
171			Ayre	[TrTrBB vl] bc	
172			Corant	[TrTrBB vl] bc	

---

[n] Parts in *Ob* Mus. Sch. D 241-4.
[o] Only the Prelude appears in *Ob* Mus. Sch. E 451; presumably the basso continuo parts were on pp. 162-3 which are missing. The parts for all seven movements of the '2^d Sett' are in *Ob* Mus. Sch. D 241-4.

Oxford, Bodleian Library Music School MSS E 451

	[Jenkins]		[Suite in B flat]ᵖ		5	
173			Fancy	[TrTrBB vl] bc		
175			Almane	[TrTrBB vl] bc		
176			Corant	[TrTrBB vl] bc		
	[Jenkins]		[Suite in E minor]ᵖ		7	
177			Fancy	[TrTrBB vl] bc		
178			Ayre	[TrTrBB vl] bc		
179			Corant	[TrTrBB vl] bc		
	[Jenkins]		[Suite in F]ᵖ		8	
179			Fancy	[TrTrBB vl] bc		
181			Ayre	[TrTrBB vl] bc		
182			Corant	[TrTrBB vl] bc		
	'Mʳ Baltzars su[i]te in Gamut'ᑫ					
187		1	Pavan	[2vln b.vl] bc	51	
188		2	Galliard	[2vln b.vl] bc	52	
188		3	Almaine	[2vln b.vl] bc	53	
190		4	Pavan Almaine	[2vln b.vl] bc	54	
190		5	Almaine	[2vln b.vl] bc	55	
192		6	Corant	[2vln b.vl] bc	56	
192		7	Corant	[2vln b.vl] bc	57	
192		8	Sarabrand	[2vln b.vl] bc	58	
192		9	Sarabrand	[2vln b.vl] bc	59	
	Mʳ Lock[e]		[The 'Broken Consort' Part 2]ʳ			
194		1ˢ	Pavan [in C minor]	[TrTrB vl] bc	1	
196		2	Ayre [in C minor]	[TrTrB vl] bc	2	
196		3	Corant [in C minor]	[TrTrB vl] bc	3	
198		4	Pavan [in C]	[TrTrB vl] bc	4	
198		5	Ayre [in C]	[TrTrB vl] bc	5	
	'A songe for 3 of Dr. Wilson. This was prict out for / ye Act. 1674'					
199			The southwinde Blowes	[3vv] bc		
	Mʳ Will: Lawes		[Dances Movements]ʳ			
201		1	Almaine [in G minor]	[TrB vl] bc	349	1655⁵
201		2	Corant [in G minor]	[TrB vl] bc	350	1651⁶/2
201		3	Almaine [in G minor]	[TrB vl] bc	351	1651⁶/2
201		4	Sarabrand [in G minor]	[TrB vl] bc	352	1651⁶/2
202		5	Almaine [in G]	[TrB vl] bc	314	
202		6	Coranto [in G]	[TrB vl] bc	315	
202		7	Coranto [in G]	[TrB vl] bc	316	
202		9ᵗ	Almaine [in C minor]	[TrB vl] bc	221	1655⁵
203		10	Ayre [in C minor]	[TrB vl] bc	222	
203		12ᵗ	Sarabrand [in C minor]	[TrB vl] bc	224	1655⁵
203		13	Almaine [in C]	[TrB vl] bc	202	

ᵖ Parts in *Ob* Mus. Sch. D 241-4.

ᑫ The index (f. i) states 'Mr. Baltzars su[i]te in G: made in A', indicating that the suite has been transposed from A to G major. Parts in *Ob* Mus. Sch. C 102 a-b.

ʳ Parts in *Ob* Mus. Sch. D 233-6.

ˢ Nos. 6-20 of the Second Part of the 'Broken Consort' appear on pp. 119-34.

ᵗ Sic: '8 none', '11 none. / Corant'.

203		15[u]	Ayre [in C]	[TrB vl] bc	204
204		16	Sarabrand [in C]	[TrB vl] bc	205
204		19[u]	Ayre [in D]	[TrB vl] bc	248
205	[H. Lawes]		Simphonye [in G minor][v]	[TrB vl] bc	
205	[H. Lawes]		Simphonye [in G][v]	[TrB vl] bc	
	[H. Lawes]		'Thes[e] 3 [Symphonies] belonge to St Johns play'[w]		
205		1	[Symphony in D minor][v]	[TrB vl] bc	
205		2^d	[Symphony in D][v]	[TrB vl] bc	
205		3^d	[Symphony in D][v]	[TrB vl] bc	
	M^r W: Lawes		[Dance Movements][v]		
206[a]			Almaine [in G minor]	[TrB vl] bc	346 1651[6]/2, 1655[5], 1662[8]
206[a]			Coranto [in G minor]	[TrB vl] bc	167
206[a]			Almaine [in D minor]	[TrB vl] bc	256
206[a]			Coranto [in D minor]	[TrB vl] bc	257
206[b]			Sarabrand [in D minor]	[TrB vl] bc	258
213	[E. Lowe?]		Pavan [in C minor][v]	[TrTrB vl] bc	
			'Made for Mr Godfrey. Octo: / 25. 1641.'		

....

219	Mr Will Lawes	Goe bleeding hart[x]	[SAB] bc	

....

237	[Dering][y]	Conceptio tua[v]	[CB] bc	1662[4]
238	[Dering]	Sancta et Im[m]aculata Virgo[v]	[TT] bc	1662[4]
239	Mr Deeringe	Qualis est Dilectus tuus[v]	[CTB] bc	1662[4]
240	Geo: Jeffreyes	Singe unto ye Lord	[TTB] bc	
241	[Jeffreys]	Prior Christus[z]	[TTB] bc	
242	[Jeffreys]	Ecce Dilectus meus[z]	[TTB] bc	
243	[Jeffreys]	Nil canitur[z]	[TTB] bc	
244	[Jeffreys?][a]	Euge Serve [bone][z]	[CTB] bc	
246	Mr. Deeringe[b] [recte Grandi]	O bone Jesu 'The 4th part is in / Medius 2^{dus} of ye 6 bookes for ye church'[c]	[ATTB] bc	G3422, 1662[4]
248	[Antonelli]	Dulcis Jesu [pie Deus][d]	[CCB] bc	
249	D^r [C.] Gibbons	Gloria Patri	[CB] bc	
		'This songe was part of his exercise / for his D^{r}Ship. [7 July 1664] & after this was a / Gloria patris of 8 partes'		

---

[u] Sic: '14 none / Corant:' and '17. 18 none'.

[v] Parts in *Ob* Mus. Sch. D 233-6.

[w] Possibly George Wilde's *Love's Hospitall* which was acted before the King and Queen on 30 August 1636 at St John's College, Oxford.

[x] Text only; laid out in table book format but no music entered.

[y] For manuscript concordances with the Dering and Jeffreys pieces see Tables 28 and 23 respectively.

[z] Duplicated on pp. 79-82.

[a] 'Euge serve bone' is not to be found in any of Jeffreys' autograph manuscripts (e.g. *Lbl* Add. 10,338, *Lcm* 920); the apparent attribution on p. 79 is therefore questionable.

[b] Attributed to 'Legrand' in the index (f. i^v).

[c] I have been unable to identify these partbooks.

[d] Incomplete.

Oxford, Bodleian Library Music School MSS E 451 333

250	Merula		Fontes et omnia	[BB] bc	M2338

253	M[r]: Deeringe	3[d] [e]	Gaudent in C[a]elis[f]	CCbc	1662[4]
255	M[r]: Deeringe	2[d]	Justus Cor suum tradidit[f]	CBbc	1662[4]
258	M[r]: Deeringe	7th	O bone Jesu[f]	CCbc	1662[4]
261	M[r]: Deeringe	8	O Domine Jesu Christe[f]	SBbc	1662[4], 1674[2]
264	M[r]: Deeringe	4	Isti sunt sancti[f]	C[CB] bc[g]	1662[4]
266	M[r]: Deeringe	5	Panis Angelicus[f]	C[CB] bc[g]	1662[4]
268	M[r]: Deeringe	6	L[a]etamini Cum Maria[f]	C[CB] bc[g]	1662[4]
	'Deeringes Songes of 5 voc:'[h]				
271		1	O bone Jesu	Cbc[g]	D1317
272		2[d]	O nomen Jesu	Cbc[g]	D1317
274		3[d]	Jesu dulcis memoria	Cbc[g]	D1317
275		4	Quando Cor visitas Nostrum	Cbc[g]	D1317
276		4	Jesu Dulcedo cordium	Cbc[g]	D1317
278			Desidero [te]	Cbc[g]	D1317
279			Jesu Decus Angelicum	Sbc[g]	D1317
281		6	Jesu sum[m]a benignitas	Cbc[g]	D1317
282		7	Ave verum Corpus	Cbc[g]	D1317
283		8	Anima Christi Sanctifica me	Cbc[g]	D1317
285		9	Vox in Rama	Cbc[g]	D1317

287	[Casati]	O dulce [nomen Jesu]	[CC] bc	C1411
289	[Casati]	Tota pulchra es	[SS] bc	C1411
293	[Casati]	Magnificate cælj	[SS] bc	C1411

	['Deeringes Songes of 5 voc:' continued][i]				
297		16	Contristatus est Rex	Cbc[g]	D1317
298		17	Omnem super quem videritis	Cbc[g]	D1317
299		18	Ave Marja	Cbc[g]	D1317

303	[Sances]	Laudemus viros [gloriosos]	[TT] bc	S768
305	[Casati]	Exultate justi	[CC] bc	C1411
307	[F.M. Marini]	Venite Gentes	[CC] bc	M672
308	[F.M. Marini]	Euge serve bone	[CC] bc	M672
309	[Filippi]	Canite tuba	[CC] bc	F733
310	[Fontei]	Laudamus Dominum	[CC] bc	F1487
312	[Fontei]	Felix victoria	[CC] bc	F1487
315	[Rovetta]	Io mi sento morir 'Italian songe for 2 meanes'	[CC] bc	R2981

---

[e] I have been unable to identify the source to which the number system refers (perhaps the '6 bookes for the church' mentioned on p. 246?). (The source for the Dering motets is *not* Playford ed., *Cantica Sacra* (London, 1662): the readings differ).
[f] Parts in *Ob* Mus. Sch. D 233-6.
[g] Short score.
[h] The first eleven pieces - here numbered 1-9 - from Dering, *Cantiones Sacrae Quinque Vocum* (Antwerp, 1617); see also pp. 297-300: space was left for nos. 10-15 (pp. 287-96) but this was later used for the three pieces by Casati.
[i] Dering (1617) continued: see pp. 271-86.

318 rev	Mr Mel[l]		'An Almaine for two' [in C minor]	TrB vl	55	

'Thes[e] 10 are Mr Davice Mell's: wch are for 4 parts, all but / the 4th wch had noe inner part sent. The Other two / parts are in the Countertenor & Tenor of my / Parchment-cover Bookes'[j]

319 rev		10	[Morisco in G minor]	TrB vl	5	1662[8]
320 rev		9	[Morisco in F]	TrB vl	70	1662[8]
321 rev		8	Tom Sharlett [in F]	TrB vl	69	1662[8]
322 rev		7	Sarabrand [in F]	TrB vl	68	1662[8]
323 rev		6	Corant [in F]	TrB vl	67	1662[8]
324 rev		5	Almaine [in F]	TrB vl	66	1662[8]
324 rev		4	Longe time [in B flat]	TrB vl	38	1662[8]
325 rev		3	Sarabrand [in G minor]	TrB vl	3	1662[8]
326 rev		2	Corant [in G minor]	TrB vl	2	1662[8]
326 rev		1	A masqinge Ayre [in G minor]	TrB vl	1	1662[8]
327 rev	Mr Jenkins	173	[Ayre in D minor]	[TrATB vl] bc[k]	17	
328 rev	Mr Jenkins	172	[Alman in D minor]	[TrATB vl] bc[k]	16	
328 rev	Mr Jenkins	171	Corant in D minor]	[TrATB vl] bc[k]	41	
329 rev	Mr Jenkins	170	Alman in D minor]	[TrATB vl] bc[k]	15	
329 rev	Mr Jenkins	169	Alman in D minor]	[TrATB vl] bc[k]	14	
330 rev	Mr Jenkins	168	Corant in D minor]	[TrATB vl] bc[k]	40	
330 rev	Mr Jenkins	167	Alman in D minor]	[TrATB vl] bc[k]	13	
331 rev	M^r [W.] Lawes	166	[Corant in D minor]	[TrB vl] bc[k]	288	
331 rev	M^r [W.] Lawes	165	[Ayre in D minor]	[TrB vl] bc[k]	287	
331 rev	M^r [W.] Lawes	164	[Ayre in D minor]	[TrB vl] bc[k]	286	
332 rev	M^r [W.] Lawes	163	[Corant in D minor]	[TrB vl] bc[k]	285	
332 rev	M^r [W.] Lawes	162	[Ayre in D minor]	[TrB vl] bc[k]	284	
332 rev	M^r [W.] Lawes	161	[Ayre in D minor]	[TrB vl] bc[k]	283	

....

333			Cum Comederis	CCAB[l]	
335	Mr Will[iam] Lawes		Gather y[ou]r rose buds	SSB	L1172-3
			1652[7], 1652[8], 1653[7], 1666[4], 1667[6], 1669[5], 1673[4], 1678[4]		
336	E[dward] L[owe]		You who the Lord adore	AAB	
			'Psal: 134. Sands translation'[m]		

....

340 rev	M^r [W.] Lawes	66	[Corant in G]	[TrB vl] bc[n]	326	
340 rev	M^r [W.] Lawes	65	[Corant in G]	[TrB vl] bc[n]	325	
341 rev	M^r [W.] Lawes	64	[Ayre in G]	[TrB vl] bc[n]	118	1655[6], 1662[8]
341 rev	M^r [W.] Lawes	63	[Pavan in G]	[TrB vl] bc[n]	324	
342 rev	Mr Jenkins	36	[Saraband in G minor]	[TrATB vl] bc[n]	52	
342 rev	Mr Jenkins	35	[Alman in G minor]	[TrATB vl] bc[o]	33	
343 rev	Mr Jenkins	34	[Corant in G minor]	[TrATB vl] bc[o]	44	
343 rev	Mr Jenkins	33	[Pavan in G minor]	[TrATB vl] bc[o]	49	
344 rev	Mr Jenkins	32	[Corant in G minor]	[TrATB vl] bc[o]	43	

---

[j] i.e. the two missing parts from *Ob* Mus. Sch. C 233-6 which was originally a set of six books.
[k] Bass viol part only in *Ob* Mus. Sch. C 236.
[l] Copied in tablebook format (i.e. the top two voice parts are reversed).
[m] Sandys (1636).
[n] Bass viol part only in *Ob* Mus. Sch. C 236.
[o] Tr & B parts in *Ob* Mus. Sch. C 233 & 236.

Oxford, Bodleian Library Music School MSS E 451   335

344 rev	Mr Jenkins	31	[Ayre in G minor]	[TrATB vl] bc[p]	32	1651[6], 1655[5], 1662[8]
344 rev	Mr [W.] Lawes	30	[Ayre in G minor]	[TrB vl] bc[p]	341	
345 rev	[W.] Lawes	29	[Ayre in G minor]	[TrB vl] bc[p]	102	1655[5]
345 rev	Mr [W.] Lawes	28	[Ayre in G minor]	[TrB vl] bc[p]	340	
346 rev	Mr [W.] Lawes	19	[Corant in G minor]	[vln b.vl] bc[q]	370	
346 rev	Mr [W.] Lawes	18	[Corant in G minor]	[vln b.vl] bc[q]	369	
346 rev	Mr [W.] Lawes	17	[Ayre in G minor]	[vln b.vl] bc[q]	73	
347 rev	[W. Lawes]		Corant [in G]	[? b.vl] bc[q]	323	
347 rev	[W. Lawes]		[Ayre in G]	[? b.vl] bc[q]	80	
347 rev	[W. Lawes]		[Ayre in G]	[? b.vl] bc[q]	320	
348 rev	Mr [W.] Lawes		Pavan [in G]	[? b.vl] bc[q]	79	
	Mr [W.] Lawes		['Sharp Ayres' in D from *The Royall Consort*]			
356 rev		6	Sarabrand	[TrTrBB vl, 2 theo] bc[r]	28	
356 rev		5	Corant	[TrTrBB vl, 2 theo] bc[r]	26	
357 rev		4	Alman	[TrTrBB vl, 2 theo] bc[r]	24	
357 rev		3	Ayre	[TrTrBB vl, 2 theo] bc[r]	23	
358 rev		2	Corant	[TrTrBB vl, 2 theo] bc[r]	25	
358 rev		1	Pavan	[TrTrBB vl, 2 theo] bc[r]	22	
359 rev		5	Sarabrand	[TrTrBB vl, 2 theo] bc[r]	32	
359 rev		4	Ayre	[TrTrBB vl, 2 theo] bc[r]	37	
360 rev		3	Corant	[TrTrBB vl, 2 theo] bc[r]	33	
360 rev		2	Ayre	[TrTrBB vl, 2 theo] bc[r]	31	
360 rev		1	Alman	[TrTrBB vl, 2 theo] bc[r]	29	
	'Mr Younges sharpe Ayres'					
363 rev		[8]	[Saraband in D]	[TrB vl] bc[s]	8	
363 rev		[7]	[Alman in D]	[TrB vl] bc[s]	7	
363 rev		[6]	[Corant in D]	[TrB vl] bc[s]	6	
363 rev		[5]	[Alman in D]	[TrB vl] bc[s]	5	
363 rev		[4]	[Saraband in D]	[TrB vl] bc[s]	4	
363 rev		3	[Alman in D]	[TrB vl] bc[s]	3	
365 rev		2	[Corant in D]	[TrB vl] bc[s]	2	
365 rev		1	[Alman in D]	[TrB vl] bc[s]	1	
	'Hudsons Ayres'					
365 rev			[Corant in F]	[TrB vl] bc[s]	73	
367 rev			[Alman in F]	[TrB vl] bc[s]	72	
367 rev			Pavan [in F]	[TrB vl] bc[s]	71	
367 rev			[Ayre & Tripla in F]	[TrB vl] bc[s]	70	
367 rev			[Ayre in F]	[TrB vl] bc[s]	47	
369 rev		5	[Corant in D minor]	[TrB vl] bc[s]	46	
369 rev		4	[Alman in D minor]	[TrB vl] bc[s]	45	
369 rev		3	[Ayre in D minor]	[TrB vl] bc[s]	43	
369 rev		2	[Corant in D minor]	[TrB vl] bc[s]	42	
369 rev		1	[Alman in D minor]	[TrB vl] bc[s]	41	

[p] Tr & B parts in *Ob* Mus. Sch. C 233 & 236.
[q] Bass viol part only in *Ob* Mus. Sch. C 236.
[r] Two treble and a bass viol part in *Ob* Mus. Sch. C 233-4 & 236; the 'two breaking Base' parts were, according to a note in C 236 f. 1[v], copied by Lowe in the missing countertenor and tenor books.
[s] Parts in *Ob* Mus. Sch. C 233 & 236.

'Mr. Younges sett'

371 rev	11	[Corant in D minor]	[TrB vl] bc[t]	11
371 rev	10	[Alman in D minor]	[TrB vl] bc[t]	10
371 rev	9	Pavan [in D minor]	[TrB vl] bc[t]	9
373 rev	8	[Saraband in D minor]	[TrB vl] bc[t]	8
373 rev	7	[Corant in D minor]	[TrB vl] bc[t]	7
373 rev	6	[Corant in D minor]	[TrB vl] bc[t]	6
373 rev	5	[Alman in D minor]	[TrB vl] bc[t]	5
375 rev	4	[Corant in D minor]	[TrB vl] bc[t]	4
375 rev	3	[Corant in D minor]	[TrB vl] bc[t]	3
375 rev	2	[Alman in D minor]	[TrB vl] bc[t]	2
375 rev	1	[Alman in D minor]	[TrB vl] bc[t]	1

'M[r] [W.] Lawes flat Ayres in D [minor]' from *The Royall Consort*

377 rev	12	[Saraband]	[TrTrBB vl, 2 theo] bc[u]	13
377 rev	11	[Corant]	[TrTrBB vl, 2 theo] bc[u]	12
377 rev	10	[Ayre]	[TrTrBB vl, 2 theo] bc[u]	10
377 rev	9	[Saraband]	[TrTrBB vl, 2 theo] bc[u]	21
379 rev	8	[Corant]	[TrTrBB vl, 2 theo] bc[u]	20
379 rev	7	[Alman]	[TrTrBB vl, 2 theo] bc[u]	19
379 rev	6	[Corant]	[TrTrBB vl, 2 theo] bc[u]	18
379 rev	5	[Corant]	[TrTrBB vl, 2 theo] bc[u]	16
381 rev	4	[Ayre]	[TrTrBB vl, 2 theo] bc[u]	15
381 rev	3	[Corant]	[TrTrBB vl, 2 theo] bc[u]	11
381 rev	2	[Ayre]	[TrTrBB vl, 2 theo] bc[u]	9
383 rev	1	Pavan	[TrTrBB vl, 2 theo] bc[u]	8

MANUSCRIPT XXXI

OXFORD, BODLEIAN LIBRARY TENBURY MSS 973-6 & 1273

A set of five partbooks containing madrigals for two to four voices and basso continuo by Italian composers.

Copied 1638-46?
Five partbooks:

---

[t] Parts in *Ob* Mus. Sch. C 233 & 236.
[u] Two treble and a bass viol part in *Ob* Mus. Sch. C 233-4 & 236; the 'two breaking Base' parts were, according to a note in C 236 f. 1[v], copied by Lowe in the missing countertenor and tenor books.

MS 973: Cantus parts to pieces 1, 6, 10 and 13-15; Alto parts to pieces nos. 2, 7-9 and 11; Tenor I parts to pieces nos. 3-5 and 12. ff. i + 12. Modern pencil foliation: ff. 1-8, followed by four unnumbered folios [9]-[12]. No music entered on ff. 1, 2^v, [9], [12]^v. Collation: one gathering of twelve.

MS 974: Cantus parts to pieces nos. 5 and 11; Alto parts to pieces nos. 13-15; Tenor II parts to pieces nos. 2-4, 6-10 and 12. ff. i + 10. Modern pencil foliation: ff. 1-6, followed by four unnumbered folios [7]-[10]. No music entered on ff. [7]^v, [10]^v. Collation: one gathering of ten.

MS 975: Bass parts to pieces nos. 1-15. ff. 12. Modern pencil foliation: two unnumbered folios [a]-[b], ff. 1-6, followed by four unnumbered folios [7]-[10]. No music entered on ff. [a], [b]^v, [7], [10]^v. Collation: one gathering of twelve.

MS 976: Tenor parts to pieces nos. 11 and 13-15; Bass II part to piece no. 12. ff. i + 4. No foliation/pagination. No music entered on f. [4]^v. Collation: one gathering of four.

MS 1273: Basso Continuo parts to pieces nos. 1-15. ff. i + 20 + i. Modern pencil foliation: one unnumbered and unruled folio at beginning and end acting as cover, ff. 1-18, followed by two unnumbered folios [19]-[20]. No music entered on ff. 1-3, 4^{r-v}, 8^v-12^v, 15^v-[20]^v. Collation: one gathering of twenty.

Paper: 315 x 190 mm. Ten staves per page (ruled with a five-stave rastrum of 108 mm span and individual staves each measuring 11.5 mm).

Watermark: pot with letters GRV.

Scribe: George Jeffreys.

No original bindings. MSS 973-6 are bound together in a modern binding; MS 1273 is unbound.

Contents of *Ob* Tenbury MSS 973-6 and 1273:

No.	Composer	Title	Scoring	Folios 973	974	975	976	Concordances 1273	
[1]	[Turini]	O misera Dorinda	CBbc	1^v	-	a^v	-	3^v	T1388
[2]	[Arrigoni]	Tu m'amasti	ATBbc	3	1	1	-	5	A2490
[3]	[Merula]	Voi che per altri ardete	TTBbc	3^v	1^v	1^v	-	5	M2348
[4]	[Grandi]	Io d'altrui?	TTBbc	4	2	2	-	5^v	G3463
[5]	[Merula]	Questo da te vorrei	CTBbc	4^v	2^v	2^v	-	5^v	M2348
[6]	[Merula]	Sempre terrò memoria	CTBbc	5^v	3^v	3^v	-	6	M2348
[7]	[Rovetta]	Piangea donna crudel	ATBbc	6	4	4	-	6^v	R2981
[8]	[Rovetta]	Quante volte giurai	ATBbc	6^v	4^v	4^v	-	6^v	R2981
[9]	[Rovetta]	Quella fede leal	ATBbc	7	5^v	5^v	-	7	R2981
[10]	[Rovetta]	Ove ch'io vada	CTBbc	8	6	6	-	7^v	R2981

[11]	[Arrigoni]	Usami pur orgoglio	CATBbc	[9]^v	[8]	[7]^v	[1]	13	A2490
[12]	[Arrigoni]	Stelle fulminatrici	TTBBbc	[10]	[8]^v	[8]	[1]^v	13^v	A2490
[13]	[Rovetta]	Credetel voi[a]	CATBbc	[11]	[9]	[8]^v	[2]^v	14	R2981
[14]	[Rovetta]	Anime pellegrine[a]	CATBbc	[11]^v	[9]^v	[9]	[3]	14^v	R2981
[15]	[Rovetta]	Udite, amanti[a]	CATBbc	[12]	[10]	[9]^v	[3]^v	15	R2981

MANUSCRIPT XXXII

OXFORD, BODLEIAN LIBRARY TENBURY MS 1005

A score to madrigals by Stefano Bernardi and Claudio Monteverdi.

Copied 1643-6?
ff. 16. Modern pencil foliation: ff. 1-16.

Paper: 285 x 390 mm. ff. 1-2: ten staves per page (ruled with a five-stave rastrum of 117 mm span and individual staves each measuring 13 mm); f. 3^{r-v}: ten staves per page (ruled with a two-stave rastrum(?) of 38 mm span and individual staves each measuring 12 mm); ff. 4-16^v: twelve staves per page (ruled with a six-stave rastrum of 126.5 mm span and individual staves each measuring 10.5-11 mm). The pages are not folded into gatherings and the staves on the left and right of each folio have been joined by hand in the middle to enable the scribe to copy stratigraphically across the whole width of the paper. No music entered on ff. 4^v-5.

Watermarks: ff. 1-3: pillars (as in *Ob* Mus. Sch. C 204, ff. 46-9); ff. 4-16: pelican?

Scribe: Stephen Bing.

Inscriptions: ff. 1-2^v (top left): 'Lib. 4º. Claudio Monteverde:' (Bing); f. 3 (top left): '1. side / A.2 &. a.4. ad imitazione / d'uno del Sig. L. M.' (Bing) and added by a later hand: 'Marenzio'; f. 3^v (top left): '2. side' (Bing); f. 3^v (top right): 'Nº. (63) 11.' (later hand); f. 5 (left): 'Concerti academici con varia [s]orte / di Sinfonie a Sei voci de Stefano / Bernardi Maestro di Capella della / academia dell illustrissimi Signori / filarmonici di Verona. Libro Primo / opera ottava. / In Venetia appresso / Giacomo Vincenti 1616'; f. 5 (right): 'Madrigals / Bernardi', and 'Nº. (63) 1.' (later hands).

No original binding (f. 5 shows signs of wear and tear due to use as an outer cover); each leaf has been guarded and bound in a modern binding with *Ob* Tenbury MSS 1006-14.

Contents of *Ob* Tenbury MS 1005:

---

[a] Score in *Ob* Tenbury 1012; see MS XXXVI below.

Folio	Composer	No.	Title	Scoring	Concordances
1	Claudio Monteverde	1	Ah dolente partita[a]	5vv	M3467
1v	Claudio Mont[everdi]	2	Cor mio mentre	5vv	M3467
2	Claudio Monteverde	4	Sfogava con le stelle	5vv	M3467
2v	Claudio Mont[everdi]	3	Cor mio non mori[b]	5vv	M3467
3			Andianne à gli'horti[b]	4vv bc	
4v	[Bernardi]		[Ohimè dov'è il mio ben?][c]	6vv bc	B2055
5v	Stefano Bernardi	1	O primavera, gioventu	6vv bc	B2055
7	B[ernardi]	2	Se mi nieghi il conforto	6vv bc	B2055
8	S[tefano] B[ernardi]	3	L[i]eti fiori e felici	6vv bc & inst.	B2055
9v	S[tefano] B[ernardi]	4	Pur venisto [*recte* venisti] cor mio	6vv bc	B2055
10v	[Bernardi]	5	Quel Rosignuol	6vv bc & inst.	B2055
12	[Bernardi]	6	Poi che si nega fede	6vv bc & inst.	B2055
13v	[Bernardi]	7	Fusti amante com'io	6vv bc	B2055
14	[Bernardi]	8	Lasso ch'io ardo	6vv bc & inst.	B2055
16	[Bernardi]	9	Dunque esser puo	6vv bc	B2055

MANUSCRIPT XXXIII

OXFORD, BODLEIAN LIBRARY TENBURY MS 1009

A score to Italian madrigals by Stefano Bernardi, Richard Dering and Carlo Gesualdo and anonymous English madrigals.[a]

Copied 1643-6?
ff. 14. Modern pencil foliation: ff. 1-14.
Paper: 305 x 405 mm. ff. 1-3v and 5r-v: twelve staves per page; ff. 4r-v, 6-14v: ten staves per page (ruled with a variety of rastra). The pages are not folded into gatherings and the staves on the left and right of each folio have been joined by hand in the middle to enable the scribe to copy stratigraphically across the whole width of the paper. No music entered on f. 10.

---

[a] The first four pieces are textless, the fifth piece is fully texted and the remainder are all partly texted.
[b] Incomplete.
[c] Final 11 bars only.
[a] It is possible that the madrigals with English texts are unidentified *contrafacta* of Italian madrigals.

Watermarks: ff. 1-3, 5: pelican?; ff. 4, 6, 8-9: pillars; f. 7: small pot with letters IDB (as in *Ob* Tenbury MS 1016); ff. 10-14: small pot with letters VI.

Scribe: Stephen Bing.

Inscriptions: f. 3: 'P. Venosa' (later pencil attribution); f. 7 (top left): 'N⁰. (63) 8,' (later hand); f. 13: 'S. Benabei' (later incorrect attribution). f. 9ᵛ originally page '19'.

No original binding; each leaf has been guarded and bound in a modern binding with *Ob* Tenbury MSS 1005-8 and 1010-14.

Contents of *Ob* Tenbury MS 1009:

Folio	Composer	No.	Title	Scoring	Concordances
1			You sylvane Nimphs[b]	6vv	
1ᵛ			Fall downe abonndant teares	6vv	
2			Whilst Daphnis w[i]th a hart	6vv	
2ᵛ			Steale on myne eyes	6vv	
3	[Veno]sa [Gesualdo]		Il sol [qual'hor] [Pt 1]	6vv	G1735
3ᵛ	[Ve]nosa		Volgi mia luce [Pt 2]	6vv	G1735
4			Phillis and her Amintas	5vv	
4ᵛ			Come gentle spring tyde	5vv	
5	[Ve]nosa		Donna se m'ancidete	6vv	G1731
5ᵛ			Phillis beholding heaven	6vv	
6			Thirsis away, Dorus away	5vv	
7			Alasse why dost thou fly me	5vv	
7ᵛ			Say love where thy abyding	5vv	
8			Awake thou best of kings	5vv	
8ᵛ			This babe was like Minerua	5vv	
9	[Dering]	2	Donna mentr[']i[o] vi miro	Cbc	
9			[*leading to*] O Bellezza vitale	5vv	
10ᵛ	Step[hano] B[ernardi]	1	Occhi ch'a la mia vita	5vv	B2066
11ᵛ	B[ernardi]	2	Lacrimosa pieta	5vv	B2066
13ᵛ	[Bernardi]	3	Piangete [e intenerite]	5vv	B2066

---

[b] The text of each madrigal is included at the head of the page, but only the initial words of each phrase are given in the music.

MANUSCRIPT XXXIV

OXFORD, BODLEIAN LIBRARY TENBURY MS 1010

A score to the Ascension anthem, 'With notes that are both loud and sweet', for two basses and basso continuo, by George Jeffreys.

Copied in 1669.
Single leaf. No foliation.
Paper: 300 x 380 mm. Marginal rulings on left and right. Recto: twelve staves, and verso: nine staves (ruled by hand).
Watermark: undetermined; E. Heawood, 'Paper Used in England after 1600 i. The Seventeenth Century to *c.*1680', *The Library*, Fourth Series, xi (1930-1), 299, Fig. 96?
Scribe: George Jeffreys.
Inscriptions: bottom right-hand corner of recto: '[16]69' (Jeffreys); bottom right-hand corner of verso: 'To all / to all / Too'(?) (Jeffreys).
No original binding; the leaf has been guarded and is bound in a modern binding with *Ob* Tenbury MSS 1005-9 and 1011-14.
Contents of *Ob* Tenbury MS 1010:

[Jeffreys]   W[i]th notes [tha]t are both loud and sweet[a]   [BBbc]

MANUSCRIPT XXXV

OXFORD, BODLEIAN LIBRARY TENBURY MS 1011

A score of three of Henry Purcell's *Sonnata's of III. Parts* (1683).

Copied 1683-5.
ff. 4. Original pagination occasionally visible: pp. 1-8.
Paper: 310 x 400 mm. Red marginal rulings. Twelve staves per page (ruled with a two-stave rastrum of 36 mm span and individual staves measuring 11 mm and 11.5 mm). The pages are not folded into gatherings and the staves on the left and right of each folio have been joined by hand in

---

[a] For concordant sources see Table 23e above.

the middle to enable the scribe to copy stratigraphically across the whole width of the paper.

Watermark: foolscap with countermark IM; Thompson (1988), Watermark XXX.

Scribe: George Jeffreys.

Inscription on f. 1: 'Mr Henry Purcell' (Jeffreys).

No original binding; each leaf has been guarded and bound in a modern binding with *Ob* Tenbury MSS 1005-10 and 1012-14.

Contents of *Ob* Tenbury MS 1011:

Trio Sonatas by Henry Purcell

Title	Page	Folio	Zimmerman No.[a]	Printed Concordance
Sonata 9	1	[1]	Z 798	P6083
Sonnatta .1.	4	[2]^v	Z 790	P6083
3^d. Sonnata[b]	6	[3]^v	Z 791	P6083

MANUSCRIPT XXXVI

OXFORD, BODLEIAN LIBRARY TENBURY MS 1012

A score of three madrigals by Giovanni Rovetta for four voices and basso continuo.

Copied 1638-46?

ff. 4. No foliation/pagination.

Paper: 300 x 390 mm. Ten staves per page (ruled with a five-stave rastrum of 117 mm span and individual staves measuring 12.5/12.5/13/12.5/13.5 mm); the pages are not folded into gatherings and the staves on the left and right of each folio have been joined by hand in the middle to enable the scribe to copy stratigraphically across the whole width of the paper. No music entered on f. [1].

Watermark: pot with letters PB.

Scribe: George Jeffreys.

Inscription on f. [1]: '3 Madrigales a 4 Rovetta -'.

---

[a] Zimmerman (1963).
[b] Number 2 in *Sonnata's of III. Parts* (1683). The incorrect numbering was probably due to a copyist's error as a comparison of the readings indicates that the manuscript was copied from the printed source (albeit carelessly).

No original binding; each leaf has been guarded and bound in a modern binding with *Ob* Tenbury MSS 1005-11 and 1013-14.

Contents of *Ob* Tenbury MS 1012:[a]

Folio	Composer	Title	Scoring	Printed Concordance
[1]v	Rovetta	Udite, amanti	CATBbc	R2981
[2]v	Rovetta	Credetel voi	CATBbc	R2981
[4]	Rovetta	Anime pellegrine	CATBbc	R2981

MANUSCRIPT XXXVII

OXFORD, BODLEIAN LIBRARY TENBURY MS 1013

A score of Alessandro Grandi's Mass for four voices and basso continuo from *Il Primo Libro de Motetti* (1610).

Copied 1642-6?
ff. 6. No foliation/pagination.
Paper: 300 x 390 mm. Ten staves per page (ruled with a five-stave rastrum of 111 mm span and individual staves each measuring 12-12.5 mm); the pages are not folded into gatherings and the staves on the left and right of each folio have been joined by hand in the middle to enable the scribe to copy stratigraphically across the whole width of the paper. No music entered on
f. [6].
Watermark: pot with letters ID; Thompson (1988), Watermark IX.
Scribe: George Jeffreys.
Inscriptions: f. [1]: 'Messa. A 4 voc Primo libo. All: Grandi' (Jeffreys); f. [6]: 'Messa a 4. Primo Lib.º All. Grandi' (later hand).
Bound with *Ob* Tenbury MSS 1004-12 and 1014 in modern binding.
Contents of *Ob* Tenbury MS 1013:

---

[a] Parts in *Ob* Tenbury 973-6 & 1273; see MS XXXI above.

Alessandro Grandi's *Messa a 4 Voci*[b]

Folio	Title	Scoring
[1]	Kyrie eleyson	TTbc
[1]	Christe eleyson	ABbc
[1]ᵛ	Kyrie eleyson	ATTBbc
	[Gloria in excelsis Deo]	
[1]ᵛ	Et in terra pax	ATTBbc
	[Credo in unum Deum]	
[3]	Patrem omnipotentem	ATTBbc
[3]ᵛ	Qui propter nos homines	ATbc
[3]ᵛ	Et incarnatus est	ATBbc
[3]ᵛ	Crucifixus	ATTbc
[3]ᵛ	Et resur[r]exit	ATTBbc
[4]	Et iterum venturus est	ATTBbc
[4]	Et in Spiritum Sanctum	ATTBbc
[5]	Sanctus	ATTBbc
[5]ᵛ	Benedictus	ATTBbc
[5]ᵛ	Agnus Dei	AAbc
[6]	Agnus Dei	ATTBbc

MANUSCRIPT XXXVIII

OXFORD, BODLEIAN LIBRARY TENBURY MS 1015

Scores to five-voice madrigals from Pomponio Nenna's *Il Settimo Libro de Madrigali* (1608) with English words.

Copied 1638-46?
ff. i + 13.
Modern pencil foliation: ff. 1-13. Each madrigal is numbered (original hand), and some also include a second redundant numbering system (from the source used in copying?).
Paper: 300 x 400 mm. Ten staves per page (ruled with a five-stave rastrum of 118 mm span and individual staves measuring 12.5/13/12.5/13/14 mm); the pages are not folded into gatherings and the staves on the left

---

[b] Printed source: *Il Primo Libro de Motetti* (Venice, 1610); *RISM* G3417.

and right of each folio have been joined by hand in the middle to enable the scribe to copy stratigraphically across the whole width of the paper. No music entered on f. 13ᵛ.

Watermarks: f. i: Norman posthorn with monogram 'D. VAULLEGARD' beneath; ff. 1-12: pot with letters GRO; f. 13: countermark 'PRINAUD'(?)

Scribe: George Jeffreys.

Inscriptions: f. 1, 'Pomponio Nenna lib: 7' (Jeffreys). A later hand has added, in pencil, on f. 3: 'Sweet Damsel' (above piece no. 4), and on f. 10: 'Mary O do not waver for then lived exiled' (above piece no. 14/13).

Bound with *Ob* Tenbury MSS 1016-18 in modern binding.

Contents of *Ob* Tenbury MS 1015:

Pomponio Nenna's *Il Settimo Libro de Madrigali*[a] 'Englished'

No.	Title [& original]	Folio
1	Let my heart then adore thee [S'egli è ver ch'io v'adoro]	1
2	The sonne one day in glory [Godea del sol i rai la mia ninfa vezzosa]	1ᵛ
3	Whom one fayr branch in closes [In due vermiglie labra]	2
4	How then shall death deprive me [Che non mi date aita]	3
5	With hands sweetly imbracing [Con le labra di rose mi rapi Filli il cor]	3ᵛ
6	Happy torments, blessed wounds [Occhi belli ch'adoro]	4ᵛ
7	Behold the starre apeareth [Suggetemi, suggete il sangue]	5
8/7	Then Peter like an exile [Havea per la sua ninfa]	6
9	If sweet Jesu to pray thee [Filli mia, s'al mio seno]	6ᵛ
-	Happy soule in thy bosome [Coridon, del tuo petto]	7ᵛ
11/10	Now death sadly attended [L'amoroso veleno serpendo]	8
10/11	Ay me my sonne sweet Jesu [Non veggio il mio bel sol]	8ᵛ
13/12	While sighes prayers and lamentings [Sospir, baci e parole]	9ᵛ

[a] *RISM* N392.

14/13	O sweet Jesu my saviour [Filli, cor del mio core]	10
16/15	Behold my soule sweet Jesu [Ardemmo insieme, bella donna]	11
17/16	His fayr eyes, on her fixed [Parean dir gli occhi suoi]	11ᵛ
2/19	Fly not, sweet Jesu [Fuggite pur, fuggite, crudel]	12ᵛ

MANUSCRIPT XXXIX

OXFORD, BODLEIAN LIBRARY TENBURY MS 1016

Scores to madrigals for one to three voices and basso continuo by Richard Dering.

Copied in the mid 1630s?
ff. 15. Pencil foliation: ff. 1-15.
Paper: 300 x 380-400 mm. Ten staves per page ruled with a two-stave rastrum of 38.5 mm span and individual staves each measuring 11.5 mm. The pages are not folded into gatherings and the staves on the left and right of each folio have been joined by hand in the middle to enable the scribe to copy stratigraphically across the whole width of the paper. No music entered on ff. 1, 15ᵛ.
Watermark: pot with letters IDB (as in *Ob* Tenbury MS 1009, f. 7).
Scribe: George Jeffreys.
Inscriptions on f. 1: 'A. 1. 2. & 3 M Deeringe./' (Jeffreys); and 'No (91) 3' (later unidentified hand).
No original binding; each leaf has been guarded and bound in a modern binding with *Ob* Tenbury MSS 1015 and 1017-18.
Contents of *Ob* Tenbury MS 1016:

Madrigals by Richard Dering

No.	Title	Scoring	Folios
-	O Donna troppo [cruda]	CTbc	1v
1	Vergine bella	Tbc	2
2	Donna mentre [i'vi miro][a]	Cbc	2v
3	Cosi dunque [morire ohime]	Tbc	2v
1	O miei giorni fugaci	TBbc	3
2	O Durezza [di ferro]	TTbc	3v
3	Legasti [anima mia]	TTbc	4
[1]	T' amo mia vita	TTBbc	4v
2	Crudelissima doglia	TTBbc	5v
3	Alme d'amor rubelle	TTBbc	6v
4	Ho visto' al mio [dolore]	TTBbc	7v
5	Felice [chi vi mira]	TTBbc	8v
6	Che veggio ohime	CTBbc	9v
7	Al fonte['al prato][b]	TTBbc	10v
8	Pargoletto'e colei	TTTbc	11v
9	Lungi dal vostro [lume]	TTBbc	12v
10	Lasso ch'io moro	TTBbc	13v
11	O dolce mio Martire	TTBbc	14v

MANUSCRIPT XL

OXFORD, BODLEIAN LIBRARY TENBURY MS 1017

A score to two madrigals by Tarquinio Merula.

Copied 1638-46?
ff. 4. Modern pencil foliation: ff. 1-4.
Paper: 295 x 395 mm. Ten staves per page (ruled with a five-stave rastrum of 118.5 mm span and individual staves each measuring 13 mm). The pages are not folded into gatherings and the staves on the left and right of each folio have been joined by hand in the middle to enable the scribe to copy stratigraphically across the whole width of the paper. No music entered on f. 1.

---

[a] Does not include the five-part concluding chorus 'O Bellezza vitale' which appears in *Ob* Tenbury 1009, f. 9; see MS XXXIII above.
[b] The final section 'Occhi ladri' is a resetting of a four-voice canzonet from Dering's *Canzonette a quattro voci* (1620).

Watermarks: pot with letters ID; Thompson (1988), Watermark IX.

Script: Stephen Bing (with some text underlay added to 'Nominativo hic' by George Jeffreys).

No original binding (f. 1 show signs of wear and tear due to use as outer cover); each leaf has been guarded and bound in a modern binding with *Ob* Tenbury MSS 1015-16 and 1018.

Contents of *Ob* Tenbury MS 1017:[a]

Folio	Composer	Title	Scoring
1[v]	Claudio Merula[b]	Nominativo hic & h[a]ec & hoc	CATBbc
3[v]	Claudio Merula[b]	Nominativo q[ui]s vel qui qu[a]e quod	CATBbc

MANUSCRIPT XLI

OXFORD, BODLEIAN LIBRARY TENBURY MS 1285a-b

A score to the anthems 'In the midst of life' and 'What praise can reach thy clemency' by George Jeffreys for four voices and basso continuo, and Michael East's anthem 'Awake and stand up' for six voices and basso continuo.

Jeffreys' anthems copied *c*.1665, and the anthem by East copied onto the spare paper sometime in the nineteenth century(?).

ff. 17. ff. [1][v]-[7] are paginated 45-56 in ink (nineteenth century) and ff. [8][v]-[17] are paginated 111-128 in pencil. ff. [1][r] and [17][v] are pasted to the card covers, and ff. [7][v] and [8][r] are glued together.

Paper: 315 x 205 mm. Red marginal rulings on left and right. ff. [1][v]-[7]: twelve staves per page ruled with a four-stave rastrum of 82 mm span and individual staves each measuring 11 mm; ff. [8][v] [17]: ten staves per page ruled with a five-stave rastrum of 118 mm span and individual staves each measuring 13.5-14 mm.

Watermark: coat of arms (Amsterdam).

Collation: A^4(A1 removed) B^4 C^2 D^6 E^2.

Scribe: George Jeffreys.

Card covers inscribed 'ANTHEM / BY / Michael Este / &[cc] / 1624.'[c]

Contents of *Ob* Tenbury MS 1285:

---

[a] Printed concordance: *RISM* M2348.

[b] Attribution at the foot of f. 4[v] in the hand of George Jeffreys.

[c] i.e. printed source: *The Sixt Set of Bookes* (London, 1624); *RISM* E10.

Folio	Composer	Title	Scoring
		1285a	
[1]ᵛ	Michael Este	Awake and stand up '1624'	6vv bc
		1285b	
[8]ᵛ	[Jeffreys]	In the midst of life[d]	AATBbc
[11]ᵛ	[Jeffreys]	What praise can reach thy Clemency[e] 'Essay 3[8]'[f]	CATBbc

MANUSCRIPT XLII

OXFORD, CHRIST CHURCH MUS. 2, 397-408 & 436

The 'Great Set' of consort music of three to six parts (score, partbooks and organbook) which includes a number of untexted five-part madrigals and motets.

Copied in the mid to late 1630s.

Mus. 2: score to three-, four-, five- and six-part works.
Mus. 397-400: partbooks to four-part works.
Mus. 401-2: two lower parts of three-part works (lacks treble-viol book).[a]
Mus. 403-8: partbooks to five- and six-part works.
Mus. 436: organbook for four-, five- and six-part works.[a]

---

[d] An annotation on f. 160ᵛ of *Lbl* Add. 10,338 states: 'This song being blotted I have transposed into my other booke'; *Ob* Tenbury 1285 is probably a remnant of this score. Another annotation on f. 164 of *Lbl* Add. 10,338 indicated that the anthem was composed in October 1657. See MS I above.

[e] An annotation on f. 154 of the *Lbl* Add. 10,338 copy of 'What praise can reach thy clemency' states: 'This song being blotted & Altered, I have transposed into my other Score Book 1665'; *Ob* Tenbury 1285 is probably a remnant of this score.

[f] Sandys (1638), Es[s]ay XXXVIII, Part 2.

[a] See also *Och* Mus. 417-18/1080 and Mus. 432/612-13; MSS L & LI below.

Mus. 2

ff. i + 303 + ii.

Modern pencil foliation: ff. 1-290, followed by thirteen unnumbered folios.

Paper: 420 x 275 mm. Marginal rulings on left and right. Two rastra used throughout in various combinations to produce distinct systems of 2-6 staves (Rastrum 1: a two-stave rastrum of 26.5 mm span and individual staves each measuring 9 mm; Rastrum 2: a three-stave rastrum of 45.5 mm span and individual staves each measuring 9 mm), all barred in advance with eight bars per system. ff. 1-47^v: sixteen rastrum-ruled staves per page, ruled with Rastrum 1 in eight two-stave blocks; ff. 48-73^v: eighteen rastrum-ruled staves per page, ruled with Rastrum 2 in six three-stave blocks; ff. 74-107^v: twenty rastrum-ruled staves per page, ruled with Rastrum 1 in five four-stave blocks; ff. 108-213^v and [301]-[302]^v: twenty rastrum-ruled staves per page, ruled with Rastra 1 and 2 in four five-stave blocks; ff. 214-[300]^v and [303]$^{r-v}$: eighteen rastrum-ruled staves per page, ruled with Rastrum 2 in three six-stave blocks. No music entered on ff. 1-49^v, 73-73^v, 107^v, 153-162^v, 195-200^v, 205^v-213^v, 284^v-290^v, nor on any of the unnumbered folios (but barred throughout with eight bars per stave group).

Collation: ff. 1-47^v: A-G^6 H^6(H6 removed)

ff. 48-73^v: J^6(J1-3 & J6 removed) K-N^6

ff. 74-107^v: O^6(O4 removed) P^4 Q^6 R^4 S^8 T^6 V^2(V2 removed)

ff. 108-213^v: X-Y^6 Z^8 Aa^6 Bb^6(Bb6 removed) Cc-Nn^6 Oo^8(O8 removed)

ff. 214-[303]^v: Pp-Qq^6 Rr^4(Rr3 removed) Ss-Fff^6 Ggg^4(Ggg1 removed).

Watermark: coat of arms of Strasbourg (the 'Strasbourg Bend') with monogram 'WR' (presumably Wendelin Riehel of Strasbourg); Thompson, (1988), Watermark L.[b]

Scribe: Stephen Bing.

Inscriptions: titles, attributions and numbering added by Henry Aldrich to ff. 108-20. Various pencil attributions (by G.E.P. Arkwright?, early 20th century).

Binding: modern. (Johann Baptist Malchair's catalogue of the Christ Church music collections (1787) - now *Lcm* MS 2125 - describes the binding of Mus. 2 as 'rugh calf'.)

Mus. 397-400

Mus. 397: ff. iii + 42 + i. Modern pencil foliation: ff. 1-41, followed by one unnumbered folio. No music entered on ff. 11, 12, 40, 41-[42]^v. Collation: A-G^6.

---

[b] See also G. Piccard, *Wasserzeichen Lilie* (Stuttgart, 1983), marks 867-83 & 885.

Mus. 398: ff. i + 42 + i. Modern pencil foliation: ff. 1-40, followed by two unnumbered folios. No music entered on ff. 41^v-[42]^v. Collation: A-G^6.

Mus. 399: ff. i + 44 + i. Modern pencil foliation: ff. 1-41, followed by three unnumbered folios. No music entered on ff. 11^v-12, 41^v-[44]^v. Collation: A-B^6 C^2 D-H^6.

Mus. 400: ff. iii + 41 + i. Modern pencil foliation: ff. 1-40, followed by one unnumbered folio. No music entered on ff. 40^v-[41]^v. Collation: A^6(A6 removed) B-G^6.

Paper: 265 x 210 mm. Marginal rulings on left and right. Eight rastrum-ruled staves per page (ruled with a two-stave rastrum of 41 mm span and individual staves measuring 12.5 & 12 mm).

Watermark: coat of arms of Strasbourg (the 'Strasbourg Bend') with monogram 'WR'.

Scribe: John Lilly.

Inscriptions: various pencil attributions (by G.E.P. Arkwright?, early 20th century).

Bindings: late 17th-century, typical Oxford/Aldrich bindings: speckled brown leather with blind-tooled motif of three pointed buds; spine inscription in gold lettering: 'FANT[asia] G 4.B[ooks]'.

Mus. 401-2

Mus. 401: ff. iii + 48 + i. Modern pencil foliation: two unnumbered folios [a-b], ff. 1-40, 40a, 41-4, followed by one unnumbered folio. No music entered on ff. [a]-[b]^r, 34, 44^v-[45]^v. Collation: A^2 B^8 C^8(C7-8 removed) D-G^8.

Mus. 402: ff. ii + 50 + i. Modern pencil foliation: two unnumbered folios [a-b], ff. 1-45, followed by three unnumbered folios. No music entered on ff. [a]-[b]^v, 34, 45^v-[48]^v. Collation: A^2 B-G^8.

Paper: 263 x 216 mm. Marginal rulings on left and right. Eight rastrum-ruled staves per page (ruled with a two-stave rastrum of 40-41 mm span and individual staves measuring 12.5 & 12 mm).

Watermark: coat of arms of Strasbourg (the 'Strasbourg Bend') with monogram 'WR'.

Scribe: John Lilly.

Inscriptions: Mus. 401, f. i: 'In these Bookes. the first seven are Mr Coperario's / the next. 27 Mr Lupo's / the next seven Mr Mico's. / the last nine. Mr Orl. Gibbons's.' (Henry Aldrich). Various pencil attributions (by G.E.P. Arkwright?, early 20th century).

Bindings: late 17th-century, typical Oxford/Aldrich bindings: speckled brown leather with blind-tooled motif of three pointed buds; spine inscription in gold lettering: 'FANT[asia] F 4.B[ooks]' (sic: first viol book and keyboard book? missing).

Mus. 403-8

Mus. 403: ff. iii + 52 + iii. Modern pencil foliation: one unnumbered folio [a], ff. 1-50, followed by one unnumbered folio (Mus. 403 contains the sixth part of the six-part works). No music entered on ff. [a]^r, 47, 49-[51]^v. Collation: A-B^6 C-D^4 E-H^6 J-K^4.

Mus. 404: ff. i + 126 + i. Modern pencil foliation: ff. 1-125, followed by one unnumbered folio. No music entered on ff. 73-6 (74-5: unruled), 94, 123, 125-[126]^v. Collation: A-C^6 D^6(D6 removed) E-H^6 J^2 K-N^6 O^2 P-V^6 X^6(X4 removed) Y^6(Y3 & Y6 removed) Z^6.

Mus. 405: ff. i + 121 + iii. Modern pencil foliation: ff. 1-121. No music entered on ff. 16, 119, 121-121^v. Collation: A^6(A5 removed) B^4 C^4(C4 removed) D^4 E^6(E6 removed) F-G^4 H-Y^6 Z^2.

Mus. 406: ff. i + 125 + iii. Modern pencil foliation: ff. 1-46, 46[a]-104, 104a-123. No music entered on ff. 72-4 (72-3: unruled), 120, 122-123^v. Collation: A^6(A5 removed) B^6 C^4 D^6 E^6(E1 removed) F^6 G^2 H-K^6 L^6(L6 removed) M^6 N^4(N1 removed) O^6 P^2 Q^6(Q6 removed) R^4 S-V^6 X^6(X5 removed) Y^6 Z^6(Z6 removed) Aa-Bb^4.

Mus. 407: ff. i + 128 + iii. Modern pencil foliation: ff. 1-54, 54a-126, followed by one unnumbered folio. No music entered on ff. 19, 72-7 (75-6: unruled), 94, 99, 124, 126-[127]^v. Collation: A^6 B^6(B5 removed) C^6 D^6(D4 removed) E^6(E6 removed) F-N^6 O^2 P-V^6 X^6(X4 removed) Y^6 Z^4.

Mus. 408: ff. iii + 124 + iii. Modern pencil foliation: ff. 1-124. No music entered on ff. 17, 18, 59, 60, 70, 73-6 (74-5: unruled), 123. Collation: A^6 B^4 C^6 D^6(D5 removed) E^6 F^4 G-J^6 K^4 L-N^6 O-P^2 Q-Z^6 Aa^2(Aa2 removed).

Paper: 263 x 214 mm. Marginal rulings on left and right. Eight rastrum-ruled staves per page (ruled with a two-stave rastrum of 40 mm span and individual staves measuring 12.5 & 12 mm).

Watermark: coat of arms of Strasbourg (the 'Strasbourg Bend') with monogram 'WR'.

Scribe: John Lilly.

Inscriptions: titles, attributions and numbering added by Henry Aldrich to ff. 1-12^v of Mus. 404-8. Various pencil attributions (by G.E.P. Arkwright?, early 20th century).

Bindings: late 17th-century, typical Oxford/Aldrich bindings: speckled brown leather with blind-tooled motif of three pointed buds; spine inscription in gold lettering: 'FANT[asia] H VI.B[ooks]'.

Mus. 436

ff. i + i (modern) + 389 + i.

Modern pencil foliation: ff. 1-125, [125a], 126-78, followed by ten unnumbered folios.

Paper: 268 x 405 mm. Marginal rulings on left and right. Eight six-line staves per page (ruled with a two-stave rastrum of 41 mm span and individual six-line staves each measuring 14 mm). No music entered on ff. 40^v-48^v, 64^v-66, 112^v-114, 116^v-123, 124^v-125a, 126-147, 148^v-149, 150^v-155, 166^v-167, 177^v-[188]^v.

Collation: each folio consists of half a sheet of paper (probably cut before binding and each folio sewn individually) with horizontal chain lines stiched along what was originally the top or bottom of a sheet; there are therefore no gatherings in the normal sense.

Watermark: coat of arms of Strasbourg (the 'Strasbourg Bend') with monogram 'WR'.

Scribe: Stephen Bing.

Inscriptions: titles and attributions added by Henry Aldrich to ff. 49-63. Various pencil attributions (by G.E.P. Arkwright?, early 20th century).

Binding: late 17th-century, typical Oxford/Aldrich bindings: speckled brown leather with blind-tooled motif of three pointed buds (no inscription on spine).

Contents of *Och* Mus. 2, 397-408 & 436:

Three-Part Works[c]

| Composer | Title | Folios | | | VdGS |
		2	401	402	No.
[Coprario]	[Fantasia]	50	[b]^v	b^v	10
[Coprario]	[Fantasia]	50^v	1^v	1^v	1
[Coprario]	[Fantasia]	51	2^v	2^v	2
[Coprario]	[Fantasia]	51^v	3^v	3^v	4
[Coprario]	[Fantasia]	52^v	5^v	5^v	9
[Coprario]	[Fantasia]	53	6^v	6^v	5
[Coprario]	[Fantasia]	53^v	7^v	7^v	6
[Lupo]	[Fantasia]	54	8^v	8^v	2
[Lupo]	[Fantasia]	54^v	9^v	9^v	3
[Lupo]	[Fantasia]	55	10^v	10^v	4
[Lupo]	[Fantasia]	55^v	11^v	11^v	5
[Lupo]	[Fantasia]	56	12^v	12^v	6
[Lupo]	[Ayre]	56^v	13^v	13^v	7
[Lupo]	[Fantasia]	57	14^v	14^v	8

[c] Lacking the treble-viol partbook.

Composer	Title				
[Lupo]	[Fantasia]	57v	15v	15v	9
[Lupo]	[Fantasia]	58	16v	16v	10
[Lupo]	[Fantasia]	58v	17v	17v	11
[Lupo]	[Fantasia]	59	18v	18v	12
[Lupo]	[Fantasia]	59v	19v	19v	13
[Lupo]	[Fantasia]	60	20v	20v	14
[Lupo]	[Fantasia]	60v	21	21	15
[Lupo]	[Ayre]	61	21v	21v	20
[Lupo]	[Fantasia]	61v	22v	22v	16
[Lupo]	[Fantasia]	62	23	23	19
[Lupo]	[Fantasia]	62v	23v	23v	17
[Lupo]	[Ayre]	63	24v	24v	18
[Lupo]	[Ayre]	63v	25v	25v	21
[Lupo]	[Ayre]	64	26v	26v	23
[Mico]	[Fantasia]	64v	27v	27v	1
[Mico]	[Fantasia]	65	28v	28v	2
[Mico]	[Fantasia]	65v	29v	29v	3
[Mico]	[Fantasia]	66	30v	30v	4
[Mico]	[Fantasia]	66v	31v	31v	5
[Mico]	[Fantasia]	67v	32v	32v	6
[Mico]	[Fantasia]	68	33v	33v	7
[O. Gibbons]	[Fantasia]	68v	34v	34v	1
[O. Gibbons]	[Fantasia]	69	35v	35v	2
[O. Gibbons]	[Fantasia]	69v	36v	36v	3
[O. Gibbons]	[Fantasia]	70	37v	37v	4
[O. Gibbons]	[Fantasia]	70v	38v	38v	5
[O. Gibbons]	[Fantasia]	71	39v	39v	6
[O. Gibbons]	[Fantasia]	71v	40v	40v	7
[O. Gibbons]	[Fantasia]	72	40av	41v	8
[O. Gibbons]	[Fantasia]	72v	41v	42v	9
[Lupo]	[Pavan]	-	42v	43v	4
[Lupo]	[Pavan]	-	43	44	3
[Lupo]	[Pavan]	-	43v	44v	1
[Lupo]	[Pavan]	-	44	45	2

Four-Part Works

| Composer | Title | Folios | | | | | VdGS |
		2	397	398	399	400	436	No.
[Bull][d]	[Fantasia]	74	1	1	1	1	1	-
[Ferrabosco II]	[Fantasia]	74v	1v	1v	1v	1v	1v	1

---

[d] The pencil attribution to Coprario in the score (Mus. 2) is incorrect and was probably taken from the misattribution in *Ob* Mus. Sch. F 568-9; see G. Dodd, 'Coperario or Bull?', *Chelys*, i (1969), 41.

[Ferrabosco II]	[Fantasia]	75ᵛ	2ᵛ	2ᵛ	2ᵛ	2ᵛ	2	2
[Ferrabosco II]	[Fantasia]	76ᵛ	3ᵛ	3ᵛ	3ᵛ	3ᵛ	3ᵛ	3
[Ferrabosco II]	[Fantasia]	77ᵛ	4ᵛ	4ᵛ	4ᵛ	4ᵛ	4ᵛ	4
[Ferrabosco II]	[Fantasia]	78	5ᵛ	5ᵛ	5ᵛ	5ᵛ	5ᵛ	5
[Ferrabosco II]	[Fantasia]	78ᵛ	6ᵛ	6ᵛ	6ᵛ	6ᵛ	6ᵛ	6
[Ferrabosco II]	[Fantasia]	79	7ᵛ	7ᵛ	7ᵛ	7ᵛ	7ᵛ	7
[Ferrabosco II]	[Fantasia]	79ᵛ	8ᵛ	8ᵛ	8ᵛ	8ᵛ	8ᵛ	8
[Ferrabosco II]	[Fantasia]	80	9ᵛ	9ᵛ	9ᵛ	9ᵛ	9ᵛ	9
[Ferrabosco II]	[Fantasia]ᵉ	80ᵛ	10ᵛ	10ᵛ	10ᵛ	10ᵛ	10ᵛ	10
[Ferrabosco II]	[Fantasia]ᵉ	81ᵛ	11ᵛ	11ᵛ	12ᵛ	11ᵛ	11ᵛ	11
[Ferrabosco II]	[Fantasia]	82ᵛ	12ᵛ	12ᵛ	13ᵛ	12ᵛ	12ᵛ	12
[Ferrabosco II]	[Fantasia]	83ᵛ	13ᵛ	13ᵛ	14ᵛ	13ᵛ	13ᵛ	13
[Ferrabosco II]	[Fantasia]	83ᵛ	14ᵛ	14ᵛ	15ᵛ	14ᵛ	14ᵛ	23
[Ferrabosco II]	[Fantasia]	84ᵛ	15ᵛ	15ᵛ	16ᵛ	15ᵛ	15ᵛ	14
[Ferrabosco II]	[Fantasia]	85ᵛ	16ᵛ	16ᵛ	17ᵛ	16ᵛ	6ᵛ	15
[Ferrabosco II]	[Fantasia]	86ᵛ	17ᵛ	17ᵛ	18ᵛ	17ᵛ	17ᵛ	16
[Ferrabosco II]	[Fantasia]	87ᵛ	18ᵛ	18ᵛ	19ᵛ	18ᵛ	18ᵛ	17
[Ferrabosco II]	[Fantasia]	88ᵛ	19ᵛ	19ᵛ	20ᵛ	19ᵛ	19ᵛ	18
[Ferrabosco II]	[Fantasia]	89ᵛ	20ᵛ	20ᵛ	21ᵛ	20ᵛ	20ᵛ	19
[Ferrabosco II]	[Fantasia]	90ᵛ	21ᵛ	21ᵛ	22ᵛ	21ᵛ	21ᵛ	20
[Ferrabosco II]	[Fantasia]	91ᵛ	22ᵛ	22ᵛ	23ᵛ	22ᵛ	22ᵛ	21
[Ferrabosco II]	[Fantasia]	92ᵛ	23ᵛ	23ᵛ	24ᵛ	23ᵛ	23ᵛ	22
[Ward]	[Fantasia]	93ᵛ	24ᵛ	24ᵛ	25ᵛ	24ᵛ	24ᵛ	1
[Ward]	[Fantasia]	94ᵛ	25ᵛ	25ᵛ	26ᵛ	25ᵛ	25ᵛ	2
[Ward]	[Fantasia]	95	26ᵛ	26ᵛ	27ᵛ	26ᵛ	26ᵛ	3
[Ward]	[Fantasia]	95ᵛ	27ᵛ	27ᵛ	28ᵛ	27ᵛ	27ᵛ	4
[Ward]	[Fantasia]	96ᵛ	28ᵛ	28ᵛ	29ᵛ	28ᵛ	28ᵛ	5
[Ward]	[Fantasia]	97	29ᵛ	29ᵛ	30ᵛ	29ᵛ	29ᵛ	6
[Jenkins]	[Fantasia]	97ᵛ	30ᵛ	30ᵛ	31ᵛ	30ᵛ	30ᵛ	1
[Jenkins]	[Fantasia]	98ᵛ	31ᵛ	31ᵛ	32ᵛ	31ᵛ	31ᵛ	2
[Jenkins]	[Fantasia]	99ᵛ	32ᵛ	32ᵛ	33ᵛ	32ᵛ	32ᵛ	4
[Jenkins]	[Fantasia]	100ᵛ	33ᵛ	33ᵛ	34ᵛ	33ᵛ	33ᵛ	3
[Coprario]	[Fantasia]	101ᵛ	34ᵛ	34ᵛ	35ᵛ	34ᵛ	34ᵛ	1
[Coprario]	[Fantasia]	102ᵛ	35ᵛ	35ᵛ	36ᵛ	5ᵛ	35ᵛ	2
[Coprario]	[Fantasia]	103ᵛ	36ᵛ	36ᵛ	37ᵛ	36ᵛ	36ᵛ	3
[Coprario]	[Fantasia]	104ᵛ	37ᵛ	37ᵛ	38ᵛ	37ᵛ	37ᵛ	4
[Coprario]	[Fantasia]	105ᵛ	38ᵛ	38ᵛ	39ᵛ	38ᵛ	38ᵛ	5
[Coprario]	[Fantasia]	106ᵛ	39ᵛ	39ᵛ	40ᵛ	39ᵛ	39ᵛ	7

ᵉ Parts 1 and 2 of a four-part version of the 'Hexachord' Fantasia *a* 5 (see below); Part 1: ut-re-mi and Part 2: la-sol-fa. Edward Lowinsky attributed the piece to Alfonso dalla Viola (*c*.1508-*c*.1573) on uncertain grounds. See E. Lowinsky, 'Echoes of Adrian Willaert's Chromatic "Duo" in 16th and 17th-Century Compositions', *Studies in Music History: Essays for Oliver Strunk* (Princeton, 1968), 211.

Five-Part Works

Composer	No.	Title[f]	\	\	\	Folios	\	\	\	\	VdGS No.	Printed Source
			2	403	404	405	406	407	408	436		
Luca Marenzio	1	Arda pur [sempre o mora]	108	–	1	1	1	1	1	49		M560
L. Marenzio	2	Rimanti in pace	108v	–	1v	1v	1v	1v	1v	49v		M557
L. Marenzio	3	Ond[']ei di morte	109	–	2	2	2	2	2	50		M557
L. Marenzio	4	Caro dolce [mio ben]	109v	–	2v	2v	2v	2v	2v	50v		M546
L. Marenzio	5	Che sei tu [se'l cor mio]	110	–	3	3	3	3	3	51		M557
Claudio Monteverde	6	Latral Parte prima[g]	110v	–	3v	3v	3v	3v	3v	51v		M3459
Ric. Mico	7	Parte Seconda[g]	111	–	4	4	4	4	4	52		
Claudio Monteverde	8	Sovra tenere herbette	111v	–	4v	4v	4v	4v	4v	52v		M3459
Cl: Monteverde	9	O com[']e gran martire	112v	–	5	5	5	5	5	53v		M3459
Horatio Vecchi	10	Clorinda [hai vinto]	113	–	5v	5v	5v	5v	5v	54		V1043
Mr Wm White	11	Diapente [Pt 1][h]	113v	–	6	6	6	6	6	54v		
Mr John Ward	12	Cor mio [deh non languire][i]	114v	–	6v	6v	6v	6v	6v	55v		

[f] The madrigals and motets in this section are all without text; attributions, titles and numbers were added by Henry Aldrich.
[g] 'Latral' is a textless version of 'La tra'l sangue e le morti egro', the second section of a three-section madrigal from Monteverdi's *Il Terzo Libro de Madrigali a Cinque Voci* (1592) ('Vattene pur crudel', 'La tra'l sangue' and 'Poi ch'ella', text by Tasso). Mico's 'Parte Seconda' is attached in two other sources (*Lbl* Egerton 2485 and *Ob* Mus. Sch. E 415-18). 'Latral' contains a central chromatic fugato on a falling subject and Mico's piece contains a fugato on a rising subject; no other connection between the two is known and no explanation of Mico's contribution can presently be offered.
[h] For Part 2, see below.
[i] Fully texted in *Lbl* Egerton 3665 only.

Composer		Title								Source
Benedetto Pal[l]avicino	13	Era l'anima [mia]	115v	-	7	7	7	7	7	56v	P793
L. Marenzio	14	Ami Tyrsi [e me'l nieghi]	116v	-	7v	7v	7v	7v	7v	57	M560
L. Marenzio	15	Deh poi ch'era	117	-	8	8	8	8	8	57v	M560
Benedetto Pal[l]avicino	16	Come vivro	117v	-	8v	8v	8v	8v	8v	58	P793
L. Marenzio	17	Quell'augellin	118	-	9	9	9	9	9	58v	M560
L. Marenzio	18	Ma gridiran [*recte* grideran per me]j	118v	-	9v	9v	9v	9v	9v	59	M560
Th: Lupo	19	Miserere [mei Domine]	119	-	10	10	10	10	10	59v	
Th: Lupo	20	O vos omnes	119v	-	10v	10v	10v	10v	10v	60	
Marenzio [*recte* Pallavicino]k	21	O doloroso [*recte* dolorosa morte]	120	-	11	11	11	11	11	60v	P796
Cl: Monteverde	22	Voi pur [da me partite]	-	-	11v	11v	11v	11v	11v	61v	M3467
Cl: Monteverde	23	Luci [seren'e chiare]	-	-	12	12	12	12	12	62v	M3467
Alfonso Ferrabosco [II]	24	Dovehouse Pavan	-	-	12v	12v	12v	12v	12v	63	
[Mico]		[Pavan]	-	-	13	13	13	13	13	63v	1
[Mico]		[Pavan]	-	-	13v	13v	13v	13v	13v	64	2
[Mico]		[Pavan]	-	-	14	14	14	14	14	-	3
[Mico?]l		[Fantasia]	-	-	14v	14v	14v	14v	14v	-	3
[Mico?]l		[Fantasia]	-	-	15	15	15	15	15	-	4

j Second section of 'Cruda Amarilli'.
k Aldrich mistakenly attributes 'O dolorosa' to 'Marenzio'.
l Attributed to Mico on grounds of position in source and style; see Dodd ed. (1980-), MICO - 1 & 4.

[Mico]	[In Nomine]	–	–	–	–	–	–	66ᵛ	–
[Ferrabosco II]	[In Nomine]	–	–	–	–	–	–	67ᵛ	3
[Ferrabosco II]	[In Nomine]	–	–	–	–	–	–	68ᵛ	1
[Ferrabosco II]	[In Nomine]	–	–	–	–	–	–	69ᵛ	2
[Ward]	[Dolce languir]ᵐ	127ᵛ	47ᵛ	47ᵛ	46aᵛ	47ᵛ	47ᵛ	101ᵛ	1
[Ward]	[La rondinella]ᵐ	128ᵛ	48ᵛ	48ᵛ	47ᵛ	48ᵛ	48ᵛ	102ᵛ	2
[Ward]	[Fantasia]	129ᵛ	49ᵛ	49ᵛ	48ᵛ	49ᵛ	49ᵛ	103ᵛ	3
[Ward]	[Fantasia]	130ᵛ	50ᵛ	50ᵛ	49ᵛ	50ᵛ	50ᵛ	104ᵛ	4
[Ward]	[Fantasia]	131ᵛ	51ᵛ	51ᵛ	50ᵛ	51ᵛ	51ᵛ	105ᵛ	5
[Ward]	[Fantasia]	132ᵛ	52ᵛ	52ᵛ	51ᵛ	52ᵛ	52ᵛ	106ᵛ	6
[Ward]	[Fantasia]	133ᵛ	53ᵛ	53ᵛ	52ᵛ	53ᵛ	53ᵛ	107ᵛ	7
[Ward]	[Fantasia]	134ᵛ	54ᵛ	54ᵛ	53ᵛ	54ᵛ	54ᵛ	108ᵛ	8
[Ward]	[Fantasia]	135ᵛ	55ᵛ	55ᵛ	54ᵛ	54aᵛ	55ᵛ	109ᵛ	9
[Ward]	[Non fu senza]ⁿ	136ᵛ	56ᵛ	56ᵛ	55ᵛ	55ᵛ	56ᵛ	110ᵛ	10
[Ward]	[Fantasia]ⁿ	137ᵛ	57ᵛ	57ᵛ	56ᵛ	56ᵛ	57ᵛ	111ᵛ	14
[Ferrabosco II]	[Fantasia]ⁿ	138ᵛ	58ᵛ	58ᵛ	57ᵛ	57ᵛ	58ᵛ	–	–
[Ferrabosco II]	[Fantasia]ⁿ	139ᵛ	59ᵛ	59ᵛ	58ᵛ	58ᵛ	59ᵛ	–	–
[Ferrabosco II]	[Pavan]	140ᵛ	60ᵛ	60ᵛ	59ᵛ	59ᵛ	60ᵛ	114ᵛ	9
[Ferrabosco II]	[Pavan]ᵒ	141	61	61	60	60	61	115	4
[Ferrabosco II]	[Pavan]	141ᵛ	61ᵛ	61ᵛ	60ᵛ	60ᵛ	61ᵛ	115ᵛ	3
[Ferrabosco II]	[Alman]	142	62	62	61	61	62	116	4

ᵐ Fantasia of madrigalian origin; title from *Lbl* Egerton 3665.
ⁿ Parts 1 and 2 of the 'Hexachord' Fantasia; Part 1: ut-re-mi and Part 2: la-sol-fa (for a four-part version, see above).
ᵒ The so-called 'Four Notes Pavan' is underlaid with Ben Jonson's text 'Hear me, O God' in the following sources: *Lbl* Add. 29,372-7, *Lbl* Egerton 2013, *Lbl* Egerton 3665, *Ob* Tenbury 1018 and *Och* Mus. 423-8.

[Jenkins]	[Fantasia]	142v	–	62v	62v	61v	61v	62v	–	8
[Jenkins]	[Fantasia]	143v	–	63v	63v	62v	62v	63v	–	9
[Jenkins]	[Fantasia]	144v	–	64v	64v	63v	63v	64v	–	11
[Jenkins]	[Fantasia]	145v	–	65v	65v	64v	64v	65v	–	12
[Jenkins]	[Fantasia]	146v	–	66v	66v	65v	65v	66v	–	14
[Jenkins]	[Fantasia]	147v	–	67v	67v	66v	66v	67v	–	10
[Jenkins]	[Pavan]	148v	–	68v	68v	67v	67v	68v	–	1
[O. Gibbons]	[In Nomine]	149v	–	69v	69v	68v	68v	69v	123v	2
[W. White]	[Fantasia]	150v	–	70v	70v	69v	69v	70v	–	2
[W. White]	[Fantasia]p	152	–	71v	71v	70v	70v	71v	–	3
[Pallavicino]	[Cor mio deh non languire]q	–	–	72v	72	71v	71v	72v	125[a]v	P793
[Coprario]	[Leno]r	–	–	19v	19v	19v	19v	19v	70v	47
[Coprario]	[Cresce in voi]	163s	–	20	20	20	20	20	71v	16
[Coprario]	[Deh cara anima mia]t	–	–	20v	20v	20v	20v	20v	72	32
[Coprario]	[Crudel perche or Corsea/Corisca]u	120v	–	21	21	21	21	21	72v	1
[Coprario]	[Io son ferito amore]	121	–	21v	21v	21v	21v	21v	73v	2
[Coprario]	[O voi che sospirate]v	163v	–	22	22	22	22	22	74v	48

p Part 2 of 'Diapente', see above.
q Textless madrigal.
r Fantasies of madrigalian origin. See Charteris (1976); ibid. (1982), 18-19; and Pinto (1981), 25.
s Incomplete.
t Fully texted in *Ob* Tenbury 940-4 and *US-SM* EL 25 A 46-51.
u Entitled 'Crudel perche' in *Ob* Egerton 2485, *Lbl* Egerton 3665, *Och* Mus. 61-6 and *US-Wc* M990 C66F4; 'Corsea' or 'Corisca' in *Och* Mus. 527-30 & 1024; and *Lbl* Add. 39,550-4 contain both titles.
v A parody of Marenzio's 'O voi che sospirate' published in *Il Secondo Libro de Madrigali a Cinque Voci* (Venice, 1581); see Kerman (1962), 44, note 1.

[Coprario]	[Per far una leggiadra vendetta]	121v	–	22v	22v	22v	22v	75v	31
[Coprario]	[Gittene Ninfe]	164v	–	23v	23v	23v	23v	76v	34
[Coprario]	[Rapina l'alma]	122v	–	24v	24v	24v	24v	77v	3
[Coprario]	[Lume tuo fugace]	123v	–	25v	25v	25v	25v	78v	4
[Coprario]	[Io piango]	165v	–	26v	26v	26v	26v	79v	5
[Coprario]	[Luci beate e care]	124v	–	27v	27v	27v	27v	80v	9
[Coprario]	[In voi moro]	166v	–	28v	28v	28v	28v	81v	8
[Coprario]	[In te mio nove sole]	167v	–	29v	29v	29v	29v	82v	6
[Coprario]	[Del mio cibo amoroso]	168v	–	30v	30v	30v	30v	83v	7
[Coprario]	[Al primo giorno *or* In un boschetto]w	169v	–	31v	31v	31v	31v	84v	10
[Coprario]	[Chi pue mirarvi *or* Non posso piu soffrire]x	170v	–	32v	32v	32v	32v	85v	11
[Coprario]	[Lucretia mia]	125v	–	33v	33v	33v	33v	86v	12
[Coprario]	[Fantasia]y	171v	–	34v	34v	34v	34v	87v	49
[Coprario]	[Fuggi se sai fuggire]	172v	–	35v	35v	35v	35v	88v	38
[Coprario]	[Occhi miei con viva speme]	126v	–	36v	36v	36v	36v	89v	46
[Pallavicino]	[O come vaneggiate donna]z	–	–	37	37	37	37	90	P793

w Entitled 'Al primo giorno' in *Lbl* Egerton 3665 and *US-Wc* M990 C66F4; and 'In un boschetto' in Mad. Soc. G 37-42.
x Entitled 'Chi pue mirarvi' in *Lbl* Egerton 3665 and *US-Wc* M990 C66F4; and 'Non posso piu soffrire' in Mad. Soc. G 37-42 (although it is possible that this is the text of the entry at the 44th semibreve).
y Untitled in all sources.
z Textless madrigal.

Composer	Title									No.
[Coprario]	[O sonno, della mia morte or Deh preg' Amore][a]	174v	-	-	-	-	-	-	90v	21
[Lupo]	[Fantasia]	-	-	37v	37v	37v	37v	37v	91v	4
[Lupo]	[Il vago][b]	-	-	38v	38v	38v	38v	38v	92v	5
[Lupo]	[Io moriro][b]	-	-	39v	39v	39v	39v	39v	93v	18
[Lupo]	[Fantasia]	-	-	40	40	40	40	40	94v	2
[Lupo]	[Fantasia]	-	-	40v	40v	40v	40v	40v	95v	11
[Lupo]	[Fantasia]	201[c]	-	41v	41v	41v	41v	41v	96v	12
[Lupo]	[Fantasia]	201v	-	42v	42v	42v	42v	42v	97v	13
[Lupo]	[Fantasia]	202v	-	43v	43v	43v	43v	43v	98v	14
[Lupo]	[Fantasia]	203v	-	44v	44v	44v	44v	44v	99v	1
[Lupo]	[Fantasia]	204v	-	45v	45v	45v	45v	45v	100v	3
[Coprario]	[Dolce mia vita][d]	173v	-	-	-	-	-	-	-	14
[Coprario]	[Passa madonna]	175	-	-	-	-	-	-	-	15
[Coprario]	[Illicita cosa]	175v	-	-	-	-	-	-	-	13
[Coprario]	[Caggia fuoco dal cielo]	176v	-	-	-	-	-	-	-	19
[Coprario]	[Ite leggiadre rime]	177v	-	-	-	-	-	-	-	25
[Coprario]	[De la mia cruda sorte]	178v	-	-	-	-	-	-	-	26
[Coprario]	[D'un si bel fuoco]	179	-	-	-	-	-	-	-	37

[a] Fantasia of madrigalian origin entitled 'O sonno' in *Lbl* Egerton 3665, *Och* Mus. 61-6 and *US-Wc* M990 C66F4; and 'Deh preg' Amore' in *EIRE-Dm* Z3.4.1-6.
[b] Fantasia of madrigalian origin; title from *Lbl* Egerton 3665.
[c] Incomplete.
[d] Fantasies of madrigalian origin.

[Coprario]	[Dove il liquido argento *or* Fuggendo mi strugge][e]	179v	-	-	-	-	45
[Coprario]	[Voi caro il mio contento]	180v	-	-	-	-	17
[Coprario]	[Alma mia tu mi dicesti]	181v	-	-	-	-	18
[Coprario]	[Fugga dunque la luce]	182v	-	-	-	-	20
[Coprario]	[Dolce ben mio]	183v	-	-	-	-	22
[Coprario]	[Qual vaghezza]	184v	-	-	-	-	23
[Coprario]	[Credemi]	185v	-	-	-	-	24
[Coprario]	[Dammi o vita mia soccorso]	186v	-	-	-	-	27
[Coprario]	[Sia maledetto amore]	187v	-	-	-	-	28
[Coprario]	[Ninfa crudele]	188	-	-	-	-	29
[Coprario]	[Nel sen della mia Margherita]	188v	-	-	-	-	30
[Coprario]	[Ohime la gioia e breve]	189	-	-	-	-	35
[Coprario]	[O misero mio core]	189v	-	-	-	-	33
[Coprario]	[Lieti cantiamo]	190v	-	-	-	-	43
[Coprario]	[Dolce tormento]	191	-	-	-	-	40
[Coprario]	[Quando la vaga flori]	191v	-	-	-	-	42
[Coprario]	[Ingiustitia d' Amore][f]	192	-	-	-	-	41
[Coprario]	[La Primavera]	192v	-	-	-	-	39
[Coprario]	[Se mi volete morto]	193v	-	-	-	-	36
[Coprario]	[Io vivo in amoroso fuoco]	194v [g]	-	-	-	-	44

[e] Entitled 'Dove il liquido argento' in *Lbl* Egerton 3665 and *EIRE-Dm* Z3.4.13; and 'Fuggendo mi strugge' in *US-SM* EL 25 A 46-51.
[f] Bass part lacking.
[g] First 31 breves only.

Six-Part Works

Composer	Title	2	403	404	405	406	407	408	436	VdGS No.
					Folios					
[Lupo]	[Fantasia]	214	[a^v]	76^v	72^v	74^v	77^v	76^v	-	1
[Lupo]	[Fantasia]	215^v	1^v	77^v	73^v	75^v	78^v	77^v	-	2
[Lupo]	[Fantasia]	217	2^v	78^v	74^v	76^v	79^v	78^v	-	3
[Lupo]	[Fantasia]	218	3^v	79^v	75^v	77^v	80^v	79^v	-	4
[Lupo]	[Fantasia]	219^v	4^v	80^v	76^v	78^v	81^v	80^v	-	5
[Lupo]	[Fantasia]	221	5^v	81^v	77^v	79^v	82^v	81^v	147^v	6
[Lupo]	[Fantasia]	222	6^v	82^v	78^v	80^v	83^v	82^v	-	7
[Lupo]	[Fantasia]	223^v	7^v	83^v	79^v	81^v	84^v	83^v	149^v	8
[Lupo]	[Fantasia]	225	8^v	84^v	80^v	82^v	85^v	84^v	-	9
[Lupo]	[Fantasia]	227^v	9^v	85^v	81^v	83^v	86^v	85^v	-	10
[Ward]	[Fantasia]	229	10^v	86^v	82^v	84^v	87^v	86^v	-	2
[Ward]	[Fantasia]	230	11^v	87^v	83^v	85^v	88^v	87^v	-	3
[Ward]	[Fantasia]	231	12^v	88^v	84^v	86^v	89^v	88^v	-	4
[Ward]	[Fantasia]	232^v	13^v	89^v	85^v	87^v	90^v	89^v	-	5
[Ward]	[Fantasia]	233^v	14^v	90^v	86^v	88^v	91^v	90^v	-	6
[Ward]	[Fantasia]	235	15^v	91^v	87^v	89^v	92^v	91^v	155^v	7
[Ward]	[In Nomine]	236^v	16^v	92^v	88^v	90^v	93^v	92^v	156^v	1
[Ward]	[In Nomine]	238	17^v	93^v	89^v	91^v	94^v	93^v	158^v	2
[Ferrabosco II]	[Fantasia]	239^v	18^v	94^v	90^v	92^v	95^v	94^v	157^v	1
[Ferrabosco II]	[Fantasia]	241	19^v	95^v	91^v	93^v	96^v	95^v	159^v	2

[Ferrabosco II]	[Fantasia]	242ᵛ	20ᵛ	96ᵛ	92ᵛ	94ᵛ	97ᵛ	96ᵛ	160ᵛ	3
[Ferrabosco II]	[In Nomine]	244	21ᵛ	97ᵛ	93ᵛ	95ᵛ	98ᵛ	97ᵛ	161ᵛ	1
[Ferrabosco II]	[Fantasia]	245ᵛ	22ᵛ	98ᵛ	94ᵛ	96ᵛ	99ᵛ	98ᵛ	-	4
[Ferrabosco II]	[Fantasia]	247	23ᵛ	99ᵛ	95ᵛ	97ᵛ	100ᵛ	99ᵛ	-	5
[Ferrabosco II]	[Fantasia]	248ᵛ	24ᵛ	100ᵛ	96ᵛ	98ᵛ	101ᵛ	100ᵛ	162ᵛ	7
[Ferrabosco II]	[Fantasia]	250ᵛ	25ᵛ	101ᵛ	97ᵛ	99ᵛ	102ᵛ	101ᵛ	163ᵛ	6
[Ferrabosco II]	[Fantasia]	251ᵛ	26ᵛ	102ᵛ	98ᵛ	100ᵛ	103ᵛ	102ᵛ	164ᵛ	8
[Ferrabosco II]	[Fantasia]	252ᵛ	27ᵛ	103ᵛ	99ᵛ	101ᵛ	104ᵛ	103ᵛ	165ᵛ	9
[Ferrabosco II]	[Fantasia]	253ᵛ	28ᵛ	104ᵛ	100ᵛ	102ᵛ	105ᵛ	104ᵛ	-	10
[W. White]	[Fantasia]	255	29ᵛ	105ᵛ	101ᵛ	103ᵛ	106ᵛ	105ᵛ	-	1
[W. White]	[Fantasia]	256ᵛ	30ᵛ	106ᵛ	102ᵛ	104ᵛ	107ᵛ	106ᵛ	-	2
[W. White]	[Fantasia]	258ᵛ	31ᵛ	107ᵛ	103ᵛ	104aᵛ	108ᵛ	107ᵛ	-	3
[W. White]	[Fantasia]	260	32ᵛ	108ᵛ	104ᵛ	105ᵛ	109ᵛ	108ᵛ	-	4
[W. White]	[Fantasia]	261ᵛ	33ᵛ	109ᵛ	105ᵛ	106ᵛ	110ᵛ	109ᵛ	-	5
[W. White]	[Fantasia]	262ᵛ	34ᵛ	110ᵛ	106ᵛ	107ᵛ	111ᵛ	110ᵛ	-	6
[Coprario]	[Fantasia]	283	35ᵛ	111ᵛ	107ᵛ	108ᵛ	112ᵛ	111ᵛ	167ᵛ	2
[Coleman]	[Fantasia]	268	36ᵛ	112ᵛ	108ᵛ	109ᵛ	113ᵛ	112ᵛ	168ᵛ	3
[Coleman]	[Fantasia]	265	37ᵛ	113ᵛ	109ᵛ	110ᵛ	114ᵛ	113ᵛ	169ᵛ	2
[Coleman]	[Fantasia]	266ᵛ	38ᵛ	114ᵛ	110ᵛ	111ᵛ	115ᵛ	114ᵛ	170ᵛ	1
[O. Gibbons]ʰ	[Fantasia]	269ᵛ	39ᵛ	115ᵛ	111ᵛ	112ᵛ	116ᵛ	115ᵛ	171ᵛ	1
[O. Gibbons]	[Fantasia]	271	40ᵛ	116ᵛ	112ᵛ	113ᵛ	117ᵛ	116ᵛ	172ᵛ	2

ʰ Anonymous in all sources but, since the works of other composers in the 'Great Set' are placed together (except in the five-part works with vocal origins), it seems reasonable to assign the whole group to Gibbons; stylistically there is nothing to argue against this suggestion. See R. Nicholson, 'A Note on Gibbons and the Anonymous 6-Part Fantasies in Christ Church Library', *Viola da Gamba Society Bulletin* (July, 1967); and Harper ed. (1982), pp. xv-xviii.

[O. Gibbons][i]	[Fantasia]	272ᵛ	41ᵛ	117ᵛ	113ᵛ	114ᵛ	118ᵛ	117ᵛ	173ᵛ	3
[O. Gibbons][i]	[Fantasia]	274	42ᵛ	118ᵛ	114ᵛ	115ᵛ	119ᵛ	118ᵛ	174ᵛ	4
[O. Gibbons][i]	[Fantasia]	275ᵛ	43ᵛ	119ᵛ	115ᵛ	116ᵛ	120ᵛ	189ᵛ	175ᵛ	5
[O. Gibbons][i]	[Fantasia]	277	44ᵛ	120ᵛ	116ᵛ	117ᵛ	121ᵛ	120ᵛ	176ᵛ	6
[O. Gibbons][i]	[Variations on 'Go from my window']	278ᵛ	45ᵛ	121ᵛ	117ᵛ	118ᵛ	122ᵛ	121ᵛ	-	-
[O. Gibbons]	[Pavan]	280ᵛ	47ᵛ	123ᵛ	119ᵛ	120ᵛ	124ᵛ	123ᵛ	-	-
[O. Gibbons]	[Galliard]	281ᵛ	48ᵛ	124ᵛ	120ᵛ	121ᵛ	125ᵛ	124ᵛ	-	-

---

[i] See note h. above.

MANUSCRIPT XLIII

OXFORD, CHRIST CHURCH MUS. 14

John Blow's autograph score of sacred and secular music by English and Italian composers.

    Copied in the mid 1670s.[a]
    ff. iv + 143 + iv.
    Original foliation: ff. 1-142 followed by one unnumbered folio [modern pencil: f. 143].
    Paper: 360 x 233 mm. Red marginal rulings on left and right. Twelve rastrum-ruled staves per page (ruled with a three-stave rastrum of 68 mm span and individual staves each measuring 12-12.5 mm). No music entered on f. [143]^v. f. ii^{r-v}: index in the hand of Johann Baptist Malchair (*c*.1787).
    Watermark: fleur-de-lys with countermark IHS.
    Collation: A-F^4 G^4(G3 removed) H-Ll^4.
    Scribe: John Blow.
    Inscription on f. 94: 'The last movement of the famous Serenato of Jacomo Carissimi. This Serenata is known by the name of I[l] Naviganti' (J.B. Malchair). (For John Blow's inscriptions see the inventory below.)
    Binding: speckled brown leather with blind-tooled motif of pointed buds.
    Contents of *Och* Mus. 14:

Folio	Composer	Title	Scoring	Printed Sources
1	Jo. Blow	Turn [th]ee unto me O Lord 'Anthem'	SATBbc	
3	Jo. Blow	How doth ye city sit solitary '3 Voc.'	ATBbc	
5^v	Jo. Blow	O Lord I have sinned[b] 'Anthem'	SATBbc	
8^v	Mat[t]hew Locke	When death shall depart us 'A Dialogue between Thirsis & Dorinda'	TBbc	1687^5, 1675^7, 1676^3
11^v	Jo. Blow	How art thou fallen from heaven	SBbc	1688^1
13	Jo. Blow	Jesus seeing the multitudes 'Anthame'	SSATBorg	
17^v	D^r. [C.] Gibbons	Sing unto the Lord O ye saints	SSATBorg	1674^2

---

[a] See Watkins Shaw (1964), 88-9.
[b] Written for the funeral of General Monck in 1670.

20ᵛ	Docter. Gibbons	The Lord said unto my Lord	SSSAbc	
23	Dʳ. [C.] Gibbons	Teach mee O Lord	SSATBbc	1674²
26	Dʳ. [C.] Gibbons	God be mercyful unto us	SSSABbc	
29	Dʳ. Child	O bone Jesu	CATBbc	
31	Dʳ. [C.] Gibbons	Ah my Soule why soe dismayd	SSBbc	
32	Dr. [C.] Gibbons	Above ye starrs my Saviour dwells	SSATBorg	
36	Dʳ. [C.] Gibbons	Laudate dominum	SSABbc	
38ᵛ	Dʳ. [C.] Gibbons	O Bone Jesu	SAABbc	
40	John Blow	Gloria patri et filio	SAbc	
41	Dʳ. [C.] Gibbons	O prayse the Lord all yee heathen	SSABbc	
42	Mʳ Wise	Awake Awake up my Glory	SATBbc	
43ᵛ	Jo. Blow	I will cry unto thee O god	SATBbc	
46	John Blow	Sing wee merrily	SSATTBbc	
51	[Rovetta]ᶜ	Io mi sento morir	CCbc	R2981
53	Alessandro Vincenti [*recte* Pesenti]ᵈ	Vano e il desio	CCbc	P1549
55ᵛ	[Crivelli]	Ah non si puo crudele	CATBbc	C4424
59	[Rovetta]	Chi vuol haver felice	CCbc	R2981
61ᵛ	[Crivelli]	Vanne mesto sospir	CATBbc	C4424
64ᵛ	[Monteverdi]	Tu dormi, Ah crudo core	CATBbc	M3494
66ᵛ	[Rovetta]	Udite'amante meraviglia	CATBbc	R2981
70	[Monteverdi]	Allume de le stelle [*recte* Al lume delle stelle]	CCTBbc	M3494
72	[Monteverdi]	Non e di gentil core	CCbc	M3494
74ᵛ	[Monteverdi]	Parlo misero	CCBbc	M3494
77	[Pesenti]	Ancor non sapev'io	TTBbc	P1549
80	[Pesenti]	Perche non mi rimiri	CTTBbc	P1549
84	[Pesenti]	Ite rose felice [*recte* felici]	CCATBbc	P1549
87ᵛ	[Rovetta]	Credetel voi che non sentite amore	CATBbc	R2981
90ᵛ	Matthew Lock	All things their certayn Periods have 'A New yeares Song'	CATBbc	
94	[Carissimi]	Amanti che diteᵉ	CCBbc	
95ᵛ	[Carissimi?]ᶠ	Il mondo tace	CCBbc	
97	[Stradella?]ᵍ	Lontani del core	CCBbc	

ᶜ Incorrect pencil attribution to 'Alessandro Vincenti'.
ᵈ Also misattribution to 'Alessandro Vincenti' (the publisher) in *Ob* Mus. Sch. C 12-19 and *Lwa* CG 63.
ᵉ Last movement of the cantata *I Naviganti* ('Sciolto hauean').
ᶠ Questionable attribution in *F-Pn* Vm⁷ 8.
ᵍ Attributed to Stradella in *Lbl* Add. 33,235 (MS XI above); not listed in Jander (2/1962).

101	[Carissimi]	Tronchi si pensiri'il vuolo	CBbc
104	Jo. Blow	Post haec audivi	ABbc
106ᵛ	Jo. Blow	In lectulo meo	ATbc
108	Jo. Blow	Paratum cor meum	SSbc
109ᵛ	Jo. Blow	Cantate domino	AAbc
111		Correte amante	CCBbc
113	John Blow	Quam diligo legam tuam	SSbc
114ᵛ	Jo. Blow	Laudate nomen domini	SSbc
117		Confitebor tibi	CCAbc
122	Jo. Blow	Salvator mundi	SCATBbc
124ᵛ	Jo. Blow	Gloria patri qui creavit nos	SCATBbc
128ᵛ	Sig: Cælo Checchelli	Dicite laudem	ATBbc 1650[1]
131	[Locke]	A Hymne O god becommeth thee	AABbc
133ᵛ	Mʳ: Lock:	O give thanks	SABbc
136	Jo. Blow	As on Euphrates shady bancks	SSBbc
139	Capt. Henry Cooke	Turn thou us O good lord	SATBbc
140ᵛ	Lock	How doth the city sit solitary	CCATBorg

MANUSCRIPT XLIV

OXFORD, CHRIST CHURCH MUS. 18

Henry Aldrich's score of sacred and secular music by English and Italian composers.

> Copied before c.1670?[a]
> ff. v + 43 + v.
> Original pagination: pp. 1-86.
> Paper: 355 x 237 mm. Marginal rulings on left and right. Twelve rastrum-ruled staves per page (ruled with a single-stave rastrum measuring 13 mm). f. i: index in the hand of Johann Baptist Malchair (c.1787).
> Watermark: fleur-de-lys with countermark IHS / LM.
> Collation: A⁴(A3 removed) B-L⁴.
> Scribe: Henry Aldrich.
> Binding: typical Oxford/Aldrich binding: speckled brown leather with blind-tooled motif of three pointed buds.

---

[a] Certainly copied before 1677 as John Blow, who received his doctorate in 1677, is described as 'Mr John Blow'.

Contents of *Och* Mus. 18:

Composer	Title	Scoring	Page	Printed Source
[Cesti?][b]	Amanti sentiti	SAbc	1	
	Pensieri quietate	Sbc	4	
	Occhi belli	SSbc	5	
[Turini]	O misera Dorinda	SBbc	7	T1388
[C. Gibbons]	Celebrate Dominum	SBbc	11	1674[2]
[Jeffreys][c]	With notes that are both loud and sweet	BBbc	13	
[Carissimi?][d]	Care salve beate	Bbc	18	
W. Lawes	Let God arise	Bbc	21	
Sig^{re} Charissimi	Lucifer coelestis	Bbc	23	1693[1]
Mr John Blow	Turne thee unto me	SATBbc	26	
Mr Orlando Gibbons	Behold thou hast made	Abc	29	1641[5]
Chr: Gibbons	How long wilt thou forget me	SSbc	32	1674[2]
	Ave maris stella	Sbc	35	
	Cur sic ploras	SBbc	37	
[Jeffreys]	Heu me miseram	SBbc	39	
[Grandi]	Oh quam gloriosus	SSbc	43	G3455[e]
	Hodie per te hominum	SSbc	46	
[Ramsey]	In guilty night[f]	STbc	48	
[O. Gibbons]	Sing unto ye Lord	BBbc	52	
H[enry] A[ldrich]	Salvator mundi	SSBbc	57	
[Jeffreys]	Erit gloria	STbc	64	1674[2]
[Grandi]	Tu dulcis es Messia	[S]Tbc[g]	66	G3439[h]
[Jeffreys]	Et ingrediar [i]	STbc	68	
[Facchi]	Quid timidi estis	S[Sbc][j]	70	F44
[Grandi]	O quam Suave est Nomen	S[Sbc][j]	74	G3422
Mr Mich: Wise	I charge you O Daughters of Jerusalem	SBbc	76	1674[2]
H[enry] A[ldrich]	I come into my garden	SBbc	77	

---

[b] Attributed to 'Sig^r. Marco [Cesti]' in *Och* Mus. 996, to 'Marco Marazzolli in *I-Bc* Q 50, to 'Luigi' [Rossi?] in *I-Fc* f I 25 and anonymous in all other concordant sources.
[c] Manuscript concordances for the Jeffreys pieces are given in Table 23.
[d] Questionable attribution to Carissimi by J.B. Malchair in *Och* Mus. 13 only.
[e] 'O quam gloriosa' in A. Grandi, *Il Sesto Libro de Motetti* (Venice, 1630); and 'O quam gloriosus' in *Lbl* Add. 31,479, see MS IX above.
[f] See Smallman (1965), 142-3; and Chan (1980).
[g] Top voice not copied.
[h] 'Tu pulchra es Maria' in A. Grandi, *Celesti Fiori... Libro Quinto* (Venice, 1619); and 'Tu dulcis es Messia' in *Lbl* Add. 31,479, see MS IX above.
[i] Incomplete.
[j] Top voice copied only.

| H[enry] A[ldrich] | O Lord our Governour | Sbc | 81 |
| H[enry] A[ldrich] | O bone Jesu | CCABbc | 83 |

MANUSCRIPT XLV

OXFORD, CHRIST CHURCH MUS. 21

A score of English madrigals, anthems and fantasies, and Italian madrigals.

The music by Orlando Gibbons and Coprario was copied in the 1620s; the other music, both English and Italian, was added in the 1630s?; and Benjamin Rogers interpolated copies of his own compositions and added various ascriptions and annotations c.1673-85.[a]

ff. ii + 184.

Paginated: pp. 1-372 (probably in the 1680s) by Johann Baptist Malchair who also supplied the index on ff. i^r and 2^r.

Paper: 355 x 220 mm. Marginal rulings on left and right. pp. 1-56, 321-72: twelve rastrum-ruled staves per page (ruled with a three-stave rastrum of 66 mm span and individual staves each measuring 12-12.5 mm); pp. 57-320: ten rastrum-ruled staves per page (ruled with a five-stave rastrum of 135 mm span and individual staves each measuring 12.5-13 mm). The music on the following pages is copied stratigraphically (i.e. copied across the whole width of the opening, verso to recto): pp. 2-17, 19-41, 57-165, 176-292, 294-313, 322-5, 328-69. No music entered on pp. 1, 18,
42-3, 293, 309, 326-7.

Watermark: coat of arms (details indistinguishable).

Collation: not possible due to the tightness of binding.

Scribes: A: unidentified (1620s)
    B: unidentified (1630s?)
    C: Benjamin Rogers

Inscription pasted to p. 1: 'Ben: Rogers his booke Aug[us]t 18. 1673 / and p[re]sented me, by Mr John Playford Stationer / in the Temple London. / This Score booke was done formerly, / by that rare Musition, M^r. Orlando Gibbons / and this book is of great value to a Composer'[b] (Benjamin Rogers). (For other inscriptions see the inventory below.)

---

[a] See J. Harper, 'Orlando Gibbons: The Domestic Context of his Music and Christ Church MS 21', *MT*, cxxiv (1983b), 767-70.

[b] The inscription gave rise to the tradition that the manuscript was copied by Orlando Gibbons; see Fellowes (rev. 2/1970), 63-4. The actual connection with Gibbons is unclear, but the

Binding: brown leather with floral tooling and the inscription 'ORL. GIBBONS / & / B. ROGERS / &.C' on the spine.

Contents of *Och* Mus. 21:

Page	Composer[c]	Title Inscription[c]	VdGS No.	Scribe	Printed Concordances
2	Orlando Gibbons	[Fantasia *a* 3]	1	A	G1998, 1648[7]
		('Fantazies of 3 parts by Orlando Gibbons')			
4	[O. Gibbons]	[Fantasia *a* 3]	2	A	G1998, 1648[7]
6	(Orlando Gibbons)	[Fantasia] 3 parts	4	A	G1998, 1648[7]
8	[O. Gibbons]	[Fantasia *a* 3]	5	A	G1998, 1648[7]
10	[O. Gibbons]	[Fantasia *a* 3]	7	A	G1998, 1648[7]
12	[O. Gibbons]	[Fantasia *a* 3]	6	A	G1998, 1648[7]
14	(Orlando Gibbons)	(Fantazie 3 pts.)	8	A	G1998, 1648[7]
16	(Orlando Gibbons)	(Fantazie 3 parts)	9	A	G1998, 1648[7]
17		'The end of M[r] / Gibbons 3 parts / for ye viols'			
18	[No music entered; barred for three parts]				
..........................[Pages missing]............................
19	[O. Gibbons][d]	[Variations 'Go from my window' *a* 6][e]	-	A	
20	[O. Gibbons]	[Fantasia *a* 6][f]	-	A	
26	[O. Gibbons]	[Fantasia *a* 6][f]	-	A	
28		('Fantazie 6 parts')			
30	Orlando Gibbons	Fancy 6 pts[f]	-	A	
42	[No music entered; barred for six parts]				
43	Pomponio Nen[n]a	S'io vivo: Anima mia 2[da] Parte		B	N384
		'4[th] Lib: 4' [title and clefs only]			
44	(Dr [C.] Gibbons)	Fant[as]ie	39	B	
		'2 trebbels and a base'			
48	[C. Gibbons]	2[d] Fantazie	40	B	
52	(Dr [C.] Gibbons)	3[d] Fantazi[e] ('3 parts')	41	B	
57	M[r] Orlando Gibbons	The Silver Swan[g] [incomplete]		A	G1994
		'M[r] Orlando Gib[b]ons his Songes of 5 Partes'[h]			
58	M[r] Orlando Gibbons	2[d] O That the learned Poetes[g]		A	G1994

---

authoritative inscriptions in the Gibbons-verse-anthem section suggest that the manuscript was closely connected with Gibbons or his circle.

[c] The ascriptions and inscriptions in round brackets were added to the manuscript by Benjamin Rogers; ascriptions and inscriptions not in brackets are in the hand of the relevant scribe.

[d] Anonymous in all sources, but its appearance with other music by Gibbons in *Och* Mus. 2, 403-8 & 436 (where works by the same composer are always grouped together, see MS XLII above) makes it reasonable to assign the work to Gibbons; stylistically there is nothing to argue against this suggestion. See Nicholson (1967); Harper (1982), pp. xv-xviii; and ibid. (1983a).

[e] Concluding section only.

[f] Possibly untexted vocal pieces (a section of the third six-part fantasia on p. 33 is labelled 'Cho.'); see Harper (1982), pp. xviii & 123.

[g] Textless except for opening incipit.

[h] *The First Set of Madrigals and Mottets of 5. Parts: apt for Viols and Voyces* (London, 1612) with important variants; see Harper (1983b), 769-70.

62	(Mr Ferrabosco) [*Recte* O. Gibbons]	(Fantazie 5 Parts) [*Recte* I waigh not Fortunes frowne nor smile][i]		A G1994
66	[O. Gibbons]	[I tremble not at noyse of warre][i]		A G1994
70	[O. Gibbons]	[I see Ambition never pleasde][i]		A G1994
72		('Fantazie 5 part')		
74	[O. Gibbons]	[I faine not friendship where I hate][i]		A G1994
78	[O. Gibbons]	[How are thou thrald, O poore despised creature?][i]		A G1994
82	[O. Gibbons]	[Farewell all Joyes][i] ('Fantasie 5 parts')		A G1994
86	[O. Gibbons]	[Daintie fine Bird which art incaged][i]		A G1994
88	[O. Gibbons]	[Faire Ladies that to Love captive are][i]		A G1994
92	[O. Gibbons]	[Mongst thousand good][i]		A G1994
96	[O. Gibbons]	[Now each flowry bancke of May][i]		A G1994
100	[O. Gibbons]	[Lais now old, that erst attempting Lasse][i]		A G1994
105	[O. Gibbons]	[What is our Life?][i]		A G1994
111	[O. Gibbons]	[Ah deere Hart, why doe you rise?][i]		A G1994
112	[O. Gibbons]	[Faire is the Rose][i]		A G1994
117	[O. Gibbons]	[Nay, let mee weepe][i]		A G1994
122	[O. Gibbons]	[Yet if that age had frosted ore his head][i]		A G1994
126	[O. Gibbons]	[Nere let the Sunne with his deceiving light][i]		A G1994
130	[O. Gibbons]	[Trust not too much faire youth][i]		A G1994
136		(Awake my soule)[i]		A
142	[Coprario]	[Fantasia *a* 5 'O voi che sospirate'][j][k]	48	A
146	[Coprario]	[Fantasia *a* 5][l]	49	A
150	[Coprario]	[Fantasia *a* 5 'Fuggi se sai fuggire']	38	A
154	[Coprario]	[Fantasia *a* 5 'In te mio novo sole']	6	A
158	[Coprario]	[Fantasia *a* 5 'Al primo giorno' *or* 'In un boschetto'][m]	10	A
162	[Coprario]	[Fantasia *a* 5 'Chi pue mirarvi' *or* 'Non posso piu soffrire'][n]	11	A
166	D^r. Ben: Rogers	Bow down thine eare O L[or]d '1677'		C
171	D^r: Ben: Rogers	I beheld and lo 'Hymnus Apocalipticus 1678'		C
176	(O. Gibbons)	See the Word is Incarnate[o] '[These] words were made by Doctor goodman De[an] of Rochester'		A
190	(O. Gibbons)	Sing unto the Lord[o] 'Psalme 30: Anthem of 5 voc: was made for Do[cto]r: Marshall'		A

---

[i] Textless except for opening incipit.
[j] Fantasies of madrigalian origin; see Charteris (1976), ibid. (1982b), 18-19, and Pinto (1981), 25.
[k] A parody of Marenzio's 'O voi che sospirate' published in *Il Secondo Libro de Madrigali a Cinque Voci* (Venice, 1581); see Kerman (1962), 44, note 1.
[l] Untitled in all sources.
[m] Entitled 'Al primo giorno' in *Lbl* Egerton 3665 and *US-Wc* M990 C66F4; and 'In un boschetto' in *Lbl* Mad. Soc. G 37-42.
[n] Entitled 'Chi pue mirarvi in *Lbl* Egerton 3665 and *US-Wc* M990 C66F4; and 'Non posso piu soffrire' in Mad. Soc. G 37-42 (although it is possible that this is the text of the entry at the 44th semibreve).
[o] Verse anthem.

200	(O. Gibbons)	This is the Record of John^p	A	
		'For St John Baptists day / This Anthem was made for Dr Laud president of Saint Johns (Oxford)'		
210	[O. Gibbons]	Oh all true faithfull h[e]arts^p	A	
		'A thanks giving for ye kings happie recoverie from a great dangerous illness'		
218	[O. Gibbons]	We praise [thee] O Father^p	A	
230	[O. Gibbons]	Great Kinge of gods^p	A	
		'This anthem was made for the King's being in Scotland' [1617]		
242	[O. Gibbons]	Glorious & powerfull god^p	A	
254	[O. Gibbons]	Lord graunt grace^p	A	
		'An Anthem for all Saints day'		
262	[O. Gibbons]	Blessed are they^p	A	
		'A Wedding Anthem first made for my Lord of Summersett'		
272	(Mr Orlando Gibbons)	Behold thou hast made my days^p	A	1641^5
		'This Anthem was made at the entretie of Doctor Maxcie Deane of Windsor the same day ye night before his death'		
282	[O. Gibbons]	O Lord in thee^q	A	
		'The Lamentation[?]: A full Anthem'		
293	[No music entered; barred for five parts]			
294	Pomponio nenna	Alm' Afflitta che fai^r	B	N386
296	Pomponio nenna	Tu mi lasci crudele^r	B	N386
298	Pomponio nenna	merce grido piangendo^r	B	N386
300	Pomponio nenna	Occhi belli^r	B	N386
302	Claud: monteverde	La piaga ch'o nel core^r	B	M3467
304	monteverde	Cor mio mentre^r	B	M3467
306	monteverde	Volgea l'anima mia^r [incomplete]	B	M3467
308	Claudio Monteverdi	Cor mio non mori^r [first three bars only]	B	M3467

..........................[Pages missing]..........................

309	[No music entered; unbarred staves]			
310	Prencipe de venosa [Gesualdo]	Balta [*recte* Belta] poiche^r 'Lib sesto'	B	G1741
314	D[r] Rogers	[Magnificat in a minor]	C	
		'Evening Short Service altogether in A re key. 1684'		
317	B. R[ogers]	[Nunc Dimittis in a minor]	C	
319	D^r: Rogers	Oh that the Salation '1684'	C	
320	Ben Rogers	Te Deum patrem colimus^s	C	
		'This Hymn is / Sung every day, in / Magdalen College Hall, Oxon, / Dinner, and Supper; / throught the year / for the after Grace, / by the Chaplains / Clarkes and Choristers / [illegible] / Composed by Benjamin / Rogers, Doctor of / Musique of the Univer[sit]y / of Oxon. / 1685.'		

---

^{p} Verse anthem

^{q} Now generally known in the adaptation by F.A.G. Ouseley to words written by Rev. H.R. Bramley: 'O thou the central orb'.

^{r} Textless five-part madrigal (opening text incipit only). A number of the Italian madrigals were annotated 'Ittalian' or Ittalian Compos[er]' by Rogers.

^{s} Now used as the Magdalen Tower Hymn.

...........................[Pages missing]...........................				
321	francis farmelow	[Concluding bars of piece for bass viol]	B	
322	[Wilbye]	Softly [O softly]^t	B	W1066
326-7	[No music entered; unbarred staves]			
328	petri philippi	Salve Regina mater misericordia^u [incomplete]	B	
...........................[Pages missing]...........................				
331	missino	anima anima [del cor mio]^v 8th [lacks opening]	B	M2897
332	[Missino]	Lungi da te ben mio^v 9th	B	M2897
335	[Missino]	Ite caldi Sospiri^v 10th	B	M2897
338	missino	O se vedeste un poco^v 11th	B	M2897
341	missino	Se'l miser cor avam[pa]^v 12th	B	M2897
342	[Missino]	arpa pur Sempre^v 13th	B	M2897
345	[Missino]	O Donna troppo cruda prima parte^v 14th	B	M2897
348	[Missino]	S'io vivo seconda parte^v 15th	B	M2897
350	[Missino]	Ma se da voi Terza parte^v 16th	B	M2897
350	[Missino]	Se l'alm'e [in me smarrita]^v 17th	B	M2897
352	[Missino]	Occhi per me [crudeli]^v 18th	B	M2897
354	[Missino]	Occhi belli^v 19th	B	M2897
356	[Missino]	Occhi lumi del cielo^v 20th [incomplete]	B	M2897
360	[Missino]	Filli filli dolce ben [mio] preposta^v 21th	B	M2897
362	[Missino]	Tirsi dolce ben mio Reposta^v 22th	B	M2897
366	Tarquinio Merula	La mia clor'e [brunetta]^w 'il primo libro'	B	M2346
368	[Merula]	Immortal margarita^w [incomplete]	B	M2346
371		[Textless fragment]	B	

MANUSCRIPT XLVI

OXFORD, CHRIST CHURCH MUS. 43

Henry Aldrich's score of sacred music by English and Italian composers.

Copied c.1680-1700.

ff. ii + 24 + ii (the score has had numerous pages roughly torn out: at least one folio was removed at the beginning, one folio was removed between ff. 16 and 17, eight folios were removed between ff. 21 and 22, and the stubs of at least sixty folios remain at the end of the volume which include fragments of Aldrich's copying).

Modern pencil foliation: ff. 1-24.

---

^{t} Textless six-part madrigal (opening text incipit only).
^{u} Textless six-part motet (opening text incipit only).
^{v} Textless five-part madrigal (opening text incipit only).
^{w} Textless four-voice madrigal (opening text incipit only).

Paper: 360 x 235 mm. Marginal rulings on left and right. Twelve rastrum-ruled staves per page (ruled with a four-stave rastrum of 93 mm span and individual staves each measuring 13 mm). No music entered on ff. 6^v, 21^v-22.

Watermark: fleur-de-lys with countermark IHS.

Collation: A^6 B^4 C^8(C7 removed) D^4 E^8(all removed) F^4(F4 removed) and stubs (gatherings of 6s).

Script: the fragments on f. 1 were copied by two unidentified scribes; the piece by Pelham Humfrey on f. 1^v was copied by Henry Bowman; and the remainder of the volume was copied by Henry Aldrich.

Binding: typical Oxford/Aldrich binding: speckled brown leather with blind-tooled motif of three pointed buds.

Contents of *Och* Mus. 43:

Folio	Composer	Title	Scoring	Printed Sources
1		[Unidentified fragments]		
1^v	[Humfrey]	How wel[l] does this harmonious meeting prove	SSBbc	
2	Sig^{re} Pietro Reggio	Miserere mei Deus	SSBbc	
7	[Monferrato]	Salve Regina	ATBbc	M3037
10	Sg^{re} Charissimi [*recte* Trabattone]^a	Anima mea in æterna dulcedine	CBbc	T1070
12	Sig^{re} Charissimi	Audite Sancti	CCBbc	C1221, 1645^2, 1656^2, 1693^1
14^v	[Sances]	Audite me divini fructus	Bbc	S768
16^v	Gio: Felice Sances	Dulcis amor Jesu	Bbc	S768
17^v	[Sances]	Lætamini in Domino	Cbc	S768
19	[Sances]	Ardet cor meum	Cbc	S768
20^v	[Sances]	Deus in adjutorium^b	CBbc	S768
22^v	Mr Mat[t]hew Locke	A voice came out of ye throne	BBbc	1688^1
23^v	[Lanier]	O Amantissime Domine	Cbc	
24	Mr Edw: Gibbons	Awake and arise^c	SSBbc	
24^v	Dr Christopher Gibbons	Gloria patri^c	CBbc	

---

^{a} Also misattributed to Carissimi in *Lbl* Add. 17,835, 30,382, 33,234, 33,235; *Ob* Mus. Sch. C 11; *Och* Mus. 621, 623-6, 1178; and *J-Tn* N-4/39.

^{b} Incomplete.

^{c} First line of music underlaid only.

MANUSCRIPT XLVII

OXFORD, CHRIST CHURCH MUS. 48

A score of sacred and secular music by English and Italian composers.

Copied *c*.1670-1710.
ff. ii + 93 + i.
Pencil pagination: pp. 1-186.
Paper: 330 x 210 mm. Red marginal rulings on left and right. Twelve rastrum-ruled staves per page (ruled with a six-stave rastrum of 126-7 mm span and individual staves each measuring 11.5-12 mm). f. i: index in the hand of Johann Baptist Malchair (*c*.1787).
Watermark: pp. 1-8: foolscap; pp. 5-186: coat of arms (Amsterdam).
Collation: A-T⁴ V⁴(V4 removed) X-Z⁴ Aa⁴(Aa2-3 removed).
Scribes: A: Richard Goodson I; B: Unidentified;[a]
          C: Henry Aldrich;   D: John Church (1675-1741)[b]
Inscriptions: loose-leaf note inserted between pp. 122 and 123: recto: 'The Piece mentioned on the other side begins with the words / They that go down to the Sea in ships / They that do business in great waters, these see the works / of the Lord / it is a solo anthem the words are translated by D^r. / Pickering from Gratiani. the Lattin words are <u>Dedit abyssus</u> / <u>Vocem Suam</u>.'
verso: 'I have often heard this piece of Music quoted by Professor / Hornsby as having struck him very much in his younger / days when he heard it performed at Durham in the / Church by a remarcable bass Voice which went down / to the deepe notes with the greates[t] clearness and force' (J.B. Malchair). (For other inscriptions see the inventory below.)
Binding: original cardboard cover.
Contents of *Och* Mus. 48:

Page	*Composer*	*Title*	*Scoring*	*Hand*	*Printed Source*
1	[Bassani]	Pulcra es amica mea	CCbc	A	
10	Bassani[c]	Ride tellus gaude caelum	CBbc	A	
20	[Bassani]	O splendida dies	CBbc	A	
27	[Bassani]	Esurientes venite	CBbc	A	
34	[Bassani]	Advolate fideles populi	CCbc	A	

....

[a] The same hand appears in *Och* Mus. 1151, ff. 1ᵛ-5; see MS LX below.
[b] By comparison with *Lbl* R.M. 27 a.1-15 & *Och* Mus. 627.
[c] Later attribution by J.B. Malchair.

42	[Sances]	Laetamini in Domino	Cbc	B	S768
47	[Sances]	Ardet cor meum	Cbc	B	S768
51	[Sances]	Audite me divini fructus	Bbc	B	S768
56	[Sances]	Dulcis amor Jesu	Bbc	B	S768
58	S^r. Pietro Reggio	Miserere mei Deus	SSBbc	B	
68	[Lanier]	O Amantissime Domine	Cbc	B	
70	Stradella^d	Sopra un'ecclesa ['Il Nerone']	Sbc	B	
79	Mr Matt: Locke	A voice came out of ye Throne	BBbc	B	1688[1]
82	M^r Ed: Gibbons	Awake and arise	SSbc	B	
84	Dr Christopher Gibbons	Gloria patri	CCBbc	B	
86	Jer. Clarke	The Lord is my strength 'A Thanksgiving Anthem June 27: 1706'^{e}	SATBorg	B	
100	Jer: Clarke	I will love thee 'A Thanksgiving Anthem'^{f}	SAABorg	B	
122	[Graziani]	They that go down to the sea^g 'Translated from Gratiani by Dr Pickering / ye Latin Song is Dedit abyssus vocem suam.'	Bbc	B	G3653
126	Antonio Fiocco	Coeli dapes	AABbc	B	
136	[d'India]	In principio creavit Deus	SMAT	B	I18
140		[Textless & incomplete]	CAATB	C	
144	Alessandro Stradella	La Ragion m'assicura^h 'Concerto grosso'	CBbc & inst	C	
150	[H. Lawes & Farrant arr. Aldrich]	Not unto us 'This Anthem is translated from two others viz. / Zadok the Priest by Mr Henry Lawes & / Lord for thy tender mercy's sake by Mr Richard Farrant.'	CATB	C	
153	[Palestrina arr. Aldrich?]^i	O Lord God of our salvation	CATTB	C	
157		Be thou exalted O Lord ^{j}	CATTB	C	
160	[Hooper]	I will magnify thee	CATTB	C	
165	[Tye]	I will exalt thee	CATB	C	1641[5]

---

^{d} Later attribution by J.B. Malchair.
^{e} On the victory at Ramillies.
^{f} On Marlborough's victory at Elixem, 23 August 1705.
^{g} Dr Pickering's *contrafactum* of 'Dedit abyssus vocem suam' from B. Graziani, *Motetti a Voce Sola* (Rome, 1652); see the inscription above.
^{h} From the cantata 'Vola, vola in altri petti'; see Gianturco & McCrickard (1991), 103-5.
^{i} Palestrina arranged by Aldrich according to a note in *Lbl* 31,399, but the Palestrina original has not been identified; see R. Shay, '"Naturalizing" Palestrina and Carissimi in Late Seventeenth-Century Oxford: Henry Aldrich and his Recompositions', *ML*, lxxvii (1996), 368-400.
^{j} Possibly an adaptation by Aldrich of an unidentified piece?

167	Blow	The Lord hear thee	SATB	D
170	Thomas Tallis	[Preces with Venite, Responses and Litany] 'Mr. Thomas Tallis his Litany-service, For men.'	ATTB	C 1641[5]
181		Proper Tunes [Psalm chants]	4vv	C

Dr Blow
D^r A[ldrich] x 3
Mr Pel Humfrey
Mr Rich Goodson
Mr Tho. Purcel
Mr Edw. Purcel
Mr Henry Purcel
M^r Fr. Withye
Dr Turner x 4
Mr Bat. Isaac
Mr Smith x 2

MANUSCRIPT XLVIII

OXFORD, CHRIST CHURCH MUS. 49

A composite score of English and Italian vocal music and English keyboard music.

Eight different sections dating from between the early seventeenth and the late eighteenth centuries (see below).
ff. iii + 122 + i.
Modern pencil pagination: pp. 1-2; original ink pagination: pp. 3-41; one unnumbered page [42]; modern pencil pagination: pp. 43, 43a, 44-243 (even-number pages numbered only); various pages reveal the remnants of original pagination systems (see below).
Binding: vellum-covered board with brown-leather spine inscribed 'MASS / BY / CARISSIMI / &.^{C}'.

Layer 1: pp. 1-43a; pp. 3-41 have the original pagination: pp. 3-41. Paper: 312 x 200 mm. Red marginal rulings on left and right. pp. 1-8: twelve rastrum-ruled staves per page (ruled with a four-stave rastrum of 82.5 mm span and individual staves each measuring 10.5-11 mm); pp. 9-43a: twelve rastrum-ruled staves per page (ruled with a six-stave rastrum of 131-2 mm span and individual staves each measuring 11-12 mm). Watermark: pp. 1-8: encircled lion(?) with countermark ID; pp. 9-43a: coat of arms (Amsterdam) with countermark CS (S reversed). Collation: not possible due to tightness of binding (twos?). No music entered on pp. 1-2, 42-43a. Scribe: Francis Smith (1690s).[a]

Layer 2: pp. 44-7. Paper: 312 x 200 mm. Red marginal rulings on left and right. Twelve rastrum-ruled staves per page (ruled with a six-stave rastrum of 130 mm span and individual staves each measuring 10.5-11.5 mm). Watermark: coat of arms (Amsterdam) with countermark JJ. Collation: a single bifolio. Scribe: William Turner II (late seventeenth/early eighteenth century).[b]

Layer 3: pp. 48-65. Paper: 312 x 200 mm. Red marginal rulings on left and right. Ten rastrum-ruled staves per page (ruled with a five-stave rastrum of 125 mm span and individual staves measuring 12/12.5/14/13.5/13.5 mm). Watermark: coat of arms (Amsterdam). Collation: not possible due to tightness of binding (A-E^2 with one removed?). No music entered on pp. 48 and 57. Script: pp. 50-6 text and music: Edward Lowe; pp. 58-65 basso continuo: Lowe, voice part and text: Francis Withey[c] (1670s). Inscription on p. 48: '2 Songes for a Countertenor alone' (Lowe).

Layer 4: pp. 66-86. pp. 68-84 have the original pagination: pp. 3-19. Paper: 312 x 200 mm. Red marginal rulings on left and right. Twelve rastrum-ruled staves per page (ruled with a four-stave rastrum of 82 mm span and individual staves each measuring 11.5-12 mm). Watermark: encircled lion(?) with countermark VI. Collation: not possible due to tightness of binding. No music entered on pp. 85-7. Scribe: unidentified (late eighteenth century).

Layer 5: pp. 88-151. Paper: 310 x 200 mm. Red marginal rulings on left and right. Ten rastrum-ruled staves per page (ruled with a five-stave rastrum of 125-6 mm span and individual staves each measuring 13.5-14 mm). Watermark: foolscap. Collation: A^{12}(A7-12 removed) B^8(B5-8 removed) C^8(C5-8 removed) D^{18}. No music entered on p. 151. Scribe: unidentified (late seventeenth/early eighteenth century). Inscription on p. 127: 'Here's a Health to ye King whom ye Crown does belong to' (Henry Aldrich).

---

[a] Francis Smith (1672-98) was a singing man at Christ Church, Oxford c.1692-6, and also worked as an artist and engraver (he was Peter de Walpergen's partner in the publication of *Musica Oxoniensis* (Oxford, 1698) for which he designed the moveable typeface). Smith was paid three times for copying music at Christ Church between 1693 and 1696; these copies survive in *Och* Mus. 1220-4 and 1246. I am grateful to Dr Robert Thompson for this information.

[b] For William Turner (1652-1740), see D. Franklin, 'Turner, William (ii)', *New Grove*, xix, 281-2; and Spink (1995), 137-45.

[c] Francis Withey (d. 1727), copyist and singing man at Christ Church, Oxford 1680-1713; see Thompson (1991).

Layer 6: pp. 152-191; pp. 160-83 have original pagination: pp. 1-24. Paper: 300 x 200 mm. Red marginal rulings on left and right. Ten rastrum-ruled staves per page (ruled with a five-stave rastrum of 125 mm span and individual staves each measuring 13-13.5 mm). Watermarks: pp. 152-9 and 184-91: coat of arms (Amsterdam); pp. 160-83: foolscap. Collation: one gathering of 20. No music entered on pp. 158-9, 191. Script: pp. 152-7 and 184-9 basso continuo: Lowe, voice part and text: F. Withey (as pp. 58-65); pp. 160-83 text and music: Charles Husbands the elder;[d] p. 190 text and music: Lowe (1670s). Inscriptions: p.179: 'Through Base in ye [illegible] 4to / page 303' (Lowe); p. 190: 'The other pt. figure 2do.' (Lowe).

Layer 7: pp. 192-99. Paper: 310 x 200 mm. Red marginal rulings on left and right. Twelve rastrum-ruled staves per page (ruled with a six-stave rastrum of 129 mm span and individual staves each measuring 10.5-11.5 mm). Watermark: coat of arms (Amsterdam) with countermark WB. Collation: a single gathering of 4. Scribe: Francis Smith (1690s).

Layer 8: pp. 200-43. Paper: 297 x 200 mm. Marginal rulings on left and right. Ten six-line staves per page (ruled with a five-stave rastrum of 115 mm span and individual staves each measuring 13-13.5 mm), an extra stave has been added by hand in the middle and occasionally also at the bottom of the pages. Watermark: pot with letters PI. Collation: A^{10} B^{12}. No music entered on pp. 200 and 243. Scribe: John Lugge (early seventeenth century).[e] Inscription on p. 211: 'play this if you [illegible due to trimming]' (Lugge).

Contents of *Och* Mus. 49:

Page	Composer	Title	Scoring	Printed Sources
3	[f]	[Mass in C: Ky, Gl, Cr, San, Ben, Ag]	CCATBbc	
44	W[illiam] T[urner]	[16 single and one double chant]	SATB	
50	Felice Sances	O quam speciosa	Abc	S768
54	Felice Sances	Quemadmodum desiderat	Abc	S768

---

[d] Identified from a note in *Och* Mus. 1151; see MS LX below. Charles Husbands (d. 1678) was a professional copyist, clerk of St George's Chapel, Windsor and Gentleman of the Chapel Royal; see Ashbee (1986), 109, 136, 143, and ibid. (1991b), 73.

[e] John Lugge (1580-after 1647) was organist of Exeter Cathedral from 1602 to the interregnum. The presence of this manuscript fascicle in Oxford may be explained by the fact that Lugge's son, Robert, was organist at St John's College, Oxford (1635-8). See S. Jeans & J. Steele ed., *John Lugge: The Complete Keyboard Works* (London, 1990); and Watkins Shaw (1991), 108-9.

[f] Attributed to Carissimi on the binding but unlikely to be authentic; see Massenkeil (1963), and Dixon (1986), 15-17.

Oxford, Christ Church Mus. 49

58	[Sances]	Solvatur lingua mea	Tbc	S768
61	[Sances]	Conditor c[a]eli	Tbc	S768

66	Mr Norris	In Jewry is God known	SATBbc	
72	Dan: Purcell	O Let my mouth be filled	SATBbc	
79	Dan Purcel[l]	My God my God look upon me[g]	Sbc	

88	Mr Portman	Rejoyce in the Lord	CCbc	
91	Mr. Hum[frey]	Wilt thou forgive	Sbc	1688[1]
94	Mr Wilkinson	Hear my Prayer o God	Cbc[h]	
96	[Humfrey]	Lord I have sinn'd	Sbc	1688[1]
99	[Blow/Humfrey]	Hark how the wakefull cheerfull Cock 'A Dialogue between 2 Penitents' 'Begun by Mr Humphreis, and finished by Dr. John Blow'	SSbc	
108	Mr. Humpheis	O! the sad day	Sbc	1688[1]
111	[Cooke]	Awake my soul 'The Morning Hymn'	Sbc	
113	[Cooke]	Sleep, downy Sleep 'The Evening Hymn'	Sbc	
115	Mr. James Hart	Where would coy Aminta run	Sbc	1684[3], 1695[17]
117	Dr. John Wilson	Stay lovely Boy	Sbc	
120	[Wilson]	Black Maid complain not 'The Answer'	Sbc	1669[5]
122	Mr. Lock[e]	When Death shall part us 'Dialogue between Thirsis and Dorinda'	STbc	1675[7], 1676[3], 1687[5]
128	Dr. John Blow	Awake my Lyre 'Davids Song to Michael at her Window. out of Mr. Cowley' 'Composed by Dr. John Blow; the words / out of Mr. Cowley's Davideis'[j]	Sbc[i]	1681[4]
133	[Hall]	Hast[e] Charon hast[e] 'tis Nol 'A Dialogue between / Oliver and Charon'	SSBbc	1685[6], 1695[17]
141	Captain Henry Cooke	As on a River[']s side	Sbc	
145		If I live to be old	Sbc	1686[4]

---

[g] Incomplete.
[h] Lacks the chorus parts found in most other sources.
[i] A reduced version of the Act Song written for the Oxford Encænia of 1678 originally for four voices, two violins and basso continuo; the solo version also appears in J. Playford ed., *Choice Ayres and Songs* Bk. 3 (London, 1681).
[j] Cowley (1656), iii, §57, 101.

147[k]	[Wise]	Old Chiron thus preach't	SBbc	W1688 & P6057, 1685[4], 1686[4]

152	[Sances]	Ardet cor meum	Cbc	S768
160	Felice Sances	Judica me Deus	C[C]bc[l]	S768
165	Felice Sances	Domine ne meminiris	C[C]bc[l]	S768
169	Felice Sances	Tota pulchra es	A[T]bc[l]	S768
175	Felice Sances	Deus in adjutorium	C[B]bc[l]	S768
179	Sances	Laudemus viros gloriosos	T[T]bc[l]	S768
184	Sances	L[a]etamini in Domino	Cbc	S768
190	[Cesti?][m]	Amante sentite	[S]A[bc][n]	

192	O. Gibbons	Behold thou hast made my days	CATTBorg	1641[5]

201	John Lugge	Miserere. Cano[n] in ye .5th.	organ
203	Jo: Lugge	Gloria tibi trinitas	organ
205	Jo: Lugge	Gloria tibi trinitas	organ
207	Jo: Lugge	Gloria tibi trinitas	organ
209	Jo: Lugge	Gloria tibi trinitas	organ
211	Jo: Lugge	Gloria tibi trinitas	organ
213	[Lugge]	Christe qui lux	organ
217	Jo: Lugge	Gloria tibi trinitas	organ
219	Jo: Lugge	In nomine	organ
226	John Lugge	Ut re mi fa sol la	organ
233	Jo: Lugge	voluntarie .3. pts	organ
237	Jo: Lugge	Voluntarie .3. pts	organ
240	Jo: Lugge	voluntary .3. & 4. pts	organ

MANUSCRIPT XLIX

OXFORD, CHRIST CHURCH MUS. 372-6

A set of five partbooks containing four- and five-part instrumental pieces (some of vocal origin) and madrigals by Diomedes Cato, Francesco Mason', Claudio Merulo and Cipriano de Rore.

---

[k] False start on p. 147; copied in full on pp. 148-50.
[l] Short-score.
[m] Attributed to 'Sig[r]. Marco [Cesti]' in *Och* Mus. 996, to 'Marco Marazzolli in *I-Bc* Q 50, to 'Luigi' [Rossi?] in *I-Fc* f I 25, and anonymous in all other concordant sources.
[n] Alto part only.

Copied in the early seventeenth century.

Mus. 372: ff. 23 + i (the final folio and the endpage are attached to the back cover). Modern pencil foliation: ff. 1-6, preceded by one unnumbered folio [a] and followed by sixteen unnumbered folios [7]-[22]. Collation: A^4 B^4(B1 removed) C-F^4. No music entered on ff. [a]$^{r-v}$, 2, 5^v-[22]^v.

Mus. 373: ff. 29. Modern pencil foliation: ff. 1-15 followed by fourteen unnumbered folios [16]-[29]. Collation: A^4(A2 removed) B^4(B1 & B4 removed) C-H^4. No music entered on ff. 1-2^v, 14^v-[29]^v.

Mus. 374: ff. 31 (the first and last folios are attached to the covers). No foliation/pagination. Collation: A^4(A4 removed) B-H^4. No music entered on ff. [1]$^{r-v}$, [2]$^{r-v}$, [14]^v-[31]^v.

Mus. 375: ff. 27 (the final folio is attached to the back cover). No foliation/ pagination. Collation: A^4(A4 removed) B-G^4. No music entered on ff. [1]-[2]^v, [14]^v-[27]^v.

Mus. 376: ff. 24 (the first and last folios are attached to the covers). No foliation/pagination. Collation: A^2 B^4(B2-3 removed) C-G^4. No music entered on ff. [1]-[2]^v, [14]^v-[24]^v.[a]

Paper: 155 x 205 mm. Marginal rulings on left and right. Five rastrum-ruled staves per page (ruled with a five-stave rastrum of 119 mm span and individual staves each measuring 12 mm).
Scribe: unidentified.
Watermark: fleur-de-lys.
Bindings: vellum with remnants of original blue ties.
Inscription on front cover of Mus. 372: '24. Fantasies. of. 3.4. &. 5. / pts.' (Stephen Bing); and 'Fantasies of / Signior Diomede Claudio Correggio / Francesco Mason Ciprian de Roro. / 3.4. & 5 Parts.' (George Holmes).
Contents of *Och* Mus. MSS 372-6:

No.[b]	Composer	Title	Folios				
			372	373	374	375	376
1	Claudio Correggio [Merulo]	[Canzona 'La Pazza'][c]	-	3	[2]	[3]	[2]
2	Francesco Mason'	[Canzona]	-	3^v	[2]^v	[3]^v	[2]^v
3	Claudio Correggio	[Canzona 'La Radivila'][c]	-	4^v	[3]^v	[4]^v	[3]^v
4	[Merulo?][d]	[Canzona]	-	5^v	[4]^v	[5]^v	[4]^v

[a] Mus. 376, f. [2]^r has G clefs and B flat 'key' signatures entered on each stave only.
[b] In Mus. 373-6; the seven pieces in Mus. 372 are numbered 1-7.
[c] Concordant printed source: C. Merulo, *Libro Secondo di Canzoni d'Intavolatura d'Organo* (A. Gardano, Venice, 1606); *RISM* M2379.
[d] No. 4 is unattributed, but Pinto (1990), 105, footnote 27, notes that the piece is 'comparable thematically and stylistically to *canzoni* accepted as works of Merulo, and should be added to the canon.'

5	Signior Diomede [Diomedes Cato]	[Ricercar]	–	6	[5]	[6]	[5]
6	Signior Diomede	[Ricercar]	–	6^v	[5]^v	[6]^v	[5]^v
7	Signior Diomede	[Ricercar]	–	7^v	[6]^v	[7]^v	[6]^v
8	Claudio Correggio	[Canzona]	–	8	[7]	[8]	[7]
9	Signior Diomede	[Ricercar]	–	8^v	[7]^v	[8]^v	[7]^v
10	Ciprian de Roro	[Untexted madrigal?]	–	9^v	[8]^v	[9]^v	[8]^v
11	Signior Diomede	[Ricercar]	1	10^v	[9]^v	[10]^v	[9]^v
12	Signior Diomede	[Ricercar]	1^v	11	[10]	[11]	[10]
13	Signior Diomede[e]	[Ricercar]	2^v	11^v	[10]^v	[11]^v	[10]^v
14	Signior Diomede	Tirsi morir volea[f]	3^v	12^v	[11]^v	[12]^v	[11]^v
15	Signior Diomede	Freno Tirsi'l desio 2 par[f]	3^v	13	[11]^v	[12]^v	[11]^v
16	Signior Diomede	Cosi morire fortunati 3 par[f] [recte Cosi moriro i fortunati]	4^v	13^v	[12]^v	[13]^v	[12]^v
17	Ciprian de Roro	[Untexted madrigal?]	5	14	[13]	[14]	[13]

MANUSCRIPT L

OXFORD, CHRIST CHURCH MUS. 417-18 & 1080

Three of a set of four partbooks of viol-consort music for three and four parts.[a]

Copied in the mid to late 1630s.

Mus. 417: ff. v + 61 + i. Modern pencil foliation: ff. 1-58, followed by three unnumbered folios [59[]-[61]. No music entered on ff. 31^v-32^v, 57^v-[61]^v. Collation: A-O^4 ?P^6(1 removed). Scribe: Stephen Bing.

Mus. 418: ff. iv + 60 + i. Modern pencil foliation: ff. 1-60. No music entered on ff. 31^v-32^v, 60^v. Collation: A-P^4. Scribe: Bing. Pencil inscription on f. ii: 'This book to be bound as it is'.

Mus. 1080: ff. v + 59 + i. Modern pencil foliation: ff. 1-60 (end-page numbered). No music entered on ff. 31^v-32^v, 51^{r-v}. Collation: A-O^4 P^4(P3 removed). Scribe: Bing (except for f. 59^v rev. which was copied by a later unidentified scribe).

Paper: 252 x 200 mm. Marginal rulings on left and right. Eight rastrum-ruled staves per page (ruled with a two-stave rastrum of 38.5 mm span and individual staves each measuring 13 mm).

---

[e] Attributed to 'Ciprian de Roro' in Mus. 372.
[f] The text, by Guarini, appears only in Mus. 372.
[a] *Och* Mus. 2 and Mus. 436 provide a score and organbook and, with the exception of the six three-part fantasies by Jeffreys, the contents of *Och* Mus. 417-18 & 1080 are duplicated in the partbooks of the 'Great Set' (*Och* Mus. 397-402, see MS XLII above).

Watermark: coat of arms of Strasbourg (the 'Strasbourg Bend') with monogram 'WR' (presumably Wendelin Riehel of Strasbourg); Thompson (1988), Watermark L.

Bindings: late 17th-century, typical Oxford/Aldrich bindings: speckled brown leather with blind-tooled motif of three pointed buds; spine inscription in gold lettering: 'FANT[asia] D 3.B[ooks]'[b] (Mus. 417-18 only, lacking on Mus. 1080).

Contents of *Och* Mus. 417-18 & 1080:

Three-Part Works

Composer	Title	Folios			VdGS
		417	418	1080	No.
[Lupo]	[Pavan]	1	1	1	4
[Lupo]	[Pavan]	1v	1v	1v	3
[Lupo]	[Pavan]	2	2	2	1
[Lupo]	[Pavan]	2v	2v	2v	2
[Lupo]	[Fantasia]	3	3	3	14
[O. Gibbons]	[Fantasia]	3v	3v	3v	1
[O. Gibbons]	[Fantasia]	4v	4v	4v	2
[O. Gibbons]	[Fantasia]	5v	5v	5v	3
[O. Gibbons]	[Fantasia]	6v	6v	6v	4
[O. Gibbons]	[Fantasia]	7v	7v	7v	5
[O. Gibbons]	[Fantasia]	8v	8v	8v	6
[O. Gibbons]	[Fantasia]	9v	9v	9v	7
[O. Gibbons]	[Fantasia]	10v	10v	10v	8
[O. Gibbons]	[Fantasia]	11v	11v	11v	9
[Mico]	[Fantasia]	12v	12v	12v	1
[Mico]	[Fantasia]	13v	13v	13v	2
[Mico]	[Fantasia]	14v	14v	14v	3
[Mico]	[Fantasia]	15v	15v	15v	4
[Mico]	[Fantasia]	16v	16v	16v	6
[Coprario]	[Fantasia]	17v	17v	17v	10
[Coprario]	[Fantasia]	18v	18v	18v	1
[Coprario]	[Fantasia]	19v	19v	19v	2
[Coprario]	[Fantasia]	20v	20v	20v	4
[Coprario]	[Fantasia]	21v	21v	21v	3
[Coprario]	[Fantasia]	22v	22v	22v	9
[Coprario]	[Fantasia]	23v	23v	23v	5
[Coprario]	[Fantasia]	24v	24v	24v	6

[b] The fourth partbook was obviously missing before Aldrich had the set bound (c.1670-80).

[Jeffreys]	[Fantasia]	25ᵛ	25ᵛ	25ᵛ	1
[Jeffreys]	[Fantasia]	26ᵛ	26ᵛ	26ᵛ	2
[Jeffreys]	[Fantasia]	27ᵛ	27ᵛ	27ᵛ	3
[Jeffreys]	[Fantasia]	28ᵛ	28ᵛ	28ᵛ	4
[Jeffreys]	[Fantasia]	29ᵛ	29ᵛ	29ᵛ	6
[Jeffreys]	[Fantasia]	30ᵛ	30ᵛ	30ᵛ	5

Four-Part Works

[Bull]	[Fantasia]	33	33	33	-
[Ferrabosco II]	[Fantasia]	33ᵛ	33ᵛ	33ᵛ	1
[Ferrabosco II]	[Fantasia]	34ᵛ	34ᵛ	34ᵛ	2
[Ferrabosco II]	[Fantasia]	35ᵛ	35ᵛ	35ᵛ	3
[Ferrabosco II]	[Fantasia]	36ᵛ	36ᵛ	36ᵛ	4
[Ferrabosco II]	[Fantasia]	37ᵛ	37ᵛ	37ᵛ	5
[Ferrabosco II]	[Fantasia]	38ᵛ	38ᵛ	38ᵛ	6
[Ferrabosco II]	[Fantasia]	39ᵛ	39ᵛ	39ᵛ	7
[Ferrabosco II]	[Fantasia]	40ᵛ	40ᵛ	40ᵛ	8
[Ferrabosco II]	[Fantasia]	41ᵛ	41ᵛ	41ᵛ	9
[Ferrabosco II]	[Fantasia]	42ᵛ	42ᵛ	42ᵛ	12
[Ferrabosco II]	[Fantasia]	43ᵛ	43ᵛ	43ᵛ	13
[Ferrabosco II]	[Fantasia]	44ᵛ	44ᵛ	44ᵛ	23
[Ferrabosco II]	[Fantasia]	45ᵛ	45ᵛ	45ᵛ	14
[Ferrabosco II]	[Fantasia]	46ᵛ	46ᵛ	46ᵛ	15
[Ferrabosco II]	[Fantasia]	47ᵛ	47ᵛ	47ᵛ	16
[Ferrabosco II]	[Fantasia]	48ᵛ	48ᵛ	48ᵛ	17
[Ferrabosco II]	[Fantasia]	49ᵛ	49ᵛ	49ᵛ	18
[Ferrabosco II]	[Fantasia]	50ᵛ	50ᵛ	50ᵛ	19
[Ferrabosco II]	[Fantasia]	51ᵛ	51ᵛ	-	20
[Ferrabosco II]	[Fantasia]	52ᵛ	52ᵛ	-	21
[Ferrabosco II]	[Fantasia]	53ᵛ	53ᵛ	-	22
[Ward]	[Fantasia]	54ᵛ	54ᵛ	-	1
[Ward]	[Fantasia]	55ᵛ	55ᵛ	-	2
[Ward]	[Fantasia]	56ᵛ	56ᵛ	-	3
[Ward]	[Fantasia]	-	57ᵛ	-	4
[Ward]	[Fantasia]	-	58ᵛ	-	5
[Ward]	[Fantasia]	-	59ᵛ	-	6

....

Absalom my son   59ᵛ rev
[*a* 6 round at the unison]

MANUSCRIPT LI

OXFORD, CHRIST CHURCH MUS. 432 & 612-13

Two partbooks and organbook to fantasies and ayres for two bass viols and organ by Coprario, Jenkins and Ward (the organbook also contains Mico's three-part fantasies).

Copied in the mid to late 1630s.

Mus. 432 Organ: ff. ii + 138 + iv. Modern pencil foliation: one unnumbered folio [a], ff. 1-110 (numbered every ten folios only between ff. 20 and 100), followed by twenty-seven unnumbered folios [111]-[137]. Paper: 255 x 409 mm. Marginal rulings on left and right. Eight rastrum-ruled six-line staves per page (ruled with a two-stave rastrum of 40.5 mm span and individual six-line staves each measuring 14 mm). No music entered on ff. [a]^r, 11^v-102^v, 109^v-[137]^v. Watermark: coat of arms of Strasbourg (the 'Strasbourg Bend') with monogram 'WR' (presumably Wendelin Riehel of Strasbourg); Thompson (1988), Watermark L. Collation: each folio consists of half a sheet of paper (probably cut before binding and each folio sewn individually) with horizontal chain lines stiched along what was originally the top or bottom of a sheet; there are therefore no gatherings in the normal sense. Scribes: ff. [a]^v-11: John Lilly; ff. 103 rev - 109 rev: Stephen Bing (apparently copied after binding).

Mus. 612 Bass Viol I: ff. iv + 48 + iv. Modern pencil foliation: ff. 1-2, 3a, 3-15, followed by thirty-two unnumbered folios [16]-[47]. Paper: 340 x 225 mm. Marginal rulings on left and right. Ten rastrum-ruled staves per page (ruled with a two-stave rastrum of 39.5 mm span and individual staves each measuring 12 mm). No music entered on ff. 8, 15-[47]^v. Watermark: encircled peacock. Collation: A-H^6. Scribe: Lilly.

Mus. 613 Bass Viol II: ff. iv + 48 + iv. Modern pencil foliation: ff. 1-16, followed by thirty-two unnumbered folios. Paper: 340 x 225 mm. Marginal rulings on left and right. Ten rastrum-ruled staves per page (ruled with a two-stave rastrum of 39.5 mm span and individual staves each measuring 12 mm). No music entered on ff. 9, 16-[48]^v. Watermark: encircled peacock. Collation: A-H^6. Scribe: Lilly.

Bindings: dark-blue morocco, richly gilt and containing the full Hatton coat of arms (azure, a chevron between three garbs or) flanked with the inscription 'CHR:HATTON DEO:ET PATRIÆ' and encircled by a riband from which hangs the ensign medallion of the Order of the Bath; see Plate 2.

Contents of *Och* Mus. 432 & 612-13:

Composer	Title	Folios			VdGS
		612	613	432	No.
[Coprario]	[Fantasia]	1	1	[a]^v	1
[Coprario]	[Fantasia]	1^v	1^v	1	2
[Coprario]	[Fantasia]	2	2	1^v	3
[Coprario]	[Fantasia]	2^v	2^v	2	4
[Coprario]	[Fantasia]	3a	3	2^v	5
[Coprario]	[Fantasia]	3a^v	3^v	3	6
[Coprario]	[Fantasia]	3	4	3^v	7
[Coprario]	[Fantasia]	3^v	4^v	4	8
[Coprario]	[Fantasia]	4	5	4^v	9
[Coprario]	[Fantasia]	4^v	5^v	5	10
[Ward]	[Ayre]	5	6	5^v	1
[Ward]	[Ayre]	5^v	6^v	6	2
[Ward]	[Ayre]	6	7	6^v	3
[Ward]	[Ayre]	6^v	7^v	7	4
[Ward]	[Ayre]	7	8	7^v	5
[Ward]	[Ayre]	7^v	8^v	8	6
[Jenkins]	[Ayre]	8^v	9^v	8^v	38
[Jenkins]	[Ayre]	9^v	10^v	9	37
[Jenkins]	[Ayre]	10^v	11^v	9^v	45
[Jenkins]	[Ayre]	11^v	12^v	10	46
[Jenkins][a]	[Ayre]	12^v	13^v	10^v	63
[Jenkins]	[Ayre]	13^v	14^v	11	44
[Mico]	[Fantasia][b]	-	-	109 rev	1
[Mico]	[Fantasia][b]	-	-	108 rev	2
[Mico]	[Fantasia][b]	-	-	107 rev	3
[Mico]	[Fantasia][b]	-	-	106 rev	4
[Mico]	[Fantasia][b]	-	-	105 rev	5
[Mico]	[Fantasia][b]	-	-	104 rev	6
[Mico]	[Fantasia][b]	-	-	103 rev	7

[a] Attributed to William Young in *DRc* D.4 but attributed to Jenkins on the strength of the attribution in *Lcm* 921; see Willetts (1967b).
[b] Three-part fantasia for treble & two bass viols and organ; score and parts in *Och* Mus. 2 & 401-2; see MS XLII above.

MANUSCRIPT LII

OXFORD, CHRIST CHURCH MUS. 510-14

A set of five partbooks containing four English sacred pieces and forty-five Italian madrigals.

First section copied *c.*1680-90; second section copied *c.*1612-19.

Mus. 510: ff. iii + 72 + iii. First section: modern pencil pagination pp. 1-96; second section: original pagination pp. 97-141 followed by three unnumbered pages [142]-[144]. No music entered on pp. 1, 5, 8-96, 141-[144].

Mus. 511: ff. iii + 72 + iii. First section: modern pencil pagination pp. 1-96; second section: original pagination pp. 97-141 followed by three unnumbered pages [142]-[144]. No music entered on pp. 1, 5, 10-96, 141-[144].

Mus. 512 & 513: ff. i + 72 + i. First sections: modern pagination pp. 1-96; second sections: original pagination pp. 97-141 followed by three unnumbered pages [142]-[144]. No music entered on pp. 1, 5, 10-96, 141-[144].

Mus. 514: ff. iii + 71 + iii. First section: modern pencil pagination pp. 1-96 (lacking 7 and 8); second section: original pagination pp. 97-141 followed by three unnumbered pages [142]-[144]. No music entered on pp. 1, 5, 9, 12-96, 141-[144].

Paper: 168 x 227 mm. First sections: six rastrum-ruled staves per page (ruled with a three-stave rastrum of 64 mm span and individual staves each measuring 13 mm) with red marginal rulings on left and right; second sections: six staves per page (ruled with a single-stave(?) rastrum of 10.5 mm span) with brown marginal rulings on left and right.

Watermarks: first sections: fleur-de-lys with countermark IHS/IC (Thompson (1988), Watermark XXXVIII); second section: foolscap?

Collations: A-J^8 in each partbook (Mus. 514 has had a leaf removed between pp. 6 and 9).

Script: first sections: Henry Aldrich; second sections: Francis Tregian?[a]

Bindings: late 17th-century, typical Oxford/Aldrich bindings: speckled brown leather with blind-tooled motif of three pointed buds; spine inscription in gold lettering: 'Z / V.B[ooks] I [*or* II-V]'.

Contents of *Och* Mus. 510-14:[b]

---

[a] See Willetts (1963); R.R. Thompson (1992); Cuneo (1995); and my comments on p. 190 above.
[b] All for five voices.

Composer	No.	Title	Pages in all books	Printed Source
[Aldrich]	I	I look for the Lord[c]	2	
[Aldrich]	II	I look for the Lord[c]	3	
	III	O pray for the peace	4	
[Tallis]	IV	O God our Father of heav'n [Litany]	6[d]	1641[5]
Fontanelli		Padre del Ciel	97	F1481
Marco da Gagliano		O Sonno, O della quet'humida ombrosa Notte Prima parte	98	G108
Marco da Gagliano		Questo [recte Ov'è'l] silentio Seconda parte	99	G108
Marco da Gagliano		L'ardente tua facella	100	G108
Marco da Gagliano		Su la sponda del Tebro humida herbosa	101	G114
Marco da Gagliano		Filli, mentre ti bacio	102	G108
Lucretio Quintiani		Dolce esca del cuor [recte mio cor] dolci Mam[m]elle Prima Parte	103	Q113
Lucretio Quintiani		Dolce d'ogni mio ben ricco tesoro Seconda Parte	104	Q113
Principe de Venosa [Gesualdo]		Cara amoroso neo Prima Parte	105	G1725
Principe de Venosa		Hai rotto e sciolto	106	G1725
Principe de Venosa		Che sentir deve il petto	107	G1725
Principe de Venosa		Candida man	108	G1725
Principe de Venosa		Non mi togliete [recte toglia (togl'il)] il ben mio	109	G1725
Principe de Venosa		All'apparir, di quelle luci ardenti	110	G1725
Principe de Venosa		Baci soavi et cari	111	G1721
Principe de Venosa		Mentre Madonna Prima Parte	112	G1721
Principe de Venosa		Ahi troppo saggia nel errar Seconda Parte	113	G1721
Principe de Venosa		Del bel de bei Vost'occhi	114	G1731
Principe de Venosa		Ahi dispietata e cruda	115	G1731
Principe de Venosa		Languisc'e moro	116	G1731
Principe de Venosa		Dolcissimo sospiro	117	G1731
Principe de Venosa		Deh, se gia fu crudele	118	G1731
Principe de Venosa		Questa crudele	119	G1735
Principe de Venosa		Moro, E mentre Prima Parte	120	G1735

[c] Aldrich's free adaptation of Tallis' 'Absterge Domine'; the second copy is a tone lower than the first.

[d] Mus. 514: pp. 7 & 8 are lacking; no music is entered on p. 9; and Tallis' *Litany* is continued on pp. 10-11.

Principe de Venosa	Quando di lui, la sospirata vita Seconda Parte	121	G1735
Principe de Venosa	Sparge la Morte	122	G1735
Principe de Venosa	Mentre gira costei	123	G1735
Principe de Venosa	Ecco. moriro dunque Prima Parte	124	G1735
Principe de Venosa	Ahi gia mi discoloro Seconda Parte	124	G1735
Tomaso Pecci	Se gl'amorosi miei Prima Parte	125	P1105
Tomaso Pecci	Cosi in gelida Seconda Parte	126	P1105
Tomaso Pecci	Amarillide mia	127	P1105
Tomaso Pecci	Perfidissimo Volto Prima Parte	128	P1105
Tomaso Pecci	Ahi che spent'e'l desio 3. Parte[e]	129	P1105
Tomaso Pecci	O Donna, troppo crud'e troppo bella	130	P1105
Tomaso Pecci	Ahi, ch'el [recte che'l] mio cor si fugge	131	P1105
Tomaso Pecci	Dolce tormento mio Prima Parte	132	P1105
Tomaso Pecci	Cosi pietosa Seconda Parte	133	P1105
Tomaso Pecci	Ch'io mora	134	P1116
Tomaso Pecci	Quel [neo, quel] Vago neo	135	P1116
Tomaso Pecci	Sospir che del bel petto di Madonna	136	P1116
Tomaso Pecci	Amor io parto Prima Parte	137	P1116
Tomaso Pecci	Ma che Vita diss'io Seconda Parte	137	P1116
Tomaso Pecci	O nelle tue sventure avventurosa Prima Parte	138	P1116
Tomaso Pecci	E pender semiviva Seconda Parte	139	P1116
Tomaso Pecci	Del piu leggiadro fiore	140	P1116

MANUSCRIPT LIII

OXFORD, CHRIST CHURCH MUS. 621

A score of sacred and secular music by English and Italian composers.

The first two sections were copied c.1670-80 and the third section was added c.1700.
ff. ii + 50 + ii.
Modern pencil foliation: pp. 1-50.
Paper: 360 x 235 mm. Red marginal rulings on left and right. ff. 1-41^v: twelve rastrum-ruled staves per page (ruled with a four-stave rastrum of 91 mm span and individual staves each measuring 11-11.5 mm); ff. 42-46^v: twelve rastrum-ruled staves per page (ruled with a four-stave rastrum of 99

---

[e] *Recte* Pt 2; the copyist crossed out 'Seconda' and inserted '3. Parte'.

mm span and individual staves each measuring 14 mm); ff. 47-50^v: sixteen rastrum-ruled staves per page (ruled with a four-stave rastrum of 72 mm span and individual staves each measuring 10.5 mm). No music entered on ff. 28^v, 46^v.

Watermarks: ff. 1-41: fleur-de-lys with countermark VI; ff. 42-46: fleur-de-lys with countermark IV; ff. 47-50: fleur-de-lys (without surround) with countermark IV.

Collation: A^{42}(?A2 removed) ?B^6(?B6 removed) C^4.

Script: ff. 1-41^v: Edward Lowe; ff. 42-6: Henry Bowman; ff. 47-50^v: Richard Goodson II.

Binding: original vellum-covered board with brown-leather spine inscribed 'MOTETS / BY / CASATI / &.^{C}'.

Inscriptions: bottom of ff. 39 and 41^v respectively: 'Isaia[h]: Chap: 38' and 'N.B: This Anthem More perfect / in a Scores [sic] by it self', in the same hand (Richard Goodson II?).

Contents of *Och* Mus. 621:

Folio	Composer	Title	Scoring	Printed Sources
1	Gasparis Casati	Bone Jesu verbum patris	CCbc	C1411
3^v	Gasparis Casati	O dulce nomen jesu	CCbc	C1411
5^v	Gasparis Casati	Tota pulchra es amica mea	CCbc	C1411
8	[Monferrato]	Regina cæli lætare	TTbc	M3037
9^v	Segnior Charissime [*recte* Trabattone][a]	Anima mea in æterna dulcedine	CBbc	T1070
11^v	[Rovetta]	Io mi sento morir	CCbc	R2981
13^v	Richard Goodson [i][b]	Carminum praese cithar[oque][c]	CATB [2 vln] bc	
20	Mr Matt Locke	When death shall part us 'A Dialogue between Thirsis and Dorinda'	TBbc	1675^7, 1676^3, 1687^5
22^v	Jo: Blowe	How art thou fallne	SBbc	1688^1
24^v	D^r [C.] Gibbons	Laudate Dominum	SSSATBbc	
27	D^r [C.] Gibbons	O Bone Jesu	SATBbc	
29	M^r Jo Blow	And I heard a great voice 'Anthem Revelation ye 19th. Verse ye first'	SATBBbc & 4 inst	

---

[a] Also misattributed to Carissimi in *Lbl* Add. 17,835, 30,382, 33,234, 33,235; *Ob* Mus. Sch. C 11; *Och* Mus. 43, 623-6, 1178; and *J-Tn* N-4/39.

[b] f. 19^v is annotated 'Richard Goodson' by Richard Goodson ii.

[c] An Oxford Act Song adapted, in part, from Carissimi's music; see Massenkeil, *New Grove*, iii, 793.

35ᵛ	Mʳ Pell Humfr[e]y	Have mercy upon me^d	CATBbc
39	John Blow	I said in the cutting off of my day	SATTBbc & 4 inst

....

42	[Bowman?]	How long wilt thou forget	SSATBbc

....

47	[G. Holmes]^e	I will love thee O Lord	SATBbc

MANUSCRIPT LIV

OXFORD, CHRIST CHURCH MUS. 623-6

A set of four partbooks containing sacred and secular music by English and Italian composers.

Copied $c.1670$-85.^a

Mus. 623 *Canto primo*: ff. ii + 53. Original ink pagination: pp. 1-104, 109-10. No music entered on pp. 97, 109-10. Collation: A-C^4 D-J^6 K^6($K5$ removed). f. i is annotated 'Medius / Cantoris', and f. ii contains an incomplete index 'Table' in the same hand (Bowman?). f. i is annotated 'Medius / Cantoris'; and f. ii contains an incomplete index 'Table' in the same hand (Bowman?).

Mus. 624 *Canto secundo*: ff. ii + 55. Original ink pagination: pp. 1-110. No music entered on pp. 95, 102-10. Collation: A^4 B^2 C^6 D^4 E^8 F^2 G^6 H^4 J^8 K^4 L^8 ($L8$ removed).

Mus. 625 *Basso*: ff. ii + 43. Original ink pagination: pp. 1-86. No music entered on pp. 13, 57, 82-6. Collation: A^4($A4$ removed) B-D^4 E-F^6 G^4 H-J^6.

Mus. 626 *Basso / pro Organo*: ff. i + 36. Original ink pagination: pp. 1-72. No music entered on pp. 69-72. Collation: A-C^4 D-G^6.

---

[d] This is the second working of this text by Humfrey which appears in the majority of the sources. The early version is to be found in *Lbl* Add. 30,932 & 33,239; see Dennison (1986), 56-63. Robert Ford's claim (1986) that the 'first version' of the anthem is not a childhood composition by Humfrey but one modelled on Humfrey's 'second version' by Richard Henman, is refuted by Dennison, ibid., 117.

[e] Later pencil attribution only in *Och* Mus. 621; attributed to George Holmes in *Lbl* Harley 7341.

[a] Possibly copied before 1677 as John Blow, who received his doctorate in 1677, is described as 'Mr John Blow'; however, this should perhaps be disregarded as Christopher Gibbons, who was awarded the Oxford D.Mus in 1663, is also described as 'Mr' (Christopher Gibbons is normally given as 'Dr Gibbons' in Restoration sources in order to distinguish him from his father).

Paper: 375 x 245 mm. Red marginal rulings on left and right. Twelve rastrum-ruled staves per page (ruled with a three-stave rastrum of 65 mm span and individual staves each measuring 11.5-12 mm).
Watermark: fleur-de-lys with countermark VI.
Scribe: Henry Bowman.
Binding: original cardboard covers annotated 'Canto primo', 'Canto secundo', 'Basso' and 'Basso / pro Organo'.
Contents of Och Mus. 623-6:

Composer	Title	Scoring[b]	Pages				Concordances
			623	624	625	626	
[Monferrato]	Salve Regina	TABbc	1	1	1	1	M3037
[Casati]	O dulce nomen Jesu	CCbc	3	2	-	50	C1411
[Casati]	Bone Jesu Verbum Patris	CCbc	5	4	-	2	C1411
[Monferrato]	Regina Cæli lætare	TTbc	7	6	-	4	M3037
[Casati]	Tota pulchra es	CCBbc[c]	8	8	3	5	C1411
[Casati]	Magnificate cæli	CCbc	10	10	-	6[d]	C1411
	In te Domine	CCbc	12	12	-	10	
Mat: Lock[e]	Agnosce, o Christiane	CBbc	14	-	2	9	1674[2]
[Cesti?][e]	Amante sentite Amor	CAbc	15	13	-	11	
[Bowman]	I'le sing of Heroes	SSBbc	16	14	4	12	B4036
	Vivo in foco Amoroso	TABbc	17	16	5	13	
	Ecco che pur baciate	TTBbc	19	17	6	14	
[Rovetta]	Quante volte giurai	TABbc	20	18	7	15	R2981
[Rovetta]	Si mi dicesti	TTBbc	21	19	8	17	R2981
[Facchi]	Questa ch'orsola	CCBbc	22	20	10	18	F45
[Monteverdi]	Vaga su spina ascosa	TTBbc	23	21	11	19	M3494
[Monteverdi]	Eccomi pronta	TTBbc	25	23	12	20	M3494
[Rovetta]	Venga dal ciel	CC/AT/2vln/Bbc	26	24	24	26	R2985
[Scarani]	Transfige mi Domine	CTBbc	30	28	28	30	S1168
[Filippi]	Vidi turbam magnum	BBBbc	32	30	30	31	F733
[Filippi]	O sacrum Convivium	TABbc	33	30	31	32	F733
[Fontei]	Et ecce sonuit	TABbc	34	32	32	33	F1487
[F.M. Marini]	O Vos omnes	ATBbc	36	34	33	34	M672
	Sanctum Redemptoris nomen	CABbc	37	35	43	35	
[Filippi]	Intuens in Cælum	TABbc	38	36	35	36	F733
[Sances]	O Crux benedicta	TABbc	39	37	36	37	F768
[Aloisi]	Quid mihi est in Cælo	TABbc	40	38	37	38	A876
[Jenkins]	Victorious time	CBbc	41	-	29	28	
[Scarani]	Jubilate Deo	TABbc	42	40	38	39	S1168
[F.M. Marini]	Anima mea, liquefacta est	CABbc	43	41	39	40	M672
[F.M. Marini]	Magnum hæreditatis	CABbc	44	42	40	42	M672
[Jenkins]	Wellcome pure thoughts	CBbc	46	-	41	29	
C. Taylor	Cantate Jehovæ	SBbc	47	-	42	41	

[b] Given in the order of the partbooks: Mus. 623-6.
[c] The vocal-bass part does not appear in any other source.
[d] Mus. 626 contains both the Basso Continuo and Cantus I parts.
[e] Attributed to 'Sig[r]. Marco [Cesti]' in *Och* Mus. 996, to 'Marco Marazzolli in *I-Bc* Q 50, to 'Luigi' [Rossi?] in *I-Fc* f I 25, and anonymous in all other concordant sources.

Composer	Title	Scoring					
[Rovetta]	Laudate pueri	T/C/2vln/bc	48	44	14	44	R2971
[Casati]	Regina cæli lætare. Alleluja	CCbc	50	46	-	43	C1411
[Martinengo]	Adoro te, laudo te	CCbc	52	48	-	47	C1411
[Casati]	O Jesu mea Vita	TTbc	53	49	-	48	C1411
[Casati]	Omnes gentes	CCbc	55	51	-	49	C1411
	When David heard	SCB	57	53	43	-	
[Ferrabosco II]	Rorate Cæli	SSB	58	54	44	-	
Felice Sances[f]	Plagæ tuæ Domine	TABbc	59	55	18	21	F768
[Facchi]	Exurgat Deus	CCBbc	61	57	20	23	F44
[Facchi]	O sacrum Convivium	CABbc	62	58	21	24	F44
[Facchi]	Audite Cæli	CCBbc	63	59	22	25	F44
[Sances]	O Domine guttæ tui	TABbc	64	60	45	51	F768
[Sances]	Magnificemus in Cantico	CCBbc	66	62	23	53	F768
Carissimi[f]	Audite Sancti	CCBbc	68	64	46	54	C1221, 1645[2], 1656[2], 1693[1]
[Sances]	Judica me Deus	CCbc	70	66	-	55	F768
[Sances]	Psalite Domino	CCbc	72	68	-	56	F768
[Sances]	Vulnerasti Cor meum	CTbc	74	70	-	59	F768
[Sances]	Tota pulchra es	TAbc	76	72	-	60	F768
[Sances]	Domine ne memineris	CCbc	78	74	-	58	F768
[Sances]	Deus in adjutorium	CBbc	80	-	48	62	F768
[Sances]	O Jesu mi dulcissime	A/CC/Bbc	82	76	49	63	F768
Carissimi [recte Trabattone][g]	Anima mea, in æterna dulcedine	CBbc	83	-	50	64	T1070
	Mortali che fate 'Chorus'	ATBbc	85	78	52	65	1686[4]
M[r]: Ed Low[e]	O how amiable 'Psal: 84'	C/C/BAT	86	78	62	-	
	How long wilt thou forget me	C/AT/B/bc	87	80	54	66	
Mr Christopher Gibbons	How long wilt you forget me 'Anthem: Psal: 13.'	S/S/BAT	88	82	58	-	1674[2]
Ed: Low[e]	O give thanks '136. Psalm'	C/C/BAT	89	83	66	-	
M[r] Wise	Blessed is he 'Psal: 41'	S/S/BAT	90	84	68	-	
	The Lord is my shepherd 'Psal: 23.'	T/AC/B/bc	91	86	55	67	
Ed: Low[e]	When the Lord turned again 'Psal: 126'	C/C/BAT	92	88	60	-	
Ed: Low[e]	O clapp your hands 'Psal: 47'	C/C/BAT	93	88	64	-	
Benj: Rogers	I will magnify thee 'Ps: 30'	C/C/BAT	94	90	78	-	
D[r]. Child	Behold how good & joyful 'Psal: 133. v.i'	C/C/BAT	95	91	80	-	
Ed: Low[e]	If the Lord himself 'Psal: 124'	C/A/BB	96	92	70	-	
M[r]. Orlando Gibbons	Glorious & powerfull God	CT/A/B	98	93	72	-	
M[r]. Orlando Gibbons	Sing unto the Lord	CT/AA/BB	100	96	74	-	

[f] Later attribution in Mus. 625 only.
[g] Also misattributed to Carissimi in *Lbl* Add. 17,835, 30,382, 33,234, 33,235; *Ob* Mus. Sch. C 11; *Och* Mus. 43, 621, 1178; and *J-Tn* N-4/39.

Mr John Blow	Turne you unto me 'Psal: 25. vers 15'	S/AT/B	102	98	76	-
[Wise]	Awake up my glory 'Ps: 57. v.9.'	S/AT/B	104	100	77	-

MANUSCRIPT LV

OXFORD, CHRIST CHURCH MUS. 732-5 & ROYAL MUSIC LIBRARY MS 24.K.3[a]

A set of four partbooks and a companion organbook containing Fantasia-Suites for violin, bass viol and organ, and Fantasia-Suites for two violins, bass viol and organ by John Coprario; and Fantasies for treble viol, bass viol and 'great Dooble Basse', and Fantasies for two treble viols, bass viol and 'great Dooble Basse' by Orlando Gibbons.

Copied in the early to mid 1630s.
Watermarks: No. 1: pot with letters PO
      No. 2: pillars
      No. 3: grapes[b]
      No. 4: indistinguishable (encircled peacock?)
Scribes: A: unidentified[c]
    B: unidentified
    C: Stephen Bing
    D: unidentified

---

[a] R.M. 24.k.3: housed in the British Library.
[b] The same grapes watermark appears in *Och* Mus. 878-80 (as Watermark No. 4; see MS LVIII below).
[c] Most of the pieces copied by Scribe A are annotated 'exd'. The scribe, who appears to have been an associate copyist of John Barnard's, also contributed to the copying of *Lcm* 1045-51 and *Ob* Tenbury 302; see Willetts (1991). Willetts, ibid., 35, has suggested that scribe 'A' (= Willetts' scribe 'B') may be John Tomkins (1586-1638), a court musician and also colleague of Bing's and Woodington's at St Paul's Cathedral. The circumstantial evidence makes this an attractive proposition. See also J. Morehen (1969), 244-304. Mention should be made of two other 'sightings' of scribe 'A': Dart & Coates ed. (2/rev. 1962), 288, considered that *Lbl* R.M. 24.k.3 was copied by Coprario; and Pinto ed. (1991), p. xvi, considered the same manuscript to be 'in the youthful hand of [William] Lawes... dating from the mid-1620s' (see also Pinto (1995), 15-16). The present writer is not in agreement with either identification, but Pinto's suggestion that scribe 'A' is William Lawes, and the 'knock-on' implications, needs careful consideration.

Mus. 732

Canto [I]: ff. 34.

Modern pencil foliation: ff. 0-34 (the back cover is foliated).

Paper: 295 x 190 mm. Marginal rulings on left and right. Ten rastrum-ruled staves per page (ff. 0-23^v and 31-32^v: ruled with a five-stave rastrum of 119 mm span and individual staves each measuring 12 mm; ff. 25-30^v: ruled with a five-stave rastrum of 117 mm span and individual staves each measuring 13.5-14 mm; f. 33^{r-v}: ruled with a five-stave rastrum of 122 mm span and individual staves each measuring 11.5-12 mm; f. 24 is not ruled; and f. 32 consists of only the top half of a folio (145 x 190 mm)). No music entered on ff. 0, (24^{r-v}), 25, 29^v-31, 32^v-33, (34^{r-v}).

Collation: A^{20} B-C^2 i D^6 E^2 F^1.

Watermarks: ff. 1, 4, 5, 8, 10, 12, 13, 16, 17, 19, 21, 22, 24, 32(?): No. 1; ff. 26, 27, 30: No. 2; f. 33: No. 3.

Script: ff. 0^v-8: A; 8^v-23, 25^v-29, 31^v-32: B; f. 33^v: C.

Inscriptions: front cover recto: 'Coperario his .2. & .3. pts / to the / Organ. / Orlando Gibbons his musique / for the Double / Base.'; front cover verso: 'John Wodenton'; f. 15^v: 'Here begineth the Songes for two viollins'.

Binding: modern vellum but the original paper covers are preserved.

Mus. 733

Canto secundoe: ff. ii + 14 + ii.

Modern pencil foliation: ff. 0-11, followed by two unnumbered folios [12]-[13].

Paper: 295 x 195 mm. Marginal rulings on left and right. Ten rastrum-ruled staves per page (ruled with a five-stave rastrum of 119 mm span and individual staves each measuring 12.5 mm). No music entered on ff. 0, 8^v-9, 11^v-[13]^v.

Collation: a single gathering of twelve with a bifolio inserted between ff. 8 and 11.

Watermark: ff. 0, 1, 4, 6, 8, 9, 11: No. 1.

Script: ff. 0^v-8, 10^v-11: B; ff. 9^v-10: C.

Inscription on front cover: 'Coperario his 2. & 3 pts / to the / Organ. / Orlando Gibbons his musique / for the Double / Base'.

Binding: modern vellum but the original paper covers are preserved.

Mus. 734

Basso: ff. i + 28 + i.

Modern pencil foliation: ff. 1-29 (the endpaper is numbered).

Paper: 295 x 195 mm. Marginal rulings on left and right. Ten rastrum-ruled staves per page (ruled with a five-stave rastrum of 119 mm span and individual staves each measuring 12 mm). No music entered on f. 1.

Collation: A²⁰ B⁸.
Watermark: ff. 1, 2, 5, 7, 9, 11, 13, 15, 17, 18, 23, 25, 27, 28: No. 1.
Script: ff. 1ᵛ-9, 16ᵛ-28ᵛ: A; ff. 9ᵛ-15: D; ff. 15ᵛ-16: B.
Inscriptions: front cover: 'Coperario. his .2. pts & .3. pts. / to the / Organ. / Orlando Gibbons his musique / for the Double / Base.'; back cover: 'Woodington' (autograph?); f. 16ᵛ: 'For two Treble Violins one Base violl & ye Organ.'
Binding: modern vellum but the original paper covers are preserved.

Mus. 735

The great Dooble Basse: ff. i + 6.
Modern pencil foliation: ff. 1-6.
Paper: 290 x 190 mm. Marginal rulings on left and right. Ten rastrum-ruled staves per page (ruled with a five-stave rastrum of 119 mm span and individual staves each measuring 12 mm). No music entered on ff. 1, 5, 6.
Collation: ff. A-C².
Watermark: ff. 1, 3, 5: No. 1.
Script: ff. 1ᵛ-4ᵛ, 5ᵛ: B; f. 6ᵛ: C.
Inscription on front cover: 'Orlando for the Double Base'.[d]
Binding: modern vellum but the original paper covers are preserved.

R.M. 24.k.3

Organ: ff. iii + 96 + iii.
Modern pencil foliation: ff. 1-47, followed by forty-nine unnumbered folios [48]-[96].
Paper: 245 x 380 mm. Marginal rulings on left and right. Eight six-line staves per page (ruled with a two-stave rastrum of 38.5 mm span and individual staves measuring 12.5 mm). No music entered on ff. 1, 47ᵛ-[96]ᵛ (most of the unused pages are barred in two-stave groupings with ten bars per line).
Collation: A-Q⁶
Watermark: No. 4.
Script: A.
Inscription on f. 31ᵛ: 'Heare begingth for 2 treble viollins ye basse violl. & ye Organ.'
Binding: black morocco bearing the arms of Charles I (front and back) and ornate gilt tooling.[e]

---

[d] I cannot agree with Richard Charteris (1975), 43-4, that the title - 'The great Dooble Basse' - on the front cover of *Och* Mus. 735 is 'almost certainly in Woodington's hand', and that scribes 'B' and 'C' (Bing) contributed to the titles and inscriptions on the paper covers of *Och* Mus. 732-4.
[e] In common with the following MSS: *Cfm* Mu 734; *Lbl* Add. 17,801 (Locke autograph); and *Ob* Mus. Sch. B 2 & 3 (W. Lawes autographs).

Contents of *Och* Mus. MSS 732-5 and *Lbl* R.M. MS 24.k.3:

Three-Part Fantasia-Suites by Coprario

No.	Title	Folios					VdGS No.
		732	733	734	735	24.k.3	
1	Fantaziæ	0v	-	1v	-	1v	1
	Allmand/Almaine	1	-	2	-	2v	
	Galliard	1	-	2	-	3	
2	Fantaziæ	1v	-	2v	-	3v	2
	Allmand/Almaine	2	-	3	-	4v	
	Galliard	2	-	3	-	5	
3	Fantaziæ	2v	-	3v	-	5v	3
	Allmand/Almaine	3	-	4	-	6v	
	Galliard	3	-	4	-	7	
4	Fantaziæ	3v	-	4v	-	7v	4
	Allmand/Almaine	4	-	5	-	8v	
	Galliard	4	-	5	-	9	
5	Fantaziæ	4v	-	5v	-	9v	5
	Almaine	5	-	6	-	10v	
	Galliard	5	-	6	-	11	
6	Fantaziæ	5v	-	6v	-	11v	6
	Almaine	6	-	7	-	12v	
	Galliard	6	-	7	-	13	
7	Fantaziæ	6v	-	7v	-	13v	7
	Almaine	7	-	8	-	14v	
	Galliard	7	-	8	-	15	
8	Fantaziæ	7v	-	8v	-	15v	8
	Allmand/Almaine	8	-	9	-	16v	
	Galliard	8	-	9	-	17	
1f	Fantaziæ	8v	-	9v	-	17v	9
	Almaine	9	-	10	-	18v	
	Galliard	9	-	10	-	19	
2	Fantaziæ	9v	-	10v	-	19v	10
	Allmand/Almaine	10	-	11	-	20v	
	Galliard	10	-	11	-	21	
3	Fantaziæ	10v	-	11v	-	21v	11
	Allmand/Almaine	11	-	12	-	22v	
	Galliard	11	-	12	-	23	
4	Fantaziæ	11v	-	12v	-	23v	12
	Almaine	12	-	13	-	24v	
	Galliard	12	-	13	-	25	

f The pieces are numbered 1-23 in R.M. 24.k.3.

5	Fantaziæ	12ᵛ	-	13ᵛ	-	25ᵛ	13
	Almaine	13	-	14	-	26ᵛ	
	Galliard	13	-	14	-	27	
6	Fantaziæ	13ᵛ	-	14ᵛ	-	27ᵛ	14
	Almaine	14	-	15	-	28ᵛ	
	Galliard	14	-	15	-	29	
7	Fantaziæ	14ᵛ	-	15ᵛ	-	29ᵛ	15
	Almaine	15	-	16	-	30ᵛ	
	Galliard	15	-	16	-	31	

Four-Part Fantasia-Suites by Coprario

1/1	Fantasie	15ᵛ	0ᵛ	16ᵛ	-	31ᵛ	1
2	Almaine	16	1	17	-	32ᵛ	
3	Galliard	16	1	17	-	33	
2/4	Fantazie	16ᵛ	1ᵛ	17ᵛ	-	33ᵛ	2
5	Almaine	17	2	18	-	34ᵛ	
6	Galliard	17	2	18	-	35	
3/7	Fantasie	17ᵛ	2ᵛ	18ᵛ	-	35ᵛ	3
8	Almaine	18	3	19	-	36ᵛ	
9	Galliard	18	3	19	-	37	
4/10	Fantasie	18ᵛ	3ᵛ	19ᵛ	-	37ᵛ	4
11	Almaine	19	4	20	-	38ᵛ	
12	Galliard	19	4	20	-	39	
5/13	Fantasiæ	19ᵛ	4ᵛ	20ᵛ	-	39ᵛ	5
14	Almaine	20	5	21	-	40ᵛ	
15	Galliard	20	5	21	-	41	
6/16	Fantasie	20ᵛ	5ᵛ	21ᵛ	-	41ᵛ	6
17	Almaine	21	6	22	-	42ᵛ	
18	Galliard	21	6	22	-	43	
7/19	Fantasie	21ᵛ	6ᵛ	22ᵛ	-	43ᵛ	7
20	Almaine	22	7	23	-	44ᵛ	
21	Galliard	22	7	23	-	45	
8/22	Fantasie	22ᵛ	7ᵛ	23ᵛ	-	45ᵛ	8
23	Almaine	23	8	24	-	46ᵛ	
24	Galliard	23	8	24	-	47	

Three-Part 'Dooble Base' Fantasies by Orlando Gibbons

1	Fantasie	25ᵛ	-	24ᵛ	3ᵛ	-	1
2	Fantasie	26ᵛ	-	25	4	-	2
3	Fantasie	27ᵛ	-	25ᵛ	1ᵛ	-	3
4	Fantasie	28ᵛ	-	26ᵛ	2ᵛ	-	4

Four-Part 'Dooble Base' Fantasies by Orlando Gibbons

5	Fantasie	31ᵛ	9ᵛ	27ᵛ	5ᵛ	-	1
6	Fantasie	33ᵛ	10ᵛ	28ᵛ	6ᵛ	-	2

MANUSCRIPT LVI

OXFORD, CHRIST CHURCH MUS. 747-9

Three of a set of four partbooks containing anthems, madrigals and motets for two to four voices and basso continuo by William Child, Richard Dering, Alessandro Grandi, George Jeffreys and Matthew Locke (the basso continuo part is lacking).

Copied in the 1640s? (with later additions).

Mus. 747: ff. 18. Original foliation: ff. 1-18. Collation: $A^2 B^4 C\text{-}D^6$. No music entered on ff. $6^{r\text{-}v}$, $14\text{-}18^v$. Scribe: unidentified; a second unidentified scribe added the piece on f. $5^{r\text{-}v}$. Vellum covers decorated and inscribed in red and black: '441 / Tenor, 4 & 5 Voyces'.[a]

Mus. 748: ff. 20. Original foliation: ff. 1-7; modern pencil foliation: ff. 8-20. Collation: $A\text{-}B^6 D^2$. No music entered on ff. 6, $12^{r\text{-}v}$, 20^v. Scribe: unidentified; the second unidentified scribe added the piece on f. $11^{r\text{-}v}$ and a third unidentified scribe added the piece on f. 6^v. Vellum covers inscribed: '441 / Medius 4, 5, and 6 voyces'.[a]

Mus. 749: ff. 20. Modern pencil foliation: ff. 1-19 followed by one unnumbered folio. Collation: $A\text{-}B^6 D^2$. No music entered on ff. 6, $12^{r\text{-}v}$, 20^v. f. 20: list of contents (later hand). Scribe: unidentified; the second scribe added the piece on f. $11^{r\text{-}v}$, and the third scribe added the piece on f. 6^v. Vellum covers inscribed: '30 / Sextus / Anthems / Rich Deering / Locke / Wm Child / Alex Grande'.[a]

Paper: 310 x 205 mm. Marginal rulings on left and right. Ten rastrum-ruled staves per page (ruled with a five-stave rastrum of 115-17 mm span and individual staves each measuring 13-13.5 mm).
Watermark: pillars.
Contents of Och Mus. 747-9:[b]

No.	Composer	Title	Scoring	Folios 747	748	749
1	Rich Deering	Justus cor suum tradidit	TB[bc]	-	1	1
2	Rich Deering	Gaudent in cælis	CC[bc]	-	1^v	1^v
3	Rich Deering	Ardens est cor meum	CB[bc]	-	2	2
4	Rich Deering	O Domine Jesu Christe	SB[bc]	-	2^v	2^v

---

[a] The inscriptions, and the fact that the covers are smaller than the pages of the manuscript, indicate that these are not the original covers (despite the fact that the composers named on the cover of Mus. 749 are correct).
[b] For the concordant sources of the Dering and Jeffreys pieces, see Tables 28 and 23 respectively.

5	Rich Deering	O bone Jesu	TT[bc]	-	3	3
6	Rich Deering	Ego dormio	BB[bc]	-	3v	3v
7	Rich Deering	Beatus vir	TT[bc]	-	4	4
8	Rich Deering	Gratias tibi Deus	BC[bc]	-	4v	4v
9	Rich Deering	Canite Jehovae	BS[bc]	-	5	5
	Rich Deering	Veni electa mea	CB[bc]	-	5v	5v
	Mr Locke	Agnosce O Christiane[c]	CB[bc]	-	6v	6v
1	Rich Deering	O quam suavis est Domine	TCB[bc]	1	7	7
2	Rich Deering	Panis Angelicus	CCB[bc]	1v	7v	7v
3	Rich Deering	Justus Germinabit sicut	TTB[bc]	2	8	8
4	Rich Deering	Isti sunt sancti	CCB[bc]	2v	8v	8v
5	Rich Deering	Qualis est dilectus tuus	TCB[bc]	3	9	9
6	Rich Deering	Gloria patri	ATB[bc]	3v	9v	9v
7	Rich Deering	Sleepe quiett Lee	MTB[bc]	3v	9v	9v
8	Rich Deering	Laetamini cum Maria	CTB[bc]	4	10	10
9	Rich Deering	Vulnerasti cor meum	TTB[bc]	4v	10v	10v
	W. Child	Come Hymen come[d]	TAB[bc]	5	11	11
	[Jeffreys]	Unto the[e] O Lord	AAB[bc]	7	13	13
	[Jeffreys]	Beatus author [*recte* auctor] seculi	AAB[bc]	7v	13v	13v
	[Jeffreys]	Lapidabant Stephanum	AAB[bc]	8	14	14
	[Jeffreys]	Ex[s]urge, quare obdormis Domine	AAB[bc]	8v	14v	14v
	[Jeffreys]	O quam gloriosum	AAB[bc]	9	15	15
	[Jeffreys]	Ecce dilectus meus	TTB[bc]	9v	15v	15v
	[Jeffreys]	Prior Christus	TTB[bc]	10	16	16
	[Jeffreys]	Christo Jesu	TTB[bc]	10v	16v	16v
	[Jeffreys]	Sing unto the Lord	TTB[bc]	11	17	17
	[Jeffreys?][e]	Euge serve bone	TCB[bc]	11v	17v	17v
	[Dering]	Cantate Domino	CCB[bc]	12	18	18
	[Dering]	Tibi laus	CTB[bc]	12v	18v	18v
		This day our sauiour Christ was born[f]	SSB[bc]	13	19	19
	Grandi[g]	O bone Jesu	TATB[bc]	13v	19v [h]	19v

[c] Later addition; printed source: Playford ed. (1674[2]).
[d] Later addition.
[e] Attributed to Jeffreys in *Ob* Mus. Sch. E 451 (basso continuo only) but not included in any of Jeffreys' autograph manuscripts (e.g. Lbl Add. 10,338, Lcm 920).
[f] Title in Mus. 748: 'A Caroll for Christmas Day'.
[g] Printed sources: G3422 & Playford ed (1662[4]).
[h] Mus. 748 contains both the Alto and Tenor II parts.

MANUSCRIPT LVII

OXFORD, CHRIST CHURCH MUS. 754-9

A set of six partbooks containing 'The Royall Consort' (new version) for two violins, two bass viols and two theorbos by William Lawes.[a]

Copied c.1653.
Six unbound partbooks: Mus. 754: *Violin 1*; Mus. 755: *2 Violin part*; Mus. 756: *1º Theorbo*; Mus. 757: *2º Theorbo*; Mus. 758: *1º Base Vyoll;* and Mus. 759: *2º Base Violl*. Each partbook consists of eighteen folios without pagination/foliation; pieces numbered: 1-66.
Paper: 305 x 205 mm. Ten rastrum-ruled staves per page with marginal rulings on left and right (ruled with either a five-stave rastrum of 119 mm span and individual staves each measuring 12.5-13 mm, or with a five-stave rastrum of 109 mm span and individual staves each measuring 12-12.5 mm) with an extra hand-drawn stave occasionally added at the foot of a page. No music entered on the versos of the final folios of each partbook.
Watermark: pot with letters NRO (or damaged RRO).
Collations: Mus. 754: A^{10} B^8; Mus. 755-9: A^{10} B^6.
Scribe: Stephen Bing.
Inscriptions in the hand of Bing: Mus. 755: after no. 21, 'The end of the first Sett.'; after no. 40, 'The end of the second sett.'; after piece 66, 'Finis Mr William Lawes / His Consort / for .2. Violins / for .2. Base Violles / & for .2. Theorboes'. Mus. 756: after piece 40, 'Finis / Mr Will[ia]m Lawes .2. Sett in .d. sol re / for .2. Violins. .2. Theorboes. and .2. / Base Violls. The Royall Consort.';[b] after piece 66, 'Finis Mr William Lawes. / His Consort. / for .2. Violins / for .2. Base Violles / and .2 Theorboes.' Mus. 757: after piece 40, 'Finis Mr. Wm Lawes. / The Royall Consort.'[b] Mus. 759: after piece 66, 'Finis Mr William Lawes / His Consort / for .2. Violins. / for .2. Base Violles / & for .2. Theorboes.' George Holmes added the annotation 'Mr William Lawes his / Royall Consort' above the first piece in partbook 759.
No original bindings (modern folder).
Contents of *Och* Mus. 754-9:

---

[a] The sources of 'The Royall Consort' divide into those with distinct tenor and bass lines (the 'old' version) and those in which the two lower parts have been transformed into 'two breakeinge Bases' (the 'new' version); the versions in *Och* Mus. 754-9 apparently represent Lawes' latest reworkings. See Lefkowitz (1960), 68-87; and Dodd (1975-6).
[b] Stephen Bing considered that 'The Royall Consort' consisted only of the d minor and D major sets.

'The Royall Consort' (New Version) by William Lawes

	No.	Title	VdGS No.
[Set in D minor]	1	Allmain	19
	2	Fantasy	1
	3	Aire [Corant]	11
	4	Allmain [Ayre]	9
	5	Allmain [Ayre]	10
	6	Corant	12
	7	Sarabrand	13
	8	Pavan	18
	9	Corant	17
	10	Saraband	14
	11	Aire	15
	12	Allmain [Ayre]	16
	13	Corant	18
	14	Corant	20
	15	Sarabrand	21
	16	Allmain [Ayre]	2
	17	Allmain	3
	18	Corant	4
	19	Corant	5
	20	Sarabrand	6
	21	Ecco	7
[Set in D]	22	Fantasy	36
	23	Allmain	38
	24	Ayre	30
	25	Corant	26
	26	Sarabrand	27
	27	Pavan	22
	28	Aire	23
	29	Ayre	24
	30	Aire	25
	31	Morrisse	41
	32	Eccho	40
	33	Ayre	29
	34	Ayre	37
	35	Allmain	31
	36	Corant	33
	37	Ayre	32
	38	Corant	39
	39	Ayre	34
	40	Sarabrand	35

[Set in A minor]	41	Ayre	43	
	42	Allmain [Ayre]	44	
	43	Allmain	45	
	44	Ayre	46	
	45	Corant	47	
	46	Saraband	48	
[Set in C]	47	Pavan	49	
	48	Ayre	50	
	49	Allmain	51	
	50	Ayre	52	
	51	Corant	53	
	52	Sarabrand	54	
[Set in F]	53	Pavan	55	
	54	Ayre	56	
	55	Allmain	57	
	56	Corant	58	
	57	Allmain	59	
	58	Corant	60	
	59	Sarabrand	61	
[Pavan in A minor]	60	Pavan	42	
[Set in B flat]	61	Pavan	62	
	62	Allmain	63	
	63	Corant	64	
	64	Allmain	65	
	65	Corant	66	
	66	Sarabrand	67	

MANUSCRIPT LVIII

OXFORD, CHRIST CHURCH MUS. 877-880

A set of four partbooks containing both printed and manuscript copies of madrigals and motets for one to six voices and basso continuo (many are incomplete).

The first two manuscript layers in Mus. 878-80, the third layer in Mus. 878 & 880 and the fifth layer in Mus. 880 were probably copied before 1646; the fourth manuscript layer in Mus. 880 appears to date from the 1650s.

Watermarks: No. 1: coat of arms
No. 2: pot with letters DIV
No. 3: pot with letters CAB
No. 4: grapes
No. 5: pot with letters ID[a]
No. 6: shield
No. 7: pot with letters RRO
No. 8: pillars with letters DI[b]

Scribes: A: unidentified
B: unidentified
C: George Jeffreys
D: Stephen Bing
E: Angelo Notari

Mus. 877

ff. i + 18 + printed matter.
No foliation/pagination.
Paper: 283 x 185 mm. Ten staves per page with red marginal rulings on left and right (ruled with a five-stave rastrum of 119 mm span and individual staves each measuring 13 mm). No music entered.
Collation: not possible due to tightness of binding (manuscript section probably A-C^6).
Watermark: No. 1 throughout.
f. [18] followed by: John Wilson, *Psalterium Carolinum....* (J. Martin & J. Allestrey, London, 1657): *Cantus Primus*.

Mus. 878

ff. i + 54 + printed matter.
Pencil foliation: ff. 1-39, followed by fifteen unnumbered folios [40]-[54].
Paper: 285 x 185 mm. Ten staves per page with marginal rulings on left and right (ff. 1-2^v, 15-18^v: ruled with a five-stave rastrum of 119 mm span and individual staves each measuring 13-13.5; ff. 3-14^v: ruled with a five-stave rastrum of 119.5 mm span and individual staves each measuring 13-13.5 mm; ff. 19-30^v: ruled with a five-stave rastrum of 124 mm span and individual staves each measuring 11.5-12 mm; ff. 31-[54]^v: ruled with a five-stave rastrum of 119 mm span and individual staves each measuring 12.5-13 mm). No music entered on ff. 10^v-12, 13-14^v, 23^v-26, 27-30^v, 38^v-39^v, [40]-[54]^v.
Collation (manuscript section): A^2 B-C^6 D-E^2 F-G^6 H^{24}.

---

[a] Thompson (1988), Watermark IX.
[b] Ibid., Watermark I.

Watermarks: ff. 2, 15, 18: No. 2; ff. 4, 5, 8, 9, 12, 13: No. 3; ff. 22, 24-6, 28: No. 4; ff. 32-39, [41], [42], [45], [54]: No. 5.

Script: ff. 1-2^v: A; ff. 3-7^v: B (music) and C (clefs & text); ff. 8-10, 12^v: D (music) and C (text); ff. 15-18: A; ff. 18^v-22^v: B (music) and C (clefs & text); f. 23: D (music) and C (text); 26^v: B (music) and C (text); ff. 31-8: E. The following folios have occasional text alternatives written in by D: ff. 3, 4, 5^v, 7^v, 8, 19, 19^v, 22^v.

Inscriptions: f. 8: 'The following Duets and solo's [sic] are imperfect for want of a Basso continuo.'; f. 15: 'These following are imperfect; one voice part out of three being not written' (late 17th-century hand?), and on the same folio below the piece: 'This is perfect' (pencil, different hand from above); f. 15^v, 'Imperfect' (same pencil hand). Various pencil attributions (by G.E.P. Arkwright?, early 20th century).

Remnants of an original pagination or numbering system on ff. 10 ('14') and 12^v ('12').

f. [54] followed by: J. Wilson, *Psalterium Carolinum: Cantus Secundus*. Walter Porter, *Mottets of Two Voyces*.... (W. Godbid, London, 1657): *Altus*; the preface - 'To all lovers of Musick' - includes corrections and annotations in Porter's hand;[c] these include the insertion of the name 'Monteverde' after the words 'my good Friend and Maestro'.

Mus. 879

ff. i + 35 + printed matter.

Pencil foliation: ff. 1-23, three unnumbered folios [24]-[26], 27-29, followed by six unnumbered folios [30]-[35].

Paper: 285 x 185 mm. Ten staves per page with marginal rulings on left and right (in red on ff. [30]-[35]^v), (ff. 1-2^v, 14-17^v: ruled with a five-stave rastrum of 119 mm span and individual staves each measuring 13-13.5 mm; ff. 3-13^v: ruled with a five-stave rastrum of 119.5 mm span and individual staves each measuring 13-13.5 mm; ff.18-29^v: ruled with a five-stave rastrum of 124 mm span and individual staves each measuring 11.5-12 mm; ff. [30]-[35]^v: ruled with a five-stave rastrum of 119 mm span and individual staves each measuring 13 mm). No music entered on ff. 10, 11-13^v, 22^v-27^v, 28^v-29^v, [30]-[35]^v.

Collation (manuscript section): A^2 B^6(B4 removed) C^6 D-E^2 F-H^6.

Watermarks: ff. 2, 14, 17: No. 2; ff. 3, 4, 9, 10, 13: No. 3; ff. 18, 19, 21, [26], 28, 29: No. 4; ff. [30], [32]: No. 1.

Script: four hands, as follows: ff. 1-2^v: A; ff. 3-7^v: B (music) and C (clefs & text); ff. 8-9^v, 10^v: D (music) and C (text); ff. 14-17: A; ff. 17^v-21^v: B (music) and C (clefs & text); f. 22: D (music) and C (text); f. 28 rev:

---

[c] By comparison with the autograph dedications in two other editions of *Mottets*: *Och* Mus. 819, and *Ob* Mus. Sch. D 349.

B (music) and C (clefs & text). The following folios have occasional text alternatives written in by D: ff. 3, 4, 5^v, 7^v, 8, 18, 18^v, 21^v.

Inscriptions: f. i^v: 'A Collection of Songs by Jefferies late Organist of Christ Church' (late 17th-century hand?); f. 8: 'N.B. the following Duets and solo's [sic] are imperfect for want of a Basso continuo'; f. 14: 'These are imperfect - one voice part out of three not being written' (late 17th-century hand?), and on same folio below the piece: 'This is perfect' (pencil, different hand from above). Various pencil attributions (by G.E.P. Arkwright?, early 20th century).

f. 21 offers evidence that the pages were severely cut down to size: the bottom of this folio is folded up rather than cut off. f. 28 is copied upside down.

The following folios reveal various redundant systems of pagination or numbering: ff. 1 ('10'), 1^v ('18' sic), 2 ('2'?), 2^v ('3'), 4 ('9'), 5 ('20'), 6-6^v ('6-7'), 7 ('3'), 7^v ('5' sic), 8-8^v ('16-17'), 9 ('19'), 9^v ('21'), 10^v ('15'), 14 ('11'), 14^v ('22'), 15 ('30'), 15^v ('23'), 16 ('26'?), 16^v ('34'), 20 ('27'), 27^v ('33'), 21 ('31'), 21^v ('29').

f. [35] followed by: J. Wilson, *Psalterium Carolinum*: *Base*. W. Porter, *Mottets*: *Bassus*; the preface includes corrections and annotations in Porter's hand.

Mus. 880

ff. i + 43 + printed matter + 41 + i.

Pencil foliation: ff. 1-43; and after printed matter: ff. 1-41.

Paper: 282 x 184 mm. Ten staves per page with marginal rulings on left and right (1st sequence ff. 1-2^v, 15-18^v: ruled with a five-stave rastrum of 119 mm span and individual staves each measuring 13-13.5 mm; ff. 3-14^v: ruled with a five-stave rastrum of 119.5 mm span and individual staves each measuring 13-13.5 mm; ff. 19-30^v: ruled with a five-stave rastrum of 124 mm span and individual staves each measuring 11.5-12 mm; ff. 31-43: ruled with a five-stave rastrum of 119 mm span and individual staves each measuring 12.5-13 mm; 2nd sequence ff. 1-23: ruled with a five-stave rastrum of 119 mm span and individual staves each measuring 12.5-13 mm; ff. 24-41: ruled with a five-stave rastrum of 117 mm span and individual staves each measuring 13 mm). No music entered on the following: 1st sequence ff. 8-14^v, 23-26, 27-30^v, 42^v-43^v; 2nd sequence ff. 34^v, 41-41^v.

Collation: manuscript 1st sequence: A^2 B-C^6 D-E^2 F-G^6 ?H^{24}(H14-24 removed?: ff. 31-41 = eleven singletons, ff. 42-3 = a bifolio, the centre of an original gathering of twenty-four?); printed matter; manuscript 2nd sequence: A^8(A8 removed) B^4 C-G^6. Gatherings A-D (2nd sequence) must originally have formed a large single gathering as follows:

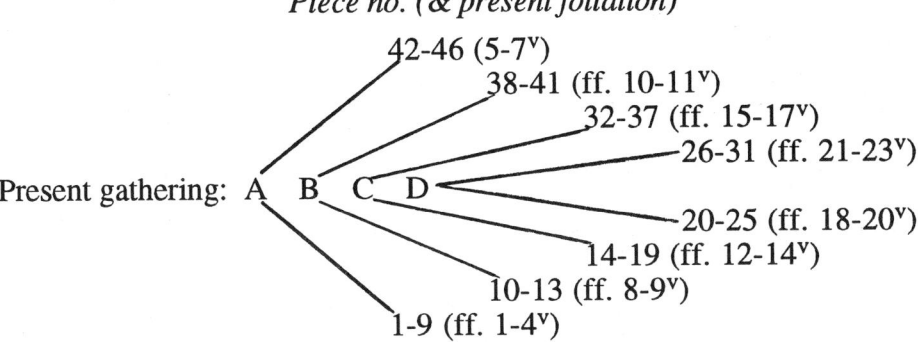

(ff. 1 and 7^v show signs of wear and tear due to use as covers.)

Watermarks: 1st sequence: ff. 2, 15: No. 6; ff. 3, 4, 6, 9, 10, 12: No. 3; f. 18: No. 2; ff. 20, 21, 24, 27, 29: No. 4; ff. 31-34, 38-40, 42: No. 5; 2nd sequence: ff. 4, 6-8, 10, 12, 15, 16: No. 7; ff. 27-29, 31, 32, 35, 39-41: No. 8.

Script: five hands, as follows: 1st sequence: ff. 1-2^v: A; ff. 3-7^v: B (music) and C (clefs & text incipits); ff. 15-18: A; ff. 18^v-22^v, 26^v: B (music) and C (clefs & text incipits); ff. 31-42: E; 2nd sequence: ff. 1-34, 35-40^v: D.

Inscriptions: f. i^v: 'Mr Jeffrey's [*sic*] Collection of Songs. Dr. Wilson's Psalterium Carolinum. Mr Walter Porter's Mottets. Through Base to the Prince of Venosas 5 parts' (late 17th-century hand?). Various pencil attributions (by G.E.P. Arkwright?, early 20th century).

f. 30 (1st sequence), bottom right-hand corner: section of paper 30 x 90 mm cut out. Page removed between ff. 7 and 8 (2nd sequence): remaining stub inscribed 'Mr Richard Re...' (illegible) by hand D.

Between the two manuscript sections: J. Wilson, *Psalterium Carolinum*: *Basso Continuo*. W. Porter, *Mottets*: *Basso Continuo*; the preface includes corrections and annotations in Porter's hand.

Bindings: late 17th-century, typical Oxford/Aldrich bindings: speckled brown leather with blind-tooled motif of three pointed buds; spine inscription in gold lettering: 'MOT 4.B[ooks] I [II, III *or* IV]'.

Contents of *Och* Mus. 877-80:

410 *Musical Patronage in Seventeenth-Century England*

No.	Composer	Title	Scoring	Folios 878	879	880	Hand	Printed Sources[d]
1	[Dering]	Justus cor suum tradidit	TBbc	1	1	1	A	1662[4]
2	[Dering]	Gaudent in cælis	CCbc	1ᵛ	1ᵛ	1ᵛ	A	1662[4]
3	[Dering]	Ardens est cor meum	CBbc	2	2	2	A	1662[4]
4	[Dering]	O Domine Jesu Christe	CBbc	2ᵛ	2ᵛ	2ᵛ	A	1662[4]
	[Dering]	Conceptio tua (Nativitas tua) 'A.2.'	CBbc	3	3	3	BC(D)	1662[4]
	[Dering]	Gratias tibi Deus 'A.2.'	CBbc	3ᵛ	3ᵛ	3ᵛ	BC	1662[4]
	[Dering]	Sancta et immaculata virginitas/ (divinitas) 'A.2.'	TTbc	4	4	4	BC(D)	1662[4]
	[Dering]	O donna troppo cruda 'A.2.'	CTbc	4ᵛ	4ᵛ	4ᵛ	BC	
	[Dering]	Ego dormio 'A 2 Basses'	BBbc	5	5	5	BC	1662[4]
	[Dering]	Veni electa mea 'A.2.'	CBbc	5ᵛ	5ᵛ	5ᵛ	BC(D)	1662[4]
	[Dering?]	Hei mihi Domine 'A.2.'	CBbc	6	6	6	BC	
	[Dering]	Anima Christi 'A.2.'	CBbc	6ᵛ	6ᵛ	6ᵛ	BC	
	[Dering?]	O sacrum convivium 'A.2.'	CBbc	7	7	7	BC	
	[Dering]	O crux ave (Jesu salve) 'A.2.'	CBbc	7ᵛ	7ᵛ	7ᵛ	BC(D)	1674[2]
		Beatus laurentius (O fælix Ecclesia) 'A.2.'	CB[bc]	8	8	-	DC(D)	
		Protector noster 'A.2.'	CC[bc]	8ᵛ	8ᵛ	-	DC	
		Propitius esto 'A.2.'	CT[bc]	9	9	-	DC	
	[Dering]	Duo seraphin 'A.2.'	TT[bc]	9ᵛ	9ᵛ	-	DC	1662[4]
		Tua Jesu dilectio 'A.1. Sola'	T[bc]	10	-	-	DC	
		Jesus auctor 'Solus'	B[bc]	-	10ᵛ	-	DC	
		Gloria tibi Trinitas 'Solus'	T[bc]	12ᵛ	-	-	DC	
5	[Dering]	O bone Jesu	TTbc	15	14	15	A	1662[4]
6	[Dering]	Panis angelicus	C[C]Bbc	15ᵛ	14ᵛ	15ᵛ	A	1662[4]
7	[Dering]	O quam suavis	C[T]Bbc	16	15	16	A	1662[4]
8	[Dering]	Justus germinabit	T[T]Bbc	16ᵛ	15ᵛ	16ᵛ	A	1662[4]
	[Dering]	Isti sunt sancti	C[C]Bbc	17	16	17	A	1662[4]
	[Dering]	Qualis est dilectus	C[T]Bbc	17ᵛ	16ᵛ	17ᵛ	A	1662[4]
	[Dering]	Tibi laus	C[T]Bbc	18	17ᵛ	18ᵛ	BC	
		O Maria (O Messia) 'A.3.'	C-Bbc	19	18	19	BC(D)	
	[Dering]	Lætamini cum Maria 'A.3.'	C[T]Bbc	19ᵛ	18ᵛ	19ᵛ	BC(D)	1662[4]
	[Dering]	Vulnerasti cor meum 'A.3.'	C[C]Bbc	20	19	20	BC	1662[4]
	[e]	Exultavit cor meum 'A.3.'	C[C]Bbc	20ᵛ	19ᵛ	20ᵛ	BC	
	[Dering]	Cantate Domino 'A.3.'	C[C]Bbc	21	20	21	BC	1662[4]
		Paratum cor meum 'A.3.'	C-Bbc	21ᵛ	20ᵛ	21ᵛ	BC	
		Confitemini Domino 'A.3. Basses'	BB[B]bc	22	21	22	BC	
		Augustine (O Messia) 'A.3.'	-TBbc	22ᵛ	21ᵛ	22ᵛ	BC(D)	
		Quemadmodum desiderat 'A.3.'	C-B[bc]	23	22	-	DC	
		I heard a voice	(-)ABbc[f]	26ᵛ	28	26ᵛ	BC	

[d] For manuscript concordances of the Dering pieces, see Table 28.
[e] Later pencil attribution to 'Dering' on uncertain grounds.
[f] Mus. 878: 'A.2'; and Mus. 879: 'A.3'.

	Ch'io non t'ami 'A 3. Voci'	[C]C-bc	31	-	31	E	
[Monteverdi]	T'amo mia vita 'A tre voci'[g]	[C]C[B]bc	32	-	31[v]	E	M3475
	Fiumi e fonti	[C]bc	-	-	31[v]	E	
	Jubilate 'A 2. Voci'	--bc	-	-	32	E	
[Monteverdi]	Ahi com'a un vago sol 'A 3. Voci'[g]	[C]C[B]bc	31[v]	-	32[v]	E	M3475
[Notari]	Occhi un tempo mia vita 'A 2. Voci'	[T]Tbc	33[v]	-	33	E	N797
	Alla vermiglia	? bc	-	-	33[v]	E	
[Monteverdi]	Crud'Amarilli	[CC]bc[g]	-	-	34	E	M3475
	Una farfalla cupida 'A 2. over 3 Voci'	-C(-)bc	34	-	34[v]	E	
	Ecco nova beltà [Pt 1][h] 'A 2. Voci.'	[C]Cbc	37[v]	-	35	E	
	Ecco le piagge amene [Pt 2][h]	[C]Cbc	37[v]	-	35	E	
	Ecco, gli Augelli [Pt 3][h]	[C]Cbc	38	-	35	E	
	Ecco rider le grazie [Pt 4][h]	[C]Cbc	38	-	35	E	
	Questo è pur 'A 2. Voci'	--bc	-	-	35[v]	E	
	Ave sanctissima 'voce sola'	-bc	-	-	36	E	
	Questa crudel[i] 'voce sola'	[C]bc	-	-	36[v]	E	
	Deh poi 'A 2.'	--bc	-	-	37	E	
	Spesso t'amo 'A 2.'	--bc	-	-	37[v]	E	
	Che fai alma 'Dialogo. à 2' [Core & Alma]	--bc	-	-	38	E	
	Interdette 'Basso solo' [Pt 1]	[B]bc	-	-	39	E	
	E s'al mio mal [Pt 2]	[B]bc	-	-	39	E	
	Usin... [Usi[g]nolo?] [Pt 3]	[B]bc	-	-	39	E	
	Gett'amor [Pt 4]	[B]bc	-	-	39[v]	E	
[Notari]	Intenerite voi 'A.2. Voci'	[C]Cbc	35	-	40	E	N797
	Quell'augellin 'A.3. Voci'	[C]C-bc	35[v]	-	40[v]	E	
	Ah non si può crudele 'A 2. Voci'	[C]Cbc	36[v]	-	41	E	
[Monteverdi]	Non è di gentil core[j] 'A 2. Voci'	[C]Cbc	36	-	41[v]	E	M3494
	Filli miranda 'A2. et a3 Voci'	---bc	-	-	42	E	

....

John Wilson, *Psalterium Carolinum The Devotions of his Sacred Majestie in his Solitudes and sufferings...* (J. Martin & J. Allestrey, London, 1657)

Walter Porter, *Mottets of two voyces for Treble or Tenor and Bass...* (W. Godbid, London, 1657)

....

---

[g] Arrangement of the original five-voice madrigal.
[h] Strophic variations on the same bass.
[i] Four sections.
[j] Variant of the published duet.

No.	Composer	Title	Scoring	Folio in 880 2nd sequence	Hand	Printed Concordances
1	[Merula]	Cum complerentur	[CATB] bc	1	D	M2338
2	[Merula]	Magnificate Dominum	[CATB] bc	1ᵛ	D	M2338
3	[Merula]	Ego flos campi	[CB 2vln] bc	2	D	M2339
4	[Grandi]	Diligam te Domine	[CCBB] bc	2ᵛ	D	G3431
5	[Grandi]	Domine ne in furore tuo	[CATB] bc	3	D	G3455
6	[Grandi]	O bone Jesu	[ATTB] bc	3	D	G3422
7	[Trabattone]	Kyrie eleison 'Litanie BVM'	[CATB] bc	3ᵛ	D	T1070
8	[Grandi]	Obaudite me	[ATTB] bc	4	D	G3417
9	[Grandi]	Vidi [speciosam]	[ATTB] bc	4ᵛ	D	G3417
42	[Tomasi]	Quasi cedrus	[CATB] bc	5	D	T922
43	[Tomasi]	O Maria [sanctissima]	[CATB] bc	5ᵛ	D	T922
44	[Tomasi]	Kyrie eleison 'Lettanie BVM'	[CATB] bc	5ᵛ	D	T922
45	[Sances]	Salve ò Christe	[CATB] bc	6ᵛ	D	S768
46	[Ferrabosco]ᵏ	Fuerunt mihi [lacrimae]	[AATT] bc	6ᵛ	D	
10	[Grandi]	Caro mea [vere est cibus]	[CATB] bc	8	D	G3417
11	[Grandi]	Congratulamini omnes	[CATB] bc	8ᵛ	D	G3417
12	[Grandi]	Cantabo Domino	[ATTB] bc	9	D	G3417
13	[Grandi]	Hic est vere Martyr	[ATTB] bc	9ᵛ	D	G3417
38	[Aloisi]	Audite gentes	[CATB] bc	10	D	A876
39	[Sances]	O Jesu mi dulcissime	[CCAB] bc	10ᵛ	D	S768
40	[Facchi]	O Jesu clementissime	[CCAB] bc	11	D	F44 as 'O Virgo prudentissima'
41	[Facchi]	Ave saluberrima	[CCAB] bc	11ᵛ	D	F44
14	[Grandi]	Benedictus Dominus	[ATTB] bc	12	D	G3417
15	[Grandi]	Heu mihi	[ATTB] bc	12ᵛ	D	G3422
16	[Grandi]	Magnum hæreditatis	[TTBB] bc	13	D	G3422
17	[Grandi]	Inter vestibulum	[CTTB] bc	13ᵛ	D	G3422
18	[Grandi]	Deus qui nos [in tantis]	[CATB] bc	14	D	G3431
19	[Grandi]	Plorabo [die ac nocte]	[CATB] bc	14ᵛ	D	G3431
32	[Trabattone]	Dicite nobis	[CATB] bc	15	D	T1070
33	[Merula]	Nominativo hic	[ATBB] bc	15ᵛ	D	M2348
34	[Merula]	Nominativo quis vel qui	[CATB] bc	16	D	M2348
35	[Merula]	Tempesta di dolcezza	[CATB] bc	16ᵛ	D	M2348
36	[Merula]	Belle ha le perle	[CATB] bc	17	D	M2348
37	[Mazzocchi]	Nigra sum	[CCBB] bc	17ᵛ	D	1643¹, 1652¹
20	[Aloisi]	Impetum [inimicorum]	[CATB] bc	18	D	A872
21	[Aloisi]	Cantate Domino	[CATB] bc	18ᵛ	D	A872
22	[Aloisi]	Dulcissime [Jesu Christe]	[CATB] bc	19	D	A872 as 'Dulcissima Christi Mater'
23	[Gallerano]	In Domino confido	[CCTB] bc	19ᵛ	D	A872
24	[Aloisi]	Attollite portas	[CTTB] bc	20	D	A872
25	[Trabattone]	Qui habitatis	[CATB] bc	20ᵛ	D	T1070

ᵏ Sometimes attributed to Ferrabosco II (e.g. *New Grove*, vi, 482) on dubious stylistic grounds; however, the piece is ascribed to Ferrabosco I in *Lbl* Egerton 3665 by a copyist who was always careful to distinguish between the two Ferrabosocos. It is therefore probably correct to ascribe the piece to the elder Ferrabosco. See R. Charteris, *'Fuerunt mihi lacrymae*: Alfonso Ferrabosco the Elder or the Younger?', *Altro Polo: Essays on Italian Music in the Cinquecento*, ed. R. Charteris (Sydney, 1990), 113-30.

26	[Trabattone]	In cælis hodie	[CATB] bc	21	D	T1070
27	[Merula]	Jesu dulcissime	[CATB] bc	21^v	D	M2338
28	[Arrigoni]	Usami pur [orgoglio]	[CATB] bc	22	D	A2490
29	[Arrigoni]	Stelle fulminatrici	[TTBB] bc	22^v	D	A2490
30	[Trabattone]	Laudate Dominum	[CATB] bc	23	D	T1070
31	[Trabattone]	Lætis nunc mentibus	[CATB] bc	23^v	D	T1070
1	Venosa	Cara [amorosa] [Pt 1]	[5vv] bc[1]	24	D	G1722-5
2	[Gesualdo]	Ma se tale [ha costei] [Pt 2]	[5vv] bc	24	D	G1722-5
3	Venosa	Hai rott'e [sciolto e spento]	[5vv] bc	24^v	D	G1722-5
4	[Gesualdo]	Se per lieve [Pt 1]	[5vv] bc	24^v	D	G1722-5
5	[Gesualdo]	Che sentir deve'l petto [mio] [Pt 2]	[5vv] bc	25	D	G1722-5
6	[Gesualdo]	In piu leggiadro [velo]	[5vv] bc	25^v	D	G1722-5
7	[Gesualdo]	Se cosi dolc'e'l duolo [Pt 1]	[5vv] bc	25^v	D	G1722-5
8	[Gesualdo]	Ma s'averra [ch'io moia] [Pt 2]	[5vv] bc	26	D	G1722-5
9	[Gesualdo]	Se taccio [il duol s'avanza]	[5vv] bc	26	D	G1722-5
10	[Gesualdo]	O com['] e gran martire [Pt 1]	[5vv] bc	26^v	D	G1722-5
11	[Gesualdo]	O mio soave ardore [Pt 2]	[5vv] bc	26^v	D	G1722-5
12	[Gesualdo]	Sento [che nel partire]	[5vv] bc	26^v	D	G1722-5
13	[Gesualdo]	Non e [questa la mano] [Pt 1]	[5vv] bc	27	D	G1722-5
14	[Gesualdo]	Ne tien [face o saetta] [Pt 2]	[5vv] bc	27^v	D	G1722-5
15	[Gesualdo]	Candida man	[5vv] bc	27^v	D	G1722-5
16	[Gesualdo]	Dall'odorate [spoglie] [Pt 1]	[5vv] bc	28	D	G1722-5
17	[Gesualdo]	E quell'arpa felice [Pt 2]	[5vv] bc	28	D	G1722-5
18	[Gesualdo]	Non mai [non cangerò]	[5vv] bc	28^v	D	G1722-5
19	[Gesualdo]	All'apparir [di quelle luci ardenti]	[5vv] bc	28^v	D	G1722-5
20	[Gesualdo]	Non mi [togl'il ben mio]	[5vv] bc	29	D	G1722-5
1	[Gesualdo]	Baci soavi e cari] [Pt 1] 'A.5. lib.2'	[5vv] bc	29	D	G1721 & G1726-9
2	[Gesualdo]	Quant'ha [di dolce amore] [Pt 2]	[5vv] bc	29^v	D	G1721 & G1726-9
3	[Gesualdo]	Madonna [io ben vorrei]	[5vv] bc	29^v	D	G1721 & G1726-9
4	[Gesualdo]	Com'esser puo [ch'io viva]	[5vv] bc	30	D	G1721 & G1726-9
5	[Gesualdo]	Gel'ha [Madonna il seno]	[5vv] bc	30	D	G1721 & G1726-9
6	[Gesualdo]	Mentre Madonna [il lasso] [Pt 1]	[5vv] bc	30^v	D	G1721 & G1726-9
[7]	[Gesualdo]	Ahi [troppo saggia nell'errar] [Pt 2]	[5vv] bc	30^v	D	G1721 & G1726-9
8	[Gesualdo]	Se da si [nobil mano]	[5vv] bc	31	D	G1721 & G1726-9
9	[Gesualdo]	Amor pace non chero	[5vv] bc	31	D	G1721 & G1726-9
10	[Gesualdo]	Si gioiso [mi fanno i dolor miei]	[5vv] bc	31^v	D	G1721 & G1726-9
[11]	[Gesualdo]	O dolce mio martire	[5vv] bc	31^v	D	G1721 & G1726-9

---

[1] The printed editions of Gesualdo's madrigal books I, II & IV do not contain a basso continuo part.

12	[Gesualdo]	Tirsi morir [volea] [Pt 1]	[5vv] bc	32	D	G1721 & G1726-9	
13	[Gesualdo]	Freno Tirs'il desio [Pt 2]	[5vv] bc	32	D	G1721 & G1726-9	
14	[Gesualdo]	Mentre mia [stella miri]	[5vv] bc	32^v	D	G1721 & G1726-9	
15	[Gesualdo]	Non mirar [non mirare]	[5vv] bc	32^v	D	G1721 & G1726-9	
16	[Gesualdo]	Questi [leggiadri odorosetti fiori]	[5vv] bc	33	D	G1721 & G1726-9	
17	[Gesualdo]	Felice primavera [Pt 1]	[5vv] bc	33^v	D	G1721 & G1726-9	
18	[Gesualdo]	Danzan [le Ninfe oneste] [Pt 2]	[5vv] bc	33^v	D	G1721 & G1726-9	
19	[Gesualdo]	Son si belle [rose]	[5vv] bc	34	D	G1721 & G1726-9	
20	[Gesualdo]	Bell'angioletta	[5vv] bc	34	D	G1721 & G1726-9	
1	[Gesualdo]	Luci serene e chiare 'A.5. lib.4'	[5vv] bc	35	D	G1735	
2	[Gesualdo]	Tall'hor [sano desio]	[5vv] bc	35^v	D	G1735	
3	[Gesualdo]	Io tacero [ma nel silenzio mio] [Pt 1]	[5vv] bc	35^v	D	G1735	
4	[Gesualdo]	Invan [dunque o crudele] [Pt 2]	[5vv] bc	36	D	G1735	
5	[Gesualdo]	Che fai [meco mio cor]	[5vv] bc	36	D	G1735	
6	[Gesualdo]	Questa crudele [e pia]	[5vv] bc	36^v	D	G1735	
7	[Gesualdo]	Hor ch'in gioia [Pt 1]	[5vv] bc	36^v	D	G1735	
8	[Gesualdo]	O sempre [crud'Amore] [Pt 2]	[5vv] bc	37	D	G1735	
9	[Gesualdo]	Cor mio [deh non piangete] [Pt 1]	[5vv] bc	37	D	G1735	
10	[Gesualdo]	Dunque [non m'offendete] [Pt 2]	[5vv] bc	37^v	D	G1735	
11	[Gesualdo]	Sparge [la morte]	[5vv] bc	37^v	D	G1735	
12	[Gesualdo]	Moro [e mentre sospiro] [Pt 1]	[5vv] bc	38	D	G1735	
13	[Gesualdo]	Quando di lui [la sospirata vita] [Pt 2]	[5vv] bc	38	D	G1735	
14	[Gesualdo]	Mentre gira [costei]	[5vv] bc	38^v	D	G1735	
15	[Gesualdo]	A voi [mentre il mio core]	[5vv] bc	39	D	G1735	
16	[Gesualdo]	Ecco moriro [dunque] [Pt 1]	[5vv] bc	39	D	G1735	
17	[Gesualdo]	Ahi gia [mi discoloro] [Pt 2]	[5vv] bc	39^v	D	G1735	
18	[Gesualdo]	Arde il mio cor	[5vv] bc	39^v	D	G1735	
19	[Gesualdo]	Se chiudete [nel core]	[5vv] bc	40	D	G1735	
20	[Gesualdo]	Il sol [qual'or piû splende] [Pt 1]	[6vv] bc	40	D	G1735	
21	[Gesualdo]	Volgi mia luce [Pt 2]	[6vv] bc	40^v	D	G1735	

MANUSCRIPT LIX

OXFORD, CHRIST CHURCH MUS. 1023

A manuscript basso continuo part to Richard Dering's *Cantica Sacra* (1618).[a]

Copied 1643-6.
ff. 12 + i. Original pagination: pp. 1-22 followed by two unnumbered pages [23]-[24].

Paper: 213 x 170 mm. Marginal rulings on left and right. Eight rastrum-ruled staves per page (ruled with a two-stave rastrum of 32 mm span and individual staves each measuring 10.5 mm). No music entered on pp. [23-4].

Watermark: encircled peacock?
Collation: A-C^4.

Script: music copied by Stephen Bing; text incipits added by George Jeffreys.

No binding (modern folder); the original paper cover survives inscribed on the front: 'Bookes Imperfect' (Jeffreys).

Contents of *Och* Mus. 1023:

Basso Continuo Part to Six-Part Motets by Richard Dering[b]

Page	Title
1	Jubilate Deo
2	Vulnerasti cor meum
3	Sancta & immaculata [virginitas]
4	Congratulamini mihi
5	Surge amica mea
6	Hei mihi Domine
7	Quae est ista [quae ascendit quasi aurora]
8	Adiuro vos [filiae]
9	Virgo prudentissima
10	Ardens est cor meum
11	Quam pulchra [es amica mea]
12	Factum est silentium
13	Panis Angelicus
14	O vos omnes
15	Cantate Domino
16	Quem vidistis [pastores]

---

[a] One of the two copies of Dering's *Cantica Sacra* at Christ Church (Mus. 881-6) lacks the basso continuo part; presumably the manuscript was copied as a replacement.
[b] *Cantica Sacra* (1618); *RISM* D1319.

17	Veni Jesu
18	Paratum cor meum
20	Jesu decus Angelicum
21	O Crux ave spes
22	[Te laudamus] Te invocamus

MANUSCRIPT LX

OXFORD, CHRIST CHURCH MUS. 1151

A score of two solo-voice motets by Giovanni Felice Sances.

Copied *c*.1670-80.
ff. 8. Modern foliation: ff. 1-8.
Paper: 325 x 213 mm. Red marginal rulings on left and right. Ten rastrum-ruled staves per page (ruled with a five-stave rastrum measuring of 125 mm span and individual staves each measuring 13-14 mm). No music entered on ff. 1, 7-8^v.
Watermark: coat of arms (Amsterdam).
Collation: A-B^4.
Script: ff. 1^v-5: unidentified;[a] ff. 5^v-6^v: Edward Lowe.
Inscription on f. 1: '2 Songes for a Base alone. / 2 for a meane alone in ye Duos. prickt by Mr Husband' (Lowe).[b]
Binding: modern vellum.
Contents of *Och* Mus. 1151:[c]

Folio	Composer	Title	Scoring
1^v	[Sances]	Audite me divini fructus	Bbc
5^v	[Sances]	Dulcis amor Jesu	Bbc

---

[a] The same scribe copied sections of *Och* Mus. 48; see MS XLVII above, Hand B.
[b] This apparently refers to *Och* Mus. 49, ff. 152-89; see MS XLVIII below.
[c] Printed source: *Motetti* (1638); *RISM* S768.

MANUSCRIPT LXI

OXFORD, CHRIST CHURCH MUS. 1155-61

A set of seven partbooks containing a variant version of Alessandro Striggio's *Il Cicalamento delle Donne al Bucato* first published in 1567.

Copied in the early seventeenth century.
Seven partbooks: *Cantus, Cantus 2s, Altus, Altus 2s, Tenor, Tenor 2s, Bassus*:
ff. i + 6 + i.
Paper: 265-75 x 200-5 mm.
No foliation/pagination. Red marginal rulings on left and right. Nine rastrum-ruled staves per page (ruled with a three-stave rastrum of 66 mm span and individual staves each measuring 13 mm). No music entered on Mus. 1155, ff. [1] (text only), [5]^v-[6]^v; Mus. 1156, ff. [1] (text only), [6]$^{r\text{-}v}$; Mus. 1157, ff. [1], [6]^v; Mus. 1158, ff. [1] (text only), [6]$^{r\text{-}v}$; Mus. 1159, ff. [1], [6]^v; Mus. 1160, ff. [1], [6]^v; Mus. 1161, ff. [1], [6]^v.
Collations: single gatherings.
Watermark: fleur-de-lys.
Scribe: unidentified (same hand appears in *Och* Mus. 78-82 and 463-7).
Inscription on f. i^r of each partbook: 'Ciccalemento di Don[n]e' or 'Il Ciccalamento Di Don[n]e, di / Alessandro striggio'; George Holmes added 'A 7. Voc.' to f. i^r of Mus. 1159.
No binding (modern folder).
Contents of *Och* Mus. 1155-61:

Alessandro Striggio's *Il Cicalamento Delle Donne Al Bucato*[a]

Title	\multicolumn{7}{c}{Folios}
	1155	1156	1157	1158	1159	1160	1161
Nella vaga stagion Prima parte a.4.	[1]^b	[1]^b	[1]^v	[1]^b	[1]^v	[1]^v	[1]^v
Buon giorno belle donne Secunda Pars a.7.	[1]^v	[1]^v	[2]^v	[1]^v	[2]^v	[2]^v	[2]^v
Ho udito anch'io Tertia Pars a.7.	[2]^v	[2]^v	[3]^v	[2]^v	[3]^v	[3]^v	[3]^v
Il Gentil huom Quarta Pars a.7.	[3]^v	[3]^v	[4]^v	[3]^v	[4]^v	[4]^v	[4]^v
Orsu stendiamo Quinta Pars a.7.	[4]^v	[4]^v	[5]^v	[4]^v	[5]^v	[5]^v	[5]^v

---

[a] Published by G. Scotto in Venice, 1567 (*RISM* S6959); the partbooks contain a variant version.
[b] Text only copied for 'Prima parte' in Mus. 1155, 1156 & 1158.

MANUSCRIPT LXII

OXFORD, CHRIST CHURCH MUS. 1178

A composite collection of vocal parts and short scores of sacred music by Italian composers.

Copied *c*.1670-80.
ff. 20. Two layers combined: ff. 1-4^v and 17-20^v form the 'outer' layer and ff. 5-16^v the 'inner' layer.
Modern pencil foliation: ff. 1-20 (5-16^v contain original pagination: pp. 1-24).
Paper: 305 x 217 mm. Red marginal rulings on left and right. Ten rastrum-ruled staves per page (ff. 1-4^v and 17-20^v ruled with a five-stave rastrum of 125 mm span and individual staves each measuring 13-14 mm; ff. 5-16^v ruled with a five-stave rastrum of 126 mm span and individual staves each measuring 12.5-13 mm). No music entered on ff. 17, 20^v.
Watermarks: ff. 1-4^v & 17-20^v: coat of arms (Amsterdam); ff. 5-16^v: foolscap.
Collation: a single gathering of twenty (the 'inner' layer was placed in the centre of the 'outer' layer).
Script: ff. 1-4^v, 17^v-20: Edward Lowe; ff. 5-16^v: unidentified.
Inscriptions: f. 14^v: 'Through base in ye thick 4to page 303' (Lowe);[a] f. 17: 'Set up thy selfe' (Lowe).
Binding: modern leather.
Contents of *Och* Mus. 1178:

Folio	Composer	Title	Scoring	Printed Source
1	[Casati]	Regina c[a]eli lætare	[C]C[bc]	C1411
2	[Rovetta]	Laudate pueri	C[T 2vln bc]	R2971
3^v	Se^{g}nior Charissime[b] [*recte* Trabattone]	Anima mea in æterna dulcedine	C[B]bc	T1070

....

[a] i.e. *Ob* Mus. Sch. MS E 451; see MS XXX above.
[b] 'Supposd to be Se^{g}nior Charissime's'. Also misattributed to Carissimi in *Lbl* Add. 17,835, 30,382, 33,234, 33,235; *Ob* Mus. Sch. C 11; *Och* Mus. 43, 621, 623-6; and *J-Tn* N-4/39.

5	Felice Sances	Judica me Deus '2 Voc'	[C]Cbc	S768
7ᵛ	Felice Sances	Domine ne memineris 'A2 Voc'	[C]Cbc	S768
9ᵛ	Felice Sances	Tota pulc[h]ra es '2 voc'	[A]Tbc	S768
12ᵛ	Felice Sances	Deus in adjutorium 'A2 voc'	[C]Bbc	S768
14ᵛ	Felice Sances	Laudemus viros '2 voc'	[T]Tbc	S768
17ᵛ	Cassatus	O Jesu mea vita	[T]T[bc]	C1411
18ᵛ	[Monferrato]	Regina cæli lætare	[T]T[bc]	M3037
19ᵛ		In te Domine	[C]C[bc]	

MANUSCRIPT LXIII

OXFORD, CHRIST CHURCH MUS. 1185

An organbook containing John Coprario's Fantasia-Suites for violin, bass viol and organ.

Copied in the mid seventeenth century.
ff. ii + 84 + ii.
Modern pencil foliation: 1-31, [32]-[81], 82, [83]-[84].
Paper: 210 x 325 mm. Marginal rulings on left and right. Six six-line staves per page (ruled with a three-stave rastrum of 76.5 mm span and individual staves each measuring 15-16 mm.) No music entered on ff. 1, 31ᵛ-[81], [84]ᵛ. The top half of f. [55] has been cut out.
Watermark: coat of arms.
Collation: A⁴ B-E⁸ F⁶ G⁴ H⁸ J⁸(J1-2 removed) K-M⁸.
Scribes: ff. 1ᵛ-31: Stephen Bing; ff. 84-81ᵛ rev: Richard Goodson II.
Inscription on f. 1: 'R. Goodson' (autograph: Richard Goodson the elder?).
Binding: brown leather with gold floral tooling and remnants of green and red ties.
Contents of *Och* Mus. 1185:

Coprario's Fantasia-Suites

Folio	No.	Title	VdGS No.
1ᵛ	1	Fancy	1
2ᵛ	1	Aire	
3	1	Galliard	
3ᵛ	2	Fancy	2
4ᵛ	2	Aire	

5	2	Galliard	
5v	3	Fancy	3
6v	3	Aire	
7	3	Galliard	
7v	4	Fancy	4
8v	4	Aire	
8v	4	Galliard	
9v	5	Fancy	12
10v	5	Aire	
11	5	Galliard	
11v	6	Fancy	13
12v	6	Aire	
13	6	Galliard	
13v	7	Fancy	14
14v	7	Aire	
15	7	Galliard	
15v	8	Fancy	15
16v	8	Aire	
17	8	Galliard	
17v	9	Fancy	8
18v	9	Aire	
19	9	Galliard	
19v	10	Fancy	7
20v	10	Aire	
21	10	Galliard	
21v	11	Fancy	6
22v	11	Aire	
23	11	Galliard	
23v	12	Fancy	11
24v	12	Aire	
25	12	Galliard	
25v	13	Fancy	10
26v	13	Aire	
27	13	Galliard	
27v	14	Fancy	9
28v	14	Aire	
29	14	Galliard	
29v	15	Fancy	5
30v	15	Aire	
31	15	Galliard	
84-81v		Fuga Del: Sr G:F: Hendel[a]	

[a] Incomplete; Allegro from Suite in E Minor.

MANUSCRIPT LXIV

OXFORD, CHRIST CHURCH MUS. 1215, FASCICLE 3

The organ part to verse anthems *a* 3 by John Ward.

Copied in the 1630s.
ff. 5. Modern pencil foliation, ff. 1, 3-5, 2.
Paper 290 x 200 mm. Ten six-line staves per page (ruled with a five-stave rastrum of 114 mm span and individual (five-line) staves each measuring 12.5-13 mm; extra line added to each stave by hand).
Watermark: small two handled pot.
Single gathering (second folio removed, stub remains). The present order of the folios is incorrect; the modern foliation indicates the original order (ff. 1-5; f. 5^v is discoloured as it originally acted as an outer cover). Original collation: A^2 B^4(B1 removed).
Scribe: Stephen Bing.
No binding.
Contents of *Och* Mus. 1215/3:

Folio	Composer	Original Order	Title
1	[Ward]	1	Praise ye Lo[rd] '103 psalme' [Pt 1]
1^v	[Ward]	2	The Lord executeth Righteousnes [Pt 2]
3	[Ward]	5	The Lord hath prepared [Pt 5]
3^v	[Ward]	6	Have mercy upon mee O god '51 psalme' [Pt 1]
4	[Ward]	7	Behold I was shapen in wickedness [Pt 2]
4^v	[Ward]	8	Turn thy face [Pt 3]
5	[Ward]	9	Deliver me from blood-guiltness [Pt 4]
2	[Ward]	3	For look how high [Pt 3]
2^v	[Ward]	4	The dayes of Man [Pt 4]

MANUSCRIPT LXV

EIRE, DUBLIN, MARSH'S LIBRARY MS Z3.4.13,[a] FOLIOS 47-59

An autograph score of George Jeffreys' six 'Fantazies of Three Parts'.

Copied before 1648 (mid to late 1630s?).
ff. 13. Modern pencil foliation, ff. 47-59.[b]
Paper 210 x 280 mm. Marginal rulings on left and right. Six rastrum-ruled staves per page (ruled with a three-stave rastrum of 73.5 mm span and individual staves measuring 13.5/13/12.5 mm). The music is copied stratigraphically across the whole width of a page-opening (verso to recto). No music entered on f. 47^r.
Watermark: grapes.
Collation: not possible due to tightness of binding.[c]
Scribe: George Jeffreys (autograph on f. 59).[d]
Contents of *EIRE-Dm* Z.3.4.13, ff. 47-59^v:

Fantazies of Three Parts by George Jeffreys

Folio	No.	Title
47^v	1	[Fantasia]
49^v	2	Fantazia
51^v	3	Fantazia
53^v	4	Fantazia
55^v	5	Fantazia
57^v	6	Fantazia

---

[a] *EIRE-Dm* Z.3.4.13 is a miscellaneous collection of loose leaf- and fascicle-manuscript scores and parts copied by a number of scribes (including Benjamin Rogers and Narcissus Marsh); see Charteris (1976), 31-2, 38, & 40-1, and ibid., (1982), 112-18. The material in this collection was probably used at Narcissus Marsh's weekly music meetings at Oxford (1666-78), but the manuscripts were not all necessarily copied specifically for the meetings: some of fascicles were copied earlier.
[b] *EIRE-Dm* Z.3.4.13 contains continuous pencil foliation: ff. 1-103.
[c] The preceding section of *EIRE-Dm* Z.3.4.13, ff. 33-46^v, which contains Narcissus Marsh's copies of basso continuo parts to fantasies by Ives, Jenkins, Ferrabosco II and Ward (inverted and reversed), has the same paper and contains the same stave-rulings as ff. 47-59. Marsh must have used-up spare paper associated with the Jeffreys' scores.
[d] f. 59^v contains roughly copied intonations and responses (concluding with the opening of the Venite) in an unidentified later hand.

APPENDIX

THE HATTON MUSIC COLLECTION

Key

+++ Definitely of Hatton provenance
++   Very likely of Hatton provenance
+   Possibly of Hatton provenance
X   Less likely to be of Hatton provenance

† Copy at Christ Church (†[1]: *unicum*; †[2]: only complete copy extant)
‡ Listed in Martin's book catalogues
* No copy in U.K. today

(1) Bought by Christopher Hatton III from Robert Martin in Nov. 1638
(2) Copy-texts for Hatton's scribes (B: Bing, J: Jeffreys, L: Lilly)
(3) Covers annotated by Bing (b), Hatton (ha), Holmes (h), or Jeffreys (j)
(4) Bound with the Hatton purchases of 1638
(5) Bound with prints used by Hatton's musicians/copyists
(6) Miscellaneous association with the Hatton collection e.g. b: binding, d: dedicatory, r: repertorial, or scribal (B: Bing, J: Jeffreys, L: Lilly)

Prints

++	G.B. Aloisi, *Coelestis Parnasus* (1628)†[1]	(2BJ)
+++	G.B. Aloisi, *Contextus Musicarum Proportionum* (1637)†‡	(1; 2BJ)
+++	G.B. Aloisi, *Corona Stellarum* (1637)†[2] ‡	(1; 2J)
++	G.G. Arrigoni, *Concerti di Camera* (1635)‡	(2BJ)
+++	A. Aux-Cousteaux, *Meslanges de Chansons* (1644)†[2]	(3ha)
+	B. Barbarino, *Madrigali* [Bk 1] (1609)†	(3b)
+	B. Barbarino, *Il Secondo Libro de Madrigali* (1611)†	(3b)
+	B. Barbarino, *Il Quarto Libro de Madrigali* (1614)†[1]	(3b)
+	B. Barbarino, *Canzonette a Una e Due voci* (1616)†[1]	(3b)
+	B. Barbarino, *Madrigali a Tre Voci* (1617)†[1]	(3h)
+	O. Bartolini, *Il Primo Libro de Madrigali* (1606)†[2]	(3b)
+	D. Bellante, *Concerti Accademici* Op. 1 (1629)†[2] ‡	(4)
++	S. Bernardi, *Secondo Libro de Madrigali* Op. 7 (1616)†	(2B)
+	S. Bernardi, *Concerti Accademici.... Libro Primo* Op. 8 (1615-16)*	(2B)
+	S. Bonini, *Lamento d'Arianna* (1613)†	(4)
+	S. Bonini, *Serena Celeste* Op. 8 (1615)†[1]	(4)
+	C. Burgh, *Hortus Marianus* (1630)†[2]	(4)
+	G. Caccini, *L'Euridice* (1615)†	(3b)

+	G. Caccini, *Le Nuove Musiche* (1615)†	(3b)
+	V. Calestani, *Madrigali et Arie.... Parto Primo* (1617)†	(3b)
+	L. Calvi ed., *Quarta Raccolta de Sacri Canti* (1629)†	(4)
+	G. Carrone, *Il Primo Libro delli Motetti* Op. 1 (1629)†[1]	(4)
+	J. de Castro, *Chant Musicale* (1597)†[1]	(3j)
+++	F. Cauda, *Catena Sacrarum Cantionum* Bk 1, Op. 3 (1626)†[1] ‡	(1)
+	E. du Caurroy, *Fantasies a III. IIII. V et VI* (1610)†[2]	(3b)
+	E. du Caurroy, *Meslanges de la Musique* (1610)†	(3b)
+	T. Cecchino, *Amorosi Concetti. Il Terzo Libro* (1616)†[1]	(3b)
+	G.M. Cesare, *Concerti Ecclesiastici* Bk 1 (1614)†[1] ‡	(4)
+++	A. della Ciaia, *Madrigali* Op. 1 (1636)†[2] ‡	(1)
+	A. Cifra, *Motecta* [Bk 1] (1614)†	(4)
+	A. Cifra, *Motecta* Bk 2 (1611)†	(4)
+	A. Cifra, *Motecta* Bk 3 (1614)†	(4)
+	A. Cifra, *Motecta* Bk 4, Op. 8 (1613)†	(4)
++	A. Cifra, *Motecta* Bk 5, Op. 11 (1616)†	(2J)
+	A. Cifra, *Scherzi et Arie* (1614)†	(4)
+	A. Cifra, *Madrigali a Cinque Voci* Bk 3 (1615)†	(4)
+	B. Cossa, *Madrigaletti a Tre Voci* Bk 1 (1617)†	(4)
+++	F. Costantini ed., *Motetti* Bk 4, Op. 12 (1634)†[1] ‡	(1)
+++	A. Cremonese, *Madrigali Concertati* Bk 1, Op. 1 (1636)†[1] ‡	(1)
+	M. Delipari, *I Baci. Madrigali* Bk 1 (1630)†[2] ‡	(4)
+	R. Dering, *Cantiones Sacrae Quinque Vocum* (1617)†	(4)
++	R. Dering, *Cantica Sacra... Senis Vocibus* (1618)†	(2BJ)
+	M. East, *Madrigals to 3. 4. and 5. parts* (1604)†	(3bj)
+	M. East, *The Second Set of Madrigals* (1606)†	(3bj)
+	M. East, *The Third Set of Bookes* (1610)†	(3bj)
++	M. East, *The Seventh Set of Bookes* (1638)†	(6d)
+++	A. Facchi, *Motetti* Bk 2 (1635)†[1] ‡	(1; 2BJ)
+++	A. Facchi, *Madrigali* Bk 2 (1636)†[2] ‡	(1)
+++	B. Ferrari, *Musiche Varie* [Bk 1] (1633)†[1] ‡	(1)
+	G. Ferrari, *Il Primo Libro de Madrigali* Op. 2 (1628)†‡	(4)
+++	G. Filippi, *Concerti Ecclesiastici* Bk 1 (1637)†[2] ‡	(1)
+	G. Fornaci, *Amorosi Respiri Musicali* Bk 1, Op. 2 (1617)†	(3b)
+++	N. Fontei, *Bizzarrie Poetiche* [Bk 1] (1635)†[1] ‡	(1)
+++	N. Fontei, *Bizzarrie Poetiche* Bk 2 (1636)†[1] ‡	(1)
+++	N. Fontei, *Melodiae Sacrae* Op. 3 (1638)†[2] ‡	(1)
+	L. Gallerano, *Ecclesiastica Armonica Concerti* (1624)†[1] ‡	(4)
+	O. Gentile, *Il Primo Libro de Madrigali* (1616)†	(3b)
++	C. Gesualdo, *Madrigali* [Bk 1] (1617 as 'Bk 2')†‡	(2B)
++	C. Gesualdo, *Madrigali* Bk 2 (1616 as 'Bk 1')†‡	(2B)
++	C. Gesualdo, *Madrigali* Bk 3 (1619)†‡	(2B)
++	C. Gesualdo, *Madrigali* Bk 4 (1616)†‡	(2B)

+	C. Gesualdo, *Madrigali* Bk 6 (1616)†‡	(5)
+++	O. Gibbons, *The First Set of Madrigals and Mottets* (1612)†	(6bd)
X	O. Gibbons, *Fantazies of III parts* (c.1620)†	(6r)
++	A. Grandi, *Il Primo Libro de Motetti* (1628)†‡	(2BJ)
++	A. Grandi, *Il Secondo Libro de Motetti* (1628)†‡	(2BJ)
++	A. Grandi, *Il Quarto Libro de Motetti* (1628)†‡	(2BJ)
++	A. Grandi, *Celesti Fiori... Libro Quinto* (1625)†‡	(2J)
++	A. Grandi, *Il Sesto Libro de Motetti* (1630)†‡	(2BJ)
X	A. Grandi, *Motetti a Voce Sola* (1628)†‡	(6)
++	A. Grandi, *Motetti... con Sinfonie* Bk 3 (1629)†	(2J)
++	A. Grandi, *Madrigali Concertati* [Bk 1] (1626)†	(2J)
+	A. Grandi, *Madrigali Concertati* Bk 2, Op. 11 (1626)†	(4)
+	J. Graswinkel ed., *Nervi D'Orfeo* (1605)†	(3b)
+	A. Gregori, *Sacrarum Cantionum* Bk 3, Op. 8 (1635)‡	(2J)
+	A. Gualtieri, *Motetti* Bk 3, Op. 10 (1630)†[1]‡	(4)
X	G. Guami, *Canzonette Francese* (1612)†[1]	(6r)
+	G. Hayne (E. Hennio), *Motetti Sacri* Op. 4 (1646)*	(2J)
+	S. d'India, *Liber Primus Motectorum* (1627)†	(4)
+	S. d'India, *Liber Secundus Sacrorum Concentuum* (1610)†	(4)
+	S. d'India, *Libro Primo de Madrigali a 5* (1610)†‡	(5)
+	S. d'India, *Libro Secondo de Madrigali a 5* (1611)†[2]‡	(5)
+	S. d'India, *Il Terzo Libro de Madrigali a 5* (1615)†[2]‡	(4)
+	S. d'India, *Il Quarto Libro de Madrigali a 5* (1616)†[2]	(5)
+	S. d'India, *Il Quinto Libro de Madrigali a 5* (1616)†	(5)
++	S. d'India, *Le Musiche* [Bk 1] (1615)†	(3h; 4)
+	S. d'India, *Le Musiche* Bk 4 (1621)†[1]	(4)
+	S. d'India. *Le Musiche* Bk 5 (1623)†[1]	(4)
+	S. d'India, *Le Musiche e Balli a 4* (1621)†[1]	(5)
+	S. d'India, *Delle Villanelle alla Napolitana* Bk 1 (1610)†	(4)
+	L. Leoni, *Sacri Flores* (1619)†	(4)
+++	A. Marastoni, *Madrigali Concertati* Op. 6 (1628)†‡	(1)
+	L. Marenzio, *Cantiones Sacrae* (1603)†	(3b)
+	L.Marenzio, *Il Primo, Secondo, Terzo, Quarto & Quinto Libro delle Villanelle et Canzonette a 3* (1610)†	(3b)
+	L. Marenzio, *Madrigali a Quatro Voci* Bk 1 (1587)†	(3b)
+	L. Marenzio, *Madrigali a Cinque Voci Ridotti in un Corpo* (1593)†	(3j)
+	L. Marenzio, *Il Primo, Secondo, Terzo, Quarto & Quinto Libro de Madrigali a Cinque Voci* (1609)†	(3j)
+	L. Marenzio, *Madrigalia a Quinque Vocum* (1601)†	(3h)
+	L.Marenzio, *Madrigali Spirituali a Cinque Voci* (1610)†	(3b)
+	L. Marenzio, *Il Quarto Libro de Madrigali a 6* (1587)†	(3b)
+	L. Marenzio, *Il Sesto Libro de Madrigali a 6* (1610)†	(3b)

+   L. Marenzio, *Il Primo, Secondo, Terzo, Quarto & Quinto Libro de Madrigali a Sei Voci* (1610)†   (3b)
+   B. Marini, *Per le Musiche di Camera Concerti* (1634)†¹ ‡   (4)
+   B. Marini, *Madrigaletti* Bk 5, Op. 9 (1635)†¹ ‡   (4)
+++ F.M. Marini, *Concerti Spirituali* Bk 1 (1637)†² ‡   (1; 2J)
+   T. Merula, *Il Primo Libro de Motetti* Op. 6 (1624)‡*   (2BJ)
++ T. Merula, *Libro Secondo de Concerti Spirituali* (1628)   (2BJ)
+++ T. Merula, *Musiche Concertate* Bk 2, Op. 10 (1635)†‡   (1; 2BJ)
+++ T. Merula, *Curtio Precipitato* Bk 2, Op. 13 (1638)†¹ ‡   (1)
+++ N. Metru, *Fantaisies a Deux Parties* (1642)†   (3ha)
+   R. Micheli, *Musica Vaga* (1615)†   (4)
+   G.L. Missino, *Tirsi Doglioso. Primo Libro* (1615)†   (3b)
+   S. Molinaro, *Concerti Ecclesiastici* (1605)†   (4)
+   F. de Monte, *Musica Sopra Il Pastor Fido* (1600)†²   (4)
+++ G. Monte dell'Olmo, *Applausi Ecclesiastici* Bk 1 (1636)†² ‡   (1)
+++ G. Monte dell'Olmo, *Sacri Affetti* Bk 2 (1637)†¹ ‡   (1)
+   C. Monteverdi, *L'Orfeo* (1615)†   (4)
+   C. Monteverdi, *Scherzi Musicali a Tre Voci* (1615)†   (3b)
+   C. Monteverdi, *Il Primo Libro de Madrigali* (1621)†‡   (4)
+   C. Monteverdi, *Il Secondo Libro de Madrigali* (1621)†‡   (4)
++ C. Monteverdi, *Il Terzo Libro de Madrigali* (1621)†‡   (2BL)
++ C. Monteverdi, *Il Quarto Libro de Madrigali* (1622)†‡   (2BL)
+   C. Monteverdi, *Il Quinto Libro de Madrigali* (1620)†‡   (4)
+   C. Monteverdi, *Il Sesto Libro de Madrigali* (1620)†‡   (4)
+   C. Monteverdi, *Concerto. Settimo Libro de Madrigali* (1628)†‡   (4)
+   G.C. Monteverdi, *Delli Affetti Musici* Bk 1 (1620)†   (4)
+   T. Morley, *The First Booke of Balletts a 5* (1595)†   (3j)
+   T. Morley, *The First Book of Consort Lessons* (1599)†   (3bj)
+   P. Nenna, *Il Primo Libro de Madrigali a 4* (1621)†²   (5)
+   P. Nenna, *Il Primo Libro de Madrigali a 5* (1617)†‡   (5)
+   P. Nenna, *Il Quarto Libro de Madrigali a 5* (1617)†‡   (5)
+   P. Nenna, *Madrigali.... Quinto Libro a 5* (1612)†   (5)
+   P. Nenna, *Il Sesto Libro de Madrigali a 5* (1618)†   (5)
++ P. Nenna, *Il Settimo Libro de Madrigali a 5* (1624)†‡   (2J)
+   C. Orlandi, *Arie a Tre Due et Voce Sola* Op. 2 (1616)†¹   (3b)
+   B. Pallavicino, *Sacrae Dei Laudes* (1605)†‡   (3h)
+   B. Pallavicino, *Il Primo Libro de Madrigali a 5* (1606)†‡   (4)
+   B. Pallavicino, *Il Secondo Libro de Madrigali a 5* (1606)†‡   (4)
+   B. Pallavicino, *Il Terzo Libro de Madrigali a 5* (1606)†‡   (4)
+   B. Pallavicino, *Il Quarto Libro de Madrigali a 5* (1607)†‡   (6)
+   B. Pallavicino, *Il Quinto Libro de Madrigali a 5* (1609)†‡   (4)
+   B. Pallavicino, *Il Sesto Libro de Madrigali a 5* (1611)†‡   (4)
+   B. Pallavicino, *Il Settimo Libro de Madrigali a 5* (1611)†   (4)

++	B. Pallavicino, *L'Ottavo Libro de Madrigali* a 5 (1612)†¹	(3h; 4)
+	S. Patta, *Motetti et Madrigali* (1614)†	(3h)
++	D. Pecci, *Sacri Modulatus* Op. 3 (1629)†¹ ‡	(2J)
+	T. Pecci, *Madrigali* (1609)†	(3b)
+	P. Philips ed., *Melodia Olympica* (1591)†	(3b)
X	P. Philips, *Il Primo Libro de Madrigali* a 6 (1604)†	(6r)
X	P. Philips, *Il Secondo Libro de Madrigali* a 6 (1603)†	(6r)
+	P. Philips, *Madrigali a Otto Voci* (1599)†	(3b)
+	G.B. Piazza, *Canzonette a Voce Sola* [Bk 2] (1633)†‡	(4)
+	F. Pio, *Liber Primus Motectorum* (1622-4)*	(2J)
+++	A. de Pisticci, *Motetti* Bk 3, Op. 6 (1633)†‡	(1)
+++	A. de Pisticci, *Motetti* Bk 4, Op. 7 (1637)†¹ ‡	(1)
+++	O. Polidori, *Motetti* Op. 13 (1636)†‡	(1)
+	W. Porter, *Motetts of Two Voyces* (1657)†	(6)
+	E. Radesca di Foggia, *Madrigali* Bk. 1 (1615)†	(3b)
+	E. Radesca di Foggia, *Canzonette Madrigali et Arie* [Bk 1] (1616)†	(3b)
+	E. Radesca di Foggia, *Il Secondo Libro delle Canzonette Madrigali et Arie* (1616)†	(3b)
+	E. Radesca di Foggia, *Il Terzo Libro delle Canzonette Madrigali et Arie* (1616)†	(3b)
+	E. Radesca di Foggia, *Il Quarto Libro delle Canzonette Madrigali et Arie* (1616)†	(3b)
+	E. Radesca di Foggia, *Il Quinto Libro delle Canzonette Madrigali et Arie* (1617)†	(3b)
X	P. Rimonte, *Parnaso Español de Madrigales* (1614)†	(6r)
++	G. Rovetta, *Madrigali Concertati* Bk 1, Op. 2 (1629)†‡	(2J)
+	G.F. Sances, *Cantade.... a Doi Voci* Bk 2 (1633)†‡	(4)
+++	G.F. Sances, *Motetti* (1638)†‡	(1; 2BJ)
+++	C. Saracini, *Musiche* Bk 5 (1624)†‡	(1)
+++	C. Saracini, *Musiche* Bk 6 (1624)†‡	(1)
+	H. Schütz, *Symphoniae Sacrae* (1629)†‡	(4)
X	L. Simonetti ed., *Ghirlanda Sacra... Libro Primo* (1630)†‡	(6)
+++	B. Tomasi, *Motecta* Op. 6 (1635)†² ‡	(1; 2BJ)
++	E. Trabattone, *Concerti* Bk 2, Op. 4 (1629)†¹ ‡	(2J)
+	R. Trofeo & G.D. Rognoni Taeggio, *Canzonette Leggiadre* (1600)†²	(4)
++	F. Turini, *Madrigali* Bk 1 (1624)†‡	(2J)
+	G.Turnhout, *Il Primo Libro de Madrigali a Sei Voci* (1589)†	(3b)
++	G. Valentini, *Secondo Libro de Madrigali* (1616)†	(3h; 6B)
+	L. Valvasensi, *Secondo Giardino d'Amorosi Fiori* (1634)†¹ ‡	(4)
+	T.L. de Victoria, *Motecta* (1603)†	(3b)
+	F. Vitali, *Concerto... Madrigali* Bk 1 (1629)†‡	(4)

+	J. Ward, *The First Set of English Madrigals* (1613)†	(3b)
+	J. Wilson, *Psalterium Carolinum* (1657)†	(6)
+	F. Wynant, *Madrigali a Cinque Voci* Bk 1 (1597)†	(4)

Manuscripts

X	British Library, London Egerton 2485	(6L)
++	Christ Church, Oxford Mus. 2/397-408/436	(6BL)
X	Christ Church, Oxford Mus. 21	(6r)
X	Christ Church, Oxford Mus. 44	(6)
X	Christ Church, Oxford Mus. 56-60	(6)
X	Christ Church, Oxford Mus. 61-7	(6)
+	Christ Church, Oxford Mus. 372-6	(3bh)
++	Christ Church, Oxford Mus. 417-18 & 1080	(6B)
+++	Christ Church, Oxford Mus. 432/612-13	(6bBL)
X	Christ Church, Oxford Mus. 459-62	(6r)
+	Christ Church, Oxford Mus. 463-7	(3b)
X	Christ Church, Oxford Mus. 510-14	(6r)
+	Christ Church, Oxford Mus. 732-5	(6B)
++	Christ Church, Oxford Mus. 754-9	(3h; 6B)
++	Christ Church, Oxford Mus. 877-880	(6BJ)
++	Christ Church, Oxford Mus. 1023	(6BJ)
+	Christ Church, Oxford Mus. 1155-61	(3h)
+	Christ Church, Oxford Mus. 1185	(6B)
+	Christ Church, Oxford Mus. 1215, fascicle 3	(6B)

BIBLIOGRAPHY

List of Music Sources Cited

Manuscript Sources

Birmingham, Barber Institute of Fine Arts, Birmingham University, MS 5002
Cambridge, Fitzwilliam Museum, MS Mu 168 [*olim* Mus. 32.G.29]
    MS Mu 734 [*olim* Mus. 24.E.13-17]
Cambridge, King's College, Rowe MS 207
    MS 321
Cambridge, Magdalene College, Pepys Library, MS 2803
Cambridge, University Library, MS Dd.6.48(F)
Carlisle Cathedral, 'Bishop Smith's Part-Song Books' (deposited in the Cumbria Record Office)
Durham, Cathedral Library, MS B.1
    MS D.4
Glasgow, University Library, Euing Music Collection, MSS Rd 58-61
King's Music Library (housed in the British Library), R.M. MS 20.h.8
    R.M. MS 24.c.10
    R.M. MS 24.d.3
    R.M. MS 24.k.3
    R.M. MSS 27.a.1-15
Lincoln, Cathedral Library, MS 1
    MSS 2-4
London, British Library, Add. MS 10,338
Add. MS 10,444
Add. MS 11,585
Add. MS 11,587
Add. MS 11,608
Add. MS 17,784
Add. MS 17,801
Add. MSS 17,816 & 30,829-30
Add. MS 17,835
Add. MSS 18,940-4
Add. MS 23,779
Add. MS 24,293
Add. MSS 27,550-4
Add. MS 29,282
Add. MSS 29,372-7
Add. MS 29,427
Add. MS 30,382
Add. MS 30,487
Add. MSS 30,826-8
Add. MS 63,852
Add. MS 31,399
Add. MS 31,428
Add. MS 31,431
Add. MS 31,434
Add. MS 31,437
Add. MS 31,440
Add. MS 31,460
Add. MS 31,472
Add. MS 31,476
Add. MS 31,477
Add. MS 31,479
Add. MS 33,234
Add. MS 33,235
Add. MS 33,236
Add. MS 36,877
Add. MSS 39,550-4
Add. MSS 40,657-61
Add. MS 53,723
Add. MS 59,869
Egerton MS 2013
Egerton MS 2485
Egerton MS 2960
Egerton MS 3665
Evelyn MS 189
Evelyn MS 211
Harley MS 1265
Harley MS 1501
Harley MS 7341

London, Guildhall Library, Gresham College Collection, MSS 469-71 [*olim* VI.3.43-5]
London, Royal Academy of Music,   MS 42
                                  MS 43
                                  MS 107
London, Royal College of Music,   MS 660   MS 1064
                                  MS 920   MS 1076
                                  MS 920A   MS 1145
                                  MS 921   MS 2033
                                  MS 995   MS 2034
                                  MSS 1045-51   MS 2039
London, St Paul's Cathedral Library,   MS Partbooks A 1
                                       MS Partbook 43.D
London, Westminster Abbey Library,   MS CG 63
                                     MS Partbooks Triforium Set 1
                                     MS Partbooks Triforium Set 2
Madrigal Society (housed in the British Library, London),   MSS G 33-6
                                                            MSS G 37-42
                                                            MSS G 55-9
Manchester, Central Public Library, Henry Watson Music Library, MS BRm 832 Vu 51
Northamptonshire Record Office,   Finch-Hatton MS 1395
                                  Finch-Hatton MS 1997
                                  Finch-Hatton MS 2398
                                  Finch-Hatton MS 3431A
                                  Finch-Hatton MS 3431B
                                  Finch-Hatton MS 3431C
Oxford, Bodleian Library,   MS Don c 57   MSS Mus. Sch. E 406-9
                            MS Mus. a 1   MSS Mus. Sch. E 415-18
                            MS Mus. c 27   MSS Mus. Sch. E 431-6
                            MS Mus. d 10   MSS Mus. Sch. E 443-6
                            MS Mus. d 16   MS Mus. Sch. E 450
                            MSS Mus. f 16-19   MS Mus. Sch. E 451
                            MS Mus. Sch. A 641   MSS Mus. Sch. F 568-9
                            MS Mus. Sch. B 2   MS Mus. Sch. F 575
                            MS Mus. Sch. B 3   MS Mus. Sch. G 612
                            MS Mus. Sch. C 9   North MS e 37
                            MS Mus. Sch. C 10   Tenbury MS 302
                            MS Mus. Sch. C 11   Tenbury MS 310
                            MSS Mus. Sch. C 12-19 Tenbury MS 335
                            MSS Mus. Sch. C 20-3   Tenbury MS 713
                            MSS Mus. Sch. C 24-7   Tenbury MS 720
                            MSS Mus. Sch. C 54-7   Tenbury MS 892
                            MSS Mus. Sch. C 81-91 Tenbury MS 926
                            MSS Mus. Sch. C 98-9   Tenbury MSS 940-4
                            MS Mus. Sch. C 100   Tenbury MSS 973-6 & 1273
                            MS Mus. Sch. C 101   Tenbury MS 1005
                            MS Mus. Sch. C 102   Tenbury MS 1009
                            MS Mus. Sch. C 203   Tenbury MS 1010
                            MS Mus. Sch. C 204   Tenbury MS 1011
                            MS Mus. Sch. D 217   Tenbury MS 1012
                            MSS Mus. Sch. D 233-6 Tenbury MS 1013
                            MS Mus. Sch. D 237   Tenbury MS 1015
                            MSS Mus. Sch. D 241-4 Tenbury MS 1016

Oxford, Bodleian Library, Tenbury MS 1017
Tenbury MS 1018
Tenbury MS 1162-7
Tenbury MS 1285

Oxford, Christ Church, Mus. 2, 397-408 & 436
Mus. 9
Mus. 13
Mus. 14
Mus. 16
Mus. 17
Mus. 18
Mus. 19
Mus. 21
Mus. 43
Mus. 44
Mus. 48
Mus. 49
Mus. 53
Mus. 55
Mus. 56-60
Mus. 61-6
Mus. 67
Mus. 68-74
Mus. 78-82
Mus. 83
Mus. 367-70
Mus. 372-6
Mus. 379-81
Mus. 417-18 & 1080
Mus. 423-8
Mus. 430
Mus. 432 & 612-13
Mus. 435
Mus. 459-62
Mus. 463-7
Mus. 473-8
Mus. 510-14
Mus. 521-4
Mus. 525
Mus. 526
Mus. 527-30 & 1024
Mus. 615
Mus. 621
Mus. 623-6
Mus. 716-20
Mus. 732-5
Mus. 736-8
Mus. 747-9
Mus. 754-9
Mus. 877-80
Mus. 996
Mus. 1004
Mus. 1005
Mus. 1013-15
Mus. 1023
Mus. 1078
Mus. 1151
Mus. 1155-61
Mus. 1178
Mus. 1185
Printed Sheet Mus. 1208
Mus. 1215

York, Minster Library, MSS M.1.S
MSS M.3.S
MSS M.5.S
MS M.93.S

Belgium, Brussels, Bibliothèque Royale de Belgique, MS II 4109
EIRE (Ireland), Dublin, Marsh's Library, MSS Z3.4.1-6
MS Z3.4.13
MS Z3.5.13
France, Paris, Bibliothèque du Conservatoire (housed in the Bibliothèque Nationale), MS Rés F 934[a]
MS Rés F 934[b]
France, Paris, Bibliothèque Nationale, MS Vm^7 8
Italy, Bologna, Civico Museo Bibliografico Musicale, MS Q 50
Italy, Florence, Biblioteca del Conservatorio, MS f I 25
Japan, Tokyo, Nanki Library, MS N-4/39
U.S.A., Chicago, Newberry Library, MS VM I A 18 J 52c
U.S.A., Los Angeles, University of California, William Andrews Clark Memorial Library, MS C 6968 M4
MS F 1995 M4

U.S.A., New York, Public Library, Mus. Res. Drexel MS 3976
MS 4302
MS 5624
U.S.A., Rochester, Sibley Music Library, Eastman School of Music, MS ML96 L814f
U.S.A., San Marino, Huntington Library, Ellesmere MSS 25 A 46-51
U.S.A., Washington D.C., Library of Congress, MSSM990 C66F4

Printed Sources

† Copy in the library of Christ Church, Oxford (†^{1}: *unicum*; †^{2}: only complete copy in existence)
‡ Listed in Robert Martin's printed catalogues
* Copy bought by Sir Christopher Hatton in 1638 from Robert Martin

E. Adriaenssen ed., *Pratum Musicum* (P.Phalèse, Antwerp, 1584) [1584^{12}]
G.B. Aloisi, *Coelestis Parnasus* Op. 1 (B. Magni, Venice, 1628†^{1}) [A872]
—— *Harmonicum Coelum* Op. 3 (B. Magni, Venice, 1628‡) [A875]
—— *Contextus Musicarum Proportionum* Op. 4 (B. Magni, Venice, 1637†‡*) [A876]
—— *Corona Stellarum* Op. 5 (B. Magni, Venice, 1637†^{2} ‡*) [A877]
G.B. Anselmi ed., *Madrigali... a 2.3.4.5. Voci* (B. Magni, Venice, 1624‡) [1624^{11}]
A. Antonelli, *Liber Primus/Secundus/Tertius Diversarum Modulationum* (B. Zannetti, Rome, 1615/1615/1616) [A1271-3]
G.G. Arrigoni, *Concerti di Camera* (B. Magni, Venice, 1635‡) [A2490]
A. Aux-Cousteaux, *Meslanges de Chanson* (R. Ballard, Paris, 1644†^{2}) [A2892]
B. Barbarino, *Madrigali* [Bk 1] (R. Amadino, Venice, 1606; 2/1609†) [B868-9]
—— *Il Secondo Libro de Madrigali* (R. Amadino, Venice, 1607; 2/1611†) [B870-1]
—— *Il Quarto Libro de Madrigali* (R. Amadino, Venice, 1614†^{1}) [B876]
—— *Canzonette a Una e Due Voci* (R. Amadino, Venice, 1616†^{1}) [B877]
—— *Madrigali a Tre Voci* (R. Amadino, Venice, 1617†^{1}) [B878]
J. Barnard ed., *The First Book of Selected Church Musick* (E. Griffin, London, 1641†) [1641^5]
O. Bartolini, *Il Primo Libro de Madrigali a Cinque Voci* (A. Raverii, Venice, 1606†^{2}) [B1141]
G.B. Bassani, *Concerti Sacri* Op. 11 (M. Silvoni, Bologna, 1692) [B1191]
D. Bellante, *Concerti Accademici* Op. 1 (B. Magni, Venice, 1629†^{2}‡) [B1712]
S. Bernardi, *Concerti Accademici.... Libro primo* Op. 8 (G. Vincenti, Venice, 1615-16) [B2055]
—— *Secondo Libro de Madrigali a Cinque Voci* Op. 7 (G. Vincenti, Venice, 1616†) [B2066]
J. Blow, *Amphion Anglicus* (W. Pearson, London, 1700†) [B2985]
—— *Go, Perjur'd Man* (T. Cross, London, n.d.) five undated editions [B2987-91]
S. Bonini, *Lamento d'Arianna* (B. Magni, Venice, 1613†) [B3498]
—— *Serena Celeste... Motetti a Una, Due, e Tre Voci* Op. 8 (B. Magni, Venice, 1615†^{1}) [B3500]
M. Borchgrevinck ed., *Giardino Novo Bellissimo... Il Primo Libro de Madrigali a Cinque Voci* (H. Waltkirch, Copenhagen, 1605) [1605^7]
—— *Giardino Novo Bellissimo... Il Secondo Libro de Madrigali a Cinque Voci* (H. Waltkirch, Copenhagen, 1606) [1606^5]
H. Bowman, *Songs, for One, Two & Three Voices* (T. Bowman, Oxford, 1677) [B4036]

W. Boyce, *Cathedral Music* (s.n., London, i/1760,† ii/1768, iii/1773†)

S. Briscoe ed.,*New Songs in the Third Part of the Comical History of Don Quixote* (S. Briscoe, London, 1696) [1696[10]]

H. Brome ed., *New Ayres and Dialogues* (M.C., London, 1678) [1678[4]]

D. Brown & T. Benskin ed., *The Newest Collection of the Choicest Songs* (T. Haly, London, 1682) [Not in *RISM*]

J. Bull, W. Byrd & O. Gibbons, *Parthenia* (W. Hole (G. Lowe), London, [1613]) [1613[14]]

C. Burgh, *Hortus Marianus* (P. Phalèse, Antwerp, 1630†[2]) [B5019]

F. Caccini, *Il Primo Libro delle Musiche* (Z. Pignoni, Florence, 1618) [C2]

G. Caccini, *L'Euridice* (G. Marescotti, Florence, 1600; 2/ G. Vincenti, Venice, 1615†) [C4-5]

—— *Le Nuove Musiche* (G. Marescotti, Florence, 1602; 3/ G. Vincenti, Venice, 1615†) [C6, C8]

G.B. Caifabri ed., *Scelta de'Motetti.... Parte Prima* (G. Fei, Rome, 1665) [1665[1]]

—— *Scelta de'Motetti.... Parte Seconda* (A.Belmonte,Rome, 1667) [1667[1]]

G.B. Caifabri ed., *Scelta di Mottetti* (V. Mascardi, Rome, 1675) [1675[3]]

V. Calestani, *Madrigali et Arie.... Parto Primo* (G. Vincenti, Venice, 1617†) [C69]

L. Calvi ed., *Quarta Raccolta de Sacri Canti* (A. Vincenti, Venice, 1629†) [1629[5]]

G. Carissimi, *Missa a Quinque et a Novem, cum Selectis Quibusdam Cantionibus* (F. Friesser, Cologne, 1665-6) [C1220]

—— *Arion Romanus* (D. Hautt jun., Konstanz, 1670) [C1221]

—— *Sacri Concerti Musicali* (V. Mascardi, Rome, 1675†) [C1222]

J. Carr & S. Scott ed., *Comes Amoris; or the Companion of Love* (N. Tompson, London, 1687) [1687[4]]

G. Carrone, *Il Primo Libro delli Motetti Op. 1* (A. Vincenti, Venice, 1629†[1]) [C1262]

G. Casati, *Il Primo Libro de Motetti Concertati Op. 1* (A. Vincenti,Venice, 1643) [C1411]

—— *Amoenum Rosarium Op. 5* (P. Phalèse, Antwerp, 1649†) [C1424]

J. de Castro, *Chant Musicale* (G. Grevenbruch, Cologne, 1597†[1]) [C1495]

F. Cauda, *Catena Sacrarum Cantionum... Liber Primus Op. 3* (B. Magni, Venice, 1626†[1] ‡*) [C1539]

E. du Caurroy, *Fantasies* (P. Ballard, Paris, 1610†[2]) [D3617]

—— *Meslanges de la Musique* (P. Ballard, Paris, 1610†) [D3616]

M. Cazzati, *Motetti a Due Voci Op. 10* (A. Vincenti, Venice, 1648) [C1589]

T. Cecchino, *Amorosi Concetti, Il Terzo Libro de'Madrigali a Una et Due Voci Op. 7* (G. Vincenti, Venice, 1616†[1]) [C1671]

G.M. Cesare, *Concerti Ecclesiastici... Libro Primo* (B. Magni, Venice, 1614†[1] ‡) [C1751]

W. Child, *The First Set of Psalmes of III. Voyces* (J. Reave, London, 1639†; 2/ J. Playford, 1650†) [C2056-7]

A. della Ciaia, *Madrigali... a Cinque Voci con Basso Continuo Op. 1* (B. Magni, Venice, 1636†[2] ‡*) [D1394]

A. Cifra, *Motecta... Liber Primus* (G. Vincenti, Venice, 1609; 5/1614†) [C2161, C2165]

—— *Motecta... Liber Secundus* (G.B. Robletti, Rome, 1609; 4/ G. Vincenti, 1611†) [C2167, C2170]

—— *Motecta... Liber Tertius* (G.B. Robletti, Rome, 1609; 5/ G. Vincenti, 1614†) [C2174, C2178]

A. Cifra, *Motecta... Liber Quartus* Op. 8 (G.B. Robletti, Rome, 1609; 4/ G. Vincenti, 1613†) [C2179, C2182]

—— *Motecta... Liber Quintus* Op. 11 (G.B. Robletti, Rome, 1612; 2/ G. Vincenti, 1616†) [C2190-1]

—— *Scherzi et Arie* (G. Vincenti, Venice, 1614†; 3/1628‡) [C2216, no third edition survives]

—— *Madrigali a Cinque Voci... Libro Terzo* (G. Vincenti, Venice, 1615†) [C2218]

A. Corelli, *Sonate a Tre* Op. 1 (Rome, 1681) [C3658]

B. Cossa, *Madrigaletti a Tre Voci, Libro Primo* (B. Magni, Venice, 1617†) [C4182]

F. Costantini ed., *Motetti.... Libro Quarto* Op. 12 (B. Magni, Venice, 1634$†^1$ ‡*) [1634^1]

A. Cremonese, *Madrigali Concertati.... Libro Primo* Op. 1 (B. Magni, Venice, 1636$†^1$ ‡*) [A933]

G.B. Crivelli, *Il Primo Libro delli Madrigali Concertati* (A. Vincenti, Venice, 1626) [C4424]

M. Delipari, *I Baci. Madrigali.... Libro Primo* (B. Magni, Venice, 1630$†^2$ ‡) [D1393]

R. Dering, *Cantiones Sacrae Quinque Vocum* (P. Phalèse, Antwerp, 1617†) [D1317]

—— *Cantica Sacra... Senis Vocibus* (P. Phalèse, Antwerp, 1618†) [D1319]

—— *Canzonette a Tre Voci* (P. Phalèse, Antwerp, 1620) [D1321]

—— *Canzonette a Quattro Voci* (P. Phalèse, Antwerp, 1620†) [D1320]

M. East, *Madrigals to 3.4. and 5. Parts: Apt for Viols and Voices* (T. East, London, 1604†) [E4]

—— *The Second Set of Madrigales* (J. Windet, London, 1606†) [E5]

—— *The Third Set of Bookes* (T. Snodham, London, 1610†) [E6]

—— *The Sixt Set of Bookes* (T. Snodham, London, 1624) [E10]

—— *The Seventh Set of Bookes* (W. Stansby & G. Latham, London, 1638†) [E11]

A. Facchi, *Motetti... Libro Sec.* (B. Magni, Venice, 1635$†^1$ ‡*) [F44]

—— *Madrigali... Libro Secondo* (B. Magni, Venice, 1636$†^2$ ‡*) [F45]

B. Ferrari, *Musiche Varie a Voce Sola* (B. Magni, Venice, 1633$†^1$ ‡*) [F265]

G. Ferrari, *Il Primo Libro de Madrigali* Op. 2 (B. Magni, Venice, 1628†‡) [F295]

G. Filippi, *Concerti Ecclesiastici.... Libro Primo* (B. Magni, Venice, 1637$†^2$ ‡*) [F733]

G. Finetti, *Motecta Binis Vocibus Concinenda... Libro Secundus* (A. Gardano, Venice, 1611; 5/ B. Magni, 1621‡) [F815, F817]

—— *Cantiones Binis Vocibus Concinendae... Liber Tertius* (B. Magni, Venice, 1613; 4/1620‡) [F820-1]

—— *Concerti Ecclesiastici* (P. Phalèse, Antwerp, 1621$†^2$) [F830]

Florido de Silvestri ed., *Concentus Sacras* (A. Fei, Rome, 1643) [1643^1]

—— *Sacras Cantiones* (L. Grignani, Rome, 1645) [1645^2]

—— *Cantiones Alias Sacras* (L. Grignani, Rome,1649) [1649^2]

—— *Sacras Cantiones* (L. Grignani, Rome, 1650) [1650^1]

—— *Sacras Cantiones... Pars Prima* (V. Mascardi, Rome, 1651) [Not in *RISM*]

—— *Sacras Cantiones.... Pars Secunda* (V. Mascardi, Rome, 1652) [1652^1]

—— *Cantiones Sacras* (J. van Geertsom, Rotterdam, 1657$†^2$) [Not in *RISM*]

—— *Sacras Cantiones* (F. Moneta, Rome, 1659†) [1659^1]

—— *Psalmos* (I. de Lazzari, Rome, 1662) [1662^2]

—— *Sacras Cantiones.... Pars Secunda* (I. de Lazzari, Rome, 1663†) [1663^1]

[A. Fontanelli], *Primo Libro di Madrigali Senza Nome a Cinque Voci* (V. Baldini, Ferrara, 1595; 2/ A. Gardano, Venice, 1603†, 4/ B. Magni, Venice, 1616‡) [F1477-8, F1480]

[A. Fontanelli], *Secondo Libro de Madrigali Senza Nome a Cinque Voci* (A. Gardano, Venice, 1604; 3/ B. Magni, 1619‡) [F1481, F1483]

N. Fontei, *Bizzarrie Poetiche* [Bk 1] (B. Magni, Venice, 1635†[1]‡*) [F1485]

N. Fontei, *Bizzarrie Poetiche... Libro Secondo* (B. Magni, Venice, 1636†[1] ‡ (*?)) [F1486]

—— *Melodiae Sacrae* Op. 3 (B. Magni, Venice, 1638†[2] ‡*) [F1487]

G. Fornaci, *Amorosi Respiri Musicali.... Libro Primo* Op 2 (G. Vincenti, Venice, 1617†) [F1522]

M. da Gagliano, *Il Primo Libro de Madrigali a Cinque Voci* (A. Gardano, Venice, 1602) [G108]

—— *Il Quinto Libro de Madrigali a Cinque Voci* (A. Gardano, Venice, 1658 [*recte* 1608]) [G114]

L. Gallerano, *Ecclesiastica Armonica de Concerti... Libro Primo* Op. 6 (B. Magni, Venice, 1624†[1] ‡) [G156]

J. van Geertsom ed., *Scelta di Motetti* (J. van Geertsom, Rotterdam, 1656) [1656[2]]

—— *XIV Motetta Duarum Vocum Sive Bicinia Sacra.... Liber Secundus* (H. de Bruyn, Rotterdam, 1661†[1]) [Not in *RISM*]

O. Gentile, *Il Primo Libro de Madrigali a Cinque Voci* (G. Vincenti, Venice, 1616†) [G1578]

C. Gesualdo, *Madrigali a Cinque Voci* [Bk 1] (V. Baldini, Ferrara, 1594; 2/ A. Gardano, Venice, 1603† & 5/ B. Magni, Venice, 1617†‡ as *Libro Secondo*) [G1721, G1726, G1729]

—— *Madrigali a Cinque Voci* [Bk 2] (V. Baldini, Ferrara, 1594; 2/ A. Gardano, Venice, 1603† & 4/ B. Magni, Venice, 1616†‡ as *Libro Primo*) [G1725, G1722, G1724]

—— *Madrigali a Cinque Voci, Libro Terzo* (V. Baldini, Ferrara, 1595; 4/ B. Magni, Venice, 1619†‡) [G1731, G1734]

—— *Madrigali a Cinque Voci, Libro Quarto* (V. Baldini, Ferrara, 1596; 2/ A. Gardano, Venice, 1604†, 4/ B. Magni, Venice, 1616†‡) [G1735-6, G1738]

—— *Madrigali a Cinque Voci, Libro Sesto* (G.G. Carlino, [Naples], 1611; 2/ B. Magni, Venice, 1616†‡) [G1741-2]

O. Gibbons, *The First Set of Madrigals and Mottets of 5 Parts* (T. Snodham, London, 1612†) [G1994]

—— *Fantazies of III Parts* (s.n., [London], n.d. [*c.*1620]†) [G1998]

P.A. Giramo, *Arie a piu Voci* (O. Beltrano, Naples, 1630) [G2503]

A. Grandi, *Il Primo Libro de Motetti* (G. Vincenti, Venice, 1610; 5/1628†)‡ [G3417, G3421]

—— *Il Secondo Libro de Motetti* (G. Vincenti, Venice, 1613; 5/1628†)‡ [G3422, G3426]

—— *Madrigali Concertati* (G. Vincenti, Venice, 1615; 6/1626†) [G3463, G3468]

—— *Il Quarto Libro de Motetti* (G. Vincenti, Venice, 1616; 5/1628†)‡ [G3431, G3435]

—— *Celesti Fiori... Libro Quinto* (B. Magni, Venice, 1619; 3/1625†‡, 4/1638†‡) [G3439, G3441-2]

—— *Motetti a Voce Sola* (A. Gardano, Venice, 1621; 2/ B. Magni, 1628†‡) [G3443-4]

—— *Madrigali Concertati... Libro Secondo* Op. 11 (A. Vincenti, Venice, 1622; 3/1626†) [G3469, G3471]

—— *Motetti... con Sinfonie... Libro Terzo* (A. Vincenti, Venice, 1629†) [G3450]

A. Grandi, *Il Sesto Libro de Motetti* (A. Vincenti, Venice, 1630†‡) [G3455]

J. Graswinkel ed., *Nervi d'Orfeo* (H.L. de'Haestens, Leiden, 1605†) [1605⁹]

B. Graziani, *Motetti a Voce Sola* [Bk 1] Op. 3 (V. Mascardi, Rome, 1652) [G3653]

B. Graziani, *Del Quarto Libro de Motetti a Voce Sola* Op. 10 (G. Fei d'A.F., Rome, 1665) [G3674]

A. Gregori, *Sacrarum Cantionum.... Liber Tertius* Op. 8 (B. Magni, Venice, 1635‡) [G3813]

L. Grignani ed., *Sacrarum Modulationum* (L. Grignani, Rome, 1642) [1642¹]

A. Gualtieri, *Motetti... Libro Terzo* Op. 10 (B. Magni, Venice, 1630†¹ ‡) [G4793]

G. Guami, *Canzonette Francese* (P. Phalèse, Antwerp, 1612†¹) [G4807]

G. Hayne (E. Hennio), *Motetti Sacri* Op. 4 (M. Phalèse, Antwerp, 1646) [H4924]

J. Hilton ed., *Catch that Catch Can* (J. Benson & J. Playford, London, 1652) [1652¹⁰]

T. Hume, *Captaine Humes Poeticall Musicke, Principally Made for Two Basse-Viols...* (J. Windet, London, 1607) [H7886]

S. d'India, *Il Primo de Madrigali a Cinque Voci* (A. Tradate, Milan, 1606; 3/ A. Gardano, Venice, 1610†‡) [I19, I21]

——— *Delle Villanelle alla Napolitana, a Tre Voci... Libro Primo* (G.G. Carlino & C. Vitale, Naples, 1608; 2/ A. Gardano, Venice, 1610†) [I22-3]

——— *Liber Secundus Sacrorum Concentuum* (A. Gardano, Venice, 1610†) [I17]

——— *Libro Secondo de Madrigali a Cinque Voci* (A. Gardano, Venice, 1611†² ‡) [I25]

——— *Il Terzo Libro de Madrigali a Cinque Voci* (B. Magni, Venice, 1615†² ‡) [I27]

——— *Le Musiche a Due Voci* [Bk 1] (R. Amadino, Venice, 1615†) [I28]

——— *Il Quarto Libro de Madrigali a Cinque Voci* (R. Amadino, Venice, 1616†²) [I29]

——— *Il Quinto Libro de Madrigali a Cinque Voci* (R. Amadino, Venice, 1616†) [I30]

——— *Le Musiche e Balli a Quattro Voci, con il Basso Continuo* (A. Vincenti, Venice, 1621†¹) [I32]

——— *Le Musiche.... Libro Quarto* (A. Vincenti, Venice, 1621†¹) [I33]

——— *Le Musiche.... Libro Quinto* (A. Vincenti, Venice, 1623†¹) [I34]

——— *Liber Primus Motectorum Quatuor Vocibus* (A. Vincenti, Venice, 1627†²) [I18]

S. Landi, *Il Secondo Libro d'Arie Musicali... ad Una Voce* (G.B. Robletti, Rome, 1627) [L532]

H. Lawes ed., *Choice Psalmes put into Musick, for Three Voices* (J. Young, London, 1648) [1648⁴]

——— *Ayres and Dialogues* (T. H[arper] / W. Godbid for J. Playford, London, 1653) [L1168}

W. Lawes, 'Gather Sweet Rosebuds' in *The Lady's Magazine* (s.n., [London], 1794) [L1172]

——— *Gather Sweet Rosebuds* (R. Bride, [London], n.d.) [L1173]

N. Legname ed., *Amilla Libro Secondo di Canzonette a Tre Voci* (A. Raverii, Venice, 1608) [1608¹⁷]

L. Leoni, *Sacri Fiori. Motetti... Libro Primo* (R. Amadino, Venice, 1606; 4/ P. Phalèse, Antwerp, 1619† as *Sacri Flores*) [L1997, L2000]

A. Marastoni, *Madrigali Concertati* Op. 6 (B. Magni, Venice, 1628†‡*) [M407]

L. Marenzio, *Il Primo Libro de Madrigali a Sei Voci* (A. Gardano, Venice, 1581; 4/1603‡) [M500, M503]

——— *Madrigali Spirituali... a Cinque Voci... Libro Primo* (A. Gardano, Rome, 1584; 4/ P. Phalèse, Antwerp, 1610†) [M525, M528]

L. Marenzio, *Il Secondo Libro de Madrigali a Sei Voci* (A. Gardano, Venice, 1584; 2/ G. Scotto, 1596, 3/ A. Gardano, 1600)‡ [M504-6]

—— *Madrigali a Quatro Voci... Libro Primo* (A. Gardano, Rome, 1585; 2/ R. Amadino, Venice, 1587†, 8/ P. Phalèse, Antwerp, 1607†) [M578-9, M585]

—— *Motecta Festorum Totius Anni... Liber Primus* (A. Gardano, Rome, 1585; 4/ P. Phalèse, Antwerp, 1603† as *Cantiones Sacrae*, 5/ A. Gardano, Venice, 1606‡ as *Mottectorum pro Festis Totius Anni*) [M494, M497-8]

—— *Il Quarto Libro de Madrigali a Sei Voci* (R. Amadino, Venice, 1587†; 5/ A. Gardano, 1605‡) [M511, M514]

—— *Il Quinto Libro de Madrigali a Sei Voci* (A. Gardano, Venice, 1591; 4/1610‡) [M515, M518]

—— *Madrigali a Cinque Voci, Ridotti in un Corpo* (P. Phalèse & G. Bellero, Antwerp, 1593†; 2/1609†) [M572-3]

—— *Il Sesto Libro de Madrigali a Cinque Voci* (A. Gardano, Venice, 1594; 4/ B. Magni, 1614‡) [M557, M559]

—— *Madrigali a Sei Voci, in un Corpo Ridotti* (P. Phalèse & G. Bellero, Antwerp, 1594; 3/1610†) [M522, M524]

—— *Il Settimo Libro de Madrigali a Cinque Voci* (A. Gardano, Venice, 1595; 3/1609‡) [M560, M562]

—— *Il Sesto Libro de Madrigali a Sei Voci* (A. Gardano, Venice, 1595; 2/1609‡, 3/ P. Phalèse, Antwerp, 1610†) [M519-21]

—— *Il Nono Libro de Madrigali a Cinque Voci* (A. Gardano, Venice, 1599; 4/1609‡) [M567, M570]

—— *Madrigalia a Quinque Vocum* [Bks 1-9] (P. Kauffmann, Nuremberg, 1601†) [M576]

—— *Il Sesto, Settimo, Ottavo et Nono Libro... de Madrigali a Cinque Voci* (P. Phalèse, Antwerp, 1609†^{2}) [M574]

—— *Il Primo, Secondo, Terzo, Quarto & Quinto Libro delle Villanelle, et Canzonette alla Napolitana, a Tre Voci* (P. Phalèse, Antwerp, 1610†) [M612]

B. Marini, *Per le Musiche di Camera. Concerti* Op. 7 (B. Magni, Venice, 1634†^{1} ‡) [M662]

—— *Madrigaletti... Libro Quinto* Op. 9 (B. Magni, Venice, 1635†^{1} ‡) [M664]

F.M. Marini, *Concerti Spirituali.... Libro Primo* (B. Magni, Venice, 1637†^{2} ‡*) [M672]

P.M. Marsolo, *Secondo Libro de'Madrigali a Quattro Voci* Op. 10 (G. Vincenti, Venice, 1614) [M756]

P. Matthysz ed., *XX. Konincklycke Fantasien, om op 3 Fiooolen de Gamba* (P. Matthysz, Amsterdam, 1648) [1648^7]

T. Merula, *Il Primo Libro de Madrigali Concertati* Op. 5 (A. Vincenti, Venice, 1624) [M2346]

—— *Il Primo Libro de Motetti* Op. 6 (A. Vincenti, Venice, 1624‡) [M2338]

—— *Libro Secondo de Concerti Spirituali* (A. Vincenti, Venice, 1628) [M2339]

—— *Madrigali et Altre Musiche Concertate... Libro Secondo* Op. 10 (B. Magni, Venice, 1633; 2/1635†‡* as *Musiche Concertate*) [M2348-9]

—— *Curtio Precipitato et Altri Capricii.... Libro Secondo* Op. 13 (B. Magni, Venice, 1638†^{1} ‡*) [M2351]

C. Merulo, *Libro Secondo di Canzoni d'Intavolatura d'Organo* (A. Gardano, Venice, 1606) [M2379]

N. Metru, *Fantaisies à Deux Parties* (R. Ballard, Paris, 1642†) [M2465]

R. Micheli, *Musica Vaga et Artificiosa* (G. Vincenti, Venice, 1615†) [M2683]

G.L. Missino, *Tirsi Doglioso. Primo Libro di Madrigali a Cinque Voci* (G. Vincenti, Venice, 1615†) [M2897]

S. Molinaro, *Concerti Ecclesiastici* (R. Amadino, Venice, 1605†) [M2937]

N. Monferrato, *Motetti Concertati... Libro Primo* Op. 3 (F. Magni, Venice, 1655; 3/ P. Phalèse, Antwerp, 1660†) [M3037, M3039]

F. de Monte, *Musica Sopra Il Pastor Fido... Libro Secondo a Sette Voci* (A. Gardano, Venice, 1600†²) [M3391]

G. Monte dell'Olmo, *Applausi Ecclesiastici.... Libro Primo* (B. Magni, Venice, 1636†² ‡*) [G2516]

—— *Sacri Affetti. Motetti a Voce Sola... Libro Secondo* (B. Magni, Venice, 1637†¹ ‡*) [G2518]

C. Monteverdi, *Madrigali a Cinque Voci... Libro Primo* (A. Gardano, Venice, 1587; 3/ B. Magni, 1621†‡) [M3453, M3455]

—— *Il Secondo Libro de Madrigali a Cinque Voci* (A. Gardano, Venice, 1590; 3/ B. Magni, 1621†‡) [M3456, M3458]

—— *Il Terzo Libro de Madrigali a Cinque Voci* (R. Amadino, Venice, 1592; 7/ P. Phalèse, Antwerp, 1615†, 8/ B. Magni, Venice, 1621†‡) [M3459, M3465-6]

—— *Il Quarto Libro de Madrigali a Cinque Voci* (R. Amadino, Venice, 1603; 5/ P. Phalèse, Antwerp, 1615†, 7/ B. Magni, Venice, 1622†‡) [M3467, M3471, M3473]

—— *Il Quinto Libro de Madrigali a Cinque Voci* (R. Amadino, Venice, 1605; 8/ P. Phalèse, Antwerp, 1615†, 9/ B. Magni, Venice, 1620†‡) [M3475, M3482-3]

—— *Scherzi Musicali a Tre Voci* (R. Amadino, Venice, 1607; 3/1615†, 5/ B. Magni, 1628‡) [M3485, M3487, M3489]

—— *L'Orfeo* (R. Amadino, Venice, 1609; 2/1615†) [M3449-50]

—— *Il Sesto Libro Madrigali a Cinque Voci* (R. Amadino, Venice, 1614; 3/ B. Magni, 1620†‡) [M3490, M3492]

—— *Concerto. Settimo Libro de Madrigali* (B. Magni, Venice, 1619; 4/1628†‡) [M3494, M3497]

—— *Madrigali e Canzonette.... Libro Nono* (A. Vincenti, Venice, 1651) [M3501]

G.C. Monteverdi, *Delli Affetti Musici, Libro Primo* (B. Magni, Venice, 1620†) [M3505]

T. Morley, *The Firste Booke of Balletts to Five Voyces* (T. East, London, 1595†) [M3697]

—— *The First Book of Consort Lessons* (W. Barley, London, 1599†) [Not in *RISM*]

P. Nenna, *Il Primo Libro de Madrigali a Cinque Voci* (A. Gardano, Venice, 1582; 2/ B. Magni, 1617†‡) [N382-3]

—— *Il Quinto Libro de'Madrigali a Cinque Voci* (G.B. Sottile, Naples, 1603; 2/ A. Gardano, Venice, 1612†) [N386-7]

—— *Il Settimo Libro de Madrigali a Cinque Voci* (G.B. Sottile, Naples, 1608; 5/ B. Magni, Venice, 1624†‡) [N392, N396]

—— *Il Quarto Libro de Madrigali a Cinque Voci* (A. Gardano, Venice, 1609; 3/ B. Magni, 1617†‡) [N384-5]

—— *Il Sesto Libro de madrigali a Cinque Voci* (G.B. Sottile. Naples, 1609; 4/ B. Magni, 1618†) [N388, N391]

—— *Il Primo Libro de Madrigali a Quattro Voci... con l'Aggiunta del Basso Continuo da Carlo Milanutio* (A. Vincenti, Venice, 1621)†² [N399]

A. Notari, *Prime Musiche Nuove* (W. Hole, London, [1613]) [N797]

C. Orlandi, *Arie, a Tre, Due et Voce Sola* Op. 2 (G. Vincenti, Venice, 1616†¹) [O107]
D. Pace ed., *Motetti.... Seconda Raccolta* (P. & G.B. Serafini, Loreto, 1646) [1646²]
G.P. Palestrina, *Motettorum Quinque Vocibus Liber Quintus* (A. Gardano, Rome, 1584; 5/ G. Scotto, Venice, 1601†) [P728, P732]
——— *Offertoria Totius Anni... Pars Prima* (F. Coattino, Rome, 1593 & A. Gardano, Venice, 1593) [P746-7]
B. Pallavicino, *Il Primo Libro de Madrigali a Cinque Voci* (A. Gardano, Venice, 1581; 2/ A. Raverii, 1606†)‡ [P773-4]
——— *Il Secondo Libro de Madrigali a Cinque Voci* (A. Gardano, Venice, 1584; 2/ A. Raverii, 1606†, 3/ A. Gardano, 1607)‡ [P776-8]
——— *Il Terzo Libro de Madrigali a Cinque Voci* (G. Vincenti & R. Amadino, Venice, 1585; 2/ A. Raverii, 1606†, 3/ A. Gardano, 1607)‡ [P779-81]
——— *Il Quarto Libro de Madrigali a Cinque Voci* (A. Gardano, Venice, 1588; 4/1607†)‡ [P785, P788]
——— *Il Quinto Libro de'Madrigali a Cinque Voci* (G. Vincenti, Venice, 1593; 4/ A. Gardano, 1609†)‡ [P789, P792]
——— *Il Sesto Libro de Madrigali a Cinque Voci* (A. Gardano, Venice, 1600; 2/1611†‡; 3/ P. Phalèse, Antwerp, 1612†) [P793-5]
——— *Il Settimo Libro de Madrigali a Cinque Voci* (R. Amadino, Venice, 1604; 3/1611†, 4/ P. Phalèse, Antwerp, 1613†) [P796, P798-9]
——— *Sacrae Dei Laudes* (R. Amadino, Venice, 1605†) [P771]
——— *L'Ottavo Libro de Madrigali a Cinque Voci* (R. Amadino, Venice, 1612†¹) [P801]
S. Patta, *Motetti et Madrigali* (B. Magni, Venice, 1614†) [P1039]
D. Pecci, *Sacri Modulatus* Op. 3 (B. Magni, Venice, 1629†¹‡) [P1100]
T. Pecci, *Madrigali a Cinque Voci* [Bk 1] (A. Gardano, Venice, 1602; 3/1609†) [P1105, P1107]
M. Pesenti, *Il Quarto Libro de Madrigali* Op. 9 (A. Vincenti, Venice, 1638) [P1549]
P. Phalèse ed., *Novi Frutti Musicali Madrigali* (P. Phalèse, Antwerp,1610†) [1610¹⁴]
——— *Florida Verba* (P. Phalèse, Antwerp, 1661†) [1661¹]
P. Philips ed., *Melodia Olympia* (P.Phalèse & J. Bellero, Antwerp, 1591†) [1591¹⁰]
P. Philips, *Il Primo Libro de Madrigali a Sei Voci* (P. Phalèse, Antwerp, 1596; 2/1604†) [P1991-2]
——— *Madrigali a Otto Voci* (P. Phalèse, Antwerp, 1598; 2/1599†) [P1994-5]
——— *Il Secondo Libro de Madrigali a Sei Voci* (P. Phalèse, Antwerp, 1603†) [P1997]
G.B. Piazza, *Libro Secondo. Canzonette a Voce Sola* (B. Magni, Venice, 1633†‡) [P2038]
F. Pio, *Liber Primus Motectorum* (A. Vincenti, Venice, 1622-4) [P2411]
A. de Pisticci, *Il Terzo Libro delli Motetti* Op. 6 (B. Magni, Venice, 1633†‡*) [P2454]
——— *Mottetti.... Libro Quarto* Op. 7 (B. Magni, Venice, 1637†¹ ‡*) [P2455]
H. Playford ed., *The Theater of Music.... The First Book* (J. Playford, London, 1685) [1685⁵]
——— *The Theater of Music.... The Second Book* (J. P[layford], London, 1685) [1685⁶]
——— *The Theater of Music.... The Third Book* (H. Playford & R. Carr, London, 1686) [1686³]
——— *The Theater of Music.... The Fourth and Last Book* (B. Motte, London, 1687) [1687⁵]
——— *Harmonia Sacra, or, Divine Hymns and Dialogues* (E. Jones, London, 1688†) [1688¹]

H. Playford ed., *The Banquet of Musick.... The First Book* (E. Jones, London, 1688) [1688[6]]
— *The Banquet of Musick.... The Second Book* (E. Jones, London, 1688) [1688[7]]
— *The Banquet of Musick.... The Fifth Book* (E. Jones, London, 1691) [1691[6]]
— *The Banquet of Musick.... The Sixth and Last Book* (E. Jones, London, 1692) [1692[8]]
— *The New Treasury of Musick* (H. Playford, London, 1695) [1695[17]]
— *Wit and Mirth: or, Pills to Purge Melancholy.... The Second Part* (H. Playford, London, 1700) [1700[4]]
J. Playford ed., [Pt 1] *A Musicall Banquet*
[Pt 2] *Musica Harmonia*
[Pt 3] *Musick and Mirth* (T.H., London, 1651) [1651[6]]
— *Musick's Recreation: on the Lyra Viol* (J. Playford, London, 1652) [1652[7]]
— *Select Musicall Ayres and Dialogues, in Three Bookes* (T. Harper, London, 1653) [1653[7]]
— *Court-Ayres* (J. Playford, London, 1655) [1655[5]]
— *Musick's Recreation: on the Viol, Lyra-way* (J. Playford, London, 1661) [1661[4]]
— *Cantica Sacra* (W. Godbid, London, 1662†) [1662[4]]
— *Courtly Masquing Ayres* (W. Godbid, London, 1662) [1662[8]]
— *Musick's Delight on the Cithren* (W. Godbid, London, 1666) [1666[4]]
— *Catch that Catch Can, or the Musical Companion* (W. Godbid, London, 1667) [1667[6]]
— *The Treasury of Musick* (W. Godbid, London, 1669) [1669[5]]
— *Musick's Recreation on the Viol, Lyra-way* (W. Godbid, London 1669) [1669[6]]
— *Cantica Sacra.... The Second Sett* (W. Godbid, London, 1674†) [1674[2]]
— *Choice Ayres, Songs, and Dialogues.... The Second Edition Corrected and Enlarged* (W. Godbid, London, 1675) [1675[7]]
— *Choice Ayres, Songs, and Dialogues.... Newly Re-printed with Large Additions* (W. Godbid, London, 1676) [1676[3]]
— *Choice Ayres and Songs.... The Second Book* (A. Godbid, London, 1679) [1679[7]]
— *Musick's Recreation on the Viol, Lyra-way* (W. Godbid & J. Playford, London, 1682) [1682[9]]
— *The Second Book of the Pleasant Musical Companion.... The Second Edition Corrected and Much Enlarged* (J. Playford, London, 1686) [1686[4]]
— *Harmonia Sacra.... The Second Book* (E. Jones, London, 1693†) [1693[1]]
J. Playford jnr ed., *Choice Ayres and Songs.... The Third Book* (A. Godbid & J. Playford jnr, London, 1681) [1681[4]]
— *Choice Ayres and Songs.... The Fourth Book* (A. Godbid & J. Playford jnr, London, 1683) [1683[5]]
— *Choice Ayres and Songs.... The Fifth Book* (J. Playford jnr, London, 1684) [1684[3]]
— *Catch that Catch Can: or the Second Part of the Musical Companion* (J. Playford jnr, London, 1685†) [1685[4]]
A. Poggioli ed., *Delectus Sacrarum Cantionum* (P. Phalèse, Antwerp, 1652†[1]) [Not in RISM]
O. Polidori, *Motetti a Voce Sola, et a Doi* Op. 13 (B. Magni, Venice, 1636†‡*) [P5024]

W. Porter, *Madrigales and Ayres* (W. Stansby, London, 1632) [P5218]
―――― *Mottets of Two Voyces for Treble or Tenor and Bass* (W. Godbid, London, 1657†) [P5219]
P. Possenti, *Canora Sampogna* (B. Magni, Venice, 1623; 2/1628‡) [P5247-8]
H. Purcell, *Sonnata's of III. Parts* (J. Playford & J. Carr, London, 1683†) [P6083]
―――― *The Songs in Amphitryon* (J. Heptinstall, London, 1690) [P5826]
―――― 'Ah me! Too Many Deaths Decreed' in *The Gentleman's Journal* (R. Parker, London, 1692) [P6001]
―――― *Fair Cloe my Breast so Alarms* (T. Cross, [London], n.d. [c.1695]) [P6028]
―――― *Orpheus Britannicus* (H. Playford, London, 1698) [P5979]
―――― *Orpheus Britannicus.... the Second Book* (W. Pearson, London, 1702) [P5983]
―――― *A Collection of the Most Celebrated Songs & Dialogues* (R. Meares, London, n.d. [c.1705]) [P5978]
―――― *Lost is my Quiet for Ever* (s.n., [London], n.d. [c.1700]) [P6050]
―――― *Lost is my Quiet for Ever* (s.n., [London], n.d. [c.1710]) [P6051]
―――― *Fair Iris and her Swain* ([T. Cross, London], n.d. [c.1710]) [P6031]
―――― *Mad Bess* (s.n., [London], n.d. [c.1720]) [P6011]
―――― *Mad Bess. A Favorite Song* (R. Birchall, London, n.d. [c.1720]) [P6012]
―――― *Bess of Bedlam* (J. Bland, [London], n.d. [c.1720]) [P6013]
―――― [*Bess of Bedlam*] (H. Andrews, [London], n.d. [c.1720]) [P6014]
―――― *Go Tell Amynta Gentle Swain* (s.n., [London], n.d. [c.1720]) [P6039]
―――― *Let Caesar and Urania Live* (s.n., [London], n.d. [c.1720]) [P6047]
L. Quintiani, *Il Primo Libro de Madrigali a Cinque Voci* (R. Amadino, Venice, 1588) [Q113]
E. Radesca di Foggia, *Canzonette, Madrigali, et Arie alla Romana... Libro Primo* (S. Tini & F. Lomazzo, Milan, 1605; 3/ G. Vincenti, Venice, 1616†) [R13, R15]
―――― *Il Secondo Libro delle Canzonette, Madrigali, et Arie alla Romana* (S. Tini, & F. Lomazzo, Milan, 1606; 2/ G. Vincenti, Venice, 1616†) [R16-17]
―――― *Il Quarto Libro delle Canzonette, Madrigali, et Arie alla Romana* (G. Vincenti, Venice, 1610; 2/1616†) [R18-19]
―――― *Madrigali a Cinque, et Otto Voci.... Libro Primo* (G. Vincenti, Venice, 1615†) [R20]
―――― *Il Terzo Libro delle Canzonette Madrigali, et Arie alla Romana* (G. Vincenti, Venice, 2/1616†) [R21]
―――― *Il Quinto Libro delle Canzonette, Madrigali et Arie* Op. 9 (G. Vincenti, Venice, 1617†) [R22]
F. Rasi, *Vaghezze di Musica per Una Voce Sola* (A. Gardano, Venice, 1608) [R290]
P. Reggio, *Songs* (s.n., [London], 1680) [R724]
P. Rimonte, *Parnaso Español de Madrigales* (P. Phalèse, Antwerp, 1614†) [R1713]
G. Rolla ed., *Teatro Musicale de Concerti Ecclesiastici* (G. Rolla, Milan, 1649; 2/1653 (enlarged)) [1649[1], 1653[1]]
R. Rontani, *Varie Musiche... Libro Quinto* Op. 9 (G.B. Robletti, Rome, 1620) [R2470]
―――― *Le Varie Musiche.... Libro Sesto* Op. 11 (G.B. Robletti, Rome, 1622) [R2471]
C. de Rore, *Il Primo Libro de Madrigali a Quatro Voci* (G. de Buglhat & A. Hucher, Ferrara, 1550; 2/ A. Gardano, Venice, 1551) [R2500-1]
C. de Rore & A. Padovano, *Madrigali a Quattro Voci... Libro Quinto* (Venice, 1561) [1561[15]]

G. Rovetta, *Madrigali Concertati.... Libro Primo* Op. 2 (B. Magni, Venice, 1629†‡; 2/1636; 4/ H. de Bruyn, Rotterdam, 1660†) [R2981-2, R2984]

―――― *Motetti Concertati* Op. 3 (A. Vincenti, Venice, 1635) [R2964]

―――― *Motetti Concertati* Op. 5 (A. Vincenti, Venice, 1639) [R2967]

―――― *Madrigali Concertati... Libro Secondo* (A. Vincenti, Venice, 1640) [R2985]

―――― *Salmi a Tre, et a Quattro Voci* Op. 7 (A. Vincenti, Venice, 1642) [R2971]

―――― *Bicinia Sacra* (P. Phalèse, Antwerp, 1648; 2/1668†) [R2975-6]

―――― *Gemma Musicalis* (M. Phalèse, Antwerp, 1649†) [R2977]

G. Sabbatini, *Sacrae Laudes Musicis Concentibus... Liber Primus* Op. 3 (A. Vincenti, Venice, 1626) [S3]

―――― *Sacrarum Laudum Musicis Conceptibus... Liber Secundus* Op. 7 (A. Vincenti, Venice, 1637) [S7]

―――― *Sacre Lodi Concerto a Voce Sola* Op. 9 (A. Vincenti, Venice, 1640) [S10]

G.F. Sances, *Cantade.... a Doi Voci... Libro Secondo, Parte Seconda* (B. Magni, Venice, 1633†‡) [S766]

―――― *Motetti* (B. Magni, Venice, 1638†‡*) [S768]

C. Saracini, *Le Quinte Musiche* (B. Magni, Venice, 1624†‡*) [S913]

―――― *Le Seste Musiche* (B. Magni, Venice, 1624†‡*) [S914]

M. Scacchi, *Madrigali a Cinque Voci*(B. Magni, Venice, 1634‡) [S1131]

G. Scarani, *Concerti Ecclesiastici.... Libro Primo* Op. 2 (B. Magni, Venice, 1630 [1641])‡ [S1168]

H. Schütz, *Symphoniae Sacrae* (B. Magni, Venice, 1629†‡) [S2287]

L. Simonetti ed., *Ghirlanda Sacra... Libro Primo* Op. 2 (B. Magni, Venice, 1625; 2/1630†(‡?), 3/1636‡) [1625^2, 2/ not in *RISM*, 1636^2]

―――― *Raccolta Terza* (B. Magni, Venice, 1630; 2/1635-6‡ as *Messa et Salmi*) [1630^1, 1636^1]

F. Smith & P. de Walpergen ed., *Musica Oxoniensis. A Collection of Songs* (L. Lichfield, Oxford (J. Walsh & J. Hore, London), 1698†) [1698^3]

A. Striggio, *Il Cicalamento del Donne al Buccato* (G. Scotto, Venice, 1567) [S6959]

G.A. Terzi, *Intavolatura di Liutto, Accomodata con Diversi Passaggi per Suonar in Concerti a Duoi Liutti, et Solo, Libro Primo* (R. Amadino, Venice, 1593) [T540]

―――― *Il Secondo Libro de Intavolatura di Liuto* (Venice, 1599) [T541]

B. Tomasi, *Motecta* Op. 6 (B. Magni, Venice, 1635†^{2} ‡*) [T922]

E. Trabattone, *Concerti... Libro Secondo* Op. 4 (B, Magni, Venice,1629†^{1} ‡) [T1070]

R. Trofeo & G.D. Rognoni Taeggio, *Canzonette Leggiadre a Tre Voci* (S. Tini & F. Besozzi, Milan, 1600†^{2}) [1600^{17}]

F. Turini, *Madrigali... Libro Primo* (B. Magni, Venice, 1621; 2/1624†‡) [T1388-9]

G. Turnhout, *Il Primo Libro de Madrigali a Sei Voci* (P. Phalèse & G. Bellero, Antwerp, 1589†) [T1435]

G. Valentini, *Secondo Libro de Madrigali* (G. Vincenti, Venice, 1616†) [V88]

L. Valvasensi, *Secondo Giardino d'Amorosi Fiori* Op. 8 (B. Magni, Venice, 1634†^{1} ‡) [V185]

O. Vecchi, *Madrigali a Cinque Voci.... Libro Primo* (A. Gardano, Venice, 1589) [V1043]

R. Vecoli, *Il Secondo Libro de Madrigali a Cinque Voci* (A. Le Roy & R. Ballard, Paris, 1586†^{2}) [V1086]

T.L. de Victoria, *Motecta* (A. Gardano, Venice, 1572; 5/1603†) [V1421, V1425]

F. Vitali, *Concerto... Madrigali... Libro Primo* (B. Magni, Venice, 1629†‡) [V2136]

J. Walsh & P. Randall ed., *The Jovial Companion* (J. Walsh & P. Randall, London, [1704])

J. Ward, *The First Set of English Madrigals* (T. Snodham, [London], 1613†) [W207]

J. Wilbye, *The Second Set of Madrigales to 3.4.5. and 6. Parts* (T. East, London, 1609) [W1066]

J. Wilson, *Cheerful Ayres or Ballads* (W. Hall, Oxford, 1660†) [W1237]

[M. Wise attrib. H. Purcell], *Old Chiron Thus Preach'd* (*s.n.*, [London], n.d. [*c.*1705]) [W1688 & P6057]

F. Wynant, *Madrigali a Cinque Voci... Libro Primo* (G. Vincenti, Venice, 1597†) [W2198]

N. Yonge ed., *Musica Transalpina* (T. East, London, 1588†) [1588[29]]

―――― *Musica Transalpina. The Second booke...* (T. East, London, 1597†) [1597[24]]

Non-Music Manuscripts

Cambridge, University Library MS Dd.III.73: William Johnson's Latin play *Valetudinarium* (ff. 23[r-v] contains the song 'Dulcis somne' copied by a different hand from that of the play-text).

Canterbury Cathedral, Bound Papers of Accounts 1576-1642 (with gaps).

―――― Fair Copy Accounts 26-47, 1617-42 (with gaps).

Dublin, Archbishop Marsh's Library MS Z2.2.3a: Narcissus Marsh's diary (20 December 1690 - 8 December 1696) (Z2.2.3b is a typescript transcription).

Hereford Cathedral Library MS R.11, xlii: Roger North's final version of 'The Musicall Grammarian' to which is appended his last musical essay, 'Memoires of Musick' (1728).

Lincolnshire County Record Office, Lincoln Cathedral Chapter Acts A.3.9, f. 254: concerning Stephen Bing's appointment as Senior Vicar Choral at Lincoln Cathedral (21 March 1667).

London, British Library Add. MSS 29,548-96: correspondence of the Hatton and Finch families; specifically:

―――― Add. MS 29,548, f. 14: permit for Lord Hatton to reside in London, signed by Oliver Cromwell (6 March 1658).

―――― Add. MS 29,549, f. 54: letter from Secretary Edward Nicholas writing from Oxford to Christopher Hatton III at Banbury (30 March 1645).

―――― Add. MS 29,550, ff. 91-3: two letters from George Jeffreys to Lady Hatton concerning, among other things, his negotiations with Colonel Barkstead over Hatton House which had been commandeered by the Parliamentarians (5 and 8 February 1649).

―――― Add. MS 29,550, f. 236[v]: letter from George Jeffreys to Lady Hatton in which he mentions his presence in Oxford during the Civil War (1665).

―――― Add. MS 29,550, f. 275: letter from George Jeffreys to Lady Hatton mentioning that Captain Cooke was teaching the Hatton children (11 December 1656).

―――― Add. MS 29,550, f. 344: Christopher Hatton III's instructions to 'honest George [Holmes]' over dealings with William Searle (29 January, 1659).

―――― Add. MS 29,551, ff. 35, 105-6 & 259: letters from George Jeffreys to Hon. Christopher Hatton IV (13 April 1663, 24 November 1664 & n.d.).

―――― Add. MS 29,552, ff. 7 & 302: letters from George Jeffreys to Hon. Christopher Hatton IV (10 January 1669 & 25 April 1670).

London, British Library Add. MS 29,552, f. 213: letter from Jeffreys to Christopher Hatton III at Thanet House which mentions in passing that his daughter has secretly married William Goode (7 February 1669).

——— Add. MS 29,552, f. 223: letter from Jeffreys to Christopher Hatton III in which he recommends his son-in-law, William Goode, for employment (1 February 1669).

——— Add. MS 29,553, ff. 226, 245 & 284: correspondence concerning the sale of the Hatton library (June-August 1671).

——— Add. MS 29,557, f. 309: letter from Jeffreys to Christopher Hatton IV in which the rector of Weldon, John Elkin, is described as 'one that has still the Presbyterian itch' (11 December 1679).

——— Add. MS 29,570, ff. 37-8: letter in the hand of George Jeffreys recopied from Hatton's draft: ff. 34-5 (14-15 August 1645).

——— Add. MS 29,571, f. 3: letter from Alice Hatton to her son, Christopher (III), who was then a student at Jesus College, Cambridge (n.d., early 1620s).

——— Add. MS 29,571, ff. 64-5 & 68: letters from Christopher Hatton IV to his wife Cecilia which mention the shipping of organ pipes to Kirby Hall (n.d., 1670s).

——— Add. MS 29,574, f. 317: letter from Charles Hatton to Christopher Hatton IV concerning the library at Kirby Hall (2 August 1694).

——— Add. MS 29,576, f. 134: letter from Charles Hatton to Christopher Hatton IV mentioning books in the library at Kirby Hall (12 October 1703).

——— Add. MS 29,577, ff. 48-9: letter from Charles Lyttelton to Hon. Christopher Hatton IV (10 December 1664).

——— Add. MS 29,586 f. 29^{r-v}: 'An Account of what goods received backe from my masters use from my cousin Thomas Holmes' in the hand of George Holmes (12 November 1661).

——— Add. MS 29,586 ff. 14 & 15: permits for Christopher, 1st Baron Hatton to reside in London, 1657 and 1658.

——— Add. MS 29,587, f. 47: 'The speech of Monsieur du Vain when he delivered the Seales to the King, translated out of French', hand of Stephen Bing (n.d.).

——— Add. MSS 32,507 and 32,509-10: draft material for Roger North's *The Life of... Francis North*.

——— Add. MS 32,514: Roger North's final manuscript version of 'The Life of Dr Jno. North'.

——— Add. MS 32,516: Roger North's draft for 'The Life of Dr Jno. North'.

——— Add. MS 32,533: Roger North's 'The Musicall Grammarian' (draft version *c*.1726).

——— Add. MS 32,536: Roger North's 'An Essay of Musical Ayre' (*c*.1715-20).

——— Add. MS 41,161: memoirs of Lady Ann Fanshawe (May 1676).

——— Add. MS 46,378 B, f. 3: autograph letter of Angelo Notari (25 May 1642).

——— Add. MS 64,883, f. 57: petition from John Woodington to Charles I (12 May 1625)

——— Egerton MS 1048, f. 186: list of Queen Henrietta Maria's musicians (*c*.1640).

——— Egerton MSS 2533-62: correspondence of Secretary Edward Nicholas including letters from Christopher Hatton III under pseudonyms (August 1648 - October 1656); specifically:

——— Egerton MS 2533, ff. 481-2: letter from Christopher Hatton III to Secretary Edward Nicholas in the hand of Stephen Bing (16/26 March 1648/9).

——— Evelyn Family Papers, John Evelyn's 'Kalendarium' [1620-1697].

London, British Library Harley MS 1911: minutes of the Corporation of Musicians (21 October 1661 - 21 September 1676).
——— Harley MS 3785, ff. 19, 20, 24, 27, 29 & 47: letters from Stephen Bing to William Sancroft, Dean of St Paul's Cathedral (1665).
——— Harley MS 5409: Anthony Wood's diary *c*.1632-60.
——— Harley MS 7019: report on the Cambridge Colleges by a Parliamentary Committee.
——— Printed Book 664.b.45: book once owned by Thomas Alston which includes a hand-written cast list for the 1632-Cambridge performance of Hausted's *The Rivall Friends*.
——— Sloane MS 1707, f. 2: Angelo Notari's astrological chart.
London, Guildhall Library MS 980/1: box of parchment rolls, from various London parishes, recording the payment of taxes.
——— St Paul's Archives MS 25,200/6: letter from Christopher Hatton III to Dean Barwick of St Paul's Cathedral concerning the placement of singing man Henry Frost (21 October 1661).
——— St Paul's Archives MS 25,473/34. p. 70: account of payments made at St Paul's Cathedral between 1 July 1699 and 31 September 1699 (including payment to John Gostling for 'pricking Anthems').
——— St Paul's Archives MS 25,632: Prebendal Surveys relating to lands and revenues of St Paul's Cathedral (1649).
——— St Paul's Archives MS 25,633/1: St Paul's Cathedral Prebendal Estates Book (1649-56).
——— St Paul's Archives MS 25,643/1: St Paul's Cathedral Accounts of the Chamberlain and Receiver General (1666-79).
——— St Paul's Archives MS 25,650/2: AcquittanceBooks containing receipts for salaries at St Paul's Cathedral (1670-1687).
——— St Paul's Archives MS 25,661/1: St Paul's Cathedral Seal Book; record of documents to which the seal of the Dean and Chapter was attached: leases, powers of attorney, presentations, etc. (1660-98).
——— St Paul's Archives MS 25,664/1: St Paul's Cathedral Muniments Book (1660-1695).
——— St Paul's Archives MS 25,707/1: St Paul's Cathedral Steward's Cash Accounts (1670-85).
——— St Paul's Archives MS 25,738/1: St Paul's Cathedral Muniments, Minute Book (1660-4).
——— St Paul's Archives MS 25,738/2: St Paul's Cathedral Muniments, Minute Book (1664-85).
——— St Paul's Archives MS 25,746: account book of the Warden of the College of Minor Canons of St Paul's Cathedral (1631-1792).
London, Public Record Office Declared Accounts of the Treasurer of the Chamber from the Audit Office (AO1) 394/72: annual accounts Michaelmas 1634 to Michaelmas 1635.
——— Exchequer Acquittance Book (E) 101/438/11: list of Queen Henrietta Maria's musicians (1630-1).
——— Exchequer Acquittance Book (E) 101/439/3: list of Queen Henrietta Maria's musicians (1634-5).

London, Public Record Office Exchequer Assignments, Probates, etc., (E) 406/50, f. 158: letter from Andrew Hatley and William Browne (executors of the will of John Jenkins, deceased) appointing Frances Lilly of Baldwins Gardens, Middlesex (widow and executor of the will of John Lilly, deceased) and Johanna Wheeler of Stepney, to be their attorney to receive all sums of money due to Jenkins from the Exchequer or Treasury Chamber (23 March 1680).

────── Exchequer Enrolments and Registers of Issues (E) 403/1801, p. 175: exchequer payment of £20 to Francis Lilly, widow and executor of John Lilly (25 September 1683).

────── Lord Chamberlain's Papers (LC) 3/2: Establishment Book.

────── Lord Chamberlain's Papers (LC) 3/33: appointments, assignments, etc.

────── Lord Chamberlain's Papers (LC) 3/39: arrears of liveries.

────── Lord Chamberlain's Papers (LC) 5/134: warrants.

────── Lord Chamberlain's Papers (LC) 5/137-45: warrants.

────── Lord Chamberlain's Papers (LC) 5/189: petitions, etc.

────── Lord Chamberlain's Papers (LC) 9/199: Debenture Book.

────── Lord Chamberlain's Papers (LC) 9/255: accounts of the Great Wardrobe.

────── Lord Chamberlain's Papers (LC) 9/341: appointments, assignments, etc.

────── Lord Chamberlain's Papers (LC) 9/389/ii: 'Liveries in Arrears & Onpayd from June 1660 to Mich[aelm]as 1667'.

────── Prerogative Court of Canterbury (PROB) 11/368/179 (*olim* 179 North), ff. 300^v-301: Stephen Bing's will.

────── State Papers, Domestic (SP) 16/215, f. 14: an anonymous letter concerning the suicide of Henry Butts, the Vice-Chancellor of Cambridge University, on 1 April 1632.

────── State Papers, Domestic (SP) 23/200 pp. 115 (14 December 1648), 117 (9 February 1648), 119 (15 December 1648), 121 (30 November 1647), 126 (26 June 1646), 137 (8 May 1646), 140 (20 March 1646), 141 (5 December 1646): representations to the Committee for Compounding made by George Jeffreys on behalf of Christopher Hatton III (pp. 126 and 141 are signed by Hatton).

────── State Papers, Domestic (SP) 23/200 p. 135: deposition signed by Christopher Hatton relating to sequestration assessments 1647-9.

────── State Papers, Domestic (SP) 23/200 p. 143: printed pass (dated 25 June 1646) issued by the Parliamentarian forces to enable Christopher Hatton III to move around freely after the fall of Oxford.

────── State Papers, Domestic (SP) 23/233, f. 87^v: representation to the Committee for Compounding made by George Jeffreys on behalf of Christopher Hatton III (4 May 1649).

────── State Papers, Domestic (SP) 28/212: report by Ralph Farmer, the Solicitor for Sequestrations (April 1643 - 1 March 1644).

────── State Papers, Domestic (SP) 28/355/1: record of rent and revenues of St Paul's Cathedral received by Parliamentarian sequestrators (2 April 1644 - 10 April 1646) and of payments authorised to Cathedral officials.

────── State Papers, Domestic (SP) 29/2, No. 58: petition of John Wilson, 'do[cto]r in musicke', to Charles II (undated [1660]).

────── State Papers, Domestic (SP) 29/33, No. 85: petition of Simon Hopper, 'violin for yo[u]r Ma[jes]ties Practice of dancinge', to Charles II (undated [1660]).

London, Public Record Office State Papers, Domestic (SP) 29/45, No. 54: petition of Thomas Lanier, 'one of yo[u]r Ma[jes]ties Serv[an]ts of the Private Musique in Ordinary', to Charles II ([November?] 1661).
—— State Papers, Domestic (SP) 99/10, p. 62: letter from Sir Dudley Carleton (the King's envoy in Venice) to Sir John Harryngton which mentions that a 'Mr Dearing' was in Rome (26 June 1612).
—— State Papers, Domestic (SP) 142/376/100: *Inquisition post mortem* of Sir Christopher Hatton II (28 June 1619).
London, Royal College of Music MS 2125: catalogue of Dean Aldrich's and Richard Goodson's music collections at Christ Church, Oxford compiled by Johann [John] Baptist Malchair (31 July 1787).
London, Westminster Abbey Muniments 33,706, 33,710, 33,714 & 33,717: Westminster Abbey Account Books (years ending Michaelmas 1673, 1676, 1679 & 1682).
—— Muniments 61,228A: the Precentor's Book.
Longleat, Whitelocke Papers, Parcel II, No. 9: material relating to the performance of James Shirley's masque *The Triumph of Peace* (performed at the Banquetting House, Whitehall on 3 February 1634).
Northamptonshire Record Office Finch-Hatton MS 170: 'Chartae Antiquae ex Originalibus accuratissime transcriptae Annis 1640-1641', Christopher Hatton III's 'Book of Seals', a collection of transcripts of early deeds with sketches of seals.
—— Finch-Hatton MS 617: an appraisal of the contents of Kirby Hall (1619-22).
—— Finch-Hatton MS 618: an appraisal of the contents of the Hattons' Westminster house (1619-22).
—— Finch-Hatton MS 642: 'A catalogue of the Lady Hattons bookes', including a section headed 'Bookes --- [illegible] Chris: Hatton had w[i]th him in Cambridge' (n.d.).
—— Finch-Hatton MS 802: plan of Kirby Hall (n.d.).
—— Finch-Hatton MS 814: rents, etc. due to Sir Christopher Hatton (I or II) (n.d.)
—— Finch-Hatton MS 841: agreement between Lord Hatton, John Clements, John Farewell and Richard Langhorne (4 February 1664).
—— Finch-Hatton MS 1407: letter from George Jeffreys to Lady Hatton (4 October 1678).
—— Finch-Hatton MS 2010: 'Articles of Agreement: beetween the Ld Hatton & Margarett Countess Dowager of Thanett' (4 July 1666).
—— Finch-Hatton MS 2044: document concerning the case between John Clements and Lord Hatton, mortgages, etc. (n.d. [1671-2]).
—— Finch-Hatton MS 2048: copy of a paper, concerning mortgages and debts, sent to John Clements by Lord Hatton (n.d., [1670s]).
—— Finch-Hatton MS 2133: list of musical instruments, organ stops, musical terms, etc., in the hand of Christopher Hatton III.
—— Finch-Hatton MS 2409: fragment of Italian verse 'Mane vado, a la guerra o soigniora' [*sic*] in the hand of George Jeffreys.
—— Finch-Hatton MS 2416: George Holmes' account of £5 travelling expenses (1 July 1647).
—— Finch-Hatton MS 2444: inventory of books, woman's clothing, house linen (including linen marked A[lice] H[atton]), upholstery, pictures of Mr and Mrs Fanshawe and Sir James Poynes, etc. (n.d.).
—— Finch-Hatton MS 2445: 'Lady Alice Hatton's inventory. March 1639'.

Northamptonshire Record Office Finch-Hatton MS 2631: letter from George Holmes to Mr Clements at his lodgings in 'Charingcrosse' (c.1660).

—— Finch-Hatton MS 2635: 'A note of clothes, etc.' in the hand of George Holmes (n.d.).

—— Finch-Hatton MS 2652: bill for printed music 'To the Right w[orshi]pfull Sir Christopher Hatton Novemb[er] 1638' from the London bookseller Robert Martin, and a quittance signed by Martin (9 November 1641).

—— Finch-Hatton MS 2657A: 'Mr Ho[l]mes his bill' (1661).

—— Finch-Hatton MSS 2659 and 2661: bills for books and bindings supplied by the London stationer William Searle, endorsed by Stephen Bing(?) (1657-60).

—— Finch-Hatton MS 3101: marriage settlement, Lord Hatton and Hon. Frances Yelverton (18 November 1675).

—— Finch-Hatton MS 3545: indenture between Sir Christopher Hatton II, Sir Edward Coke and Francis Needham, declaring Corfe Castle and Hatton House for the use of Sir Edward Coke and his wife Elizabeth, and concerning the dispersal of other Dorset estates (24 November 1608).

—— Finch-Hatton MS 3713 A & B: notes on the settlement of the affairs of Sir Christopher Hatton I after his death (n.d., [c.1598]).

—— Finch-Hatton MS 3845: letter to Christopher Hatton IV from his lawyer, Richard Langhorne, advising a second marriage 'with a fortune of 8,000*l*. or thereabouts' (13 October 1673).

—— Finch-Hatton MS 3921: letter from George Jeffreys to Lady Hatton (10 March 1655).

—— Finch-Hatton MSS 3981-4, 3987, 3989, 4000, 4002 & 4011: documents relating to Hatton's fines and sequestrations (1645-8).

—— Finch-Hatton MS 4016: 'A Cattalogue of some Manuscripts of my Masters taken at Moulton Parke Aprill 15th 1633' in the hand of George Jeffreys.

—— Finch-Hatton MS 4017: catalogue of manuscripts and printed books, grouped according to format, in William Dugdale's hand (n.d.).

—— Finch-Hatton MSS 4019-23: short lists of books in the Hatton collection.

—— Finch-Hatton MS 4025: catalogue of manuscripts and printed books in the Hatton collection in the hand of Stephen Bing (n.d.).

—— Finch-Hatton MS 4106: catalogue of Christopher Hatton III's debts (1642).

—— Finch-Hatton MS 4180: fragment of a letter from George Jeffreys (to Lady Hatton?) concerning a purchase from Lord Cardigan (n.d.)

—— Finch-Hatton MS 4287: 'Books lent to Dr Stillingfleet, Deane of St Paules out of ye MSS belonging to ye L[or]d Hatton' (23 December 1683) and notes as to which had been returned (5 August 1705).

—— Finch-Hatton MS 4841: requisition ordering books to be taken from Kirby Hall to the Parliamentarian garrison at Rockingham Castle 'for the publick [use]' (27 January 1644 NS).

Oxford, Bodleian Library Ashmole MS 38: a poetic miscellany compiled by Nicholas Burghe (1630s?).

—— Autograph MS C 19: receipts of payments (f. 147: Angelo Notari (1619); ff. 148-9: Thomas Lupo (1619 & 1647); ff. 150-1: Henry Cooke for boys of the Chapel Royal (15 June 1665 & 26 May 1665)).

—— Bankes Papers, Bundle 38/29: includes licences for Lady Elizabeth Hatton to reside in London.

Oxford, Bodleian Library Bodley MS 878: papers relating to the formation of the library of Christopher Hatton III, including lists of books offered to or purchased by him in England and France, letters to him from e.g. Peter Gunning, bills, etc. (c.1646-9).

—— Carte MS 74, f. 301: petition from Christopher Hatton III to King Charles II to become 'Tresorer of your Royall Household' (n.d.).

—— Donation MS b 9: the 'Wybard Manuscript' of prose by Donne and verse and prose by Carew etc. (1630s).

—— Hatton MSS 113-16 (*olim* Junian MSS 22-4 & 99): four volumes of Anglo-Saxon Homilies donated to the Bodleian Library by Christopher Hatton IV in 1675.

—— Lister MS 36, ff. 129-30^v: letter from Henry Aldrich, Dean of Christ Church, Oxford, to Dr Martin Lister, Old Palace Yard, Westminster (12 September 1695).

—— Mus. MS e 17: notes for a projected history of music made by Thomas Ford, chaplain of Christ Church, Oxford (1708-11).

—— MS Mus. Sch. C 203*[R]: 'The Catalogue of Musicke-Bookes giuen by Dr. Heather', parchment roll (n.d., c.1627).

—— MS Mus. Sch. C 204*[R]: 'A Catologue (sic) of All the Books wch belong now to ye Musick School 1682', parchment roll.

—— MS Rawlinson B 121: list of fees paid to musicians for performing at ceremonies associated with the conferring of dignities at the Oxford Court (1644-5).

—— Rawlinson MS Poet 62, f. 14^{r-v}: poem 'Welcome on shore' by Martin Lluellyn, 'To my L[or]d Hatton at Calais' [1646].

—— Tanner MS 102, ff. 1-69: Anthony Wood's 'Life' 1632-72.

—— Tanner MS 130, ff. 17 & 19: letters from Michael Honywood, Dean of Lincoln, to William Sancroft, Dean of St Paul's Cathedral (1666).

—— Tanner MS 130, f. 106: letter from William Sancroft, Dean of St Paul's Cathedral, to Stephen Bing (20 September 1665).

—— Tanner MS 466, ff. 1-39: manuscript copied by Willian Sancroft, includes carols by William Cartwright (f. 32^v) and Martin Lluelyn (ff. 32 & 33).

—— Wood MS D.19 (4): Anthony Wood's 'Notes on the Lives of Musicians' (c.1688 with later additions)

Oxford, Christ Church Disbursement Books 1641-4, 1658-92.

—— Library Records 2: John Hinton's 'CATALOGUS Librorum omnium in Bibliotheca Ædis Christi' (1665).

—— Library Records 12: three catalogues of the music collection at Christ Church: Burney (November 1778); Boyce (before 1778); and anonymous (?late-18th century).

—— Library Records 15: the earliest extant catalogue of the music collection at Christ Church (1717) with 'A Catalogue of Mr Goodson's Books... 1747' added at the end (reversed).

—— Library Records 31: an alphabetical catalogue of the printed music in the Christ Church collection compiled by Henry Havergal (1846).

Oxford, Merton College Register (1567-1731).

Works Printed Before 1800

H. Aldrich, *Elementa Architecturae Civilis* (Oxford, 1789)

Anonymous, *Maria Triumphans* (St Omer, 1635)

Anthems to be Sung at the Celebration of Divine Service, in the Cathedral Church of the Holy and Undivided Trinity in Dublin (Dublin, Trinity College R.f.53; 1662)

J. Batchiler, *The Virgin's Pattern: in the Exemplary Life, and Lamented Death of Mrs Susanna Perwich* (London, 1661)

[J. Brooksbank], *The Well-Tuned Organ* (London, 1660)

C. Burney, *A General History of Music* (London, 1776-89), 4 vols

[T. Carew], *Select Psalmes of a New Translation* ([London], 1655)

W. Cartwright, *Comedies, Tragi-Comedies, with other Poems* (London, 1651)

Clarendon, Edward Hyde 1st Earl of, *The History of The Rebellion and Civil Wars in England Begun in the Year 1641* (Oxford, 1702-4), 3 vols

J. Clifford, *Divine Services and Anthems* (London, 1663; rev. 2/1664)

A. Cowley, *Poems: Viz. I. Miscellanies.II. The Mistress, or, Love Verses.III. Pindarique Odes. And IV. Davideis.Or a Sacred Poem of the Troubles of David* (London, 1656)

E. Dering, *A Declaration... with his Petition to the House of Commons* (London, 1644)

—— *A Discourse of Proper Sacrifice* (Cambridge, 1644)

W. Dugdale, *The Antiquities of Warwickshire Illustrated* (London, 1656)

—— *The History of S$^{t.}$ Pauls Cathedral in London* (London, 1658)

[W. Dugdale], *The Life of that Learned Antiquary, Sir William Dugdale, Kt. .... Published from an Original Manuscript* (London, 1713)

T. D'Urfey, *New Poems, Consisting of Satyrs, Elegies, and Odes: Together with a Choice Collection of the Newest Court Songs* (London, 1690)

T. Flatman, *Poems and Songs* (London, 1674)

T. Fuller, *The History of the Worthies of England* (London, 1662)

[J. Gauden], *Eikon Basilike, The Pourtraicture of his Sacred Majestie in his Solitudes and Sufferings* [London, 1649]

J. Hall, *Holy Obseruations Lib. 1. and Some Few of David's Psalms Metaphrased for a Taste of the Rest* (London, 1607)

C. Hatton [J. Taylor], *The Psalter of David with Titles and Collects According to the Matter of Each Psalme* (Oxford, 1644)

R. Hatton, *Ovid's Walnut-Tree Transplanted* (London, 1627)

P. Hausted, *The Rivall Friends, a Comedie* (London, 1632)

—— *Ten Sermons, Preached upon Severall Sundayes and Saints Dayes* (London, 1636)

—— *Ad Populum, or A Lecture to the People* (Oxford, 1644)

J. Hawkins, *A General History of the Science and Practice of Music* (London, 1776; repr. 1875)

G. Herbert, *The Temple. Sacred Poems and Private Ejaculations* (Cambridge, 1633)

[R. Herrick], *His Noble Numbers or his Pious Pieces* (London, 1647)

R. Herrick, *Hesperides: or, The Works both Humane & Divine* (London, 1648)

N. Hookes, *Amanda, a Sacrifice to an Unknown Goddesse* (London, 1653)

H. L'Estrange, *The Alliance of Divine Offices* (London, 1659)

M. Lluelyn, *Men-Miracles.With other Poems* ([Oxford], 1646)

T. Mace, *Musick's Monument* (London, 1676)

R. Martin, 'Libri Musici', *Catalogus Librorum ex Italia* ([London], 1633)

—— 'Libri Musici', *Catalogus Librorum ex Roma, Venetiis aliisque Italiae* ([London], 1635)

—— 'Libri Musici Varii', *Catalogus Librorum ex Praecipus Italiae Emporoiis* ([London], 1639)

—— 'Libri Musici', *Catalogus Librorum e Diversis Europae Regionibus* ([London], 1640)

R. Martin, 'Libri Musici', *Catalogus Librorum ex Praecipuis Italiae Emporiis* ([London], 1650)
J. Misheu, *Ductor in Linguas, the Guide into Tongues* (London, 1617)
T. Morley, *A Plaine and Easie Introduction to Practicall Musicke* (London, 1597)
J. Norris, *Collection of Miscellanies* (London, 1687)
R. North, *The Life of the Right Honourable Francis North, Baron of Guilford* (London, 1742)
J. Playford, *A Catalogue of All the Musick-Bookes that have Been Printed in England, Either for Voyce or Instruments* (London, [1653])
—— *A Breefe Introduction to the Skill of Musick* (London, 1654; 10/1683 & 12/1694 as *An Introduction to the Skill of Musick*)
T. Randolph, *The Jealous Lovers. A Comedie Presented to their Gracious Majesties at Cambridge* (Cambridge, 1632)
—— *Poems, with The Muses' Looking-Glass and Amyntas* (Oxford, 1638)
G. Sandys, *Paraphrase upon the Psalmes of David* (London, 1636)
—— *A Paraphrase upon the Divine Poems* (London, 1638)
[R. Scrope & T. Monkhouse ed.], *State Papers Collected by Edward, Earl of Clarendon, Commencing from the Year MDCXXI, Containing the Materials from which his History of the Great Rebellion was Composed* (Oxford, 1767-86), 3 vols
C. Simpson, *The Division-Violist* (London, 1659)
W. Sympson, *De Accentibus Hebraicis* (London, 1617)
J. Taylor, *Of the Sacred Order and Offices of Episcopacy* (Oxford, 1642)
—— *A Discourse of The Liberty of Prophesying* (London, 1647)
[J. Taylor], *A New and Easie Institution of Grammar* (London, 1647)
J. Taylor, *The Great Exemplar of Sanctity and Holy Life* ([London], 1649)
—— *The Golden Grove, or, A Manuall of Daily Prayers and Letanies* (London, 1655)
E. Walker, *Historical Discourses, Upon Several Occasions* [1664] (London, 1705) reissued as *Historical Collections... Relating to the... Rebellion and Civil War of England* (London, 1707)
A. Wood, *Athenae Oxoniensis: An Exact History of All the Writers and Bishops who have had their Eductaion in the University of Oxford. To which are added the Fasti, or Annals, of the said University* (London, 1691), 2 vols (3rd edn, with additions by P. Bliss (London, 1813-21), repr. New York & London, 1967)

Works Printed After 1800

H. Abbey, 'Sir Peter Leycester's Book on Music', *Journal of the Viola da Gamba Society of America*, xx (1984), 28-44
J. Adair, *By the Sword Divided: Eyewitnesses of the English Civil War* (London, 1983)
P. Allsop, 'Problems of Ascription in the Roman *Simfonia* of the late Seventeenth Century: Colista and Lonati', *MR*, l (1989), 34-44
—— *The Italian 'Trio' Sonata: From its Origins Until Corelli* (Oxford, 1992)
J.R. Anthony, *French Baroque Music from Beaujoyeulx to Rameau* (London, rev. 2/1978)
J. Aplin, 'Sir Henry Fanshawe and Two Sets of Early Seventeenth-Century Part-Books at Christ Church Oxford', *ML*, lvii (1976), 11-24
G.E.P. Arkwright, 'An English Pupil of Monteverdi', *The Musical Antiquary*, iv (1913), 236

G.E.P. Arkwright, *Catalogue of Music in the Library of Christ Church, Oxford* (London, 1915-23), 2 vols
A. Ashbee, 'The Four-Part Consort Music of John Jenkins', *PRMA*, xcvi (1969-70), 29-42
—— 'A Further Look at Some of the Le Strange Manuscripts', *Chelys*, v (1973-4), 24-41
—— 'Towards the Chronology and Grouping of Some Airs by John Jenkins', *ML*, lv (1974), 30-44
—— 'Instrumental Music from the Library of John Browne (1608-91), Clerk of the Parliaments', *ML*, lviii (1977), 43-59
—— 'John Jenkins, 1592-1678: the Viol Consort Music in Four, Five and Six Parts', *EM*, vi (1978), 492-500
—— *Records of English Court Music*, vol. i (Snodland, 1986)
    vol. iii (Snodland, 1988)
    vol. iv (Snodland, 1991a)
    vol. v (Aldershot, 1991b)
    vol. viii (Aldershot, 1995)
—— *The Harmonious Musick of John Jenkins. Volume One: The Fantasias for Viols* (Surbiton, 1992)
A. Ashbee, R. Thompson & J.P. Wainwright eds, *Index of Manuscripts Containing Music for Viols*, VdGS (forthcoming)
P. Aston, 'George Jeffreys', *MT*, cx (1969), 772-6
—— 'George Jeffreys and the English Baroque' (D.Phil. dissertation, University of York, 1970)
—— 'Tradition and Experiment in the Devotional Music of George Jeffreys', *PRMA*, xcix (1972-3), 105-15
—— 'Jeffreys, George', *New Grove*, ix, 583-6
G.E. Aylmer, *The King's Servants* (London & Boston, 1961; rev. 1974)
G. Baker, *The History and Antiquities of the County of Northampton* (Northampton, 1822-41), 2 vols
E.S. de Beer ed., *The Diary of John Evelyn* (London, 1955), 6 vols
W.G. Bell, *The Great Plague in London in 1665* (London, 1924; rev. 2/1951)
J. Bennett & P. Willetts, 'Richard Mico', *Chelys*, vii (1977), 24-46
K. Bergdolt, 'The Sacred Music of George Jeffreys' (Ph.D. dissertation, University of Cincinnati, 1976)
J. Bergsagel, 'Danish Musicians in England 1611-14: Newly-Discovered Instrumental Music', *Dansk Aarbog for Musikforskning*, vii (1973-6), 9-20
J.A. Bernstein, 'Lassus in English Sources: Two Chansons Recovered', *JAMS*, xxvii (1974), 315-25
—— 'Philip Van Wilder and the Chanson in Tudor England', *MD*, xxxiii (1979), 55-75
—— 'An Index of Polyphonic Chansons in English Manuscript Sources, c.1530-1640', *RCRMA*, xxi (1988), 21-36
L. Bianconi, 'Gesualdo, Carlo', *New Grove*, vii, 313-24
—— *Music in the Seventeenth Century*, trans. D. Bryant (Cambridge, 1987)
T. Birch ed., *The Court and Times of Charles I* (London, 1848), 2 vols

P. Bliss ed., [Anthony Wood] *Athenae Oxoniensis: An Exact History of all the Writers and Bishops who have had their Eductaion in the University of Oxford* (London, 1813-21), 4 vols

—— [Anthony Wood] *Fasti Oxoniensis* (London, 1815)

J.R. Bloxam, 'Chaplains, Clerks and Organists', *The Magdalen College Register*, (Oxford, 1857), ii

S. Boorman, 'Notari, Porter and the Lute', *Lute Society Journal*, xiii (1971), 28-32

S. Boyer & J. Wainwright, 'From Barnard to Purcell: the Copying Activities of Stephen Bing', *EM*, xxiii (1995), 620-48

P. Brett, 'East [Easte, Est, Este], Michael', *New Grove*, v, 801-2

C.M. Briquet, *Les Filigranes*, ed. A.H. Stevenson (Amsterdam, 1968), 4 vols

J. Bunker Clark, 'Adrian Batten and John Barnard: Colleagues and Collaborators', *MD*, xxii (1968), 207-29

M. Burden ed., *The Purcell Companion* (London, 1995)

J. Caldwell, 'Phillips, Arthur', *New Grove*, xiv, 659

C. Carlton, *Charles I: The Personal Monarch* (London, 1983)

H. Carter, 'Peter de Walpergen, Punchcutter and Typefounder, 1646(?)-1703', *Guttenberg Jahrbuch* (1965), 48-52

M. Chan, 'John Hilton's Manuscript British Library Add. MS 11608', *ML* lx (1979), 440-9

—— 'The Witch of Endor and Seventeenth-Century Propaganda', *MD*, xxxiv (1980), 205-14

—— 'A Mid-Seventeenth-Century Music Meeting and Playford's Publishing', *The Well Enchanting Skill: Music, Poetry, and Drama in the Culture of the Renaissance: Essays in Honour of F.W. Sternfeld*, ed. J. Caldwell, E. Olleson & S. Wollenberg (Oxford, 1990), 231-44

R. Charteris, 'Autographs of John Coprario', *ML*, lvi (1975), 41-6

—— 'Consort Music Manuscripts in Archbishop Marsh's Library, Dublin', *RCRMA*, xiii (1976), 27-63

—— 'John Coprario's Five- and Six-Part Pieces: Instrumental or Vocal?', *ML*, lvii (1976), 370-8

—— *John Coprario: A Thematic Catalogue of his Music with a Biographical Introduction* (New York, 1977)

—— 'Four Caroline Part-Books', *ML*, lix (1978), 49-51

—— *A Catalogue of the Printed Books on Music and Music Manuscripts in Archbishop Marsh's Library, Dublin* (Clifden, 1982a)

—— 'A Postscript to *John Coprario: A Thematic Catalogue of his Music with a Biographical Introduction* (New York, 1977)', *Chelys*, xi (1982b), 13-19

—— 'The Huntington Library Part-Books, Ellesmere MSS EL 25A 46-51', *The Huntington Library Quarterly*, l (1987), 59-84

—— '*Fuerunt mihi lacrymae*: Alfonso Ferrabosco the Elder or the Younger?', *Altro Polo: Essays on Italian Music in the Cinquecento*, ed. R. Charteris, Frederick May Foundation for Italian Studies (Sydney, 1990), 113-30

J.L. Chester ed., *The Marriage, Baptismal, and Burial Registers of the Collegiate Church or Abbey of St Peter, Westminster*, Publications of the Harleian Society, x (London, 1876)

G.H. Chettle, rev. P. Leach, *Kirby Hall, Northamptonshire*, English Heritage (London, 1986)

I. Cheverton, 'Captain Henry Cooke (c.1616-72): The Beginnings of a Reappraisal', *Soundings*, ix (1982), 74-86

A. Clark ed., *The Life and Times of Anthony Wood* (Oxford, 1891-1900), 5 vols

J.V. Cockshoot, 'Alfonso Ferrabosco (ii)', *New Grove*, vi, 482-4

E. Cole, 'In Search of Francis Tregian', *ML*, xxxiii (1952), 28-32

―――― 'Seven Problems of the Fitzwilliam Virginal Book', *PRMA*, lxxix (1952-3), 51-64

J.M. Cowper ed., *The Register Booke of the Parish of St. George the Martyr within the Citie of Canterburie* (Canterbury, 1891)

C. Coxon, 'A Handlist of the Sources of John Jenkins' Vocal and Instrumental Music', *RCRMA*, ix (1971), 73-89

M. Crum, 'A Seventeenth-Century Collection of Music Belonging to Thomas Hamond, a Suffolk Landowner', *Bodleian Library Record*, vi (1957), 373-86

―――― 'Early Lists of the Oxford Music School Collection', *ML*, xlviii (1967), 23-34

―――― 'The Consort Music from Kirtling, Bought for the Oxford Music School from Anthony Wood, 1667', *Chelys*, iv (1972), 3-10

W.H. Cummings, *Purcell* (London, 1881; 2/1896)

A. Cuneo, 'Francis Tregian the Younger: Musician, Collector and Humanist?', *ML*, lxxvi (1995), 398-404

J.P. Cutts, *Roger Smith, his Book: Bishop Smith's Part-Song Books in Carlisle Cathedral Library*, American Insititute of Musicology (Stuttgart, 1972)

R.T. Daniel & P. le Huray, *The Sources of English Church Music 1549-1660*, Early English Church Music, supplement i (London, 1972), 2 vols

R.T. Dart see R. Thurston Dart

E. David & M. Lussy, *Histoire de la Notation Musicale* (Paris, 1882)

M. Dean-Smith, 'Playford', *New Grove*, xv, 1-4

P. Dennison, 'The Sacred Music of Matthew Locke', *ML*, lx (1979), 60-75

―――― 'Bowman, Henry', *New Grove*, iii, 136-7

―――― 'Cooke, Henry', *New Grove*, iv, 710-11

―――― *Pelham Humfrey* (Oxford, 1986)

G. Dixon, *Carissimi* (Oxford, 1986)

―――― 'Purcell's Italianate Circle', *The Purcell Companion*, ed. M. Burden (London, 1995), 38-51

F. Dobbins, '"Doulce Mémoire": A Study of the Parody Chanson', *PRMA*, xcvi (1969-70), 85-102

G. Dodd, 'The Coperario-Lupo Five-Part Books at Washington', *Chelys*, i (1969), 36-40

―――― 'Coperario or Bull?', *Chelys*, i (1969), 41

―――― 'William Lawes: Royall Consort Suite No. 9 in F', *Chelys*, vi (1975-6), 3-9

―――― *Thematic Index of Music for Viols*, The Viola da Gamba Society (London, 1980-)

S.R. Dunlap, *The Poems of Thomas Carew* (Oxford, 1949)

C. Egerton, 'The Horoscope of Signor Angelo Notari (1566-1663)', *The Lute*, xxviii (1988), 13-18

A. Einstein, 'The Elizabethan Madrigal and *Musica Transalpina*', *ML*, xxv (1944), 66-77, & ibid., xxvi (1946), 273

W. McC. Evans, *Henry Lawes, Musician and Friend of Poets* (New York, 1941)

H.C. Fanshawe, *The History of the Fanshawe Family* (Newcastle-upon-Tyne, 1927)

E.H. Fellowes, *Orlando Gibbons and his Family* (2/London, 1951; rev. 1970)

I. Fenlon, 'La Diffusion de la Chanson Continentale dans les Manuscripts Anglais entre 1509-1570', *La Chanson à la Renaissance*, ed. J.-M. Vaccaro (Tours, 1981), 172-89
―――― 'Michael Honywood's Music Books', *'Sundry sorts of music books' Essays on The British Library Collections Presented to O.W. Neighbour on his 70th Birthday*, ed. C. Banks, A. Searle & M. Turner (London, 1993), 183-200
C.D.S. Field, 'Musical Observations from Barbados, 1647-50', *MT*, cxv (1974), 565-7
―――― 'Fantasia-suite', *New Grove*, vi, 392-3
―――― review of John Jenkins, *Consort Music for Viols in Four Parts*, ed. A. Ashbee, and William Lawes, *Consort Sets in Five Parts*, ed. D. Pinto, *ML*, lxii (1981), 98-103
M.E. Finch, *The Wealth of Five Northamptonshire Families* (London, 1956)
C.H. Firth & R.S. Rait, *Acts and Ordinances of the Interregnum, 1642-1660* (London, 1911), 3 vols
M.M. Foot, *The Henry Davis Gift: A Collection of Bookbindings* (1978-83), 2 vols
R.F. Ford, 'Minor Canons at Canterbury Cathedral: The Gostlings and their Colleagues', Ph.D. dissertation, University of California, Berkeley, 1984)
―――― 'Henman, Humfrey and *Have mercy*', *MT*, cxxvii (1986), 463-6
K. K. Forney, 'Antwerp's Role in the Reception and Dissemination of the Madrigal in the North', *Atti del XIV Congresso della Società Internazionale di Musicologia: Transmissione e Recezione delle Forme di Cultura Musicale (Bologna, 27 August - 1 September 1987)*, i, 239-53
N. Fortune with I. Fenlon, 'Music Manuscripts of John Browne (1608-91) and from Stanford Hall, Leicestershire', *Source Materials and the Interpretation of Music: A Memorial Volume to Thurston Dart*, ed. I. Bent (London, 1981), 155-68
J. Foster, *The Register of Admissions to Gray's Inn, 1521-1889* (London, 1889)
―――― *Alumni Oxonienses: The Members of the University of Oxford, 1500-1714* (Oxford, 1891-2), Early Series, 4 vols
D. Franklin, 'Turner, William (ii)', *New Grove*, xix, 281-2
J.A. Fuller Maitland & W. Barclay Squire, 'Introduction', *The Fitzwilliam Virginal Book Edited from the Original Manuscript* (London and Leipzig, 1894-9), i, pp. v-xi
[C. de Gamaches], *Mémoires de la Mission des Capucins*, ed. A. de Valence (Paris, 1881)
P. Gaskell, *A New Introduction to Bibliography* (Oxford, 1972)
C. Gianturco & E. McCrickard, *Alessandro Stradella (1639-1682): A Thematic Catalogue of his Compositions*, Thematic Catalogue Series 16 (New York, 1991)
M.A.E. Green ed., *Calendar of the Proceedings of the Committee for Compounding, &c., 1643-1660* (London, 1889-92; 2/Nendeln, Liechtenstein, 1967), 5 vols
P. Gregg, *King Charles I* (London, 1981)
D. Griffiths, *A Catalogue of the Music Manuscripts in York Minster Library* (York, 1981)
L. Hamessley, *The Reception of the Italian Madrigal in England: A Repertorial Study of Manuscript Anthologies ca. 1580-1620* (Ann Arbor, 1990)
―――― 'The Tenbury and Ellesmere Partbooks: New Findings on Manuscript Compilation and Exchange, and the Reception of the Italian Madrigal in Elizabethan England', *ML*, lxxiii (1992), 177-221
W. Hamper ed., *The Life, Diary and Correspondence of Sir William Dugdale* (London, 1827)
G. Hampshire ed., *The Bodleian Library Account Book 1613-1646*, Oxford Bibliographical Society (Oxford, 1983)

J. Harley, *Music in Purcell's London: the Social Background* (London, 1968)

J. Harper, 'Introduction', *Orlando Gibbons: Consort Music*, Musica Britannica xlviii (London, 1982), pp. xv-xxix

—— 'The Distribution of the Consort Music of Orlando Gibbons in Seventeenth-Century Sources', *Chelys*, xii (1983a), 3-22

—— 'Orlando Gibbons: The Domestic Context of his Music and Christ Church MS 21', *MT*, cxxiv (1983b), 767-70

W.O. Hassall, 'The Books of Sir Christopher Hatton at Holkham', *The Library*, Fifth Series, v/1 (1950), 1-13

W.C. Hazlitt ed., *Poeticall and Dramatic Works of Thomas Randolph*, i (London, 1875)

E. Heawood, 'Paper Used in England after 1600: i. The Seventeenth Century to c.1680', *The Library*, Fourth Series, xi (1930-1), 263-99

—— 'Further Notes on Paper Used in England after 1600', *The Library*, Fifth Series, ii (1947-8), 119-49

—— *Watermarks Mainly of the 17th and 18th Centuries* (Hilversum, 1950; 2/Amsterdam, 1970)

P. Heitz, *Les Filigranes des Papiers Contenus dans le Archive de la Ville de Strasbourg* (Strasbourg, 1902)

E.B. Helm, 'Italian Traits in the English Madrigal', *MR*, vii (1946), 26-34

R.R. Herber ed., rev. C.P. Eden, *The Whole Works of the Right Rev. Jeremy Taylor, D.D., Lord Bishop of Down, Connor, and Dromore: With a Life of the Author, and a Critical Examination of his Writings* (London, 1847-54), 10 vols

A. Hiff, *Catalogue of Printed Music Published Prior to 1801 now in the Library of Christ Church, Oxford* (Oxford, 1919)

W.G. Hiscock, *A Christ Church Miscellany* (Oxford, 1946)

—— *Henry Aldrich of Christ Church 1648-1710* (Oxford, 1960)

Historical Manuscripts Commission, *Fifth Report of The Royal Commission on Historical Manuscripts* (London, 1876)

—— *Calendar of the Manuscripts of the Most Hon. The Marquis of Salisbury Preserved at Hatfield House, Hertfordshire* (London, 1904), x

J.G. Hoffman, 'The Puritan Revolution and the "Beauty of Holiness" at Cambridge: The Case of John Cosin, Master of Peterhouse and Vice-Chancellor of the University', *Proceedings of the Cambridge Antiquarian Society*, lxxii (1982-3), 94-105

P. Holman, 'George Jeffries and the *Great Dooble Base*', *Chelys*, v (1973-4), 79-80

—— 'The English Royal Violin Consort in the Sixteenth Century', *PRMA*, cix, (1982-3), 39-59

—— *Four and Twenty Fiddlers: The Violin at the English Court 1540-1690* (Oxford, 1993)

I. Holst ed., *Henry Purcell 1659-1695: Essays on his Music* (London, 1959)

A. Hughes-Hughes, *Catalogue of MS Music in the British Museum* (London, 1906-9; rev. 1964-6), 3 vols

C.W. Hughes, 'Porter, Pupil of Monteverdi', *MQ*, xx (1934), 278-88

L. Hulse, 'Christopher 1st Baron Hatton (1605-1670): Musical Patron and Collector', unpublished paper presented at the Fourth Biennial Conference on Baroque Music at Royal Holloway and Bedford New College (University of London), July 1990

—— 'The Musical Patronage of Robert Cecil, First Earl of Salisbury (1563-1612)', *JRMA*, cxvi (1991), 24-40

L. Hulse, 'The Musical Patronage of the English Aristocracy *c*.1590-1640' (Ph.D. dissertation, University of London, 1993)
C. Hurst, *Catalogue of the Wren Library of Lincoln Cathedral: Books Printed before 1801* (Cambridge, 1982)
W.H. Husk (rev.), 'Holmes, George', *New Grove*, viii, 657
J. Irving, 'Matthew Hutton and York Minster MSS M 3/1-4 (S)', *MR*, xliv (1983), 163-77
J. Izon, 'Italian Musicians at the Tudor Court', *MQ*, xliv (1958), 329-37
W.A. Jackson ed., *Records of the Court of the Stationers' Company 1602-1640* (London, 1957)
O. Jander, *A Catalogue of Manuscripts of Compositions by Alessandro Stradella*, The Wellesley Edition Cantata Index Series, iv (1960; rev. 2/1962)
S. Jayne, *Library Catalogues of the English Renaissance* (Berkeley, 1956; rev. 2/Godalming, 1983)
S. Jeans & J. Steele ed., *John Lugge: The Complete Keyboard Works* (London, 1990)
A.V. Jones, *The Motets of Carissimi* (Ann Arbor, 1982), 2 vols
M.F. Keeler, *The Long Parliament* (Philadelphia, 1954)
J.P. Kenyon, *Stuart England*, The Pelican History of England vi (London, 1978; 2/1985)
J. Kerman, 'Master Alfonso and the Elizabethan Madrigal', *MQ*, xxxviii (1952), 222-44
―――― *The Elizabethan Madrigal: a Comparative Study* (New York, 1962)
F. Kidson, 'John Playford, and 17th Century Music Publishing', *MQ*, iv (1918), 516-34
A.H. King, *Some British Collectors of Music c.1600-1960* (Cambridge, 1963)
R. Klakowich, '*Scocca pur*: Genesis of an English Ground', *JRMA*, cxvi (1991), 63-77
D.W. Krummel, *English Music Printing, 1553-1700* (London, 1975)
―――― 'Venetian Baroque Music in a London Bookshop', *Music and Bibliography: Essays in Honour of Alec Hyatt King*, ed. O. Neighbour (London, 1980), 1-27
H.C. de Lafontaine, *The King's Musick* (London, 1909)
J.F. Larkin ed., 'Royal Proclamations of King Charles I 1625-46', *Stuart Royal Proclamations*, ii (Oxford, 1983)
R. Latham & W. Matthews ed., *The Diary of Samuel Pepys*, (London, 1970-83), 11 vols
M. Laurie, 'The Chapel Royal Part-Books', *Music and Bibliography: Essays in Honour of Alex Hyatt King*, ed. O. Neighbour (London, 1980), 28-50
M. Lefkowitz, *William Lawes* (London, 1960)
―――― 'The Longleat Papers of Bulstrode Whitelocke: New Light on Shirley's *Triumph of Peace*', *JAMS*, xviii (1965), 42-60
P. le Huray, *Music and the Reformation in England 1549-1660* (London, 1967; 2/Cambridge, 1978)
―――― 'Lowe, Edward', *New Grove*, xi, 287-8
R. Lemon & M.A.E. Green ed., *Calendar of State Papers, Domestic Series* [1547-1660] (London, 1856-72)
W. van Lennep, *The London Stage 1660-1800* (Carbondale, Illinois, 1965)
F.J. Levy, 'How Information Spread Among the Gentry, 1550-1640', *Journal of British Studies*, xxi (1982), 11-34
J. Lindt, *The Paper-Mills of Berne and their Watermarks* (Hilversum, 1964)
N. Linnell, 'Michael Honywood and Lincoln Cathedral Library', *The Library*, Sixth Series, v (1983), 126-39
J. Loftis ed., *The Memoirs of Anne, Lady Halkett and Ann, Lady Fanshawe* (Oxford, 1979)

H. Love, *Scribal Publication in Seventeenth-Century England* (Oxford, 1993)

E. Lowinsky, 'Echoes of Adrian Willaert's Chromatic "Duo" in 16th and 17th-Century Compositions', *Studies in Music History: Essays for Oliver Strunk* (Princeton, 1968), 183-238)

L.C. Loyd & D.M. Stenton ed., *Sir Christopher Hatton's Book of Seals*, Northamptonshire Record Society, xv (London, 1950)

R. Luckett, 'Music', *The Diary of Samuel Pepys*, ed. R. Latham & W. Matthews (London, 1983), x, 258-82

M. Mabbett, 'Italian Musicians in Restoration England (1660-90)', *ML*, lxvii (1986), 237-47

W. MacCaffrey, 'Place and Patronage in Elizabethan Politics', *Elizabethan Government and Society: Essays Presented to Sir John Neale*, ed. S.T. Bindoff, J. Hurstfield, & C.H. Williams (London, 1961), 95-126

W.D. Macray, *Annals of the Bodleian Library, Oxford, A.D. 1598 - A.D. 1867* (London, 1868; 2/enlarged: Oxford, 1890 & repr. 1984)

W.D. Macray ed., *Calendar of the Clarendon State Papers Preserved in the Bodleian Library* [1649-57] (Oxford, 1869-76), ii & iii

―――― *Clarendon's The History of the Rebellion and Civil Wars in England* (Oxford, 1888), 6 vols

F. Madan, *Oxford Books: A Bibliography of Printed Works Relating to the University and City of Oxford or Printed or Published there* (Oxford, 1912-1931), 2 vols

F. Madan, H.H.E. Craster and N. Denholm-Young ed., *Summary Catalogue of Western MSS in the Bodleian Library* (Oxford, 1895-1937), 5 vols

―――― *A New Bibliography of the Eikon Basilike of King Charles the First with a Note on the Authorship*, Oxford Bibliographical Society Publication, New Series, iii (1950)

A.R. Maddison, 'Lincoln Cathedral Choir, A.D. 1640 to 1700', *Associated Architectural Societies' Reports and Papers*, xx/1 (1889), 41-55

―――― 'Lincoln Cathedral Choir A.D. 1700-1750', *Associated Architectural Societies' Reports and Papers*, xx/2 (1889), 213-26

H. Marryat & U. Broadbent, *The Romance of Hatton Garden* (London, 1930)

G. Massenkeil, 'Über die Messen Giacomo Carissimi', *AnMc*, i (1963), 28-37

―――― 'Carissimi, Giacomo', *New Grove*, iii, 785-94

A.G. Matthews, *Walker Revised* (Oxford, 1948)

W.R. Matthews & W.M. Atkins, *A History of St Paul's Cathedral* (London, 1957)

R. McGrady, 'Captain Cooke: A Tercentenary Tribute', *MT*, cxiii (1972), 659-60

W.C. Metcalfe, *A Book of Knights Banneret, Knights of the Bath and Knights Bachelor made Between the Fourth Year of King Henry VI and the Restoration of King Charles II* (London, 1885)

E.H. Meyer, *English Chamber Music* (London, 1946); rev. with D. Poulton as *Early English Chamber Music* (London, 1982)

P. Millard ed., [Roger North] *General Preface and Life of Dr John North* (Toronto, 1984)

L.J. Mills, *Peter Hausted, Playwright, Poet and Preacher*, Indiana University Publications Humanities Series, xii (Bloomington, 1944)

L.J. Mills ed., *Peter Hausted's The Rival Friends*, Indiana University Publications Humanities Series, xxiii (Bloomington, 1951)

C. Monson, 'Thomas Myriell's Manuscript Collection: One View of Musical Taste in Jacobean London', *JAMS*, xxx (1977), 419-65

C. Monson, *Voice and Viols in England 1600-1650* (Ann Arbor, 1982)
G.C. Moore Smith ed., 'The Academic Drama at Cambridge: Extracts from College Records', *Malone Society Collections*, ii/2 (n.p., 1923), 192-3
G.C. Moore Smith, 'Some Unpublished Poems of Thomas Randolph', *Palaestra*, cxlviii (1925), 244-57
J. Morehen, 'The Sources of English Cathedral Music *c*.1617-*c*.1644' (Ph.D. dissertation, University of Cambridge, 1969)
—— 'Barnard, John', *New Grove*, ii, 165-6
O. Neighbour, 'Orlando Gibbons (1583-1625): The Consort Music', *EM*, xi (1983), 351-7
A. Nelson, *Records of Early English Drama: Cambridge* (Toronto, 1989), 2 vols
A. Newcomb, 'Secular Polyphony in the 16th Century', *Performance Practice: Music Before 1600*, New Grove Handbook in Music (London, 1989), 222-39
J. Nichols, *The Progresses, Processions, and Magnificent Festivities of King James the First, his Royal Consort, Family, and Court* (London, 1828), 4 vols
R. Nicholson, 'A Note on Gibbons and the Anonymous Six-Part Fantasies in Christ Church Library', *Viola da Gamba Society Bulletin* (July 1967)
A. Obertello, *Madrigali Italiani in Inghilterra* (Milan, 1949)
G. Ornsby ed., *The Correspondence of John Cosin, Together with other Papers Illustrative of his Life and Times*, Surtees Society lii & lv (London, 1869-72)
W. Osthoff ed., *Composizioni Vocali Profane e Sacre (Inedite)* (Milan, 1958)
C. Ozanne, 'Contemporary Accounts of the Explosion at Castle Cornet, December 1672', *Report & Transactions* [of] *La Société Guernesiaise*, xi (1930), 41-54
G. Parry, *The Trophies of Time: English Antiquarians of the Seventeenth Century* (Oxford, 1995)
J.M. Patrick ed., *The Complete Poetry of Robert Herrick* (New York, 1963)
I. Payne, 'The Handwriting of John Ward', *ML*, lxv (1984), 176-88
—— 'British Library Add. MSS 30,826-28: A Set of Part-Books from Trinity College Cambridge?', *Chelys*, xvii (1988), 3-13
L.L. Peck, '"For a King not to be bountiful were a fault": Perspectives on Court Patronage in Early Stuart England', *Journal of British Studies*, xxv (1986), 31-61
—— *Court Patronage and Corruption in Early Stuart England* (London, 1990)
L.L. Peck ed., *The Mental World of the Jacobean Court* (Cambridge, 1991)
P.A.J. Pettit, *The Royal Forests of Northamptonshire: A Study in their Economy, 1558-1714*, Northampton Record Society, xxiii (1968)
I. Philip, *The Bodleian Library in the Seventeenth and Eighteenth Centuries* (Oxford, 1983)
G.A. Philipps, 'Crown Musical Patronage from Elizabeth I to Charles I', *ML*, lviii (1977), 29-42
G. Piccard, *Wasserzeichen* (Stuttgart, 1977-87)
D. Pinto, 'William Lawes' Music for Viol Consort', *EM*, vi (1978), 12-24
—— 'The Fantasy Manner: the Seventeenth-Century Context', *Chelys*, x (1981), 17-28
—— 'William Lawes at the Siege of York', *MT*, cxxvii (1986), 579-83
—— 'The Music of the Hattons', *RCRMA*, xxiii (1990), 79-108
—— 'Introduction', *William Lawes: Fantasia-Suites*, Musica Britannica lx (London, 1991), pp. xv-xix

D. Pinto, *'for ye violls': The Consort and Dance Music of William Lawes* (Richmond, 1995)

—— 'The True Christmas: Carols at the Court of Charles I', *William Lawes (1602-1645): Essays on His Life, Times and Work*, ed. A. Ashbee & L. Hulse (forthcoming)

P. Platt, 'Richard Dering: An Account of his Life and Work' (B.Litt. dissertation, University of Oxford, 1951-2)

—— 'Dering's Life and Training', *ML*, xxxiii (1952), 41-9

—— 'Perspectives of Richard Dering's Vocal Music', *Studies in Music* i, University of Western Australia (1967), 56-66

—— 'Dering [Deering, Dearing, Diringus etc], Richard', *New Grove*, v, 382-3

H.R. Plomer, 'A Cavalier's Library', *The Library*, Second Series, v (1904), 158-72

G. Pollard & A. Ehrmann, *The Distribution of Books by Catalogue* (Cambridge, 1965)

W.R. Powell ed., *The Victoria History of the County of Essex* (London, 1966), v

D.C. Price, *Patrons and Musicians of the English Renaissance* (Cambridge, 1981)

J. Pulver, *A Biographical Dictionary of Old English Music* (London, 1927; rev. 1968)

E.F. Rimbault ed., *The Old Cheque Book of the Chapel Royal* (London, 1872)

R.J. Roberts, 'Sir Christopher Hatton's Book-Stamps', *The Library*, Fifth Series, xii (1957), 119

M. Rogers, *William Dobson 1611-46, National Portrait Gallery* (London, 1983)

G. Rose, 'Pietro Reggio: A Wandering Musician', *ML*, xlvi (1965), 207-16

L. Rostenberg, 'Robert Scott, Restoration Stationer and Importer', *The Papers of the Bibliographical Society of America*, xlviii (1954), 49-76

Royal Commission on Historical Monuments, *An Inventory of the Historical Monuments in the City of Cambridge* (London, 1959), 2 vols

B. Schofield & R. Thurston Dart, 'Tregian's Anthology', *ML*, xxxii (1951), 205-16

P. Scholes, *The Puritans and Music in England and New England* (London & New York, 1934)

A. Searle, 'Julian Marshall and the British Museum: Music Collecting in the Later Nineteenth Century', *British Library Journal*, xi (1985), 67-87

K. Sharpe, 'The Image of Virtue: The Court and Household of Charles I, 1625-1642', *The English Court from the War of the Roses to the Civil War*, ed. D. Starkey (London, 1987), 226-60

—— *Politics and Ideas in Early Stuart England: Essays and Studies* (London, 1989)

H.W. Shaw see H. Watkins Shaw

R. Shay, 'Henry Purcell and "Ancient" Music in Restoration England' (Ph.D. dissertation, University of North Carolina, Chapel Hill, 1991)

—— '"Naturalizing" Palestrina and Carissimi in Late Seventeenth-Century Oxford: Henry Aldrich and his Recompositions', *ML*, lxxvii (1996), 368-400

J.D. Shute, 'Anthony à Wood and his MSS Wood D 19 (4) at the Bodleian' (Ph.D. dissertation, International Institute of Advanced Studies, Clayton, Missouri, 1979)

B. Smallman, 'Endor Revisited: English Biblical Dialogues of the Seventeenth Century', *ML*, xlvi (1965), 137-45

W. Sparrow Simpson, *The Chapter and Statutes of the College of the Minor Canons in Saint Paul's Cathedral, London* (London, 1871)

W.L. Spiers, 'The Note-Book and Account Book of Nicholas Stone', *Walpole Society*, vii (1918-19)

I. Spink, 'Walter Porter and the Last Book of English Madrigals', *AcM*, xxvi (1954), 18-36
—— 'An Early English Strophic Cantata (Porter's *Farewell*)', *AcM*, xxvii (1955), 138-40
—— 'Angelo Notari and his *Prime Musiche Nuove*', *MMR*, lxxxvii (1957), 168-77
—— 'The Musicians of Queen Henrietta-Maria: Some Notes and References in English State Papers', *AcM*, xxxvi (1964), 177-82
—— 'The Old Jewry *Musick-Society*: A Seventeenth Century Catch Club', *Musicology*, ii (1967), 35-41
—— 'Notari, Angelo', *New Grove*, xiii, 333
—— 'Porter, Walter', *New Grove*, xv, 137
—— *Restoration Cathedral Music 1660-1714* (Oxford, 1995)
J.H. Srawley, *Michael Honywood, Dean of Lincoln (1660-81): A Story of the English Church in Critical Times* (Lincoln, 1950; 2/1981)
F.W. Sternfeld, 'Cavalli and Purcell', Correspondence, *JRMA*, cxvi (1991), 324-5
E.M. Thompson ed., *Correspondence of the Family of Hatton, Being Chiefly Letters Addressed to Christopher First Viscount Hatton, A.D. 1601-1704*, Camden Society (London, 1878), 2 vols
R. Thompson, 'English Music Manuscripts and the Fine Paper Trade, 1648-1688' (Ph.D. dissertation, University of London, 1988)
—— 'George Jeffreys and the *Stile Nuove* in English Sacred Music: A New Date for his Autograph Score, British Library Add. MS 10338', *ML*, lxx (1989), 317-41
—— 'The Sources of Locke's Consort *for seaverall friends*', *Chelys*, xix (1990a), 16-43
—— 'Manuscripts of the Civil War Period?', unpublished paper presented at Study Day on Music 1550-1650, Oxford, May 1990 (1990b)
—— '"Francis Withie of Oxon" and his Commonplace Book, Christ Church, Oxford, MS 337', *Chelys*, xx (1991), 3-27
R.R. Thompson, 'The "Tregian" Manuscripts: A Study of their Compilation', *British Library Journal*, xviii (1992), 202-4.
R. Thurston Dart, 'Tregian, Francis', *Grove's Dictionary of Music and Musicians* (5th edition, London, 1954), viii, 539
—— 'The Printed Fantasies of Orlando Gibbons', *ML*, xxxvii (1956), 342-9
R. Thurston Dart & W. Coates ed., *Jacobean Consort Music*, Musica Britannica ix (London, 2/rev. 1962)
R. Thurston Dart & R. Marlow, 'Tregian, Francis', *New Grove*, xix, 126
M. Tilmouth, 'King, William', *New Grove*, x, 67.
C.G.C. Tite ed., [Thomas Smith] *Catalogue of the Manuscripts of the Cottonian Library 1696* (Cambridge, 1984)
H. Trevor-Roper, *Catholics, Anglicans and Puritans: Seventeenth-Century Essays* (London, 1987)
F.B. Tupper, *The History of Guernsey and its Bailiwick* (2/Guernsey, 1876)
H.D. Turner, 'Five Studies of the Aristocracy, 1689-1714' (M.Litt. dissertation, University of Cambridge, 1965)
—— 'Charles Hatton: A Younger Son', *Northamptonshire Past and Present*, iii (1965-6), 254-61
—— 'Viscount Hatton and the Government of Guernsey, 1670-1706', *Société Guernesiaise Report and Transactions 1969*, xvi (1970), 415-26

E. Van Tassel, 'Purcell's *Give Sentence*: Two Purcell Discoveries - 1', *MT*, cxviii (1977), 381-3

F.J. Varley, *The Siege of Oxford: An Account of Oxford During the Civil War 1642-6* (London, 1932)

E. Veevers, *Images of Love and Religion: Queen Henrietta Maria and Court Entertainments* (Cambridge, 1989)

J. Venn & J.A. Venn, *The Book of Matriculations and Degrees: A Catalogue of those who have been Matriculated or been Admitted to any Degree in the University of Cambridge from 1544 to 1659* (Cambridge, 1913)

────── *Alumni Cantabrigienses: A Biographical List of all Known Students, Graduates and Holders of Office at the University of Cambridge, from the Earliest Times to 1900* (Cambridge, 1922-54), 10 vols

E. Vogel, A. Einstein, F. Lesure & C. Sartori, *Bibliografia della Musica Italiana Vocale Profana Pubblicata dal 1500- al 1700* (Pomezia, 1977), 3 vols

J.P. Wainwright, 'A Study of Five Related English Manuscripts Containing Italian Music: British Library Additional Manuscripts 31,434, 31,440 and 31,479; Madrigal Society Manuscripts G. 55-9; and Christ Church, Oxford Manuscripts 877-880' (M.Phil. dissertation, University of Cambridge, 1986)

────── 'Civil War Oxford: a Centre for the Dissemination of Italian Music in England?', unpublished paper presented to the Viola da Gamba Society, London, February 1987

────── 'George Jeffreys' Copies of Italian Music', *RCRMA*, xxiii (1990), 109-24

────── 'The Musical Patronage of Christopher, First Baron Hatton (1605-1670)' (Ph.D. dissertation, University of Cambridge, 1993), 2 vols

E. Walker, 'An Oxford Book of Fancies', *Musical Antiquary*, iii (1912), 65-73

J. Walker ed., [John Aubrey] *Letters Written by Eminent Persons in the Seventeenth and Eighteenth Centuries, to which are Added Lives of Eminent Men* (London, 1813)

P. Walls, 'The Origins of the English Recitative', *PRMA*, cx (1983-4), 25-40

────── 'The Influence of the Italian Violin School in 17th-Century England', *EM*, xviii (1990), 575-87.

A.W. Ward & A.R. Waller ed., 'The Drama to 1642', *The Cambridge History of English Literature*, vi (Cambridge, 1932)

G.F. Warner ed., *The Nicholas Papers: Correspondence of Sir Edward Nicholas*, Camden Society (London, 1886-92), 2 vols

H. Watkins Shaw, 'Extracts from Anthony à Wood's *Notes on the Lives of Musicians Hitherto Unpublished*', *ML*, xv (1934), 157-62

────── 'John Blow', *MT*, xcix (1958), 542-4

────── 'A Contemporary Source of English Music of the Purcellian Period', *AcM*, xxxi (1959), 38-44

────── 'A Cambridge Manuscript from the English Chapel Royal', *ML*, xlii (1961), 263-7

────── 'The Autographs of John Blow', *MR*, xxv (1964), 85-95

────── 'Aldrich, Henry', *New Grove*, i, 234-6

────── 'Blow, John', *New Grove*, ii, 805-12

────── 'Bing, Stephen', *New Grove*, ii, 723

────── 'Goodson, Richard', *New Grove*, vii, 531

────── 'Gostling, John', *New Grove*, vii, 565

────── *The Bing-Gostling Part-Books at York Minster: A Catalogue with Introduction*, Church Music Society, The Royal School of Church Music (London, 1986)

Watkins Shaw, *The Succession of Organists of the Chapel Royal and the Cathedrals of England and Wales from c.1538* (Oxford, 1991)

J.A. Westrup, *Purcell* (London, 1937; rev. 4/1980)

—— 'Foreign Musicians in Stuart England', *MQ*, xxvii (1941), 70-89

—— 'Domestic Music under the Stuarts', *PRMA*, lxviii (1942), 19-53

J. Whenham, *Duet and Dialogue in the Age of Monteverdi* (Ann Arbor, 1982), 2 vols

P. Willetts, 'Sir Nicholas le Strange and John Jenkins', *ML*, xlii (1961a), 30-43

—— 'Music from the Circle of Anthony Wood at Oxford', *British Museum Quarterly*, xxiv (1961b), 71-5

—— 'A Neglected Source of Monody and Madrigal', *ML*, xliii (1962), 329-39

—— 'Tregian's Part-Books', *MT*, civ (1963), 334-5

—— 'Sir Nicholas Le Strange's Collection of Masque Music', *The British Museum Quartlerly*, xxix (1965), 79-81

—— 'John Lilly, Musician and Music Copyist', *Bodleian Library Record*, vii (1967a), 307-11

—— 'Autograph Music by John Jenkins', *ML*, xlviii (1967b), 124-6

—— 'Musical Connections of Thomas Myriell', *ML*, xlix (1968), 36-42

—— *The Henry Lawes Manuscript* (London, 1969a)

—— 'Autographs of Angelo Notari', *ML*, l (1969b), 124-7

—— 'The Identity of Thomas Myriell', *ML*, liii (1972), 431-3

—— 'Myriell, Thomas', *New Grove*, xiii, 6

—— 'Stephen Bing: a Forgotten Violist', *Chelys*, xviii (1989), 3-17

—— 'John Barnard's Collections of Viol and Vocal Music', *Chelys*, xx (1991), 28-42

—— 'John Lilly: A Redating', *Chelys*, xxi (1992), 27-38

J. Wilson ed., *Roger North on Music* (London, 1959)

J.K. Wolf & E.K. Wolf, 'Rastrology and its use in Eighteenth-Century Manuscript Studies', *Studies in Musical Sources and Style: Essays in Honor of Jan La Rue*, ed. E.K. Wolf & E.H. Roesner (Madison, 1990), 237-91

J.K. Wood, 'Two Latin Play Songs', *RCRMA*, xxi (1988), 45-52

W.L. Woodfill, *Musicians in English Society from Elizabeth I to Charles I* (Princeton, 1953)

F.B. Zimmerman, *Henry Purcell (1659-1695): An Analytical Catalogue of his Music* (London, 1963)

—— 'Purcell's "Service Anthem", *O God, Thou Art my God* and the B-flat Major Service', *MQ*, l (1964), 207-14

—— *Henry Purcell, 1659-1695: His Life and Times* (Philadelphia, 1967; rev. 2/1983)

INDEX

Aldrich, Henry 26-7, 36-9, 42-3, 67, 78, 160, 166, 188, 191, 199, 204, 368-70, 374-8, 389-91
Aston, Peter 154, 159
Aubrey, John 16

Banister, John 196
Barnard, John 59, 61-2, 65, 89, 107, 109
  First Book of Selected Church Musick 157
Bianconi, Lorenzo 207
Bing, Stephen 32-5, 52-114, 160-9
  career 59-61, 90-1, 99-100, 103-6, 108-10, 112-14
  handwriting 52-4, 57-9
  at Oxford 90-2
Blow, John 205-6, 366-8
Bowman, Henry 199, 239-42, 251-3, 282-4, 321-6, 375, 391-6

Carissimi, Giacomo 199
Cartwright, William 172-3
Charles I 11-12, 80-2, 171-2
Charles II 195-6
Charteris, Richard 63
Child, Simon 264
Christ Church, Oxford 30-45, 209-10
Church, John 376-8
Clarendon, 1st Earl of (Edward Hyde) 16
Cooke, Captain Henry 25, 196, 198-9
Coprario, John 81-2

Davenant, William 16
Dering, Sir Edward 10, 171
Dering, Richard 158, 161-2, 178-85
Dobson, William 17
Dugdale, William 10, 12, 16

East, Michael 10, 40n.
Evelyn, John 17-19, 198
Exeter House Chapel 15, 18, 149-50

Fanshawe, Lady Anne 16
Fanshawe, Sir Henry 65, 189
Fanshawe, Sir Thomas 5, 12

Ford, Robert 108

Gibbons, Orlando 6, 25, 187-8
Glasgow, Euing Music Collection R.c.28 30-1
Goodson I, Richard 43, 160, 188, 199, 264-7, 304-15, 376-8
Goodson II, Richard 200, 297-300, 304-13, 419-20
Gunning, Peter 14-15, 18, 145, 149-50, 225
Gostling, John 106, 121
Gostling, William 121

Hatton, Charles 23
Hatton I, Sir Christopher 3
Hatton II, Sir Christopher 5-6, 27-8
Hatton III, Christopher, 1st Baron 6-22
  as antiquarian 10. 12, 21
  at Cambridge 6-10
  career 10-12, 19-21
  as Comptroller of King's Household 15-16
  debts 11, 19-20
  exile in Paris 17-18
  Governor of Guernsey 20-1
  music collection 25-45, 425-30
  at Oxford 11-17
  patronage of High Church clergymen 13-15
  The Psalter of David 14
  return to England 19
Hatton IV, Christopher, 1st Vicount 22
Hatton, Lady Elizabeth (née Montagu) 18-19, 50
Hatton, Richard 7, 115
Hatton, Sir Robert 7
Hatton, Sir Thomas 7, 11
Hatton House (Ely Place) 3, 5
Hausted, Peter 7-10, 13
  The Rivall Friends 8-10, 150
Hawkins, John 119, 170-1
Hayes, Philip 264, 297
Henrietta Maria, Queen 17, 172, 174-6
Holmes, George 32-5
Honywood, Michael 59, 105-6
Hume, Tobias 6

Humfrey, Pelham 196-7
Husbands, Charles 300-2, 314-15, 378-82
Husbands, William 200, 264-7
Hutton, Matthew 314-15

Italian music 25, 85-9, 92-9, 121-32, 156-9, 195-207

Jeffreys, George 18, 21, 32-5, 60, 92, 115-59, 160
  assessment of 154-9
  at Cambridge 7-10
  career 115-20
  compositions 132-54, 158-9
  at Oxford 116, 118-19
Jenkins, John 49-50, 89

King, Gregory 21
Kirby Hall 5, 19, 26n.

Laud, Archbishop William 90, 172
Lawes, Henry 95-6, 173
Lawes, William 88, 101-2, 267-74
  'The Royall Consort' 101-2
Le Strange, Sir Nicholas 89
Lilly, John 46-52, 66-7, 79, 89-90, 102
Lluelyn, Martin 173
Locke, Matthew 197-8
Lowe, Edward 46, 60, 101, 103, 119, 297-300, 302-15, 320-36, 378-82, 391-3, 416, 418-19
Lugge, John 378-82

Malchair, Johann Baptist 43, 67, 160, 376-8
manuscripts:
  Lbl Add. MS 10,338: 133-53, 217-32
  Lbl Add. MSS 17,816 & 30,829-30: 141-4, 233-5
  Lbl Add. MSS 27,550-4: 102, 235-8
  Lbl Add. MS 29,282: 154, 238-9
  Lbl Add. MS 29,372-7: 64
  Lbl Add. MS 29,427: 85
  Lbl Add. MS 30,382: 239-42
  Lbl Add. MS 31,434: 95-9, 123, 242-4
  Lbl Add. MS 31,440: 165, 191-4, 244-51
  Lbl Add. MS 31,460: 251-3
  Lbl Add. MS 31,479: 125-31, 254-60
  Lbl Add. MS 33,234: 260-4
  Lbl Add. MS 33,235: 264-7
  Lbl Add. MSS 40,657-61: 88-9, 267-74
  Lbl Add. MS 59,869: 275-9
  Lbl Egerton MS 2485: 89-90, 279-82
  Lbl Egerton MS 2960: 282-4
  Lbl Egerton MS 3665: 85, 190-1
  Lbl Evelyn MS 189: 183-5, 285
  Lbl R.M. MS 24.k.3: 61-4, 396-400
  Lcm MS 920: 153-4, 286-8
  Lcm MS 920A: 154, 288-90
  Lcm MS 1045-51: 62-3
  Lcm MS 1145: 89
  Lcm MS 2033: 183-5, 290-1
  Lcm MS 2034: 183-5, 292-3
  Lcm MS 2039: 183-5, 293-7
  Lgc Mus. MSS 469-71: 102
  Lsp MS Partbook A 1: 110
  Lsp MS Partbook 43.D: 110-12
  Lwa MS Partbooks Triforium Set 1: 109
  Lwa MS Partbooks Triforium Set 2: 108-9
  Madrigal Society MSS G 55-9: 125-31, 254-60
  NRO Finch-Hatton MS 2652: 28-9
  Ob Mus. Sch. MS C 9. 297-300
  Ob Mus. Sch. MS C 10. 300-2
  Ob Mus. Sch. MS C 11: 302-4
  Ob Mus. Sch. MSS C 12-19: 304-13
  Ob Mus. Sch. MSS C 24-7: 314-15
  Ob Mus. Sch. MSS C 54-7: 316-18
  Ob Mus. Sch. MS C 87: 102-3, 319-20
  Ob Mus. Sch. MS C 204: 60, 116, 321-6
  Ob Mus. Sch. MS E 451: 326-36
  Ob Tenbury MS 302: 62-3, 89
  Ob Tenbury MSS 973-6 & 1273: 123-5, 336-8
  Ob Tenbury MS 1005: 93, 338-9
  Ob Tenbury MS 1009: 93, 339-40
  Ob Tenbury MS 1010: 154, 341
  Ob Tenbury MS 1011: 116, 341-2
  Ob Tenbury MS 1012: 123, 342-3
  Ob Tenbury MS 1013: 123, 343-4
  Ob Tenbury MS 1015: 123, 344-6
  Ob Tenbury MS 1016: 131-2, 346-7
  Ob Tenbury MS 1017: 93, 123, 347-8
  Ob Tenbury MS 1285: 141, 348-9

Index 469

Och Mus. 2, 397-408 & 436 'The Great Set': 66-90, 349-65
Och Mus. 14: 205-6, 366-8
Och Mus. 18: 204, 368-70
Och Mus. 21: 187-8, 370-4
Och Mus. 43: 374-5
Och Mus. 44: 188
Och Mus. 48: 376-8
Och Mus. 49: 378-82
Och Mus. 56-60: 189
Och Mus. 61-7: 64, 85, 188
Och Mus. 78-82: 187
Och Mus. 372-6: 187, 382-4
Och Mus. 417-18 & 1080 'The Bing Set': 66-90, 384-6
Och Mus. 432 & 612-13 'The Hatton Set': 66-90, 387-8
Och Mus. 459-62: 150
Och Mus. 463-7: 187
Och Mus. 468-72: 152
Och Mus. 510-14: 191, 389-91
Och Mus. 621: 391-3
Och Mus. 623-6: 393-6
Och Mus. 732-5: 61-4, 396-400
Och Mus. 747-9: 184, 401-2
Och Mus. 754-9: 100-2, 403-5
Och Mus. 877-80: 160-9, 405-14
Och Mus. 1023: 91, 415-16
Och Mus. 1151: 416
Och Mus. 1155-61: 187, 417
Och Mus. 1178: 418-19
Och Mus. 1185: 419-20
Och Mus. 1215: Fascicle 3: 64, 421
Y MSS M.1.S: 106-7
EIRE-Dm MS Z3.4.13, ff. 47-59ᵛ: 151-2, 422
US-NYp Drexel MS 4302: 190-1
US-NYp Drexel MS 5624: 80
US-R MS ML96 L814f, fascicle 3: 80, 151
Marsh, Narcissus 151-2
Marshall, Julian 121
Martin, Edward 13, 18
Martin, Robert 28-30
Mell, Davis 147
Monson, Craig 65
Morgan, Charles 199, 260-4
Myriell, Thomas 64-6, 85, 150-1, 188-9

Newport-Hatton, Lady Elizabeth 3, 189, 191

Newport(-Hatton), Sir William 3
Nicholas, Sir Edward 17, 100
North, Roger 48, 50
North family 50-1, 102-3, 126-7, 319-20
Notari, Angelo 98, 162-5, 191-4, 244-51
  Prime Musiche Nuove 164-5

Oliphant, Thomas 120, 140, 218, 233
Ouseley, Sir Frederick 121
Ouseley, Sir Frederick Arthur Gore 121
Oxford Court 11-12, 16-17, 127-9, 169-77

Pepys, Samuel 195
Perwich, Susanna 100
Pett, Peter 147
Phillips, Arthur 172
Pinto, David 5, 36, 63, 88, 95, 120, 172, 187-8
Porter, Walter 165-6
Purcell, Henry 107-8, 112, 206-7

Quartermaine, Thomas 109

Randolph, Thomas 7-8
  The Jealous Lover 8
  The Maskque of Vices 150
Reggio, Pietro 129, 192
Rogers, Benjamin 188, 370-4

St Michael's College, Tenbury 121
Sancroft, William 59, 104
Smith, Francis 200, 378-82
Spencer, Robert 127
Spink, Ian 166

Taylor, Jeremy 13-14
Thompson, Robert 93, 126, 143, 147, 150-1, 157-8
Tregian, Francis 85, 190-1, 389-91
Tucker, William 109
Turner, William 378-82

Ward, John 65-6, 188-9
Warren, Joseph 121, 243
Warren-Horne, Edmund 120, 218-19
Watkin Shaw 59
Westrup, Sir Jack 198
Whenham, John 163

Willetts, Pamela 46, 53-4, 57-9, 63,
    91, 96, 192
Wilson, John 165-6
Withey, Francis 200, 378-82
Wood, Anthony 14, 16, 42, 115, 119,
    147, 178-9
Woodington, John 61-3, 397-8

Yonge, Nicholas 64-5